D1559852

U.S. Intelligence and the Nazis

This book is a direct result of the 1998 Nazi War Crimes Disclosure Act. Drawing on many documents declassified under this law, the authors demonstrate what U.S. intelligence agencies learned about Nazi crimes during World War II and about the nature of Nazi intelligence agencies' role in the Holocaust. It examines how some U.S. corporations found ways to profit from Nazi Germany's expropriation of the property of German Jews. This book also reveals startling new details on the Cold War connections between the U.S. government and Hitler's former officers.

At a time when intelligence successes and failures are at the center of public discussion, *U.S. Intelligence and the Nazis* also provides an unprecedented inside look at how intelligence agencies function during war and peacetime.

Richard Breitman, professor of history at American University, is the author or coauthor of seven books and more than forty articles. One of his books, *The Architect of Genocide: Himmler and the Final Solution*, won the Fraenkel Prize for Contemporary History, and another, *Official Secrets: What the Nazis Planned, What the British and Americans Knew*, was a finalist for the National Jewish Book Award in Holocaust Studies. Breitman serves as editor of the scholarly journal *Holocaust and Genocide Studies*.

Norman J. W. Goda is an associate professor of History at Ohio University. He is the author of *Tomorrow the World: Hitler, Northwest Africa and the Path to America* and numerous scholarly articles. He is currently completing a book entitled *Tales from Spandau: Cold War Diplomacy and the Nuremberg War Criminals*.

Timothy Naftali, an associate professor at the University of Virginia's Miller Center of Public Affairs, directs the Presidential Recordings Program and the Kremlin Decision-Making Project. Coauthor of *"One Hell of a Gamble": Khrushchev, Castro and Kennedy, 1958–1964*, he is currently completing *Khrushchev's Cold War and Blindspot: The Secret History of U.S. Counterterrorism*. Naftali was most recently a consultant to the 9/11 Commission.

Robert Wolfe was the senior research specialist for more than thirty years for the National Archives' massive captured German and World War II war crimes trial records, as well as for the records of the postwar occupation of Germany and Austria. His publications include *Americans as Proconsuls: U.S. Military Government in Germany and Japan, 1944–52,* and *Captured German and Related Records*.

MOST SECRET

March 20, 1942.

It has been learned from a most secret source that on November 24, 1941, the Chile n Consulate, in Prague, made the following statement regarding German legislation for Jews:-

"An order published in Berlin regarding Jews abroad has been adopted in the Protectorate. Here is a full translation:-

"A Jew habitually residing abroad cannot be a German citizen. The Jew loses German nationality immediately this order comes into force, whether he is abroad or whether he was established outside Germany prior to this order. The fortune of a Jew who loses German nationality – in accordance with this order – belongs to the Reich. Likewise the Reich seizes the fortunes of Jews who, on the date of this order – and stateless and originally had German nationality although they habitually have their residence outside Germany. The fortune which the Reich obtains in this manner will serve to solve the questions in connection with Jews....."

Another recent order is as follows:-

"It is strictly prohibited for Jews: to transfer their movable goods or any of their property, installations in their departments, personal effects, claims to other goods, without special permission for each article, issued by the competent German authority. Contraveners, sellers, purchasers or intermediaries in illegal acts are subject o severe penalty.

Neither can the Jews conceal, hide, deposit or decrease the value of any of their property. It is particularly prohibited to transfer, sell, make gifts of, employ or give in custody to other persons their property or deeds.

All the sales effected after the 10th October of such property should be notified to the Jewish Community Office giving exact details of the name of the purchaser and seller, list of valuable articles etc. etc. In the case of a gift the dates should be given. Penalties for contravention are equally severe.....

The Jewish problem is being partially solved in t e Protectorate, as it has been decided to eradicate all the Jews and send some to Poland and others to the town of Terezin, w ilst looking for a more remote place.

The German triumph will leave Europe freed of Semites. Those who escape with their lives from this trial will certainly be deported to Siberia, where they will not have much opportunity to make use of their financial capabilities.

In proportion to the U.S.A. increasing its attacks on the Reich, Germany will expedite the destruction of Semitism, as she accuses international Judaism of all the calamities which have befallen the world.

The exodus of the Jews from the Reich has not had the results prophesied by the enemies of Germany: on the contrary: they have been replaced by Aryans with obvious advantage to everything and in everything, except in the usury line in which they are past masters."

British translation of an intercept from the Chilean Consul in Prague to his headquarters in Santiago. A discussion of this document begins on page 17. The document itself is in NA, RG 226, entry 210, box 386, folder 6.

U.S. Intelligence and the Nazis

Richard Breitman
American University

Norman J. W. Goda
Ohio University

Timothy Naftali
University of Virginia

Robert Wolfe
U.S. National Archives and Records Administration

CAMBRIDGE UNIVERSITY PRESS
Cambridge, New York, Melbourne, Madrid, Cape Town, Singapore, SãoPaulo

Cambridge University Press
40 West 20th Street, New York, NY 10011-4211, USA

www.cambridge.org
Information on this title: www.cambridge.org/9780521852685

First published by the National Archives Trust Fund Board for the Nazi War Crimes and Japanese
Imperial Government Records Interagency Working Groups, Washington, DC.
First published by Cambridge University Press 2005

Printed in the United States of America

A catalog record for this publication is available from the British Library.

Library of Congress Cataloging in Publication Data
U.S. intelligence and the Nazis /   Richard Breitman . . . [et al.].
    p.   cm.
  Includes bibliographical references and index.
ISBN 0-521-85268-4 – ISBN 0-521-61794-4 (pbk.)
      1. World War, 1939–1945 – Secret service – United States. 2. World War, 1939–1945 –
Military intelligence – United States. 3. World War, 1939–1945 – Secret service – Germany.
4. World War, 1939–1945 – Collaborationists – Germany. 5. Holocaust, Jewish (1939–1945).
I. Title: United States intelligence and the Nazis. II. Breitman, Richard, 1947–

D810.S7U75 2004
940.54′85–dc   2004044870

ISBN-13 978-0-521-85268-5 hardback
ISBN-10 0-521-85268-4 hardback

ISBN-13 978-0-521-61794-9 paperback
ISBN-10 0-521-61794-4 paperback

History Matters

Contents

Preface

THIS BOOK HAS its own unusual history. The four co-authors all served as consulting historians for the Nazi War Criminal and Imperial Japanese Records Interagency Working Group (IWG), a small government organization created to implement the 1998 Nazi War Crimes Disclosure Act. Working closely with the IWG and with archivists at the U.S. National Archives, we helped with the declassification of approximately 8 million pages of U.S. government records; we examined a significant portion of those records; and over the course of five years we wrote about what we considered the most significant topics illuminated by newly declassified records.

Part of the purpose of the Nazi War Crimes Disclosure Act of 1998 was to release to the public the remaining archival secrets about U.S. government policies concerning Nazi war crimes and criminals during and after World War II. Some members of the IWG—Thomas Baer, Richard Ben-Veniste, Elizabeth Holtzman, and its first chair Michael Kurtz—decided that independent historians with some expertise in the areas covered by the act were in a better position to assist in contextualizing the new material than were government historians employed by the various affected agencies. We have thus not written as government historians—three of us continue to hold university appointments—but rather as independent scholars. We requested and received the freedom to select our own topics and to adopt our own interpretations. We did not think we could credibly present our versions of history unless we had intellectual independence.

The original version of our report was published in limited circulation by the National Archives Trust Fund. Cambridge University Press recognized that the authors' expertise served as the basis for a study of U.S. intelligence and the Nazis; private publication might reinforce the point that this work is *not* an official history, based on sources inaccessible to others. Anonymous peer reviewers for Cambridge were kind enough to suggest that our work might have some continuing value. (The Cambridge work was not initiated or sponsored by the IWG.) This expanded book contains a rewritten introduction, a new conclusion, and minor corrections in chapters and notes.

We would like to acknowledge all those who made both versions of this work possible. The IWG consisted (as of this writing, it still consists) of seven high-level government agency representatives and three "public" members, appointed by President Clinton and continuing under President Bush. The public members—Thomas Baer, Richard Ben-Veniste, and Elizabeth Holtzman—were particularly generous with their time and their suggestions for improvements in our work. The first chair of the IWG, Michael Kurtz, helped the historians establish the preconditions for successful independent scholarly work. His successor, Steven Garfinkel, drew upon his decades of experience with the process of declassification to help the historians gain access to the agency records they needed. IWG executive director Larry Taylor helped get resources and solve problems. Kristine Rusch edited the manuscript superbly and ironed out differences among the authors. The National Archives and Records Administration supplied a staff of able archivists to the IWG—staff director Dave van Tassel, William Cunliffe, Dick Myers, and for a time, Greg Bradsher and Steve Hamilton. Without these outstanding archivists our work would not have been possible.

Gerhard L. Weinberg chaired a group of distinguished outside experts (Historical Advisory Panel) who supplied advice and specific comments to their colleagues. We are grateful to all of them—Rebecca Boehling, the late James Critchfield, Ed Drea, Carol Gluck, Peter Hayes, Robert Hanyok, Linda Goetz Holmes, Christopher Simpson, Barry White, and Ron Zweig—for their time, patience, and suggestions. Robert Hanyok also contributed his expertise on the topic of signals intelligence with a piece we included as an appendix.

Eli Rosenbaum, director of the Office of Special Investigations of the Department of Justice, generously allowed the authors to interview him and OSI staff historians. Their expertise was invaluable, even when we did not see the subject the same way.

Several researchers hired by the IWG—Paul Brown, Miriam Kleiman, Robert Skwirot, and Eric Van Slander—assisted us in finding and organizing records, and Paul Browne contributed a piece of one chapter. Brenda Jones made countless photocopies for us, allowing us to organize our materials.

At Cambridge University Press, Lewis Bateman showed great enthusiasm for this project and pushed it over the various obstacles. All of those listed have improved what we wrote; of course, we are responsible for what problems may remain.

Richard Breitman
Norman J. W. Goda

N
W — E
S

Circular
Watertower

Angerburg

World-War
Russo-German
Cemetary, marked
by large wooden
cross.

Ski-jump

300 m

Bath-house

200 m

Restaurant
"Jägerhöhe"

Schwanzeit-see

300 m

Headquarters
O.K.W.

Foreign
Office

"Steinort"
Ribbedrop
not
Gross-
Steinort)

Barracks

Angerburg

Harschen

6-9 km

Numeiten (indicated
on good map)
Farm-house
for visitors
(eg. Ritter)

R.R. sidings with trains of Goering,
Himmler, and Foreign Office, latter
reffered to as "Westfalen".

Nearest anti aircraft is at Angerburg.

At great personal risk, Fritz Kolbe (code named "George Wood"), a German Foreign Office official, provided Allen Dulles, the OSS operative in Bern, with critical wartime information on the military, intelligence, economic, and political affairs of both Gemany and Japan. He also gave Dulles documentary evidence regarding the persecution of Jews in Hungary and Italy.

At an August 1943 meeting with Dulles, Kolbe drew a map (see previous page) showing Hitler's headquarters at Rastenburg (the "Wolf's Lair"); Ribbentrop's residence nearby; the Wehrmacht headquarters; and siding tracks for Himmler's, Göring's, and Ribbentrop's special trains. In September, Kolbe provided Dulles with a printed map (above), on which he identified the location of the Wolf's Lair with an X. Together, these two items provided concrete information for possible Allied operations. These maps, released under the Nazi War Crimes Disclosure Act of 1998, are in NA, RG 226, entry 190C, folder 19, box 1.

U.S. INTELLIGENCE
AND THE NAZIS

Introduction

⟫◆⟪

NEARLY SIXTY YEARS after World War II, the American public and media continue to investigate parts of its legacy—troubling questions of conscience and history. Who knew what about the Holocaust, and when? Was it possible for the Allies to rescue some Jews from the Holocaust, or was that notion a myth, as one scholar recently put it?[1] Some U.S. businesses collaborated with the Nazi state before and during World War II. What was the extent of these activities, and what was the result? What happened after the war to those who had perpetrated wartime atrocities?

In the 1980s Josef Mengele, whose name has become a symbol of the evil of Auschwitz, became the object of an international manhunt, even though, as it turned out, he had died in Brazil shortly before then. Like the Mengele case, the French trial of Klaus Barbie, the "Butcher of Lyon," raised questions long after the war about how some Nazi war criminals managed to escape postwar justice. U.S. Army intelligence had used and protected Barbie, a known Nazi war criminal, in return for assistance in the Cold War. Under what circumstances were other Nazi war criminals used directly or indirectly by U.S. intelligence agencies after the war?

All these questions remain pertinent for various reasons—not just for those who are fixated with the past. Genocide and "ethnic cleansing" are still part of human existence. In the current struggle against terrorism, the notion of recruiting intelligence assets from among previous foes remains a powerful urge. Can we learn practical lessons from World War II experiences?

Launching a wave of destruction that threatened Western civilization, Nazi Germany sought to annihilate its self-defined racial enemies physically and culturally, eradicating their presence from Europe and from history itself. Leading Nazi officials feared that "weaker" contemporaries and subsequent generations might not understand the "necessity" of their actions, so they tried to conceal their genocidal policies as well as the corpses of many of their victims.

Nevertheless, many of Nazi Germany's secrets leaked. Underground organizations, intelligence officials of governments-in-exile, and some anti-Nazi

Germans all supplied important information about Germany to Britain and the United States during World War II. Britain and the United States also developed their intelligence channels to get at the innermost secrets of the Nazi regime. Allied intelligence organizations made unprecedented efforts during the war to learn about their German intelligence rivals, believing that such knowledge would help them win the war more quickly. After the war, they continued to gather such intelligence, hoping to prevent the resurgence of a Nazi threat in Allied-occupied Germany. All these intelligence-related documents represented a storehouse of valuable historical information.

Yet World War II scholars and students of postwar intelligence have long found it difficult to use this information effectively. Although many millions of pages of intelligence compiled by agencies of the U.S. government were previously declassified and made available in the National Archives, specific categories of this intelligence information were withheld or withdrawn from public view, rendering American intelligence information fragmentary and at times opaque.

Some of the best intelligence about Nazi policies and activities acquired by the U.S. government during World War II, for example, came from foreign sources, especially from Great Britain. But to maintain good relations with foreign governments and organizations, information supplied by foreign governments was automatically excluded from regular declassification practices and was exempted even under the Freedom of Information Act. Intelligence "sources and methods" was another privileged category, and the details related to these issues were blacked out (redacted) or entirely withheld. Existing laws also allowed certain World War II–era information to remain classified for national security and privacy considerations. Relevant information about the activities of Nazis or Nazi collaborators after World War II was inaccessible for other reasons. The act of revealing sources cuts against the grain of what intelligence services do.

Spurred by Senator Michael DeWine of Ohio and Congresswoman Caroline Maloney of New York, in 1998 Congress passed the Nazi War Crimes Disclosure Act. Designed to address moral and historical imperatives, this law obliged the CIA, the U.S. Army, and the FBI to declassify operational information on their recruitment among Nazi and collaborationist veterans in the early Cold War. It also created a new organization, the Nazi War Criminal and Imperial Japanese Records Interagency Working Group (IWG), to implement and oversee a declassification effort that turned out to be the largest targeted declassification in American history.

The volume of documents declassified under the Nazi War Crimes Disclosure Act (an estimated 8 million pages) proved too large for us to examine all of them. But acting as historical consultants to the IWG, we have looked closely at hundreds of thousands of pages of recently opened records of the Office of Strategic Services (OSS)—the ancestor of the CIA—and at a good portion of an even larger collection of new FBI records.[2] We have drawn more selectively upon very large collections of new U.S. Army Intelligence records and State

Department records. We have used an unprecedented collection of documents from the CIA. Finally, we were able to work with small but important collections from the National Security Agency and some other agencies such as the Office of Naval Intelligence.

At times our research strategy was determined or influenced by external constraints, such as which records had been located and which collections or files had been delivered to the National Archives or declassified up to that time. We began with a sense that we should write about new and significant findings. Of course, our ability to recognize new and significant documents in a vast pipeline of records depended in part upon our previous knowledge. Different researchers might well have found and selected different subjects. Over time we looked to broaden our initial selection of topics.

In this book we have tried to demonstrate that newly declassified documents, particularly when combined with previously available documents, allow us to add to, or even revise, our understanding of certain aspects of the Holocaust, of the looting of assets by Nazi Germany and its allies, and of perpetrators of war crimes or acts of persecution. Unlike many other studies of World War II–era intelligence,[3] we concentrate not on military intelligence, but on political intelligence: not on what made the greatest difference at the time, but often what slipped by and in retrospect seems more important than contemporaries recognized.

We have begun to describe how Allied intelligence organizations reacted to the Holocaust and other war crimes during and soon after the war. We also examine the activities and interactions of intelligence organizations from five Allied or pro-Western governments or communities: the Polish government-in-exile, the Jewish Agency for Palestine, the United States, Great Britain, and West Germany.

The Polish underground gathered information about the vast array of Nazi crimes and murders in Polish territory, including the extermination of millions of Jews in special camps equipped with gas chambers and crematoria. This information reached the Polish government-in-exile in London, and much of it was passed to Britain and the United States. Although they had all the evidence in front of them, Polish government officials did not sufficiently recognize the distinctions Nazi Germany made between Poles and Jews. For the Nazis, the Jews were the prime enemy—the moving force behind most opposition to Germany— which justified an extraordinary effort to eradicate them across Europe. The Polish government-in-exile highlighted the persecution of Poles.[4] Nonetheless, they recognized the inherently murderous character of Nazi rule and supplied much detailed evidence to Britain and the United States.

The Jewish Agency for Palestine understood Nazi goals and tried, under terrible constraints during the war, to counteract them in limited ways. Kept at arm's length by the Western Allies, the Jewish Agency had neither the resources nor the legitimacy of a government. But it, too, gathered intelligence about Nazi Germany and tried to arrange the escape or rescue of some remnants of Jewish communities in Axis Europe, tasks it saw as directly related. Other Jewish organizations—the Bund, the World Jewish Congress, the Joint Distribution Committee, and Agudas Israel—also carried out rescue and relief efforts and ran into similar problems. Their activities forced them to have contacts with some Nazi officials, and these contacts created or increased some Allied suspicions about their loyalty to the Allied cause.

Much remains to be learned about the wartime reactions of American and British intelligence agencies to the Holocaust. The raw evidence is now available for systematic study of OSS, the FBI, and various American military intelligence organizations. Evidence presented here suggests that some American intelligence officials understood Nazi goals and methods for Jews and other persecuted groups, but others clearly did not. Unlike the Jewish Agency, American intelligence agencies did not view World War II and the Holocaust as closely related. Although American intelligence organizations gathered information about a vast range of conditions in Nazi territories, in satellite countries, and even in neutral countries, there are relatively few signs of special intelligence efforts to secure information about the fate of Jews in occupied Europe until President Roosevelt established the War Refugee Board in January 1944. There was more attention to gathering evidence about the perpetrators of what were called atrocities or war crimes (later to be called crimes against humanity), but a great deal of information about what we have come to call the Holocaust came in from other places or was accumulated incidentally—it came in with other matters considered more significant to the war effort.

Since Nazi Germany's policies of genocide, exploitation, and looting were central elements of the regime, some may judge in retrospect that there was at least a partial intelligence failure—a failure to grasp one of the central political goals of the enemy. And, given the range of evidence about specific elements of the Holocaust presented below, it seems that this failure had less to do with collecting information than with recognizing its significance.

On the other hand, American and British intelligence scrutinized their intelligence rivals in Nazi Germany and in the process turned up incriminating evidence about a range of German intelligence organizations and officials. New evidence we have drawn upon here, when combined with previously known documents, indicates that German intelligence organizations, particularly the foreign intelligence branch of the SS Security Service (*Sicherheitsdienst* or SD), were very much part of the Nazi apparatus of persecution and extermination. The ideological conformity required by Hitler and his key subordinates forged a cooperative effort among the SS, the police, and German intelligence organizations that is visible today through detailed historical research. To loyal Nazi intelligence officials, gathering information for the war was directly related to helping Hitler to eliminate what he considered his most dangerous enemy—the Jews.

The central German military intelligence organization known as the Abwehr, subordinate to the High Command of the Armed Forces, certainly contained numerous individuals of conscience—even some leading figures of the anti-Nazi resistance. But the Abwehr as an organization could hardly escape the constraints or the criminality of the Nazi regime. The valiant individuals who resisted at best won small victories. We have gone to some length to describe new evidence about Nazi intelligence organizations because it casts light upon the connections between intelligence gathering and Nazi Germany's war against the Jews.

After the end of World War II, thousands of war criminals were prosecuted in different countries. Thousands of others escaped prosecution for reasons that had little or nothing to do with American postwar policies. But a good number of former German intelligence personnel, some of them members of criminal organizations such as the SS or the Gestapo, had special advantages.

The Army Counterintelligence Corps (which was the largest American intelligence organization in the immediate postwar period), the CIA, and the American-sponsored organization under General Reinhard Gehlen that became the basis of the West German Secret Service found it desirable to make postwar intelligence use of a substantial number—at least some dozens—of their former intelligence or police enemies. The notion that they employed only a few "bad apples" will not stand up to the new documentation.

Some American intelligence officials could not or did not want to see how many German intelligence officials, SS officers, police, or non-German collaborators with the Nazis were compromised or incriminated by their past service. Many of those with dubious pasts were eager to sell their knowledge and their services. A good number convinced some Western government and intelligence officials that they could be useful, often against a growing Communist threat. Once they had secured a foothold in postwar Europe, they generally found protection against criminal prosecution, which by the late 1940s was winding down. Others, unable or unwilling to succeed in the new Europe, unreconstructed Nazis or Nazi allies notorious for their crimes, found protection only in South America or the Middle East.

Hindsight allows us to see that American use of actual or alleged war criminals was a blunder in several respects. Granted, some intelligence activities involve a degree of secrecy and messiness which strain conventional moral standards, but there was no compelling reason to begin the postwar era with the assistance of some of those associated with the worst crimes of the war. Lack of sufficient attention to history—and on a personal level, to character and morality—established a bad precedent, especially for new intelligence agencies. It also brought into intelligence organizations men and women previously incapable of distinguishing between their political/ideological beliefs and reality. As a result, they could not and did not deliver good intelligence. Finally, because their new "democratic convictions" were at best insecure and their pasts could be used against them, some could be blackmailed by Communist intelligence agencies. Thus they represented a potential security problem. The new Communist enemy (against whom they were supposed to be useful) could and in some cases did recruit them as double agents. The extent of this security problem did not become evident to American and West German intelligence until the 1960s.

Perhaps we still need to ponder this chapter in history. At a time when there is renewed emphasis on the need for recruiting agents and informants among the enemies of the United States, the lesson of the postwar intelligence use of former Nazis and collaborationist officials is that it is better not to have some kinds of assistance.

We also need to learn from what we did not find—and we have made some effort to do this in our chapters. Some claims about vast conspiracies involving the American government and Nazi war criminals or the intelligence use of some big-name Nazis in the postwar period turned out to be completely unfounded. The hiring of Nazi criminals, for the most part, occurred on an ad hoc basis, rather than by grand design. And legends and concoctions about certain high-level criminals such as Heinrich Müller, head of the Gestapo, whose fate remained obscure at the end of the war, flourished best in a climate of suspicion and secrecy. The opening of OSS, CIA, and FBI records on Müller will not sway those determined to believe in conspiracy theories, but they should convince those who are willing to base conclusions on the evidence.

Can we learn from history? Some people are optimists, others not. But in a sense we have no choice but to make use of the past. The limitations of our knowledge and the complexity of our problems mean that we inevitably borrow from past experience—individual and collective—in efforts to understand and choose among our options. Is Saddam Hussein another Hitler? Was the Baath regime like the Nazi regime? Can Iraq become a democracy as West Germany did? We cannot begin to answer such explicit or implied questions soundly unless we understand the past in some depth. The real question is not whether we will make use of our past to deal with the present, but rather how well we will do so. To do it well, we need all the documents, particularly the kinds declassified by the IWG.

This work is neither an official history nor an exclusive one. All the documents used here are available to other researchers. We have done our best to give careful citations in our notes—which, for a time, will serve others as entrée into new collections. Those willing to carry out archival research will undoubtedly make their own discoveries in these declassified documents and in related records at the National Archives. The importance of the newly declassified records can best be measured after years of archival research by a wide community of researchers and writers.

Notes

1. William D. Rubenstein, *The Myth of Rescue: Why the Democracies Could Not Have Saved More Jews from the Nazis* (London: Routledge, 1997).

2. All documents cited in National Archives, Record Group 226, entries 210–219, were declassified under the Nazi War Crimes Disclosure Act. We have also mentioned in the text the declassification of some significant documents in other entries of RG 226.

3. Among which the largest and most famous is probably F. H. Hinsley et al., *British Intelligence in the Second World War*, published by Cambridge University Press.

4. David Engel, *In the Shadow of Auschwitz: The Polish Government-in-Exile and the Jews, 1939–1942* (Chapel Hill: University of North Carolina Press, 1987) and *Facing a Holocaust: The Polish Government-in-Exile and the Jews, 1943–1945* (Chapel Hill: University of North Carolina Press, 1993).

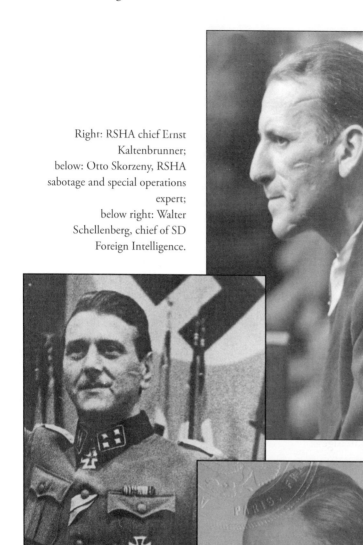

Right: RSHA chief Ernst Kaltenbrunner; below: Otto Skorzeny, RSHA sabotage and special operations expert; below right: Walter Schellenberg, chief of SD Foreign Intelligence.

1

OSS Knowledge of the Holocaust

Richard Breitman
with Norman J. W. Goda

INFORMATION ABOUT NAZI SHOOTINGS of Jews started to leak out shortly after they began during World War II. At first, however, U.S. media coverage indicated that large numbers of people in different Nazi-occupied countries were suffering terribly, and there was little distinction between the fate of Jews and that of other groups. In any case, the military situation and the fate of friends and relatives on the battlefronts were the central collective concerns in the United States. The Allies seemed to be struggling to cope with one Axis conquest after another in the early phases of the war. Given this focus, many Americans did not recognize what we have come to call the Holocaust even after an Allied statement in December 1942 that Nazi Germany was carrying out a policy of mass extermination of Jews.

Did American intelligence officials know more, or know earlier? The small office of the Coordinator of Information (COI), and its successor, the new Office of Strategic Services (OSS), both headed by General William J. Donovan, attempted to capture as much information as possible about Nazi Germany, particularly about its military, economic, or sociopolitical weaknesses. As a by-product, the COI and OSS accumulated substantial intelligence about Nazi measures against Jews.

In memoirs and other retrospective accounts, however, a number of former OSS officials have disclaimed recognition of the Holocaust at the time. For example, William J. Casey, stationed in the OSS London office from October 1943 on (and later director of the CIA in the Reagan administration), commented in his memoirs:

I'll never understand how, with all we knew about Germany and its military machine, we knew so little about the concentration camps and the magnitude of the Holocaust. We knew in a general way that Jews were being persecuted, that they were being rounded up in occupied countries, and deported to Germany, that they were brought to camps, and that brutality and murder took place at these camps. But few if any comprehended the appalling magnitude of it. It wasn't sufficiently real to stand out from the general brutality and slaughter which is war. There was little talk in London about the concentration camps except as places to which captured agents and resistants were deported if they were not executed on the spot. And such reports as we did receive were shunted aside because of the official policy in Washington and London to concentrate exclusively on the defeat of the enemy.[1]

Casey's last comment suggests that lack of awareness of the Holocaust went beyond the OSS and into the upper ranks of the American and British governments.

Arnold Price fled Nazi Germany during the 1930s and landed in the Research and Analysis (R&A) branch of the OSS in 1942, where, among other things, he gathered biographical information about influential Germans. Price recalled:

We remained ignorant of the Holocaust. Yes, I saw our map of Nazi concentration camps, but none was identified as a death camp. We received no real information on the "final solution." I am surprised that I did not give it any thought as I had early on always believed that the Nazis were out to do away with the Jews.[2]

Price's "we" referred to himself and his colleagues in R&A.

Another OSS R&A man, Arthur Schlesinger, Jr., later became an eminent figure in government and the academy. He recalled:

I have asked myself and I have asked R&A colleagues when any of us first became aware of a policy of mass murder as something qualitatively different from the well-recognized viciousness of the concentration camps. OSS presumably received the best possible intelligence, and German-Jewish refugees would have been the last people inclined to ignore or discount reports of a Final Solution.

Yet my recollection is that, even in the summer of 1944 as we received with horror the mounting flow of information about the camps, most of us were still thinking of an increase of persecution rather than a new and barbaric policy of genocide . . . I cannot find R&A colleagues who recall a moment of blazing revelation about the Final Solution.[3]

All three OSS men describe a common pattern of being unaware of genocide, but Price and Schlesinger cautiously limit it to the Research and Analysis branch.

Scholarly studies about the OSS and the Holocaust have revealed that two young American Jews working in OSS Research and Analysis—Abraham Duker and Charles Irving Dwork—not only recognized the Holocaust as it was happening, but also tried to gather systematic information about it. What later became known as the Duker-Dwork collection in the United States National Archives represents probably the largest single cluster of OSS information about the Holocaust. But Duker and Dwork represented the exceptions that proved the rule. They were upset that more senior officials in Research and Analysis did not give sufficient weight to Nazi genocide—or even recognize it for what it was. Few, if any, of those in R&A had the clearance to gain access to the most highly classified OSS documents. Duker and Dwork had to search for documents about the fate of Jews from other sections of the OSS and from outside the agency.[4]

With few exceptions, OSS R&A documents have been declassified for some time—the majority for more than five decades. OSS documents recently declassified under the Nazi War Crimes Disclosure Act of 1998 and other records from the Secret Intelligence branch and field offices abroad supply more specific information about the Holocaust. They do not indicate what the mythical "average" OSS official in Washington knew about the Holocaust. In this sense, the evidence presented here does not contradict the recollections of Casey, Price, Schlesinger, or others. But it adds to our knowledge of how and when top-secret information leaked out of Nazi Germany and provides additional detail about particular events, sites, and perpetrators. These documents represent another perspective on how much information about the Holocaust was available to some American intelligence officials who were in the right place geographically and organizationally. Initially, the right place was New York, partly because of a British connection there. But the British effort to gain access to foreign diplomatic reports began elsewhere.

The Diplomatic Pouches

A recent biography of the now notorious Anthony Blunt, wartime official in MI-5 (the British equivalent of the FBI) and Soviet spy, discloses that Blunt and others figured out ways to gain access to sealed diplomatic pouches of neutral diplomats stationed in Britain:

> At ports, the couriers would be persuaded to hand their bags over to Port Security, who would put them into a safe. "Blunt's people would open the back of the safe," a colleague recalled, and take out the bags and examine them. At airports, flights would be "delayed," and the couriers once again would be persuaded to hand over their bags for "security," "giving him time for his cronies to open the bags, open the envelopes, read everything in them, photograph some of them if need be, and put it all back so nobody would know a thing." Blunt's department collaborated with the post office to develop special methods for opening the seals on the bags and repairing them without trace.

Blunt found that MI-6 (British secret intelligence service) was also collecting its own information from foreign embassies abroad, presumably by similar means.[5]

In his memoirs, MI-6 agent H. Montgomery Hyde discussed some isolated British successes at opening diplomatic pouches at the Gibraltar station, and he alluded to ways of temporarily separating a diplomatic courier from his pouch and photographing the contents at censorship stations in Bermuda and the

Caribbean. The FBI, he said, put such methods into practice after he suggested them.[6] Perhaps so: FBI records do contain some copies of foreign diplomatic reports sent across the Atlantic, but they contain markings indicating that they were of British origin.[7] In any case, OSS records contain a very large quantity of foreign diplomatic despatches sent across the Atlantic. Most of them indicate that they were obtained from a "most secret" source, which is a British designation. A number of them specifically state that they were given to the British Security Coordination Office in New York, and went from there to the OSS.[8]

A batch of these British-copied diplomatic despatches arrived before the United States formally entered the war—an indicator of the friendly British-American intelligence relationship. Because some British intelligence officials, especially William Stephenson, were heavily invested in making the COI work,[9] the COI may have been the first and preferred recipient of this type of prized British diplomatic intelligence.

Sometimes the prize was dubious. Diplomats stationed in Germany and other European posts during World War II varied widely in ability, political orientation, and access to inside information. Many diplomatic reports were partially or wholly inaccurate. It is usually difficult to discern whether even the better despatches had any impact at the time. But at least they were copied, translated, and distributed to a few officials who might have had official interest.

Some largely accurate information about the Holocaust can be gleaned from those diplomatic reports that came into British and then American hands. For example, in late August 1941, the Mexican minister to Portugal, J. M. Alvarez del Castillo, drew extensively from an Italian newspaper report (in the *Giornale d'Italia*) about German behavior in Russia following the German invasion, as follows:

> Almost every morning in the Russian cities occupied by Axis troops, men and women are shot by military squads for the commission of acts of sabotage during the previous night.
>
> These mass assassinations of innocent and defenceless men and women (especially the latter) in Russia, on the trivial pretext that they have committed sabotage, shows the moral, or amoral, state of the Reich.

This report seems to have been derived from Italian observers at the front, who may not have recognized that SS and police units did far more such killing than the regular army. The general thrust of the story was accurate nonetheless.

After describing the German Blitzkrieg in the East and commenting that Germany did not seem to be making quick enough progress to win a decisive victory, Alvarez returned to his moral concerns:

> In the occupied countries the tragic number of victims who—on the pretext that they have carried on communist propaganda, that they belong to the Jewish

race, or that they have committed acts of sabotage—are inhumanly sacrificed, grows incessantly. These are the patriots of the nations that are suffering German oppression, who are guilty of nothing more than being arbitrarily considered as suspect by the occupying authorities. By these methods of classic criminality Nazism is rapidly bringing upon itself humanity's repudiation of its doctrine, its philosophy and its morals . . .[10]

Alvarez's open condemnation of Nazi killings shows that intelligent contemporaries could see through pretexts and rationalizations to the essence of Nazi policy and methods.

Gonzalo Montt Rivas

The Chilean consul in Prague, Gonzalo Montt Rivas, was closer to the ghettos and killing sites in the East and had even better sources of inside information. Montt unwittingly became a repeated supplier of information to British and American intelligence about Nazi measures against Jews. Ideologically and politically, Montt was diametrically opposed to Alvarez: Nazi Germany could not have found a better South American advocate of its anti-Jewish policy.

In 1940 Germany requested the closure of Chilean consulates in Paris, Brussels, the Hague, Copenhagen, and Prague. (After the German annexation of Bohemia and Moravia in March 1939, Prague was no longer capital of a country.) The Chilean consul general in Hamburg, Eugenio Palacios Bate, took charge of the work of the closed consulates, but in 1941 he was able to reopen the consulate in Prague. It appears that Nazi attitudes toward Chile transcended diplomatic neutrality—they were characterized as friendly—and the former Chilean consul in Prague, Montt, was able to resume his post in spite of the fact that all other foreign diplomats had been forced to leave.[11]

Montt was a forty-eight-year-old career diplomat who had previously served in Bolivia, Brazil, Paraguay, Uruguay, Britain, and the United States. He also fought in the Paraguayan army during the Chaco War and was awarded a decoration. He went on to have a very successful career after the war, serving as the Chilean delegate to the United Nations and ambassador to Egypt.[12] His activities during the Nazi era have never been studied.

Montt's reports from Prague, most of which are newly declassified, reveal considerable access to the thinking of Nazi officials. In June 1941 he quoted passages from a lecture given by Karl Hermann Frank, the number-two Nazi official in the Protectorate (Bohemia-Moravia): "The Reich has once again manifested its firm intention . . . of Germanizing all territories within its 'living space.' And experience has shown that the only practical means of achieving this object is to eliminate the native inhabitants, replacing them with its own co-nationals."[13] In September 1941, Montt reported the establishment of the Warsaw ghetto and forecast a similar solution for Jews in the Protectorate. He traced a host of new restrictions forced upon Czech Jews and characterized these restrictions as returning Jews to their status of several centuries earlier. He found it unsurprising that Germany had taken such steps: the "Jewish element" in Britain, the United States, and Russia had launched the war against Germany, hoping to destroy the Christian world, annihilate gentiles, and achieve world domination. Only then would their Messiah come.[14] One could hardly distinguish Montt's beliefs from the Nazi worldview.

On November 1, 1941, Montt accurately reported intensified Nazi evacuations of Jews from the Protectorate and Germany itself to Lodz and other ghettos in the General Government (the Nazi administrative unit for about two-thirds of Poland). All Jews from Luxembourg had already been transferred east; that country was now "free from Semites." Montt added,

> I always draw your attention to these Jewish questions as I have the impression that the [Nazi] intention is to get rid of the Jews at all costs, and one way would be by sending them to our countries, which I hope and trust our Government will not permit, and which our people would not tolerate, as [the Jews] are useless for agricultural or mining work, which is what should be increased in our Hemisphere . . . They are all propagators of communism, bolshevism and other physical and moral vices.[15]

Montt noted other brutal Nazi policies. In mid-November, he reported various executions of Czechs accused of subversive activities: Reich authorities were "determined to drown in blood every attempt, every plot, and every act or word, which threatens the security of the Great[er] Germany . . ." To Montt, Germany was determined to Germanize the Protectorate, and, unfortunately for the Czechs, they fell within Germany's political orbit. He continued, "The history of the whole of Europe is made up of struggles of this kind. Some races disappear, being absorbed or destroyed by others more numerous, stronger, more intelligent, or possibly more fortunate."[16] Montt seemed to have little sympathy for the people and the country to which he was originally sent.

In late November 1941, Montt sent word to the Foreign Ministry about local German press coverage of a recent agreement among Chile, Uruguay, Paraguay, Brazil, and Bolivia not to accept illegal Jewish immigrants. If Jews had not received proper exit visas from their country of origin, they would not be allowed in. Montt added a warning about recent Jewish efforts to obtain Chilean visas from the consulate in Prague. Some of these Jews had claimed that their relatives or acquaintances in Santiago had succeeded in getting the Foreign Ministry to authorize visas for them. As far as he was concerned, however, even a "baptized" Jew remained a Jew: "Baptismal water can cleanse original sin, but not the filth accumulated during centuries in ghettos everywhere."[17]

Montt's most revealing despatch came when Nazi Germany targeted Jews who had already left German territories. According to the Eleventh Decree to the Reich Citizenship Law announced and published on November 25, 1941, Jews living abroad could no longer be German subjects, and all remaining assets of German Jews residing abroad automatically and immediately were forfeited to the Reich. Expropriation, more than denaturalization, was the goal of this measure.[18]

A day *before* the Eleventh Decree was issued, on November 24, 1941, Montt translated a portion of it for the benefit of his government. "The Jew [residing abroad] loses German nationality immediately . . . The fortune which the Reich obtains in this manner will serve to solve the questions in connection with Jews . . ." He then quoted a portion of another recent order in the Reich Protectorate of Bohemia-Moravia, barring unauthorized transfer or sale of property by Jews after October 10.[19]

These two specific regulations moved Montt to summarize Nazi policy in general:

> The Jewish problem is being partially solved in the Protectorate, as it has been decided to eradicate all the Jews and send some to Poland and others to the town of Terezin, whilst looking for a more remote place. . . .
>
> The German triumph [in the war] will leave Europe freed of Semites. Those [Jews] who escape with their lives from this trial will certainly be deported to Siberia, where they will not have much opportunity to make use of their financial capabilities.
>
> In proportion to the U.S.A. increasing its attacks on the Reich, Germany will expedite the destruction of Semitism, as she accuses international Judaism of all the calamities which have befallen the world.
>
> The exodus of the Jews from the Reich has not had the results prophesied by the enemies of Germany: on the contrary: they have been replaced by Aryans with obvious advantage to everything and in everything, except in the usury line in which they are past masters.[20]

Although lacking details of most of the logistics of the Final Solution, in his last paragraphs this Chilean diplomat managed to capture the gist of Nazi goals on the Jewish question. Two months before the Wannsee Conference, he was able to forecast the Nazi destruction of "Semitism," the clearing of Jews from Europe. Montt did not perceive broad Nazi objectives to be vague rhetoric or metaphor— a conclusion reinforced by his reference to Jews who escaped with their lives to Siberia. Nazi Germany was pursuing a policy of genocide.

Montt's report of Nazi objectives was so plain that his comment about Nazi reactions to American criticism seems a little askew. Nazi Germany would hardly adopt a policy of extermination simply as a result of American hostility toward Germany. On the other hand, it might blame the United States for its need to resort to the harshest measures, and it might possibly accelerate the timing of killing measures intended in any case.

Montt's statement that Terezin (Theresienstadt) would serve as a temporary collection site for Czech Jews showed knowledge of specific plans first discussed

SECRET

R/5114

FROM: RIVAS G. MONTT,   TO: MINISTER FOR FOREIGN AFFAIRS,
      CHILIAN CONSUL,   SANTIAGO, CHILE
      PRAGUE

DATE: Sept.6th, 1941 (Spanish)

ANTI-JEWISH MEASURES IN WARSAW AND PRAGUE

"In WARSAW the Jews have been concentrated in a single quarter of the city, that is to say, there has been a return to the mediaeval 'ghetto'. This Jewish city within the Polish capital has some 500,000 inhabitants; 40% of them work as artisans, shoemakers, cabinet-makers, tailors and mechanics. The German authorities supplied many of them with the means of setting up their workshops.

"The example of WARSAW shows that some solution can be found for this aspect of the Jewish problem. There is no reason why similar action should not be taken in the Protectorate. What has been done so far is incomplete: the Jews are forbidden to go to cinemas and cafés .. but they always manage to evade these regulations, and carry on dishonest trading (black markets of all kinds); they also spread fantastic lies about the REICH and provoke the Aryans by their arrogance. A search of the houses and apartments occupied by Jewish families shows that these PRAGUE Hebrews, far from suffering in any way from the war, had managed to get hold of large quantities of foodstuffs, preserves, clothing, shoes, etc.

"The time has therefore come to put a stop to such behaviour. The Jews are now forbidden to enter public and private libraries; the reproduction in any form of music by Jewish composers is prohibited; punishment for infringement of the regulations is a maximum fine of 5000 Kr. and 15 days' imprisonment. All typewriters owned by Jews must be registered. They must also register their furs. This last measure is no doubt due to the intention to requisition all skins, which are required to line the coats of the German soldiers fighting in RUSSIA.

"Henceforth the PROTECTORATE Jews will have to wear a yellow star over the left breast and will not be allowed to go about in PRAGUE or the interior without police permission.

"....The Jews are returning to the position in which they found themselves centuries ago. It is not to be wondered at that the REICH is taking these measures against the Israelites, seeing that it is in reality the dominant Jewish element in GREAT BRITAIN, U.S.A. and RUSSIA which brought about this war against GERMANY; when the Christian element has been destroyed and the 'Gentiles' have been annihilated, the Jews hope that their expected Messiah will come, to make the 'chosen people' the rulers of the world."

B.6.11.41   London (2) New York (2) Trinidad (1) Jamaica (1)
MF   G.F. CZECHOSLOVAKIA

11/1/00 SP 12LK15s   6389

Report from Gonzalo Montt Rivas, the Chilean consul in Prague, to the Minister of Foreign Affairs, intercepted and translated by the British and passed on to U.S. authorities [NA, RG 65, 62-65008-24-1-(1–100), boxes 26–27, folder–Secret Intercepts-South America].

among high Reich Security Main Office (RSHA) officials in Prague on October 10. Reinhard Heydrich, head of the RSHA, had spoken at a press conference that same day, releasing selected information about the Jewish question to sympathetic journalists.[21]

While Hitler was secluded at his East Prussian headquarters during much of the summer and fall of 1941, and Himmler was either at his own headquarters nearby or touring sites near the front where his SS and police were in action,[22] Heydrich went to Prague. Hitler appointed him as Reich Protector of Bohemia-Moravia on September 27. From that point on, Heydrich operated not only as Himmler's key subordinate on Jewish matters, but also as an independent authority in the Protectorate. He reported some matters directly to Martin Bormann in order to inform Hitler, and he had at least one private meeting with Hitler (on October 25), at which he apparently gave a presentation.[23] During this time, Hitler continually ranted about removing the "Jewish menace" in the Protectorate and elsewhere.[24] Himmler also explained to Slovakian government officials that he wished to help them solve the Jewish problem.[25] Heydrich was well versed in what was expected, and he was in control of operations in at least one key region.

The various despatches from Montt in Prague to the Foreign Ministry in Santiago, Chile, were misread in one respect—Montt's name was frequently garbled. Although at least one of Montt's despatches has his name typed at the bottom,[26] most have only a signature—really a barely legible scrawl. If one knows that Gonzalo Montt was the consul in Prague, one can make the signature out—with difficulty. It is invariably *G. Montt*, with the *G* resembling an *E* and the last *t* appearing uncrossed.

Many of the British intelligence translations of Montt's despatches given to COI simply do not name the Chilean diplomat—they give only his post—but there are some exceptions. A British report of September 13, 1941, passing along the Chilean despatch of June 24, 1941, gave the Chilean the name E. Morin.[27] A British report of February 4, 1942, summarizing the Chilean despatch of November 15, 1941, listed him as E. C. Conti.[28] The signature actually looks more like E. C. Conti than like Montt, but no one with the name Conti ever served as a Chilean diplomat.[29] The man in Prague was always the same: Montt.

The errors in reading the signature confirm that British intelligence got access to Montt's actual paper despatches. Radio messages would have given the name—in code, to be sure—but even garbled British decoding would have produced a more consistent version of Montt's name.

Montt's November 24, 1941, despatch came to the West in early 1942 (the United States received a copy from the British on March 20, 1942) very early in the flow of information about the Holocaust. A set of Chilean reports from Prague, Montt's among them, went from the British office in New York to David Bruce, who had just become head of the new Secret Intelligence branch of the Coordinator of Information.[30] Bruce apparently directed copies to those who might be interested in the contents. A handwritten note on the British/Chilean despatch of November

24 indicates that William Kimbel, an administrative assistant to director William J. Donovan, received a copy. No information has been found to suggest how Kimbel reacted—or whether he did anything else with this document. Nor is there anything to demonstrate that Donovan himself saw this information.

FBI copies of selected despatches from Montt were forwarded to Assistant Secretary of State Adolf Berle and Byron S. Huie, Jr., an intelligence analyst in the Board of Economic Warfare. Nelson Rockefeller, who headed the independent Coordinator of Inter-American Affairs, received a copy of at least the report about Jews being deported to the General Government.[31] The reasoning for sending it to Rockefeller seemed to be that Montt's fears of Jews trying to seek entry into Western Hemisphere countries might materialize; therefore, those in charge of Latin American policy should be informed about potential Nazi actions.

Some of the Chilean despatches about economic conditions in Bohemia-Moravia and the availability of food and raw materials were sent by Bruce to Secretary of the Treasury Henry Morgenthau, Jr.[32] Morgenthau, who was friendly with Donovan,[33] was perhaps the most prominent Jew in the Roosevelt administration and the one high government official who might have reacted vigorously and quickly to the report about Nazi policy toward the Jews. Ironically, he did not receive a copy of what is in retrospect Montt's most important despatch.

In Britain the Chilean report fit into a pattern of other completely reliable intelligence information about Nazi genocidal policy, and it may have strengthened British intelligence conclusions about Nazi policy toward Jews across the continent. In the United States, where there was less in the way of relevant and trustworthy intelligence information in early 1942, there is no sign that this Chilean report had an impact, beyond possibly reinforcing fears about an influx of Jewish refugees into the Western Hemisphere.

Despite Montt's clear articulation of the Reich's genocidal intentions, his November 24 despatch had limited impact upon Western governments at the time. It prompted no Western action to warn potential Jewish victims. Why would any British or American official pay particular attention to the views of an unknown Chilean diplomat in Prague, who adopted Nazi rhetoric so freely? Perhaps there was a gap between rhetoric and reality. In addition, for many Americans and Britons inside and outside of government, the central, overriding concern during 1939-1945 was the war itself—not the barbaric policies that accompanied it. No single document—no matter how powerful—could change the dominant perception within a new American intelligence organization that it had to concentrate on ways to help win the war.

Early OSS Sources

At its birth on June 13, 1942, the OSS consisted of a little more than eight hundred employees.[34] Some branches, such as Research and Analysis as well as Secret Intelligence and Special Operations, were carried over from the COI and then expanded; others had to be created. In mid-1942, the OSS did not yet have officials in key listening posts near Germany such as Switzerland and Sweden. It had to rely partly on outside assistance.

The COI had established the Oral Intelligence Unit in August 1941 in New York to collect first-hand information from refugees and others returning home from enemy territory.[35] A large number of individuals who experienced Nazi abuses during the 1930s managed to enter the United States by 1941. Their impressions of the country they had left and their accounts of their experiences provided not only unique details, but also general information of value to subsequent generations.[36] Some OSS interviews of these immigrants and refugees remained classified until recently, apparently because they listed the names of individuals and their interviewers.

In the period 1942–44, it was quite unusual for Jews to escape Nazi territory and make their way into the United States—or even to give detailed testimony to American officials abroad. But there are some interesting exceptions which produced good historical evidence. One case will have to suffice here.

Forty-nine-year-old Joseph Goldschmied had been a citizen of Czechoslovakia before the Nazis dismembered it. He was married to an American. The Swiss government arranged an exchange in which first his wife and son and then Goldschmied himself were extricated from danger in mid-1942. He left Prague twelve days after Heydrich was assassinated, then spent nearly a week in a police camp in Berlin. After a railway trip through France to Spain, he eventually sailed on the *Drottningholm*, one of the exchange ships crossing the Atlantic. Interviewed after his arrival in New York in July 1942, he dictated and wrote an extremely detailed, twenty-six-page, single-spaced picture of his experiences from the time Germany occupied Prague until his departure.

Goldschmied had worked for the Bohemian Union Bank in Prague. He gave a vivid account of the process of organized robbery that followed the German occupation, including the takeover of his bank by the Deutsche Bank. His report covered, among other things, Nazi repression after the assassination of Heydrich, the activities of the Czech resistance, illegal listening to foreign radio broadcasts, the attitudes of German soldiers in Prague, economic conditions and forced labor practices in the Protectorate of Bohemia-Moravia, conditions and attitudes in Berlin, and the behavior of the Gestapo.

Goldschmied went into greatest detail about Nazi measures against Czech Jews, and he was able to trace over time shifts in Nazi strategy—from expropriation and forced emigration measures to forced labor and deportations, and from deportations to annihilation. The report began with the claim that the SS and Gestapo had been entrusted with the task of annihilating the Jews. He ended as follows:

Of the 48,500 Jews still living in Prague before the occupation, approximately one half [were] deported [by] the day of my departure. Everything was carried through upon direct orders from Berlin, where they had had a good deal of practice before. From the small towns almost all Jews were deported, in Prague only those could remain who were married to an Aryan. Later transports went to Theresienstadt, a garrison about one hour from Prague . . . Later on Theresienstadt was used only as a transit place. After three days the Jews were sent on to Poland . . . Men and women were separated and many died of starvation. Reports coming in indirectly from Poland give heartbreaking details. If Hitler remains true to his program of destroying all European Jewry—he will have achieved that goal soon and most countries will be depleted of Jews.[37]

OSS interviewer Emmy Rado described him as intelligent, perceptive, and objective, in spite of what he had gone through. Goldschmied must have convinced Rado that he knew that Nazi Germany was carrying out Hitler's threat to destroy the Jewish people; she rated his lengthy account credible.

Additional information about the Holocaust came to the OSS around that time from a series of three letters or articles by an unidentified journalist, or possibly by an official of the Office of War Information. The author was in Lisbon in June 1942 and "on the German frontier"—probably Switzerland or Vichy France—in November 1942. These three letters were declassified well before the Nazi War Crimes Disclosure Act. Some historians have used them previously, considering them good sources, despite some inaccuracies and gaps.[38]

It is difficult to be precise about the origin of these letters because of their handling in the post-World War II period. Before they were sent to the National Archives, the author's and recipient's names were blacked out, and the documents were photocopied. The originals apparently no longer exist, so the redactions cannot be removed now.

The IWG has now declassified a large number of additional letters on a wide variety of topics. This related set of documents is scattered within a particular entry of OSS records. Although the unidentified authors and foreign locations vary, the additional letters, like the three discussed above, are virtually all addressed the same way: "Dear A——." The traces of a capital A are visible in the blacked-out name in some letters; a final n appears in others. In one case the censor (fortunately) slipped up entirely, and the name appears in its entirety: Allen.[39]

We deduce that Allen Dulles, while stationed in the COI's New York office, began the practice of soliciting detailed reports from journalists or other contacts who were stationed or traveling abroad. These background reports on conditions in locations throughout the world continued to flow into OSS New York even after Dulles went to Switzerland in November 1942 to head the OSS office there.[40] The three-part series of articles on the topic "Nazi extermination of Jews," addressed to Dulles, also went to OSS Secret Intelligence in New York, which makes it important evidence in a study of what the OSS knew and when.[41] Only the author is unknown.[42]

The first letter from Lisbon, dated June 28, 1942, specified that Nazi Germany had made the Jews into a special case—they were beyond persecution:

Germany no longer persecutes the Jews. It is systematically exterminating them.

The new racist policy, which in cold, calculated cruelty surpasses the horrors of Magdeburg or Carthage, was revealed to me at Lisbon by a British officer who escaped the hell of the Himmler ghetto in Warsaw . . . According to the officer, who was caught in Warsaw and hidden by Jews until his escape fourteen days ago, as the Jews die, disappear or are executed, new Jews are brought into the ghettos to replace them from Austria, Germany, Moravia, Bohemia, and elsewhere, keeping the maximum at the destruction centers. Eventually all Jews within the grasp of Greater Germany will be rounded up and routed to Poland, deprived of all rights, robbed, practically undressed, herded [?] into the "epidemic districts" then starved, terrorized or executed. . . .

In a recent visit to the governor [of the General Government] during April, Herr Himmler complained that Jews were not disappearing fast enough to please the Fuehrer. Himmler then laid down a sort of ultimatum to Berlin's representative. . . .

Firstly: Virtual extermination of all Jews must be accomplished before a specified date, known to the Aryan chiefs.

Secondly: All Polish secret organizations must likewise be exterminated.

Thirdly: All Jewish business, mainly black market groups, must be immediately wiped out by execution.

Fourthly: One more million Poles must be transported to Germany to work, forming part of the most colossal slave drive in history.

Himmler's records confirm that he visited the Warsaw ghetto on the evening of April 17, 1942; Gestapo officials executed more than fifty Jews in Pawiak Prison that same evening.[43] There is no confirmation that Hitler or Himmler issued a formal order in April 1942 requiring the rapid elimination of all remaining Jews in the General Government, but it is not improbable—similar things were ordered later. The British officer who escaped from the Warsaw ghetto to Lisbon knew what he was talking about. There may be further British documents about this escapee, but if so, they have not been released.

The second article by the same author, dated November 7, 1942, was equally pointed:

The exact date when Hitler decided to wipe the [J]ews from the surface of Europe in the most literal sense of the word, namely by killing them, is unknown. Evacuations and deportations accompanied by executions date as far back as the Polish campaign [fall 1939], but the organized wholesale slaughter of whole communities and trainloads of [J]ews appears to have been practiced not before the German attack on Russia. . . .

When the Red armies flooded back from the Baltic countries there began at once an all out hunt of "[J]ews" and "communists." Since there were hardly any communists left—most of them followed the red army—the [J]ews had to bear the brunt of the orgy of revenge which followed the communist reign in the Baltic countries. Many [J]ews had, indeed, been unwise enough to associate themselves too closely with the communist regimes, apparently hoping that they would protect them against Hitler. Their miscalculation hastened their destruction. Lithuanian and Latvian fascists ably assisted by special SS detachments massacred within a few days tens of thousands of Jews in Lithuania and Latvia alone.

This orgy of bloodshed, which in a way can be described as a genuine pogrom, was the signal for the general massacer [*sic*] of Jews in all three Baltic countries, in Poland, White-Russia and the Ukraine. As long as it was possible Lithuanians and Latvians were used as executioners, but even the most bloodthirsty among them soon got tired of the job and left it to the genuine professionals from Germany.

But even in the following months Lithuania and Latvia, the scene of the "real pogroms" remained one of Himmler[']s favorite execution grounds. Whatever happened there could, if necessary, be blamed on the local anti-[S]emites and on the [J]ewish communists commis[s]ars who had been the cause of this anti-[S]emitism.

This account of Nazi-incited pogroms, followed by more organized and systematic mass shootings, captured the general pattern in Latvia and Lithuania.

The third article, dated November 15, 1942, continued the woeful story of Nazi executions in the Baltic States, tracing, on the basis of information from an eyewitness, one train of Wesphalian Jews deported to Riga, who were executed batch by batch in a ditch dug in a forest on the route to Kaiserwald. The author went on to discuss similar executions, carefully prepared, elsewhere. But he concluded with a mention of the very latest methods, whose details were still unknown: gassing in trains (a slight error; it was vans) and electrocution in water basins, which was an inaccurate report. If these methods proved technically feasible, "there is every reason to assume that they will finally replace the old methods." The author did not have up-to-date information about the construction of extermination camps using gas chambers and crematoria, but the level of detail about mass shootings in the East, the first phase of the Holocaust, was quite impressive.

Dulles himself most likely did not have access to these letters before he left New York for Switzerland (the first letter was delayed, the second written while he was en route, the third after his arrival). Whether or not he received them in Switzerland, he got similar information after his arrival there on November 10, 1942. Drawing from various sources, Dulles quickly became well informed about the Holocaust.

Allen Dulles in Switzerland
Allen Welsh Dulles, forty-nine years old in 1942, was perfectly qualified for his role as an intelligence official in Switzerland concerned primarily with Nazi Germany. Of upper-class birth and Princeton education, Dulles pursued

successful careers in diplomacy and law—both closely tied to European affairs. He had served as a young diplomat in Switzerland during World War I, at the peace conference in Paris in 1919, and in Germany in the immediate postwar period. He was friendly with two leading German Social Democrats, Rudolf Hilferding and Rudolf Breitscheid, both of them to die at the hands of the Nazis. He held some negative stereotypes of Jews, but in 1921 he was directly involved in efforts to expose the now infamous *Protocols of the Elders of Zion* as a forgery. He was unable to persuade the State Department to denounce the document publicly. In April 1933, Dulles took time out from his legal career to serve again as a diplomat on disarmament matters, during which time he went back to Germany and had a face-to-face discussion with Hitler. As a successful corporate lawyer, Dulles spent much time with German clients and lawyers. As strains developed between Germany and the West during the late 1930s, Allen Dulles, in contrast with his elder brother, John Foster, became more and more convinced that Nazi Germany could not be allowed to expand at will. Shortly after Pearl Harbor and Germany's declaration of war on the United States, he began to work for the COI.[44]

By the time the COI became the OSS in 1942, high officials had recognized the value of having a well-stocked base in neutral Switzerland, nearly surrounded by the Axis powers, prepared to defend itself if attacked, but otherwise steering a delicately balanced course. Switzerland had so many economic links with both Germany and Italy that there was bound to be leakage of information through corporate channels. Prominent exiles from Nazi Germany in the country still had lines of information into Berlin. The Swiss government, the International Red Cross, and the Bank of International Settlements might each yield some Nazi secrets if the right people plied their officials. Dulles had just the right qualifications. He almost left for Switzerland too late—the journey was strewn with obstacles, and Dulles barely made it across the French border before Germany shut off this route in response to the Allied invasion of French North Africa.[45]

Dulles was given the cover of being special assistant to the American minister in Bern, Leland Harrison. Dulles had regular contact with Embassy officials, including Harrison; he even used some State Department codes when his own facilities for communication with Washington were overloaded. Although Dulles quickly found and developed his own sources of information about Nazi Germany, he was aware of, and occasionally drew on, information from the legation and consulates. It turned out that legation and consular officials had very good sources of their own with regard to the Holocaust.

In the summer and fall of 1942, individual private reports about the Nazi policy of mass extermination of the Jewish "race" reached Jewish sources in Switzerland. The most famous report originated with an anti-Nazi German industrialist, Eduard Schulte, whose huge company, Georg von Giesches Erben, ran a zinc rolling mill in the town of Auschwitz.[46] Schulte gave the report to his business associate Isidor Koppelmann, who contacted Benjamin Sagalowitz, a press officer for the Jewish community of Zurich. Sagalowitz went to Gerhart

Riegner, representative of the World Jewish Congress in Geneva. In early August, Riegner outlined the Nazi Final Solution, the use of gas chambers and a poison gas based on prussic acid to exterminate 3.5 to 4 million Jews. Keeping the name of his source secret, Riegner asked American and British diplomats to send this information to their governments, and also to give it to officials of the World Jewish Congress in both countries.[47]

American diplomats in Geneva and Bern sent Riegner's telegram to the State Department. The desk officers in the European Division and the refugee specialists discounted this telegram, and the State Department declined to pass it on to Rabbi Stephen Wise, president of the American Jewish Congress. The State Department summarized this information for the OSS in Washington as "a wild rumor inspired by Jewish fears."[48]

But Wise later got the information from London colleagues and brought it to the attention of Undersecretary of State Sumner Welles. Welles then ordered an investigation. Harrison received a triple priority instruction from Undersecretary of State Welles to investigate Riegner's sources and the accuracy of his information. As part of that process, on October 22, Harrison met with Riegner and his colleague from the Jewish Agency for Palestine, Richard Lichtheim; he even induced Riegner to give him the name of his German industrialist in a sealed envelope. Riegner and Lichtheim presented Harrison with a set of documents, nearly thirty pages including the industrialist's information and other independent sources. Their cover sheet on the packet of documents indicated that, in keeping with deliberate Nazi policy, four million Jews were on the verge of complete annihilation by a number of methods, including: starvation; ghettos; slave labor; deportation under inhumane conditions; and mass murder by shooting, poisoning, and other means. Harrison and other American diplomats collected much more information about the Holocaust than actually went to Washington.[49] After Harrison notified Welles that he was convinced of the accuracy of the information, Welles privately confirmed Riegner's telegram to Wise. Wise quickly held a press conference in late November to publicize the information.[50]

The refugee specialist at the State Department, Robert Borden Reams, complained in an internal memorandum that Wise should never have publicized the information he had received from Riegner (and which Undersecretary Welles had privately confirmed):

> It should again be stressed that all of these reports are unconfirmed. It is obviously impossible to secure confirmation of German activities in the various occupied countries . . . It cannot be doubted that the Jewish people of Europe are oppressed and it is certain that considerable numbers of them have died in one way or another since the war started. Whether the number of dead amounts to tens of thousands, or, as these reports state, to millions is not material to the main problem . . . Our main purpose is the winning of the war and other considerations must be subordinate thereto.[51]

Reams was hardly the only one in government who felt that way, but he was unusually blunt in stating that he wanted relevant information about the Holocaust to be disregarded. He did not want Rabbi Wise to stir up demands for some kind of government action that might interfere with the war effort.

On December 8, Rabbi Wise and a number of other American Jewish representatives presented some of the evidence about the Holocaust, including Riegner and Lichtheim's documents, to President Roosevelt at the White House. The president said that the government was familiar with most of the facts, but that it was hard to find an appropriate course of action. The Jewish leaders asked for an official government statement denouncing Nazi policy, and FDR agreed. Independently, pressures mounted in London for a similar British statement. On December 17, the United States, Britain, and a number of other Allied governments (overriding objections from the State Department and the British Foreign Office) formally recognized that Nazi Germany was pursuing a policy of extermination of the Jewish people. But American and British refugee policies were not otherwise changed for some time.[52] There was a major difference between recognizing information and taking action on the basis of it.

The exchanges between Bern and Washington indicate how much basic information about the Holocaust was available and accepted by American diplomats in Switzerland by the late fall of 1942, when Allen Dulles arrived. Dulles would have been a poor intelligence man if he had not learned quickly about the State Department's interaction with the legation in Bern over Nazi policy toward Jews. He was in Switzerland when the Allied governments issued their December 17 statement, which was based in part on the information and evidence the legation had provided. He would likely have known that State Department bureaucrats were unhappy that the legation had allowed Riegner to send information to Wise, and even unhappier when Wise publicized this information. All these events help to explain why certain kinds of Holocaust information did not go through OSS channels. Dulles did not need to reconfirm the obvious, especially because it was politically sensitive in Washington.

Later, Nazi Germany supplied some solid evidence of its intended actions against Jews. On February 24, 1943, Hitler commemorated the 22nd anniversary of the naming of the Nazi Party with a speech in which he again promised that the war would lead to the annihilation of the Jews. The German press published an account under the headline *The Destruction of the Jews*, suggesting a sharpening of Nazi policy.[53] This kind of propaganda offensive had several different rationales. Nazi leaders used anti-Semitic themes generally to try to convince people in Allied countries that the Jews were forcing them to carry on a costly war. But Hitler's "prophecy" at this time was partly an effort to show progress toward a fundamental Nazi goal, despite the recent catastrophic defeat at Stalingrad. Just as importantly, it incriminated Germans by giving them a sense of extreme measures (while requiring their complete loyalty), without revealing exactly what had happened and was still happening to Jews deported from Germany.[54]

On February 27, Berlin SS and police began a roundup of a planned total of fifteen thousand Jews, largely those working in factories but including those who were married to Christians and had been previously exempt. As the roundup continued into early March, targeted Jews were confined in the Jewish Community's administration building in the Rosenstrasse. The spouses of some of those arrested flocked to the site and began a demonstration. Meanwhile, other Jews learned of the roundup in advance and went into hiding.[55]

Dulles learned of these Berlin events from Dr. Visser t'Hooft (to whom Dulles gave the code number 474), a Dutch theologian who was first secretary of the World Council of Churches and was based in Bern. Visser t'Hooft's sources in Berlin indicated that the SS was trying to remove all Jews from the capital by mid-March:

> It is definitely expected that these methods of rapid and total extermination of the Jews in Germany will be extended in the coming weeks to other German regions, and very likely also to the occupied territories. Instead of deporting the Jews to Poland and having them killed in that country, the new policy is to kill them on the spot.

The last portion—regarding killing on the spot—was clearly inaccurate, but the report tracked important events almost as they occurred.[56]

If his recollections are accurate, Visser t'Hooft had grasped the thrust of Nazi policy toward the Jews since sometime in early 1942. The decisive event for him was hearing a Swiss businessman tell what he had witnessed during a trip to Russia. German officers had invited him to observe a mass killing of Jews—men, women, and children machine-gunned as they lay in prepared mass graves. After hearing of this incident, Visser t'Hooft closely followed subsequent reports about Nazi actions against Jews.[57]

Dulles had a long talk with Visser t'Hooft to discover his sources about the Berlin roundup. A Swede, likely Hugo Cedergren of the YMCA, had recently been to Berlin and had the information from a Protestant pastor whose wife was non-Aryan, as well as from an official at the Swedish legation in Berlin. Dulles told Visser t'Hooft that this was a matter in which Minister Harrison took a deep interest. On the other hand, Dulles said that the information was not fully verified, and that unspecified proposed Allied measures to hinder this new program did not seem at all practical. Dulles wrote up his conversation with Visser t'Hooft for Harrison, who responded that Riegner had given American Consul Paul Squire some additional reports about the disappearance of Jews in the privileged category, including Riegner's own uncle.[58]

The two senior American officials traded information and scrutinized sources, both of them recognizing the sensitivity of this matter in Washington. (State Department officials had earlier prohibited Harrison from allowing private individuals like Riegner to send information through diplomatic channels, but Harrison told Dulles that this prohibition no longer applied to Dulles' means of communication.)⁵⁹ Dulles also reported the public protests by the affected spouses of some of the Jews detained. A month later British press attaché Elisabeth Wiskemann told Dulles that one of her sources had confirmed Visser t'Hooft's account of the arrest of "half-Jews"; she also reported that many religious people in Berlin were hiding Jews.⁶⁰ Some of Dulles' information about Nazi measures against Jews in Berlin went from the OSS to the White House.⁶¹

Sometimes Washington asked Dulles to investigate allegations that the Nazis were sparing specific Jews for their own purposes. FBI Director J. Edgar Hoover received a quotation allegedly from Ilya Ehrenburg's book *The Great War for the Fatherland*, published in the Soviet Union in 1942, which indicated that Nazi anti-Semitism was a lie: "They have their own Jews whom they spare. These Jews have on their passports two letters, *W.J.*, meaning 'worthy Jew.'" Hoover asked Donovan to look into this, even though he was skeptical. Donovan asked Dulles (among others), who could not confirm that there were such markings on passports, although he did mention that the Nazis had given some Jews marked identity cards. Donovan quickly told Hoover of reports of two isolated cases, but said that the British had never heard of the practice and considered it improbable.⁶²

When he had impeccable sources about actions against Jews, Dulles did not hesitate to tell Washington. In October 1943, after Berlin ordered a roundup of the Jews in Rome, the German consul Eitel Friedrich Möllhausen dissented; he asked Hitler and Foreign Minister Ribbentrop for instructions. Dulles later received a copy of Möllhausen's cable and decided to send it verbatim to Washington through a special means of transmission. The original document allowed Washington to see just how German officials lobbied. Möllhausen had written:

> Obersturmbannfuehrer Kappler has been commissioned from Berlin, to seize the 8,000 Jews resident in Rome and take them to northern Italy where they are to be liquidated. General Stahelm [Stahel], city commander of Rome, said that this action is to be permitted only with the approval of the German Foreign Minister. I am personally of the opinion that it would be better business to transport the Jews to Tunis for work on fortifications.⁶³

By the time he received this document, Dulles knew that the roundup of Jews in Rome had been carried out, even if it turned out to be only partly effective.⁶⁴

On at least one occasion Dulles cast a cable to OSS Washington in such a way that it revealed his basic understanding of Nazi policy against Jews. In an early March 1943 discussion of Hungary's "straddling" (shifting slightly away from its alliance with Germany), Dulles mentioned Hungarian anti-Semitic speeches and discrimination against Jewish professionals, but pointed out that Hungary had taken in seventy thousand Jewish refugees from Poland, Croatia, and Slovakia. This balancing act was part of a reported Hungarian strategy to hold off German pressure: "[Hungarian officials] felt that if they barked at the Jews, biting them would not be necessary. Had the blocking of Germany been tried by Hungary, there would have perished in the latter country eight hundred thousand Jews."[65] Under these circumstances, Dulles did not want to be too critical of Hungary's Jewish policy. He believed that wherever Germany extended its control, Jews would be eliminated.

Dulles had a number of advantages in recognizing the scope of Nazi policy. The legation in Switzerland had gathered much relevant information before he arrived. Dulles quickly chose a naturalized American named Gero von Gaevernitz as his chief assistant. Born and raised in Germany, Gaevernitz had excellent contacts among the anti-Nazi resistance. His mother was of Jewish origin, and he would have been very sensitive to any news about measures against German Jews. Dulles also used a number of informants who possessed a clear understanding of the Final Solution, including Eduard Schulte, the original source of information for Riegner's telegram.

Given the level of reporting from Dulles and other OSS officials in Europe, the Secret Intelligence branch of the OSS hardly lacked basic information about the Holocaust. In addition, it received information in Europe and in the United States from Jewish organizations such as the Jewish Labor Committee.[66] The Polish underground and the Polish government-in-exile also contributed substantial, detailed information.

In one now-famous case, both Polish channels and the Jewish Labor Committee were involved in getting to the OSS the horrifying eyewitness account of Polish courier Jan Karski, who secretly visited the Warsaw ghetto.[67] A leader of the Bund (a Polish party closely allied with the Jewish Labor Committee), who was among the doomed in the Warsaw ghetto, had given Karski a message to carry to the West:

> What is happening to us is altogether outside the imagination of civilized human beings. They [in the West] don't believe what they hear. Tell them that *we are all dying*. Let them rescue all those who will still be alive when the Report reaches them. We shall never forgive them for not having supplied us with arms so that we may have died like men, with guns in our hands.[68]

This moving document reached OSS hands. How widely it was distributed within the organization and how much attention and credibility it generated are open to question.[69]

The Extermination Camps: Allied Information and Conclusions

If Dulles was well aware of Nazi policy toward Jews, he probably did not know much about the means and sites of mass murder. To be sure, he learned that conditions in the concentration camps in Germany were horrifying. One report from a prisoner at Dachau who escaped into Lucerne estimated that one thousand of four thousand Polish priests imprisoned there during 1942–43 had died as a result of mistreatment and inadequate food.[70] But the OSS and the FBI lacked early evidence about the internal conditions and workings of the camps, especially the extermination camps; their best sources arrived later.

The operations of the Nazi extermination camps were so secret that even transports to the camps were reported in heavily coded language.[71] Although information on the extermination camps reaching the West was fragmentary by nature, it allowed for more general conclusions.[72] Newly released records declassified by the IWG suggest that the OSS did not actively seek information on concentration or extermination camps. Ordered late in the war to assemble specific information on German war crimes and criminals for the purpose of arrest and prosecution, the OSS seems to have done relatively little in this regard, even when valuable information fell into its lap.

Information on the extermination camps was available in London. The murderous nature of Belzec was known in London as early as April 1942, and that of Treblinka as early as July.[73] *The Jewish Chronicle* reported on Chelmno's gas vans in the summer of 1942, as well.[74] Information on Auschwitz-Birkenau was received in London and Washington during 1942 and 1943, partly thanks to British intercepts and partly due to the Polish underground.[75] The British picked up a decode in November 1942 indicating that guards at Auschwitz would need six hundred gas masks. In 1942, through intercepted and decoded German radio messages, they were able to follow jumps and falls in the registered Auschwitz Jewish population as well as in the number of Jews deported by rail to Auschwitz, which was a far higher number than registered Jews. Polish underground reports on Jewish extermination activities at Auschwitz also reached London in the fall of 1942, and reports on new crematoria reached London in March 1943. The most famous and most detailed report on Birkenau remains that of escapees Rudolf Vrba and Alfred Wetzler, parts of which were available in London and Washington from mid-June 1944 as Hungary's Jews were transported there.[76]

An account written by a Polish agent code named "Wanda" in October 1943 and forwarded to the Polish government-in-exile in January 1944 was handed directly to the Americans—to the Military Attaché in March 1944 and to the OSS in April. "Up to September 1942," it said,

468,000 non-registered Jews have been gassed in Oswiecim [Auschwitz]. Between September 1942 and the beginning of June 1943 there arrived approximately 60,000 Jews from Greece . . . about 50,000 Jews from Slovakia and the Protectorate, approximately 60,000 Jews from Holland, Belgium and France, 6,000 from Chrzanow and 5,000 from Kety, Zywiec, Sucha, Slemien and vicinity. Two per cent of these people are alive today . . . Each convoy arriving in Oswiecim is unloaded; men are separated from women, and then packed haphazard, in a mass (mainly women and children) into cars and lorries and taken to the gas chamber in Brzezinka [Birkenau]. There they [are] suffocated with the most horrible suffering lasting 10-15 minutes, the corpses being . . . cremated . . . At present, three large crematoria have been erected in Brzezinka, for 10,000 people daily, which are ceaselessly cremating bodies and which the neighboring population call "the eternal fire" . . .

As from 20.6.1943 mass convoys have been arriving in the Oswiecim camp (Brzezinka), including: one convoy from Nice (870 persons), one convoy with more than 500 persons from Berlin, 800 people from Salonika. Two convoys with 1,600 persons from Brandenburg, one convoy from Sosnowiec, one convoy from Lublin, containing 391 people. These convoys contained 80% Jews and 20% Gypsies from Greece and southern France. Possibly 10% of these people have remained alive in the camp, the remaining 90% were immediately taken to the gas chambers and gassed . . ."

The report that contained Wanda's account noted that the Poles "asked that the report be given publicity."[77] It was never made public.

Most reports on camps came to the OSS from British intelligence, and they have long been declassified. A Polish political escapee named Szadowski, who had been at the Auschwitz main camp from June 1940 to March 1942 and then at Birkenau until his escape in 1943, reported in person to British intelligence in October 1944.[78] According to his British interrogator, "Szadowski . . . shows surprisingly accurate knowledge of conditions in Oswiecim and his account tallies perfectly with all the information at our disposal." Szadowski's detailed account was thus compared with many other accounts received by the British. Yet Szadowski seems to have been interrogated mostly on mundane issues like barrack size, the camp barbers, availability of cigarettes, and the location of horse stables. Szadowski surely had much to say on Birkenau's gas chambers and crematoria, but his account of these amounts to a half-page of a twenty-five-page report. Since his report was based on interrogation, one must assume that this was the interrogator's choice.[79]

In November 1944, the British interrogated an escaped former officer-cadet of the Polish Air Force named Henryk Rygiol, whose family still lived near Birkenau. Rygiol had been interned in Auschwitz and used as a rail worker. The tales of other inmates supplemented his own observations to British intelligence—observations which included the murder of 450,000 Hungarian Jews from May to July 1944. "Twenty-one ovens were burning day and night," reported Rygiol, a fact which he said "could be confirmed by anyone in the area." Rygiol also reported on other atrocities such as attacks by dogs on female prisoners, and he named a number of perpetrators, including the Commandant Rudolf Höss. Rygiol's inflated claim that up to 7 million Jews had been killed at Auschwitz might have detracted from his other comments concerning German atrocities there. The maps provided from his interrogation, in any event, were of strategic targets such as the detention camp at Mylowitz, used as a collection point for the movement of Polish workers to France. Of the three detailed diagrams provided by Rygiol for British intelligence, none was of Birkenau.[80] Rygiol's interrogation reinforces other historians' comments that strategic concerns at the Auschwitz complex, not the mass extermination of Jews, were of top importance to the Allies.[81]

Similarly, when U.S. intelligence assembled data on Germany's victims, the driving force was strategic. The OSS borrowed information from French intelligence on the use of labor from the Dora concentration camp to assemble German V-2 rockets; it studied German documents seized by French agents from Natzweiler-Struthof, which contained statistics on the death of inmates there. The OSS learned from various sources that air raids over prisoner of war camps caused considerable loss of life among prisoners, including fifty-two killed on the night of February 2, 1945, at Stalag XIII B.[82] The OSS studied the numbers, locations, and health conditions of Russian, Polish, French, Dutch, Belgian, Yugoslav, and Italian slave laborers in Germany, who, it was thought, could support Allied operations through sabotage if supplied with weapons via parachute. The OSS assembled detailed statistics and locations for each national group of slave laborers in Germany. It concluded that advance "OSS . . . organizers . . . would be sufficient to create strong foreign worker nuclei to which quantities of arms could be dropped."[83]

The OSS was very cool to the idea of using eager Jews from Palestine either as commandos or as agents in southeastern Europe, even though the Jewish Agency offered everything from personnel to organizational structure.[84] Jews who were not prisoners were not part of the OSS' strategic thinking, and Jewish camp prisoners were not either. In the view of the OSS, there was no serious military need to study the camps where Jews were held.

Toward the end of the war, lower-level Allied intelligence officials undertook studies intended to convey a sense of the German camp system as a whole. This effort was mainly a British one, with the OSS simply receiving British reports. These reports were flawed, possibly because those who compiled the reports, as a result of bureaucratic compartmentalization, lacked access to the best intelligence then available.

One case in point is a newly declassified "List of German Concentration Camps." Compiled by the German and Austrian Intelligence Branch of Britain's primary information agency, the Political Warfare Executive (PWE), the List was revised every few months based on collected intelligence. The version of the List in recently declassified OSS records is dated June 21, 1944 (three months after the previous update), and it lists 144 camps.[85] In war information made publicly available, PWE played down the plight of Europe's Jews.[86] The June 1944 List should be seen in this context. It contained the peculiar comment that

> reliable information is hard to obtain. In the German Press individual camps have never been mentioned by name . . . The reports of even inmates of the camps need interpretation. Inmates may not be told the correct name of the camp to which they are taken and may identify it by a railway station.[87]

The report also acknowledged confusion as to the nature of the concentration camp system itself: "There are several types of camp which may be confused with concentration camps, but should probably not be included on a list of concentration camps." These other types, though, included not extermination camps but work camps (*Arbeitslager*) and prison camps (*Straflager*).

Theresienstadt was the only camp out of 144 on the PWE list where the notation "for Jews" was included. Chelmno was simply noted as being 64 kilometers northwest of Lodz. Oswiecim (Auschwitz) was included in the list with no special distinction at all, and Brzezinki (Birkenau) was said to be "possibly associated with Oswiecim."[88] Death camps Belzec, Sobibor, and Treblinka, all shut down by this time, were still thought to be in operation but received no special distinction beyond their location.[89]

Given what information was available from other sources by mid-1944, the List of Concentration Camps seems inept. British analysts surely knew the German press contained nothing on extermination camps in Poland, but they also knew that one could look in other places, most of which were in London, for information such as escapee reports and intercepts. The OSS knew this too.

Britain's most comprehensive wartime analysis of concentration camps, written by the British secret intelligence service, MI-6, was completed in April 1945 as an appendix to a chapter in *The German Basic Handbook*. Parts of the report were used at the Nuremberg trials of the major war criminals later that year. The appendix on concentration camps is thirty-six pages long and includes enormous detail, broad attempts at analysis, and its own sub-appendix that attempts to list every known German camp, including transit camps, labor camps, and so on— more than three hundred in all. The detail is such that MI-6 surely began work on the concentration camp appendix much earlier than April 1945; the appendix can thus be seen as an inventory of what British intelligence understood (or chose to say) about the camp system in the later part of the war, and perhaps as what the OSS understood, too. The OSS does not seem to have ever undertaken such a study on its own.[90]

MI-6 failed to comprehend the aims of the German camp system. The report included no information from escapees, the Polish underground, intercepts, or censorship. Key parts of the appendix were based on sources from liberated western camps such as Drancy in France, while for the East it depended on Soviet radio broadcasts regarding camps recently liberated in Poland. None of it seems to have been built on what had been learned about Belzec and Treblinka via the Polish underground, and none of it came from detailed intercepts or reports on Auschwitz-Birkenau that had reached London. Perhaps the appendix foreshadowed official thinking about Jewish displaced persons in 1945, according to which Jewish refugees, despite their statelessness and the horrors of their wartime experience, were to receive no preferential treatment.[91]

The appendix noted that "the Concentration Camp system is coeval with the Nazi regime," but it never acknowledged that Jews were the primary victims of the same regime.[92] MI-6's analysis of concentration camps incorrectly sewed Jews into the broad quilt of Nazi Germany's many racial and political enemies:

> The victims [of concentration camps] are . . . of two kinds. The first consists of persons considered dangerous to the régime: Jews, anti-Germans from the occupied countries, members of oppositional political groups who have tried to make friendly contacts with prisoners of war, Germans who have had sex-relations with members of "Helot" races such as Jews or Poles, disgruntled German workers who have grumbled once too often, listeners to foreign broadcasts, and, in general, "politically unreliable" individuals. The second kind includes persons believed to have committed robberies with violence, black-market swindlers, officials who have been denounced as bribe-takers, racketeers or alleged racketeers of various species, and other non-political offenders.

British analysts had a clear sense of group badges worn by camp inmates.[93] But it was also known at the time that throughout the concentration camp system Jews were hardly on a par with German racketeers. Otherwise, badges would not have been needed at all. Yet the appendix argues that "reports indicate a practice of discriminating racially, as regards both discipline and living conditions, against other people besides the Jews."[94]

MI-6 analysts acknowledged in the concentration camp appendix that a "Death Camp System" existed (it counted eleven death camps in all) and that in 1942 the death toll among all German prisoners in Europe rose drastically as a result.

> There are certain camps which function mainly, if not exclusively, as centres for the mass extermination of prisoners . . . a report that the death-rate of the Concentration Camps as a whole rose during 1942 to 12 per cent per month does not appear to be exaggerated.

The statement by Vrba and Wetzler that "on principle only Jews are gassed," was ignored in this appendix.[95] Instead MI-6 erroneously tied the entire system of camps—extermination camps included—to the labor needs of the Reich and the need to move local populations far from potential bases of resistance. It reads:

> During the latter half of 1942, the transportations from the western camps into Poland grew, and were only partly offset by the despatch to German camps of Polish and Russian contingents. Deportations were part of the system. Thus in 1942 Jugoslav "political" prisoners were to be found confined in Norway. (Out of 900 sent to Narvik in July, 550 had died, mainly of disease and neglect, by October of that year). But the intake of fresh inmates in the west was also increasing. Despite the transportations to Poland, the evidence points to no permanent depletion of numbers elsewhere.

At one point MI-6 even explained the purpose of German camps in Poland as the accommodation of runoff from camps in Germany itself:

> The size of those [camps] in Germany, indeed, may partly have been kept down by means of systematic deportations of their surplus to the great camps of Poland.
> The [death] camps served as a "pool" or reservoir which could be used to smooth out irregularities in the supply of their human material from the rest of Europe.

Most of the information for the appendix seems to have come from Belzec and Maidanek, and though Auschwitz-Birkenau and Chelmno were mentioned briefly as death camps, so were camps that were not death camps at all, such as Gusen (near Linz) and Neuengamme (near Hamburg). Sobibor did not appear at all in a list of more than 330 camps. Neither, astonishingly, did Treblinka, about which a great deal had been known in London for three years.

Death camp victims, said the appendix, were of two types. Large parts were "unwanted populations" belonging to "Helot races," namely Poles and Jews. MI-6 did not distinguish between the two, and the appendix reveals no sense that Nazism viewed the Jews as a singular threat, rather than as just "unwanted" people. The intelligence analysts overlooked twelve years of apocalyptic anti-Semitic rhetoric coming from Berlin[96] and numerous reports of exclusively Jewish transports from all over Europe to Poland. MI-6 did not acknowledge Jews as the primary victims of the extermination camps.

Certain populations, according to MI-6, were killed simply because they represented unwanted mouths to feed or because they were in the way, occupying areas needed for German colonization. The second category of death camp victims, according to the report, were "worked-out" victims of all nationalities condemned to death because they were no longer fit or were security liabilities after their labor on certain sensitive projects, such as V-2 rockets. MI-6 also misunderstood, to a degree, the methods of human extermination. "From Majdanek," said the report, came the now familiar account of the disinfectant-gas chamber where prisoners were murdered by "so-called cyclone" (Zyklon) gas. Yet MI-6 also believed errant reports that electrocution in a metal-floored shower installation was the primary means of execution at Belzec.

It is hard to fathom how analyses of this nature could have misrepresented so many aspects of the German system this late in the war. A great deal of information was readily available on extermination camps and also on the singling out of Jews for mass murder. After the war, when war criminals were arrested en masse, this information was used to assemble names. In May 1945, British Military Intelligence (MI-14) handed the OSS a list of over five hundred German concentration camp officers, compiled "during a period of several years," so that these men could be arrested if encountered. Most of the names came from western camps liberated by the Allies such as Mauthausen, Dachau, Buchenwald,

Natzweiler, and Flossenbürg. None came from Treblinka, Sobibor, Belzec, or Chelmno, but 102 of the names—roughly 20 percent—were from Auschwitz, and many of these had been learned as early as September 1942.[97]

On December 15, 1944, William Donovan relayed instructions from the War Department that the OSS was to help the Judge Advocate General Division with the assembly of names and evidence for eventual war crimes arrests and prosecution.[98] But with the war in Europe at a crucial stage—the Germans would launch the second Ardennes offensive the following day—the OSS does not seem to have done much in this regard using its own records.

In all, newly released OSS records concerning German camps reflect the strategic priorities of the war and thus confirm earlier historical findings regarding Allied intelligence and the Holocaust. The OSS was able to assemble hard-to-find information on German camp prisoners for strategic projects, as its detailed work on slave laborers in Germany shows. The OSS does not seem to have taken much detailed interest in German camps as they concerned the extermination of Jews. The "Wanda" report mentioned above was not sought by OSS officials—it fell into the OSS' lap. Information assembled on Auschwitz, such as it was, was gathered by British interrogators, not American ones. The OSS seems to have undertaken no general study concerning the German extermination of its Jewish prisoners.

Notes

1. William J. Casey, *The Secret War Against Hitler* (Washington, DC: Regnery Gateway, 1986), 218, quoted in Raul Hilberg, *Perpetrators, Victims, Bystanders: The Jewish Catastrophe 1933–1945* (New York: Harper Collins, 1992), 254.

2. Arnold H. Price, *My Twentieth Century: Recollections of a Public Historian* (Tübingen: Universitas Verlag Tübingen, 2003), 87.

3. Arthur M. Schlesinger, Jr., *A Life in the Twentieth Century: Innocent Beginnings, 1917–1950* (Boston: Houghton Mifflin, 2000), 307.

4. Shlomo Aronson, "Preparations for the Nuremberg Trials: The O.S.S., Charles Dwork, and the Holocaust," *Holocaust and Genocide Studies* 12, no. 2 (1998): 266–70; Barry M. Katz, "The Holocaust and American Intelligence," in *The Jewish Legacy and the German Conscience: Essays in Memory of Rabbi Joseph Ascher*, 297–307, ed. Moses Rischin and Raphael Ascher (Berkeley, CA: Judah L. Magnes Museum, 1991).

5. Miranda Carter, *Anthony Blunt: His Lives* (New York: Farrar, Straus, and Giroux, 2001), 273–74.

6. H. Montgomery Hyde, *Secret Intelligence Agent* (New York: St. Martin's Press, 1982), 33–34, 104–05.

7. For a sample, Rivas G. Montt [*sic*], Chilean Consul, Prague, to Minister of Foreign Affairs, Santiago, Chile, 6 Sept. 1941, NA, RG 65, 62-65008-24-1-(1–100), boxes 26–27.

8. In at least one case, William Stephenson personally solicited Donovan's reaction to Argentinian diplomatic reports from Berlin. See British Security Coordination (Bill) to William J. Donovan, 27 June 1942, NA, RG 226, entry 210, box 400, folder 9085. For documents that clarify Q (the designation for British Security Coordination), see To Q, 13 July 1942, NA, RG 226, entry 210, box 326, folder–British Data; and Allen W. Dulles to David Bruce, 17 July 1942, NA, RG 226, entry 92, box 103, folder 9452.

9. Donovan was selected Coordinator of Information on June 17, 1941, and formally appointed on July 11, after opposition from the Office of Naval Intelligence and G-2 (Army Intelligence) had been overcome. British intelligence officials had lobbied heavily for the establishment of a unified American intelligence organization and for Donovan's appointment as director. Stephenson fed Donovan other prized intelligence. See Thomas F. Troy, *Donovan and the CIA: A History of the Establishment of the Central Intelligence Agency* (Frederick, MD: University Publications of America, 1984), 43–70, 83; and more generally: Troy, *Wild Bill and Intrepid: Donovan, Stephenson, and the Origin of CIA* (New Haven, CT: Yale University Press, 1996).

10. COI distribution, 26 Sept. 1941, based on despatch of 25 Aug. 1941, NA, RG 226, entry 16, box 3, folder 450-494, document 468.

11. Mario Barros Van Buren, *La Diplomacia Chilena en la Segunda Guerra Mundial*, (Santiago, CL: Empresa Editora Arquen, 1998) 83, 118–20. Montt's name is listed in Fritz Berber, ed., *Jahrbuch für Auswärtige Politik* 6, (1940):11. Our thanks to Gerhard Weinberg for this reference.

12. *Diccionario Biografico de Chile* (Santiago: Empresa Periodística Chile) eighth edition, 1950–52, and twelfth edition, 1962–64. We are grateful to Pascale Bonnefoy for the references.

13. [British] Summary, 13 Sept. 1941, of Chilean despatch, 24 June 1941, copy in NA, RG 226, entry 16, box 32, folder 7000-7377, document 7346.

14. Montt to Foreign Minister, 6 Sept. 1941, Chilean National Archives, Ministerio de Relaciones Exteriores de Chile, vol. 149 (1941), file E 3-10-1-1. Translated copy in NA, RG 65, 62-65008-24-1, boxes 26–27.

15. Conti [Montt] to Minister of Foreign Affairs, Santiago, Chile, 1 Nov. 1941. Translated copy of "Evacuation of Jews from Bohemia and Moravia" in NA, RG 65, 62-65008-24-178-156, box 27, folder–Secret Intercepts-South America.

16. [British] Intelligence report, 4 Fcb. 1942, regarding Chilean despatch from Prague, 15 Nov. 1941, copy in NA, RG 226, entry 16, box 49, folder 11250-11300, document 11280. The consul is incorrectly identified as E. C. Conti. For explanation of the mistake, see below.

17. Montt to Minister of Foreign Affairs, 6 Sept. 1941, Chilean National Archives, Ministerio de Relaciones Exteriores de Chile, vol. 149 (1941), file E 3-10-1-1. Translated copy of "Anti-Jewish Measures in Warsaw and Prague" in NA, RG 65, 62-65008-24-1-(1–100), boxes 26–27, folder–Secret Intercepts-South America.

18. This decree is published by H. G. Adler, *Der verwaltete Mensch: Studien zur Deportation der Juden aus Deutschland* (Tübingen: Mohr, 1974), 500–04. For analysis, see Martin Dean, "The Development and Implementation of Nazi Denaturalization and Confiscation Policy up to the Eleventh Decree to the Reich Citizenship Law," *Holocaust and Genocide Studies* 16, no. 2 (2002): 217–42.

19. See the British translation dated 20 Mar. 1942 in NA, RG 226, entry 210, box 386, folder 6. The diplomat's name is not given in the British version. The Spanish original may be found in the Chilean National Archives.

20. See the British translation NA, RG 226, entry 210, box 386, folder 6.

21. See Notizen aus der Besprechung am 10.10.41 über die Lösung von Judenfragen, copy in United States Holocaust Memorial Museum (USHMM), RG 48.005, roll 3. There is a reference to the press conference in Peter Witte et al., eds., *Der Dienstkalender Heinrich Himmlers 1941–42* (Hamburg: Christians, 1999), 231n26.

22. Ian Kershaw, *Hitler: 1936–1945: Nemesis* (London: Penguin, 2000), 420; Richard Breitman, *The Architect of Genocide: Himmler and the Final Solution* (Hanover, NH: University Press of New England, 1991), 170–214.

23. Heydrich Fernschreiben for Lammers, for Bormann, 9 Oct. 1941, NA, RG 242, T-120, roll 1026, frames 406029-34; Hitler's appointment schedule, NA, RG 242, T-84, roll 387, frame 516. On October 21 Himmler had discussed with Heydrich his "Vortrag b. Führer."

24. Kershaw, *Nemesis*, 488.

25. See Witte, et al., *Dienstkalender Heinrich Himmlers*, 241n61, referring to a discussion among Himmler, Tiso, Tuka, and Mach on 20 Oct. 1941.

26. Montt to Foreign Ministry, 18 Oct. 1940, vol. 148 (1940), Chilean National Archives.

27. NA, RG 226, entry 16, box 32, document 7346.

28. NA, RG 226, entry 16, box 49, folder 11250-11300, document 11280.

29. We are grateful to Pascale Bonnefoy for this information.

30. Nelson D. Lankford, *The Last American Aristocrat: The Biography of David K. E. Bruce, 1898–1977* (Boston: Little, Brown, 1996), 125–28.

31. Conti [Montt] to Minister of Foreign Affairs, Santiago, Chile, 1 Nov. 1941. Translated copy of "Evacuation of Jews from Bohemia and Moravia," in NA, RG 65, 62-65008-24-156, box 27, folder–Secret Intercepts-South America. Also, J. Edgar Hoover to Adolf A. Berle and Huie, 1 May 1942, ibid.

32. See Montt's despatches of November 18 and 20, 1941, dated 20 and 23 Mar. 1942, NA, RG 226, entry 210, box 386, folder 6.

33. See Troy, *Donovan and the CIA*, 40, 61–62.

34. Ibid., 152.

35. Ibid., 91.

36. See the collection of interviews conducted by the OSS Division of Oral Intelligence in NA, RG 226, entry 210, boxes 258, 261, and 264.

37. Rado to Buxton, 8 Aug. 1942, NA, RG 226, entry 210, box 258, folder 2.

38. Richard Breitman, *Official Secrets: What the Nazis Planned, What the British and Americans Knew* (New York: Hill and Wang 1998), 129; Witte, et al., *Dienstkalender Heinrich Himmlers*, 401n44.

39. From Beirut to Dear Allen, 17 Feb. 1943, NA, RG 226, entry 16, box 330, folder 31750-31903, document 31770.

40. These letters all seem to be in NA, RG 226, entry 16. Some of those of intelligence value were copied to other agencies.

41. The first letter does not state that it is part of a series of articles, but the second one notes it is the second article (although the first one had not yet arrived in New York), and the third one notes it is the third article. NA, RG 226, entry 16, boxes 252, 257, and 259, documents 26896, 27275, and 27428.

42. Richard Breitman previously speculated that the author was Gerald M. Mayer, who represented the Office of War Information post in Switzerland and worked closely with Dulles there; see Breitman, *Official Secrets*, 129. Mayer's itinerary roughly corresponds with the author's, but the wider series of "Dear Allen" letters raises other possibilities. Mayer was not the only former or active journalist in Europe who took an interest in Nazi persecution of Jews.

43. Witte, et al., *Dienstkalender Heinrich Himmlers*, 400, 400n43.

44. We have drawn this portrait generally from Peter Grose, *Gentleman Spy: The Life of Allen Dulles* (Boston: Houghton Mifflin, 1994), 1–145.

45. On Dulles' trip, see Grose, *Gentleman Spy*, 148–51.

46. Staight to Dolbeare, 30 Nov. 1943, NA, RG 226, entry 107, box 3, folder 43–Rocket Weapons.

47. Walter Laqueur and Richard Breitman, *Breaking the Silence: The German Who Exposed the Final Solution* (Hanover, NH: University Press of New England for Brandeis University Press, 1994), 115–49.

48. To OSS R&A from Harrison, 11 Aug. 1942, NA, RG 226, entry 4, box 1, folder 2–Bern.

49. See the account in Richard Breitman and Alan M. Kraut, *American Refugee Policy and European Jewry, 1933–1945*, (Bloomington: Indiana University Press, 1987), 153–57.

50. Laqueur and Breitman, *Breaking the Silence*, 156–60. State Department experts (like those in the British Foreign Office) resisted the conclusion that Nazi Germany was pursuing a systematic policy of mass extermination of Jews, or that the Allied governments should

publicly denounce it. This debate has been studied in detail by a number of previous historians (see n. 52 below), most recently by Breitman, *Official Secrets*, 141–54.

51. Reams to Travers, 15 Dec. 1942, NA, RG 59, file 52D-408, box 3, folder–Bermuda Conference Background. Quoted in Breitman, *Official Secrets*, 173.

52. The period between August 1942 and the Allied Declaration of December 17, 1942, is recognized as a critical learning period in all of the following works, each of which has somewhat different interpretations about the period of inaction that followed: Arthur D. Morse, *While Six Million Died: A Chronicle of American Apathy* (1968; Woodstock, NY: Overlook Press, 1983); Henry L. Feingold, *The Politics of Rescue: The Roosevelt Administration and the Holocaust, 1938–1945* (New Brunswick, NJ: Rutgers University Press, 1970); Saul S. Friedman, *No Haven for the Oppressed: United States Policy Toward Jewish Refugees, 1938–1945* (Detroit: Wayne State University Press, 1973); Monty N. Penkower, *The Jews Were Expendable: Free World Diplomacy and the Holocaust* (Urbana: University of Illinois Press, 1983); David S. Wyman, *The Abandonment of the Jews: America and the Holocaust, 1941–1945* (New York: Pantheon, 1984); Richard Breitman and Alan M. Kraut, *American Refugee Policy and European Jewry, 1933–1945* (Bloomington: Indiana University Press, 1987).

53. On the speech, see Nathan Stoltzfus, *Resistance of the Heart: Intermarriage and the Rosenstrasse Protest in Nazi Germany* (New York: W. W. Norton, 1996), 207.

54. David Bankier, "The Use of Antisemitism in Nazi Wartime Propaganda," in *The Holocaust and History: The Known, the Unknown, the Disputed, and the Reexamined,* ed. Michael Berenbaum and Abraham J. Peck (Bloomington: Indiana University Press in association with the United States Holocaust Memorial Museum, 2002), 48.

55. Stoltzfus, *Resistance of the Heart*, 209–48. Many aspects of these events have been revised, on the basis of German documents, by Wolf Gruner, "The Factory Action and the Events at the Rosenstrasse in Berlin: Facts and Fictions about 27 February 1943—Sixty Years Later," *Central European History* 36, no. 2 (2003): 179–208. Dulles' intelligence sources were too imprecise—they were wrong about some details—to resolve issues now disputed among historians, but two different informants, discussed below, suggested that SS officials in Berlin had a radical view about eliminating the remaining Jews. These sources also support the view that public protest and sheltering of Jews who went into hiding helped to frustrate SS hopes.

56. Bern to Secretary of State for OSS-SI, 10 Mar. 1943, NA, RG 226, entry 134, box 171, folder 1079.

57. Walter Laqueur, *The Terrible Secret: Suppression of the Truth about Hitler's "Final Solution"* (Boston: Little, Brown, 1980), 99.

58. Undated Visser t'Hooft report, L. H. to A. W. D., 13 Mar. 1943, and A. W. D. for the Minister, 15 Mar. 1943, NA, RG 84, Records of the Foreign Service Posts of the Department of State, American Legation Bern, General Records 1942–48, Economic Section, box 13, 1943, 840.1 Jews.

59. Harrison's handwritten addendum, in L. H. to A. W. D., 13 Mar. 1943, Ibid.

60. Harrison, Legation [Dulles] to Secretary of State [SI], 1 Apr. 1943, NA, RG 226, entry 134 Washington Registry: Radio and Cables Files, box 171, folder 1079. See also Stoltzfus, *Resistance of the Heart*, 244. On Wiskemann's letter [15 Apr. 1943—B arrived from Berlin

on 13 Apr.] to Dulles, see NA, RG 226, entry 210, box 376, folder 5. Those with one Jewish parent who were treated as Jews because of their identification with the Jewish community were among those rounded up. There is some evidence of more far-reaching plans to deport all whom the Nazis considered half-breeds (*Mischlinge*), which were not carried out. See Stoltzfus, *Resistance of the Heart*, 203–07.

61. Grose, *Gentleman Spy*, 179.

62. SI to Drum, Bern, 16 Mar. 1943, and Burns, Bern to SI, 5 Apr. 1943, NA, RG 226, entry 134, box 165, folder 1057; and NA, RG 226, entry 134, box 171, folder 1079, D-27 to Bern, document CD16945. Hoover to Donovan [undated], and Donovan to Hoover, 5 Apr. 1943, NA, RG 65, 65-43015-37x.

63. This document came from the anti-Nazi official in the German Foreign Office, Fritz Kolbe, one of Dulles' best sources. See Bern to SI, 30 Dec. 1943 (IN 8021 and 8020), NA, RG 226, entry 210, box 463, folder 2. For the most recent account of Fritz Kolbe's espionage work, based in part on newly declassified material, see Greg Bradsher, "A Time to Act: The Beginning of the Fritz Kolbe Story, 1900-1943," *Prologue: Quarterly of the National Archives and Records Administration* 34, no. 1 (2002): 7–26.

64. See chapter 3.

65. Bern to Secretary of State, 2 Mar. 1943, NA, RG 226, entry 134 Washington Registry, Radio and Cables Files, box 171, folder 1079, D-27 from Bern, 16 June 1942–31 July 1943, document CD15751.

66. Arthur Goldberg to Dulles, 20 July 1942, and Goldberg to Bowden, 2 Sept. 1942, NA, RG 226, entry 134, box 98, document 10641B.

67. See Breitman, *Official Secrets*, 148, 288n41.

68. For this eloquent document, NA, RG 200, National Archives Gift Collection, Duker/Dwork Papers, box 11, folder 107–Report . . . Polish National Council (quoted at greater length in Breitman, *Official Secrets*, 149).

69. It is worth noting that Abraham Duker and Charles Dwork salvaged this copy for the Research and Analysis Branch of the OSS, and that other copies have not been found in the OSS collection.

70. Memorandum on the Visit of L [Lunders] on Jan. 14 [report dated 15 Jan. 1942], NA, RG 226, entry 210, box 375, folder 4, document WN 13,925.

71. Peter Witte and Stephen Tyas, "A New Document on the Deportation and Murder of Jews during 'Einsatz Reinhard' 1942," *Holocaust and Genocide Studies* 15, no. 3 (2001): 468–86.

72. See Breitman, *Official Secrets*, 94; Martin Gilbert, "What Was Known and When," in *Anatomy of the Auschwitz Death Camp*, ed. Yisrael Gutman and Michael Berenbaum (Bloomington: Indiana University Press in association with the United States Holocaust Memorial Museum, 1994), 539–52; Miroslav Karny, "The Vrba and Wetzler Report," ibid., 553–68. Also Yitzak Arad, *Belzec, Sobibor, Treblinka: The Operation Reinhard Death Camps* (Bloomington: Indiana University Press, 1987): 349ff.

73. Arad, *Belzec, Sobibor, Treblinka*, 349–51.

74. Bernard Wasserstein, *Britain and the Jews of Europe 1939–1945* (London: Institute of Jewish Affairs; New York: Oxford University Press, 1979), 150. See also Laqueur, *Terrible Secret*, 74ff, 219–23.

75. See Breitman, *Official Secrets*, 115–17. Martin Gilbert mentions a report dated Apr. 18, 1943, written in London by a member of the Polish underground, and adds that the report made little impression in London since it was never made public. Martin Gilbert, *Auschwitz and the Allies*, (New York: Holt, Rinehart, and Winston, 1981), 130.

76. Karny, "The Vrba and Wetzler Report," 558–62. For the text see Rudolf Vrba and Alfred Wetzler, *The Extermination Camps in Auschwitz (Oswiecim) and Birkenau in Upper Silesia* [Vrba–Wetzler Report] (Washington, DC: Executive Office of the President, War Refugee Board, n.d.). Available in photocopy format at the United States Holocaust Memorial Museum Library.

77. For the report see F. L. Belin to Dr. William L. Langer, 10 Apr. 1944, and enclosed "Description of the Concentration Camp at Oswiecim," NA, RG 226, document 66059, identical with Military Attaché report 20 Mar. 1944, NA, RG 165, box 3138, folder–Poland 6950. In fact, the report, while overestimating the numbers in some cases, such as Greece (only 36,151 Jews arrived from 20 Mar. 1943 to 16 May 1943), was remarkably accurate on others. The total for Jews arriving from Holland, Belgium, and France from September 1942 to June 1943 was 66,378. For calculations see Danuta Czech, *Kalendarium der Ereignisse im Konzentrationslager Auschwitz–Birkenau 1939–1945* (Reinbek bei Hamburg: Rowohlt, 1989). This report from Wanda is also discussed in Richard Breitman, "Auschwitz Partially Decoded," in *The Bombing of Auschwitz: Should the Allies Have Attempted It?* ed. Michael J. Neufeld and Michael Berenbaum (New York: St. Martin's Press, 2000), 33. See also See Richard Breitman, "Auschwitz and the Archives," *Central European History* 18 (1985): 371–72.

78. "Oswiecim Concentration Camp," dated by hand 26 Oct. 1944, NA, RG 226, entry 16, document 98885.

79. This suggestion is borne out by the analysis in Laqueur, *Terrible Secret*, 66–7. Poles were in fact interrogated by British military intelligence officers, though one wartime Polish emissary would later comment that his Foreign Office interrogators had little interest in what he had to say about Poland's Jews.

80. Report No. PWIS (H)/ LDC / 469, NA, RG 226, entry 190, box 801, folder 17.

81. See especially Dino A. Brugioni, "The Aerial Photos of the Auschwitz–Birkenau Extermination Complex," in *Bombing of Auschwitz*, 52–4.

82. OSS Paris Report, No. FF–4777, 5 Mar. 1945, NA, RG 226, entry 190, box 784, folder 10. Natzweiler-Struthof (in Alsace) was liberated on November 23, 1944.

83. HQ & HQ Detachment, Office of Strategic Services, European Theater of Operations, United States Army (Main) APO 413, 3061/406, 9 Jan. 1945, Written By Gerald Miller, Chief–SO Branch, NA, RG 226, entry 190, box 784, folder 10. See also Supreme Headquarters/Allied Expeditionary Force/G-3 Division (Main), SHAEF/17240/25/Ops (C), GCT/370-15/Ops (C) 14 Feb. 1945, NA, RG 226, entry 190, box 784, folder 6.

84. See chapter 2.

85. On PWE's reluctance to report on the mass murder of Jews, see Breitman, *Official Secrets*, 102–3, 155–58.

86. On Foreign Minister Anthony Eden's role, see Arieh J. Kochavi, *Prelude to Nuremberg: Allied War Crimes Policy and the Question of Punishment* (Chapel Hill: University of North Carolina Press, 1998), 141–42. There was more Jewish emphasis in the wake of the declaration in

1942. Breitman, *Official Secrets*, 159.

87. The Polish exile press and the English language Jewish Press, which contained numerous reports, are not mentioned.

88. "P.W.E. German and Austrian Intelligence, List of German Concentration Camps," 21 June 1944, NA, RG 226, entry 190, box 801, folder 17.

89. Himmler decided on the liquidation of the three Reinhard camps in March 1943. Belzec was closed in July, Treblinka in November, Sobibor in December. Arad, *Belzec, Sobibor, Treblinka,* 370–76.

90. The report is part of a larger work by MI-6 on the German police system and is titled "Appendix to Chapter VI–Concentration Camps," located in NA, RG 65, 65-47826-12-330, boxes 50–52.

91. Arieh J. Kochavi, *Post-Holocaust Politics: Britain, the United States, and Jewish Refugees, 1945–1948* (Chapel Hill: University of North Carolina Press, 2001), 32ff.

92. "Appendix to Chapter VI–Concentration Camps," located in NA, RG 65, 65-47826-12-330, boxes 50–52, 1.

93. Ibid., 23.

94. Ibid., 10.

95. Vrba–Wetzler Report, 16.

96. Jeffrey Herf, "Anti-Semitism as Hatred and Explanation: Goebbels' Major Public Statements," paper presented at German Studies Association, Annual Meeting, October 2001, Washington, D.C.

97. MI-14, War Office, "German Concentration Camp Personalities," NA, RG 226, entry 190, box 801, folder 17.

98. Donovan to List S, 15 Dec. 1944, NA, RG 226, entry 190, box 536, folder 124.

2

Other Responses to the Holocaust

Richard Breitman

THE FIRST OFFICIAL RECOGNITION that Nazi Germany was pursuing a war of extermination against the Jews—the Allied Declaration of December 17, 1942—generated public and media criticism that Britain and the United States were not doing anything to halt the slaughter. During a late March 1943 trip to the United States, British Foreign Minister Anthony Eden engaged in preliminary discussions in preparation for a joint American-British conference on refugee problems. This conference, scheduled to take place in Bermuda in April 1943, was arranged in part to show that the two governments *were* working on saving lives.

The State Department and the Bermuda Conference

Rabbi Stephen Wise of the American Jewish Congress and Joseph M. Proskauer of the American Jewish Committee met with Eden while he was in the United States and asked him for an Allied declaration calling upon Hitler to permit Jews to leave Nazi-occupied Europe. Eden rejected this idea as "fantastically impossible," also repudiating their hope of shipping food to starving Jews in Europe. In a meeting later that day with high State Department officials, Eden warned that Hitler might take the Allies up on an appeal to release large numbers of Jews, and that there were not enough ships and means of transportation in the world to handle them.[1] (German U-boats, in fact, were destroying Allied ships in the Atlantic faster than new ships could be built: an Allied invasion of North Africa in the fall of 1942 suffered from insufficient shipping.)[2]

Eden's dismissal reduced the chance of an Allied appeal to Hitler. On April 7, Undersecretary of State Sumner Welles, who favored some specific schemes to evacuate Jews from the Balkans, told the Jewish leaders that only President Roosevelt could reverse the unfavorable attitude within the government regarding an appeal to Hitler to release Jews.

A newly declassified document suggests that the idea of an appeal to Hitler was still alive going into the Bermuda Conference. A few days before the conference, the head of the Visa Division in the State Department, Robert C. Alexander, told FBI official S. S. Alden that President Roosevelt had had some difficulty finding someone to head the American delegation to the Bermuda Conference. In his memo of the conversation Alden noted:

> Mr. Alexander further advised in the strictest confidence that the tentative plan was to ask Hitler, through neutral intermediaries, to release several million Jewish refugees presently in occupied territory. If Hitler refused, his moral position would be further aggravated. I asked Mr. Alexander if, in the event [Hitler] agreed, the United States and the other nations represented at the Bermuda Conference would not be faced with an inescapable obligation to immediately care for several million people, and [Alexander] agreed that such was the case.[3]

The two men expressed concern that the Nazis might offer to interrupt or reduce the Final Solution in order to embarrass or hinder the Allies, who could not handle a huge flow of refugees.

This account of a private conversation casts new light on tensions and significant divisions of opinion on the American side. Alexander worked closely with and under Breckinridge Long, assistant secretary of state for Special War Problems. From the start of the war, Long supported one barrier after another to refugees applying to enter the United States; he did not want the Bermuda Conference to relax these immigration restrictions, and he did not want an Allied appeal to Hitler to let Jews leave Nazi territories. Long was in charge of preparations for Bermuda, and not coincidentally, his friend Harold Dodds, a conservative Republican who was president of Princeton University, ended up as chair of the American delegation. The second member of this delegation was Scott Lucas, a Democrat senator from Illinois, who resisted any rescue project that might impinge on the war effort. The third member was Representative Sol Bloom, a Democrat from Brooklyn, who was chair of the House Foreign Affairs Committee. Long indicated at the time that he felt Bloom would be easy to handle.[4] Passed over was Representative Samuel Dickstein, another American Jew who was chair of the House Committee on Immigration and Naturalization. Dickstein had considerable expertise on refugee matters but was a sharp critic of Long's policies.

Though he was no Dickstein, Bloom declined to be a stand-in for Long.[5] According to the minutes of Bermuda Conference meetings, Bloom strongly advocated an Allied appeal for the release of Jews. After Richard Law, chair of the British delegation, opened on April 20 by criticizing extravagant suggestions, such as dealing with Hitler to release vast numbers of Jews, Bloom recommended at least seeing what could be achieved through private negotiations. Bloom suggested that the Allies give Nazi Germany a target number—the number of refugees per month the Allies could handle. Dodds reminded Bloom that the official policy of the U.S. government forbade any kind of negotiations with Nazi Germany. The British delegates and the American delegation secretary, Robert Borden Reams, then joined Dodds in criticizing Bloom's proposal. The minutes noted that another "extended argument" ensued before the discussion moved on.[6]

Bloom had very little room to maneuver at Bermuda. In his opening statement, Law explicitly raised the specter of Nazi Germany agreeing to release a million or two Jews, sending spies among them and overwhelming Allied shipping capacity. The Allies could not issue a blanket appeal because Hitler might accept it. But to work out practical arrangements on a smaller scale meant that somebody would have to negotiate with Nazi Germany. The Allied policy of "unconditional surrender" announced in January 1943, however, virtually precluded any talks but surrender negotiations. If Bloom pushed a public appeal, he ran into British refusal; when he supported negotiations, he ran afoul of the U.S. and British support for the policy of unconditional surrender, designed in part to reassure the Soviet Union that the West would not strike a deal with Germany. Alexander had spoken to Alden about the possibility of Bermuda delegates looking for neutral intermediaries to appeal to Hitler, but what neutral party would undertake this role without Allied backing?

Would a widely publicized appeal have moved Hitler to release Jews? In retrospect, the idea seems a complete illusion. Nonetheless, it might have influenced attitudes in Nazi satellite countries, which, after Nazi military setbacks, were beginning to doubt Germany's chances in the war, and it might have encouraged neutral countries to accept more of those Jews who were able to reach their borders. A wide public appeal would also have alerted many countries and citizens to the true nature of Nazi Germany's aims. The recently declassified FBI document does not reveal new opportunities for rescue, but it permits better understanding of some U.S. officials' hostile attitudes toward rescue, which also interfered with less ambitious rescue and relief options.

Bloom was not the kind of politician who generally led solitary crusades. Did he have some encouragement from Undersecretary of State Welles (or even President Roosevelt?), who was more positive than most State Department officials about relief and rescue opportunities? The evidence is circumstantial, but the possibility exists. Bloom's comments at the conference were consistent with what Alexander had told Alden a week earlier.

The International Committee of the Red Cross

Could a neutral organization such as the International Committee of the Red Cross (ICRC), based in Geneva, have appealed for the release of Jews from Nazi territories? The Red Cross was able to arrange some shipments of food parcels to Theresienstadt and some ghettos, but it was unable to obtain information about the fate of deported Jews. It was also unwilling to issue a public condemnation of Nazi killings of Jews on the grounds that it would be taking sides against a single belligerent and compromising both its neutral status and its ability to do practical humanitarian work for POWs and non-Jews who were suffering.[7]

During late 1942 and 1943, the World Jewish Congress lobbied repeatedly for Red Cross support for a number of proposals, such as an effort to appeal to neutral countries to open their borders to escaping refugees, an inquiry into the fate of deported Jews, and verbal support for Allied relief measures targeting the suffering populations of occupied Europe. The ICRC declined to enter discussions with the World Jewish Congress on these matters.[8] In May 1943, the Washington delegate of the ICRC sent to Geneva a list of specific actions proposed by the World Jewish Congress. Although the original letter is not available in the National Archives, a copy of the response from ICRC Secretary General Jean Suchard, dated June 24, 1943, is among the documents recently declassified by the IWG. Suchard painted a bleak picture:

> We can only confirm [our previous view that it is] . . . quite impossible for us either to make protests or to take action as the World Jewish Congress frequently demands of us.
>
> The German authorities will tolerate no intervention whatsoever regarding the Jewish question, and again quite recently we have come up against a blunt refusal even over the question of relief work, which we were attempting to extend to certain Jewish workers camps in Silesia, similar to that which we have undertaken for the internees in Theresienstadt.
>
> . . . Dr. Tartakower [of the World Jewish Congress] proposes a vast plan for feeding the Jewish population of Europe—the means being furnished by the United Nations: he does not take into account however, these measures resulting from the economic war, which prohibit all transfer of food to the belligerent countries of Europe; only parcels for prisoners of war and civilian internees are permitted. The case of Greece is the sole exception which the Allies have been willing to make to this rule, which has been strictly observed up till now.

Suchard explained that the World Jewish Congress should submit its plan to the Allies enforcing this blockade, and also get the support of the American Red Cross. The national organizations were not under the control of the International Committee. He concluded with a postscript:

> If there is an apparent contradiction between our cable of 28th December, 1942, to the World Jewish Congress . . . and our present attitude, it is essential to make it quite clear that the situation has considerably modified since the time when the cable was sent: the authorizations which we then possessed no longer exist, and we regret to have to add that it is in part due to the protests which appeared in the international press, causing a definite tightening-up in the attitude of the occupying authorities, and which have thus resulted in an aggravation of the situation of the deported Jews.[9]

Those opposed to public pressure for action on behalf of potential victims and refugees frequently asserted that publicity had somehow intensified Nazi persecution of Jews. In retrospect, however, the claim seems to be based on a complete misunderstanding of Nazi policy.

A month later, the ICRC went as far as it was willing to go in the way of a public appeal. It sent a telegram to all the belligerents, with copies to the national Red Cross organizations, and also published the text in the August 1943 issue of the *International Journal of the Red Cross*. The telegram read:

> Faced with the horrors, sufferings and injustices of war, the guiding principle of the International Committee of the Red Cross has always been to make clear its moral position and its wish to bring [succor] by deeds rather than by words. . . .
>
> The International Committee of the Red Cross wishes yet again to entreat the belligerent powers whatever military considerations dictate to respect man's natural right to be treated according to the law, without arbitrariness and without being held to account for actions he bears no responsibility for. It also requests the powers not to resort to unwarranted acts of destruction and above all not to pernicious forms of warfare banned by international law.

An ICRC historian concluded that this text did not have unfortunate consequences, but it also did not create much of a stir.[10]

"Dogwood" and Anti-Nazi Germans

One Central European and Balkans intelligence network linked to the OSS supplied substantial information about the Holocaust; some of its informants also recommended more active Allied responses. But this network, code named "Dogwood," turned out to have fatal security flaws, which ultimately discredited even the worthwhile intelligence and contacts it supplied. Historian Barry Rubin reconstructed the general story of the Dogwood network on the basis of less extensive documentation.[11] The discovery and full declassification of additional intelligence reports, especially a complete narrative history by one of the key participants in Dogwood, reveal more links to the Holocaust and greater detail about the activities of a number of anti-Nazi Germans and Austrians.

Dogwood's creator was Alfred Schwarz, a thirty-nine-year-old Czech Jew who had lived in Istanbul for more than fifteen years. An engineer who sold and installed heavy industrial machinery, Schwarz had represented a number of machinery manufacturing firms, among them the Chicago Pneumatic Tool Company. After the war broke out, he volunteered to work for British intelligence in Istanbul and for Czech intelligence (operating out of Jerusalem) without pay. By mid-1943, he already knew the espionage trade. Earlier that year he had liquidated his firm, devoting himself full-time to wartime problems and plans for postwar reconstruction. He had good language skills and intimate knowledge of the heavy industry sectors in Czechoslovakia, Germany, and Austria. Two OSS officials who met him were also impressed with his broad command of economic, social, political, and military matters in Central Europe. One of them thought him too good to be true—he must be a German spy. But his loyalty to the Allies turned out to be genuine, and he was brought into the OSS in July 1943.[12]

Taking over the office of an agent for the Cunard Cruise Line, which had little business during the war, Schwarz was initially insulated from other OSS officials and operations in Istanbul. He reported only to Archibald Coleman, an old friend of William Donovan, director of the OSS. Coleman took on the code name "Cereus," Schwarz became "Dogwood," and most of Dogwood's agents and informants were named after trees, flowers, plants, herbs, or spices.

Working with a number of anti-Nazi German émigrés in Istanbul,[13] Schwarz had already developed some well-placed contacts in Germany and satellite countries. In reports about a range of political, economic, and military matters, they had also passed along information of mixed quality about the Holocaust. Schwarz gave some of these earlier reports to Coleman after he joined the OSS.

An informant named Wurm, reporting details of Slovakian politics, extensively covered Slovakian efforts to resolve its "Jewish problem" through legislation and deportations. While in Hungary, Wurm was able to learn that deported Jews went to three locations—Birkenau, Podleski-Medzirici (relatively near Sobibor), and Sobibov (Sobibor)—but thought that these were way stations to other eastern execution sites, where all except those Jews capable of hard labor were shot in mass graves. He left no doubt that Slovak officials were eager to cooperate with Nazi Germany in getting rid of Jews permanently.[14]

On a July 1943 trip to Istanbul, the (now famous) anti-Nazi resistance leader Helmuth James von Moltke presented two key Dogwood men with a detailed but largely inaccurate and previously unknown account of the Warsaw ghetto uprising, in which tenacious Jewish fighters were equipped with the most up-to-date weapons.[15] This claim must have reached the High Command of the Armed Services from SS sources seeking to explain why it took them so long to suppress the Jewish revolt in the Warsaw ghetto; Moltke apparently believed it and passed it on. Moltke's report further indicated that twelve hundred to fifteen hundred Germans defected to the Jewish side during the battle because of their rejection of further massacres and atrocities in the name of the German people. This was wishful thinking on the part of those who wanted to salvage some honor for Germans. Moltke did accurately report that transports of Jews from the Warsaw ghetto had gone to "annihilating institutes" (presumably, the German term was *Vernichtungsanstalten*) in Poland.[16]

A separate report written one month later (but reaching an American diplomat in Istanbul in January 1944) filled in the details about one "annihilating institute." The supplier of the report was described as a reliable Jew in Istanbul. Nothing in the document clearly labels it a Dogwood report, but it likely came from Schwarz. The original source of the information was a Jew named David Milgrom, originally from Lodz, who had spent 1940 and 1941 in Warsaw.[17] Although deported from Czestochowa to Treblinka in the fall of 1942, Milgrom was able to join a small group of Jews assigned to sorting the clothing of Jews who were gassed. Although kept away from the area of the gas chambers, Milgrom heard a first-hand description from two boys who temporarily crossed over to the barracks for the Jewish workers. Milgrom related:

> The naked people who were brought there were herded into those barracks, and told that they are going to be bathed. When a batch of them was inside, poison gas was let in. Those still outside naturally tried desperately to back away when they realized what was going on inside. Then the SS and the Ukra[i]nians with their bloodhounds went into action and forced them in. The cries we had heard came from such crowds at the moment of entering. When a batch was inside the door was closed and remained so for fifteen minutes. When it was opened again, everyone inside was dead. Now the 500 Jews employed there had to throw the corpses into the fire-ditch which stretched beyond the fence into the death-camp. Those 500 Jews were in terrible condition of physical and psychic decay. They also got very little food, and ten or twelve committed suicide daily. From their "work" they all emitted a penetrating cadaverous smell, and it was this smell which betrayed our two informants, who were discovered among us and marched away by guards.[18]

Remarkably, after less than a week in this hell, Milgrom and two companions were able to escape. Two of the three reached Warsaw, and Milgrom went on to Cracow, where he obtained "Aryan" papers. Eventually, he contacted Slovakian smugglers who helped him cross the border. He wrote up his experiences in late August 1943. If they came into the hands of the Dogwood network, then Schwarz had a clear sense of how the Final Solution was being pursued.

Coleman met five times with Josef W. Rüdiger, the assistant general manager of the large Semperit manufacturing firm in Austria, who was based in Istanbul. Semperit was involved in the manufacture of natural and artificial rubber in locations from Duisberg to Cracow.[19] Rüdiger had previously told Schwarz (in June 1943) that Germany had become much more dependent upon the manufacture of artificial rubber, some of which was to be produced at "Ausspitz" in Moravia. (Perhaps Schwarz or one of his subordinates did not hear Rüdiger precisely, but someone knew enough to write in a correction—Oswiecim, the Polish name of Auschwitz.)[20] In August, Rüdiger indicated that the Auschwitz area in Upper Silesia (correct this time) was becoming the most important German war arsenal, and that it ought to be "flattened even at great risk." This report mentioned that the concentration camp of sixty-five thousand people, including thirty-two thousand Jews, supplied labor for new factories, and that twenty-two hundred SS men served as guards there.[21] In September, Rüdiger again suggested bombing Germany's sources of raw materials, especially oil fields and Buna factories. The OSS in Washington was impressed enough by this source to have the Research and Analysis branch prepare a questionnaire about Buna, which was later sent to Istanbul for Rüdiger.[22]

Giving Rüdiger the code name "Stock," Coleman considered him a highly valuable source after he revealed detailed information about the V-1 planes and

V-2 rocket program, which turned out to be 92 percent accurate. Rüdiger also developed an intelligence link with his corporate superior Franz Messner, who, like Rüdiger, was a native Austrian with a Brazilian passport. Messner ("Cassia") then developed his own intelligence and sabotage chain.[23] It later turned out, however, that Rüdiger's office associate and friend was a Gestapo agent, who probably was the cause of Messner's arrest by the Gestapo in Budapest in mid-1944.[24]

At the beginning of October 1943, OSS Washington alerted field offices that the most important function of the Secret Intelligence branch was to penetrate Germany to obtain specific intelligence, and that nearby neutral countries or countries occupied by Axis troops offered the best opportunities.[25] The Dogwood network fit this mold precisely. The head of OSS Istanbul, Lanning "Packy" Macfarland, alerted OSS Washington: "For the last two months we have been building up an independent group for penetration into the Reich. This group is well set up now, and starting to attain results."[26]

OSS Washington was quick to follow up with a request for more information. Macfarland asked to go to Washington and to meet with William Donovan personally; Donovan arranged for him to receive top air priority and said he was urgently needed. On October 30, Macfarland promised to give further details in person about "our Nazi penetration group [which] is getting in touch with top-notch Axis economic and military officials and former diplomats; some are renowned. Proceeding very well under the close surveillance of my assistant [Coleman]."[27] When Macfarland reached Washington, he radioed Istanbul to ask for the latest information about Coleman's Hungarian contact. Macfarland arranged for Coleman to meet with Donovan and himself in Cairo in late November; Coleman was to bring all his data along.[28]

This flurry of activity at the highest levels of the OSS resulted directly from an effort authorized by the Joint Chiefs of Staff to detach one or more of the satellite nations from the Axis. After OSS Istanbul drew up a memorandum on the Hungarian situation, the Joint Chiefs authorized the OSS to investigate the chance of persuading Hungary to break its alliance with Germany.[29]

There was also an initial burst of interest—but ultimately strong opposition in Washington—to Moltke's December 1943 effort through some of the Dogwood operatives to bring about some form of cooperation between the Western Allies and the anti-Nazi opposition in Germany. Moltke went to Istanbul, hoping to speak directly to an American he could trust. He left Istanbul disappointed. Still, Washington continued to value the intelligence extracted by Dogwood in Istanbul. At the end of the year, OSS Washington notified Macfarland in Istanbul: "Our political intelligence is being accorded markedly increased interest on the part of civilian departments of the government. Isn't it possible for the German field to yield more of your famous flowers?"[30] Moltke ("Camelia") became unavailable shortly afterwards: the Gestapo arrested him for unrelated reasons on January 19, 1944.[31]

The pressure from Washington for results helps to explain some OSS decisions in Istanbul that soon led to disaster. The first mistake was Coleman's decision to make use of a known Hungarian smuggler named Andre Gyorgi (aka Bandi Grosz). Grosz, code named "Trillium," came to Coleman's attention through Teddy Kollek, head of the Jewish Agency for Palestine's intelligence group in Istanbul. Kollek (much later to become the mayor of Jerusalem) explained that Grosz had helped to smuggle gold coins into Germany, which were then used to finance the escape of Jews to Turkey and other neutral countries. Kollek considered Grosz untrustworthy (to wit, "a double-crossing rat"), but he was also a good smuggler who worked on the side for others, including Hungarian intelligence and the General Staff of the Hungarian army.[32]

Coleman did not put much stock in intelligence delivered by Grosz. When Grosz brought a report that Germany and the Soviet Union had conducted separate peace negotiations in Bulgaria, with positive results, Coleman commented that this was typical of "leaks" stage-managed by the German Foreign Office. He rated the intelligence D-4: both the messenger and the message were unreliable.[33] He also thought that Grosz had little opportunity to gain insight into Dogwood's activities. But intelligence and political needs worked in Grosz's favor. The OSS wanted to contact the Hungarians secretly, and Grosz, acting for the Hungarian chief of staff, was no less eager to find a channel to American officials. Grosz and his sponsor in Hungarian intelligence, Col. Otto Hatz, however, tipped the Germans off about a potential Hungarian break with the Axis.[34] Germany had time to prepare to occupy Hungary with its own troops, and it did so on March 19, 1944.

American intelligence problems in Istanbul went deeper than Grosz, who was, from the beginning, regarded as a risk. As Coleman became seriously ill in late December 1943, Macfarland took over supervision of Dogwood. Schwarz, a man of strong will and great faith in his own judgment, decided to exploit this situation, maneuvering Coleman out of the picture. Macfarland allowed Schwarz even freer reign than he had enjoyed before.[35] An investigation by an outside OSS official in August 1944 disclosed that Coleman had warned Schwarz repeatedly against using his old friend Fritz Laufer, another Czech of Jewish background, for intelligence purposes. But Schwarz ignored the advice, considering Laufer (code named "Iris") one of his best agents.[36] Laufer, however, turned out to be a Sicherheitsdienst (SD) agent who helped destroy Dogwood's usefulness. By July 1944, the whole Dogwood network was in shambles, and OSS Istanbul had little left in the way of an intelligence network.

After Coleman recovered and wrote a long report on this debacle, OSS officials asked him a number of questions. The last one was: "How does the 'Brand Mission' fit into the above picture?"[37] Coleman said he knew nothing about this mission. Since some of Dogwood's people were involved in Brand's mission, this question still lingers for historians.

The Brand Mission

In May 1944, while rounding up Hungarian Jews for deportation to Auschwitz-Birkenau, Adolf Eichmann allegedly offered to spare Hungary's Jews in return for ten thousand trucks and other needed commodities from the Western Allies to be used by Nazi Germany only against the Soviet Union. Eichmann used Joel Brand, a Hungarian Jewish activist, to convey the offer of "Jews for trucks" to Western officials in Istanbul. Eichmann held Brand's wife hostage in Budapest. At the same time, the SD officials in Budapest sent another intermediary, none other than Grosz (Trillium in the Dogwood network), along with Brand to contact Western officials about the possibility of Germany reaching a separate peace with the West.

Were these Nazi feelers a hoax or a real chance to prevent, or at least delay, the last stage of the Holocaust? Lacking conclusive evidence, historians have divergent viewpoints.[38] Israeli historian Yehuda Bauer has taken the Brand-Grosz mission as a serious offer because Himmler was allegedly behind these feelers; by May 1944 Himmler might have been willing to break with Hitler. But Himmler's willingness to stage a coup and halt the Holocaust was never tested, according to Bauer, because British government officials, and to a lesser extent, their American counterparts, had no interest in pursuing a deal for Jewish lives. Besides the formidable political and military risks of bargaining with Nazi Germany, the rescue of Jews did not enjoy high priority for Western governments.[39]

Bauer's interpretation shifts moral responsibility for the last phase of the Holocaust partly to the Western Allies. (Although the Soviet Union was in a better geographical position to try to intervene, Stalin's regime showed not the slightest interest in doing so.) Newly declassified evidence about Brand's mission can inform the debate about what the West might have done in response to the Holocaust in Hungary. One example is the first postwar debriefing of Rudolf Kasztner, one of the Jewish representatives in Budapest involved in contacts with Nazi officials there. Although this document in FBI files does not identify Kasztner by name, he fits the description of the source: "a Hungarian Jew who arrived in Switzerland on April 18 [1945, who] acted as a go-between in negotiations conducted by the SS with various Jewish organizations in Switzerland..." Kasztner described Eichmann as running a tight ship in Hungary. If any of his SS subordinates had accepted bribes, Eichmann would have had them shot.

The one apparent exception was SS-Hauptsturmführer Dieter Wisliceny, who had taken bribes while serving in Slovakia during 1943. Knowing this, Hungarian Zionist and other leading Hungarian Jews hoped that money might stop the death factories. They therefore commissioned Kasztner to contact German authorities after Germany took control of Hungary. Wisliceny introduced Kasztner to Eichmann's subordinate, Hermann Krumey, who in turn arranged for a meeting with Eichmann. Eichmann demanded and received an advance of 6.5 million pengoes in Hungarian currency before he would negotiate. Afterwards, he insisted that he was not interested in money, but he did want ten thousand trucks.

This debriefing of Kasztner, now available in FBI records, supplies important background to the missions of Brand and Grosz in Istanbul. In particular, it clarifies that the initial idea of striking a bargain for lives came from Hungarian Jews who had learned (and misinterpreted) what had occurred in Slovakia earlier. Eichmann expanded and exploited this initiative.[40]

There is also some new information about Brand's traveling companion Grosz. Hermann Krumey was among a trio of Nazi officials who briefed Grosz before he left for Istanbul. According to a newly declassified OSS document obtained from the British, two SD men, Otto Klages and Fritz Laufer (Dogwood's "Iris"), plus Krumey, gave Grosz instructions. He was to bring about a meeting between high American and British officers with two or three high SD officials in a neutral country. He was to use Zionist contacts—both Brand and Grosz had had past dealings with Jewish Agency officials—to bring about this meeting. If, however, the Zionist connection failed, Grosz had another channel: after all, he was part of Dogwood. So Grosz could reach American officials one way or another.[41] This event suggests that Eichmann's men in Budapest and the SD were working together, not at cross-purposes, as some historians had believed.

In Istanbul, Grosz was met with suspicion and hostility. American intelligence officials had by now discovered from various sources that the Nazis had thoroughly penetrated the Dogwood network and that much of the intelligence Dogwood and his subordinates had collected was planted. An American counterintelligence officer quickly excoriated Grosz:

> This man has been an unscrupulous double-agent. He has worked for most of the intelligence organizations operating in Istanbul, but has been faithful to none, so far as we can see. He is a Jew [he was actually a convert to Catholicism] and has Hungarian-Jewish support. With this he has attempted to go to Palestine . . . We have a great deal of interest in this interrogation [which the British will carry out] . . . *We expect that easy methods will be used at first but that there will be no hesitation in using methods of whatever degree of stringency may be required to get results. The man definitely deserves no consideration on our part but we are concerned in getting out of him what he knows and what he has blown to the Germans.*[42]

Grosz's reputation eliminated any possibility that Western intelligence officials would listen to the messages Brand and Grosz brought with them. Grosz represented a source of danger, and in their eyes Brand was at best an unknowing accomplice. After discussions with Jewish officials in Istanbul and an initial debriefing by British intelligence officials, Brand and Grosz crossed the border into British-held Syria, trying to reach Palestine. Suspicious of both men and the offers they carried, British officials grilled them in Aleppo, and later sent them to Cairo for more extensive interrogation.

Quite independently, but almost simultaneously, the Morale Operations branch of OSS Cairo proposed to launch a publicity campaign directed toward

Jews in Hungary and Romania, inciting them to fight against their collaborationist regimes and the Nazis. Proposed articles and leaflets, allegedly stemming from the Hungarian underground, urged:

> We, Catholic Hungarians, with faith in God and mindful of the [T]en [C]ommandments, took up the fight against the gangsters of Hitler, and we fight with every available means. Many of our underground organizations were killed during the first days of our fight, but we gain a dozen new soldiers for every martyr. . . .
>
> What are you doing, Jewish brothers?
>
> Are you going to join our fight like men, or will you go to your death without opposition, like a bunch of sheep? Our lives are not in jeopardy like yours—we are only fighting for our country. Your days are numbered, and you know that after the most terrible humiliations and degradations, your destination is—Poland!
>
> You are facing the inevitable—so why don't you fight?
>
> You know that you are sentenced to death; why not at least take a Nazi beast with you?
>
> —St. Stephan's League[43]

Another appeal, titled "Fight, Jew, Fight," was to come from a Jewish organization called Son of Samson:

> Are we the cowards, the lice, the scum the Nazis say we are; or are we men, like the Warsaw heroes?! . . .
>
> There are 850,000 of us, we can do untold damage to Hitler, and if some of us will have to go down fighting, at least we will not die in vain like the heroes of the Warsaw ghetto. By fighting hard, we will hasten the liberation, and at least some of our loved ones will escape Poland's extermination plants.[44]

Whatever its potential disadvantages in motivating Hungarian Jewish resistance, the draft did not mince words. Another branch of the OSS had recognized that the Nazis had a policy of genocide for the Jews.

OSS Cairo sent this unusual proposal to Washington, where the OSS Planning Group emphatically rejected it and proposed to use Donovan's authority against it. OSS Washington told Cairo that the matter "involves matters undoubtedly unknown to you and too complex to enumerate."[45] Perhaps that was an allusion to Brand's mission and Allied attempts to discern what Nazi motives lay behind it.

OSS counterintelligence in Washington, despite wanting more information about Brand and Grosz, soon concluded that the Nazi offer to trade Jewish lives for trucks was meant to cause the Allies embarrassment: "Roosevelt is the chief target, for the Nazis claim that he is impeding the war effort by his attempts to rescue Jews."[46]

News of Eichmann's offer through Brand was leaked to the press in late June, and the British government publicly rejected it. Nonetheless, officials of the American War Refugee Board were open to the possibility of using Jewish negotiations with Nazi officials to delay further deportations and killings. Officials of the Jewish Agency for Palestine, as well as other Jewish organizations, were also willing to try to save the last large component of European Jewry.

So negotiations—not between Nazi officials and the West, but between Nazi officials and Jewish representatives—started again, despite the fact that Brand and Grosz had failed and were kept out of action. As a result of these meetings, first in Budapest between SS official Kurt Becher and Rudolf Kasztner, and then on the border of Switzerland, 1,684 Hungarian Jews were sent first to Bergen-Belsen and later to freedom in Switzerland as a sign of Nazi "good faith."[47]

The Allies never gave Nazi Germany trucks or other needed commodities, but questions remain about the original Nazi offer. Who gave the signal to send Brand and Grosz to Istanbul, and why? The following aftermath of the story, unknown until discovered among documents recently declassified by the IWG, suggests new answers.

On November 13, 1944, a German officer named Karl Marcus deserted and surrendered to Free French troops in France. After his release in Paris, Marcus established contact with British officers and convinced them he had valuable information. Marcus had served as assistant to Kurt Jahnke, a veteran German intelligence official who was a regular advisor to Walter Schellenberg, head of SD Foreign Intelligence. Marcus represented himself as Jahnke's envoy to the West.

British officials had no interest in pursuing Marcus' (or Jahnke's) idea that Britain should abandon the idea of fighting until Germany was destroyed, and that instead Britain should work with Germany to counteract Soviet influence. But they recognized that Marcus had a great deal of information about German intelligence operations. With the express permission of Prime Minister Winston Churchill, Marcus was brought to England at the beginning of 1945 and given various code names.[48]

British intelligence officials interrogated Marcus repeatedly. After giving a wealth of information about specific individuals and intelligence operations, especially in Britain and Ireland, Marcus revealed that Joel Brand's mission was approved by Schellenberg himself, and that its main purpose was to split the alliance against Germany.[49]

Schellenberg lacked jurisdiction over what the Nazis called the "Final Solution" of the Jewish question; there is no way he could have legitimately offered to stop mass murder of Jews. (And despite Eichmann's alleged offer to Brand to stop the deportations and killing, the trains of Jews from Hungary to Auschwitz continued while Brand was in Istanbul.) But if the purpose of sending Brand and Grosz to Istanbul was to sow dissension among the Allies, Eichmann would have surely gone along with Schellenberg's maneuver.

The OSS and the Jewish Agency for Palestine

The Jewish Agency for Palestine was among those institutions that suffered from the collapse of Dogwood and Allied suspicions of Brand and Grosz. As a result, it became harder for the Jewish Agency to develop a mutually beneficial relationship with the OSS. The Jewish Agency nonetheless produced evidence of Nazi war crimes. Because in the past many key documents remained classified, this story has always been hazy.

In August 1943, Moshe Shertok, head of the Political Bureau of the Jewish Agency for Palestine, went to Istanbul and met with one of Schwarz's Dogwood operatives in the hope of creating a connection with American intelligence. Although the Jewish Agency was already cooperating with British intelligence, the British government was unlikely to support Zionist political objectives at the end of the war, whereas the United States might. Schwarz indicated to Coleman that the Jewish Agency wanted to earn American goodwill, and after the war it would want to be able to point to its wartime contributions to the Allied cause.[50]

In Istanbul, Teddy Kollek, a Jewish Agency intelligence operative, was in charge of getting information about Jews in occupied countries, smuggling funds to them, and working out any possible rescue and relief measures. Kollek joined Schwarz's Dogwood network, receiving the code name "Gerbera"; Coleman described him as very intelligent, serious, and absolutely reliable.[51] Kollek represented the first known direct link between Jewish Agency intelligence and the OSS. But if Kollek turned over a lot of intelligence to Dogwood, most of these reports are no longer in the files.

At the end of December 1943, Irving Sherman, an official in the OSS New York office, recommended sending an American named Herbert Katzki to Istanbul to exploit Jewish sources better. Katzki had received OSS training but had never been used. He had previously worked in Europe (especially in Lisbon) for the American Jewish Joint Distribution Committee, and Sherman considered him a natural for contacting Jewish escape networks.[52] By the time Katzki arrived, however, he had additional functions assigned.

On January 22, 1944, President Roosevelt established a War Refugee Board to help "rescue the victims of enemy oppression in imminent danger of death" and to "provide relief and assistance consistent with successful prosecution of the war." The Board also arranged to have the State Department send out a forceful cable to its embassies, legations, and consulates, making it plain that this humanitarian work was now part of their jobs.[53] Later that month, OSS Istanbul was contemplating joint activities with the Jewish Agency, sending some agents into Bulgaria and Romania under OSS jurisdiction.[54] The climate for such activities had improved. The War Refugee Board asked the OSS to lend it Katzki for its operations based in Istanbul, and the OSS agreed, though Katzki also carried out intelligence work there.[55] From this point on, the War Refugee Board became the main sponsor of rescue and relief operations in the Balkans; it worked with the Jewish Agency, but also with other Jewish organizations.

In an early-February letter to Lord Moyne, the British Minister-Resident in the Middle East, Shertok proposed to have the Jewish Agency organize Jews in the Balkans and southeastern Europe "to take advantage of such opportunities as may arise for fighting the enemy and saving themselves from a possible doom." Shertok pointed to sporadic Jewish attempts at resistance in the ghettos of Poland, which had occurred without outside encouragement and with little in the way of arms, resulting in heavy casualties on the Nazi side. Those who were left should be organized, equipped, and trained for guerrilla warfare. He recommended activity in four countries: Bulgaria, Romania, Hungary, and Slovakia. Greece and Yugoslavia were omitted, he said, because Jews were already part of guerrilla forces there. But the leadership had to come from Jews in Palestine, so far underutilized by the Allies.[56]

The prospect of sending Palestinian Jews into southeastern Europe to create Jewish fighting forces there did not inspire great enthusiasm among some British officials in Cairo or in London, who felt that such action might have adverse repercussions upon Britain's position in Palestine after the war. British forces did, however, drop four Jewish parachutists into Yugoslavia in March. One of them was the now-famous Hannah Szenes, who was captured when she crossed into Hungary in June. (She was executed at Hitler's orders in November.) Other Hungarian infiltrators suffered a similar fate. After initial British rejection and some delay, Jewish Agency parachutists working with the British had some success organizing resistance in Bulgaria, Romania, and Slovakia.[57]

The Jewish Agency had hoped to send a thousand people into southeastern Europe; the British used thirty-two.[58] The Jewish Agency kept pushing for a separate intelligence relationship with the OSS, partly to employ its additional men and women, and partly to earn American goodwill. But American military officials had reservations about using Jewish agents. In mid-June, one American officer had warned the OSS:

> If occasions arise where the interest of the Jewish Agency and the United States conflict, we can expect that subject, as an agent, will work against our interest. . . .
>
> From a security standpoint, it is a dangerous policy to recruit and use double agents of this type, even when the dual capacity is fully apparent. The only justification is the successful gathering of intelligence or the successful accomplishment of operations which could not otherwise be carried out.[59]

On the same day this letter was written, a prominent official of the Jewish Agency, stopped at a border check in Egypt, was found to have notes about Jewish candidates for infiltration missions in Europe; the notes also contained names of OSS and British intelligence officers and personnel.[60] This discovery not only set off alarms about security but also raised the possibility that the Jewish Agency was seeking to penetrate OSS through the joint operations.

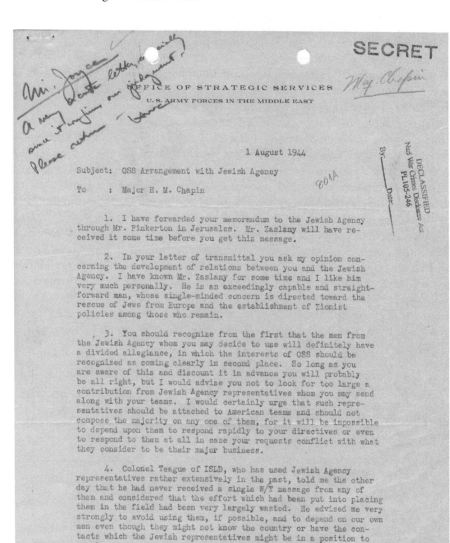

OFFICE OF STRATEGIC SERVICES

U. S. ARMY FORCES IN THE MIDDLE EAST

1 August 1944

Subject: OSS Arrangement with Jewish Agency

To   : Major H. M. Chapin

1. I have forwarded your memorandum to the Jewish Agency through Mr. Pinkerton in Jerusalem. Mr. Zaslany will have received it some time before you get this message.

2. In your letter of transmittal you ask my opinion concerning the development of relations between you and the Jewish Agency. I have known Mr. Zaslany for some time and I like him very much personally. He is an exceedingly capable and straightforward man, whose single-minded concern is directed toward the rescue of Jews from Europe and the establishment of Zionist policies among those who remain.

3. You should recognize from the first that the men from the Jewish Agency whom you may decide to use will definitely have a divided allegiance, in which the interests of OSS should be recognized as coming clearly in second place. So long as you are aware of this and discount it in advance you will probably be all right, but I would advise you not to look for too large a contribution from Jewish Agency representatives whom you may send along with your teams. I would certainly urge that such representatives should be attached to American teams and should not compose the majority on any one of them, for it will be impossible to depend upon them to respond rapidly to your directives or even to respond to them at all in case your requests conflict with what they consider to be their major business.

4. Colonel Teague of ISLD, who has used Jewish Agency representatives rather extensively in the past, told me the other day that he had never received a single W/T message from any of them and considered that the effort which had been put into placing them in the field had been very largely wasted. He advised me very strongly to avoid using them, if possible, and to depend on our own men even though they might not know the country or have the contacts which the Jewish representatives might be in a position to supply.

5. Not long ago a document was found in the car of a Jewish

- 1 -

First page of a note from Stephen Penrose of OSS Cairo to his colleague in Washington claiming that the Jewish Agency is too self-interested to be a suitable partner for joint operations (Penrose to Chapin, 1 Aug. 1944, re. OSS arrangement of Jewish Agency, NA, RG 226, entry 190, box 172, folder 1281–Jewish Agency).

Shortly afterward, Reuven Zaslani, a member of the Political Department of the Jewish Agency and the liaison from the Haganah to the British army, went to Allied headquarters at Bari, Italy, and agreed on a draft of a formal agreement with OSS officials at Bari.[61] Stephen Penrose of OSS Cairo then commented that Zaslani was capable and straightforward, but his "single-minded concern is directed toward the rescue of Jews from Europe and the establishment of Zionist policies among those who remain." Reviewing the incident of the seized notes about the OSS, Penrose cautioned OSS official Howard Chapin at Bari and OSS Washington that the Jewish Agency might use any joint operations now as claims at a postwar peace conference for further American assistance toward a Jewish state.

> You will probably think from the above that I am an anti-Semite as well as a cynic. I am not the first, although my experiences during the past three or four years may have made me the second . . . I am not strongly in favor of your proceeding very far with the Jewish Agency . . . but I do not wish to influence you [Chapin] unduly.

In a postscript, he added, "Their motto is 'us first'—'you second' (or third)."[62] Elsewhere, Penrose declared that from the time of his arrival in the Middle East, he had fought the idea of recruiting Jewish Agency personnel for intelligence missions.[63]

Army security officials were even more negative, citing proof that some representatives of the Jewish Agency had been used by German intelligence (Grosz was the obvious example on everyone's mind). Counterintelligence Corps (CIC) officers in Cairo believed that the greatest mistake made by Allied intelligence was to presume that any Jew was anti-Nazi and anti-Axis. The CIC believed that Jews would deal with Nazi Party officials and German intelligence, and sell out Allied contacts, agencies, and operations if it served their cause.[64] The American consul general in Jerusalem also weighed in against using the Jewish Agency operatives.[65]

The Jewish Agency had some OSS supporters. Carl Devoe in the Labor Section of the OSS said that the Jewish Agency had turned over useful intelligence reports based on interviews with refugees en route to Palestine. These reports contained economic data that aided the selection of targets for bombing. The Jewish Agency was aware, Devoe said, that there would be no American quid pro quo. Lewis Leary, chief of OSS Secret Intelligence for the Middle East, still favored careful cooperation with the Jewish Agency, pointing out both that the British had already used such men and women for operations in the Balkans, and that the OSS would control radio communications.[66]

Teddy Kollek of the Jewish Agency continued to believe that Zionist representatives who had had contact with Nazi officials in Hungary and Slovakia possessed useful information that the Allies might develop. Kollek sent Penrose a list of such Zionist officials: the top two Hungarian names were Rudolf Kasztner and Haynal Brand (wife of Joel Brand). Zaslani went to Cairo to brief Penrose on what they and others might accomplish with Allied backing.[67]

As the debate within the OSS stretched out to the end of 1944, the Jewish Agency raised another possibility, suggesting that it be allowed it to use Switzerland as a base to reach those Jews left in Germany and Austria, as well as the inmates of Theresienstadt. The author (probably Teddy Kollek)[68] of a new proposal now tried to turn the abortive Brand mission into an advantage. He stated that Nazi officials such as Krumey (Eichmann's man), Laufer, and Klages (both SD Foreign Intelligence) had used Brand and were still contacting other Jewish officials, such as Rudolf Kasztner in Budapest. Although these Nazi officials wanted to negotiate on various matters such as relief or exchange of Jews, contact with the Nazis might yield highly useful intelligence for the Allies. Nazis who had taken part in persecuting and exterminating Jews were among the fanatics who might likely go underground after Germany's defeat. The Allies would need information about such criminals, some of whom would seek refuge outside Germany. Switzerland was now a better vantage point than Istanbul to develop these Jewish Agency links with Nazi officials.

According to the same memorandum, the Allies had neglected another option to shorten the war. There were British and American plans to reach Allied POWs in Nazi camps and to incite uprisings or sabotage by foreign laborers in Germany. In late September 1944, Allied planes dropped 250,000 incendiary weapons in the section of Frankfurt-Mainz with a high concentration of workers. General Eisenhower, in a radio broadcast translated into several languages, appealed to foreign workers to bring the war to an earlier conclusion through sabotage.[69] But nothing had been worked out to reach Jews interned in labor camps, who might also take part in an uprising coordinated with the Allied invasion of Germany. Switzerland was the best base for clandestine efforts into Germany's camps, and the Jewish Agency wanted to send people there with Allied support.[70]

OSS Washington sent the Jewish Agency's proposal for a Swiss base to Irving Sherman in the New York office. Sherman, something of an expert on Jewish issues, told Allen Dulles he thought the OSS should move forward at once:

> The Intelligence Section of the Jewish Agency has been very effective. They have succeeded in maintaining regular contact with key individuals in various Axis countries . . .
>
> The problems peculiar to the Jews, and consequently to the Jewish Agency [have] necessitated their having close liaison with some important Nazi and Gestapo individuals. I know that important contacts are maintained through Switzerland and know of important negotiations even now taking place there.

Sherman recommended transferring Herbert Katzki from Istanbul to Switzerland, where he could again work both for the War Refugee Board and the OSS, and could serve as liaison to the Jewish Agency.[71] Dulles, who apparently had not received the Jewish Agency's detailed memo, cautioned Sherman against working "too closely with Kantar [code name for the Jewish Agency] at this stage" since its primary objective was to use the OSS to facilitate the movement of refugees to Palestine. But he expressed willingness to cautiously try "Ardent" (Katzki) or someone else.[72]

By late February 1945, Zaslani and Penrose had both gone to Washington, where they resumed contact. Lewis Leary in Cairo again lobbied for OSS cooperation with the Jewish Agency. But the military situation had changed: the movement of Allied troops toward the heart of Germany had reduced the need for internal uprisings to bring about Germany's defeat. Sensing as much, the Jewish Agency sought other opportunities for collaboration with the OSS. Emissaries from Palestine, working with local Jewish officials and communities still remaining in liberated territories, could assist OSS operations there, identify German agents and saboteurs, collect evidence about war criminals, and trace them. They could also help the Americans strengthen democratic influences in newly liberated countries. Infiltration of agents into areas still controlled by Germany—Austria in particular—was mentioned, but now it was subordinate to other goals.[73]

In early March, Penrose cleared Katzki's trip to Switzerland, nominally again for the War Refugee Board, but also for the purpose of a liaison between the OSS and the Jewish Agency.[74] Then he notified Dulles of the proposed limited relationship:

> We are willing to receive from [the Jewish Agency], with absolutely no commitments on our part, information which they will freely turn over to us. It has been definitely decided on a high level that we are to offer no assistance, financial or otherwise, to the advancement of their interests in the belief that this would help our own operations. We will not bring [the Jewish Agency] representatives to Switzerland . . . for it is our belief that such activity on their part would only be a cover to their political interests.[75]

This tentative decision meant that the OSS was not willing to give cover (such as working for the War Refugee Board) to anyone from the Jewish Agency.

As Katzki was en route, OSS officials in Washington sharpened their opposition. First, high-level officials finally rejected the plan to send Jewish agents into southeastern Europe as part of American teams. Whitney Shepardson, chief of Secret Intelligence in Washington, sided with Penrose, concluding that there was more to be lost than to be gained in collaboration on these operations, and that the Jewish Agency had not been really helpful enough in previous efforts. (It appears that a negative report from Lieutenant Jules Konig, who visited Palestine and met with some of the proposed candidates, influenced this decision.)[76] Then the same calculation reduced the scope of the proposed collaboration in Switzerland: any overt collaboration was to be avoided, mainly because "they always exploit any possible connection to their own advantage." The OSS would gladly take whatever intelligence the Jewish Agency could provide, but this was to be a one-way flow of information with nothing given in return.[77]

A subsequent letter by Stephen Penrose explained that Konig's negative report had an impact, but even more decisive was the Jewish Agency's suggestion (called a prerequisite) that the OSS bring a Jewish Agency man inside its organization to make the liaison work. This proposal again raised the specter of Jewish Agency penetration of the OSS, which high OSS officials emphatically rejected.[78] So a one-way flow of information from the Jewish Agency to the OSS was all that remained.

Jewish Agency for Palestine War Crimes Documentation

Shortly before the end of the war in Europe, the Political Department of the Jewish Agency began to organize its information about war crimes against Jews according to the names of individual perpetrators. For each of the individuals in a long alphabetized file, Jewish Agency officials drew on information obtained from survivors or witnesses, most or all of whom had reached Palestine. The individual sources were each given numbers, and next to each specific action attributed to a perpetrator were the numbers of potential witnesses.

SS and Police Leader Friedrich Katzmann "was charged with the extermination of Jews in eastern Galicia. He planned all proceedings against the Jews and supervised the strict carrying out of the orders." Source numbers 74 and 83 were prepared to testify that, in the middle of November 1941, Katzmann ordered all Jews to move into a ghetto, and that during this transfer some fourteen thousand elderly Jews were taken away and simply executed. Numbers 84 and 72 had information about Katzmann's inspections of the Janowska camp, during which he sometimes personally killed inmates.[79]

Although Katzmann was a high-ranking perpetrator, there were many files on lowly gendarmes or members of the German municipal police sent to occupied territories, and some German soldiers were included. Individuals who served in what is today Poland were the main subjects, but there was also coverage of some towns in conquered areas of the Soviet Union. It may be that the Jewish Agency compiled a broader geographical range of files and covered non-Germans as well as Germans.[80]

Some of the summaries were mildly exculpatory. Dr. Nagel, head of the Sipo (Security Police) and SD section dealing with Jews in Lvov, was involved in the first deportation from the ghetto; but higher authorities considered him too lenient. He was transferred in July 1942.[81] Other reports contained unusual information—events that did not fit known patterns. For example, SS-Hauptsturmführer Novak, who headed the Gestapo in Sosnowice (Poland), started the persecution of Jews there. At the end of 1940, he arranged deportation of some Jews, mostly intellectuals or those suspected of political activities or offenses against regulations, to "the Oswiecim extermination camp."[82] At that time, Auschwitz was not yet an extermination camp, but some Jews were sent to what started as a concentration camp for Poles, and hardly any survived. Similarly, a report on the extermination of the Jews of Tarnów indicated that sixty prominent Jews were arrested and sent to Oswiecim at the beginning of 1941, never to return.[83]

When there were enough survivors with good memories or documents for particular locations, Jewish Agency officials combined their information into reference works. The name files comprised detailed information about individual crimes and had even provided physical descriptions of the perpetrators—to aid their recognition and arrest. But the reference files tried to provide an understanding of the events in particular localities—the process of destruction as it developed over time.

What must be the earliest history (or mini-history) of the extermination of the Jews in Lvov was prepared on June 5, 1945. The ten-page document pointed out that, as soon as German troops took Lvov, Ukrainians in the city denounced Jews who had cooperated with Soviet authorities during the period of Soviet occupation, 1939-41. Those Jews were arrested, gathered near the municipal building, and beaten by the Germans and local inhabitants. Later, local inhabitants, especially from the villages nearby, ravaged the Jewish quarter and beat Jews who stood in the way of their robbery. Starting on July 1, a pogrom was organized; German police, soldiers, and local Ukrainians all took part. Many of those arrested were tortured and killed. On July 2, Dr. Levy, chief rabbi of Lvov, traveled to see Archbishop Sheptytsky (of the Uniate Church) to plead for his intercession, but on his return trip Levy was attacked by Ukrainians, taken to the local prison, and shot by a German army officer. More than twelve thousand Jews were killed in the first weeks of the German occupation of Lvov. The report described the establishment of a ghetto in fits and starts, the use of some Jews in labor camps, the killings on site, and the deportations to Belzec beginning in August 1942.[84]

The Jewish Agency's report on Tarnów traced the refusal of the Jewish council (Judenrat) to cooperate with deportations in June 1942. A number of its members were killed, and German authorities were forced to organize deportations themselves with the aid of SS extermination brigades, the German Schutzpolizei (municipal police), the Criminal Police, Polish police, and local Hitler Youth members. When the ghetto was finally liquidated in September 1943, a number of visitors—including the now notorious Amon Goeth, commandant at Plaszow, who had dealings with Oskar Schindler—arrived from Cracow. The Tarnów study detailed Goeth's personal involvement in murder:

> Goeth inspected the people lined up on the square and sent all those who appeared frail, old or for any other reason unfit for work, as well as mothers with children, to the railway station for deportation to Belzec. Several women who were found hiding their children among their baggage were shot by Goeth and his assistants. . .

... [As for] women and small children, who had not complied with orders [i.e., got out of the lorries], the SS fired at them. Among the shooting party were Goeth, Grunoff, Palten, and Rommelmann.[85]

In general, these studies contained a great deal of material of historical value, some hard-to-find nuggets about chronology and specific events, and some useful information for potential war crimes purposes.

It is hard to determine whether all this work—files on at least 569 individual perpetrators—contributed to the arrest or prosecution of anyone.[86] The individual sources of information are listed only by code number, and the identification list is not in the files. Some of the same individuals may have testified later in war crimes proceedings, but it would be impossible to determine from the information available in the National Archives.

The Jewish Agency apparently supplied a microfilm copy of these records to the OSS, which printed hard copies at some later date on thick paper. These paper records later became part of the collection of war crimes records assembled by American prosecutors at the Nuremberg trials. At some later date they arrived at the National Archives, where they were declassified long ago, but were otherwise ignored. They had been tightly tied together in bundles with rope (apparently of the 1940s era); the thick paper had curled into tight cylinders, and one needed to use two hands to unwind and read each page. The paper was brittle and unmanageable. But archives curators took over in 2002, making a better copy that is available for research today.

There were many reasons why the Allied governments prosecuted only a small percentage of those who committed murder and other crimes during the Holocaust. It was a huge task, and there were many practical obstacles. But one of the problems was accumulating specific evidence about exactly what each perpetrator did when, and where. Perhaps what came for free to the OSS was not properly appreciated.

Notes

1. Richard Breitman, *Official Secrets: What the Nazis Planned, What the British and Americans Knew* (New York: Hill and Wang 1998), 182.

2. Gerhard L. Weinberg, *A World at Arms: A Global History of World War II* (New York: Cambridge University Press, 1994), 380, 384.

3. Memorandum for Mr. Ladd, 13 Apr. 1943, NA, RG 65, 64-23000–Bermuda Conference on Refugees, box 16.

4. Henry L. Feingold, The *Politics of Rescue: The Roosevelt Administration and the Holocaust, 1938–1945* (New Brunswick, NJ, 1970), 195.

5. Influenced by the meager results of the Bermuda Conference, Jewish activists at the time and historians have judged Bloom harshly. See, for example, Richard Breitman and Alan M. Kraut, *American Refugee Policy and European Jewry, 1933–1945* (Bloomington: Indiana University Press, 1987), 139–40; Henry L. Feingold, *Bearing Witness: How America and its Jews Responded to the Holocaust* (Syracuse, NY: Syracuse University Press, 1995), 83; Monty N. Penkower, *The Jews Were Expendable: Free World Diplomacy and the Holocaust* (Urbana: University of Illinois Press, 1983), 108.

6. Morning Conference, 20 Apr. 1943: Confidential Memorandum for the Chairman, NA, RG 59, 52D-408 Misc. Subject Files, 1942–1947, box 3, folder–Bermuda Conference Minutes.

7. Jean-Claude Favez, *The Red Cross and the Holocaust*, trans. and ed. John and Beryl Fletcher (New York: Cambridge University Press, 1999), 78–79, 103.

8. Favez, *Red Cross*, 79–80.

9. The 28 Dec. 1942 cable is not available in the National Archives. Suchard to Peter, 24 June 1943 re. Intervention of the World Jewish Congress, censorship copy in NA, RG 226, entry 191, box 4, folder 44–Censorship-Greece.

10. Favez, *Red Cross*, 89–90.

11. Barry Rubin, *Istanbul Intrigues* (New York: McGraw-Hill, 1989). See also some key documentation reprinted in *USA und deutsche Widerstand*, ed. Jürgen Heideking and Christof Mauch (Tübingen: Francke Verlag, 1993), 40–69.

12. Arch F. Coleman to Maj. Lee M. Sharrar, Narrative Account of the Organization and Activities of the "Dogwood Project–Istanbul Mission," 5 Dec. 1944, 1–2, NA, RG 226, entry 214, box 6, folder WN24849-24859, document WN24851 [hereafter cited as Coleman Report]. Also, Coleman's earlier assessment (of Dogwood) in Report on Field Conditions, Istanbul, 2 May–14 Sept. 1944, NA, RG 226, entry 210, box 536, folder 1.

13. In September 1943, Ernst Reuter, Gerhard Kessler, Hans Wilbrandt, and Alexander Rüstow founded a German Freedom Movement in Istanbul. All but Wilbrandt were academics. See *USA und deutsche Widerstand*, 41–43. Two young German physicians, Peter Ladewig and Werner Laqueur, worked in Schwarz's office. Ladewig was considered part Jewish by the Nazis, and Laqueur was Jewish. See Coleman Report, 4.

14. Bericht Wurm, 20–26 Apr. 1943, NA, RG 226, entry 137, box 23, folder 160, envelope 3A, part 2.

15. The July 9, 1943, report is identified only as WRu-OKW; this abbreviation meant Wilbrandt and Rüstow from an OKW source. NA, RG 226, entry 137, box 23, folder 160, envelope

3A, part 2. A later document, a 14 Sept. 1943 report from Cereus on the basis of information from Hyacinth [Dr. Hans Wilbrandt] through Dogwood [Schwarz], specifically identified Moltke as the source of the July 9 report, which covered a number of other subjects in addition to the Warsaw ghetto uprising. See Cereus (13), Hyacinth via Dogwood, 8 Sept. 1943, NA, RG 226, entry 137, box 23, folder 160, envelope 3A, part 2. For additional evidence of Moltke's trip to Istanbul and his meeting with Wilbrandt and Rüstow, see Helmuth James von Moltke, *Letters to Freya*, trans. Beata Ruhm von Oppen (New York: Knopf, 1990), 317, 317n1.

16. WRu-OKW, 9 July 1943, NA, RG 226, entry 137, box 23, folder 160, envelope 3A, part 2.

17. Melbourne to Secretary of State, 13 Jan. 1944, NA, RG 59, CDF-740.00116 E.W. [European War] 1939/1311 2/3/TLPS/TL.

18. Ibid.

19. Coleman Report, 10.

20. Riediger [*sic*], (Stock) Report of 10 June 1943, NA, RG 226, entry 137, box 23, folder 160, envelope 3A, part 2.

21. Only the second page of this report from Rüdiger survives—it left Cairo on 29 Sept. 1943, copy in NA, RG 226, entry 146, box 246, folder 3437.

22. Report from Stock/Periwinkle through Cereus, 7 Sept. 1943, NA, RG 226, entry 137, box 23, folder 160, envelope 3A, part 2. OSS to Macfarland, Istanbul, 19 Jan. 1944, NA, RG 226, entry 134, box 288, folder 1651.

23. Coleman Report, 10–11.

24. Irving Sherman, Report on My Istanbul Mission, 24 Aug. 1944, NA, RG 226, entry 210, box 369, folder 7.

25. OSS Washington to Gustav, Cairo, 1 Oct. 1943, NA, RG 226, entry 134, box 252, folder 1521.

26. Macfarland was then in Cairo for consultations. Gustav, Cairo to OSS, From 550 [Macfarland] to 154 [Shepardson] re. Penetration into the Reich, 8 Oct. 1943, ibid.

27. OSS to Gustav, Cairo, Carib and 154 to 550, 9 Oct. 1943; Gustav, Cairo to OSS, Macfarland to Buxton, 11 Oct. 1943; OSS to Gustav, Cairo, Donovan to Toulmin, 23 Oct. 1943, all in NA, RG 226, entry 134, box 252, folder 1521. Quote from Macfarland, Istanbul to OSS, 30 Oct. 1943, NA, RG 226, entry 134, box 288, folder 1652.

28. OSS to Macfarland, Istanbul, From 550 [Macfarland], 7 Nov. 1943, NA, RG 226, entry 134, box 288, folder 1652–Dispatches; Macfarland, Istanbul, to OSS, From 550: Attention, Cereus, 10 Nov. 1943, ibid.

29. OSS to Macfarland, from Carib and 154, 22 Nov. 1943; OSS to Macfarland, 9 Dec. 1943, both in NA, RG 226, entry 134, box 288, folders 1651 and 1652.

30. The story of Moltke's Dec. 1943 feeler, which the OSS called the "Herman Plan," is already well covered in scholarly literature. See *USA und deutsche Widerstand*, 52–67, for key documents. The section of the Coleman Report on Moltke contains much misinformation about the man and his motives. For the quote, OSS to Macfarland, Istanbul, 31 Dec. 1943 re. the German Field, NA, RG 226, entry 134, box 288, folder 1652–Satellite nations of Axis and Hungary.

31. Moltke, *Letters to Freya*, 385.

32. Coleman Report, 14–16.

33. Source: Cereus (35); Subsource Trillium via Dogwood, 24 Sept. 1943, re. Rumors of Russo-German Peace Negotiations, NA, RG 226, entry 137, box 23, folder 160, envelope 3A, part 2.

34. Coleman Report, 16, 18–20, 23–24.

35. Coleman Report, 27–31.

36. Sherman's Report on My Istanbul Mission, 24 Aug. 1944, NA, RG 226, entry 210, box 369, folder 7, document WN14753.

37. Coleman Report, 62.

38. See discussion of varying historical interpretations in Richard Breitman and Shlomo Aronson, "The End of the Final Solution? Nazi Plans to Ransom Jews in 1944," *Central European History* 25, no. 2 (1992): 177–80.

39. Yehuda Bauer, *Jews for Sale? Nazi-Jewish Negotiations, 1933–1945* (New Haven, CT: Yale University Press, 1994), esp. 119–195.

40. Military Intelligence Report from unidentified Information Group, 17 May, 1945, on SS Organizations in Hungary Responsible for Jewish Persecution, copy in NA, RG 65, 65-47826-249, box 63.

41. Grosz met with two SD men and one Security Police official (Jeschke) in Budapest on May 15, 1944. The next day he met with two SD men and one of Eichmann's subordinates (Krumey). Both meetings involved discussions of Grosz's (and Brand's) mission in Istanbul. Extract of British interrogation of Grosz in Aleppo, Syria, 6–22 June 1944 (S.I.M.E. Report 3), NA, RG 226, entry 210, box 447, folder 10, document WN16145. The full interrogation of Grosz is already available at the Public Record Office at Kew: FO 371/42811.

42. X-2 report for week ending 3 June 1944, NA, RG 226, entry 108A, box 141, folder DX 010 1944. Emphasis is in the original document.

43. The original title was the Calvin League, which was struck out. Perhaps someone remembered that Calvin was not Catholic.

44. Hungarian Jews, NA, RG 226, entry 92, box 552, folder 15, document 31957. This document, declassified well before 1998, was called to my attention by Daniel Davis, to whom I am grateful.

45. Wilson to Director, Strategic Services, 15 June 1944 re. MO plan for Jews in Hungary and Romania, in NA, RG 226, entry 92, box 552, folder 15, document 31957.

46. OSS to Ustavic, London, 7 July 1944, re. Brand Plan, NA, RG 226, entry 134, box 245, folder 1499–Wash-Sect-R&C 75.

47. Breitman and Aronson, "End of the Final Solution?" 193–202; Tuvia Friling, "Nazi–Jewish Negotiations in Istanbul in mid-1944," *Holocaust and Genocide Studies* 13, no. 3 (1999): 405–36.

48. OSS despatch, at the request of the chief of MI-6, 28 Dec. 1944, entitled Nazi Attempt to Contact British; Buxton's Memoranda for the Secretary of State and the Joint Chiefs of Staff, 16 Jan. 1945, both in NA, RG 226, entry 210, box 364, folder 2.

49. Dictionary Information about the UK and Eire: Interrogation No. 25 re. Jahnke, undated, NA, RG 226, entry 109, box 66, folder XX11587-11599.

50. Report on the Desirability of our Co-operation with the Jewish Agency, 27 Oct. 1943 [from

Dogwood and Cereus], NA, RG 226, entry 210 (A1-171), box 20, folder 11.

51. Coleman's assessment in Report on Field Conditions, Istanbul for the period 2 May to 14 Sept. 1944, NA, RG 226, entry 210, box 536, folder 1; also Coleman Report, 14.

52. Sherman to Beale, 31 Dec. 1943, re. Herbert Katzki, NA, RG 226, entry 214, box 7, folder WN25844-25850, document WN25846.

53. Executive Order 9417, quoted in Breitman and Kraut, *American Refugee Policy*, 191; on the cable, 191–92.

54. Macfarland to Lt. Col. Vala Mocarski, OSS Cairo, 31 Jan. 1944, NA, RG 226, entry 215, box 4, folder WN25940-25949.

55. Hughes to Shepardson, from Donovan to Macfarland, 17 Mar. 1944, re. Herbert Katzki to Istanbul, NA, RG 226, entry 214, box 7, folder WN25833-25843. On Katzki's work for OSS, see Sherman to Dulles, 17 Jan. 1945, re. Intelligence Section of the Jewish Agency, NA, RG 226, entry 210, box 241, folder WN9432/001-9890/048, document WN9446.

56. Shertok to the Minister-Resident in the Middle East, Cairo, 7 Feb. 1944, re. Jewish resistance in the Balkans, copy in NA, RG 226, entry 215, box 4, folder WN25940-25949.

57. For British reaction, see Bernard Wasserstein, *Britain and the Jews of Europe 1939–1945* (New York: Oxford University Press, 1979), 289–94; also Dina Porat, *The Blue and the Yellow Stars of David: The Zionist Leadership in Palestine and the Holocaust*, (Cambridge, MA: Harvard University Press, 1990), 224–25. For a summary of the results of the missions and information about those involved, see Porat, 225–28.

58. Porat, *Blue and Yellow Stars*, 228.

59. Major C. T. S. Keep to Mr. Penrose, Cairo, 13 June 1944, re. Sample security opinion for men recruited from the Jewish Agency, NA, RG 226, entry 190, box 172, folder 1281–Jewish Agency.

60. CIC Cairo Report to A. C. of S., G-2, U. S. A. F. I. M. E., 13 June 1944, re. translation of notes found on a prominent member of the Jewish Agency, ibid. The man was not named in this document.

61. Proposed Cooperative Arrangement between SI Central European Section OSS and Jewish Agency Intelligence Service, 21 July 1944; Chapin to Penrose, 24 July 1944, re. Jewish Agency Intelligence Service Proposed Agreement, both in NA, RG 226, entry 190, box 172, folder 1281–Jewish Agency.

62. Penrose to Chapin, 1 Aug. 1944, re. OSS arrangement of Jewish Agency, ibid.

63. Penrose to Wisner, memorandum from Wisner previously dated 17 and 19 Aug. 1944, 24 Aug. 1944, NA, RG 226, entry 210, box 252, folder 6, document 10250/5.

64. Kennedy to Toulmin, 7 Aug. 1944, re. Jewish Agency, NA, RG 226, entry 190, box 172, folder 1281–Jewish Agency.

65. Mentioned in Leary to Shepardson, Notes on Cooperation with the Jewish Agency, 15 Mar. 1945, NA, RG 226, entry 215, box 4, folder WN25940-25949, document WN25946.

66. Devoe to Penrose, 16 Sept. 1944, re. Report on meeting with officials of Jewish Agency, NA, RG 226, entry 215, box 4, folder WN25940-25949; Leary to Chief, SICE, 16 Mar. 1945, re. Mission in near East, Accomplishments and Personal Conclusions; and Leary to Shepardson, 6 Mar. 1945, re. proposed cooperation between the Jewish Agency and OSS in penetrating

Austria, both in NA, RG 226, entry 215, box 4, folder WN25940-25949, document WN25946.

67. Kollek to Penrose, 31 Oct. 1944, re. Zaslani trip to Cairo, NA, RG 226, entry 215, box 4, folder WN25940-25949.

68. Kollek had by this time been transferred from Istanbul to Jerusalem. On 14 Dec. 1944 he wrote Penrose on several matters and said that he was attaching a suggestion about activities that could be organized in Switzerland. Kollek to Penrose, 14 Dec. 1944, NA, RG 226, entry 215, box 4, folder WN25940-25949.

69. Christof Mauch, *The Shadow War Against Hitler: The Covert Operations of America's Wartime Secret Intelligence Service*, trans. Jeremiah Riemer (New York: Columbia University Press, 2003), 176.

70. Jewish Agency for Palestine, Switzerland as Base of Operations, 11 Dec. 1944; a handwritten note indicates that it was sent to Whitney Shepardson in Washington, NA, RG 226, entry 215, box 4, folder WN25940-25949. The Jewish Agency had apparently learned from its previous rebuff that it had to deliver more that was of intelligence value to the OSS if it wanted American sponsors. In January, Kollek promised an increase flow of material, and he delivered a thirteen-page memo on "Jewish Terrorist Gangs in Palestine," which one OSS official found worthwhile.

71. Sherman to Dulles, 17 Jan. 1945, re. Intelligence Section of the Jewish Agency, NA, RG 226, entry 210, box 241, folder 3–WN9432/001-9890/048, document WN9446.

72. Bern to OSS, from 110 to 154 and 209 [Shepardson and Sherman?] 17 Feb. 1945, re. Kantar, NA, RG 226, entry 134, box 192, folder 1219–IN D–27 SI Bern Jan.–Mar. 1945.

73. Zaslani to Shertok, 27 Feb. 1945, re. Jewish Agency for Palestine, document WN25946; Leary to Shepardson, 26 Feb. 1945, re. Swiss Plan from Jewish Agency, document WN25946; Leary to Shepardson, 6 Mar. 1945, re. Proposed Cooperation between the Jewish Agency and OSS in penetrating Austria, document WN25946; Unsigned [Zaslani] Suggestions for Joined Activities in South–Eastern European Countries, 27 Feb. 1945; all in NA, RG 226, entry 215, box 4, folder WN25940-25949, and RG 226, entry 190, box 172, folder 1281.

74. Penrose to Sherman, 10 Mar. 1945, re. Kantar, NA, RG 226, entry 210, box 241, folder 3, document WN9439/009.

75. Penrose to 110 [Dulles], 22 Mar. 1945, re. [Ardent], NA, RG 226, entry 214, box 7, folder WN25833-25843, document WN25837.

76. Penrose to Leary, 20 Mar. 1945 re. Jewish Agency Plan, NA, RG 226, entry 215, box 4, folder WN25940-25949; Washington to Aldrich and Leary, Maddox, Caserta, for Ulmer, Bari from 154 [Shepardson] and Penrose, 21 Mar. 1945, NA, RG 226, entry 190, box 172, folder 1281. Konig submitted a preliminary report on March 5 (Konig Preliminary Report, 5 Mar. 1945, cover sheet 6 Mar. 1945, see Konig to Chief, SICE, 16 Mar. 1945). Leary sent his own summary on March 15 (Leary to Shepardson, 15 Mar. 1945, NA, RG 226, entry 215, box 4, folder WN25940-25949, document WN25946), and Konig sent a supplement on March 16 (Konig to Chief, SICE, 16 Mar. 1945, NA, RG 226, entry 215, box 4, folder WN25940-25949, document WN25946).

77. Penrose to Leary, 20 Mar. 1945, re. Jewish Agency Plan, NA, RG 226, entry 215, box 4, folder WN25940-25949, document WN25946.

78. Leary to Shepardson, 15 Mar. 1945, notes on cooperation with the Jewish Agency; Penrose to Leary, 30 Mar. 1945, re. the decision on cooperation with the Jewish Agency, both in NA, RG 226, entry 215, box 4, folder WN25940-25949, document WN25946.

79. Katzmann, Brigadeführer SS, NA, RG 238, entry 52D, box 15, folder–Immhof-Katzmann.

80. Here I cover only those copies that ended up in American hands. The original files are said to be in the Haganah archives in Israel.

81. From the Jewish Agency re. Dr. Nagel and Novak, dated 10 and 30 May 1945, NA, RG 238, entry 52D, box 15, folder–Mons-Novak.

82. Ibid.

83. Report titled "The Extermination of the Jews of Tarnov" from the Jewish Agency for Palestine, 28 May 1945, NA, RG 238, entry 52D, box 16, folder–Reports-Extermination of the Jews of Sosnowiec, Bendzin and vicinity, etc.

84. Report titled "The Extermination of the Jews in Lvov" from the Jewish Agency for Palestine, 5 June 1945, NA, RG 238, entry 52D, box 16, folder–Krueger-Kuehnlein; Misc. Reports.

85. Report titled "The Extermination of the Jews of Tarnov" from the Jewish Agency for Palestine, 28 May 1945, NA, RG 238, entry 52D, box 16, folder–Reports-Extermination of the Jews of Sosnowiec, Bendzin and vicinity, etc.

86. Alphabetical list of criminals, undated, from the Jewish Agency for Palestine, NA, RG 238, entry 52D, boxes 15 and 16, folder–Misc., Alphabetical List.

3

Case Studies of Genocide

Richard Breitman
with Robert Wolfe

EXISTING NAZI GOVERNMENT and party documents do not reveal the full intentions and crimes of Nazi officials. Some incriminating matters were never put in writing, while others were camouflaged with euphemisms or vague allusions. Some highly sensitive documents were lost or intentionally destroyed as Germany's military fortunes deteriorated.

A number of Nazi secrets, however, leaked out at the end of the war when Nazi officials talked. In other cases, Allied intercepting and decoding operations picked up German radio messages. This chapter contains one case study using each type of intelligence. These two new cases, the result of material declassified under the Nazi War Crimes Disclosure Act, help to reveal how far the Nazis went to commit murder and to conceal their crimes.

The "Selection" of Elite Czech Children

Nazi efforts to Germanize Czech territory involved more than bringing German settlers into the Protectorate of Bohemia-Moravia or seizing Czech assets. The SS was prepared to destroy the Czech nation. The main lines of Nazi policy were laid out in German documents long since declassified, but one newly declassified Allied interrogation of an SS officer stationed in Prague yields striking and ghastly details of a previously unknown plan to murder talented Czech children.

In September 1940, Reinhard Heydrich, head of the Reich Security Main Office (RSHA), wrote a memo for the files about the need to conduct a racial census in the Protectorate. Like his boss, Reichsführer SS Heinrich Himmler, Heydrich was convinced that a certain percentage of the Czech population was of Germanic stock and therefore valuable—suitable for Germanization, absorption into the German people. What percentage of Aryan blood qualified a person as valuable? In marginal cases, one could also look at subjective qualities, such as behavior. But only a racial census of the population could supply baseline data for determining who could stay and who must go. Those Slavs considered

CSDIC(WEA)
BAOR
31 Aug 46

APPENDIX TO FR 92

Georg BÜGELSACK

SECRET

APPENDIX

PLAN FOR THE EXTERMINATION OF CZECH CHILDREN

A. HISTORY AND ORGANISATION

1.   In 1941 Ostubaf KÜNZEL received an order from HITLER via Gruf HEYDRICH, to work out details of a plan for the liquidation of those Czech children who on account of their personality, physical excellence and high intelligence seemed likely to become future leaders of Czech national life. KÜNZEL planned this operation in conjunction with HEYDRICH, and later Oberf BIHMANN, and with the Secretary of State for the Protectorate, K H FRANK. The plan finally decided on was as follows:-

2.   Permission was requested from the Czech President, Dr HACHA, for commissions of German doctors to tour the Protectorate with a view to X-raying all Czech children, allegedly in order to discover and prevent the spread of tuberculosis. The operation was outwardly of a purely medical nature and was to be carried out in co-operation with the Czech local authorities. Accordingly it received HACHA's support.

3.   About 1942, three separate commissions of three or four members each were formed. The heads, KÜNZEL, PREUSS and ULRIAK, were all SS officers who pretended to be doctors; they wore civilian clothes. The commissions toured the entire Protectorate. The heads called on the local Czech mayors and requested them to assemble the children in the school building. Here X-ray photographs were taken of each child. The children also underwent a brief examination as to racial characteristics and were given an intelligence test.

4.   Results of these examinations were collated and sent to Ostuf Dr med HUSSMANN in PRAGUE, who had established an office in the Hradschin under the cover-name of "Röntgenkommission". HUSSMANN was assisted by Oschaf BENDER, Oschaf STUTZ and Rotf BÖHM. The results obtained by the "medical" commissions were entered on a card-index, each child receiving a separate card.

5.   The process of liquidation was planned in the following manner: The local Czech authorities would be furnished with nominal rolls of children who, it would be claimed, needed hospital or medical treatment for TB. The authorities would be requested to inform the parents of this fact and to cause the children to be sent to German Youth Hostels and convalescence centres. From here it was planned to send the victims to special extermination camps. In due course, the parents were to be informed that their children had died of TB.

6.   Prisoner states that this order was never given, but the work of the unit was not wasted. When the Russians were approaching the borders of CZECHOSLOVAKIA, large numbers of Czech youths, specially earmarked for extermination, were despatched to exposed sectors of the front. They were officially given the job of building fortifications; Prisoner, states, however, that the true intention was to cause their death. This purpose has, according to Prisoner, largely been achieved.

7.   Prisoner states that about 1942/43 the SS Rasse- und Siedlungsamt Aussenstelle BÖHMEN und MÄHREN" was set up in CZECHOSLOVAKIA. The HQ (Hauptdienststelle) was at Marakstr 5, PRAGUE. Provincial offices (Dienststellen) were set up in various towns of the Protectorate.

8.   The complete card-index prepared by the "Röntgenkommission" was transferred to the Hauptdienststelle and was kept by one of the sub-departments known as "Kartei". The officials of the Dienststellen

Part of a report from British interrogation of Georg Büglesack describing Nazi plans to murder gifted Czech children (CSDIC Final Report on Georg Büglesack, July 1946, NA, RG 65, 105-9666, box 156, Appendix 1 dated 31 Aug. 1946, 1).

unsuitable, Heydrich wrote, could not remain in Bohemia: he set himself a goal of evacuating them somewhere yet to be determined.[1]

In January 1941, Himmler proceeded with this policy by ordering German officials to arrange for school-based physical examinations of Czech children. Otto Hofmann, chief of the SS Race and Settlement Main Office, suggested that while these exams would produce statistics on racial composition, school physicians would undoubtedly make mistakes and even submit false reports to shield as many children as possible. Recommending more effective examinations by the X-ray team within his office, he reported that he had ordered SS-Sturmbannführer Ermin Künzel to Prague.[2]

The thirty-three-year-old Künzel had served in the Race and Settlement Office since 1934, rising to SS-Obersturmbannführer while leader of the regional office in Prague. He served a brief period in the Waffen-SS in 1942, but suffered a relapse of tuberculosis and was discharged. Apart from this stint, he remained in Prague and other SS Race and Settlement outposts. Among other things, he supervised a program labeled "Acceptance of applicants capable of Germanization" (*Zulassung eindeutschungsfähiger Bewerber*).[3] Available German documents do not clarify what was intended for Künzel's rejects.

In September 1946, British military police arrested Georg Bügelsack, another former Race and Settlement official from Prague, who supplied information to the British about Künzel that was later given to the FBI. Bügelsack had served as chief of staff in the Prague Race and Settlement office in mid-1944. Although he had not been there in the early years of Nazi occupation, he had heard a great deal from colleagues who had stayed in Prague throughout. Bügelsack explained that the original plan in Prague was for

> local Czech authorities to be furnished nominal rolls of children who . . . needed . . . treatment for TB . . . and to inform the parents that . . . the children would be sent to German Youth Hostels and convalescence centers . . . From here it was planned to send the victims to special extermination camps. In due course the parents would be informed the children had died of TB.[4]

This clandestine extermination plan resembled the carefully camouflaged "euthanasia" program carried out in Germany and some German-occupied territories to dispose of those persons considered genetically deficient because of actual or perceived physical or mental impairments.

The term "euthanasia" was itself camouflage—these individuals were not terminally ill. Some of them had conditions or diseases merely suspected to be hereditary. This so-called euthanasia program, authorized directly by Hitler, was not an SS operation: officials of Hitler's private chancellery directed operations from an office at Berlin's Tiergartenstrasse 4, hence the program's code name "T-4." Through the summer of 1941, more than seventy thousand Germans labeled as defective through this process had already been gassed.[5]

Their relatives were given false information that they had died as a result of diseases.

Künzel's secret plan, as reported by Bügelsack, diverged from T-4 in two respects. First, this program was directly in the hands of the SS. Second, the goal of the SS was not to kill those people labeled defective but "to liquidate Czech children who on account of their personality, physical excellence and high intelligence seemed likely to become future leaders of Czech national life."[6] If the Czech nation was to disappear, then the future Czech leaders had to die. Bügelsack identified Heydrich, State Secretary Karl Hermann Frank, and an SS-Oberführer Weihmann as the high authorities behind this plan.[7] It would appear that Künzel kept them satisfied. Künzel's superior in the Race and Settlement Office, Otto Hofmann, pressed for his promotion because Künzel had undertaken "wide-ranging activities, especially in the area of racial policy . . . which were not only valued but esteemed by Heydrich."[8]

Bügelsack claimed that all the exams were conducted and selections made, but the order to kill the children never arrived. Perhaps Heydrich's assassination in mid-1942 disrupted arrangements, created new priorities, or removed the one person who would not have shied away from the ramifications. Nonetheless, Bügelsack asserted that the work of examining and classifying Czech children was not "wasted." In the late stages of the war, as Soviet troops approached Czechoslovakia, large numbers of Czech youths, particularly those who had been marked for extermination, were sent to exposed sectors of the front, allegedly to build fortifications. But the true intention of these assignments was to bring about their death, which frequently occurred.[9]

Bügelsack's account helps to explain what the Chilean consul in Prague, Gonzalo Montt Rivas, wrote in September 1941: Bohemia-Moravia was to be Germanized. Sometimes stronger peoples simply eliminated weaker ones, a process repeated throughout history.[10] This time, Montt guessed wrong.

<hr>

The study of past plans for mass murder may decrease the chances of future occurrences. The more evidence we have, the better the chance that we will learn. A second case study of genocide draws upon Allied signals intelligence uncovered and declassified by the IWG and subsequently also made available at the Public Record Office (Kew) in the United Kingdom. These new documents offer a clearer picture of German activities in Italy in the summer and fall of 1943, including the effort to deport and exterminate the Jews of Rome.

New Documents on the Holocaust in Italy
On July 23, 1943, in response to rumors about a plot to overthrow Mussolini's government, Herbert Kappler set up a short-wave radio in his office in Rome and established contact with his superiors in Berlin.[11] Technically a police attaché

within the German Embassy in Rome, the thirty-six-year-old Kappler was placed with German diplomats as a cover. In actuality, he reported not to the German Foreign Office, but to officials of departments IV (the Gestapo) and VI (SD Foreign Intelligence) of the RSHA.

Kappler's radio connection to Berlin came just in time. Two days later, a palace coup in Italy unseated Mussolini and installed Marshal Pietro Badoglio in office. Anxious authorities in Germany wanted immediate information about the situation, and Kappler used his radio to describe the maneuvers of the Badoglio government, the Italian military, and the Vatican, as well as to report on the status of trusted Fascist officials.

After Italy secretly negotiated an armistice with the Allies and the British and Americans landed troops in southern Italy, Germany responded by rushing large numbers of troops and some policemen into Italy, and by taking control of the capital. Italy was no longer a German ally, but an occupied country—and a battleground.

Finding himself at the focal point of attention in Europe, Kappler relied heavily on radio communication; it gave him independence from Italian (and local German) officials. Radio was also a means to reach Ernst Kaltenbrunner, chief of the RSHA, and even Heinrich Himmler. Although some mail went by courier and some phone calls may have been made, from early September until late October 1943 Kappler and various RSHA and SS authorities in Germany exchanged radio messages each day. These messages provide a running log of SS and police reactions to, and activity during, the Italian crisis; they also include small but revealing bits of information about the first stage of the Holocaust in Italy.

While many radio messages between Kappler and authorities in Germany have not survived or have not yet surfaced, other transmissions were intercepted and quickly deciphered by British intelligence.[12] Translations were distributed within days, and some American intelligence officials were among the recipients. Using documents declassified by the IWG, we can now understand more fully what British and American intelligence learned at the time.[13]

In postwar testimony during his own trial and again later at the trial of Adolf Eichmann, Kappler explained that just after the liberation of Mussolini he had received a phone call from Himmler's office with very good and bad news. He was promoted to SS-Obersturmbannführer and awarded the Iron Cross decoration. In the same call he learned that Himmler wished to proceed with the arrest and deportation of the Jews of Rome. (Kappler did not state who called him.)

The timing of the call mattered because Kappler claimed that he then delayed carrying out Himmler's order. He had misgivings about carrying out this action under the eyes of Pope Pius XII and an unsupportive Italian population. During the rest of September, he hoped to show his superiors that it would be more profitable to exploit Rome's Jews. The latest historical study, Robert Katz's *The Battle for Rome*, essentially accepts Kappler's version.[14] So did a 1948 Italian military tribunal, which convicted Kappler for other things, but not for deporting Jews from Rome.[15]

The decodes of SD messages (hereafter called SD decodes) and some older evidence raise substantial doubts about Kappler's testimony. During the days before September 12, Himmler was obsessed with the rescue of Mussolini from his Italian captivity. Infuriated by a refusal from General Karl Student, commander of an air corps, to divide his parachute troops to try to free Mussolini, Himmler ordered the rescue of Mussolini with the use of all available SS and police forces; all other activities were to be deferred. Himmler's instructions went to Walter Schellenberg, head of SD Foreign Intelligence, who radioed them to Kappler.[16] Himmler's telephone logs include nothing about a phone call to Kappler in mid-September 1943.[17] New and old sources suggest that any orders for deportations of Jews came later than September 12. Rome was not even under full German control then.

Perhaps the key is to look more closely at the date and manner of Kappler's promotion, which Kappler connected with Himmler's order. It turned out that in February 1944 the RSHA learned for the first time of this promotion and inquired how it had come about. The response was that Karl Wolff, Highest SS and Police Leader for Italy, had suggested it to Himmler in the early days of Italy's effort to desert Germany, and that Himmler had accepted the idea. When he was asked about the date of the promotion, Himmler (in March 1944) wanted it to coincide with the day of Mussolini's liberation—September 12, 1943. So the paperwork was backdated.[18]

Karl Wolff met with Himmler on the afternoon and again on the evening of September 15; he probably suggested the promotion at that point.[19] It does not appear that Himmler or his office notified Kappler of the promotion, and the RSHA did not know about it, so that left Wolff. Along with some trusted Italian Fascists, Wolff flew from Germany to Rome on September 17, and Kappler was instructed to have his party met at the airport. Wolff reported his arrival to Himmler the next day. He had begun work in collaboration with General Ricci, newly installed head of a Fascist militia in Rome.[20] Wolff immediately ordered the transfer to Rome of a hundred policemen from a German police battalion in northern Italy, giving Kappler the nucleus of a force of his own. He also used Waffen-SS units to reorganize the Fascist militia.[21] All these forces would be important during the next month, since Kappler recognized that he could not depend upon the Italian police to cooperate in deporting Jews. In fact, the general unreliability of Italian police in Rome forced Kappler to take some Roman police officials into custody.[22]

Wolff did one other thing that is of interest in the present context: he handed out decorations to at least two German officials; they received the War Cross for Merit.[23] Wolff was the one who arranged for Kappler's promotion. Would he not want to pass the news to Kappler at the first opportunity? Was Wolff the one who informed Kappler orally about Himmler's order to deport the Jews of Rome? If Kappler's testimony about hearing about his promotion and the order to deport Jews simultaneously is accurate, it incriminates Wolff. If Kappler's testimony is inaccurate, it suggests that Kappler heard about the order later and did not seek to delay its implementation.

On September 24, Kappler warned Berlin that Spanish diplomats were about to leave Rome on a special train, and that the Vatican had sold Spanish, Argentinian, Portuguese, and Mexican visas to Jews trying to escape Rome on this train.[24] Whether the Vatican had actually done what Kappler reported is doubtful. In any case, no known independent evidence confirms the sale of visas to Jews. But Kappler's warning that some Jews were escaping, and his promise to find out who the purchasers of visas were, cast doubt on his postwar testimony of resisting Himmler's order. By this time, certainly, Kappler was familiar with Himmler's goal of deporting Italian Jews to their deaths. On September 25, the RSHA circulated a list of Jews of various nationalities who could now be deported from different locations—Italian Jews were first on the list.[25]

On September 26, Kappler met with two leading Italian Jews, Dante Almansi, president of the Union of Italian Israelite Communities, and Ugo Foa, president of the Jewish Community of Rome, to demand fifty kilograms of gold from the Jewish community of Rome within forty-eight hours. If they failed, two hundred Jews would be deported to Germany. Kappler's postwar testimony was that he turned to extortion as an alternative to deportation—he hoped to show his superiors how profitable it would be to exploit Rome's Jews.[26] Historian Susan Zuccotti summarized Kappler's explanation, but expressed great skepticism, and she later dismissed it entirely.[27]

Robert Katz maintained that Kappler was afflicted by "Rome fever" and concerned about maintaining security in the capital. Katz found indications of Kappler's pessimism reflected in his radio messages; perhaps they did reflect Kappler's private view that roundup and deportation of Rome's Jews would be problematic. Katz also plausibly claimed that Kappler tried at least to postpone the roundup of Jews because it might endanger or disrupt the arrest and deportation of more than fifteen hundred Carabinieri, who were deemed a security risk.[28]

The decodes do not conclusively establish Kappler's motivation. They do show that he was concerned about a rise in anti-German sentiments among the Italian population; his measures against the Jews of Rome were adding to the problem.[29] Nonetheless, he collected the gold and, as the decodes reveal, shipped it off to Kaltenbrunner at his RSHA office on October 7.[30]

In an October 6 radio message decoded by the British,[31] Kappler alerted Wolff, who had returned to Germany, that SS-Hauptsturmführer Theodor Dannecker had arrived in Italy with orders to seize all Jews quickly and ship them off "to Germany." In the rest of the message, whose interception or decoding was partly garbled, Kappler warned that German officials in Rome were going to Field Marshal Kesselring, commander of the German Army in Italy, to suggest that the Jews could be better used as laborers in Italy.[32]

In his postwar testimony, Kappler claimed that Dannecker had arrived with authorization signed by Gestapo chief Heinrich Müller to deport the Jews and to draw on all available police, a sign that Kappler's foot-dragging had failed.[33] In actuality, Dannecker's arrival in Rome in early October seems to mark the point when those German officials in Italy who disagreed with Berlin about the Final Solution began to act. German Foreign Office records indicate that the main lobbyist against deportation was the German consul in Rome, Eitel Friedrich Möllhausen, who was the senior Embassy diplomat in the absence of Ambassador Rahn. Möllhausen contacted Foreign Minister Joachim von Ribbentrop on October 6 to try to cancel the deportations. According to a document later smuggled into Switzerland by an anti-Nazi official in the German Foreign Office, Möllhausen also addressed this message to Hitler.[34] The text suggested that General Rainer Stahel, the German commandant of Rome, was opposed to deportation; it was ambiguous about Kappler's view. Möllhausen's cable specified that he was about to go to Kesselring to reverse any deportation order: he had not already done so.[35]

There is no doubt about Möllhausen's courageous initiative. Kappler, however, sent mixed signals. While awaiting resolution from above, Kappler passed along to Berlin another report that a businessman named Morini from Alessandria was traveling around Italy helping to smuggle Jews into Switzerland.[36] Kappler sent this report to help his superiors shut down this activity, again suggesting that if Kappler were opposed to deporting the Jews of Rome, it was only because he had concerns about whether he could pull it off without the full support of the German authorities in Italy and in the face of hostile Italian public opposition.

On the evening of October 7, Karl Wolff met with Hitler in the Führer's headquarters.[37] Whatever his own views, Wolff knew Hitler well enough not to recommend lesser punishment for Italian Jews. Hitler's comments are undocumented. It is likely that both men were aware that the deportation of Italian Jews was politically sensitive, and that neither particularly wanted to assume direct responsibility for it. In a conflict between SS and military authorities, however, Hitler must have known how to tip the balance without leaving much trace of his involvement. On October 11, Kaltenbrunner sent Kappler a very firm order that undoubtedly reflected both Hitler's and Himmler's view:

> It is precisely the immediate and thorough eradication of the Jews in Italy which is the special interest of the present internal political situation and the general security in Italy. To postpone the expulsion of the Jews until the Carabinieri and the Italian army officers have been removed can no more be considered than the idea mentioned of calling up the Jews in Italy for what would probably be very improductive [sic] labour under responsible direction by Italian authorities. The longer the delay, the more the Jews[,] who are doubtless reckoning on evacuation measures[,] have an opportunity by moving to the houses of pro-Jewish Italians of disappearing completely. [Garbled word—Einsatzkommando?] Italy [has been] instructed in executing the RFSS orders to proceed with the evacuation of the Jews without further delay.[38]

This message survives only because of British interception; we have no other evidence of Kaltenbrunner's intervention. Kappler could now have no doubts that he was expected to fulfill orders regardless of difficulties or repercussions. The next day Kaltenbrunner added a sweetener with his message that Kappler had been awarded not only the Kriegsverdienstkreuz First Class, but also the Iron Cross Second Class.[39]

Kappler's preparations for the action of October 16 in Rome do not appear in the decoded messages to Berlin. But when 365 SS and police managed to round up 1,259 Jewish men, women, and children, and imprison them within a military school near the Vatican, Kappler quickly sent off a radio report that same evening (and by courier later). His tone was slightly defensive—he had planned as well as possible, all available German police were used, the Italian police were unreliable, and it had not been possible to cordon off whole blocks in an open city to prevent Jews from escaping. Above all, the Italian public had resisted passively, and there were some instances of active opposition.[40] The results, he seemed to be implying, were as good as possible under difficult circumstances. Whether his superiors would rejoice in the seizure or bemoan the number of those not apprehended (about 6,800), he did not know.[41]

Kappler's men screened the Jewish prisoners, releasing non-Jews arrested by mistake, Jews in mixed marriages, and some other special cases, such as Jews from countries where Germany had not yet started deportations. The Vatican Secretariat of State sought to influence the German ambassador to save these innocent people and to win the release of converts to Catholicism, but without success. About 250 people, non-Jews or part-Jews not deemed Jewish under Nazi standards, were released—not because of Vatican efforts, but because their arrest had been a mistake.[42] On October 18, the remainder left Rome on a train numbered X70469. Wilhelm Harster, Commander of the Security Police and SD for Italy, requested that Kappler radio Vienna and Prague (as well as Berlin) to arrange relief of the police escort when the train arrived there. Harster's radio message specified the ultimate destination of the transport: Auschwitz. British intelligence read that quite clearly.[43] Dannecker also used Kappler's radio to report to his office (and thus to Eichmann) the departure of 1,007 Jews (actually 1,002) accompanied by a detachment of guards under SS-Oberscharführer Arndze, who had two copies of a list of the passengers.[44] Upon their arrival at Auschwitz, all but 196 Jews on the transport were immediately gassed; only fifteen of the 196 were to survive the war.[45]

On October 21, Dannecker's men headed off to Florence under the temporary command of SS-Untersturmführer Eisenkolb; Dannecker himself was ill.[46] They all had done what they could in Rome under the circumstances. But Kappler was not finished explaining to his chiefs his problems in Rome. On October 27, in response to a message that some of his earlier transmissions had been garbled, Kappler retransmitted an earlier assessment: for a long time the Vatican had been helping Jews to escape, and the population of Rome was turning increasingly anti-German, fearing that seizures of Italian laborers might follow the roundup of Jews. Kappler urged better German propaganda and more use of pro-German Italians to sway Italian public opinion.[47]

Kappler's assessments were a combination of his own perceptions and his own excuses for a job very partially accomplished by Nazi standards. The action of October 16 captured about fifteen percent of the total Jewish population in Rome. The Final Solution in Italy took a toll of about 6,800 Jews—only about 20 percent of the total, but more than Nazi officials might have seized in the face of open defiance and public opposition from the Vatican. Still, it is worth noting that Kappler would hardly have agreed with one recent author that Pius XII was "Hitler's Pope."[48] As far as Kappler was concerned, the Vatican represented a hostile influence. That was undoubtedly what his superiors felt, too.

Kappler might have taken comfort in his superiors' appreciation of his situation if he had been able to listen in on an October 16 conversation between Heinrich Müller, head of the Gestapo, and a German Foreign Office bureaucrat named Eberhard von Thadden. Their topic of discussion was implementation of the "solution to the Jewish Question" in newly occupied territories. Thadden pointed to the escape of most Danish Jews in early October 1943. To avoid repeating that failure, he argued, future actions against Jews should be carried out with sufficient planning and force so that serious political complications could be minimized. Conceding that the RSHA had learned something from events in Copenhagen, Müller responded that for the duration of the war it would not be possible to raise

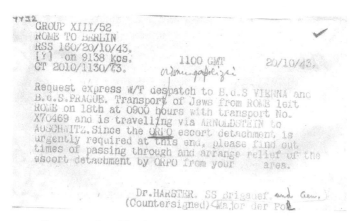

British intercept of a message from Theodor Dannecker to Eichmann reporting the transport of over a thousand Roman Jews to Auschwitz (Dannecker to RSHA IV B 4, 21 Oct. 1943, decode 7754, NA, RG 226, entry 122, Misc. X-2 Files, box 1, folder 5–Italian Decodes).

forces sufficient to carry out actions in one blow (*schlagartig*). The only recourse was to do as well as possible with the forces that were available. Reflecting the view of the Foreign Office, Thadden specifically argued that the influence of the Catholic Church in Italy made it important to strike rapidly there. But Müller stuck to his old approach: the purge of Jews would have to begin behind the line of battle in the south and spread to the north. There were not enough forces to do it any other way. Nonetheless, Thadden noted that Müller apparently was concerned about the planned seizure of eight thousand Jews in Rome—an action that was in progress as they spoke. Müller referred to it as an order from Hitler (*Führerbefehl*).[49] Kaltenbrunner had given Kappler firm instructions on October 11 because the order had come from the highest possible authority.

The Allies, the Vatican, and the Jews of Rome

Could the Allies have used information obtained from the SD decodes to try to save some Italian Jews? This question is linked to a broader debate about what can or cannot be done with intelligence during a war. Every use of intelligence carried risks to intelligence gathering, but there were ways of using information publicly without revealing specific sources. Of course, few people in the fall of 1943 had access to information classified as "Most Secret."

According to author Robert Katz and more recently Michael Phayer, German Embassy personnel opposed to the deportation of Rome's Jews contacted the German ambassador to the Vatican, Baron Ernst von Weizsäcker, who notified the Vatican of the impending roundup.[50] Although a number of monasteries and convents opened their gates to Jews seeking to go underground, there is apparently no evidence that the Vatican issued a warning or ordered Vatican institutions to offer sanctuary. There was no surge of Jewish sanctuary seekers before the roundup of October 16.[51]

Would anyone else warn the Jews of Rome? Almansi and Foa, the two Jewish leaders, did not do so—they hoped for the best from Kappler—but they got only misleading information from him. British intelligence was not in the practice of talking publicly about what it was gleaning from German radio messages. The anti-Nazi German diplomat Albrecht von Kessel later claimed to have warned some of Rome's Jews that they would be exterminated, but his words met only disbelief.[52]

There is nothing to suggest that Franklin Roosevelt received information about Nazi intentions in Italy in time to influence the outcome of events in Rome on October 16. The president did receive a translation of Möllhausen's appeal to Ribbentrop and Hitler, but only by way of a copy smuggled to Allen Dulles in Switzerland, some two months after the event.[53]

Winston Churchill had a better chance of gaining access to timely information about the Holocaust in Italy, but nothing in the intelligence files of the prime minister's office indicates that he learned of the plan for a Final Solution there.[54] Two days after the SD message of October 6 from Kappler to Wolff announcing Dannecker's arrival in Rome and clearly revealing Dannecker's mission in Italy,

Churchill happened to discuss with his War Cabinet the idea of issuing another public statement denouncing Nazi atrocities. Perhaps if the Allies publicly committed themselves to punishing those who carried out atrocities, massacres, or killings, it would deter future crimes. Foreign Minister Anthony Eden dissented from Churchill's proposal, arguing: "I am most anxious not to get into the position of breathing fire and slaughter against War Criminals and promising condign punishment, and a year or two hence having to find pretexts for doing nothing."[55] Churchill ultimately got his way, and the Moscow Declaration of November 1, 1943 (emanating from the Moscow Conference attended by the British and Soviet foreign ministers and the American secretary of state), threatened to punish war criminals. However, the Moscow Declaration made no mention of the murder of Jews and offered no warning to those still in danger of being deported.[56]

Punishment and Responsibility

What ultimately happened to the perpetrators of the Final Solution in Italy? RSHA chief Ernst Kaltenbrunner was included among the major war criminals tried by the International Military Tribunal at Nuremberg. The prosecutors did not know, one assumes, about his order of October 11, 1943, or they would have used it as evidence against him. Nonetheless, there was enough other evidence to secure a conviction and his execution.

The fate of Theodor Dannecker, head of the deportation experts in Italy, remained obscure for some time after the war. (In 1985, Holocaust scholar Raul Hilberg was only willing to claim that Dannecker was believed to have died in U.S. custody.)[57] Actually, newly declassified documents reveal that Dannecker went into hiding to help organize Nazi resistance to an Allied occupation of Germany. Before doing so, he instructed his wife to poison their two children. (One of the children died; the other was rescued by outside intervention.) Dannecker led a small band of Nazis in the Black Forest and then migrated to Bad Tölz. Benefitting from a tip, American forces captured him, jailed him, and interrogated him. Dannecker conceded having played a role in deportations of Jews from several countries, and he admitted to being in Italy from September 1943 until February 1944. Given time to write his life history, he hanged himself in his cell in December 1945. He did not write about his Italian activities.[58]

Herbert Kappler was captured by British forces and interrogated at some length in June 1945 about his recruitment of intelligence operatives, his treatment of political prisoners, and his plans for resistance to the Allied occupation of Italy. His interrogators apparently did not ask Kappler questions about Nazi policy regarding Jews, and Kappler did not volunteer any information about it. Was this lack of attention to Kappler's role in the Holocaust the result of lack of interest or lack of familiarity with the most relevant intelligence records? Without further information, it is impossible to judge. The interrogator assessed Kappler as an intelligent, ruthless man, with the mentality and mannerisms of the "cold, correct Prussian militarist," who was prepared to justify his actions in Rome, partly blaming orders from his superiors Karl Wolff and Wilhelm Harster. It is not clear from files currently available whether he blamed them for the roundup of October 16. The interrogator, who considered Kappler's testimony reliable, suggested that it might be appropriate to try him as a war criminal.[59]

Kappler was turned over to Italian authorities and tried in 1948 by an Italian military tribunal. Published accounts indicate that the court found insufficient evidence to convict Kappler for his role in deporting Jews from Rome—though he was sentenced for extorting gold from its Jewish community. Kappler was convicted, however, for directing the execution of 335 prisoners in the Ardeatine Caves on March 24, 1944, as a reprisal against acts of sabotage by Italian partisans. Some were selected because they were Jews. Kappler had claimed that Wilhlem Harster had ordered him to include Jews among the victims, but Wolff placed blame for this decision on Kappler himself.[60] Kappler remained for many years in an Italian prison. In 1977, he escaped and made his way to West Germany, which refused to extradite him. He died not long afterwards.

Kappler was not the only one responsible for reprisals in Italy. According to Kappler, Karl Wolff arrived in Rome on the evening of March 24, 1944, and complained that the execution at the Ardeatine Caves was not nearly enough; he wanted to blow up a section of the city dominated by Communists. Wolff's account in London in November 1946 had been quite different. According to Wolff, when he arrived, the executions had already been carried out on the basis of an order that came directly from the Führer to the Fourteenth Army. Kappler had taken the initiative to reach the specified number of executions by including some Jews. Kappler was suffering so much from the psychological burden of carrying out the shootings that Wolff did not give him any trouble.[61] American intelligence officials had independent evidence implicating Wolff in other German reprisals in Italy, but never used it in any proceedings against him.[62]

Wolff had the distinct advantage of having helped to arrange an early surrender of German forces in northern Italy, and of having done so with Allen Dulles in a secret deal Dulles called Operation Sunrise.[63] Although Dulles had made no promise of immunity to Wolff, he had been impressed with the man and spoke up for him afterwards. Wolff nonetheless had a number of postwar difficulties. Around the world people were shocked by photos of corpses and survivors from concentration and extermination camps. In this climate, there was no way for Himmler's former chief of staff—one of the highest ranking SS officers to survive—to escape imprisonment. Wolff was moved from one internment camp to another and regularly interrogated. He almost was named as one of the major defendants at the International Military Tribunal at Nuremberg, but he was ultimately passed over.[64]

In early 1946, Wolff was diagnosed as paranoid and was confined in a mental institution: he thought he was pursued by Jewish demons. In 1947, he recovered enough to testify for the defense in the American Zonal trial of officials of the SS

Economic-Administrative Main Office, which had overseen the concentration and extermination camps. In the course of cross-examination, the prosecutors confronted Wolff with two documents indicating that he had helped arrange deportations of Jews to Treblinka. Afterwards, Wolff met privately with the judges in their chambers, disclaiming any responsibility for the extermination program. The next day, he reappeared at the trial and added to his previous testimony. At the end of the trial, the three judges conferred among themselves, concluding that there was insufficient evidence to indict Wolff for participation in Operation Reinhard (the code name for the extermination program under the General Government in Poland). According to an affidavit prepared in 1962 by one of the three American judges, the bench was partially influenced by the fact that Wolff had "distinguished himself inasmuch as he initiated armistice negotiations . . . that led to the capitulation of the German Armed Forces in Italy and thus saved many thousands of lives of Allied and German soldiers during the last days of the war; [and] that these negotiations were initiated by General Wolff against Hitler's will . . . "[65] Evidence presented below indicates that this was an exceedingly generous interpretation of Wolff's accomplishments and motives at the end of the war.[66]

Wolff was not yet home free. The British proposed to try him together with Field Marshal Kesselring. But they changed their plans and instead held a little-publicized trial in Hamburg in 1949, in which Wolff's partners in Operation Sunrise wrote affidavits or testified on his behalf. He was convicted, but on appeal his sentence was reduced to the time he had already served in internment, the de facto equivalent of an acquittal. After the Eichmann trial, however, West German prosecutors turned up evidence that Wolff had helped to speed deportations of Jews to Treblinka. In 1962, he was convicted and sentenced to fifteen years, of which he served ten.[67]

Wilhelm Harster, Commander of the Security Police and SD in Italy, was captured and interrogated immediately after the war. Harster did not have to answer interrogators' questions about directing transports of Italian Jews to Auschwitz; there apparently were no such questions.[68] But Harster had earlier served as commander of the Security Police in the Netherlands. He was turned over to the Dutch, who tried him for his crimes there, convicted him, and gave him a twelve-year sentence, of which he served six. Afterwards he became a civil servant in Bavaria.[69]

For numerous prominent Nazi officials, the availability of top-quality intelligence regarding their crimes in Italy played no part in their treatment or their fate after the war. These Nazis benefited to some degree from the fact that information available to Allied intelligence analysts in 1943 was not available for postwar prosecutions because the wartime British decoding operation at Bletchley Park remained secret until the 1970s.

The SD decodes and other documents declassified in 2000 or later do not revolutionize our understanding of the Holocaust in Italy. The main reason for this is that Kappler's report of October 16 survived in paper form and became known to historians in the 1950s; evidence from the decodes fills in the picture around it. If decodes of later messages turn up, and if they contain details of how police in other cities prepared for and carried out deportations, that would be striking new information, but there is little prospect of such sources appearing.

At present, the new sources allow us to see a significant difference of opinion between the RSHA and SS authorities in Italy on one side and some German diplomats on the other. They help us to discount self-serving, exculpatory postwar testimony. In combination with other sources, they permit us to connect Karl Wolff and especially Ernst Kaltenbrunner to the Holocaust in Italy much more directly than has been done before. And they reinforce our understanding of the hierarchy involved in the Final Solution: in cases of difficulty, authorization came from the very top, Hitler himself.

An important facet of the new information is that it shows how Italian public opinion—or what Kappler reported as his perception of it—related very directly to how much he tried to do. Relatively late in the war, when German forces were stretched thin, Nazi officials really needed outside help or at least a neutral environment in order to carry out the Final Solution. The climate in Italy was not favorable for an efficient implementation of this policy. With regard to Herbert Kappler, there is little reason to dissent from the assessment made by British and American intelligence analysts during the war: Kappler was a powerful figure in Italy, but he was always pessimistic.[70]

Notes

1. Richard Breitman, *The Architect of Genocide: Himmler and the Final Solution* (New York: Knopf, 1991), 138.
2. Hofmann to Himmler, 17 Nov. 1941, Künzel SS Officer File, NA–BDC, RG 242, A-3343, SSO, roll 226A.
3. Künzel SS Officer File, ibid.
4. CSDIC Final Report on Georg Bügelsack, July 1946, NA, RG 65, 105-9666, box 156, Appendix 1 (dated 31 Aug. 1946), 1.
5. On the euthanasia program, see Henry Friedlander, *The Origins of Nazi Genocide: From Euthanasia to the Final Solution* (Chapel Hill: University of North Carolina Press, 1995).
6. CSDIC Final Report on Georg Bügelsack, July 1946, NA, RG 65, 105-9666, box 156, Appendix 1 (dated 31 Aug. 1946), i.
7. Ibid.
8. Hofmann to Schmitt, 16 Mar. 1942, Künzel SS Officer File, NA–BDC, RG 242, A-3343, SSO, roll 226A.
9. CSDIC Final Report on Georg Bügelsack, July 1946, NA, RG 65, 105-9666, box 156, Appendix 1 (dated 31 Aug. 1946), i.
10. On Montt generally, see chapter 1.
11. The remainder of this chapter is adapted from an article by Richard Breitman, "New Sources on the Holocaust in Italy," *Holocaust and Genocide Studies* 16, no. 3 (2002): 402–14. Kappler's radio transmitter was later moved into the German Embassy after Germany occupied Italy and Kappler could dispense with his cover. British intelligence report "German Policy Towards Italy," undated, but apparently late October 1943, copy in NA, RG 226, entry 171A, box 80, folder 891–Washington X-2 PTS 158.
12. F. H. Hinsley, et al., *British Intelligence in the Second World War: Its Influence on Strategy and Operations*, vol. 3, pt. 1 (New York: Cambridge University Press, 1984), 487.
13. The IWG and the National Archives opened these records in June 2000. The Public Record Office at Kew later opened the British collection of these messages, which covers a longer period of time. The first decode in the surviving American collection is from August 3, 1943. The British intelligence report cited in n. 11 above draws on material that is not in the American collection, and Hinsley's appendix (see n. 12) lists a longer run of decodes. What has been released in the United States is in NA, RG 226, entry 122, Misc. X-2 Files, box 1, folder 5–Italian Decodes.
14. Robert Katz, *The Battle for Rome: The Germans, the Allies, the Partisans, and the Pope* (New York: Simon and Schuster, 2003), 61–71. At one point, Katz claims that the SD decodes support his interpretation, which is not our view. On these events and Kappler's testimony, see also the sources in note 15.
15. Meir Michaelis, *Mussolini and the Jews: German–Italian Relations and the Jewish Question in Italy, 1922–1945* (New York: Oxford University Press, 1989), 352–55; Richard Lamb, *War in Italy, 1943–1945: A Brutal Story* (New York: De Capo Press, 1996), 40; Susan Zuccotti, *The Italians and the Holocaust: Persecution, Rescue, and Survival* (New York: Basic Books 1987), 109–11, 300n7.

16. Schellenberg to Rome, 8 Sept. 1943, decode 5498; Höttl to Rome, 10 Sept. 1943, decode 5696; Kappler to Berlin, 12 Sept. 1943, decode 5763; Schellenberg to Rome, 12 Sept. 1943, decode 5797; all in NA, RG 226 entry 122, Misc. X-2 Files, box 1, folder 5–Italian Decodes.

17. Copy in NA, RG 242, T-84, roll 26. Telephone log begins on frame 370834.

18. Vermerk, 12 Feb. 1944, Betr. SS-Sturmbannführer Herbert Kappler; and Brandt to von Herff, 20 Mar. 1944; in NA–BDC, RG 242, A-3343, SSO roll 152A.

19. Himmler's appointment log, 15 Sept. 1943, NA, RG 242, T-84, roll 25.

20. Höttl to Kappler, 17 Sept. 1943, decode 6153; Wolff to Himmler, 18 Sept. 1943, decode 6253, both in NA, RG 226, entry 122, Misc. X-2 Files, box 1, folder 5–Italian Decodes.

21. Wolff to Mussolini, 18 Sept. 1943, decode 6260; Kappler to Harster via Berlin, 18 Sept. 1943, decode 6261; ibid.

22. Rome to Berlin, 23 Sept. 1943, decode 6671, ibid.

23. Rink, Roehm to Berlin, 19 Sept. 1943, decode 6345, ibid.

24. Kappler to Berlin, 24 Sept. 1943, decode 6728, ibid.

25. Raul Hilberg, *The Destruction of the European Jews*, rev. and definitive ed., vol. 2, (New York: Holmes and Meier, 1985), 669. If Kappler had not received word about the Final Solution in Italy earlier, this RSHA circular directed German officials in Italy to start at once with Italian Jews.

26. Michaelis, *Mussolini and the Jews*, 354–55, and Richard Lamb, *War in Italy*, 40.

27. Zuccotti, *Italians and the Holocaust*, 111. But in *Under His Very Windows: The Vatican and the Holocaust in Italy* (New Haven, CT: Yale University Press, 2000), 53ff., Zuccotti states that Kappler received orders on September 25 and engaged in a policy of deception with the Jewish leaders. That later view is consistent with Breitman's, based largely on his reading of the decodes.

28. Katz, *Battle for Rome,* esp. 61–62, 68–70, 76.

29. Kappler to Berlin, 29 Sept. 1943, decode 6921, NA, RG 226, entry 122, Misc. X-2 Files, box 1, folder 5–Italian Decodes.

30. Kappler to Berlin, 5 Oct. 1943, decode 7185; and Kappler to Berlin, 7 Oct. 1943, decode 7256, ibid.

31. This message was decoded the next day. This decode (cited in note 32 below), in combination with the decode of October 20 (cited in note 43 below) made it plain that the purpose of shipping Jews to Auschwitz was to eliminate them.

32. Kappler to Wolff, 6 Oct. 1943, decode 7244, NA, RG 226, entry 122, Misc. X-2 Files, box 1, folder 5–Italian Decodes.

33. Michaelis, *Mussolini and the Jews*, 362.

34. Hilberg, *Destruction of the European Jews*, vol. 2, 671–72; Michaelis, *Mussolini and the Jews*, 363; Bern (Dulles) to OSS, 30 Dec. 1943, and Bern (Dulles) to Director OSS, 30 Dec. 1943, NA, RG 226, entry 210, box 463, folder 2–P.B.K. 1, Aug. 1943–Apr. 1944, documents 1496–97. Katz, *Battle for Rome*, 78–81, discussed this document in detail, indicating that it infuriated Ribbentrop and led to Möllhausen's recall.

35. Michaelis expressed bewilderment about the chronology; he thought Möllhausen had acted ten days earlier. But the newly available sources do not support that version. See Michaelis,

Mussolini and the Jews, 363n1. Zuccotti's chronology, in *Under His Very Windows*, 156–57, is more elaborate. Möllhausen tried shortly after September 25 to prevent deportations, then sent telegrams to the Foreign Ministry on October 6–7 only to receive word that he was not to get involved. Finally, he tried to work through Baron von Weizsäcker, German ambassador to the Vatican, who notified the Vatican of what was impending. The decodes and other recently declassified information do not contradict Zuccotti's account, but they do not supply confirmation, either. Katz' *Battle for Rome*, 78–85, is based on the decodes and an earlier version of Breitman's work; the chronology matches his.

36. Nothing else is known about Morini. It is possible that this report was a garbled version of the activities of Settimo Sorani, an official of the Jewish assistance organization Delasem. Sorani sometimes used cover names. Kappler to Berlin, 10 Oct. 1943, decode 7412, NA, RG 226, entry 122, Misc. X-2 Files, box 1, folder 5–Italian Decodes. On Sorani and Delasem, see Zuccotti, *Under His Very Windows*, 176, 181–86.

37. Hitler's appointments for 7 Oct. 1943 in NA, RG 242, T-84, roll 387. Katz's account, *Battle for Rome*, 61–85, omits any discussion of Wolff's role.

38. Kaltenbrunner to Kappler, 11 Oct. 1943, decode 7458, NA, RG 226, entry 122, Misc. X-2 Files, box 1, folder 5–Italian Decodes. Also reprinted in Katz, *Battle for Rome*, 77.

39. Kaltenbrunner to Kappler, 12 Oct. 1943, decode 7512, NA, RG 226, entry 122, Misc. X-2 Files, box 1, folder 5–Italian Decodes. Katz, *Battle for Rome*, 61, has the decoration awarded in September.

40. Rome to Berlin, 16 Oct. 1943, decode 7668, NA, RG 226, entry 122, Misc. X-2 Files, box 1, folder 5–Italian Decodes.

41. NA, RG 242, Records of the Reich Leader of the SS and Chief of the German Police, T-175, roll 53, frames 2567133–34. We can compare the full German original with the British interception, cited in note 40.

42. Katz, *Battle for Rome*, 104–13; Zuccotti, *Under His Very Windows*, 155.

43. Harster to Berlin, via Rome, 20 Oct. 1943, decode 7732, NA, RG 226, entry 122, Misc. X-2 Files, box 1, folder 5–Italian Decodes.

44. Dannecker to RSHA IV B 4, 21 Oct. 1943, decode 7754, ibid.

45. Zuccotti, *Italians and the Holocaust*, 123–25.

46. Kappler to Harster, via Berlin, 23 Oct. 1943, decode 7834, NA, RG 226, entry 122, Misc. X-2 Files, box 1, folder 5–Italian Decodes.

47. Rome to Berlin, 26 Oct. 1943, decode 7927, NA, RG 226, entry 122, Misc. X-2 Files, box 1, folder 5–Italian Decodes.

48. John Cornwell, *Hitler's Pope: The Secret History of Pius XII* (New York: Viking, 1999).

49. Summary of the meeting dated 11 Oct. 1943 in German Foreign Office records, copy in NA, RG 242, T-120, roll 2720, frames E 420790–93.

50. Robert Katz, *Black Sabbath: A Journey Through a Crime Against Humanity*, (New York: Macmillan 1969), 25–27, 139; Katz, *Battle for Rome*, 80. Katz's latest study also has Princess Pignatelli meeting with the Pope on October 16 to plead for his intervention; see *Battle for Rome*, 103. Michael Phayer, *The Catholic Church and the Holocaust, 1930–1965* (Bloomington: Indiana University Press, 2001), 99

51. Zuccotti, *Under His Very Windows*, 175–201. Following Italian scholar Michael Tagliacozzo,

Michaelis states that 477 Jews were sheltered within the Vatican and another 4,238 within monasteries and convents. Although he questions statistics compiled by Catholic authorities that indicate somewhat larger numbers of Jewish refugees given sanctuary, Zuccotti mainly emphasizes that the demand for sanctuary increased dramatically after the round-up of October 16 and that Catholic institutions inside and outside Vatican territory acted independently and often spontaneously. There was no coordinated Vatican policy.

52. Phayer, *Catholic Church and the Holocaust*, 99. We found no contemporary evidence to confirm von Kessel's claim, but Katz's *Battle for Rome*, 52, 78–79, is persuasive.

53. See Bern (Dulles) to OSS, 30 Dec. 1943, and Bern (Dulles) to Director OSS, 30 Dec. 1943, NA, RG 226, entry 210, box 463, folder 2–P.B.K. 1, Aug. 1943–Apr. 1944, documents 1496–97. Möllhausen's cable is discussed in chapter 1.

54. Information courtesy of Stephen Tyas, who searched the intelligence files of the Prime Minister's Office available at the Public Record Office, Kew. In daily digests of information from intercepts, Churchill did receive some items about the SD in Italy later in October.

55. Martin Gilbert, *Auschwitz and the Allies* (New York: Holt, Rinehart, and Winston, 1990), 158–59.

56. Richard Breitman, *Official Secrets: What the Nazis Planned, What the British and Americans Knew* (New York: Hill and Wang, 1998), 215.

57. Hilberg, *Destruction of the European Jews*, vol. 3, 1093.

58. NA, RG 319, IRR, entry 134B, box 669, folder XE 009228, Theodor Dannecker.

59. CSDIC Interrogation report of SS-Obersturmbannführer Herbert Kappler, 8 June 1945, copy in NA, RG 226, entry 194, Washington and Field Station Files, box 63, folder 280–London X-2 PTS 73.

60. Zuccotti, *Italians and the Holocaust*, 300n27, and Hilberg, *Destruction of the European Jews*, vol. 3, 1098; CSDIC Interrogation of Kappler, 8 June 1945, NA, RG 226, entry 194, Washington and Field Station Files, box 63, folder 280–London X-2 PTS 73; Voluntary Statement by PW LD 1513 Gen d. Waffen-SS Karl Wolff, 2 Dec. 1946 (London), copy in NA, RG 498, entry 47752 ETO-MIS-Y, box 127, folder 4–British/PWIS/LDC 5 Reports (Interr.) PW Karl Wolff formerly General. Katz, *Battle for Rome*, 223–56, offers a blow-by-blow account of the events.

61. Voluntary Statement by Wolff, 2 Dec. 1946, NA, RG 498, entry 47752 ETO-MIS-Y, box 127, folder 4–British/PWIS/LDC 5 Reports (Interr.) PW Karl Wolff formerly General.

62. Wolff to Oberbefehlshaber Südwest, 29 Dec. 1944, NA, RG 226, entry 92 COI/OSS Central Files, box 619, folder 2-33787.

63. Operation Sunrise is discussed in chapters 5 and 12.

64. Bradley F. Smith and Elena Agarossi, *Operation Sunrise: The Secret Surrender* (New York: Basic Books, 1979), 189.

65. Affidavit of Judge F. Donald Philips, 11 Dec. 1962, Allen Dulles Papers, obtained through Freedom of Information Act by Max Holland. We are grateful to him for his assistance.

66. See chapter 4.

67. Brendan Simms, "Karl Wolff—Der Schlichter," in *Die SS: Elite unter dem Totenkopf; 30 Lebensläufe*, ed. Ronald Smelser and Enrico Syring (Paderborn: Schöningh, 2000), 452–53. Information on the length of sentences is from Henry Friedlander, to whom we are grateful.

68. CSDIC Interrogation of SS-Gruppenführer Wilhelm Harster, 20 May 1945, NA, RG 226, entry 194, Washington and Field Station Files, box 63, folder 6–London X-2 PTS 73.

69. Hilberg, *Destruction of the European Jews*, vol. 3, 1096.

70. OSS Report "German Policy Towards Italy" (n.d., late 1943), NA, RG 226, entry 171A Washington X-2 Personalities Files, box 80, folder 891–Washington X-2 PTS 158; British Report "The Sicherheitsdienst–Recent Developments," 9 Oct. 1943, copy in NA, RG 226, entry 108B, box 286, folder–Special Studies RIS Reports. Both reports draw heavily on the British decodes of SD messages.

4

Nazi Espionage:
The Abwehr and SD Foreign Intelligence

Richard Breitman

DURING THE WAR, the Allies viewed German intelligence as a military and political weapon that they could neutralize if they knew enough about it. At the end of the war, Nazi spies, saboteurs, and intelligence officials might have helped diehard Nazis resist the Allied occupation of Germany or prepare for a future struggle, so even in the postwar period the Allies tried to capture German intelligence personnel and to understand the structure of German intelligence organizations. British and American intelligence officials, often working together, were able to fill gaps in their knowledge.

The IWG declassified a small quantity of new Allied material about small German intelligence organizations, such as the Research Office (Forschungsamt), an interception, wiretapping, and decoding service under the nominal supervision of Hermann Göring. The Research Office monitored some of the most sensitive internal Nazi operations, wiretapping uncooperative Catholic priests and Protestant pastors who were or were going to be persecuted. Foreign diplomats in Berlin were another regular target for wiretaps.[1] British and American intelligence paid greater attention to the Abwehr, SD Foreign Intelligence, and the Gestapo.[2]

The Abwehr
Allied officials initially thought of the Abwehr as the premier German intelligence service. The Abwehr was a top-heavy and generally inefficient military intelligence organization of more than twenty-one thousand officials in 1941, not including informants and other sources. Two particularly good studies of the Abwehr have enriched our understanding of this organization, but both of them were written decades ago.[3] Documents declassified by the IWG reinforce some points sketched lightly in these studies and help to fill in details and individual case histories from the storehouse of information assembled by Allied intelligence.

A newly declassified November 1945 Allied intelligence file, "Bibliography of the GIS" (German Intelligence Service), reviewed the major types of sources used to compose "a detailed and complete picture of the Abwehr." It includes more than 200,000 deciphered radio telegrams, captured German documents, interrogations of captured Abwehr personnel, and reports from Allied agents or double agents. Shortly after November 1942, the accumulation of different Allied sources reached a critical mass so that "by the time of [the Abwehr's] dissolution and the fall of its head [Admiral Wilhelm Canaris] in the spring of 1944 there was no important activity which it directed unknown to us."[4]

One Allied breakthrough came through a stroke of luck. On November 8, 1942, Allied troops that had just landed in North Africa captured an Abwehr official, a Major Wurmann, stationed there. Convinced that Germany's war effort was already hopeless, Wurmann told his British interrogators a great deal about the structure and operations of the organization, also offering his assessments of key personalities. Since this information was relevant to American counterintelligence efforts, British officials in London passed copies to the FBI.[5] It was declassified in 2003.

Weekly reports about the activities of Abwehr officials and agents were compiled and distributed during the last two years of the war.[6] It is probably not an exaggeration to maintain that Allied intelligence understood the Abwehr better than its own high officials did. Apart from giving new details about specific Abwehr activities, newly declassified Allied intelligence records yield fuller understanding of the Abwehr's leaders, bureaucrats, and field operatives. They also provide some new information about the anti-Nazi resistance, a small quantity of information about war crimes, and a general sense of the relative ineffectiveness of the organization.

Wilhelm Canaris

Allied intelligence analysts in the Counter-Intelligence War Room, London, recognized that the Abwehr was never representative of the High Command of the Armed Services (OKW). One source held the German Army General Staff to be scornful, calling the Abwehr the "Canaris Family Limited Liability Company" after its chief, Admiral Wilhelm Canaris.[7]

Executed in April 1945 as an alleged conspirator in the plot to assassinate Hitler, Canaris has sometimes been portrayed as a mainstay of the anti-Nazi resistance in Germany.[8] Newly declassified records, however, support a revised picture of Canaris as an experienced spymaster who was at times paralyzed or restrained by conflicting sentiments.[9] One new source about Canaris is a very detailed July 1945 British interrogation of his nephew, Constantin Canaris, who himself commanded Security Police and SD forces in Belgium and northern France. In 1934 Wilhelm Canaris had told his nephew that Hitler's upbringing had made him ruthless and intolerant of established rules of law and justice, but that he might grow out of this attitude. In 1937 the elder Canaris described Hitler as a mixture of a fanatic and dreamer who could prove quite dangerous for Germany. Canaris' deputy, General Hans Oster, alerted Constantin Canaris in 1938 that Hitler intended to take Germany to war. Admiral Canaris also told his nephew that the Munich Pact would not last because Hitler was bent on war. The younger Canaris knew that Hitler had no longer wished to see Admiral Canaris during 1943, and that Himmler and Bormann were intriguing against him. (Some of the reasons are set out below.) Constantin Canaris did know that his uncle had kept a diary, and that after the arrest he heard that it reflected his uncle's "defeatist sentiments."[10]

Uncomfortable with the ideologues of the Nazi regime, Canaris lacked a clear strategy for dealing with them, other than picking a number of high-level subordinates who were equally or even more unsympathetic to Nazism.[11] Such a group had practical difficulties and sometimes disagreements of principle with the SS. A number of related Office of Strategic Services (OSS) documents, newly declassified, give a clearer picture of Canaris' reaction to the Holocaust at a relatively early stage.

On November 30, 1941, Nazi forces under Higher SS and Police Leader Friedrich Jeckeln, and Latvian auxiliaries under Viktor Arajs, massacred approximately fourteen thousand Jews outside the city of Riga. Most of the victims that day were Latvian Jews marched out of the Riga ghetto to a prepared killing ground some eight kilometers from the city, but the first victims were some one thousand German Jews, who had just arrived in Riga the previous night on a train from Berlin. German and Latvian Jews alike were forced to strip and enter pits dug days earlier, where they were shot, one group after another. This horrific slaughter marked the beginning of the liquidation of the Riga ghetto.

In a 1982 study about Hitler's role in the Holocaust, British scholar Gerald Fleming unearthed several sources concerning the actions of a German army colonel named Walter Bruns, who had served on the bridge inspectorate in Riga. In postwar testimony Bruns claimed he had tried to stop the slaughter of Riga's Jews before it started. When he learned of the plans for impending liquidation, Bruns allegedly tried to persuade an administrative officer named Altemeyer to postpone them. After this failed, he then wrote a report which he submitted to the Army High Command. Fleming found some evidence, in the form of letters and recollections by associates of Colonel Bruns long after the war, that Bruns' report reached Admiral Canaris. Canaris allegedly went to Hitler to complain about the massacre, but Hitler angrily accused Canaris of getting soft: "I *have* to do it [mass murder the Jews], because after me no one else will!"[12] Canaris then sent a top-secret message to Abwehr headquarters in Riga, warning that attendance at "interrogations" or "maltreatments" (euphemisms for the mass shootings) was unworthy of an Abwehr officer.[13]

Fleming's account was based on the letters and recollections of a number of different people such as Bruns' subordinate Captain Schultz-Dubois—some as late as 1980—who had partial or second-hand information. Fleming did not believe that Bruns had seen the executions outside Riga—only that his two subordinates did. Perhaps Bruns and Schultz-Dubois later claimed that they and others had done more to protest than was really the case. There were no contemporary sources to verify that Hitler and Canaris ever discussed the murder of the Jews. Neither man survived the war to give his version.

The most detailed history of the Holocaust in Latvia includes nothing about Bruns or Canaris.[14] Heinz Höhne, author of a biography of Canaris published in 1976, could not have drawn on Fleming's research, and his general portrait of Canaris was that the intelligence chief responded feebly to the fundamental political and moral issues of his day.[15] Although any encounter between Hitler and Canaris over the fate of the Jews would have to be considered noteworthy, the recent, well-researched biography of Hitler by Ian Kershaw omits this episode.[16] In general, few other historians have given Bruns' or Canaris' reported exchange with Hitler space or weight. Perhaps the sources seemed too doubtful.

Walter Bruns

Declassified documents, however, offer a better picture of Colonel (later Brigadier-General) Bruns. Captured by the British on April 8, 1945, Bruns told an interrogator a couple of weeks later about his November 1941 experience with Werner Altemeyer, staff director for the German-appointed mayor of Riga.[17] Citing an order by the Führer as authorization, Altemeyer said he intended to deport Jewish men but to execute all women and children at Skirotawa, outside Riga. Bruns said he himself witnessed the mass murder of some ten thousand German and Latvian Jews, and later that day he sent out two of his officers to serve as additional witnesses. He then sent a report to headquarters about these happenings, and his officers signed on as witnesses.[18]

An even better account of events materialized the next day. Bruns was among the many German prisoners whose conversations with fellow POWs were surreptitiously tape-recorded and then transcribed by British intelligence. These transcripts contain a rich trove of information about the attitudes of German officers and soldiers and SS, especially during the last two years of the war. Candid and unconstrained expressions of opinion about Hitler, the German war effort, and the Holocaust are relatively hard to find in most German sources, but they are common in these transcripts.

In an excerpt of one such discussion that occurred on April 25, 1945, which was passed to the OSS, Bruns stated,

> As soon as I heard these Jews were to be shot on Friday [that is, he heard on Friday, November 28 that they were to be shot] I said that they had made themselves very useful in the area under my command . . . In short, all these [Jewish] women were employed in a useful capacity. I tried to save them. I told that fellow Altenmeyer (?), whose name I will always remember and who will be added to the list of war criminals: "Listen to me, they represent valuable man-power."
>
> "Do you call Jews valuable human beings, sir?"
>
> I said: "Listen to me properly, I said 'valuable *man-power*.' I didn't mention their value as human beings."

He said: "Well, they're to be shot in accordance with the Führer's orders!"
I said: "Führer's orders?"
"Yes," whereupon he showed me his orders.

. . . When I arrived those pits were so full that the living had to lie down on top of the dead; then they were shot and, in order to save room, they had to lie down neatly in layers. Before this, however, they were stripped of everything at one of the stations—here at the edge of the wood were the three pits they used that Sunday [November 30] and here they stood in a queue 1.5 [kilometers] long which approached step by step—a queuing up for death. As they drew nearer they saw what was going on. About here they had to hand over their jewelry and suitcases. All good stuff was put into the suitcases and the remainder thrown on a heap. This was to serve as clothing for our suffering population—and then, a little further on they had to undress and, 500 [meters] in front of the wood, strip completely; they were only permitted to keep on a chemise or knickers. They were all women and small two-year-old children. Then all those cynical remarks! If only I had seen those tommy-gunners, who were relieved every hour because of over-exertion, carry out their task with distaste, but no, [instead there were] nasty remarks like: "here comes a Jewish beauty!" I can still see it all in my memory: a pretty woman in a flame-coloured chemise.[19]

In the taped conversation Bruns explained that, after his own distressing experience, he had sent two of his men there because he wanted additional eyewitnesses: he had asked them to write up a report without telling them in advance what it was for. Receiving their account, he added a cover memorandum and personally took it to an officer named Jacobs at the Army High Command.

According to Bruns, Jacobs said,

"I have already two complaints sent me by Engineer 'Bataillone' from the Ukraine." There they shot [the Jews] on the brink of large crevices and let them fall down into them [this was the method used at Babi Yar]; they nearly had an epidemic of plague, at any rate a pestilential smell. They thought they could break off the edges [of the ravine] with picks, thus burying them. That loess there was so hard that two Engineer "Bataillone" were required to dynamite the edges; those "Bataillone" complained. Jacobs had received that complaint. He said: "We didn't quite know how to tell the Führer. We'd better do it through Canaris." Canaris had the unsavoury task of waiting for the favourable moment to give the Führer certain gentle hints.

In these conversations Bruns was not trying to impress his British captors; he was speaking in some heat to fellow German POWs and, in the process, giving more details—details that can be checked against other sources.

Bruns explained that his report had some repercussions in Riga, even though it did not stop the killing. After about two weeks Altemeyer triumphantly showed

TOP SECRET

C. S. D. I. C. (U.K.)

G. G. REPORT

X?75.1536

IF THE INFORMATION CONTAINED IN THIS REPORT IS REQUIRED FOR FURTHER DISTRIBUTION, IT SHOULD BE PARAPHRASED SO THAT NO MENTION IS MADE OF THE PRISONERS' NAMES, NOR OF THE METHODS BY WHICH THE INFORMATION HAS BEEN OBTAINED

S.R.G.G.1158(C)

The following conversation took place between:-

CS/1952 - Generalmajor BRUNS (Heeres-Waffenmeisterschule I, BERLIN) Captd GÖTTINGEN 6 Apr 45

and other Senior Officer PW whose voices could not be identified.

Information received: 25 Apr 45

TRANSLATION

BRUNS: As soon as I heard these Jews were to be shot on Friday I went to a 21-year old boy and said that they had made themselves very useful in the area under my command, besides which the Army MT park had employed 1500 and the 'Heeresgruppe' 800 women to make underclothes of the stores we captured in RIGA; besides which about 1200 women in the neighbourhood of RIGA were turning millions of captured sheepskins into articles we urgently required: ear-protectors, fur caps, fur waistcoats, etc. Nothing had been provided, as of course the Russian campaign was known to have come to a victorious end in October 1941! In short, all these women were employed in a useful capacity. I tried to save them. I told that fellow ALTEMEYER(?) whose name I shall always remember and who will be added to the list of war criminals:"Listen to me, they represent valuable man-power!" "Do you call Jews valuable human beings, sir?" I said:"Listen to me properly, I said 'valuable man-power'. I didn't mention their value as human beings." He said:"Well, they're to be shot in accordance with the FÜHRER's orders!" I said:"FÜHRER's orders?" "Yes", whereupon he showed me his orders. This happened at SKIOTAWA(?), 8 km. from RIGA, between SIAULAI and JELGAVA, where 5000 BERLIN Jews were suddenly taken off the train and shot. I didn't see that myself, but what happened at SKIOTAWA(?) - to cut a long story short, I argued with the fellow and telephoned to the General at HQ, to JAKOBS and ABERGER(?), and to a Dr.SCHULTZ who was attached to the Engineer General, on behalf of these people; I told him: "Granting that the Jews have committed a crime against the other peoples of the world, at least let them do the drudgery; send them to throw earth on the roads to prevent our heavy lorries skidding." "Then I'd have to feed them!" I said:"The little amount of food they receive, let's assume 2 million Jews - they got 125 gr. of bread a day - if we can't even manage that, the sooner we end the war the better." Then I telephoned, thinking it would take some time. At any rate on Sunday morning I heard that they

/2

DISTRIBUTION

BY C.S.D.I.C. (U.K.)

CLASSIFICATION CANCELLED OR CHANGED TO
BY AUTHORITY OF

APR

M.I.19.a War Office (56 copies)
N.I.D. Admiralty (9 copies)

Secretly recorded conversations of German POWs, such as the translation above, yielded information about the Holocaust not found in other sources [CSDIC (UK) G. G. Report S. R. G. G. 1158(C), 25 Apr. 1945, copy in NA, RG 226, entry 108A, Washington Registry SI Branch Field Files, box 145, folder S. R. G. G. 1129-1245].

him an order prohibiting mass shootings on that scale in the future—future killings were to be carried out more discreetly. We do not know exactly what order Altemeyer received from whom, but independent sources confirm the thrust of Bruns' comments. In a radio message on December 1, 1941, Reichsführer SS Heinrich Himmler summoned Higher SS and Police Leader Jeckeln to meet him in his East Prussian headquarters. After the war Jeckeln testified that at this private meeting Himmler told him that shooting was too complicated an operation—it was better to use gas vans.[20] Bruns' report had raised problems that reached Himmler's level.[21]

Did Admiral Wilhelm Canaris take Bruns' complaint directly to Hitler? Without any direct contemporary record of a conversation, the historian seeks other indications. Did Canaris subsequently act as if Hitler had rebuked him and prohibited any interference on the Jewish question? Another document in recently declassified OSS records, a translation of a captured German document, suggests that he did.

On December 10, 1941, Canaris gave a lecture in Berlin to the heads of Abwehr field offices. (The same lecture was apparently read again at an unidentified officers' conference ten days later.) Point number five read:

> Abwehr has nothing to do with persecution of Jews. The Ast's [Abwehrstelle's] duties are to be carried out in a humane, respectable, correct and soldierly manner. *Activity against Jews is no concern of ours.* We have nothing to do with it, hold ourselves aloof from it, do not criticize.[22]

On the one hand, Canaris did not want to get his organization involved—implicated—in mass murder. On the other hand, criticism or open opposition to Nazi policy against Jews would only bring trouble for the Abwehr, because Hitler himself was the driving force behind this policy. It seems highly likely that Canaris was drawing upon direct (and very recent) experience in giving these instructions. So this speech and this document may be seen as supporting evidence for Bruns' remarks and, to a lesser extent, for Fleming's reconstruction of the encounter between Canaris and Hitler.

It certainly took some personal courage for any German official to raise doubts with Hitler about Nazi policy toward the "Jewish question." Canaris was also willing to quietly approve when certain Abwehr officials assisted individual Jews.[23] But as much as he disliked Nazi killings of innocent civilians, knowledge that the Nazi regime was engaged in mass murder did not shake his allegiance to his country or to the regime. In the same speech on December 10, 1941, he encouraged Abwehr officials to work loyally with the Gestapo and SD on intelligence matters and urged every man to "stick to his guns for victory."[24] A later conference between Abwehr and Security Police officials in Prague tried to work out joint arrangements for efficient handling of cases of suspected espionage against Germany.[25] In other words, Canaris managed to separate his aversion to what we have come to call the Holocaust from his commitment to the German war effort. We have a better grasp of his attitude and behavior as a result of these new documents.

Anti-Nazi Dissidents in Abwehr

A good number of anti-Nazi dissidents were able to find cover in the Abwehr. Some enjoyed the protection of men such as General Oster, but others simply found their way into niches through their own personal contacts or happenstance. Although these men were not typical of Abwehr officials, their activities partially redeemed the Abwehr for some Western intelligence officials. In other cases, the Abwehr seemed only marginally different from its more sinister counterpart, SD Foreign Intelligence.

One unusual Abwehr story concerns defector Otto August Walter John, interrogated in November 1944 by MI-5, the British equivalent of the FBI.[26] Whatever his achievements during the war, John became quite important after the war. Appointed the first head of the West German Office for the Protection of the Constitution, (1950-1954), John claimed to have been kidnapped by East German agents in 1954; he returned to West Berlin in December 1955. Others charged that he was actually an East German agent, and he was tried and convicted of treason in West Germany in 1956.[27] Although John later wrote extensive memoirs, he hardly cleared up the many questions about his past. The 1944 interrogation, declassified by the IWG, represents his first detailed account of his path to the anti-Nazi resistance and to the British. It also offers the earliest test of his credibility.

Born in 1909 in Marburg, John came from a well-to-do and well-connected Protestant family. He studied law and originally hoped to become a diplomat, but his refusal to join the Nazi Party made a diplomatic career seem unlikely. He took some additional training in air law and then was appointed as a counsel to Lufthansa, where he was named assistant to the general manager. He soon became friendly with Klaus Bonhöffer, whose brother Dietrich, a distinguished theologian, was an early organizer of anti-Nazi resistance. In 1942, John became the principal legal representative of Lufthansa and one of its chief administrators. In the fall of 1943, John was on the point of being drafted into the military, but his contacts in the Abwehr managed to get him appointed to the Abwehr field office in Stettin, which protected him.

John claimed that by 1938 he had become a close collaborator of Klaus von Dohnanyi, brother of Dr. Hans von Dohnanyi, a judge and high official (and strong anti-Nazi) in the German Justice Ministry. John said that he persuaded the Dohnanyis that the conservative military and political elements opposed to Nazism needed support from the former Social Democratic Party and trade unions to govern in a post-Nazi Germany. The key to John's utility in the anti-Nazi resistance seems to have been his friendship with Prince Louis-Ferdinand Hohenzollern of Prussia, second son of the Crown Prince and grandson of the former Kaiser Wilhelm II. John, in effect, became an intermediary for the restoration of the monarchy, a goal to the liking of conservative politicians such as Carl Goerdeler, former mayor of Leipzig, and anti-Nazi officers led by General Ludwig Beck, former chief of the Army General Staff. At the same time, he retained links with the left.

In late 1944, John accurately identified to MI-5 many people known today to have been involved in resistance to the Nazi regime,[28] but MI-5 was not at all impressed, let alone satisfied, with John's testimony. Although John had contacted British officials on business trips to Madrid and Lisbon and passed along messages from Goerdeler, he had never delivered any intelligence to Britain that gave it military or political advantages. After his relations with British contacts deteriorated, John claimed that Goerdeler gave him the task of contacting General Eisenhower, but no one at the American Embassy in Madrid would vouch for his efforts to do so.

John made an unfavorable impression on his British interrogator, a Captain F. Basett, who thought that a barrister surely should have been able to do better. A muddled account was a sign of lack of candor. The interrogator also saddled John with the failings of the conservative anti-Nazi group within the government and military, whose nationalism made them unwilling to break completely with the Nazi regime or accept the Allied terms of unconditional surrender. John claimed that he had tried to convince Goerdeler to abandon the notion of negotiating a compromise settlement with the Allies and instead to throw himself upon their mercy, but there was no independent evidence to verify his disagreement with Goerdeler. Basett left open several disquieting possibilities: (1) John was actually an SD agent; (2) the SD, which might have penetrated the resistance, allowed John to develop contacts with the West to see whether he and his sponsors could get the Allies to make any concessions; and (3) John had actually done much more for the Abwehr than he admitted.

Despite these suspicions, gifted radio propagandist Sefton Delmer, director of a British program designed to subvert German morale, soon found use for John in the British Political Warfare Executive. After the war ended, John testified in one of the American zonal war crimes trials and then found himself proposed as a compromise candidate for the Office for the Protection of the Constitution in Chancellor Konrad Adenauer's first West German government. He apparently had neither too much nor too little intelligence experience.[29]

Other anti-Nazis in the Abwehr, such as the very well-informed Hans Bernd Gisevius, contacted American intelligence during the war. Gisevius worked with Allen Dulles and Gero von Gaevernitz. The native German Gaevernitz had personal or professional ties with a number of figures in the Abwehr. Gaevernitz thought highly of one of Gisevius' collaborators, Eduard Waetjen, a lawyer who had served in the Abwehr and whose sister had married into the Rockefeller family.

Waetjen's legal practice in Germany had involved salvage cases for German Jewish businessmen facing near complete expropriation during the 1930s. In one case of an airplane manufacturer imprisoned and forced to sell his business, Waetjen went to a "fixer," a Romanian national named Izadore Lazarus who passed himself off as an American named Lane. Lazarus paid at least RM 40,000 to Hermann Göring; the manufacturer was released and got approximately half a million marks as compensation for the loss of his business.[30]

If Waetjen seemed out of sympathy with fundamental Nazi goals during the 1930s, he later became actively anti-Nazi and supplied OSS in Bern with a series of reliable intelligence reports.[31] Since his track record was good, Gaevernitz later suggested Waetjen might be useful for postwar American intelligence purposes:

> Even before the war Waetjen worked with anti-Nazi resistance forces and was in touch with the Gördeler group. During the war Waetjen collaborated with the group in the German Abwehr under General Oster, which became sort of a clearing house for anti-Nazi activities. As early as 1942 Waetjen established contact with the O.S.S. in Switzerland. He traveled repeatedly, under great personal risk, from Germany to Switzerland and back and during the years 1942-1945 rendered very valuable services to the Allied cause.
>
> He has numerous connections in the business world in Europe, especially Germany, Austria, Italy, and in the Near East, particularly Turkey. Through his Turkish connections he is in contact with certain anti-Russian groups in Persia, Georgia and Turkestan. His connections might be of use.[32]

There is no evidence that the OSS' successors recruited Waetjen, but they found others.

In the second half of 1945, American intelligence officials in Germany and Austria not infrequently used cooperative ex-Abwehr officers for counterintelligence purposes. Both the counterintelligence branch of the OSS (X-2) and the U.S. Army's Counterintelligence Corps selected some Abwehr men to uncover subversive activities or continued intelligence work by Nazi loyalists; some also reported on Communist activities. An Abwehr officer code named "Java," who had worked on mail censorship and had been arrested for disloyalty to the Nazi regime, was a good source on Abwehr personalities and potential hideouts. "Culprit," who had worked in Stuttgart and Budapest, was allowed to reestablish a textile business in Feuerbach, where he was assigned to investigate reports about continued intelligence work by his former colleagues. "Zigzag," who had done Abwehr counterintelligence work in Berlin, now found twenty-four surviving members of the Abwehr and RSHA: nine were held by the Russians; one was already a prisoner of the United States; twelve were living in Berlin; two lived outside Berlin. The U.S. Army Counterintelligence Corps made two arrests as a result of Zigzag's research, which was then extended to higher SS officers.[33]

A subsequent document noted Zigzag's background without qualms:

Zigzag is a man of long Abwehr and Gestapo experience who has been an outstandingly successful penetration agent here in Berlin since September 1945. He was recruited from a POW cage near Heidelberg and today may be considered a reliable agent. We might add [that] Zigzag is a lawyer by profession, and always worked with the Abwehr III or counterintelligence staff . . .[34]

In general, Abwehr veterans were not disqualified for postwar American intelligence employment, as long as they had the right political views or powerful sponsors. Would the same latitude be extended to former members of the SD and Gestapo?

SD Foreign Intelligence

The SS Security Service (*Sicherheitsdienst* or SD) dabbled in foreign intelligence during the mid-1930s,[35] but SD Foreign Intelligence—the SS' main espionage weapon—was formed just before the war broke out. The first head of SD Foreign Intelligence, Heinz Jost, was ineffective. He tried to work with other government agencies such as the Propaganda Ministry and the Economics Ministry, but their cooperation was grudging. Jost sent representatives into various neutral countries to recruit informants there, but did not accomplish much else. In July 1941, Reinhard Heydrich, head of the RSHA, arranged for a young and ambitious lawyer, Walter Schellenberg, to become deputy chief under Jost. By one account, Schellenberg gained Canaris' support (as well as Heydrich's) to take over from Jost, who left in September 1941. Schellenberg gained full title to the office only after Heydrich's death.[36]

Schellenberg is best known today through his postwar book *The Labyrinth*, a skeletal autobiography—part espionage tale, part insider's history of Nazi Germany.[37] Schellenberg apparently wrote it to distance himself from Nazi crimes, portraying himself as a moderate on the war and as a mere intelligence specialist and indicating that his expertise could be useful to Britain and the United States in the postwar period. A combination of older documents and new ones declassified by the IWG allows historians to perceive his real wartime course.

Schellenberg had a significant career in the Nazi movement well before the war. He had entered the Nazi Party and the SS in 1933, quickly earning attention as an SD ideological instructor, a function close to Himmler's heart.[38] Schellenberg also served a stint in the Gestapo, where he rose to head of its counterintelligence section and also served as legal advisor and adjutant to Heydrich.[39] His counterintelligence work involved liaison with the Abwehr, giving him experience he soon applied within SD Foreign Intelligence.

In late 1941, Schellenberg reorganized SD Foreign Intelligence and brought in much new blood—nearly a complete turnover. There is a newly declassified, unconfirmed report that Martin Bormann was friendly with Schellenberg and saw SD Foreign Intelligence as a more suitable intelligence vehicle than either

Foreign Minister Joachim von Ribbentrop's special bureau or Rudolf Hess' special service—the latter completely discredited after Hess' flight to England in May 1941. But it seems that Schellenberg had only a short period to produce results or Himmler might simply have abolished the organization.[40]

Despite Hitler's minimal regard for intelligence reports, Schellenberg's timing was favorable. Up to that point Nazi Germany had been able to prevail through diplomacy, intimidation, and military force, but its years of complete military domination were at an end. Acquiring and using accurate information about Germany's enemies, spreading disinformation, and carrying out sabotage behind enemy lines became necessary weapons in a long world war.

Schellenberg showed talent in maneuvering through Nazi Germany's bureaucratic jungle. He managed to bring about a truce with the Foreign Office and other government agencies and acquired more resources: SD Foreign Intelligence expanded substantially. The assassination of Heydrich in May 1942 brought Schellenberg into more frequent personal contact with Himmler, who took over leadership of the RSHA for a six-month period after Heydrich's death.[41] Schellenberg used proximity to his advantage. He arranged for important incoming signals intelligence and despatches to go to Himmler. They were passed on to the Foreign Office only after Himmler had read them and decided whether or not to withhold them.[42]

It is possible that British intelligence was better informed than Ribbentrop. They intercepted and deciphered an estimated ten percent of SD intelligence reports and some related Abwehr messages. British intelligence analysts were aware, in any case, that Himmler was much attached to SD reports. A September 1943 British analysis of the SD, based largely on intercepts of SD messages, stated:

> Reports are passed to [Himmler], and assignments received from him on a surprising variety of subjects . . . In January 1942 a report on Salgado and the Green Shirt movement is passed to him for a decision; in December 1942 it is "considered essential" that he should be informed of the Cossack question: he received constant reports on the development of the SD's Persian enterprise; he is asked for a decision about the German minority in Hungary: he demands an urgent interim report on the invention of a new gas incendiary bomb: on the success of sabotage in North Africa. In addition, whenever there is an important development of a more obvious kind, the SD is required to furnish an immediate report for the Reichsführer: a governmental change in Spain in August 1941, the French crisis in November 1942, the murder of Darlan, the murder of General Lukoff in Sofia . . . His personal interest in the SD's work is a subject of comment in Abwehr circles.[43]

Another British analysis, based on intercepted and decoded SD messages between Rome and Berlin, mentioned that SD headquarters had insisted: "more important than any practical task is a constant supply of immediate reports to

Himmler." Himmler, in a telegram to Schellenberg (not intercepted by the British), commented proudly that the Führer was very satisfied with SD Foreign Intelligence reports.[44]

Under such circumstances, SD Foreign Intelligence could hardly divorce itself from the goals and methods of the SS. An undated British intelligence report, probably mid-1943, described the SD as organically linked to German police forces and chiefly concerned with police work and politics.[45] That description may have been too narrow, but it caught a good part of the reality, even for SD Foreign Intelligence.

Having moved from the Gestapo to SD Foreign Intelligence, Schellenberg saw nothing amiss with taking in others from the same background. At the start of 1944 he appointed Dr. Martin Sandberger, a lawyer who had served as chief of one of the Einsatzkommandos operating in the Baltic States during 1941-42, as his chief administrator. Sandberger was something close to Schellenberg's deputy chief, a position that did not formally exist.[46]

Other SD men in Italy carried out functions that involved "police work." Guido Zimmer, an official in SD Foreign Intelligence, went to Genoa in the fall of 1943, where he tracked Jews down, and then did much the same in Milan. He also obtained political information from abroad and built a network of agents who could supply Germany with intelligence if the Allies overran Italy.[47] In German-occupied countries there was not much separation between intelligence work and policies directed at Germany's perceived racial enemies. The very structure of the RSHA, which encompassed both the Gestapo and SD Foreign Intelligence, made it easy for officials to be shifted from one function to another. High security police positions outside Germany normally involved authority over the SD as well.

By early 1943, SD Foreign Intelligence consisted of about two thousand people—a substantial force. Schellenberg appointed his own personal representatives in each of the major countries where the SD operated.[48] He recruited an inner circle of advisors with considerable intelligence experience, perhaps to give him different perspectives on what his increasingly large team produced. A key figure was the World War I spymaster and Far Eastern specialist Kurt Jahnke, known for independent views.[49] According to his postwar testimony, Schellenberg found that Jahnke had worked to prevent war with England, that the Gestapo had suspicions about him, and that he considered Ribbentrop (for whom he had worked) an idiot—near perfect credentials! Schellenberg arranged for Jahnke to receive a monthly salary of RM 2,000 and privileged access to rationed goods.[50]

During 1943, SD Foreign Intelligence became more of a factor in the major issues of Nazi policy. In June 1943, SD agents in Argentina were told in a coded radio message (newly declassified by the IWG): "please consider penetration Brazil, Panama, USA, and Canada, with all means and by all routes, the main tack in order to receive political and military reports about the conditions and intentions of the enemy powers."[51]   Berlin subsequently asked agents to gather information about whether President Roosevelt and his partisans wanted a long war to aid his reelection in 1944, and whether American morale was adequate to the burden of several more years of war.   At the same time, Berlin was interested in whether "authoritative circles in the USA have any thought at all of an understanding with Germany within a reasonable time.   Such a possibility would be given, for example, after the breakdown of a last attempt for an American-Russian understanding or after the successful repulsion of an Allied invasion attempt."   This was one of many "questions" posed by Berlin about disagreements among the Allied Powers and differences of opinion within the American public that might impair FDR's foreign policy course.[52]   These guidelines and inquiries reflected Schellenberg's own assessment of Allied vulnerabilities.

SD agents in South America responded to such prodding with optimistic assessments that bore little correspondence to reality.   They reported Argentinian diplomats' views that General Eisenhower would seek peace if reassured that German claims were restricted to Europe—if Germany would waive claims to Africa.   Eisenhower also reportedly believed that an Allied military campaign against the Nazi "fortress Europe" would be too costly.[53]   Another report attributed political significance to the fact that Eisenhower was supposed to have been friendly to captured German officers; the agent declared him anti-Semitic as well.[54] Such intelligence was worse than useless: it only strengthened illusions in Berlin that Germany could avoid or escape the vise beginning to tighten on both sides.

If SD Foreign Intelligence failed to grasp Germany's real situation, the German Foreign Office was worse.   Foreign Minister Ribbentrop made obvious blunders, such as ignoring a report in September 1942 that the Americans and British would soon land troops in North Africa.   This misstep was reported to Hitler after the prediction turned out to be accurate.   Some high Foreign Office officials believed that their boss was incompetent and arrogant.   When Foreign Office State Secretary Martin Luther said as much through an intermediary to Schellenberg, he passed Luther's comments along to Himmler, who brought about Luther's arrest.   Luther's Germany Division within the Foreign Office was dissolved, and Ribbentrop appointed a weaker man as state secretary.[55]

Schellenberg's would-be foreign policy was more flexible and experimental than Ribbentrop's—or Hitler's.   He understood that the risk of failure in extended war on two fronts was unacceptably high. He was willing to strike a bargain with either the West or the Soviet Union if the terms were right. He managed to meet an American businessman turned intelligence official in Stockholm in November 1943, where he cautiously (and apparently without authorization) offered Himmler's support for a compromise peace.   If Schellenberg could strike a deal with the West, fine; then he could try to sell it to Himmler.   If not, he hoped to use the evidence of bargaining with the West to turn the Soviet Union against the West.   Schellenberg invited the American, Abram Hewitt, to come to Germany for further negotiations. Nazi propagandists could have used a captive American negotiator very effectively. High OSS officials wisely ordered Hewitt to decline, and Hewitt was forced to leave Stockholm as a result of his unauthorized contact with an unsavory Nazi official.[56]

To prove his bona fides, Schellenberg also gave Hewitt another message for Washington: the Gestapo was "onto" Allen Dulles' espionage work in Bern. They were feeding him false information from informants, and they had broken his codes.[57] Both items turned out to be essentially false—apparently designed to disrupt Dulles' effective operations. Dulles made little secret of what he was doing, but he was good at separating valuable informants from Nazi plants, and his codes were never broken. He recognized Schellenberg's ploy.[58]

Schellenberg and the Abwehr
Himmler initially was willing to take intelligence from wherever he could get it. Over time Schellenberg persuaded him that the Abwehr was riddled with problems. Himmler initially shied away from confrontation with the High Command of the Armed Services, which protected Admiral Canaris, because Himmler was not sure that Hitler would support him if the two intelligence organizations came to blows. But signs of the Abwehr's vulnerability began to accumulate.

One significant weakness was evidence that Canaris' deputy General Oster and some of his subordinates had rescued seven Jewish families by listing them as agents, sending them to Switzerland, and even salvaging $100,000 of their assets by cloaking it as financing for intelligence activities. The Abwehr's paymaster protested, but Canaris backed Oster. According to one well-informed, newly declassified British intelligence report, this incident was the primary reason for Oster's downfall.[59]

In April 1943, Hans von Dohnanyi was arrested; he had worked under General Oster in the Abwehr, and Oster tried to protect Dohnanyi, a fellow member of the anti-Nazi underground who was of part-Jewish ancestry. Dohnanyi, too, was implicated in the transfer of the seven Jewish families to Switzerland. First, Oster was placed under house arrest; then his access and responsibilities were curtailed.[60]

While the Gestapo conducted surveillance of Oster, other problems in the Abwehr surfaced. Several Abwehr officials in Turkey defected to the Allies in late 1943 and early 1944. An enraged Hitler gave the Abwehr to Himmler, and Himmler decided to incorporate it into SD Foreign Intelligence. Details were worked out in a series of high-level conferences in March and early April 1944. Schellenberg, in effect, got a separate Military Office staffed by Abwehr personnel within his organization. He then imposed SD control at various levels.[61]

Schellenberg's Foreign Policy
Himmler continued to believe that expansion of the SS and police empire would solve many of Germany's problems. In early 1944, after he had brought about the SD's absorption of the Abwehr, Himmler reportedly said to Schellenberg: "I

feel like a big snake which has just swallowed an ox and is still working it down his throat [i.e., Admiral Canaris], and now all I have in front of me is a rabbit [Ribbentrop] whose turn will come as soon as I have digested the ox." In his inner circle Schellenberg raised the idea of extracting the intelligence service from the RSHA, where it lay within chief Ernst Kaltenbrunner's jurisdiction and where it suffered from the stigma attached to the Gestapo. One option was to move foreign intelligence into the Foreign Office, but only if Ribbentrop were removed.[62] Some knowledgeable officials began to speak about Schellenberg as Ribbentrop's successor.[63] But Ribbentrop managed to hang on, in part because he aligned his own views so closely with Hitler's.

Himmler reportedly had one area of flexibility in plotting the course of the war. According to former Abwehr official Eduard Waetjen, Himmler's foreign policy strategy in early 1944 was to intensify the struggle against the Soviet Union, if possible, through a joint operation with the Japanese (who had not attacked the Soviets) and to convince the West that weakening or destroying the Soviet Union was in their interest. The West might then agree to a compromise peace. Waetjen also said that Himmler was still faithful to Hitler, but hoped to succeed him. High OSS officials, drawing upon a range of other sources, thought Waetjen's analysis of Himmler and the Nazi political situation had "the ring of truth."[64]

Schellenberg acted as though Himmler would accept something along these lines. Schellenberg assumed that the alliance against the Axis powers could not hold together indefinitely. One side or the other would abandon the declared Allied policy of unconditional surrender by Germany and its allies, given the right encouragement. He also thought he could probably entice the West to negotiate with Himmler (and vice versa). Neither assumption turned out to be accurate.

By the fall of 1944 Schellenberg became more inventive in approaching the West. He had some leeway to operate—he could always claim he was trying to cause trouble among the Allies—but he did not have Hitler's or Himmler's approval, and Kaltenbrunner was likely to oppose whatever Schellenberg tried. Defector Carl Marcus, closely associated with Jahnke in Schellenberg's inner circle, gave British intelligence a mixed assessment of him in early 1945. Schellenberg had seen for some time that the war would reach a disastrous conclusion unless something was changed. He saw Hitler, Bormann, and Propaganda Minister Joseph Goebbels as the main obstacles to German negotiations either with the West or with the Soviets: he and Himmler could have obtained satisfactory terms for Germany in a separate peace.[65]

Schellenberg, however, wanted his own trusted officials to handle any overtures to the West. He helped to scuttle a proposal from Wilhelm Harster, commander of the Security Police and SD in Italy, to use an Italian industrialist named Marinotti as a secret envoy, because Schellenberg and Harster were not on good terms. Harster's operation, code named "West-Wind," was rejected at the highest levels of the RSHA.[66]

The idea of using an Italian as an intermediary to launch German negotiations with the West in Switzerland, however, remained alive. In a November 1944 meeting of RSHA foreign intelligence officials in Verona called by the SD expert on Switzerland, Klaus Huegel, Guido Zimmer suggested contacting Allied intelligence in Switzerland through Baron Luigi Parrilli, formerly the representative of the Kelvinator and Nash companies in Italy. Parrilli had worked with Zimmer, but he also had contacts with Italian partisans. Other German officials backed this approach through Parrilli, and after considerable delay they received approval in principle from Berlin. In mid-February 1945 they also got support from Karl Wolff, Highest SS and Police Leader in Italy. Parrilli's mission was code named "Operation Wool."[67]

Another German emissary preceded Parrilli in getting Dulles' attention. In January 1945, Hans Wilhelm Eggen, Schellenberg's economic representative in Switzerland, met with American diplomat Frederick R. Loofborough. Eggen first took a hard line: Germany had no choice currently but to fight to the end, even if all Germans were killed. The result then would be the triumph of Bolshevism over all of Europe. But he suggested a meeting in Switzerland between Schellenberg and Dulles to avert such disaster. Schellenberg, he said, could bring Dulles proof that the Russians were not playing fair with the West. Loofborough quickly sent a report of this conversation to Dulles, who mused about the possibility of finding someone within the SS willing to sell out on a big scale.[68]

Lacking clearance from Himmler, Schellenberg at first hesitated and held back from authorizing Operation Wool. But Parrilli showed up to see Dulles in late February 1945 anyway. As an Italian with major assets, he had his own reasons for wanting to avoid a German scorched-earth policy in northern Italy. In negotiations with Dulles' assistant Gero von Gaevernitz, Parrilli reported that he was working for Zimmer in the SD and that German authorities were interested in sparing northern Italy from a horrible fate. Though skeptical, Gaevernitz asked for evidence of high-ranking German support—Zimmer by himself meant little. Dulles believed that German military forces in northern Italy were nervous. There had been some informal talks between Italian partisans and the Germans, with the Germans seeking some assurance that they would not be attacked if they should withdraw from Italy. The Germans offered to refrain from destroying Italian factories and power plants in return. But through his contacts Dulles learned that the Italian partisans firmly opposed such a deal.[69]

On March 3, 1945, Zimmer, Parrilli, and Eugen Dollmann, Himmler's representative in Italy, met with OSS official Paul Blum in Lugano, Switzerland. This meeting set the stage for a visit by Karl Wolff and his adjutant to Dulles himself on March 8. Wolff had not yet concluded that all was lost, but he had convinced himself of the value of opening a line to the West.[70] With that move by Wolff, the Americans had no need for Schellenberg. Still, even in early April Schellenberg apparently passed word through General Henri Guisan, commander of the Swiss army, that he was willing to meet with Dulles for the purpose of halting the fighting on the western front (while continuing the war in the East).[71]

The details of on-again, off-again bargaining between Dulles and Karl Wolff during March and April 1945 (and the misunderstandings on both sides) have been revealed previously. Wolff was unwilling to take extreme risks, and that in any case he had very little influence on Field Marshal Albert Kesselring and General Heinrich Vietinghoff, who would not agree to surrender army forces until the military situation forced their hand (and after Hitler's suicide had become known). Dulles and Wolff finally brought about a German surrender in Italy, but it came late: the fighting in Italy stopped on May 2. What might have been a boon to Allied forces in Italy turned out to be a saving of only five days before the end of the war in Europe. According to historians Bradley F. Smith and Elena Agarossi, the lives saved were limited in number—and mostly Italian and German.[72]

Unable to lead Himmler into separate peace discussions against Hitler's will, Schellenberg found other ways to sanitize his own record, particularly using neutral contacts to intervene on behalf of groups of concentration camp prisoners. Schellenberg first met with Himmler's friend Jean-Marie Musy, former federal president of Switzerland. On January 22, 1945, Schellenberg ordered a subordinate named Franz Göring to obtain the release of specific Jewish families from different concentration camps and turn them over to Musy on the Swiss border at Constance, an arrangement Himmler had reportedly approved in principle. By his own newly declassified account, Göring was able to track down some of his targets, but never found the whereabouts of others.

Göring also learned that Musy and Himmler had discussed a broader plan to release all remaining Jews in German concentration camps. Musy had met with Dr. Isaac Sternbuch, representative of an Orthodox Jewish rescue organization, Vaad Hatzalah, based in Montreux, Switzerland. Sternbuch allegedly told Musy that all released Jews would be sent to the United States after only a brief stay in Switzerland. Himmler had supposedly consented to this plan in order to improve Germany's image—and his own. In return, Sternbuch's organization had to give Musy 5 million Swiss francs, the money allegedly to be used to relieve the suffering of German civilians.[73] Schellenberg commented in his own mini-history: "Considerations of internal politics made him [Himmler] bring up the question of a quid pro quo, often in an ugly way."[74] This was little more than a veiled statement that Himmler did not dare to go through with such a deal unless he could demonstrate to Hitler or other hard-liners clear benefits for the war effort.[75]

Ironically, Himmler's "rabbit" Ribbentrop was experimenting with a similar option in early March 1945. Ribbentrop sent a diplomat named Fritz Hesse to Sweden with Ribbentrop's own draft of Germany's negotiating position. Sooner or later, Germany would have to surrender on one front. The West had a strong interest in seeing that Germany did not surrender to the Soviet Union.

In return for Western acceptance of a separate peace, Germany was prepared to release 400,000 Jews still in the Reich. With the aid of Werner Dankwort and Heinz Thörner of the German Embassy in Stockholm, Hesse made contact with Swedish banker Marcus Wallenberg to pass along this message, and he also met directly with Iver Olsen, representative of the American War Refugee Board in Stockholm. The German diplomat and the American official cast their discussion as an exchange of views on humanitarian issues, not as any kind of political negotiation. But articles in the Swedish press about Hesse's peace mission brought about his abrupt recall to Germany. The publicity apparently enraged Hitler and other hard-liners.[76]

Ribbentrop himself spoke with Swedish Count Folke Bernadotte along similar lines: if the West showed no consideration for Germany, it would go Bolshevist. Ribbentrop alerted Bernadotte (who later informed Schellenberg) to his private channel to Stockholm (Hesse). Schellenberg thought that Bernadotte had taken Ribbentrop's comments as an insult. The combination of Hesse's "humanitarian concern" and Ribbentrop's threat of Germany becoming Bolshevist was a bit much.[77]

In his postwar account Schellenberg alluded to another problem—he, Göring, and Musy faced formidable competition within the SS itself. Kurt Becher, an SS officer with close ties to Himmler and with experience extorting Jewish assets in Hungary, was involved in direct negotiations with Hungarian Jewish activist Rudolf Kasztner and through him with Saly Mayer, representative of the American Jewish Joint Distribution Committee in Switzerland. These contacts predated Schellenberg's and Göring's efforts with Musy.[78] In Wildbad, on January 15, 1945, Musy urged Himmler to arrange a "generous" solution to the Jewish question. Himmler then told Musy about the ongoing negotiations with Saly Mayer, which came as a complete surprise to Musy. Himmler and Musy agreed that Musy should try to determine (in Himmler's inimitable prose) "who is it who really had a connection with the American government. Is it the rabbinical Jew or is it the Joint?"[79] The OSS received an intelligence report that Himmler had asked Musy whether better treatment of the Jews and other refugees would help modify Western public opinion toward him.[80]

Himmler wanted Musy's negotiating partners in Switzerland, Sternbuch's group (linked to the Agudas Israel World Organization), to pay a hefty sum because he was trying to assess these two channels that "world Jewry" had to the Allied Powers. It never entered his mind that neither one had even a remote chance of arranging major shipments of Jewish refugees to the United States.

In his mid-January 1945 memo for the files, Himmler wrote that he told Musy to seek tractors and machinery, rather than money, in exchange for Jews. But as late as February 6 Musy asked Sternbuch (who asked the American War Refugee Board) for SF 5 million to be deposited in an account in Musy's name—Himmler would not insist on goods, Musy said. War Refugee Board representative Roswell McClelland concluded: "Himmler must be interested in negotiating for something more important to him and to the Nazis than the release of the Jews . . . Musy is even in closer contact with Schellenberg than with Himmler and . . . Schellenberg is very willing to assist in such questions as the Jewish [one] . . . "[81]

Schellenberg's side came out second best in the battle of the two Swiss connections. McClelland was authorized to play along with Becher if it meant saving some lives: he even met once in person with him in Switzerland. As a result, some American money was deposited in a blocked account in Switzerland as a sign of American interest; in return, Becher, Kasztner, and Mayer brought about the release of 1,684 Jews from Bergen-Belsen to Switzerland. Schellenberg, Göring, and Musy managed to release 1,210 Jews from Theresienstadt, in return for which Sternbuch allegedly paid SF 5,000, or by another report $13,000.[82] But no one on the American side wanted to deal with Musy, let alone Schellenberg. Perhaps it was because the United States alerted the British and the Soviet Union after the first transfer of funds: the Soviets responded that such negotiations were neither feasible nor permissible.[83]

Friends of Julius Streicher, Nazi gauleiter and editor of the rabidly anti-Semitic newspaper *Der Stürmer*, reportedly sent a protest to Hitler and Himmler about the release of Jews from Theresienstadt. Hitler later insisted that no Jews be released unless he gave authorization and Germany got something concrete in return.[84] Musy was undeterred, telling American diplomat Sam Woods that on his forthcoming trip to Berlin he would take up with Himmler the release of seventy thousand more Jews. Musy believed that if Himmler were granted safe haven somewhere, he would come to terms. Musy also offered the by now popular argument that Germany needed a strong central government to prevent chaos and Communism.[85] Schellenberg's strategy of seeking political objectives with the West through playing on fears of Communism *and* negotiating for the turnover of Jews had taken on independent life.

Schellenberg was also active in the northern theater. He and Göring linked up with Himmler's Finnish masseur Felix Kersten and with Count Bernadotte, who was the point man of a Swedish humanitarian initiative. They successfully lobbied for the release of Scandinavian prisoners brought to a camp at Neuengamme, as well as some Jews and other prisoners from Buchenwald, Bergen-Belsen, and Ravensbrück.[86]

Göring also tried to arrange for orderly turnover of all prisoners in these camps to Allied forces, but internal opposition from Kaltenbrunner and Müller turned out to be too strong.[87] Musy told American War Refugee Board representative McClelland that Himmler had originally wanted political-military concessions, such as agreeing to leave prisoners in fifteen major concentration camps and not march them away until they collapsed in exchange for a guarantee that there would be no Negro occupation troops in Germany. Musy claimed he overcame their resistance. Himmler and Schellenberg in the end had only one condition— that the SS guards and administrative personnel of the camps be treated as soldiers and regular prisoners of war (and not shot on the spot).[88] Despite these efforts, each camp went its own way, and some camp inmates were "evacuated"—sent on death marches—even as Allied troops approached. But Schellenberg had been a key part of a group that accomplished something: he had Göring, Bernadotte, and, to a lesser extent, Musy to vouch for his efforts.

Schellenberg really believed in preparing for all options: he had a forged American passport prepared with his photo.[89] In the end, he found a safer course. After Hitler's suicide, Admiral Dönitz became chancellor and appointed Schellenberg as German envoy to Sweden, allegedly in order to negotiate (with Sweden) evacuation of German troops from Norway. Schellenberg flew to Stockholm on May 4 and received a Swedish passport from authorities there. He came under the protection of Bernadotte, with whom he had just worked on humanitarian projects.[90] There his rewriting of history began.

In June 1945, Schellenberg composed an abbreviated autobiography that anticipated the tone and interpretation of his book *The Labyrinth*. He alleged that he had worked early for a compromise peace and against a two-front war, efforts that led Hitler and Kaltenbrunner to threaten to imprison him for defeatism. Yet Himmler, an exception to the whole corrupt government setup, frequently listened sympathetically to Schellenberg's arguments. Only his indecision doomed Schellenberg to failure.[91]

Schellenberg even fashioned an account of how he and Himmler planned to kill Hitler in early April 1945—the gist of the story was leaked to the *Daily Express* when Schellenberg was brought to London in July 1945 for extended interrogations (Schellenberg was first interrogated at Frankfurt). It turned out that even by his own account Schellenberg hesitated to voice this goal explicitly and Himmler refused to endorse it in Schellenberg's presence, let alone commit to do it personally. Schellenberg conjectured that Himmler had arranged for Hitler to be poisoned by his doctors.[92] But it never happened.

Britain and the United States were more interested in what Schellenberg had to say about possible Nazi resistance and continued intelligence activity after the surrender. On July 11, 1945, the Counter-Intelligence War Room in London reassured Allied Headquarters that, according to Schellenberg, Nazi plans for underground intelligence activity never matured. His information was consistent with their other sources on this point, and he had given so many details of his office's work that they accepted the thrust of his testimony.[93]

The best thing Schellenberg had going for him after the war was that he had developed the right internal enemies. British and American intelligence had independent information that Schellenberg was on the opposite side of an RSHA faction led by chief Ernst Kaltenbrunner, Gestapo chief Heinrich Müller, Otto Ohlendorf (SD domestic intelligence), and sabotage/specialist operations man Otto Skorzeny, most of them obvious war criminals.[94]

British and American intelligence had access to several types of independent sources about Schellenberg: decoded radio messages of the SD Foreign Intelligence, wartime information from one or more key defectors and British penetration agents, and postwar interrogations of other key officials in SD Foreign Intelligence who gave more complete or more accurate testimony than Schellenberg himself.

The new material declassified by the IWG allows us to write a much better history of Schellenberg and SD Foreign Intelligence; however, there are strong indications that additional information resides in unreleased British files. An FBI agent brought to Frankfurt in July 1945 noted that British intelligence had more to go on than he did:

> The Special Interrogator sent down from the War Office in London, a Mr. Johnson . . . Johnson is a man who has made a study of Schellenberg for the past five years and has had a penetration Agent in close contact with the man for some time. In fact he knows Schellenberg almost as well as he knows himself.[95]

How long did British intelligence have a penetration agent working with Schellenberg or the SD? Who was he? To the best of our knowledge, British files on any agent in contact with Schellenberg have not yet been released.[96]

Notes

1. A German POW who had served in the Forschungsamt gave a very detailed account of its activities, which cannot be covered here. See "Research Bureau" of German Air Ministry as a Secret Intelligence Information Service, 18 June 1945, copy in NA, RG 226, entry 210, box 70, folder 299. Additional information about contacts between the Forschungsamt and SD Foreign Intelligence are in Statement by Klaus Huegel, 10 July 1945, NA, RG 226, entry 119A, London X-2 PTS Files, box 54, folder 1583–Huegel.

2. The Gestapo is treated in chapter 6; the activity of the German army's Foreign Armies East intelligence organization under General Reinhard Gehlen is treated separately in chapter 14.

3. David Kahn, *Hitler's Spies: German Military Intelligence in World War II* (New York: Macmillan, 1978) and Heinz Höhne, *Canaris: Hitler's Master Spy*, trans. J. Maxwell Brownjohn (1976; New York, 1999). Kahn's work covers more than just the Abwehr; Höhne's study is as much organizational history as biography.

4. Saint, London to Saint, Washington, 28 Nov. 1945 re. Bibliography of the GIS, NA, RG 226, entry 190, box 392, folder 570–Incoming Memos 1141-1228.

5. Early information from Wurmann is in NA, RG 65, 65-37193-EBF 34, box 125.

6. British fortnightly summaries for specific regions were passed to U.S. Naval Intelligence. See Record Group 38, CNSG Library, box 74, U.S./U.K Intelligence Exchange. For weekly summaries, code named CIRCLE in OSS, see NA, RG 226, entry 210, box 9, folders 1–3.

7. War Room Monthly Summary No. 2, 16 May 1945, copy in NA, RG 226, entry 109, Washington Registry Intelligence Files, box 26, folder XX7260-XX7289.

8. Karl Heinz Abshagen, *Canaris*, trans. A. H. Broderick (London: Hutchinson, 1956).

9. This is Höhne's portrait in *Canaris: Hitler's Master Spy*.

10. CSDIC Interrogation Report on SS-Standartenführer Canaris, Constantin, 12 July 1945, NA, RG 226, entry 171, Washington X-2 Personality Files, box 22, folder 344–Washington X-2 PTS 85, document 40.

11. One of them was his deputy, General Hans Oster, who *was* a key figure in the anti-Nazi resistance.

12. Gerald Fleming, *Hitler and the Final Solution*, trans. James Porter (Berkeley: University of California Press, 1984), 80–87.

13. Fleming, *Final Solution*, 82.

14. Andrew Ezergailis, *The Holocaust in Latvia, 1941–1944: The Missing Center* (Riga: Historical Institute of Latvia in association with the United States Holocaust Memorial Museum, 1996).

15. Höhne, *Canaris: Hitler's Master Spy*.

16. Ian Kershaw, *Hitler, 1936–1945: Nemesis* (New York: W. W. Norton, 2000).

17. Detailed Interrogation Report: Notes on German Atrocities, 29 Apr. 1945, NA, RG 498, entry 47752 ETO-MIS-Y, box 93, folder 22-39. The interrogator, who wrote a summary of Bruns' various comments about atrocities he had seen, appraised Bruns as a mild-mannered "bureaucratic" officer who was anti-Nazi and eager to cooperate with the Allies. Both the source and the information were judged reliable (B-2).

18. Bruns' account diverged from Fleming's reconstruction on some particulars, including the

fact that Bruns witnessed some of the killings.

19. CSDIC (UK) G.G. Report S.R.G.G. 1158(C), 25 Apr. 1945, copy in NA, RG 226, entry 108A, Washington Registry SI Branch Field Files, box 145, folder S.R.G.G. 1129-1245.

20. Richard Breitman, *Official Secrets: What the Nazis Planned, What the British and Americans Knew* (New York: Hill and Wang, 1998), 84.

21. Altemeyer told Bruns that his report was apparently the cause of the new orders. Detailed Interrogation Report, 29 Apr. 1945, NA, RG 498, entry 41752 ETO-MIS-Y, box 93, folders 22-39–6824 DIC/MIS/CI.

22. This document, dated 10 Dec. 1942 (copy 15 Mar. 1945), was found in the files of the Belgian office of the Abwehr, copy in NA, RG 226, entry 119A, London X-2 PTS Files, box 25, folder 636–London X-2 PTS 8 Captured Documents. Emphasis in original document.

23. One example is covered in Höhne, *Canaris: Hitler's Master Spy*, 466. As many as five hundred Jews from the Netherlands were sent to South America, allegedly as agents.

24. NA, RG 226, entry 119A London X-2 PTS Files, box 25, folder 636–London X-2 PTS 8 Captured Documents.

25. Summary of report drawn up by Abwehr II C 2 for a conference in Prague on 18 May 1942, translated copy in NA, RG 226, entry 109, box 57, folder XX10660-10687, document XX 10673.

26. MI-5 Interrogation, 8 Nov. 1944, copied to Major I.I. Milne of S.I.S., 14 Nov. 1944, copy in NA, RG 226, entry 210, box 304, folder 8. This interrogation may not yet be available in the United Kingdom.

27. I am grateful to Professor David Meier of Dickinson State University, ND, for sharing his unpublished manuscript on the postwar tribulations of Otto John. David A. Meier, "Spies, Lies, and a Berlin Mystery: The Case of Otto John," [2002].

28. Some of the individuals, meetings, and events mentioned in his account appear, more or less in the same light, in historian Peter Hoffmann's massive and reliable *The History of the German Resistance 1933–1945*, trans. Richard Barry (Cambridge, MA: MIT Press, 1977).

29. This at least is the interpretation of Professor Meier (see n. 27).

30. Irving H. Sherman to Hugh Wilson re. Lee Lane, 17 July 1943, NA, RG 226, entry 110 Field Intelligence Reports: Theater Officer Correspondence, box 53, folder 526–The Lane Project.

31. See Walter Laqueur and Richard Breitman, *Breaking the Silence: The Germans Who Exposed The Final Solution* (Hanover, NH: University Press of New England for Brandeis University Press 1994), 213. See also chapter 5.

32. Saint to Saint, Amzon, 11 July 1946, NA, RG 226, entry 213, box 12, folder 12. This recommendation seems to have been originally written during mid-1945. It did not prevent Waetjen from running into trouble with suspicious American officials outside OSS, and even Gaevernitz had some difficulty establishing his bona fides in the postwar period. See Laqueur and Breitman, *Breaking the Silence*, 237–38.

33. X-2 Report, Wiesbaden, 1 Oct. 1945, for Sept 1945, NA, RG 226, entry 210, box 100945, folder 3. Memorandum: Berlin GIS Personnel Uncovered by Zigzag to SCI Amzon, 31 Oct. 1945, NA, RG 226, entry 213, box 2, folder 7.

34. AB16, Saint, Berlin to AB 24 Saint, Amzon, 9 Jan. 1946, NA, RG 226, entry 213, box 1, folder 6.

35. For the most detailed account of how the SD became involved in foreign intelligence, see Katrin Paehler, "Espionage, Ideology, and Personal Politics: The Making and the Unmaking of a Nazi Foreign Intelligence Service," (PhD diss. American University, forthcoming).

36. George C. Browder, "Walter Schellenberg—Eine Geheimdienst Phantasie," in *Die SS: Elite unter dem Totenkopf; 30 Lebensläufe*, ed. Ronald Smelser and Enrico Syring (Paderborn: Schöningh, 2000), 424.

37. Walter Schellenberg, *The Labyrinth: Memoirs of Walter Schellenberg, Hitler's Chief of Counterintelligence*, trans. Louis Hagen (1956; New York: DeCapo, 2000).

38. I owe this information to Katrin Paehler. On Himmler's stress of ideological instruction within the SS, see Richard Breitman, "Gegner Nummer Eins," in *Ausbildungsziel Judenmord? "Weltanschauliche Erziehung" von SS, Polizei und Waffen-SS im Rahmen der "Endlösung,"* ed. Jürgen Matthäus, Konrad Kwiet, Jürgen Förster, and Richard Breitman (Frankfurt am Main: Fischer Taschenbuch, 2003), 21–34.

39. Browder, "Walter Schellenberg," 422.

40. Eighth Detailed Interrogation on SS-Sturmbannführer Dr. Klaus Huegel, 26 June 1945, NA, RG 226, entry 119A, box 71, folder 1829. On the reorganization, Fifth Detailed Interrogation Report on Huegel, 14 June 1945, NA, RG 226, entry 174, box 39, folder 307–Huegel, Klaus Dr. Huegel said that Himmler gave Schellenberg a one-year trial. The source on Bormann and Schellenberg is the [British] Interrogation Report No. 2 on Karl Marcus, alias Martenhofer [later code named "Dictionary"], Public Record Office KV 2/64. I am grateful to Stephen Tyas for a copy of this document.

41. Eighth Detailed Interrogation Report on Dr. Klaus Huegel, 14 June 1945, NA, RG 226, entry 174, box 39, folder 307–Huegel, Klaus Dr. The comment about Schellenberg's having frequent contact with Himmler is confirmed by entries in Himmler's office logs.

42. Fourth Detailed Interrogation Report on Dr. Klaus Huegel, 10 June 1945, NA, RG 226, entry 174, box 39, folder 307–Huegel, Klaus Dr.

43. Himmler and the Sicherheitsdienst (R.I.S. 16), 27 Sept. 1943, Public Record Office HW 19/347. I am grateful to Stephen Tyas for a copy of this document.

44. Appendix, Group 13, Sept. 1943, PRO HW 19/347. Stephen Tyas kindly provided a copy of this document.

45. Abwehr and SD, copy in NA, RG 226, entry 119A, box 24, folder 635.

46. Extract of SIS Interrogation of Carl Marcus, Feb. 1945, PRO KV 2/94. I am grateful to Stephen Tyas for a copy of this document. Himmler to Schellenberg, 5 Dec. 1942, NA, RG 242, T-175, roll 129, frame 2655073.

47. The details of Zimmer's activities are revealed for the first time in the transcription of his shorthand notebooks, NA, RG 263, Guido Zimmer Name File.

48. Eighth Detailed Interrogation on Huegel, 26 June 1945, NA, RG 226, entry 119A, box 71, folder 1829.

49. Extract of SIS Interrogation of Marcus, Feb. 1945, PRO KV 2/94. I am grateful to Stephen Tyas for a copy of this document.

50. Jahnke and the Jahnke-Büro, Appendix 15 to Final Report on the Case of Walter Schellenberg, copy in NA, RG 65, 100-00-103569–Bulky 39, box 4.

51. Berlin to Argentine, 6 June 1943, [INCA 60], NA, RG 38, entry CNSG Library, box 79,

folder 382413 CNSG–German Clandestine (2 of 3).

52. Berlin to Argentine, 12, 15, 17 June 1943 [INCA 83], folder 2 of 3; Berlin to Argentine, 12–13 Aug. 1943, [INCA 178]; both in NA, RG 38, entry CNSG Library, box 79, folder 382413 CNSG–German Clandestine (2 of 3).

53. Argentine to Berlin, 7 Aug. 1943, NA, RG 38, entry CNSG Library, box 80, folder 382414 German Clandestine Translations–Argentina to Berlin (2 of 3).

54. Ibid. This information supposedly came from the first secretary at the American Embassy in Argentina.

55. Fourth Detailed Interrogation Report on Huegel, 10 June 1945, NA, RG 226, entry 174, box 39, folder 307–Huegel, Klaus Dr. On Luther generally, see Christopher R. Browning, *The Final Solution and the German Foreign Office: A Study of Referat D III of Abteilung Deutschland 1940–43* (New York: Holmes and Meier, 1978); the section on Luther's ouster (113–14) is based on sources with a more benign interpretation of Schellenberg's motives. In any case, Luther and Ribbentrop had longstanding disagreements; the incident described here was the coup de grace.

56. See Richard Breitman "A Deal with the Nazi Dictatorship: Himmler's Alleged Peace Emissaries in Fall 1943," *Journal of Contemporary History* 30, no. 4 (1995): 411–30.

57. OSS to Bern, Carib for 110, 29 Mar. 1944, NA, RG 226, entry 134, box 165, folder 1056–Out D. 27 Bern, March–June 1944.

58. Dulles was nonplused when Washington told him of this message, stating that Schellenberg undoubtedly knew something of his operation and would like to know a lot more. Bern to OSS-SI, For Carib, 3 Apr. 1944, NA, RG 226, entry 134, box 191, folder 1214.

59. German I.S.-Recent Developments (15 Sept. 1943–15 Oct. 1943), copy in NA, RG 226, entry 194, box 60, folder 260. This operation, known as Unternehmen 7 or V7, began to leak when the Gestapo arrested one of the participants, Wilhelm Schmidhuber, who talked. See Höhne, *Canaris: Hitler's Master Spy*, 507.

60. Eighth Detailed Interrogation Report on Huegel, 26 June 1945, NA, RG 226, entry 119A, box 71, folder 1829. See also Hoffmann, *History of the German Resistance*, 294.

61. Eighth Detailed Interrogation Report on Huegel, 26 June 1945, NA, RG 226, entry 119A, box 71, folder 1829; Fifth Interrogation Report on Huegel, 14 June 1945, NA, RG 226, entry 174, box 39, folder 307; Camp 020 Interim Interrogation Report on SS Standf. Martin Sandberger, 8 July 1945, NA, RG 226, entry 119A, box 33, folder 871.

62. Camp 020 Interim Interrogation Report on SS Standf. Martin Sandberger, Oct. 1945, NA, RG 226, entry 119A, box 33, folder 871.

63. Fourth Detailed Interrogation Report on Huegel, NA, RG 226, entry 174, box 39, folder 307–Huegel, Klaus Dr.

64. Bern to OSS-SI, Washington, 5 Mar. 1944, NA, RG 226, entry 134, box 219, folder Breakers—Jan.–Mar. 1944; Washington, SI to Bern, 7 Mar. 1944, NA, RG 226, entry 134, box 298, folder 1701–Bern, Mar. 1944.

65. This June 1945 extract of an interrogation of Marcus on 3 Feb. 1945 was recently declassified in the United Kingdom. See PRO KV 2/94. I am grateful to Stephen Tyas for discovering it and sending me a copy.

66. Sixth Detailed Interrogation Report on Huegel, 21 June 1945, NA, RG 226, entry 119A, box

71, folder 1828.

67. Ibid.

68. Meeting of 493 with Hans Ecken [*sic*] of the SS, 15 Jan. 1945, and 110 to Sasac and Saint, Washington, London, Paris, 18 Jan. 1945, both in NA, RG 226, entry 214, box 7, folder 38–WN25833-25843. On Eggen generally, see NA, RG 263, Hans Eggen Name File.

69. Details of Zimmer's interaction with Parrilli are Zimmer's diaries in NA, RG 263, Guido Zimmer Name File. For Parrilli's interaction with Gaevernitz and Dulles' views, see Bradley F. Smith and Elena Agarossi, *Operation Sunrise: The Secret Surrender* (New York: Basic Books, 1979), 68–80.

70. Smith and Agarossi, *Operation Sunrise*, 81–82.

71. Bern to OSS Washington, 5 Apr. 1945, re. Schellenberg, NA, RG 226, entry 210, box 364, folder 2.

72. Smith and Agarossi, *Operation Sunrise*, 184–91.

73. Franz Goering, "Extract from my diary concerning the release of persons from German concentration camps," NA, RG 226, entry 109, box 45, folder 261, XX9626 (11-13-45).

74. Schellenberg's draft autobiography, 10 June 1945, p. 10, NA, RG 226, entry 125A, box 2, folder 21–Schellenberg. The manuscript is thirty-five legal-size pages, single-spaced.

75. Franz Goering, "Extract from my diary concerning the release of persons from German concentration camps," NA, RG 226, entry 109, box 45, folder 261, XX9626 (11-13-45).

76. CSDIC/WEA [British] Preliminary Interrogation Report on Gesandschaftsrat Heinz Karl Eduard Thorner, undated, copy in NA, RG 226, entry 125, box 28, folder INP-83 Thorner. Johnson to Secretary of State, 7 Mar. 1945, NA, RG 59, Central Decimal File, 848.48 Refugees, 3-745 KFC (Records of the Department of State Relating to the Problems of Relief and Refugees in Europe Arising from World War II and Its Aftermath, 1938–1949, M 1284, roll 55). Olsen, who worked for OSS as well as the War Refugee Board, met directly with Hesse on March 8 with the understanding that he could exchange views only on humanitarian issues. See Johnson to Secretary of State, 11 Apr. 1945, NA, RG 59, Central Decimal File, 740.0011, E. W. 4-1145 (Records of the Department of State Relating to World War II, 1939–1945, M 982, roll 216). Meredith Hindley, "Negotiating the Boundary of Unconditional Surrender: The War Refugee Board in Sweden and Nazi Proposals to Ransom Jews, 1944–1945," *Holocaust and Genocide Studies* 10, no. 1 (1996): 52–77, sets Hesse's meeting with Olsen into a broader context of Nazi peace feelers.

77. Schellenberg's draft autobiography, 10 June 1945, NA, RG 226, entry 125A, box 2, folder 21, 8–9.

78. See Richard Breitman and Shlomo Aronson, "The End of the Final Solution? Nazi Attempts to Ransom Jews in 1944," *Central European History* 25, no. 2 (1992): 177–203.

79. Himmler's Niederschrift, 18 Jan. 1945, NA, RG 242, Records of the Reich Leader of the SS and Chief of the German Police, T-175, roll 188, frame 2643519.

80. Activities of Musy; Nazi Plans for Escape, 3 Feb. 1945, NA, RG 200, box 29, folder 361.

81. Niederschrift, NA, RG 242, Records of the Reich Leader of the SS and Chief of the German Police, T-175, roll 118, frame 2643519. Roswell McClelland, Sternbuch-Musy-Himmler-Jewish Affair, Confidential Memo, 6 Feb. 1945, private possession of Richard Breitman.

82. These events are covered in considerable detail in Yehuda Bauer, *Jews for Sale? Nazi-Jewish*

Negotiations, 1933-1945 (New Haven, CT: Yale University Press, 1994), 216–38. Bauer's general interpretation is that the German initiatives emanated from Himmler, who was working in opposition to Hitler; Becher and Schellenberg followed his lead. But Schellenberg's and Göring's accounts indicate that they (and Musy) took the initiative, that they persuaded Himmler to go along, only to find him backsliding as soon as opposition or trouble materialized. For an alternative to Bauer's interpretation, see Richard Breitman and Shlomo Aronson, "The End of the Final Solution?"

83. On the Soviet reaction see George Warren to Joseph Grew, 15 Feb. 1945, Edward R. Stettinius Papers, University of Virginia, Collection 2723, box 745, folder War Refugee Board.

84. Legation, Bern to London, 26 Feb. 1945 re. Musy–Himmler negotiations, NA, RG 84, entry American Legation Bern, American Interests Section, box 94, 840.1 Jews.

85. 224 [D'Oench] to 110 [Dulles], 8 Mar. 1945; 224 to 110, 29 Mar. 1945, both in NA, RG 226, entry 210, box 66, folder 276–New York.

86. Bauer, *Jews for Sale?*, 242–249.

87. This story is told in great detail in Göring's diary extract, NA, RG 226, entry 109, box 45, tab 1, and Schellenberg's draft autobiography, NA, RG 226, entry 125A, box 2, folder 21–Schellenberg. For scholarly accounts, see Steven Koblik, *The Stones Cry Out: Sweden's Response to the Persecution of the Jews, 1933–1945* trans. David Mel Paul and Margareta Paul (New York: Holocaust Library, 1988); and Raymond Palmer, "Felix Kersten and Count Bernadotte, A Question of Rescue," *Journal of Contemporary History*, 29 no. 1 (1994): 39–51.

88. McClelland's conversation with Musy concerning his most recent trip to Germany, 9–10 Apr. 1945, private possession of Richard Breitman.

89. Discussion of the false passport in Ayer to Director FBI, 8 June 1945, NA, RG 65, 100-103569-1, box 2. The passport itself is to be found in NA, RG 65, 65-47826, EBF 397, box 59.

90. Summary of [British] Interrogation of Schellenberg by Maj. Scott-Harston, 12 Oct. 1945, copy in NA, RG 226, entry 109, box 45, folder 261 XX9620-XX9639, document 9626.

91. An English translation of Schellenberg's autobiography, compiled during his stay in Stockholm, June 1945 NA, RG 226, entry 125A, box 2, folder 21–Schellenberg.

92. "Himmler and I Planned to Kill Hitler," *Daily Express*, 25 July 1945, copy in NA, RG 65, 100-103569-1, box 2. Schellenberg convinced the American Assistant Military Attaché in Stockholm that Himmler had poisoned Hitler. See Rayens to Bissell, 30 May 1945, NA, RG 226, entry 119A, box 26, folder 29.

93. War Room Telegram of 11 July 1945, copy in Saint, London to Washington, 13 July 1945, NA, RG 226, entry 88, box 645, folder–Incoming Plan Saint London July.

94. See Ustavic, London to OSS, SI, 14 Feb. 1945, based on highly confidential information from British intelligence, NA, RG 226, entry 210, box 554, folder 78.

95. Frederick Ayer, Jr. to Director FBI, 6 July 1945, NA, RG 65, 100-100-103569-1, box 2.

96. Stephen Tyas provided this information.

5

Follow the Money

Richard Breitman

IN THEIR SEARCH TO UNCOVER key relationships in the Watergate affair, journalists Carl Bernstein and Bob Woodward were advised to "follow the money." Recently declassified interrogations of individuals who took part in SD financial manipulations offer some new evidence about how SD Foreign Intelligence acquired and spent funds. These interrogations reveal interesting intelligence contacts, including some through which particular individuals found ways to exploit the Holocaust. In this case we need not only to follow the money, but also to inspect it.

Operation Bernhard

In postwar interrogations, Walter Schellenberg distanced himself from a substantial RSHA operation to counterfeit and distribute British pounds and, to a lesser extent, American dollars. It was RSHA chief Ernst Kaltenbrunner's work, not his own, he claimed, and he had little recollection of the personnel involved.[1] Code named "Operation Bernhard," the counterfeiting operation included a group of Jewish inmates at Sachsenhausen concentration camp coerced into forgery. Journalistic accounts in the last half-century, written partly on the basis of interviews or recollections and partly from declassified documents, have since revealed many details of this program.[2] Recently declassified documents make it possible to fill in gaps, eliminate some errors or distortions, and trace the activities of some key Nazi personnel.

According to one new account, the German counterfeiting machinery was set into motion in 1940, when Dr. Alfred Langer of the RSHA forgery shop learned that his unit was assigned to produce counterfeit British currency. He was told his shop would have no trouble getting needed raw materials, allegedly because the order for the scheme came from Hitler himself.[3]

A wartime British intelligence report gave a more detailed and probably more accurate version of how German counterfeiting work began. An Abwehr analyst secretly in contact with British intelligence stated that the Abwehr, acting partly on the advice of Helmuth James von Moltke, legal advisor to

OKW (High Command of the Armed Services) and a leader of the anti-Nazi resistance, had refused to get involved with manufacturing British currency, as did the Reichsbank. But the SD went ahead despite warnings about violation of international law.[4]

Langer's initial supervisor, Alfred Naujocks, a man with verve but lacking education and any technical knowledge, could not manage the operation.[5] His first effort to produce British pounds foundered on the inability to develop paper of passable quality. Also in trouble with Reinhard Heydrich for eavesdropping on the RSHA chief's private peccadillos, Naujocks was demoted in the fall of 1940 and was later sent to the eastern front with a Waffen-SS unit.[6]

Although a Sturmbannführer Dörner replaced Naujocks, nothing much happened. Some private German firms experimented at counterfeiting. SS-Hauptsturmführer Bernhard Krüger went off to Paris, probably to gather foreign documents that he could use as models for counterfeiting.[7] But as yet, there was no urgency to the preparations.

The decision to resume production of counterfeit pounds under Operation Bernhard came sometime after Heydrich's assassination in mid-1942, at a time when Germany's shortage of foreign exchange was already hampering imports of materials needed for war production. It appears that Heinrich Himmler authorized the operation, particularly because he needed a reliable source of foreign exchange for espionage activities abroad.[8] Trying to shield Himmler (and himself) at the end of the war, Schellenberg failed to mention Himmler's involvement to the Allies.

In any case, Krüger, whose first name, Bernhard, was borrowed as a code name for the operation, assembled a team of skilled forgers and engravers. Jewish prisoners at various concentration camps who had relevant experience were identified with the use of a punch-card system furnished by DEHOMAG (Deutsche Hollerith Maschinen Gesellschaft, AG), in peacetime an IBM subsidiary. The inmates were transferred to Sachsenhausen, where they were isolated from the rest of the camp.[9]

Two of the workers, Georg Kohn and Jack Papler, recalled after the war that on December 1, 1942, all the necessary installations were complete.

> Now Sturmbannfuehrer Ber[n]hard Krueger, accompanied by 2 Oberscharfuehrers, appeared and told us we had to print English pounds. He threatened us that we all would be killed in case we did not keep tight ... In February 1943 [after numerous tests] everything was settled and the printing was started.[10]

Another worker, Adolf Burger, wrote that the total value of notes produced by the end of the war was more than £134 million, of which about 8 percent (more than £10 million) were considered good enough for distribution.[11] Counterfeit notes were produced in three different grades. The lowest grade, suitable for deceiving only the unobservant, was apparently meant to be dropped over England in a scheme to undermine confidence in British currency. But the decline of the Luftwaffe made this idea impractical.

In late 1942, Swiss officials and the American Express Company in Zurich stumbled across £10,000 counterfeit, apparently a distribution of the early test notes. Some of the forgeries were deemed so masterful that they had to be the work of a government or people formerly employed in a government mint: they were not detected in Switzerland, but only when they reached the Bank of England. The person who passed these notes was an Austrian based in Croatia named Rudolf Blaschke. When arrested, Blaschke identified the source of the disputed currency as Friedrich Schwend. An American diplomat with no small experience in the world of intelligence quickly concluded (correctly) that both Blaschke and Schwend were German agents.[12]

The key distributor, Schwend, was well prepared for his role. After marrying a woman of some means, he engaged in illegal exchanges of genuine foreign currencies in Asia and the Americas during the 1930s. He lived for a time in the United States. By 1938, he had accumulated about $50,000 and a residence in Abbazia, a popular resort in northern Italy just across the border from Fiume.

During the first part of the war, the Abwehr engaged Schwend to locate hidden foreign currency. He got into trouble repeatedly in Croatia, and the German Embassy complained. After the Abwehr dropped him in the spring of 1942, Schwend and Blaschke launched a new scheme, trying to sell bogus German submarine plans to British agents in Trieste. The Italians caught Schwend and turned him over to German authorities at the Brenner Pass; then he was imprisoned at Klagenfurt. But selling fake military secrets was not exactly treason. At first, the Gestapo merely wanted to ensure that Schwend did not return to Italy.[13]

One journalistic account, however, had Schwend in serious jeopardy of losing his life, only to be rescued by an old acquaintance, Willi Gröbel. Gröbel allegedly came to Klagenfurt, explained to Schwend how he planned to distribute counterfeit currency for the SD, and offered to arrange Schwend's release from prison if he would take part. Schwend agreed, but asked for a cut of the profits.[14] Whether or not the two struck a deal, the Gestapo soon concluded that there was no evidence of treason against Schwend, and they allowed him to return to Italy.

Schwend and Gröbel now began work for SD Foreign Intelligence.[15] According to an RSHA official, Schwend was entrusted with a special mission for Himmler that evolved into Operation Bernhard. He was selected in part because of his financial influence and experience—and his accomplishments as a crook.[16] The head of the Munich office of SD Foreign Intelligence found a former Jewish art dealer named Georg Spitz, who agreed—under the threat of arrest and deportation—to work with Schwend and Gröbel. They recruited a number of others to distribute the pounds and purchase needed items.[17]

Although the Swiss and the West knew about the counterfeiting threat relatively early, they could do little to prevent the use of foreign currency in areas

SECRET

Report :

Of the merchant Georg KOHN, Hirschberg/Rsgb. Jaegerstreet - former inmate of 9 german concentration-camp (KL)

and of the painter JACK PLAPLER Kassel, Muellergasse 3, former inmate of 6 german concentration-camp.

Since the end of July 1942 we were employed in a
Special - Secret - Commando.
We think it our duty to report about this to the American authorities, since the following statement may be of great importance :

In 1942 we stayed in the concentration-camp Ravensbrueck. At the end of July in the same year, all the Jews were taken out of their beds during night and graphical professions were asked for. We reported, in order to get out of the severe camp, and on 20.8.42 w were transferred to Sachsenhausen. 3 days after our arrival 20 Jews came to Sachsenhausen, who had been in protective custody in the camp of Buchenwald. Some days later we had to fall out on the parade-ground and a Sturmbannfuehrer of the SD examined us. He said we were going to be employed in a printing office in block 19. After this block 19 had carefully been isolated from the remaining camp, printing machines actually did arrive. On 1.12.42 all the installations were finished. Now Sturmbannführer Berhard Krueger accompanied by 2 Oberscharfuehrers, appeared and told us we had to print English pounds. He threatened us that we all would be killed in case we did not keep tight. SD Obersturmbannfuehrer Doerner from the office Berlin-Dellbrueck-street in the most severe form repeated the same words.

Paper needed for the forged banknotes was supplied from West-phalia Hahnemehle. Before putting the banknotes into production they made 105 paper-tests. In February 1943 everything was settled and the printing was started. The capacity per month was to be one million. For reasons, easily accounted for, we sabotaged the works and therefore could not finish the asked for issue. Thereupon 20 more Jewish concentration-camp-inmates were added to our group. The finished notes were sorted into 1, 2, and 3, choice needled and made used looking. What was below their choice should be used to be dropped over England. The falsified notes were sent to Berlin every week to be put into circulation abroad. Five,-ten,-twenty,- and fifty-pount-notes were produced. In spite of conscientiousness ordered by the SD falsifications can be recognized by an expert easily, both from the paper and from the printing. Anyway we were ready to give mor information to an expert at any time desired. 20 notes of each serie "choice-pieces" had to be given to the Sturmbannfuehrer for his personal use.

Towards the end of 1943 our department was enlarged by the inclusion of block 18 and new SD people took over. The leaders were Hauptscharfuehrer Kurt Werner, and Helmuth Beckmann, besides that 14 more SS man came into our barracks. In January 1944 additional 80 Jews from Auschwitz arrived. The Sturmbannfuehrer told us, that we would have to do other things still. Block 18

SECRET

Two concentration camp survivors, forced to participate in a counterfeiting scheme, describe their experience creating fake currency and other documents (X-2 Interrogation of Georg Kohn and Jack Papler, 6 July 1945, re. German printing of British and American money, NA, RG 226, entry 108A, box 287, LWX-29).

outside their control, which began on a large scale after July 1943. Bills of £5, £10, £20, and £50 were printed.[18] This forged currency was sometimes used to pay the SD's local agents.[19] It was exchanged against legitimate Hungarian, Croatian, or Italian currency or used to make purchases of needed goods or tangible assets—arms and munitions, uniforms, gold, and jewels (the last two could be sold or held in the event of a "rainy day"). This currency traffic was a real boon—an important source of foreign exchange for the RSHA.

Schwend did his best to monopolize distribution of the counterfeit pounds through his own network, finally winning the cooperation of a high RSHA official, Josef Spacil. When Schwend wanted currency, say £1 million, Spacil received a coded telegram asking for 1,000 kilograms of "steel." Spacil's subordinate saw that Schwend's courier received the notes and kept the books. When the merchandise was shipped to the Reichsbank, Schwend's account would be credited. Schwend took a cut of 30 percent for himself.[20]

After the war Schellenberg called Schwend a swindler because he disposed of the notes largely in territories occupied by Germany and because he satisfied Kaltenbrunner's most luxurious wishes.[21] (By his own testimony, Schellenberg knew only Schwend's code name, "Wendig"; his real name was unknown.)[22] But the largest consumer of foreign exchange within the RSHA was SD Foreign Intelligence. In short, Schellenberg's empire rested partly on a huge pile of counterfeit pound notes produced by concentration camp labor. Whether or not Schellenberg promoted Operation Bernhard, he certainly knew much about it.

Postwar testimony indicated that there was an incident of theft—private appropriation of counterfeit notes—in Greece in late 1943. Thereafter, RSHA chief Kaltenbrunner himself had to authorize specific Bernhard operations.[23] But an Abwehr analyst and British informant (code named "Artist") gave a more detailed and more plausible account of the missing notes. A Greek experienced in currency arbitrage was given a supply of counterfeit pounds so realistic that the Bank of Greece verified their authenticity. He believed them to be genuine and exchanged some at a Swiss bank without any difficulty; he then carried on further exchanges. When he learned that another Swiss bank declared some of his notes to be forged, he stopped operations and took a loss on his inventory. The Gestapo then arrested him, supposedly for espionage, but the real reason for his arrest was that, having learned that the currency was fraudulent, he refused to carry on with exchanges.[24]

SD radio messages exchanged between Rome and Berlin during the fall of 1943 already show some traces of Schwend's operations in Italy. (Gröbel was killed at that time in an ambush by partisans.) In the confusing weeks following the Badoglio government's agreement to an armistice with the West and the German occupation of much of Italy, Schellenberg's office inquired about the balance of intelligence funds still available in Rome—in English pounds, U.S. dollars, Italian lira, and gold pieces. The largest foreign exchange balance was £2,550, followed by $5,250. A later message from SD Foreign Intelligence in Berlin (Wilhelm

Höttl) complained that Kaltenbrunner had given central control of the pounds question to Schwend.[25] So Schellenberg may have had some justification for his postwar claim that this project was more Kaltenbrunner's than his own.

An early 1945 operation to produce dollars, which were technically more difficult, failed: the quality was so low they were never circulated. As the Red Army approached Sachsenhausen in 1945, the prisoners dismantled and packed up the counterfeiting equipment and notes, moving them first to Mauthausen concentration camp and then to a smaller camp near Redl-Zipf. The prisoners were shipped to Ebensee, where they were to be killed. American forces arrived first, and 142 men who did the work for the largest counterfeiting operation in history were saved. Nazi officials dumped much of what was left of the money, along with numerous documents about the operation, into the depths of Lake Töplitz in large sealed crates. But a German army captain in Austria surrendered a truck with twenty-three boxes of British currency valued at £21 million.[26]

In early May 1945, U.S. Army Captain George J. McNally, Jr., a former Secret Service agent who had specialized in counterfeiting cases and was now working as a financial expert for Supreme Headquarters Allied Expeditionary Force in Frankfurt, came across traces of Operation Bernhard. In the course of his detailed investigation, McNally brought in British officials to inspect the SD's handiwork, which had caused the British much trouble. During the summer and fall of 1945, American, British, and French officials interrogated a number of Nazis and camp prisoners who had been involved in the operation. Counterfeit currency went back to the Bank of England, and McNally wrote his final report in early 1946.[27]

The distributors of the Nazis' British currency had already found a path into the postwar intelligence world. Arrested after the war ended, Schwend at first admitted nothing. But Georg Spitz advised him to confess, cooperate, and seek immunity. OSS X-2 (counterintelligence) officials took charge of Schwend, who led them to locations where he had buried gold and jewelry—the gold alone was worth about $200,000.[28] That cooperation earned him some goodwill. Until November 1945, the OSS used him on "bird-dog" operations to flush out others who were wanted. His code name, appropriately, was "Flush." Schwend supposedly wrote a history of Operation Bernhard for OSS, but the manuscript has not survived.[29]

Eric Timm, the chief of the OSS X-2 office in Munich, decided that Schwend, Spitz, and others in the Bernhard distribution network could be useful penetration assets for postwar Nazi resistance activities. Their past was no barrier. In a sense it was an asset because they were logical contacts for Nazis seeking to resuscitate their movement. Spitz supplied the OSS and its successor, the SSU, with financial information about the German Red Cross and about separatist movements in Bavaria. Schwend gathered data about the Czech intelligence service and alleged exploitation of Jewish refugees by the Soviet Union. But by 1947, in spite of continuing American intelligence contacts, Spitz came under a cloud for his role in wartime art looting in the Netherlands and postwar black market activities, and he was dropped as an American agent.[30]

By that time Schwend, too, was in trouble—again. A 1946 raid turned up evidence that surviving counterfeiters at Merano were still active. Schwend also came under suspicion of defrauding the Gehlen Organization.[31]

Schwend and his wife went to Italy in 1947 and soon emigrated to Peru. He contacted American authorities in 1959 to complain that, while in CIC confinement during 1945, he had money and property confiscated and never returned; in short, he had been robbed. In the mid-1960s, he nominally worked as the manager of a Volkswagen service garage in Lima, but his side activities were more interesting. American officials learned that a "Friedrich Schwalm" was involved in counterfeiting American dollars and trafficking in arms. He had allegedly bought himself protection in Peru by establishing contacts with some important politicians. This information was enough for the CIA to identify Schwalm as Schwend, who was described as "a completely unscrupulous person who thrives on intrigue and illicit schemes."[32]

Did he have a powerful sponsor? On November 30, 1966, the military aide to the president of Costa Rica publicly claimed that Fidel Castro was flooding Costa Rica with counterfeit dollars, an operation he compared to Nazi Germany's use of counterfeit pounds. The situation was all the more troubling because many Costa Ricans had purchased dollars as protection against the deteriorating national currency.[33] Another report suggested that Schwend had been involved with former Gestapo official Klaus Barbie in Peru to eliminate leftist politician Victor Paz Estanssoro.[34] Still another source indicated that Schwend was the head of ODESSA (a secret organization of former SS officers still committed to the cause). In any case, ODESSA possessed some plates to produce counterfeit U.S. dollars that apparently emanated from Schwend.[35] He had finally learned to turn out a better American product.

In 1972, Schwend was arrested in Peru after the murder of a wealthy businessman. The investigation turned up evidence that Schwend had blackmailed Peruvian officials, sold information, and violated currency laws. Later, he was convicted of smuggling currency out of the country and was sentenced to two years in prison. Deported to West Germany in 1976, Schwend ultimately returned impoverished to Peru, where he died in 1980.[36] It was an inconspicuous end for a man who had extended important Nazi intelligence connections into postwar American ones.

The Swiss Barrack Connection

Wooden barracks at some concentration camps (apparently Sachsenhausen and Dachau) were manufactured in Switzerland and transported to Germany. As a pure business transaction, this 1941 deal did not make sense. Nazi Germany, for example, had to supply some of the wood to the Swiss Wood Syndicate—a quasi-governmental enterprise—because the Swiss lacked a sufficient supply of timber. Moreover, some finished barracks were damaged in transport to Germany. Author

Schraga Elam has suggested that Nazi Germany must have had non-economic motives for the deal that remain unclear.[37] When combined with previously released documents in the National Archives, the newly declassified testimony of an SD official responsible for economic espionage casts new light upon the Swiss barrack connection. It is now apparent that Walter Schellenberg had intelligence needs in Switzerland, and this barrack contract gave him connections and even financial resources there.

Schellenberg's business manipulator in Switzerland was Hans Wilhelm Eggen, twenty-nine years old in 1941. Born into a well-connected family, Eggen had trained as a lawyer, entered the business world, and served in the SS Leadership Office as a liaison to the Reich Economics Ministry. He owned and managed Waren-Vertriebs, an import-export concern based in Berlin, which was largely a front for the SS. A wealthy, handsome man who liked to drink and live it up, Eggen apparently had a remarkable ability to make others like and trust him. In March 1945 he had dinner and a long after-dinner conversation with a U.S. diplomat, feeding him a steady stream of false intelligence. The diplomat found him thoroughly reliable.[38]

Eggen had wide-ranging business and political contacts, particularly in the Balkans and Switzerland. Such versatility brought him into the horizons of SD Foreign Intelligence. Eggen and Schellenberg became friendly in the fall of 1941.[39]

Shortly afterwards, Eggen received instructions from the Waffen-SS and the SS Economic-Administrative Main Office to purchase, through his firm, barracks (referred to as "hutments" in some of the English-language documents) made in Switzerland.[40] Eggen contacted Lieutenant-Colonel Henry Guisan, who happened to be the son of the commander-in-chief of the Swiss army. Henry Guisan introduced Eggen to several Swiss business and intelligence contacts, and on December 18, Eggen was able to meet with Walter Stampfli, one of Switzerland's seven Federal Councilors who headed the Swiss government. Stampfli welcomed a contract for barracks that promised to bring Switzerland an estimated 13 million Swiss francs and new jobs, but he could not agree to the proposed commission of 4.5 percent, which he said was too high. On January 22, 1942, the contract was signed nonetheless. The first shipment of barracks arrived in April 1942, and Germany paid in kind, with a delivery of 50 tons of raw iron. The relationship was established, but not yet optimal.[41]

Eggen found two well-connected Swiss associates. One was Paul Holzach-Meier (usually called "Holzach"), a businessman with experience in the wood industry, who had been arrested—and acquitted—for commercial fraud and was in need of a new position. The other was Dr. Paul Meyer-Schwertenbach, who had a law degree and side-career as a writer of detective novels (under the pen name Wolf Schwertenbach). Meyer-Schwertenbach had married and divorced a wealthy Swiss woman, receiving a generous settlement. His second marriage also brought him substantial wealth, and he acquired a castle near Kreuzlingen, on the shores of Lake Constance. But his wealth and connections were only the beginning of his assets: Meyer-Schwertenbach also held an important post in Swiss military intelligence.

At some point, probably in mid-1942,[42] Eggen, Holzach, and Meyer-Schwertenbach formed a joint Swiss-based venture that was largely a paper corporation, allegedly to negotiate the terms of the remaining barrack contract. When the first shipment of barracks arrived damaged, Meyer-Schwertenbach went to Berlin to examine the problem, which suggests that he already had a business relationship with Eggen at that point.[43] Their firm, Interkommerz, seems to have received the commission on what remained of the barrack deal and apparently also collected the profits. Later, in August 1943, Interkommerz was formally registered as a Swiss corporation.[44] With two of the three principals Swiss, it apparently qualified as a Swiss firm. Holzach was chairman of the board of directors, but Eggen was in control for the duration of the war.

Interkommerz served as a front for the SD in Switzerland. According to the head of Schellenberg's economic espionage branch, Dr. Hans Martin Zeidler, Eggen probably took additional cash on his trips to Switzerland, which gave Schellenberg financial resources to use there for intelligence purposes.[45] The SD Foreign Intelligence chief also quickly gained unusual access to high Swiss authorities.

Schellenberg and Colonel Roger Masson, the head of Swiss intelligence, exchanged some information and met in Waldshut on September 8, 1942. Impressed by the younger SD intelligence leader, Masson apparently thought he could extract benefits for Switzerland from this contact. As a result, Schellenberg was even able to meet with Swiss commander-in-chief Guisan in March 1943.

There is no evidence that Schellenberg or Eggen funneled payments to Masson. But Holzach carried an identity card signed by Masson that listed him as a captain in Swiss intelligence. At least one report described him as gathering political and military intelligence for Eggen—which meant for Schellenberg. Meyer-Schwertenbach, who frequently operated out of the Hotel Schweizerhof in Zurich and was able to tape-record telephone conversations there, was overheard to praise Hitler.[46] Masson certainly showed unusual latitude in allowing Holzach and Meyer-Schwertenbach free reign. Whether Switzerland had gained enough accurate intelligence to justify the risk of high Swiss officials being compromised is doubtful, and Masson came under much criticism after the end of the war.[47]

Through Interkommerz, Eggen, Holzach, and Meyer-Schwertenbach found various ways to assist the German cause. They apparently tried to persuade another Swiss firm to export tires to Germany—or to let Interkommerz do so—a deal that British authorities caught wind of and persuaded Swiss authorities to block. But a deal for a hundred tons of lead apparently went through. Holzach's explanation to British authorities in Switzerland was deemed unsatisfactory, and both he and Interkommerz were soon placed on the proclaimed list of neutral firms doing business in Axis countries and therefore barred from Allied markets. In August

1944, Holzach went to Germany and reportedly brought back to Switzerland some considerable quantities of securities held by the Hermann Göring Works.[48]

In late 1944, Meyer-Schwertenbach told a U.S. diplomat that he was still working "almost" exclusively for Swiss intelligence, and that Paul Holzach was one of his agents. In March 1945 he told another U.S. diplomat that one of his intelligence functions had been to maintain contact with Himmler's group.[49] Eggen and Schellenberg certainly qualified as Himmler's men. Meyer-Schwertenbach's "almost" was a telling sign that he had found an authorized way to mix his intelligence work and private ventures.

After German troops invaded Hungary in March 1944 and brought about the creation of a more cooperative Hungarian government, Holzach quickly found a way to get into Budapest—one of the first Swiss to receive permission.[50] There is some sign that he played a role in helping to arrange the Nazi-authorized release of several influential Hungarian Jewish families in return for the SS takeover of their ownership of the Manfred Weiss Works. In a January 1945 conversation with an American diplomat, Eggen claimed credit for this deal.[51]

In late 1944 and early 1945, Schellenberg sought "humanitarian" releases of Jews or other prisoners primarily to gain credit and open a dialogue with the West, but Himmler insisted on Germany's receiving material or financial compensation for any releases of Jews—to protect him against charges of defeatism or disloyalty. Himmler's economic specialist in Hungary, Kurt Becher, and Schellenberg then competed to arrange releases of Jews to Switzerland.[52] The principals of Interkommerz were more than happy to provide a service—to hold some of the cash that could be extorted from Jewish sources. Himmler allegedly approved one deal that brought about the release of Hungarian Jewish industrialist Leopold Aschner from Mauthausen Concentration Camp in return for a payment of SF 100,000; the money was deposited (in the name of Herbert Kettlitz, one of Becher's subordinates) in trust with Holzach at Interkommerz. If the claimants to the deposit disappeared or the paperwork was lacking, the principals of Interkommerz might become the real beneficiaries after the war.[53]

Because of the postwar investigation of Masson's contacts with Schellenberg, as well as legal disputes over the assets of Interkommerz, some of these relationships came to light shortly after the war; others may be found in documents declassified years ago. In a recently declassified set of interrogations we find that Schellenberg's economic espionage chief, Dr. Hans Martin Zeidler, supplied the name of one previously unknown beneficiary of Eggen's "commission": Dr. Heinrich Rothmund, perhaps the most controversial figure in World War II Switzerland.

A tall, broad-shouldered, athletic man, Rothmund was fifty-one years old when World War II began. In the 1920s he constructed the Federal Swiss Police office that dealt with aliens. He infused the Swiss Alien Police with his ideology, which was based on the notion that foreigners were difficult to assimilate and that Swiss naturalization requirements must be tightened to prevent foreign "inundation" of the country. Rothmund headed the Police Section of the Federal Justice and

Police Department throughout the 1930s and the war. In this capacity he helped
to determine Swiss refugee policy, and his police were primarily responsible for
its enforcement. His power grew to the point that he was frequently called the
"eighth Federal councilor."[54]

Rothmund had well-established views about the particular dangers Jews posed
to Switzerland. If immigrants generally were undesirable, Eastern European Jews
were the worst of the lot. But German Jews suffered too from the prejudices of
Rothmund and his police. German Jews seeking to flee early Nazi discrimination
and persecution and enter Switzerland were denied the status of political refugees
unless they were seeking asylum in Switzerland because of their political activities.
Concerned that Nazi Germany was ridding itself of Jews by encouraging illegal
Jewish immigration into Switzerland, the Swiss government, according to the
Swiss minister in Berlin, was determined to prevent the "judaicization" of
its country. Rothmund was heavily involved in direct negotiations between
Switzerland and Germany in 1938 to prevent large numbers of Jews from arriving
at Swiss borders.[55] After numerous proposals and counterproposals, German
authorities agreed to a Swiss proposal—Germany decided to stamp the passports
of German (and Austrian) Jews with an indelible *J*.[56]

During the early portion of World War II the Swiss Alien Police expelled Jews
whom they found had illegally entered Switzerland. Despite Swiss efforts to tighten
border controls, attempts at illegal entry continued and sometimes succeeded. In
early August 1942, the Swiss government decided to tighten implementation of
earlier regulations: expulsions of foreign civilian refugees would take place on a
larger scale even if such expulsions would place their lives in jeopardy. (By this
time there were plenty of reports reaching Switzerland about Nazi killings of Jews
on a vast scale.) Rothmund quickly ordered Swiss borders hermetically sealed and
reinforced earlier instructions: Jews in flight did not qualify as political refugees.[57]

One could hardly argue that Schellenberg and Eggen bribed Rothmund to
assist Nazi Germany in the Final Solution when he was already highly cooperative
of his own accord. Rothmund had maintained over a long period of time his view
that Jews posed a threat to Switzerland and had done what he could to block the
entry of Jewish refugees. But if Rothmund indeed benefited from Schellenberg's
largesse, it gave him more resources to do what he wanted to do, to assert his
influence. It was no secret that Rothmund, separated from his wife and eager to
live on a grand scale, could use the money.[58]

In a manuscript written shortly after he was captured, Zeidler identified
Rothmund as a critical figure in the barrack deal:

> The connection was set up between S.S. Brigadeführer Schellenberg and the Chief
> of the Swiss Foreign Police (Fremdenpolizei) Rothmund, through the Warenver-
> triebsgesellschaft in Berlin, proprietor Eggen. The reason for this connection was a
> large barrack business . . . which was continually causing difficulties, for either the
> prices did not agree or the dates for delivery were not adhered to. Through this I

naturally came into close contact with Herr Eggen. I now learned from him that a very important connection was involved, from which much was to be gained.[59]

During two subsequent interrogations, Zeidler named Rothmund as a key party in the barrack deal and said that Eggen gave SF 60,000 of the commission to Rothmund. (The first time Rothmund was identified as the head of Swiss intelligence—was Zeidler thinking of Masson?—but several months later, Zeidler repeated the claim that Rothmund was owed SF 60,000, and that Eggen probably took this cash with him to Switzerland. This time Zeidler correctly identified Rothmund as head of the Swiss Alien Police.) He also correctly named Holzach and Meyer-Schwertenbach as the main Swiss beneficiaries of the barrack deal.[60]

Rothmund's name has come up in previous discussions of this deal, but he has been described as an obstacle to Eggen, who needed frequent entry into Switzerland. On at least two occasions Rothmund raised objections to allowing Eggen in again to do business.[61] But these seem to be the exceptions—situations where Eggen and his Swiss partners were creating too many complications, setting Rothmund against Masson, who was overly committed to the relationship with Schellenberg.[62] Most of the time Eggen had no difficulty getting in, and by his own account he traveled to Switzerland every couple of months.[63]

Although Zeidler is the sole source of information about the link between Eggen and Rothmund, circumstantial evidence supports it. At the end of the war Eggen asked for asylum in Switzerland. Although his request was denied and he was arrested, he was particularly well treated there, receiving frequent furloughs and conducting business transactions while incarcerated.[64] After the war, Rothmund seems to have encouraged the activity of a number of holding companies that were camouflaged German undertakings. According to a January 1946 British intelligence report passed to the Americans, one of the prime instigators was Dr. Kurt Heinrich Brunner, who was a college friend of Rothmund. Rothmund intervened with the Swiss Federal Council to assist Brunner's projects in order to help Germany.[65] According to a recently published account, Rothmund also facilitated the emigration of some wanted Nazi officials to Argentina during 1947 and 1948.[66]

The evidence of a financial arrangement among Schellenberg, Eggen, and Rothmund is not solid enough at this point for scholars to accept with confidence, but it is certainly enough to warrant additional research into the relationship between Hans Wilhelm Eggen and Heinrich Rothmund.

Operation Bernhard and the Swiss Barrack Connection were different in some ways, but both operations were marked by a blend of official and private larceny characteristic of Nazi Germany. Far from distancing itself from the criminal features of the Nazi regime, SD Foreign Intelligence depended upon such financial machinations to fund its own activities. Schellenberg could no more escape this taint than he could separate himself from the SS. There was no such thing as pure intelligence in Nazi Germany.

Notes

1. Report on Interrogation of Walter Schellenberg, 27 June–12 July 1945, copy in NA, RG 319, IRR, entry 134B, box 195, Walter Schellenberg (3 of 8).
2. Among them, Walter Hagen (Wilhelm Höttl), *Unternehmen Bernhard* (Wels: Verlag Welsermühl, 1955); and Anthony Pirie, *Operation Bernhard* (New York: Morrow, 1962).
3. Translation of Report, 22 June 1945, by Dr. Albert Langer . . . on the Technical Section of Amt VI of the RSHA, copy in NA, RG 226, entry 109, box 66, folder XX11587-99.
4. Memorandum from Wilson on the Tricycle/Artist group, 20 Nov. 1943, NA, RG 226, entry 119, box 23, folder 177A. "Tricycle" was the German agent/British double agent Dusko Popov. "Artist," who provided the information about forged currency, was a Dane named Johnny Jebsen who worked in the Abwehr but also carried out private business. Based in Lisbon, Jebsen was kidnapped by Gestapo agents there in late 1944 and taken back to Germany. He was executed at Sachsenhausen in the last days of the war. Information from Stephen Tyas.
5. Translation of Report, 22 June 1945, by Dr. Albert Langer . . . on the Technical Section of Amt VI of the RSHA, copy in NA, RG 226, entry 109, box 66, folder XX11587-99.
6. Purportedly, he was punished because he spied on Heydrich to avenge his demeaning assignment to supervise "Salon Kitty," a brothel set up to eavesdrop on its mainly foreign diplomatic clients. But Heydrich also conducted "inspection visits" there. Naujocks' version of his interaction with Heydrich is in MI-5 Interim Interrogation Report on the Case of Alfred Naujocks, copy in Saint, London to Saint, Washington, 27 Nov. 1944, NA, RG 226, entry 108B, box 314, folder 2082, XX-3980.
7. Direction Generale de Etudes et Reserches Service de Documentation/Mission de Liaison SM a la 3eme Armee SMJ 3, no. 937, 25 July 1945, [Gaullist intelligence] Report, given to U.S. authorities on production of counterfeit moneys and counterfeit documents by the AMT VI F of RSHA, copy in NA, RG 65, 65, 65-47826-232 EBF 33 (2 of 2), box 62.
8. CI Interim Interrogation Report No. 47, U/Stuf Guenther, Rudolf, 6 Feb. 1945 [1946], NA, RG 65, 65-56600, box 185. Guenther was private secretary and bookkeeper for Josef Spacil, a high official in the RSHA involved in Operation Bernhard.
9. Krüger had served as Naujocks's deputy. On the operation at Sachsenhausen, see Alan Levy, "Adolf Burger: The Forger as a Work of Art; Ex-counterfeiter Documents his Holocaust History," *The Prague Post*, 1 Nov. 2000; also Adolf Burger, *Des Teuffels Werkstatt: Die Geldfälscherwerkstatt im KZ Sachsenhausen* (Fischerhütte: Verlag Neues Leben, 2000). Other inmates included accountant Oskar Stein (Skala), notorious forger Solly Smolianov, Jacob Goldglass, Heinrich Fajermann, and others. See the account compiled by War Department civilian Eric A. Harris of OSS 2677th Regiment, dated 22 June 1945, a Secret Service document released by the Treasury Department in May 2000.
10. X-2 Interrogation of Georg Kohn and Jack Papler, 6 July 1945, re. German printing of British and American money, NA, RG 226, entry 108A, box 287, LWX-29. The French intelligence report (see n. 7) indicates that two workers who became ill were killed in order to assure their silence.
11. Interrogation of Walter Schellenberg, 27 June–12 July 1945, NA, RG 319, IRR, entry 134B, box 195, Walter Schellenberg (3 of 8), 27. Digest of information on Josef Spacil of RSHA

II from reports on Kaltenbrunner, Schellenberg, Ohlendorf, Duesterberg, Wischmann, and Schulz, 20 July 1945, NA, RG 226, entry 119A, box 40, folder 1086; Burger, *Teuffels Werkstatt*, 137–38.

12. See the set of documents in NA, RG 59, box 4969, CDF-841.5158/38-41, especially Samuel Woods to Secretary of State, 15 Jan. 1943 re. counterfeit English bank notes.

13. Auszug aus den Akten Friedrich Schwendt, NA, RG 242, T-120, roll 5781, frame FH297319-55.

14. "Geld wie Heu," *Stern*, 22 Aug. 1959.

15. Auszug aus den Akten Friedrich Schwendt, NA, RG 242, T-120, roll 5781, frame FH297319-55.

16. CI Interim Interrogation Report No. 47, U/Stuf Guenther, Rudolf, 6 Feb. 1945 [1946], NA, RG 65, 65-56600, box 185.

17. Winston Scott to Sir Edward Reid, 13 June 1945 re. RSHA Financial Operations, NA, RG 226, entry 190, box 366, folder 402. On Spitz's background and involvement, see NA, RG 263, George Spitz Name File.

18. The French report (see n. 7) indicates that production of notes was small until July 1943.

19. Elyesa Bazna, the Albanian valet of the British ambassador to Turkey, was rewarded for his espionage coup, Operation Cicero, with counterfeit pounds.

20. CI Interim Interrogation Report No. 47, U/Stuf Guenther, Rudolf, 6 Feb. 1945 [1946], NA, RG 65, 65-56600, box 185.

21. Memorandum from Wilson regarding the Tricycle/Artist group, 20 Nov. 1943, NA, RG 226, entry 119, box 23, folder 177A.

22. Interrogation of Schellenberg, 27 June–12 July 1945, NA, RG 319, IRR, entry 134B. box 195, Walter Schellenberg (3 of 8).

23. Digest of information on Josef Spacil of RSHA II from reports on Kaltenbrunner, Schellenberg, Ohlendorf, Duesterberg, Wischmann, and Schulz, 20 July 1945, NA, RG 226, entry 119A, box 40, folder 1086–Spacil.

24. Memorandum from Wilson regarding the Tricycle/Artist group, 20 Nov. 1943, NA, RG 226, entry 119, box 23, folder 177A.

25. Hammer (Berlin) to Rome, 2 Oct. 1943, Decode no. 7067; Rome to Berlin, 12 Oct. 1943, Decode no. 7510; and Berlin to Rome, 21 Oct. 1943, Decode no. 7760, all in NA, RG 226, entry 122, boxes 1 and 2, folder 5–Italian Decodes.

26. Kevin C. Ruffner, "On the Trail of Nazi Counterfeiters," *Studies in Intelligence* (2002), 44.

27. Ruffner, "On the Trail," 43-45.

28. Michaelis to C.O. X-2, Germany, 20 July 1945, copy in NA, RG 226, entry 119A, box 39, folder 1070–Friedrich Schwend. Ruffner, "On the Trail," 48.

29. Ruffner, "On the Trail," 48.

30. Ibid., 50-51

31. Ibid., 51.

32. According to one report, he was wanted for having ordered one SD agent to murder another in Italy during 1944. Cables of 12 Dec. 1966 and 19 Aug. 1969, Memo for CIA Deputy Director for Plans, NA, RG 263, Friedrich Schwend Name File, vol. 2.

33. The Reuters press release of 1 Dec. 1966 is in NA, RG 263, Fritz Venceslav Schwend Name

File, vol. 2.

34. Memo from Acting Chief [office excised], 9 Mar. 1983, NA, RG 263, Fritz Venceslav Schwend Name File, vol. 2.

35. Regional Security Officer, Lima to Chief Foreign Operations, 29 Apr. 1965, NA, RG 263, Fritz Venceslav Schwend Name File, vol. 1.

36. Ruffner, "On the Trail," 53.

37. Shraga Elam, "Schweizer Qualitäts-Holzbaracken für die SS-Schergen," in Sebastian Speich, et al., *Die Schweiz am Pranger: Banken, Bosse und die Nazis* (Vienna: Ueberreuter, 1997), 132–40.

38. Basic biographical information on Eggen is in Hans Rudolf Fuhrer, *Spionage gegen die Schweiz: die geheimen deutschen Nachrichtendienste gegen die Schweiz im Zweiten Weltkrieg, 1939-1945* (Frauenfeld: Huber, 1982), 79. For the subjective impression, 15 Jan. 1945 Meeting of #493 with Hans Ecken [*sic*] of the SS, NA, RG 226, entry 214, box 7, folder 38.

39. Third Interim Report on Dr. Hans Martin Zeidler, 6 Nov. 1945 and Special [British] Interrogation Report on Dr. Hans Martin Zeidler, SIR 20, 29 Mar. 1946, copy in NA, RG 65, file 65-56411-1, entry A1-136P, box 37.

40. Ibid. Zeidler was not in charge of the economic branch of SD Foreign Intelligence at the time this deal was made. The figures he gave (SF 5 million) about the size of the deal are too low. The first delivery of barracks cost SF 5.5 million. It is likely that Zeidler, who assumed his post in June 1942, learned of a portion of the deal still outstanding.

41. Elam, "Schweizer Qualitäts-Holzbaracken," 133–34.

42. Interkommerz was added to the Swiss Commercial Register on 6 Aug. 1943, but Zeidler suggests that it was operating informally earlier. A 1944 background report on Paul Holzach-Meier drawing upon individuals acquainted with him supports that claim. See Report of 8 Mar. 1944 on Paul Holzach-Meier, NA, RG 84, American Legation, Bern, Economic Section, Safehaven, 1942–1949, box 45–Interkommerz.

43. Zeidler mentions only the commission, but Elam suggests the profits. Zeidler implies that Eggen, Holzach, and Meyer-Schwertenbach linked up before 1943. On Meyer-Schwertenbach's trip to Berlin, see Elam, "Schweizer Qualitäts-Holzbaracken," 134.

44. See Report of 8 Mar. 1944 on Paul Holzach-Meier, NA, RG 84, American Legation, Bern, Economic Section, Safehaven, 1942–1949, box 45–Interkommerz.

45. Special Interrogation Report on Dr. Hans Martin Zeidler, 29 Mar. 1946. On the specific purpose, see below.

46. Woods to Harrison, 13 Nov. 1944; Blum to Bach, 12 Oct. 1945; extracts from legation file on Holzach and Schwertenbach, 6 Sept. 1944; all in NA, RG 84, American Legation, Bern, Safehaven, box 45–Interkommerz.

47. On this subject, see Pierre Braunschweig, *Geheimer Draht nach Berlin. Die Nachrichtenlinie Masson-Schellenberg und der schweizerische Nachrichtendienst im Zweiten Weltkrieg* (Zürich: Neue Zürcher Zeitung, 1989). Also, Fuhrer, *Spionage gegen die Schweiz*, 79–80.

48. Strictly Confidential Report, 6 Sept. 1944, from #1924, NA, RG 84, American Legation Bern, Safehaven, box 45–Interkommerz. Holzach's wife reportedly gave the same information: see Harrison to U.S. Political Advisor on German Affairs, 7 Feb. 1947, in ibid.

49. Extracts from legation file on Holzach and Schwertenbach, 6 Sept. 1944; and Woods to Harrison, 13 Nov. 1944; both in NA, RG 84, American Legation, Bern, Economic Section,

Safehaven, box 45–Interkommerz. In Swiss intelligence, Schwertenbach had earlier been in charge of ferreting out subversive elements in Switzerland and of managing personal security for General Guisan, the Swiss commander-in-chief. See Sebastian Speich, "Die diebischen Elstern vom Armee-Geheimdienst," in *Die Schweiz am Pranger*, 143. On Meyer-Schwertenbach's claim to be the official Swiss liaison with Himmler's group, see 224 (Loofbourow) to 110 (Dulles), 16 Mar. 1945, NA, RG 226, entry 210, box 66, folder 276. Meyer-Schwertenbach is referred to by his nickname "Wolf."

50. British Commercial Secretariat to Reagan (American Commercial Attache, Bern), 20 Apr. 1944, and British Consulate General, Zurich to Reagan, 26 May 1944; NA, RG 84, American Legation, Bern, Safehaven, box 45–Interkommerz.

51. 15 Jan. 1945 Meeting of #493 with Hans Ecken [*sic*] of the SS, NA, RG 226, entry 214, box 7, folder 38.

52. See chapter 4.

53. In the inevitable postwar dispute over this money, Becher supplied an affidavit saying that Kettlitz had no claim to the funds, which, he said, according to Kasztner, should go to the Geneva Office of the Jewish Agency for Palestine. See P. R. Larke, British Legation, Bern, to American Legation, 28 Sept. 1948, NA, RG 84, American Legation, Bern, Safehaven, box 45–Interkommerz.

54. Alfred A. Hässler, *The Lifeboat is Full: Switzerland and the Refugees, 1933–1945*, trans. Charles Lam Markmann (New York: Funk and Wagnalls, 1967), 7–8, 108.

55. Hässler, *Lifeboat is Full*, 10, 30–53. The most recent account of these negotiations is Independent Commission of Experts—Switzerland—Second World War, *Switzerland and Refugees in the Nazi Era*, (Bern: BBL/EDMZ, 1999), 75–85.

56. In these negotiations Rothmund had supported a requirement of a German visa for travel to Switzerland. He did not particularly like the idea of the *J* because he knew that German officials also wanted to limit the travel of Swiss Jews into Germany, and that Switzerland would not be able to discriminate by similarly marking the passports of Swiss Jews.

57. Hässler, *Lifeboat is Full*, 81–82.

58. Ibid., 108–9.

59. Untitled, undated ms. [June 1945], Copy in NA, RG 226, entry 119A, box 55, folder 1617.

60. Third Interim Report on Dr. Hans Martin Zeidler, 6 Nov. 1945 and Special [British] Interrogation Report on Dr. Hans Martin Zeidler, SIR 20, 29 Mar. 1946, copy in NA, RG 65, 65-56411, Sec. 1, entry A1-136P, box 37.

61. Elam, "Schweizer Qualitäts-Holzbarracken"; and Sebastian Speich, "Die diebischen Elstern vom Armee-Geheimdienst," both in Speich, et al., *Die Schweiz am Pranger*, 138 and 144.

62. See, for example, Fuhrer, *Spionage*, 87.

63. 15 Jan. 1945 Meeting of #493 with Hans Ecken [*sic*] of the SS, NA, RG 226, entry 214, box 7, folder 38.

64. Elam, "Schweizer Qualitäts-Holzbarracken," 138.

65. Saint, London to Saint, Washington, 21 Jan. 1946, NA, RG 226, entry 109, box 56, folder XX10560-XX10579.

66. See Uki Goñi, *The Real Odessa: Smuggling the Nazis to Perón's Argentina* (London: Granta, 2002), 143–59.

6

The Gestapo

Richard Breitman
with Norman J. W. Goda and Paul Brown

The proper picture of the Gestapo is that of a legal gang of ruthless and vicious killers, whose brain was supplied largely by the shrewd, 100% Nazi SD . . . The Gestapo is the most likely home of the war criminal in the RSHA.[1]

DURING WORLD WAR II, Allied intelligence services gathered considerable information about the Gestapo, but they lacked enough unimpeachable documentary evidence to give a clear overview of the organization and the functions of individual Gestapo offices. At the end of the war they sought to extract from captured documents useful information about how the Gestapo had worked. A small collection of Gestapo intelligence and counterintelligence files remained classified until the IWG opened it in 2000. This "Himmler Collection" is described below.

Although the Gestapo was quickly indicted—and soon convicted—as a criminal organization at Nuremberg, Allied intelligence officials made at least temporary arrangements with some surviving Gestapo officials who could supply useful information. Those Gestapo men who had specific information about important decisions or policies of the Nazi regime and those who had specialized in counteracting Communist espionage had particular intelligence value in the immediate postwar years. While some Gestapo men were tried and convicted, others who cooperated with Allied intelligence were overlooked—or had their sentences commuted. Still others escaped or were never definitively identified as having died by the end of the war. Public, media, and Western government perceptions of a job left undone—locating important Gestapo officials and bringing them to justice—began to gel in the 1960s and intensify in the early 1980s.

This chapter includes case studies of Gestapo officials with different fates. Some of those who disappeared, such as Gestapo chief Heinrich Müller, have remained shrouded in mystery or controversy. Newly declassified State Department records reveal a belated and ultimately unsuccessful effort by the United States and West Germany to bring another high Gestapo official named Walter Rauff to justice. The final case study, based largely on declassified CIA records, is that of Adolf Eichmann's subordinate Alois Brunner, who escaped to Syria after World War II.

The Himmler Collection

The Gestapo was a political police that sought to eradicate all actual and potential opposition to the Nazi regime. Using pseudo-legal devices such as preventive detention and protective custody, the Gestapo pursued individuals, organizations, and groups considered inherently hostile to the Nazi regime and subjected them to mistreatment, torture, or incarceration regardless of their actual behavior. Because of the criminal nature of the organization, Gestapo personnel intentionally destroyed many files near the end of the war. Other Gestapo records were destroyed in Allied bombing attacks or lost in the confusion of Germany's collapse. Most of what survived and was captured by the United States or Britain was declassified during the 1950s, but some holdings were withheld for security reasons.[2] The recent declassification of some original Gestapo records deepens our understanding of the organization.

The so-called Himmler Collection, newly declassified by the IWG, is an amalgamation of over nine thousand pages of intelligence and counterintelligence files kept by Gestapo sections dealing with enemy groups and with counterintelligence.[3] Included, for example, are secret Gestapo lists of suspected enemy agents, traitors, and Allied pilots who had escaped from captivity, as well as periodic reports and instructions for dealing with perceived security threats that it sent to police posts across the country. Since the Abwehr was absorbed by the RSHA in 1944, some Abwehr counterintelligence documents, such as lists of suspicious persons in Denmark, are also included in the files.

Occasional new information about the Holocaust and other war crimes crops up in these newly declassified Gestapo records. For example, German counterintelligence believed that a Danish Jew named Hugo Rothenberg, with the help of a Swedish businessman named Tuschmann, helped Jews and political refugees to flee from Denmark to Sweden. But Rothenberg had high-level protection. Hermann Göring, wounded in the Beer Hall Putsch of November 1923, had fled to Sweden with Rothenberg's assistance. A grateful Göring continued to protect Rothenberg during the war. As a result of Göring's goodwill, the Gestapo decided not to intervene against Rothenberg, a fact now verified in the Gestapo index of suspicious people in Denmark.[4]

Some German counterintelligence documents found in the Himmler Collection illuminate or complement other newly declassified or previously available Allied intelligence documents. For example, previously available OSS records contain numerous documents supplied by the Polish government-in-exile. Polish agents and informants throughout Europe were able to gather a great deal of sensitive political, economic, and military information; the Polish government-in-exile in London passed much on to Britain and the United States, including some key information about the Holocaust in late 1942.[5] Newly declassified OSS records contain some additional information supplied by Polish sources in London. For example, the chief diplomatic advisor to Polish Prime Minister Sikorski gave American intelligence in London details about the thrust of Nazi occupation policies in Poland and specific measures in the districts of Lublin and Zamosc: the Gestapo and Ukrainian police massacred aged and infirm Poles, tore young children from their parents and sent them to Germany to be raised as Germans, and deported able-bodied Polish men and women to labor camps.[6] The Polish government-in-exile wanted Britain and the United States to be aware of these crimes.

The Himmler Collection reveals the other side of this picture. It contains, for example, some of what the Gestapo was able to uncover about Polish intelligence activities on the continent and about Polish information being sent to London. At the beginning of the war, Gestapo officials believed they had neutralized the Polish intelligence service, even though they recognized that the intelligence elite had escaped from Poland in late 1939. In 1942, however, they uncovered a cache of Polish intelligence documents in Prague and were surprised to see that Polish agents and informants had gathered detailed military information and smuggled it to London, via Budapest and Istanbul. The Poles had tracked German military trains to the eastern front and identified Order Police battalions sent to conquered areas early in the German campaign against the Soviet Union. In October 1941, Police Battalion 303 went to Zhitomir, Battalion 311 to Kiev, 310 to Lemberg, and 208 to Bialystok. In addition, another seventeen such battalions were stationed in the German-occupied General Government (most of Poland), according to Polish intelligence information. Such battalions of Order Police often carried out executions of Jews and other civilians under the cover of anti-partisan warfare. Polish agents also gathered detailed information about the morale of German soldiers in the East.

After uncovering a sample of the information the Poles had reported, Gestapo officials concluded in 1942 that Polish intelligence activity represented a very serious danger to Germany. As late as June 6, 1944, Heinrich Müller set up a special unit called Sonderkommando Jerzy, designed to root out the Polish intelligence network in western and southwestern Europe.[7]

Another captured Gestapo document found in OSS records offers a broader view of Gestapo and Abwehr counterintelligence work. In mid-1942, German counterintelligence officials were not terribly concerned about the French or Belgian intelligence services, were aware of increasing Swiss intelligence activity, and had established that the Poles and Japanese were cooperating on intelligence matters in a number of European locations. Gestapo officials recognized that they had very little information about the work of U.S. or British agents ("very cleverly camouflaged"), but, amazingly, they seemed not terribly concerned. Conversely, they regarded Hungary's intelligence service as one of their most serious opponents, even though Hungary was Germany's ally and there was a formal agreement between the two that no espionage was to be carried out against each other.[8]

In short, the Gestapo was concerned about those intelligence services it knew from the prewar period. Germany, Finland, Hungary, and Japan had all shared an antipathy toward the Soviet Union, which had led to some intelligence exchanges among them. Past experience as well as present information suggested that these intelligence organizations had dangerous capabilities, and their alliances or political ties with Germany were not warm enough to overcome Gestapo concerns that Germany might become the target of their intelligence activities. With regard to Britain and the United States—certainly two of Nazi Germany's most dangerous intelligence enemies—the Gestapo did not know enough about their intelligence work to voice specific concerns.

Reprisals in Denmark

A newly declassified postwar interrogation of Higher SS and Police Leader Günther Pancke, the top SS and police official for Denmark, offers insight into German police actions and general Nazi occupation policy in Denmark.[9] On December 30, 1943, Pancke, Reich Plenipotentiary for Denmark Werner Best, and General von Hanneken attended a meeting at Hitler's headquarters. After Best minimized security problems in Denmark and backed use of an SS and police court to punish acts against the German occupation, Hitler intervened:

> Up to now all disturbances and fights for freedom which have been punished by military courts have ensured that their perpetrators go down in history as national heroes . . . It is not in the interests of the Reich to create national heroes in other countries, and I therefore forbid all legal proceedings against people who commit acts which damage the German war effort, especially in Denmark. In the future reprisals are to be taken: if a factory which is working for German interests is blown up, then a factory working for purely Danish interests will be blown up in the same way . . . If a German is shot on the street, five Danes are to be shot in the same way. This method of reprisals should have particular effect on the intellectual wire-pullers who are behind resistance organizations. The SD and the Sipo usually know exactly that these people are active against us, but cannot prove their hostile activity . . .

Through such reprisals on the scale of five Danes for every German, Hitler believed, sabotage and murder against Germans would diminish and ultimately disappear. Whitney R. Harris, part of the American prosecution at the International Military Tribunal at Nuremberg, described these "Danish clearing murders" as a method of terror in which innocent Danes were assassinated.[10]

After the war, Pancke told Allied interrogators that he had reduced the scale of reprisals ordered by Hitler. When the end was near, in January 1945, he and Best decided to disregard Hitler's orders entirely and restart the use of legal proceedings in cases of sabotage.

Some intercepted top-level German Foreign Ministry conversations with Nazi officials in Denmark contain additional information about German police actions near the war's end. In late February 1945, Foreign Minister Ribbentrop informed the German legation in Copenhagen (and, through it, Werner Best) that Himmler had just consulted with Hitler, who decided against the immediate shooting of Danish hostages as a reprisal for Danish terrorism and sabotage. Germany's declining military situation apparently caused Himmler to recommend a policy that appeared less arbitrary to the Danes, and Hitler went along.

But Hitler still insisted on severe punishment. Every act of terror had to be dealt with as quickly as possible through rapid trial by a special police tribunal and an immediate execution of the sentence. In retaliation for an attack on a German sentry in Copenhagen, ten Danish terrorists were tried and executed. Best complied with this policy by setting up a police structure and set of trial regulations, and he reserved for himself the right to grant clemency.[11] This suggests that with Hitler increasingly isolated, Best believed he could get away with reducing the scale of reprisals near the end of the war.

Interrogations of Gestapo Officials

British and American interrogators wanted a clear picture of the Gestapo and how its structure and functions changed over time. They particularly wanted to know about Gestapo counterintelligence work against Allied intelligence organizations. Information about postwar underground Nazi activities or sabotage was another high intelligence priority. By the second half of 1945, Britain and the United States were also interested in what information the Gestapo had accumulated about Communist espionage in Europe. Most captured Gestapo officials tried to avoid self-incrimination; clever ones sensed what their interrogators wanted and gave it to them, thereby avoiding or passing quickly over more uncomfortable and more dangerous subjects. The regular work of the Gestapo involved activities judged criminal by Western standards—and German law before 1933. Yet many Gestapo officials had committed even more horrendous crimes outside Germany.

The Einsatzgruppen

There was a close link between the Gestapo and killing operations outside Germany. The Einsatzgruppen—battalion-sized mobile units used to carry out mass executions in many occupied areas in Eastern Europe—frequently took personnel from the Gestapo and the SS intelligence unit, the SD. The Einsatzgruppen and their successors reported through regular Gestapo communication channels to Müller and Heydrich. Based on reports from the field, the Gestapo compiled and distributed periodic summaries of executions carried out in different locations by the Einsatzgruppen.[12] Shooting more than one million Jews and other people in

-13-

APPENDIX "E" (contd)   XX-8555

     I gave the Reichsfuehrer to understand that in J uly 43 I had asked to be released to the Waffen SS and I should be glad if I could hand over my job in DENMARK to someone else. I asked again if I could not be allowed to go the Waffen SS as Haupsturmfuehrer, but he said me that I had my duty to do.

     At 1200 hrs the following day the meeting took place; we were invited to a meal with the Fuehrer.

     The following were present: The Fuehrer, Generalfeldmarschall KEITEL, General JODEL, General SCHMUNDT, General von HANNEKEN, Dr. BEST, a foreign ambassador, HIMMLER, Dr. KALTENBRUNNER, and myself. There were at the most twelve people.

     After the meal, the Fuehrer asked Dr. BEST about the general situation in DENMARK. BEST gave a favourable and truthful report about the general economic position and also said that the political situation did not call for alarm, despite the increase of hostile actions. Dr. BEST stressed that the development of the political situation in DENMARK was dependant on the general military position of the Reich. Finally, he reported that the SS and Police court which had been decided upon him and by me was operating quickly against any acts perpetrated against the interests of the Reich and Wehrmacht. The Danes, added Dr. BEST, were in agreement with this legal handling of punishable offences.

     The Fuehrer interrupted BEST with"Up to now all disturbances and fights for freedom which have been punished by military courts have ensured that their perpetrators go down in history as national heroes, whereas all the many people who have been killed by direct reprisal measures have been completely forgotten by the mass of the people". The Fuehrer cited the example of the French occupation of the Rhineland which resulted in the disappearance of Rhineland citizens.

     As opposed to that, men like Andreas HOFER, PALM, SCHLAGETER, etc, had become national heroes. "It is not in the interests of the Reich to create national heroes in other countries, and I therefore forbid all legal proceedings against people who commit acts which damage the German war effort, especially in DENMARK. In the future reprisals are to be taken: if a factory which is working for German interests is blown up, then a factory working for purely Danish interests will be blown up in the same way. If a German is shot on the street, five Danes are to be shot in the same way."

     "This method of reprisals should have particular effect on the intellectual wire-pullers who are behind the resistance organisations.The SD and the Sipo usually know exactly that these people are active against us, but cannot prove their hostile activity because they hold themselves aloof from all action. Through reprisals, if these people are afraid for their lives, the support of saboteurs, and therefore of sabotage and murder committed against Germans, will become less and will eventually be entirely prevented".

     The Fuehrer then asked what I had done to combat sabotage and murder and I replied that the tactics of the Sipo in DENMARK in penetrating the sabotage groups through Danish V-men, and in interrogating individual saboteurs were having good success in wiping out the whole group. The Danes were very talkative and boasted about their deeds of heroism,and when arrested easily gave away their comrades. I considered the legal proceedings against the Danes to be just and full of results, and was less inclined to the other kind of reprisals without a legal trial for the accused. I suggested further that death sentences could be mitigated if no further crimes of that nature took place.

     The Reichsfuehrer had made several signs to me to be quiet, when the Fuehrer interrupted angrily, and said:"You will keep my orders. Legal proceedings are forbidden, and reprisals are to be carried out as I have ordered."

Transcript of an interrogation of Günther Pancke, revealing Hitler's orders for revenge against Danish resistance to Nazi occupation (Field Interrogation Report of Günther Pancke, 6 July 1945, copy in NA, RG 226, entry 109, box 36, folder XX8540-XX8559).

the East required Gestapo coordination and supervision. Other Gestapo officials under Adolf Eichmann planned the deportations of millions of Jews and other groups to ghettos and extermination centers.

British and American intelligence officials had some sense of the connection between the Gestapo and the Einsatzgruppen. By the middle of the war Allied intelligence officials knew that the Einsatzgruppen had carried out some executions, including mass shootings of Jews. An undated (late 1943) American intelligence analysis of the RSHA in occupied countries noted that Einsatzgruppen rounded up Jews, Communists, and enemy officials in newly occupied areas; they also investigated political espionage and worked against partisans.[13]

But immediately after the war, Allied intelligence officials and war crimes investigators often lacked detailed information about who had done what in the Einsatzgruppen. Einsatzgruppen radio communications were not regularly decoded and read by British or American intelligence during the war. A copy of the Gestapo's Einsatzgruppen reports was apparently captured in September 1945 as part of a substantial cache of records in Berlin, but no one read or recognized the significance of these documents until a considerably later date—they were still not available for the International Military Tribunal at Nuremberg.[14] British and American analysts were more interested in the Gestapo's deployment of agents and in their instructions in the event of Germany's defeat than in what Einsatzkommandos did during the war.[15]

Harro Andreas Wilhelm Thomsen

Many postwar interrogations, including several of Gestapo official Harro Andreas Wilhelm Thomsen, concentrated on understanding relationships among the Gestapo's various departments. For example, Thomsen explained that officials in department IV A handled subjects categorized as hostile to the state, such as particular opposition groups, religious organizations, Freemasons, and Jews. Officials in IV B advised on policy in particular regions, especially in occupied areas; their expertise was primarily geographical. Reports on the Jewish question had to reach both sections. Thomsen added:

> From 1939 Obersturmbannführer Eichmann, the Referent [desk officer or specialist in charge], to all intents and purposes dictated policy on this question [Jews]. He dealt directly with the Chef d Sipo [Heydrich, later Kaltenbrunner] and with Himmler, and never passed on [information] to the other Referents. He was an expert on Jewish problems and "was right not to share his [information]," for such operations as the "evacuation" of Jews from occupied territory were secret. (Reports on "Evacuation" went under the heading "weather reports," and were "camouflaged.")[16]

If Eichmann kept his information to himself, then the functional and regional offices of the Gestapo could hardly have cooperated on Nazi Jewish policies. But it was convenient for Thomsen and other Gestapo officials, once in Allied hands, to know little about Nazi policies toward Jews.

Eichmann had vanished, and there was not much risk in laying so much blame on his shoulders. In short, Thomsen's account was a mixture of accurate and mendacious testimony. There were other exceptions to the Gestapo's distribution of information, so intelligence analysts concluded that the rules of collaboration between Gestapo IV A and IV B were clear, but they were not applied well.[17] They did not probe for more detailed information about Nazi Jewish policy.

Stefan Rowecki

Where there was less jeopardy of self-incrimination, Thomsen was forthcoming. For example, Thomsen was involved in Gestapo interrogations of Polish Brigadier-General Stefan Rowecki, a Polish resistance leader captured by the Nazis in June 1943. By this time Germany had experienced serious military setbacks; Himmler and other high Nazi officials were looking for ways to reverse the situation. One possibility was to recruit Poles to help Germany fight against the Soviet Union, and Rowecki was a prominent figure.

Gestapo interrogations of Rowecki were considered so important that officials in Berlin had to send a progress report every evening to Himmler's headquarters. In spite of all this attention, Rowecki gave the Gestapo little, refusing to say or do anything that might be considered "dishonourable." He was sent to Sachsenhausen concentration camp. After the Warsaw Uprising in August 1944, he was executed in a Nazi reprisal.[18] Such information adds to our understanding of how Himmler and other Nazi leaders responded to political and military pressures later in the war.

Hans Merz

Another captured Gestapo man interrogated by the British in Cairo was an agent named Hans Merz, who managed to penetrate a Polish underground organization called Sword and Plough (Miecz i Plug). He and other double agents tried to steer Polish resistance fighters in an anti-Soviet direction. In March 1943, Merz sent his Nazi superiors a plan to dispatch one of Sword and Plough's leaders to Polish General Anders in the Middle East and persuade Anders to send officers to Poland to organize resistance against the Soviets. But the plan, in conflict with Himmler's goal of eradicating Poles in the Lublin district, was rejected, and Merz barely escaped being court-martialed.[19] The cases of Rowecki and Merz suggest that Nazi officials were not willing to concede much to win Polish support.

Horst Kopkow

Gestapo official Horst Kopkow, who had gone into hiding at war's end, gave much information of historical value after his capture in the fall of 1945; only now have these documents became declassified. Kopkow had been part of a group of officials who fled Berlin to the north, and part of the group met on May 4, 1945, with Himmler in Flensburg. By this time Hitler had committed suicide, Admiral Dönitz had formed a new government, and Himmler, dismissed from offices by Hitler shortly before his death, was grappling to find a new role. Based on what he heard from a colleague named Quetting, Kopkow summarized Himmler's final instructions to some fifteen senior SS officers, including some in charge of underground resistance:

> Himmler gave those present to understand that total military defeat was a fact ... He himself had voluntarily resigned his post as Home Minister [Interior Minister] so that he would not be in the way of any new Government ... Himmler presumed that according to the situation the possibility might exist that the Allies would leave a small preserve, which was believed to be the area north of the Kiel Canal, to a still existing German Government and that this zone might be regarded as a breeding ground for a possible new and modest reconstruction. The hammer must replace the sword in this area and everyone must be called up and start immediately with the rebuilding of Railways and Industries. I also remember that Quetting repeated Himmler[']s references to the Police itself, whereby the Gestapo in its present structure was to go into the background or even disappear completely.[20]

This is the only source we have on Himmler's last speech.

Kopkow received much more attention from British intelligence than Thomsen because he had dealt directly with Communist activities in Germany; although not in charge of counterintelligence work, he was well informed about that, too. He provided details about how the Soviet Union recruited agents in Germany, which Communist espionage rings were still operating, and which agencies or offices individual agents reported to. He also revealed exactly which German officials had contributed to the discovery and destruction of the famous Communist "Red Orchestra" network throughout Europe, and he offered some details about how these Communist agents had obtained valuable intelligence. British authorities interrogated Kopkow at length at least four times.[21]

British interrogators warned Kopkow that his prospects depended on how fully he cooperated, and that his statements would be checked against those of his captured staff. As a result, he gave very detailed information, sometimes accompanied by his own spin. His interrogator noted:

> One thing is very obvious, and runs like a red thread through the whole statement[;] that is[,] K's antipathy towards the U.S.S.R. He is not only through his East Prussian upbringing biased against them, but also through his whole career he was to 90% engaged on work against Communism ...

Kopkow claimed that Russian agents were instructed to continue work in territory liberated by British forces. In other words, he tried to convince the British that they had an immediate problem with Communist espionage. The interrogator wondered:

> Is Kopkow deliberately trying to throw suspicion between the English and the Russians or is he genuinely telling matter of facts . . . ? The most probably [sic] answer to this question seems, that a conflict between the USSR [and Great Britain] would suit him down to the ground. All the same it is probable that the stories he is telling are true, only they have a normal explanation and nothing hostile towards England; but this would not enter the anti-Russian biased brain of K.

The interrogator, on the whole, thought Kopkow's accounts useful and reliable, a good window into methods used by the Gestapo. He recommended that Kopkow be interned.

Kopkow was brought to the United Kingdom for further interrogation—that much is certain. Then the trail becomes murky. According to War Office records, Kopkow died of bronchopneumonia in June 1948, shortly after his arrival.[22] Another Gestapo official named Walter Huppenkothen heard from a British officer that Kopkow died in the fall of 1947. Then Huppenkothen got conflicting stories from those involved with war crimes prosecution. He believed that the British faked Kopkow's death as camouflage for his work for British intelligence.[23] The evidence to confirm this claim is not yet available, but it seems plausible. Kopkow's knowledge of Communist espionage methods and his hatred of the Soviets were likely assets by 1948.

In 1959, a CIA official requested one of the 1945 interrogations of Kopkow. The request form did not indicate Kopkow's death; he was listed as a citizen of Germany (with a question mark). He was described as a former Abwehr official with knowledge of Communist activities. Linking Kopkow to the Abwehr was completely inaccurate, but the organization was far less of a stain than the Gestapo. Either this was sloppy work, or it would not do in 1959 to have Kopkow identified as a Gestapo official. The CIA file on Kopkow was closed at this point.[24] The German War Graves Commission reports that he adopted the family name Cordes or became Kopkow-Cordes; he died in Gelsenkirchen on October 13, 1996.[25] The most likely explanation for a false War Office document about his death nearly forty years earlier is that he worked for British intelligence.

Martin Sandberger
Some ex-Gestapo officials escaped closer scrutiny of their wartime activities—at least temporarily—by feeding their interrogators useful information. Buying time sometimes meant escaping prosecution because the zeal to prosecute Nazi war criminals diminished after early trials succeeded and after the threat of a postwar resurgence of Nazism diminished.

Martin Sandberger had served in various RSHA positions, but was a prime candidate for prosecution and punishment because he headed an Einsatzkommando which, following directly on the heels of the German army invading the Soviet Union, eliminated Jews and other Nazi targets in the Baltic states. In detailed interrogations by British intelligence, Sandberger discussed this experience, but he described his functions in such a way that minimized his culpability. He spent most of his time in Estonia, so he avoided discussing what his unit did in Latvia and Lithuania. In Estonia, to be sure, he received an order to kill Estonian Jews, but he claimed he did not carry it out. Higher SS and Police Leader Jeckeln later found out that many of these Jews had been interned in a camp in Pskov, and he had most of them shot without Sandberger's knowledge, according to Sandberger.

What really distinguished Sandberger's career was his later service as head of administration for SD Foreign Intelligence. From early 1944 he reported directly to Walter Schellenberg, and as a member of his chief's inner circle, he had access to a great deal of sensitive information that British intelligence wanted and got. Sandberger's interim interrogation runs thirty legal-size pages, single-spaced. His interrogator reported:

> Throughout his confinement at Camp 020, Sandberger has been the essence of politeness, correctness and co-operation; he has often volunteered information, and there has been no evidence of willful retention of any kind on his part. The only doubtful period in Sandberger's history is 1941-43 when he was K.d.S. [Kommandeur der Sicherheitspolizei] in Tallinn; there is, however, no evidence of particular criminal actions on his part, and it is therefore reasonable to suppose that this account of his activities there does, to a large measure, represent the truth. The factual information supplied by Sandberger on personnel and organization is considered to be reliable . . . Sandberger's main desire at present is to return to the legal profession for which he originally trained.[26]

He did go to court, but not as an attorney.

After American troops turned up a surviving copy of the Einsatzgruppen reports, Sandberger was directly and fatally implicated. (Holocaust expert Raul Hilberg concluded that Sandberger's Einsatzkommando and its Estonian helpers shot 440 Jews between September 26 and 29, 1941, sparing members of the Jewish council and physicians.)[27] One of the defendants in the American zonal trial of Einsatzgruppen officials, Sandberger was convicted and sentenced to death. General Lucius Clay confirmed the sentence, resisting political pressures, in 1949. But a clemency board under the U.S. High Commissioner for Germany, John J. McCloy, commuted his sentence to life imprisonment in 1951. In 1953 Sandberger was released from prison.[28]

Missing and Escaped Gestapo Officials

Heinrich Müller

Some Gestapo officials, such as Eichmann, managed to assume false identities and to escape from Germany. Persistent news stories in respectable publications as late as 2001 have alleged that the wartime head of the Gestapo, Heinrich Müller, also survived and came to be an intelligence asset for one or more U.S. government agencies, particularly the CIA. According to an article in *The Sunday Times of London*, for example, Lord Greville Janner said that the Americans should now reveal all because "it is beginning to look as if he [Müller] sold his knowledge about Soviet secrets in exchange for his life."[29] The trail of newly declassified records on Müller turns out to be a long one, but it scotches this particular conspiracy theory.[30]

Months before the fall of Berlin, Anglo-American counterespionage officers began their postwar planning. Using Allied lists of Nazi intelligence officers, the SHAEF G-2 Counter Intelligence (CI) War Room supervised the hunt for the remnants of Germany's military and police intelligence services. Initially, the chief concern of the officers of the CI War Room was that Nazi intelligence units would survive the war and, financed with looted assets, launch paramilitary operations in the Bavarian Alps. Intelligence reaching the War Room in the last months of the war did not mention Müller as a possible leader of postwar Nazi operations, but given his command of the Gestapo, Müller remained an important man to capture.

On May 27, 1945, the CI War Room issued a statement about its priority targets for interrogations. At the top of the list were Nazi intelligence officials involved in foreign intelligence. Next in priority were security police and SD units in occupied countries. Gestapo officials came farther down the target list. The War Room instructed interrogators of captured RSHA officers to ask: "Where are: Schellenberg, Ohlendorf, Mueller, Steimle, Sandberger?"[31] (All but Müller were subsequently located and interrogated.) A War Room fortnightly report covering the period ending June 18, 1945, stated that no leading officials of the Gestapo had yet been arrested, and "it seems clear from most reports that Müller remained in Berlin after the collapse."[32] His fate was contrasted with that of other Gestapo personalities who fled south. A separate OSS counterintelligence report at the end of the month repeated that no high-ranking Gestapo officials had yet been captured and that Müller had remained in Berlin.[33] A War Room summary for Supreme Headquarters Allied Expeditionary Forces, dated July 11, mentioned that only two important Gestapo officials had been captured so far; Müller was not found.[34]

A War Room monthly summary in late July 1945 reported that SD Foreign Intelligence officials had largely surrendered, while most Gestapo officials remained at large. Müller's fate was still unknown: "Some of our evidence, though it is by no means conclusive, suggests that Mueller himself may have remained in Berlin until the last . . . [while] the greater part of [the Gestapo] collected itself at

Hof, near Munich, and at Salzburg and Innsbruck."[35] A War Room intelligence arrest target list, dated August 21, commented that an "H. Mueller, head of the Gestapo" was "last reported Berlin, Apr. 1945."[36] A later revision to the target list reported the arrest of several Gestapo officials, including Walter Huppenkothen, who was part of the team of Gestapo officials responsible for tracking down the Communist Red Orchestra. But not Heinrich Müller.[37]

In September 1945, RSHA official Friedrich Wilhelm Heinrich Malz stated to British intelligence that Himmler had ordered many Gestapo officials to help in the defense of Berlin. One of them was Heinrich Müller, "whom Malz thinks is certainly killed as he spent the last days of Berlin (from about 23 Apr 45) in the Reichs [*sic*] Chancellery as Kaltenbrunner's deputy."[38] In November 1945, Kurt Pomme, who had been adjutant to Reinhard Heydrich, claimed that Müller had died when the Russians entered Berlin. In the same month, Horst Kopkow said that Müller had stayed in Berlin to the last.[39]

Schellenberg, a bitter rival of Müller, was the initial source of speculation that Müller had been turned by the Soviets. When interrogated by OSS in 1945, Schellenberg claimed that Müller had been in friendly radio contact with the Soviets, and Schellenberg's postwar memoirs contain verbatim exhortations from 1943 by Müller on Stalin's superiority to Hitler as a leader.[40] SS men close to Müller considered such rumors unfounded and illogical. Müller's immediate superior, Ernst Kaltenbrunner (Chief of the RSHA), later insisted under Allied interrogation that Müller could never have embraced the Soviets. Similarly, in a 1959 CIA interrogation Heinz Pannwitz, Müller's subordinate who ran the Gestapo team that pursued the Communist espionage network known as the Red Orchestra, called the notion that Müller had been turned "absolutely absurd."[41]

The Allies found many Heinrich Müllers in occupied Germany and Austria, but not the right one. Heinrich Müller is a common German name. Documentation on some of them is included—one might say mistakenly jumbled together—in the "Gestapo" Müller Army Intelligence (Investigative Records Repository or IRR) file, which the National Archives released in 2000. Part of the problem for U.S. record-keepers stemmed from the fact that some of these Müllers, including Gestapo Müller, did not appear to have middle names. An additional source of confusion was that there were two different SS generals named Heinrich Müller. In at least one instance, an index card purporting to collate information on Gestapo Müller, which was prepared by an American official after the war, actually contains two different birth dates, as well as data about a third man of the same name. A Heinrich Müller was held briefly at the Altenstadt civilian internment camp in 1945.[42] Another killed himself along with his wife and his children in April 1946.[43]

In the initial period after the Nazi surrender, U.S. counterintelligence attempted to track down all leads to Müller. Information reached U.S. Army Intelligence that Gestapo Müller had taken the assumed name Schwartz or Schwatzer and had gone south from Berlin with another Gestapo official, Christian A. Scholz. But no clear indication that either man left Berlin was ever found.[44] In 1947, British and American authorities twice searched the home of Gestapo Müller's mistress Anna Schmid for clues, but found nothing suggesting that Müller was still alive.[45] With the onset of the Cold War and the shift of intelligence resources to the Soviet target, U.S. intelligence presumed that Gestapo Müller was dead.

The dramatic Israeli abduction of Adolf Eichmann from Argentina in May 1960 created new interest in Nazi war criminals and particularly in Müller. (Eichmann himself speculated during his Jerusalem trial that Müller survived the war.) In July 1960, the West German office in charge of gathering information on war criminals charged local police authorities in Bavaria and Berlin to investigate. The West Germans were skeptical about the proposition that Müller was working for the Soviets, but did think it possible that Müller was corresponding from somewhere with his family or possibly with his former secretary, Barbara Hellmuth. All of these West German citizens were closely watched, and in May 1961 the Bavarian police asked the U.S. occupation forces to put Müller's relatives and Hellmuth under surveillance. Anna Schmid, Müller's former mistress, told West German investigators that she had not seen Müller since April 24, 1945, when he gave her a vial of poison and then disappeared. Her efforts to find him in the subsequent days and weeks had been fruitless.[46]

According to various witnesses interviewed by the West German police in 1961, the last time Müller was seen alive was the evening of May 1, 1945, the day after Hitler's suicide. Several eyewitnesses placed Müller at the Reich Chancellery building that evening and recounted his refusal to leave with the breakout group that night. Hans Baur, Hitler's pilot and an old friend of Müller's, recounts Müller as saying, "We know the Russian methods exactly. I haven't the faintest intention of . . . being taken prisoner by the Russians." Another claimed that Müller refused to leave with the rest of Hitler's entourage and was overheard saying "the regime has fallen and . . . I fall also." He was last seen in the company of his radio specialist, Christian A. Scholz. And while the bodies of others that remained that night were recovered and identified, no one in the final group witnessed the death of Müller or Scholz.[47]

West German authorities pursued three major leads in an effort to confirm Müller's death and burial in Berlin in 1945. First, there was the testimony of Fritz Leopold, a Berlin morgue official who had reported in December 1945 that Müller's body was moved (along with many others) from the RSHA headquarters at Prinz Albrecht Strasse (2000 feet from the Chancellery) for reburial in a local municipal cemetery on Lilienthalstrasse (Berlin-Neukölln) in the western half of the city. Leopold was later deemed an unreliable source, but the burial was officially registered with the Berlin authorities and a headstone was placed at Müller's grave which read, "Our loving father Heinrich Müller—Born 28 April 1900—Died in Berlin May 1945." A second story came from Müller's ex-subordinate Heinz Pannwitz, who had been captured by the Soviets and returned to West Germany in 1957, whereupon he told the West German Secret Service (BND) that his Soviet interrogators revealed to him that "your Chief [Müller] is dead." The body, they said, had been found in a subway shaft a few blocks from the Chancellery with a bullet through the head and with its identity documents intact.[48]

Walter Lueders, a former member of the German civilian fighters (*Volkssturm*), maintained that he had headed a burial detail in the summer of 1945. Of the hundreds of bodies buried by the detail, only one, said Lueders, wore an SS general's uniform, and it was found in the garden of the Reich Chancellery with a large wound in the back. Though the body had no medals or decorations, Lueders recalled with certainty that the identity papers were those of Gestapo Müller. It was moved to the old Jewish Cemetery on Grosse Hamburgerstrasse in the Soviet Sector, where it was placed in one of three mass graves. In fact, in 1955, the German Armed Forces Information Office inquired with district authorities in East Berlin and received confirmation that Gestapo Müller was buried at the Grosse-Hamburgerstrasse cemetery in 1945. Since the grave was a mass grave, however, there was no actual plot.[49]

The CIA started its involvement in the hunt for Müller at roughly the same time as the West German search, albeit from a different source base. The January 1961 defection and interrogation of a Polish intelligence officer brought Western counterintelligence tips that led to several Soviet and Polish agents active in the West, including George Blake, a mole in the British MI-6; Harry Houghton, a clerk in the British navy; and Heinz Felfe, a high level West German intelligence officer. The defector surely was Lieutenant Colonel Michal Goleniewski, the Deputy Chief of Polish Military Counter Intelligence until 1958, who had also operated as a mole for the KGB in the Polish service. In recounting his work as an interrogator of captured German officials in Poland from 1948 to 1952, Goleniewski revealed information about the fate of some Nazis. He had heard from his Soviet supervisors that sometime between 1950 and 1952 the Soviets had picked up Müller and taken him to Moscow.[50] There was little with which to evaluate this claim, and some reason to be skeptical of this hearsay. Pannwitz, after all, had recently dismissed as "nonsense" to CIA interrogators the idea that Müller worked for the Soviets, while claiming that his own Soviet interrogators repeatedly said that Müller was dead.[51]

In the aftermath of the Eichmann trial, the West German weekly *Stern* ran two articles by journalist Peter Staehle that appeared in January and August 1964. Staehle said that having followed a path after the war that included the Soviet Union, Romania, Turkey, and South Africa, Müller then became a senior police official in Albania before fleeing for South America.[52] From the start, the CIA suspected that Staehle's articles were a "plant"—part of a "clever bit of [disinformation] work" to mislead the public as well as intelligence agencies.[53] The CIA checked and disproved Staehle's claim that Müller was in fact an Albanian police official named Abedin Bekir Nakoschiri.[54] The BND and CIA also discovered that Staehle had failed to get his articles printed in the more respected weekly *Die Zeit* because he had reportedly lied about his sources.[55]

In May 1970, a Czech defector, very likely Ladislas Bittman, a disinformation specialist himself, weighed in.[56] Bittman said that the *Stern* article was planted from Prague in order to neutralize rumors that Müller might in fact be in Czechoslovakia. Bittman added for good measure that within Czech intelligence circles, it was common knowledge that the KGB had used Nazi war criminals for intelligence purposes and that key sections of Nazi archives had also been captured by the Soviets for use in "operational aims."[57]

These comments caught the eye of the CIA's Counter-Intelligence (CI) Staff, headed by the legendary James Angleton. Angleton must have recognized two possibilities. If Müller really had been in the USSR or elsewhere in Eastern Europe, and if he had taken RSHA central files with him (many of which had indeed vanished after the war), then the Soviets might be able to use this information against some prominent West Germans. It was crucial to discover what had happened, not necessarily to Müller, who well might have been dead in any case, but to the files. The opposite scenario, that Müller had died in Berlin, was equally significant: Angleton also had a special interest in Soviet disinformation.

The CI Staff undertook a thoroughgoing inquiry of Müller starting in late 1970. It resulted in a forty-page brief, "The Hunt for 'Gestapo Mueller,'" which was circulated as an internal report of the Directorate of Plans in December 1971. A memo in the file dated December 9, 1971, explaining the purpose of the report states:

> Our principal original objective in preparing the attached study of the Mueller case was to produce a training aid illustrating the vagaries and pitfalls of protracted investigations. In the past, Mueller had been viewed mainly as a missing war criminal. As the material was collected, however, we became aware of another important possibility: that Mueller had defected to World War II Soviet counterintelligence (SMERSH) and had taken with him a large assortment of files. (The central files of the German National Security Service (RSHA), of which Mueller was de facto chief . . . in the last weeks of the war, were never recovered by the Western Allies . . .) If SMERSH actually seized Mueller and the best part of the RSHA records, Soviet capabilities to control important Germans and some other Europeans would far exceed those heretofore attributed to them.[58]

The report ended on a note of skepticism. "No one appears to have tried very hard," it said,

> to find Mueller immediately after the war while the trail was still hot, either in the West or the East . . . The presumption is that Allied officials searching for Mueller soon stumbled over the . . . holdings of his effects and the . . . burial record and

considered these sufficient proof that he was dead . . . There is little room for doubt, however, that the Soviet and Czech services circulated rumors to the effect that Mueller had escaped to the West. These rumors were apparently floated to offset the charges that the Soviets had sheltered the criminal . . . There are strong indications but no proof that Mueller collaborated with [the Soviets]. There are also strong indications but no proof that Mueller died [in Berlin]. . . One thing appears certain. Mueller and Scholz had some special reason for entering the Berlin death trap and remaining behind in the Chancellery. If their object was to carry out a memorable and convincing suicide, they really bungled the job.[59]

More information about Müller might still emerge from secret files of the former Soviet Union. But currently available records of the War Room as well as other records in the National Archives indicate that Müller most likely died in Berlin in early May 1945. Müller, who apparently wanted to die fighting, would not at all have minded having the Allies struggle to figure out what had become of him.

Walter Rauff
Another severely incriminated Gestapo official, Walter Rauff, fell into American hands at the end of the war, but he was able to escape. His postwar travels have been recounted previously, but newly declassified documents add details to Rauff's postwar intelligence activities. They also show that no serious effort was made to extradite and punish Rauff until several decades after 1945.

As historians have shown, Rauff was one of a number of German officials who sought to surrender German forces in Italy to the Allies near the end of the war.[60] Cardinal Ildebrando Schuster, Archbishop of Milan, had told Rauff that Allied forces in Italy would leave the takeover of northwest Italy to Italian partisan forces, and that Marshal Graziani of the Italian Social Republic (Mussolini's rump regime) would fight the partisans till the very end. Schuster thought that an Allied takeover of the area instead would spare senseless bloodshed and destruction, which could only benefit Bolshevism. Rauff got a go-ahead from his SS and police superior Wilhelm Harster and used Schuster's secretary Don Giuseppe Bicchierai to contact Allen Dulles in Switzerland.[61] But the British as well as Italian partisans both firmly rejected Schuster's initiative, and Dulles concurred. Within a short time Dulles was involved in other negotiations with Karl Wolff's emissaries to surrender all German forces in Italy. So Rauff and two subordinates simply surrendered on April 30, 1945.[62]

According to Lieutenant Colonel Stephen Spingarn, chief of the Counterintelligence Corps (CIC), Rauff was "most uncooperative during interrogation . . . His contempt and everlasting malice towards the Allies [are] but lightly concealed. [Rauff] is considered a menace if ever set free, and failing actual elimination, is recommended for life-long internment."[63] But Rauff found his way to a postwar career nearly as adventurous as his prewar and wartime activities.

Rauff officially joined the NSDAP in May 1937, but he supported the Nazis well before then.[64] In April 1938 he joined the SS. Reportedly a close friend of Reinhard Heydrich, Rauff was immediately assigned to SD headquarters in Berlin.[65]

In September 1941, as German forces were overrunning the western Soviet Union, Rauff initiated an important invention in the technology of genocide. In charge of the Security Police division that controlled motor vehicles, Rauff asked one of his subordinates if exhaust gas could be channeled back into a closed compartment in a van carrying passengers. Getting a positive response, Rauff arranged for the acquisition and conversion of vans, which were then sent to the eastern front as substitutes for execution squads. Although these "mobile gas chambers" were not without problems (they broke down frequently),[66] they were widely used in Soviet territories to liquidate Jews. One van was also used to kill Jews at the Semlin camp outside Belgrade, and parked vans were continuously used at the Chelmno extermination camp in German-annexed Polish territory.[67]

In the summer of 1942, as commander of a Security Police detachment in North Africa, Rauff flew from Munich to Field Marshal Erwin Rommel's headquarters at Tobruk, reportedly in order to discuss the liquidation of Jews in Cairo once it was captured by the German Africa Corps.[68] Disgusted with the idea, the "Desert Fox" apparently refused to discuss the matter and sent Rauff on his way.[69] Later the same year, Rauff was in charge of an SD detachment in Tunis, where he was responsible for rounding up some 4,500 Jews for slave labor.[70] His superiors recommended him for a high decoration.[71]

With Italy's defection from the Axis in September 1943, Rauff was ordered to Bolzano for a meeting with SS-Brigadeführer Dr. Wilhelm Harster, commander of all Security Police and SD forces in Italy. Shortly thereafter, Harster appointed Rauff as chief of the Security Police and SD in northwestern Italy. Rauff established his headquarters in Milan and set about organizing the Nazi security apparatus there. Rauff's men, several of whom had served with him in Africa, were responsible for meting out particularly brutal reprisals for acts of resistance to German occupation forces. One of his chief subordinates in Italy was SS-Hauptsturmführer Theodor Saevecke, who had also served as Rauff's deputy in North Africa.[72]

In December 1946, Rauff, together with several other prisoners, escaped from American internment at Rimini, Italy. Rauff later claimed that he was aided in his escape by a Catholic priest in Naples, who helped him to make his way to Rome. Throughout 1947 and much of the following year, Rauff successfully eluded efforts to recapture him by hiding out in the convents of the Holy See, apparently under the protection of Bishop Alois Hudal.[73]

In July 1948 the Syrian government sent Captain Akram Tabarr (alias Dr. Jean Hamsi) to Rome to recruit military and police specialists, especially Germans. The Gehlen Organization, the West German intelligence organization, reported that Tabarr hired Rauff as his representative in Rome with instructions to recruit German specialists for work in Syria.[74]

Eager to begin a new life, Rauff and his family left Italy for Syria in November 1948. A few months later, Colonel Husni al-Za'im, chief of staff of the Syrian Army, led a successful coup against President Shukri Kuwatli. The coup came about as the result of public and military discontent with the humiliating defeat of the Syrian military by the Israelis in 1948. The new Syrian government looked to hire out-of-work German military and police specialists in order to prepare the nation for future confrontation with the State of Israel.

One CIA report credited Rauff with "a leading role in the German experts group in Syria prior to and during Za'im's regime."[75] As a result of German army general Hyazinth von Strachwitz's influence with Za'im, Rauff was appointed as a "commissioner of security with the special task of reorganizing Syrian intelligence." According to Strachwitz, Rauff helped model the Syrian secret police, the *Deuxieme Bureau*, along the lines of the Gestapo. The former SS officer may also have served as an advisor to the Syrian military, as he was reportedly close to General Medani, chief of Syrian military intelligence.

Following the Za'im coup, Reinhard Gehlen considered Rauff's value as a potential intelligence operative in Syria. In the end, however, the CIA believed that the Gehlen Organization "used its influence, as far as this was possible, to prevent serious and reliable former German military officers from taking part in the adventurous scheme of going to Syria."[76]

Za'im's military dictatorship was highly unpopular. Following a successful coup d'état in August 1949, another Syrian officer, Sami al-Hinnawi, seized power in Damascus. On the day of the coup, Rauff was arrested and reportedly charged with "terrorism." The Syrians claimed Rauff had employed torture devices in order to extract information from people (presumably Jews) suspected of being connected with a "Jewish bombing incident."[77]

According to one CIA report, the new Hinnawi government arrested Rauff because members of the Syrian military leadership disliked him and resented his influential position as an advisor to Za'im. Another report stated that Rauff was suspected of involvement in "aiding the Syrian Communist movement."[78] For whatever reason, the former SS officer was forced to flee Syria in the aftermath of the coup that toppled Za'im. After a brief stay in Beirut, Lebanon, Rauff returned to Italy in late 1949. Rauff decided his best course of action was to emigrate with his family to South America.

As a young naval officer aboard the cruiser *Berlin*, Rauff had spent some time in South America and Spain during the interwar years.[79] In 1949, Rauff and his family settled in Ecuador, where they remained for nearly ten years. The CIA received what it regarded as "authoritative" information that Rauff settled in the Ecuadorian capital, Quito, where he found work as a salesman for the Parke-Davis and Bayer corporations. The CIA suspected that Rauff was organizing an intelligence network in Quito but could not confirm it. Based on the information contained in its file, the CIA apparently never thoroughly investigated Rauff's activities in Ecuador.

Rauff apparently moved from Ecuador to Chile in October 1958. According to one unconfirmed CIA memorandum, the former SS officer was accused of "organizing vague international operations against Jews" during his first years in Chile. In 1959 Rauff was granted permanent residency status in Chile. In April 1960 Rauff felt secure enough in his new life to take a trip to West Germany with his wife. He apparently traveled on a Chilean passport under the name of Herman Julius Walter Rauff Bauermeister, and was in no way hindered in his travel by West German authorities.[80]

One year later, in April 1961, Rauff's name emerged during the Eichmann trial in Israel, which led authorities in West Germany to request his extradition from Chile. Chilean authorities arrested Rauff in December 1962 in the town of Punta Arenas. Five months later, the Supreme Court of Chile ruled that Chile's statute of limitations on murder (fifteen years) had expired, and since Rauff had broken no Chilean laws during his stay there, he could not legally be extradited. In July 1974, CIA sources reported that Rauff was living in the town of Porvenir in Tierra del Fuego, where he was ostensibly engaged in raising livestock.

Around the same time, the French newspaper *Le Monde* ran a story that Rauff was serving as chief of the Chilean Intelligence Service, the *Direccion de Inteligencia Nacional* (DINA).[81] Rauff once again became an international press sensation. It appears that as late as March 1976 the CIA was not clear on exactly what, if any, connections existed between Walther Rauff and the Chilean government. A report contained in the CIA file reflected the view that Rauff had "no known history of political activities in Chile, or association with illicit groups." The report went on to say that Rauff was viewed by his neighbors as ". . . a highly respected member of the community who is living out his old age quietly . . ."[82]

When President Salvador Allende and his Popular Unity government were overthrown in 1973 in a coup led by General Augusto Pinochet, Rauff found a friend and a cause he could serve. During Pinochet's iron-fisted rule, which lasted from 1973 to 1990, Rauff was allegedly involved in the torture and deaths of many Chileans who opposed Pinochet's regime.[83] A CIA report, heavily redacted to protect intelligence sources, hints at such involvement, describing Rauff as "working within" the Chilean Interior Ministry.[84]

In August 1983, the U.S. Department of State inquired what, if any, connection the CIA had with Walther Rauff. The CIA undertook what was described as "an intensive search of the files and indices" of the Agency's Directorate of Operations. A CIA officer advised the Agency's Office of the General Counsel that the State Department could be informed that: "a review of Rauff's file indicated no association or utilization of . . . [him] by this Agency."[85]

Rauff's presence in Chile for a quarter century generated significant international criticism and repeated calls for his extradition. (The following sketch of outside efforts is based largely on materials previously declassified: it is far from comprehensive.) Dissatisfied with the Chilean Supreme Court's 1963 decision, various West German governments asked Chile to extradite Rauff. But the government of Christian Democrat Eduardo Frei, the Marxist government of Salvador Allende, and the dictatorship of Augusto Pinochet all allowed the 1963 Supreme Court decision to stand.[86]

On April 12, 1983, Nazi-hunter Simon Wiesenthal sent President Ronald Reagan a personal telegram thanking Reagan for quoting him in a recent speech to the American Gathering of Jewish Holocaust Survivors. Wiesenthal also pointed out that Rauff was living undisturbed in Chile: "No regime including the present one [Pinochet] has acted on West Germany's request for his extradition." Wiesenthal asked President Reagan to get involved.[87]

Although Wiesenthal later claimed that the United States did little with his suggestions,[88] his telegram helped to generate American efforts. State Department legal adviser Donald Koblitz visited West Germany in December 1983 to confirm that West German authorities were still interested in prosecuting Rauff. The state prosecutor in Hannover, Rauff's hometown, was eager to move ahead; he assessed Chile's opposition to extradition as entirely political. Koblitz also consulted with Wolfgang Walter, chief of the West German Ministry of Justice's international section. Walter called the Rauff case one of the last great outstanding war crimes cases for West Germany. If the United States wanted to put pressure on the Pinochet government, Bonn would eagerly cooperate. Walter regarded the United States as the only country in a position to influence Chile to deport Rauff.[89] Neither the United States nor West Germany made public the serious diplomatic measures that were under discussion.

On January 20, 1984, Nazi-hunter Beate Klarsfeld arrived in Santiago to launch a loud and conspicuous campaign. During the next three weeks, Chilean police arrested Klarsfeld twice, once for leading a demonstration outside Rauff's home. On February 1, while Klarsfeld was still in Santiago, Israel entered the fray when David Kimche, Israel's Director of Foreign Affairs, stopped in Santiago on his way to Australia. The U.S. Embassy in Santiago thought the timing "more than accidental" and feared that the Chilean government would perceive it as an international conspiracy. Actually, the Israelis had cautioned Klarsfeld that a public campaign might spoil their efforts, but Klarsfeld insisted that only a frontal approach had any chance against entrenched views of the Chilean government.[90]

The European Parliament passed a resolution on February 19 calling upon Chile to hand over Rauff. The Chilean Minister of the Interior complained to the international press at a conference that the Rauff case had been transformed into a political cause designed to accuse the Chilean government of refusing to take steps that could lead to punishment of a person accused of war crimes. United States Ambassador James D. Theberge lamented after this press conference that the Chilean government "seems convinced that the campaign being mounted in other countries is more anti-Pinochet than pro-justice." Never sanguine about resolving this issue, Theberge had advised against pressing Chile to hand over Rauff: an American effort to dislodge Rauff would damage general U.S. interests in Chile, he said.[91]

Latin American specialists in the State Department were also cool. Langhorne A. Motley, Assistant Secretary of State for Inter-American Affairs, claimed that the West Germans were not pursuing the issue and had not asked for U.S. help; he also denied that the United States had particular political leverage or any legal role to play. If the United States were to become involved, then it should be in a supporting role for a West German demarche. The West Germans, who had the legal claim to Rauff, should take the initiative. Even so, an American push on Rauff would "inject a new issue into our already strained relations," creating "a bilateral issue where none existed before."[92]

The decision whether or not to engage Chile lay with Lawrence Eagleburger, the Undersecretary of State for Political Affairs.[93] Eagleburger had previously served as ambassador to Yugoslavia and as assistant secretary of state for European Affairs; he would later serve as secretary of state under President George H. W. Bush and would spearhead the trial of Balkan war criminals in December 1992.[94] He did not hesitate in early 1984: the United States would ask the West Germans to claim Rauff again, and the United States would back the West German request with a clear, unambiguous verbal demarche in Santiago. Secretary of State George Shultz signed onto this decision and gave it high priority, telling the embassies in Bonn and Santiago that congressional inquiries and a strong request from Simon Wiesenthal to President Reagan were driving U.S. interests:

> After careful review we believe that it would serve the interests of justice to advise the FRG [Federal Republic of Germany] that the U.S. would support its request to the Government of Chile for Rauff's deportation . . . We recognize that the FRG . . . has already gone to considerable lengths to pursue the case . . . [but if the West Germans would approach Santiago again] we would be prepared to support this request and approach the Chileans urging that they comply . . . We believe that if anything is to be done, it should be done quickly. We are concerned that Israeli approaches in the last few weeks may precipitate a formal and irreversible Chilean stand . . . [This] may be the last, and perhaps the best opportunity to allow German justice to close this case.[95]

In mid-February 1984, Simon Wiesenthal met with President Reagan and expressed satisfaction with State Department efforts to bring Rauff to justice. A White House spokesman confirmed that "it is longstanding United States policy to see that Nazi war criminals are brought to justice . . . [and that] the United States is prepared to offer appropriate assistance to see that justice is done."[96]

The government of Christian Democratic Chancellor Helmut Kohl moved quickly, perhaps to make amends for blunders on related issues.[97] The West German judicial system had wanted Rauff for decades. On February 29, 1984,

West German Ambassador Hermann Holtzheimer called on Mario Barros, Director General of the Chilean Ministry of Foreign Affairs to request Rauff's deportation—an easier legal procedure than extradition, and one that would bypass the Chilean Supreme Court. West German police officers could arrest Rauff and transfer him to the Federal Republic at Bonn's expense. Barros responded coolly that only new facts concerning crimes Rauff committed since Chile's 1963 court decision would influence the case. He suggested that Holtzheimer submit a note verbale to the Foreign Ministry, but for the time being, Rauff's deportation was simply not in the Chilean public interest. Holtzheimer described Chile's position as nonsense (*Augenwischerei*): Rauff was still a German citizen, and he had obtained his residence permit in Chile under false pretenses. The decision to deport or not to deport was political. Holtzheimer also warned that the Israelis, the Americans, the British, the French, and private Nazi hunters like Wiesenthal would all line up against Chile on this matter, but Barros was unfazed.[98]

The Chilean Ministry of Foreign Affairs responded sharply to the West German note verbale a week later, but launched its sharpest remarks against the United States. Chilean Foreign Minister Jaime del Valle called U.S. support for the West Germans "disconcerting, illogical, unacceptable, and absurd." Why should Pinochet overrule a twenty-one-year-old Supreme Court decision in order to arbitrarily bring about deportation of a man accused of no crimes in Chile? (It was more than a little curious that the Pinochet government endorsed the sanctity of a Supreme Court decision of a regime that it had overthrown by force.) The American Ambassador observed that the Chilean foreign minister's anger reflected frayed nerves and deepening hostility of the Chilean government to foreign interference.[99] The State Department dropped the matter for the time being.

On the morning of May 14, 1984, Walter Rauff died at his home of heart failure. One of Nazi Germany's worst perpetrators of crimes against humanity was able to escape justice through a combination of circumstances: American negligence in the immediate postwar period; active assistance from certain officials of the Catholic Church; and longstanding protection by several different Chilean governments, particularly President (and dictator) Augusto Pinochet. International efforts to force Rauff to answer for his crimes during the last two decades of his life were insufficient to reverse earlier mistakes and to overcome political resistance in Chile.

Alois Brunner

In March 2003, an American documentary film entitled *Alois Brunner: The Last Nazi* was released, reflecting widespread interest in the fate of a key war criminal who was never caught. His crimes had been brought before courts, but he had never personally appeared there. His entire postwar career was shrouded by fog and deception.[100]

Born in 1912 in the Austrian Burgenland, Brunner joined the Nazi Party illegally in 1931 and joined the SS on October 10, 1939. From 1939 he served as Eichmann's secretary in the Zentralestelle für jüdische Auswanderung, whose task it was to force Jews from the Reich. In this capacity he organized forced deportations of 47,000 Austrian Jews to ghettos and death camps. Transferred to Salonika in March 1943, Brunner oversaw the deportation of 43,000 Jews from Greece in two months. In June 1943 he took over the Drancy camp, the assembly point for Jews to be deported from France. In fourteen months he sent roughly 24,000 Jews to the East. He also directed a special commando unit to arrest Jews in Nice and bring them to Drancy, and he paid French collaborators for each Jew arrested. As late as July 1944, he organized a sweep for hidden Jewish children in France, which located and deported 250 minors as well as the last Jewish convoy from Paris on August 17, 1944.

Brunner's movements at the end of the war will likely remain a mystery. His Army IRR file, if there ever was one, is now gone, and his CIA Name File is very thin. In 1960, in the aftermath of the Eichmann capture, a number of unconfirmed sources, including the West German weekly *Der Spiegel*, suggested that Brunner was living in Damascus under the alias Dr. Georg Fischer. The Israeli and Austrian governments both requested his extradition from Syria in 1961.[101] The CIA made inquiries around that time. Certain records suggested that Brunner was hanged in the Soviet sector of Vienna in 1946, but his name popped up sporadically in Austria until 1948. "[If] he was not . . . executed," said one CIA analysis in May 1961, "but was in the hands of the Soviets, it raises the speculation that he might have become a Soviet agent."[102]

The best evidence suggested that Brunner was in Damascus. He was said to have suffered disfiguring wounds from a package bomb attack in September 1961, possibly sent by an Israeli intelligence agent.[103] The CIA also gained information on Brunner while watching another Nazi official, Franz Rademacher. Rademacher, the author of plans to send Europe's Jews to Madagascar and to deport Jews en masse from Western Europe, had been tried by West German authorities in 1952, found guilty, and sentenced to three and a half years in prison. On his appeal, a new trial was ordered, but rather than face it, Rademacher fled to Damascus in 1954. By 1957 the CIA learned that Rademacher was using the alias F. Bartholome Rosello and that he was establishing business contacts in western Europe for a Syrian import-export firm. According to his CIA Name File, Rademacher also reestablished his contacts with Brunner, and the two maintained a friendship. Rademacher and Brunner worked as advisers to the Syrian Ministry of the Interior.[104] West German sources thirty years later indicated that Brunner had helped to train Kurdish guerrillas operating against Turkey.[105]

The CIA turned up more information on Brunner during the Eichmann trial while monitoring the communication of Hans Rechenberg of Munich, a former Nazi propaganda official who had taken it upon himself to help the Eichmann family financially, to provide positive propaganda on the Eichmann trial, and to help Eichmann's West German defense attorney, Robert Servatius. In February and March 1962, Rechenberg and Servatius had tried to get Rademacher to testify on Eichmann's behalf or at least to provide evidence, but Rademacher refused even to meet Servatius secretly in Cyprus. The reason, he said, was the recent attempt on his friend Brunner's life, and the fact the he himself could get kidnapped.[106] In the meantime, Rademacher had begun spying on Syria for another foreign government (the name of which is redacted), providing information on Syrian politics to his handlers through the open mail. The Syrian government discovered Rademacher's activities and arrested him in 1964. Realizing that Rosello was Rademacher, the West German government requested his extradition, and the Syrians complied two years later. Rademacher was tried again in 1968 and sentenced to five years three months, all of which was waived. Yet while looking into Rademacher's activities, the CIA confirmed that he had been connected with a circle of Germans, including Brunner, who had direct or indirect connections with a number of intelligence services including the Soviets, the Algerian FLN, and the Egyptians.[107]

Another impetus to find and extradite Brunner in the 1980s was triggered by evidence uncovered by Nazi-hunters and journalists. In the summer of 1982, Serge Klarsfeld traveled to Syria posing as a Nazi sympathizer and managed to phone Brunner before the Syrian authorities deported him. In March 1983, Robert Fisk of the *Times of London* located Brunner's residence in Damascus despite denials by Syrian authorities that Brunner was in the country. The Anti-Defamation League (ADL) pressed the Austrian and German governments to make representations with the Syrian authorities. Austrian authorities recounted that they had asked Damascus for Brunner during the Eichmann trial in 1961 but that the Syrian government had denied Brunner's presence there. But by October, Austrian Foreign Minister Leopold Graz told members of the ADL that Austria would work "expeditiously and forthrightly" to secure Brunner's arrest. A month earlier, the West German government announced that it, too, would make efforts to secure Brunner in light of a warrant for his arrest recently ordered in Cologne.[108]

The West German government acted in December 1984, conveying a formal note to the Syrian Foreign Ministry requesting Brunner's handover, though no formal extradition treaty existed between Syria and the Federal Republic. The U.S. Embassy (which claimed to have a reliable source in the West German Embassy in Syria) reported, "Brunner is known to be protected in Syria by armed guards, presumably from the Syrian intelligence services. In the past, our source added, Brunner has done work on behalf of the Syrian intelligence services in training Kurdish guerrillas who operate from Syria against Turkey." But the West German source did not hold out much hope for Syrian compliance even though Bonn repeatedly reminded Syrian officials of the request. The official Syrian position remained that no one by the name of Alois Brunner (or Georg Fischer) lived in Syria.[109]

By the summer of 1985, more information had surfaced on Brunner's whereabouts through the West German magazine *Bunte*, which carried an interview with Brunner. The article not only noted Brunner's street address on Rue Haddad in Damascus, but also his comment that he "had no bad conscience" over his role in the extermination of Europe's Jews. The State Department then decided to become directly involved. The Austrian government, concerned with appearing too closely linked with the Americans, rejected American diplomatic support, but the West Germans welcomed the possibility of a U.S. demarche in Damascus just as they had in Santiago.[110] George Shultz hoped that the *Bunte* article, with its specific information as to Brunner's presence, could "be helpful in pressuring the Syrians, since they have told others . . . that Brunner was not in Syria." He ordered the U.S. Ambassador in Damascus, William L. Eagleton, Jr., to make the point that

> the U.S. firmly supports the [West German] request for the extradition of Alois Brunner [of] December 18, 1984 . . . In the view of the U.S., Brunner's crimes are among the most serious and appalling of those committed during the war; he is widely considered to be among the most wanted Nazis still at large . . . We believe it is imperative that Brunner be brought to justice. [Syrian government] assistance in this regard would be viewed by all of the governments and peoples involved as a wise and just act. Brunner's continued presence in Syria, on the other hand, will serve only to prolong negative international attention to his presence in Syria.[111]

This particular American demarche, however, was never delivered in Damascus, despite the West German hope that it would be of some help after the Syrians rebuffed subsequent German inquiries. As was the case in Latin America, Embassy officials on the spot did not wish to see the Brunner issue jeopardize their more urgent concerns. "Having our plate full with negative demarches involving terrorism, hostages and missiles," said Ambassador Eagleton in December 1985, "we have not found an ideal time to raise the Brunner issue here.[112] Brunner's *Bunte* interview seems to have taken place without Syrian government approval. According to U.S. Embassy contacts in Bonn, the Syrians moved Brunner after it appeared.[113]

The West Germans continued their efforts. Bonn tried throughout 1987 with a number of diplomatic notes and statements, even to Foreign Minister Sharā to get the Syrian government to change its mind, but to no avail. Syrian interlocutors either made no comment at all or continued to deny that Brunner was in the country. The most dramatic West German step came in January 1988, when Foreign Minister Hans-Dietrich Genscher raised the Brunner issue with President Hafez al-Assad himself during Genscher's visit to Damascus. Genscher's demarche was a surprise to Assad, who denied knowing Brunner's whereabouts. It was also a shock to the West German Embassy, which expected that Genscher, a superior diplomat who had wanted a smooth visit, would not raise such a touchy subject traditionally left to lower-level officials. The Syrian Ambassador to Bonn, Suleyman Hadad, even protested to the West German Foreign Ministry insisting—according to a U.S. paraphrase—that Genscher's raising of the issue was "inappropriate, in bad taste, and 'just isn't done.'"[114]

Genscher risked Assad's ire because the West Germans, according to their U.S. contacts in Damascus and Bonn, were especially well informed by this time. Eagleton reported that "there is no question . . . regarding Brunner's presence in Damascus. The Germans know where he lives and who sees him. Brunner arrived in Damascus from Egypt . . . and appears to have had some sort of consulting role for a few years after that with some unspecified security organization. Throughout the Assad regime, however, Brunner has essentially been under house arrest in Damascus."[115]

The West German Foreign Ministry had even considering buying Brunner's extradition with a cash reward to the Syrians, as the French had done with Klaus Barbie in Bolivia, but the West German Embassy advised against it, since in its estimation, the cost would be prohibitive. "Damascus," reported the U.S. Embassy in Syria, after speaking with German sources, "is too embarrassed to admit his presence and has a perverse sense of pride which would prohibit turning the former Nazi over to any [W]estern authority, since this would be perceived locally as giving in to Israeli pressures. Brunner is old and frail and the Syrians are confident that nature will eliminate the issue in the not too distant future."[116]

According to American Embassy sources in Damascus in 1990, Austrian President Kurt Waldheim made an effort during his trip to Damascus in 1988 to secure Brunner's arrest. The Austrians, like the West Germans, had been trying since 1984 to secure Brunner, but Waldheim's placement on the U.S. watch list for his wartime activities in the Balkans might have prompted him to make an effort on his own. In any event, the Syrian government did not change its story.[117]

There was a brief hope after the Gulf War of 1991 that Syria's participation in the U.S.-led anti-Iraqi coalition might make it possible to raise the Brunner issue again, this time with success. Senators Ted Kennedy and Daniel Moynihan raised American hopes in the summer of 1991. The State Department replied, "We hope to use the opportunity afforded by our successful prosecution of the Gulf War, and our contacts with the Syrian government that emerged from it, to make progress towards resolution of many of the issues of importance to us, including this one."[118]

In December 1991, Beate Klarsfeld appeared in Damascus with a false passport and protested outside the Syrian Ministry of the Interior in December 1991. After her immediate deportation, she held a press conference at the European Parliament in Strasbourg in January 1992, attacking the Syrian government.

The date and circumstances of Brunner's ultimate demise are not clear. By the end of 1992, the National Security Agency intercepted statements to the effect that Brunner had died, though it was clear that since the Syrians never admitted his presence in the country, there would be no official death announcement.[119] The hope that Brunner was alive and could still be brought to justice, however, remained. In March 2001, he was tried in absentia in the Paris Court of Assizes.

It was the second such trial for Brunner in France, the first having taken place in 1954 before the Permanent Court of the Armed Forces, where Brunner received two death sentences. If Brunner were still alive in 2001, he would have been eighty-eight years old.

The story of how Alois Brunner escaped from Europe—and from justice—after World War II is too sketchy to assign responsibility to individuals, organizations, or governments. On the other hand, Brunner's apparent ability not only to remain in Syria for decades, but even to apply his Gestapo experience there, is, in effect, a Syrian endorsement of Nazi cruelty and anti-Semitism even in the late twentieth century.

Notes

1. Undated Report, Sections of the RSHA possibly involved in War Crimes, copy in NA, RG 226, entry 119A, box 57, folder 1632. The report seems to have been compiled by American intelligence analysts in London.
2. Declassified documents are available in NA, RG 242, T-175.
3. NA, RG 242, Himmler Collection, entry 27, boxes 1–8.
4. For the file card on Rothenberg, see NA, RG 242, entry 27, box 2, file card A 1090. For the general story of Göring and Rothenberg, see Bent Blüdnikow, *So mom de slet ikke eksisterede: Hugo Rothenberg og kampen for de tyske joder* (Copenhagen: Samleren, 1991).
5. E. Thomas Wood and Stanislaw M. Jankowski, *Karski: How One Man Tried to Stop the Holocaust* (New York: J. Wiley, 1994); Darius Stola, "Early News of the Holocaust from Poland," *Holocaust and Genocide Studies* 11, no. 1 (1997): 1–27. More generally, David Engel, *In the Shadow of Auschwitz: The Polish Government-in-Exile and the Jews 1939–1942* (Chapel Hill: University of North Carolina Press, 1993).
6. Deuss to Morse, 15 Feb. 1943, NA, RG 226, entry 16, box 293, folder 29586.
7. Mitteilungsblatt der Gruppe IV E, Jg. 1942, nr. 7, redated 19 June 1943, NA, RG 242, entry 27, box 4, folder 6.
8. Gestapo IV E Account of the Security Conference at Berlin, 15–17 June 1942, attached to Saint, London to Saint, Washington, 9 Dec. 1944, NA, RG 226, entry 210, folder 5–XX 4224.
9. Field Interrogation Report of Guenther Pancke, 6 July 1945, copy in NA, RG 226, entry 109, box 36, folder XX8540-XX8559.
10. Ibid. See also Whitney R. Harris, *Tyranny on Trial: The Trial of the Major German War Criminals at the End of World War II at Nuremberg, Germany, 1945–1946* (Dallas: Southern Methodist University Press, 1954; 1999), 216–19. We are grateful to Kevin C. Ruffner for this reference used in his unpublished paper "The Fog of War: OSS and the Clearing Murders."
11. Circle Report, 31 May 1945, German Countermeasures Against Danish Acts of Resistance, NA, RG 226, entry 210, folders 001-009 and 011. The date suggests that it took Allied cryptographers several months to break the top-level German diplomatic code and read these messages.
12. Ronald Headland, *Messages of Murder: A Study of the Reports of the Einsatzgruppen of the Security Police and the Security Service, 1941–1943* (Rutherford, NJ: Fairleigh Dickinson University Press, 1992), 40–43.
13. The RSHA in Occupied or Neutral Countries, NA, RG 226, entry 171A, box 78, folder 886.
14. They were later used for the American zonal trial of Einsatzgruppen officers. Headland, *Messages of Murder*, 13–14.
15. See, for example, the Preliminary Interrogation Report on Leonhard Halmanseger, 7 Sept. 1945, and attached documents, NA, RG 226, entry 119A, box 53, folder 1563. Also, Saint, London to Saint, Washington, 4 June 1945, War Room Monthly Summary No. 2, NA, RG 226, entry 109, box 26, folder XX7260-XX7289.

16. NA, RG 226, entry 109, box 59, folder XX10820-XX10839.
17. Saint, London to Saint, Washington, 14 Feb. 1946, with final report on SS-Sturmbannführer Harro Andreas Wilhelm Thomsen, 24 Jan. 1946. This report drew on several interrogations of Thomsen in November 1945 and some other sources. NA, RG 226, entry 109, box 59, folder XX10820-XX10839.
18. Ibid.
19. OSS copy of Security Summary, Middle East No. 162 (Published by S.I.M.E., Cairo), 30 Dec. 1943, NA, RG 226, entry 108, folder 453, no. 3 cont.
20. Fourth Interim Report on Horst Kopkow, appendix 3, p. 36, NA, RG 263, Horst Kopkow Name File.
21. NA, RG 263, Horst Kopkow Name File.
22. Fourth Interim Report, p. 19. On Kopkow and the UK, PRO WO 309-248. This information in PRO WO 309/248, comes courtesy of Stephen Tyas.
23. Manuscripts written by Walter Huppenkothen, Oct.–Dec. 1948, attached to 7970 CIC Group to Commanding Officer CIC Group VI, 7 Jan. 1949, in NA, RG 319, IRR, entry 134B, Walter Huppenkothen.
24. NA, RG 263, Horst Kopkow Name File.
25. Volksbund Deutsche Kriegsgräberfürsorge (Beate Kalbhenn) letter of 5 June 2002 to Stephen Tyas.
26. Interim Camp 020 Report on Martin Sandberger, Oct. 1945, NA, RG 226, entry 119A, box 33, folder 870.
27. Raul Hilberg, *Perpetrators, Victims, Bystanders: The Jewish Catastrophe 1933–1945* (New York: Harper Collins, 1992), 97.
28. Raul Hilberg, *The Destruction of the European Jews*, rev. and definitive ed., vol. 3, (New York: Holmes and Meier, 1985), 1105; Frank M. Buscher, *The U.S. War Crimes Trial Program in Germany, 1946–1955* (New York: Greenwood Press, 1989), 166.
29. Henry Weinstein, "New Questions Arise on the Fate of Gestapo Chief," *Los Angeles Times* 26 Feb. 2001; "US May Have Used Gestapo Chief as Cold War Warrior," *Sunday Times of London* 8 Apr. 2001; Charles Fenyvesi and Dal Gilgoff, "Secrets in the Archives," *U.S. News and World Report* 7 May 2001. The Simon Wiesenthal Center asked Congress for a full investigation of the Müller case, according to a press release of 26 Feb. 2001.
30. A longer version of this section on Müller was published by Timothy Naftali, Norman J.W. Goda, Richard Breitman, and Robert Wolfe, "The Mystery of Heinrich Müller: New Materials from the CIA," *Holocaust and Genocide Studies* 15, no. 3 (2001): 453–67. Though the *HGS* article is longer, the version here contains some new evidence.
31. War Room Publication, G.I.S. Priorities for Interrogation, 27 May 1945, and War Room Publication, Tactical Interrogation of Members of the RSHA, 21 May 1945, NA, RG 226, entry 119A, box 22, folder 621.
32. W.R.C. 3 Fortnightly Report for the period ending 18 June 1945, NA, RG 226, entry 119A, box 25, folder 639.
33. Progress Report, X-2 Branch, 1–30 June 1945, attached to Saint, London to Saint, Stockholm, 13 July 1945, NA, RG 226, entry 125A, box 7, folder 76.
34. Copy in Saint, London to Washington, 13 July 1945, NA, RG 226, entry 88, box 645,

folder–Incoming Plain Saint London July.

35. War Room Monthly Summary No 4, 23 July 1945, NA, RG 226, entry 119A, box 24, folder 629.

36. NA, RG 226, entry 119A, box 22, folder 621.

37. Arrest Target List—Revision Note, 1 Nov. 1945, NA, RG 226, entry 122, Tab 6.

38. Saint, London to Saint, Washington, 5 Feb. 1946, with copy of Preliminary CSDIC Interrogation of Malz, 3 Sept. 1945, NA, RG 226, entry 109, box 58, folder 10702-10730.

39. Saint, London to Saint, Washington, 19 Apr. 1946, with copy of British interrogation of Pomme, 12 Nov. 1945. The comment on Müller is on p. 5 of appendix 2. Also, Field Interrogation Report on Horst Kopkow, part 2, p. 1, copy in NA, RG 263, Horst Kopkow Name File.

40. Excerpts from the interrogation of Schellenberg are in memo 201-742896 of 10 Feb. 1965, NA, RG 263, Heinrich Müller Name File, vol. 1. Walter Schellenberg, *The Labyrinth: Memoirs*, trans. Louis Hagen (New York: Harper, 1956), 319–20.

41. For Kaltenbrunner's interrogation, see the excerpts in memo 201-742896 of 10 Feb. 1965, NA, RG 263, Heinrich Müller Name File, vol. 1. On Pannwitz, see [CIA/EUR] to Chief, EE and Chief SR, [A]-44835, 24 Sept. 1959, NA, RG 263, Heinrich Müller Name File, vol. 1.

42. Two consecutive index cards, probably prepared in 1946, are reproduced in Gestapo Müller's IRR File; they give two birth dates, the correct date and 7 June 1896. Card #2 contains the misinformation that Heinrich Müller was being detained at Civilian Internment Enclosure #10, Altenstadt. It is quite possible that a Heinrich Müller was there, but neither of those two whose birth dates were listed. The U.S. Army did not list any further dealings with the Altenstadt Müller. NA, RG 319, IRR, entry 134B, Heinrich Müller.

43. See the note by the Intelligence Bureau, C. C. G. (British Element), Bad Oeynhausen to G-2 (CI), USFET, 23 May 1946, in NA, RG 319, IRR, entry 134B, Heinrich Müller. There is also a reference to this information in "Subject: Müller, Heinrich," 5 May 1961, the same U.S. Army consolidated report that lists Müller as having been in Altenstadt in December 1945. This report was easily dismissed because Gestapo Müller's wife and children were still alive.

44. See the cards photocopied in NA, RG 319, IRR, entry 134B, Heinrich Müller.

45. CIA Directorate of Plans, "The Hunt for 'Gestapo Mueller,'" a counterintelligence brief issued Dec. 1971, [hereafter cited as "Hunt for Gestapo Mueller"] p. 12, NA, RG 263, Heinrich Müller Name File, vol. 2. The origins of this brief are explained below.

46. See Landeskriminalamt Baden-Württemberg, Sonderkommission Zentrale Stelle, Tgb. Nr. SK. Zst. III/I-79/60, 29 July 1960 to Barnett at the U.S. Consulate, NA, RG 319, IRR, entry 134B, Heinrich Müller; Landeskriminalamt Baden-Württemberg Sonderkommission Zentrale Stelle, SK Zst. I/1-79/60 to Zentrale Stelle Ludwigsburg, 27 Feb. 1961, ibid. The U.S. Army helped for ninety days beginning in May 1961 with the surveillance of Müller's father and children, but this surveillance yielded no results.

47. The witnesses, questioned in connection with a West German police investigation in 1961, are quoted in "Hunt for Gestapo Mueller," 16, 18.

48. [CIA/EUR] to Chief, EE and Chief SR, [A]-44835, 24 Sept. 1959, NA, RG 263, Heinrich Müller Name File, vol. 1.

49. See the lengthy German police reports of 1960 and 1961 submitted to U.S. Army

Counterintelligence and contained in NA, RG 319, IRR, entry 134B, Heinrich Müller. Fainter copies of these reports were made available by the Army to the CIA in 1970 and are included in the CIA's Müller file: NA, RG 263, Heinrich Müller Name File. See also, "Hunt for Gestapo Mueller," 33.

50. Memo [A]-744, 10 May 1961, NA, RG 263, Heinrich Müller Name File, vol. 2. The defector's name is redacted, but Tim Naftali has identified him as Goleniewski.

51. To: Chief, EE, Chief SR A [excised] [excised/excised]/Operations Further [excised] Reports on Rote Kapelle Personalities, 24 Sept. 1959, NA, RG 263, Heinrich Müller Name File, vol. 1. The informant is revealed by name as Pannwitz in "Hunt for Gestapo Mueller," 14–16.

52. "Gestapo-Müller lebt in Albanien," *Stern*, January 1964; "Die Spur führt nach Südamerika," *Stern*, 16 Aug. 1964. The latter article in full is in NA, RG 263, Heinrich Müller Name File, vol. 1.

53. On the possibility of disinformation, see [CIA/EUR] dispatch [A]-13564 CS, 31 Jan. 1964, ibid.

54. Ibid.

55. [CIA/EUR] to Chief, EE, [A]-63831, 5 Feb. 1964, ibid.

56. Staff memorandum, 9 Dec. 1970, in ibid. This is a debriefing of a defector with inside knowledge of Czech intelligence and KGB active measures. The 1971 "Hunt for 'Gestapo Mueller,'" p. 38, further identifies this source as an apparently reliable Czechoslovak defector. The name of this defector is redacted. However, the information that this defector provided and the timing of this defection strongly suggest that this source was Ladislas Bittman.

57. Memo [A]-19267, 9 Dec. 1970, in ibid.

58. The 9 Dec. 1971 memo is in NA, RG 263, Heinrich Müller Name File, vol. 2.

59. Ibid.

60. Rauff was head of Sipo and SD for northwestern Italy.

61. On these maneuvers, see Fourth Detailed Interrogation Report on Klaus Huegel, 10 June 1945, NA, RG 226, entry 174, box 39, folder 307. On Schuster and Bicchierai, see Bradley F. Smith and Elena Agarossi, *Operation Sunrise: The Secret Surrender* (New York: Basic Books, 1979), 57–59.

62. Interrogation Report on SS-Standartenführer Rauff Walther. CSDIC/SC/15AG/SD 11, 29 May 1945, NA, RG 263, Walter Rauff Name File.

63. Ibid. We must note that Army Intelligence (IRR) destroyed its file on Rauff. Christopher Simpson had obtained a partial copy of it through a FOIA request and graciously made it available to us.

64. Rauff's SS file reflects the fact that he received the coveted "Old Fighter's" award, indicating his involvement with the Nazis prior to Hitler's appointment as chancellor in January 1933. See Rauff SS Officer File, NA–BDC, RG 242, A-3343, SSO, roll 010B.

65. Heydrich had also been forced to leave the German Navy for dishonorable actions.

66. British intelligence and OSS captured some of the documents about the use of gas vans, including August Becker's May 1942 letter to Rauff giving a litany of complaints about breakdowns and technical problems, but suggesting adaptations. NA, RG 226, entry 119A, box 25, folder 639.

67. Christopher R. Browning, *Fateful Months: Essays on the Emergence of the Final Solution* (New

York: Holmes and Meier, 1985), 60–65.

68. Rauff's flight is mentioned in a British analysis of decoded German messages about Einsatzkommandos. At the time (Nov. 1942) British intelligence was still grappling to figure out what these units did. See ZIP/IS/1 23 Nov. 1942, copy in NA, RG 226, entry 119A, box 25, folder 637. The source for Rauff's discussion with Rommel is a postwar source, cited immediately below. Rauff could have arranged for the conversion of vehicles into gas vans, as he had done in Europe.

69. Memorandum Dr. Voss and his friends, 9 Feb. 1954, Rauff, NA, RG 263, Walter Rauff Name File. This information may originate with the State Department. The document paraphrases "The Ambassador," but does not supply the source of the ambassador's information. During the war, SS-Standartenführer Dr. Wilhelm Voss was director of the armaments industrial complex at Skoda, in the Reich Protectorate [today the Czech Republic]. The CIA identified Voss as "head of the German Advisory Group in Egypt," actively engaged in promoting German investment in aircraft manufacturing in Egypt. According to a separate CIA document, Voss was closely associated with Dr. Wilhelm Beissner, a fellow SS officer with alleged links to the *Institut für Gegenwartsforschung* under Friedrich Wilhelm Heinz. Beissner was allegedly responsible for introducing Otto Skorzeny to influential persons in Egypt in the early 1950s. NA–BDC, RG 242 A-3343, SSO, roll 212B; Activities of Certain German Experts in Egypt, 16 Feb. 1954, and untitled note card, 15 June 1953, NA, RG 263, Friedrich Beissner Name File.

70. Daniel Carpi, *Between Mussolini and Hitler: The Jews and the Italian Authorities in France and Tunisia* (Hanover, NH: University Press of New England, 1994), 233–37.

71. Karl Wolff recommended Rauff for the German Cross (in silver) in June 1944. Wolff was only one of several senior officers who desired to see Rauff decorated. The German ambassador in Rome, Rudolf Rahn, and General von Arnim also voiced approval for the award. The award apparently was not bestowed. In April 1944, Rauff did receive the War Service Cross First Class (with swords), a significant non-combat medal. Rauff SS Officer File, NA–BDC, RG 242, A-3343, SSO, roll 010B.

72. In June 1999 an Italian tribunal found Saevecke guilty of ordering the execution of fifteen Italian partisans in 1944 and sentenced him to life imprisonment.

73. English translation of Exhibit "H" (sworn statement of Hermann Julius Walter Rauff Bauermeister, Santiago, Chile, 5 Dec. 1962, *SS Col. Walter Rauff: The Church Connection 1943–1947*, (Los Angeles: Simon Wiesenthal Center, May 1984). Rauff claimed that his family left the Soviet zone of Germany with the help of the Catholic Church.

74. Hyazinth von Strachwitz, a former Wehrmacht general who served as a senior advisor in Damascus, estimated that there were fewer than fifty Germans employed in Syria during the late 1940s, dropping to about thirty by early 1954. As late as the summer of 1950, agents of the Syrian government were actively attempting to recruit former German Army and Waffen-SS officers in Germany. Both Otto Skorzeny and his adjutant, Karl Radl, met with a Syrian agent in Munich in December 1949 to discuss the possibility of working in Syria. Apparently neither of these officers accepted an offer to work for the Syrians. See NA, RG 319, IRR, entry 134B, Rudolf Dirnagel.

75. "Background Information on German Military Experts in Syria," 23 February [19]54, NA,

RG 263, Walter Rauff Name File.

76. Gehlen Organization Report, dated 2 Nov. 1949, on German military experts in Syria (Questions from "20"), ibid.

77. Excerpt of a report dated 2 Sept. 1949, ibid.

78. Official Dispatch. Chief, Foreign Division T, dated 13 June 1950, NA, RG 263, Walter Rauff Name File.

79. Rauff had served in South America and Spain during 1925–1926. See Rauff SS Officer File, NA–BDC, RG 242, A-3343, SSO, roll 010B.

80. Bauermeister was Rauff's mother's maiden name. "Herman Julius Walter Rauff Bauermeister" was the name Rauff used when he appeared in a Chilean court on 5 December 1962 to answer charges in his extradition hearing. Rauff possibly obtained identity documents in the name of Bauermeister as early as 1947 through his contacts in the Catholic Church.

81. In the aftermath of the 1973 coup d'état that brought Pinochet to power, DINA was formed. From its inception, the organization functioned as a secret police and was engaged in the repression of dissidence within Chile and revenge on its enemies abroad. DINA was responsible for countless human rights violations including illegal arrests, executions, torture, and forced disappearances of opponents of Pinochet's regime. Colonel Manuel Contreas was the director of DINA. DINA was dissolved in 1977.

82. Report, dated Oct. [19]74, NA, RG 263, Walter Rauff Name File.

83. More than three thousand people died or disappeared (and are presumed dead) in the political violence that marked Pinochet's seventeen-year rule.

84. Report to the chief of CIA Latin American Division, dated 13 Apr. 1976, NA, RG 263, Walter Rauff Name File.

85. Memorandum from Non-Disclosure Litigation Office DO/IMS to Office of General Counsel (CIA), dated 13 Sept. 1983, ibid.

86. Simon Wiesenthal claims that Allende might have worked to hand Rauff over, had he not been deposed and murdered in September 1973; see Wiesenthal, *Justice not Vengeance*, trans. Ewald Osers (New York: Grove Weidenfeld, 1989), 63.

87. Wiesenthal to Reagan, 12 Apr. 1983, State Department, Central Foreign Policy Archives, Rauff Materials, IP 10. For the Reagan speech, see *Public Papers of the Presidents of the United States, Ronald Reagan, Book 1: January 1–July 1, 1983*, (Washington, DC: United States Government Printing Office, 1984), 523–25.

88. Wiesenthal, *Justice not Vengeance*, 63.

89. Memo by Donald Koblitz, Attorney Adviser, 22 Dec. 1983. "Memorandum of Conversation with Hannover Prosecutor and FRG Justice Ministry Officials." NA, RG 59, Central Foreign Policy Files, Western Hemisphere Posts, Rauff Materials, GX-24A. The actual discussions took place on 1 Dec. 1983.

90. For Klarsfeld in Santiago, see Theberge to Secretary of State, No. 0186, 2 Feb. 1984; Theberge to Secretary of State, no. 0972, 9 Feb. 1984; Theberge to Secretary of State, no. 1189, 21 Feb. 1984, all in NA, RG 59, Central Foreign Policy Files, Western Hemisphere Posts, Rauff Materials, U.S. Embassy B.

91. Theberge to Secretary of State, no. 3679, 1 June 1983 and no. 1189, 21 Feb. 1984, NA, RG 59, Western Hemisphere Posts, Rauff Materials, IP-15. For relations between the U.S.

and Chile in these years, see Paul E. Sigmund, *The United States and Democracy in Chile* (Baltimore: Johns Hopkins University Press, 1993); and David R. Mares and Francisco Rojas Aravena, *The United States and Chile: Coming in From the Cold* (New York: Routledge, 2001).

92. Langhorne A. Motley to Lawrence Eagleburger, undated, NA, RG 59, Central Foreign Policy files, Rauff Materials.

93. Handwritten note to Ambassador Theberge, 6 Feb. 1984, NA, RG 59, Central Foreign Policy Files, Western Hemisphere Posts, Rauff Materials, GX-25.

94. Michael P. Scharf, *Balkan Justice: The Story behind the First International War Crimes Trial since Nuremberg* (Durham, NC: Carolina Academic Press, 1997).

95. Secretary of State to U.S. Embassies in Bonn, Santiago, Tel Aviv, 17 Feb. 1984, NA, RG 59, Central Foreign Policy Files, Western Hemisphere Posts, Rauff Materials, GX-16.

96. Secretary of State to all American Republics Diplomatic Posts, no. 9539, 17 Feb. 1984, NA, RG 263, Records Released under the Nazi and Japanese War Crimes Disclosure Acts, CIA Subject File, folder–Nazis in South America, vol. 2. Wiesenthal claims credit for influencing Chancellor Helmut Kohl to make another request to the Chilean government; see Wiesenthal, *Justice not Vengeance*, 63–64.

97. West Germany had failed to claim jurisdiction in the case of Klaus Barbie, and Kohl had given a speech in Israel's Knesset that was heavily criticized by the West German left. Dennis L. Bark and David R. Gress, *A History of West Germany*, vol. 2, *Democracy and its Discontents 1963–1990* (Cambridge, MA: Blackwell, 1993), 423–24.

98. This information was obtained by the U.S. Embassy in Santiago from Holtzheimer himself. See Secretary of State to U.S. Embassy Bonn, no. 066327, 7 Mar. 1984, NA, RG 59, Central Foreign Policy Files, Rauff Materials, IP-52.

99. For a copy of the West German note, see DB Santiago, Nr. 48/84 "Nota Verbal" 1 Mar. 1984, NA, RG 59, Central Foreign Policy Files, Western Hemisphere Posts, Rauff Materials. For the text of the Chilean reply, see Chilean Foreign Ministry Note, no. 02251, 8 Mar. 1984, NA, RG 59, GX-8A. Secretary of State to U.S. Embassy, Ottawa, no. 075093, 14 Mar. 1984, NA, RG 59, Central Foreign Policy Files, Rauff Materials, IP-63.

100. See also Georg M. Hafner and Esther Schapira, *Die Akte Alois Brunner*, (Frankfurt, 2000).

101. http://www.diplomatiquejudiciare.com.

102. Munich to Director, 25 Apr. 1961, NA, RG 263, Alois Brunner Name File; Chief Munich Operations Group to COS Germany, 10 May 1961, NA, RG 263, Alois Brunner Name File.

103. [Excised] to Director, 25 Sept. 1961, NA, RG 263, Alois Brunner Name File. CIA information was incomplete on this attack, and initial reports suggested that Brunner had been killed. Other sources, however, suggested that the Syrians had moved him to a number of different hospitals and planned to give him a new identity.

104. Director to [excised], 13 Mar. 1958, NA, RG 263, Franz Rademacher Name File; [excised] to [excised], 20 Apr. 1961, NA, RG 263, Franz Rademacher Name File.

105. U.S. Embassy Damascus (Eagleton) to Secretary of State, No. 00319, 16 Jan. 1985, NA, RG 59, N-111.

106. Chief Munich to Chief EE, 21 May 1962, NA, RG 263, Franz Rademacher Name File.

107. CIA Summary of 10 Mar. 1965, ibid.
108. Fact sheet from B'nai B'rith enclosed in Senator Arlen Specter to George Shultz, 3 July 1985, NA, RG 59, CC-97.
109. U.S. Embassy Damascus (Eagleton) to Secretary of State, No. 00319, NA, RG 59, N-111.
110. State Department (Whitehead) to U.S. Embassy Vienna, No. 230898, 27 July 1985, NA, RG 59, N-153.
111. Shultz to U.S. Embassies Bonn, Vienna, Paris, No. 335422, 10 Nov. 1985, NA, RG 59, N-156.
112. Eagleton to U.S. Embassy Bonn, No. 00679, 31 Jan. 1986, NA, RG 59, N-159. See also U.S. Embassy Bonn (Burt) to U.S. Embassy Damascus, 03327, 30 Jan. 1986, NA, RG 59, N-158.
113. Eagleton to Secretary of State, No. 00557, 28 Jan. 1988, NA, RG 59, N-185.
114. U.S. Embassy Damascus (Eagleton) to Secretary of State, No. 00557, 28 Jan. 1988, ibid.
115. Eagleton to Secretary of State, No. 07006, 9 Dec. 1987, NA, RG 59, N-184.
116. Ibid.
117. U.S. Embassy Damascus (Craig) to Secretary of State, No. 04168, 10 July 1990, NA, RG 59, N-209.
118. Frederick Vreeland, Department of State, Asian Affairs, to Senator Kennedy, 1 May 1991, NA, RG 59, GT-14; Lawrence Eagleburger to U.S. Embassy Damascus, NA, RG 59, GT-7. According to West German sources, in 1990 Brunner was living in the mountain resort village of Slenfe. U.S. Embassy Damascus (Craig) to Secretary of State, No. 04168, 10 July 1990, NA, RG 59, N-209.
119. NSA intercept paraphrases, Shipment 1, Dec. 1991, 3/OO/49603-91; Shipment 2, Jan. 1992, 2/OO/1488-92. Klarsfeld was in Syria owing to a sighting of Brunner being taken to a hospital in October 1991. Secretary of State (Ross) to U.S. Embassy Damascus, Dec. 1991, NA, RG 59, GT-2.

7

Banking on Hitler: Chase National Bank and the Rückwanderer Mark Scheme, 1936-1941

Norman J. W. Goda

WITH CHASE NATIONAL BANK ASSISTANCE, the Nazi government earned dollars in the United States through the sale of special German marks—known as Rückwanderer ("returnee") marks—to U.S. residents of German descent.[1] The currency scheme began in the late 1930s and lasted until the June 1941 executive order freezing German assets. Newly declassified FBI records offer a far more detailed picture of how and why the Nazi regime gave Germans abroad generous terms to move back to Germany and how they financed these subsidies through seized Jewish assets.

The Development of the Rückwanderer Mark Scheme

After Hitler came to power and began to re-arm, Germany continued to import large quantities of American goods. In 1939 alone, for example, Germany imported 197 million Reichsmarks worth of American foodstuffs, raw materials, and finished goods (including lead, copper, aluminum, and oil) while exporting RM 125 million worth of goods to the United States. It needed dollars to finance its trade deficit.[2] The Reich Ministry of Economics (RWM) under Hjalmar Schacht experimented with several ways to acquire dollars through its subsidiary office, the Reich Office for Foreign Exchange Control, created in December 1933 and led by Dr. Hans Hartenstein.[3] A sure method of raising dollars lay in selling marks to Germans who wished to return to Germany temporarily or permanently, or to Germans living abroad who simply wished to purchase goods there.

The problem lay in fair compensation in marks for Germans who wished to exchange dollars. On March 16, 1935, the Reich Office for Foreign Exchange Control ordered Germans returning to the Reich to sell their liquid assets to the German National Bank (Reichsbank) within ten days at the current rate of exchange.[4] But the dollar had depreciated precipitously. Whereas Germans who had relocated to the United States in the 1920s could purchase U.S. currency at about RM 4.10 to the dollar, upon their return in 1935 they were able to receive only RM 2.48 per dollar.

To compensate, the Reichsbank allowed returnees to Germany to exchange 50 percent of their dollars at a rate of RM 4.10 per dollar.[5] The Reichsbank paid this favorable rate from blocked accounts once owned by refugees who had fled Germany, most of whom were Jews. Emigrating Jews lost the better part of their remaining assets through a 25 percent flight tax or through the freezing of their liquid wealth in blocked accounts over which they would no longer have control.[6] Just as the German government set the exchange rate at which it would trade marks for dollars, it purchased these blocked marks at the low rate of two to three cents per mark before trading them for dollars at set exchange rates. "The German government," the FBI would note later, "thereby netted a profit in dollars of nearly 90 percent."[7]

News of the favorable exchange rate caught the attention of entrepreneurs involved in foreign exchange markets, particularly Indiana native and Wabash college graduate Roy Frazier Potts, once a U.S. consular official in Rio de Janeiro and later an employee of the National City Bank of New York; and Hans Ziegra, a native German and Nazi Party member, and a close acquaintance of Potts also living in Rio.[8] The two concocted a plan ostensibly matching Jews who wished to leave Germany but could not leave with their assets with Germans who wished to return and could use the same assets, exchanging the property between the two. Ziegra and Potts would charge a commission for their service. Nothing came of this idea until May 1936, and Potts blamed its ultimate failure on the 25 percent tax that Jews had to pay on their capital before leaving.[9]

A month earlier, Ziegra and Potts had founded their own company, the New York Overseas Corporation, specifically for the purpose of exchanging German-Jewish and German-American property. Ziegra served as president and Potts as executive vice president.[10] A relatively early Nazi Party member who had some clout with German government agencies,[11] Ziegra procured a temporary special exchange permit that allowed New York Overseas to transfer up to $400,000 at a RM 2.48 rate and up to $400,000 at a RM 4.10 rate for returning German immigrants. The Reichsbank could thus build a balance of $800,000 while New York Overseas could profit from arbitrage in blocked marks.

The experiment was successful. New York Overseas handled 312 returnee applications.[12] The *New York World Telegram* even carried the story in June 1936 "American and Nazi Cut Red Tape on Marks for Homesick Germans," while the contract was in force.[13]

In July 1936, a new arrangement regularized the Rückwanderer mark trade. Returning immigrants could change 100 percent of their devalued U.S. currency into so-called Rückwanderer marks at the rate of RM 4.018 per dollar.[14] To increase the flow of foreign exchange, three banking institutions in the United States that were well connected in Berlin formed a consortium and received a special permit from the Reich Office for Foreign Exchange Control to facilitate the exchange. The three banks were: the New York Overseas Corporation, which had negotiated the original permit and now hoped to amass a fortune in commissions; Robert C. Mayer & Co., a partnership in New York handling German transactions in the United States, which had forwarded Rückwanderer applications to New York Overseas during the original permit but now wanted full commissions for itself; and the J. Henry Schroder Banking Corporation, a British bank involved in international trade with a chartered office in New York. Ziegra had discussed his original exchange plans with this bank and had used it for deposits during the first permit.[15]

The German government authorities expected that a new 5 percent commission directly paid by the German government would encourage the three permit holders to find German Rückwanderers in the United States, where Berlin had few contacts. Potts' brother Joseph, who acted as Treasurer for New York Overseas, testified accurately in 1941 that the Germans were more interested in foreign exchange than they were in the returnees themselves. The Reich Office for Foreign Exchange Control would pay only a 2 percent commission for Rückwanderers with less than $2,500 to convert. But the licensed financial houses did not complain at first—they saw a chance to make a significant profit, particularly with German power on the rise and German unemployment on the wane.[16]

The license holders would hand over roughly 3 percent of their 5 percent commission to wholesalers who would help locate German-Americans willing to emigrate. These wholesalers tended to be import-export companies or brokerage houses with ties to the German-American community. The three permit holders could do their own wholesaling if they wanted, but wholesalers such as Hans Utsch & Co., Robert Hautz & Co., Amerop Travel Service, the Hamburg Amerika Line, and even the American Express Company did most of the wholesale business themselves. Below the wholesalers were retailers, companies with day-to-day contacts in the German-American community, such as local travel bureaus.[17]

A German resident or citizen in the United States responding to an advertisement and wishing to repatriate could apply to the Reich Office for Foreign Exchange Control through a local retailer. The prospective immigrant had to obtain from the German consulate (for a $4 fee) a declaration of suitability (*Unbedenklichkeits-Erklärung*) after completing a questionnaire declaring his or her place of birth, occupation, number of children, and previous service to Germany, such as army service in World War I. The prospective immigrant would also declare his or her assets and debts and the amount of liquid assets to be converted.[18] The retailer would forward the entire application to the wholesaler, who would make sure the paperwork was in order. The application was then forwarded to one of the three permit holders, which would then forward a copy of the application to its office in Berlin. From there it went to the Reich Office for Foreign Exchange Control along with a request that the applicant's liquid assets be converted at the preferential rate.

Once permission was granted, the applicant would give the retailer the dollars that he or she wished to change. The money would then be forwarded to the wholesaler, and then to one of the permit holders, where it was deposited in a New York account of the German Gold Discount Bank. The Gold Discount Bank was a subsidiary and clearinghouse of the Reichsbank, which also liquidated the assets of Jewish firms in Germany whose owners had fled the country.[19] In the United States, the Gold Discount Bank's largest accounts were at the J. Henry Schroder Bank, the Bank of Manhattan, and Chase National.[20] The Reichsbank could then use the dollars in these accounts for German dollar purchases.

Chase Elbows In

How Chase National's New York Headquarters learned of the program is a mystery, but it came to the attention of the Foreign Department in August 1936, shortly after the permit was issued to New York Overseas and the others. Joseph C. Rovensky, the vice president of the Chase's Foreign Department in New York, immediately cabled Chase's representative in Berlin, Ernest H. Kuhlman, "to find out whether Chase Bank could not also participate in this business." Kuhlman arranged a meeting with Hans Hartenstein, but he did not get far, at first. "Mr. Kuhlman," Hartenstein asked, "why does the big Chase bank want to be in this particular line of business? This is small business. Why do you want to be in it?"[21]

Hans Ziegra, who along with Potts had created the entire Rückwanderer business network in the United States, had no intention of allowing Chase to move in. Ziegra told Hartenstein that Chase National had no German expertise (despite their office in Berlin) and that the inclusion of Chase would ultimately harm the interests of the Reich.[22]

On August 25, 1936, Rovensky cabled Kuhlman from New York and directed: "Be emphatic. Insist [on the] same privilege as Schroder and the other two who guarantee payment of 4.018 marks." At the same time, Chase tried to influence German banking officials directly. The breakthrough did not take long. Kuhlman's telegram of August 26 contained a single, celebratory line: "CHASE ADDED TO PRIVILEGED THREE." In an explanatory letter to his superiors of September 3, 1936, Kuhlman explained:

> The only reason why we were added to the inner circle is because we (or rather you) knew too much and Hartenstein, who only handles financial matters, knew enough about our leading position in commercial matters not to take a chance of having us go to the top . . .[23]

The "privileged three" were not happy that an elephant had stepped into their garden. Potts was furious that Chase had even learned about the Rückwanderer arrangement, and in early September he urged Ziegra to make forceful protests to Hartenstein about Chase's addition to the consortium.[24]

In August 1936, New York Overseas, which could not accept or hold deposits itself, was negotiating with another major bank, Chemical Bank and Trust, to handle the domestic and overseas banking procedures for its Rückwanderer business.   Officers in Chemical's Foreign Department were therefore very interested in the Rückwanderer mark program and seem to have been willing to take a commission of less than 0.5 percent for the handling of what they expected would be a ballooning business. "The general opinion prevails," said E. O. Detlefsen of the Foreign Department at Chemical, "that if [the rate of exchange] should be increased to about [RM] 4.30 to the dollar, the volume in all probability could be doubled."[25] The expectation that the Gold Discount Bank would set up and maintain a very large account with Chemical was part of the thinking in New York Oversees, too.

In mid-August 1936, Chemical's Foreign Department officers in New York enlisted Ziegra to approach officers of the Gold Discount Bank to open an account with them in New York. But Chemical's representative in Berlin, Hermann A. Kollmar, who was involved in numerous schemes to attract Nazi business, commented to Detlefsen that he was "frankly, not greatly impressed by the gentleman [Ziegra]." On August 20, 1936, he told his superiors in New York that Chemical should use its own prestige and Kollmar's own connections to secure the Gold Discount Bank account, and not Ziegra.[26] Chemical's officers in New York simply wanted a deal with the Germans before it was too late.

But by this time Chase National had already bullied its way into the Rückwanderer business. Chemical Bank and Trust failed to open the coveted Gold Discount Bank account, and New York Overseas watched a potentially massive part of its business slide to Chase National. Money designated for the Gold Discount Bank in the New York Overseas account at Chemical went to the Gold Discount Bank account at the Bank of Manhattan instead, which became the conduit for Rückwanderer mark deposits for New York Overseas, Robert C. Mayer, and, after it joined the consortium, the Deutsche Handels- und Wirtschaftsdienst.

Chemical Bank and Trust was left with a tiny 0.25 percent commission paid by New York Overseas for its trouble in transferring Rückwanderer dollars from its own account to the Gold Discount Bank's account at Bank of Manhattan. By the time the operation shut down nearly five years later, Chemical held a mere $150,000 in Rückwanderer money.[27] Others got much more.

In September 1936, Potts and Ziegra of New York Overseas imagined ways to increase business. Potts wrote Ziegra on September 9 to inform his German interlocutors as follows:

> In the field of publicity, we will perform the most valuable services for the Reich . . . We have reached German and English language newspapers and magazines all over the country . . . For our publicity we have engaged Publicity Associates, Inc., probably the best publicity firm in the world . . . They are the ones who handled

the worldwide publicity (really propaganda) for Haile Selassie and Ethiopia for many months . . . Everyone knows how successful the Ethiopian publicity was. Ethiopia had, and still has, the sympathy of practically the entire world.

It would also have another very important and desirable consequence. It would be marvelous propaganda for the Reich and would offset the prejudiced, Jewish-inspired anti-German propaganda of which you saw some first-class examples when you were here. Germany badly needs this sort of assistance here. There is evidently no organized German effort to combat the almost universal anti-German propaganda. This would be the best kind of pro-German propaganda because it would be indirect, disguised, and would not proceed from an official source. The American public reacts very unfavorably to the kind of direct government propaganda that is used in Europe. The result of our constant hammering would be not only good for the Rueckwanderer business; it would create a friendly feeling toward the Third Reich, with incalculable benefits in international trade and politics.[28]

But Potts' predictions were overblown. Despite the high hopes, money trickled in slowly. Part of the reason was that few Germans wished to return to a continent menaced by darkening clouds of war. Cutthroat competition within the consortium in 1936 did not help, particularly after August 1936, when a fifth member, Deutsche Handels- und Wirtschaftsdienst International Commerce Service, was added to the circle of licensed institutions. This was a German-owned brokerage company located in the same building as the German General Consulate in New York.[29] New York Overseas tried to outbid its competitors with an exchange rate of RM 4.05 instead of RM 4.018. Chase tried rate cutting, too, which brought a rebuke from the Reich Office for Foreign Exchange Control.[30]

The remedy for slow business, insofar as the five licensed consortium members were concerned, was for the RWM to offer higher conversion rates to prospective returnees and higher commissions to the American banks. On May 1, 1937, Potts wrote to Ziegra in Berlin:

It will be a pity if the [Ministry] does not make some change in the regulations which will enable them to reap the benefit of all the Rueckwanderer money that would come into Germany if more favorable terms were offered to the public and to the agents . . . Could you not take this opportunity to call on Marwede, Hartenstein and perhaps even Dr. Schacht to urge them in Germany's own interest to give this matter their most serious attention and take some immediate action?

Potts also tried to impress on the Germans the need to cut the other institutions out, leaving New York Overseas as the sole handler of the Rückwanderer business.[31]

German financial officials were willing, however reluctantly, to experiment with higher exchange and commission rates. In September 1937, the conversion rate was raised to a full RM 4.10 per dollar for returnees, and the commission rate was raised from 5 percent to 7 percent on all amounts transferred, not just those of $2,500 or more. It was understood that 4 to 5 percent of the commission would go to the wholesalers and retailers. "I anticipate," wrote Dr. Daniel of the Reich Office for Foreign Exchange Control, "that this increase will bring about greater activity in the Rueckwanderer business and that in the future it will be possible to count on considerably greater transfers of Devisen [foreign exchange]."[32]

Though a considerable number of Germans in the United States were willing to gamble with their savings, most remained less willing, prompting consternation in the RWM. As J. Henry Schroeder's representative in Berlin reported to his home office in early February 1938, "As far as the North American Rueckwanderer business is concerned, the RWM is considering a radical change if the increase in volume which the RWM had expected after they had raised the commission, has not materialized."[33]

Disappointed in the licensed firms, whose increased commission was supposed to induce them and their subagents to find more business, the RWM "even thought of throwing the business wide open so that every American bank or firm could bring in Rueckwanderer."[34] Indeed, there were American suitors. By May 1938, a short time after the German expansion into Austria, more than forty U.S. companies, including American Express, had applied to the German government to take part in the Rückwanderer business.[35] By July 1938, the RWM seriously considered raising the conversion rate for Rückwanderer marks from RM 4.10 to RM 4.20. Though the new rate never went into effect, U.S. banking representatives in Berlin understood that Nazi Germany urgently needed dollars. At Chase National in New York, Rovensky was informed as follows from his representatives in Berlin:

> Germany is making definite efforts to interest these people [Germans living abroad] in returning by making a special conversion rate for dollars . . . In this way Germany pays off its foreign obligations at cheap rates and has, at the same time a fair proportion of dollars left over from the transaction. . . .
>
> The German authorities allow us a commission of 7 percent (in dollars) for each "Rueckwanderer" so that, even though a large part [4 percent] goes to agents and sub-agents who locate the Rueckwanderer originally, such transactions are definitely profitable.[36]

On November 9, 1938, a wave of orchestrated violence terrorized Jews across Germany. Synagogues were burned, Jewish shops were destroyed, and Jews were beaten and arrested all over Germany and its new Austrian and Sudeten areas in an event that became known as the "Night of Broken Glass" (*Reichskristallnacht*). High Nazi officials decided several days later to impose a RM 1 billion penalty upon German Jews to repair the damage that they themselves suffered. The majority of the American public was appalled at the anti-Jewish pogrom, and President Franklin Roosevelt recalled the U.S. ambassador to Germany.

While German Jews tried to escape a new level of state-sponsored terror (120,000 Jews would flee Germany virtually penniless from November 1938 to September 1939),[37] German financial officials and American banks dickered over the commission from the sale of marks from the swelling accounts of appropriated Jewish assets. On November 30, 1938, the German Economics Ministry hosted a meeting of the five permit holders. While the representatives from Chase, Schroder, and the others suggested the Germans raise the exchange rate to RM 5 per dollar, irritated RWM representatives suggested lowering the five permit holders' commission from 7 percent to 4 percent. The Germans also insisted on assurances that no one involved in the Rückwanderer business on any level be Jewish.[38]

Following the meeting, Chase appealed to the German Economics Ministry not to reduce the 7 percent rate. As matters then stood, Chase paid its subcontractors up to 4 percent out of the 7 percent, out of which these agencies placed advertisements to attract Rückwanderers in the first place. "The resulting difference," argued Chase, "in no wise appears excessive in consideration of the specially trained personnel . . . for the carrying out of the Rueckwanderer business. Doubtless a reduction of the commission would have a detrimental effect upon the present working procedure . . . which naturally is not in harmony with the interests of Germany."[39] Chase's argument worked. The settled rate in 1939 was RM 4.10 to the dollar with the commission remaining at 7 percent.

At the same time, the American banks worked to keep an especially low profile for their business with Germany following the November 9 pogrom. After the Germans raised the idea of having the Reich Office for Foreign Exchange open an office in New York to speed the approval and conversion process for prospective returnees, Henry Drath, Chase's assistant representative in Berlin, shot the idea down:

> [Because of] the present strong anti-German attitude [in the United States] . . . a minimum of publicity [must] be given to the Rueckwanderer business . . . The opening of a Devisenstelle branch in New York [would] cause a storm of indignation, the extent of which is hardly to be overlooked. In such a case, the Rueckwanderer business would undoubtedly be shown up in detail for all sides with the result that Germany would suffer only disadvantages.[40]

In fact, Dr. Marwede, RWM specialist in charge of transfer of immigrant assets, had already rejected the idea of such representation in New York, though not from any consideration of what the American public would think. Public representation in New York by the Reich Office for Foreign Exchange would make it necessary, Marwede told Drath privately, to open up the Rückwanderer business to the many U.S. firms that wanted to receive the commissions. As matters stood now, the German government paid commission on only 40 percent of the dollars changed by returning Germans because 60 percent of those returning changed their money on their own.[41]

Utterly unbothered by recent events in Germany, Chase Foreign Department Second Vice President Alfred Barth hosted a meeting of the consortium on February 15, 1939, in New York to discuss ways to cut into the imagined 60 percent mentioned by Marwede. At Barth's urging, all members of the consortium agreed that German consulates throughout the United States should refer prospective Rückwanderers to *them* for currency conversion, rather than allowing them to convert their dollars on their own. Chase National quickly informed the German government of this bold resolution.[42]

When war broke out between Germany and the forces of Poland, Great Britain, and France, J. Henry Schroder Bank, which had been incorporated in Great Britain, decided to drop out of the Rückwanderer mark business, leaving four permit holders.[43] The business itself also dipped since few individuals—rates of exchange and Nazi theories of *völkisch* struggle notwithstanding—wanted to return to a country at war. But after the smashing German victory in France in June 1940, German-American interest rose to a level never before seen. Of the nearly $9 million of foreign exchange built up for the Germans by Chase alone between September 1936 and June 1941 ($503,031 of it commissions), over $3.5 million of the total—well over 30 percent—came in the six months between December 1940 and June 1941.[44] New York Overseas and the Deutsche Handels- und Wirtschaftsdienst made over 50 percent of their Rückwanderer mark sales after June 1940.[45] Numerous Germans in the United States, in other words, believed that the war was practically won and a new order in Europe would ensue.[46] Assistant Attorney General Wendell Berge pointed out, "The Rückwanderer program [from 1940 to 1941] was the German government's principal source of foreign exchange in the United States."[47] The deposit figures for the Gold Discount Bank account at Chase National Bank along with the percentage of total foreign exchange represented by these deposits are seen in figure 1. The deposits and commissions for each of the five permit holders for the entire period 1936-1941 are shown in figure 2. If the executive order of June 14, 1941, freezing German assets in the United States had not terminated this program, the totals would have been higher.[48]

How much did Nazi Germany benefit from the Rückwanderer mark scheme? Twenty-one million dollars (equal to over RM 52 million) was not a huge amount. Germany gained more foreign exchange through its conquests and seizures in Poland, France, and so on. Yet the sum remained significant, especially in light of the German effort to repurchase dollar bonds and buy German branch plants of American companies.[49] Even in 1943 the Gold Discount Bank could muster but RM 1.95 million worth of Swiss francs.[50] In other words, the German war economy continued to suffer from critical shortages of foreign exchange. Having found $21 million in *dollars* helped Germany more than the absolute value of the money.

FIGURE 1. Rückwanderer business at Chase National Bank, November 1940 to June 14, 1941

Month	Total deposits (US$)	Deposits from Rückwanderer dollars (US$)	Percentage of Rückwanderer deposits to total deposits
Nov. 1940	7,834,800	270,100	3.45
Dec. 1940	1,191,300	155,800	13.08
Jan. 1941	724,200	330,100	45.58
Feb. 1941	1,319,800	646,600	48.99
Mar. 1941	1,195,900	860,700	71.97
Apr. 1941	1,042,400	677,600	65.00
May 1941	1,137,100	766,700	67.43
Jun. 1-Jun. 14, 1941	238,400	170,200	71.39

Source: Report by H. J. Bruninga, 20 May 1942, NA, RG 65, 65-7267-78-1665, box 96, 124.

FIGURE 2. Deposits and commissions of Rückwanderer scheme permit holders

Permit Holder	Number of Applications	Dollars deposited to Golddiskontbank (US$)	Commissions (US$)
Chase National	4588	8,993,181.84	503,031.00
J. Henry Schroder	857	2,788,772.00	113,900.00
Robert C. Mayer	2055	4,448,160.00	307,389.00
Dt. Handels-und W.	1800	3,600,000.00	232,980.00
NY Overseas	1182[a]	2,677,933.90	103,559.00
Total	**10,482**	**22,508,047.74**	**1,260,859.00**

Sources: For total figures on number of applications and amounts paid between May 22, 1936, and June 14, 1941, see report by H. J. Bruninga, May 20, 1942, NA, RG 65, 65-7267-78-1665, box 96, 107; Hoover to Attorney General, August 21, 1942, NA, RG 65, 65-7267-83-1717, box 98; D. M. Ladd to Hoover, August 11, 1942, NA, RG 65, 65-7267-84-1724, box 98. Note that 429 of the applications were submitted by Germans living in Canada and Latin America. Figures on individual permit holders' commissions are the following: J. Henry Schroder Banking Corporation, report by H. J. Bruninga, September 16, 1941, NA, RG 65, 65-7267-64-1283, box 91; New York Overseas Corporation, report by H. J. Bruninga, May 5, 1942, NA, RG 65, 65-7267-75-1636, box 95; Robert C. Mayer & Co., report by H. J. Bruninga, July 15, 1942, NA, RG 65, 65-7267-81-1714, box 97. Deutsche Handels- und Wirtschaftsdienst figures approximate. Report by H. J. Bruninga, May 20, 1942, NA, RG 65, 65-7267-78-1665, box 96, 190.
[a]This number is for both permits.

The FBI Investigation of Chase National Bank

Although some information about the Chase-German cooperation was publicly available, the FBI's discovery of the Rückwanderer mark scheme was in part coincidental.[51] In November 1939, a normally reliable source used by the U.S. Office of Naval Intelligence reported that the German government had $6 million in gold within the United States to be used for espionage purposes.[52] The money was to be distributed by the German General Consulate in New York under Consul General Dr. Hans Borchers to other German consulates in the United States, then to German agents. Following this lead, the FBI began to chart the German General Consulate's primary bank account at Chase National Bank with the help of Sherrill Smith, a vice president at the bank. The tale of the $6 million for espionage turned out to be false. But the FBI continued to watch the General Consulate's Chase account while tracing, via serial number and again with Sherrill Smith's help, all $1000 bills withdrawn from Chase National by German consular personnel.[53]

Discoveries were interesting. The German Consulate made large dollar payments in 1939 to J. P. Morgan Company so the Hamburg Amerika Line could purchase—at below face value—5.5 percent interest coupons on German debts from the Dawes and Young Plan Loans. The coupons, which Morgan had urged its investors to purchase before the Nazis began to make electoral gains, were set to mature in December 1939.[54] Since the German government would not pay its debt to U.S. bearers, this (legal) arrangement allowed J. P. Morgan to salvage something.[55] FBI agents also followed leads to Robert C. Mayer & Co., one of the five permit holders in the Rückwanderer business. In April 1940, through a source close to Mayer & Co.'s president, August T. Gausebeck, it was learned that this company had funneled significant donations in small, untraceable five- and ten-dollar cash denominations to the notorious anti-Semitic radio priest, Father Charles Coughlin.[56] Mayer & Co. also expressed the intention to donate $500,000 to the 1940 Republican presidential campaign in small amounts through its employees in accordance with campaign finance laws. It appeared that the German government was secretly trying to make trouble for the Roosevelt administration.

The FBI's discovery of the Rückwanderer mark program did not come until October 1940—four years after the program had begun. A memorandum originating from the FBI's Chicago field office reported that prosperous Chicago Germans were being urged to liquidate their dollars and to invest in special "Reichwander [sic] marks." The FBI's Chicago agents knew that Friedrich Heinicken, one of the most conspicuous Nazis in Chicago with close ties to the German consulate as well as to the pro-Nazi German American Bund, operated the Chicago office of a Rückwanderer wholesaler, Hautz & Co. Upon searching Heinicken's office one night and studying the local account of Hautz & Co., the FBI discovered that many of Hautz & Co.'s checks were being written to the Chase National Bank in New York.[57]

The expected German victory in Europe increased money flow from wholesalers to Chase. "Representatives approach investors," FBI Director J. Edgar Hoover was told in late October, "and indicate to them that Germany will undoubtedly win the war . . . and that marks will undoubtedly increase many times in value . . ." The news sparked immediate attention in Washington, where it was understood that the 1939 Neutrality Act, which prohibited loans and gifts to belligerent nations, was likely being violated. In addition, the Johnson Debt Default Act of 1934 prohibited loans and gifts to states defaulting on American-held debts. Hoover, Attorney General Robert Jackson, and Treasury Secretary Henry Morgenthau reacted immediately and an extensive investigation began.[58] W. S. Deveraux, Special Agent-in-Charge in Chicago, thought about purchasing Rückwanderer marks himself until he discovered that the German Consulate would have to approve his application.[59] The real information was in New York, anyway. The entire picture would emerge only slowly, and a complete image would not emerge until after August 1941, when the Rückwanderer case was put before a federal grand jury.[60]

Newly declassified FBI records reveal that the FBI had confidential help from officials within the Foreign Department of Chase National, specifically Carl Weis (Assistant Cashier in the Foreign Department) and Leo Kelly (Assistant Manager of the Foreign Department). Both men allowed FBI agents to examine files in the bank during certain evenings without the knowledge of other Foreign Department officials or other senior figures at the bank.[61] FBI agents were especially interested in very active Chase accounts of pro-German wholesalers and retailers who had roots in the German-American community. Hautz & Co., Hans Utsch & Co., and Amerop Travel Services were among the most active wholesalers, and they sent most of the Rückwanderer applications they received to Chase National Bank.

Hans Utsch was a naturalized American citizen who remained well connected in Berlin financial circles. His commercial credit department was managed by Hans Richter, a former director at the J. Henry Schroder Bank, whose father was then a director at Dresdner Bank in Germany (an institution with its own dubious wartime past).[62] Utsch & Co.'s most recent venture was the financial backing of a new import export firm known as the Foram Management Corporation, which did business between South American companies and Germany. The president of Foram Management was none other than Roy Frazier Potts, the executive vice president of New York Overseas, who could evidently use his Rio connections.[63]

At the same time, Utsch was especially interested in the Rückwanderer trade. He had tried and failed to become one of the permit holders in 1936,[64] but in May 1939, Utsch & Co. had purchased all stock in New York Overseas from Potts, thereby assuming 100 percent ownership and the potential to earn the lion's share of the 7 percent commissions on Rückwanderer transfers that he managed.[65] Hoover concluded that "this man [Utsch] is a bad actor and runs several outfits involving clandestine Nazi activities, all of which have frozen funds . . . He collects and sends money to Germany, and has been engaged in sending mining accessories to South America . . . Utsch also sends stuff to all firms in South America that have been placed on the black list."[66] Throughout, Utsch angled for a monopoly of overseas business of the German American Bund, which included Rückwanderers or others who sent gift remittances and packages to Germany.[67] Like Chase National Bank and J. Henry Schroder Bank, Hans Utsch & Co. would remain a significant New York financial entity after the war.

The FBI, however, was interested primarily in the individual Germans in the United States who had purchased or would purchase Rückwanderer marks. To some degree this interest delayed the formation of a comprehensive picture and hindered the grand jury investigation of the entire trade. New York Special Agent-in-Charge B. E. Sackett reported to Hoover on November 23, 1940, that Chase National had about 3,500 Rückwanderer applications on file dating from 1937.[68] Sackett informed his fellow Special Agents-in-Charge throughout the country: "In filing an application to purchase these German marks, it is necessary for the applicant to obtain an affidavit from the nearest German Consulate certifying to his acceptance by the German government to reestablish permanent residence on Germany . . . " The application itself, explained Sackett, "is tantamount to an oath of allegiance to the German government."[69] Hoover agreed. After Germany and the United States were at war, over a year after the original discovery of the Rückwanderer scheme, the FBI director noted the use of the assembled data. "The fact that these people applied for or actually purchased Rueckwanderer marks," he said, "is in itself a very strong indication of where their sympathies may lie," and "vigorous investigative effort . . . will undoubtedly result in the ultimate internment of many of the alien purchasers of Rueckwanderer marks."[70]

In other words, the FBI investigation did not eliminate the Rückwanderer program in the United States immediately after discovering it, nor did it try to do so. Though Hoover asked the Attorney General's office for a legal opinion as to whether the practice violated federal law,[71] the FBI's investigation focused on the counterintelligence value of the information garnered from Chase sources to smoke out Nazi spies or saboteurs. Virtually each and every purchaser of Rückwanderer marks became the subject of an individual FBI surveillance file. By January 1941, nightly visits to the Chase bank by twenty-two special agents had resulted in a 281-page list of 2,800 purchasers all over the United States. The list was forwarded to every FBI field office from Albany to San Francisco.[72] This practice was repeated periodically with more names added to more lists, so that there were 7,300 names by May 1941.[73] Files were opened on each purchaser by the relevant field office, with the names also referred to local police "for appropriate investigative attention."[74] Local police were asked for background "with reference to any subversive activities in which [purchasers] may be involved." If relevant information were to turn up, then the FBI would keep the purchaser on another list "for possible future custodial detention."[75] Hoover added in late December 1940 that since naturalized purchasers ostensibly intended to leave the United States, then perhaps their American citizenship could be revoked or prevented, too.[76] Hoover complained in March 1942 that many individual cases had been wrongly closed based on local police investigations that had been "quite superficial." He ordered the field offices to review all case files of individuals who had purchased Rückwanderer marks and to conduct their own investigations through the use of confidential informants. The Department of Justice saw matters similarly. After the German declaration of war on the United States, it informed Alien Enemy Hearing Boards that they were to take the purchases of Rückwanderer marks into account when judging aliens because "a purchaser . . . has made dollars immediately available to the German government in the United States and has transferred all or part of his savings to Germany." Thus, "it is reasonable to conclude that a purchaser of these marks . . . has an interest in a German victory."[77]

In April 1942, FBI Assistant Director P. E. Foxworth asked for and received from Hoover a hundred additional agents to complete between 2,000 and 3,000 Rückwanderer cases that had yet to receive sufficient attention in New York. Foxworth had estimated that 130 workdays would be needed simply to examine 3,500 un-copied applications taken the previous year from Robert C. Mayer and the Deutsche Handels- und Wirtschaftsdienst.[78] Regardless of workload, the FBI followed up each case. For the FBI, the lists "served as a very lucrative source of information in connection with the Internal Security Program."[79]

Was the information of use? Rückwanderer information in many cases provided the first entrée into more derogatory information on German aliens and naturalized Germans disloyal to the United States.[80] In Newark, for example, eleven Germans were arrested while celebrating Hitler's birthday in April 1942.[81] In August, the FBI raided 150 German homes "looking toward," as Special Agent-in-Charge J. F. Sears reported to Hoover, "the internment of alien purchasers and denaturalization of citizen purchasers, in accordance with your instructions."[82] Though thirty-five of the targets had already returned to Germany, sixty possessed contraband such as guns and Axis propaganda material, leading to denaturalization proceedings.[83] On a higher level, August T. Gausebeck of the Robert C. Mayer Company, who had sold Rückwanderer marks while financing the broadcasts of Father Coughlin, was also interned as an enemy alien, though the Swiss government intervened on his behalf through the State Department to secure his release.[84]

By February 1944, the files of 547 would-be Rückwanderers working in defense-related industries were forwarded to Army and Navy intelligence, and fifty-three of these were ordered discharged from their employment by the War Department.[85] The case of Heinrich Claus is not atypical. Claus, who had purchased a sizable sum ($5,000 worth) of marks through Hautz & Co. via Chase National, was foreman in the machine shop of the Brewster Aeronautical Corporation on Long Island, which built aircraft for the U.S. Navy. Blinded by potential commissions, Foreign Department officials at Chase National had never contemplated connections such as this. The FBI did. It forwarded such information to the Office of Naval Intelligence, the Department of State, and the Department of the Treasury.[86] Indeed, as early as July 1941 the War Department had reported that the Rückwanderer mark business was one of the most important sources of foreign exchange used to pay for subversive activities (espionage and propaganda) in the United States and elsewhere.[87] Among the most famous internees were two of the eight German saboteurs who had arrived in the United States via submarine in June 1942. Both had purchased Rückwanderer marks while in the country previously.[88]

By the fall of 1942, it became clear that about a third of the over 10,000 Germans who had bought Rückwanderer marks had already returned to Germany to claim their new bank accounts.[89] But by February 1944, the FBI had apprehended 997 German aliens who had purchased Rückwanderer marks. Of the 997 apprehended, 441 were jailed on the order of the Attorney General.[90] Thirty-five naturalized citizens of German origins had their citizenship revoked as a result of investigations that started with the lists of Rückwanderer mark purchasers.[91]

The FBI's surveillance had a significant drawback. The Rückwanderer trade continued for nine of its busiest months, from October 1940 to the executive order of June 1941 freezing German assets. The Justice Department surely could have moved against the Rückwanderer mark scheme at any time while it was still in progress. Though a strike would have left the Bureau with far fewer names of possible subversives, it also would have stopped the Germans from building significant amounts of foreign exchange, to say nothing of commissions for Chase, Utsch, and the rest. By the day of the freezing order, Chase National itself had handled 4,588 Rückwanderer applications, helping the German government to garner nearly $9 million in foreign exchange, while making $503,000 in commissions for itself and its subagents. Out of this amount, the FBI watched while the Germans garnered over $3.4 million through Chase National alone, paying that bank $237,000 in commissions.[92] The assumption might have been, however, that while more Germans would not walk into a closed trap, there would always be time to prosecute.

The Failure to Prosecute Chase National and its Associates

The possibility of a Department of Justice prosecution of Chase National and the rest of the Rückwanderer consortium developed very slowly. The FBI asked the Attorney General's Office for legal opinions on the Rückwanderer practice on December 7, 1940, and again on January 4, 1941. The Department of Justice did not respond until June 4, 1941, nearly six months after the original request. In the meantime, complaints arose within the Treasury Department that it was "shocking that nothing is being done by Justice." Secretary of the Treasury Henry Morgenthau drafted a letter to Attorney General Jackson saying that "the proportions of this problem appear enormous" and that since the practice violated the Johnson and Neutrality Acts, "the matter ought to be turned over, it seems to me, for grand jury action."[93] Hoover explained some of the potential difficulties: "Should any action be taken . . . there would have to be a determination of who is responsible; that is . . . as to what the responsibility is of the purchaser, what the responsibility of his agent, such as R. E. Hautz & Co., and what the responsibility of the bank, such as the Chase National Bank, in these transactions."[94]

To prove that the practice violated the Johnson and Neutrality Acts, the FBI had to determine whether the dollar sales constituted a loan to the German government. In April 1941, the Treasury Department reported that the Gold Discount Bank was indeed a complete Reichsbank subsidiary under the direction of the Reichsbank president himself.[95] The history of the practice was hard to determine, as well. Not until July 1941—after the executive freezing order—did the FBI discover that the Rückwanderer practice began in 1936, that it originated with the New York Overseas Corporation, and that other financial institutions such as J. Henry Schroder were involved.[96] Whether the Bureau fully comprehended at that time that the marks were paid out of blocked Jewish accounts is equally unclear. In any event, the Jewish connection was not mentioned before the grand jury inquiry.

On May 12, 1941, Winthrop W. Aldrich, the Chairman of the Board of Directors at Chase National, addressed a letter to Morgenthau claiming that though "it is extremely important that American banks should cooperate . . . with the Administration . . . it is difficult, in the absence of action by the United States government to control assets owned by German, Italian, and Japanese nationals." In an attached memorandum explaining Chase National's business with regard to these states, Aldrich explained the Rückwanderer marks business in the most innocuous terms: "We have received from German residents of the United States desirous of returning to Germany to take up permanent residence there, dollars which were credited to the account of the Deutsche Golddiskontbank for the purpose of conversion into marks to be paid to those emigrants upon their arrival to Germany." Aldrich failed to mention the recruitment of emigrants through wholesalers like Hautz and Utsch or Nazis such as Heinicken, let alone the commissions earned by Chase National by acting as an agent for the German government. Evidently he was completely unaware of the cooperation of his own subordinates at Chase National with the FBI.[97]

In June 1941, George A. McNulty, Chief of the Department of Justice's Criminal Division, finally reported that Attorney General Jackson considered the Rückwanderer mark scheme a possible violation of federal law. A grand jury investigation, he announced, would ensue with a view toward the prosecution not of the purchasers of Rückwanderer marks, but of the brokers. Legal opinions within the Justice Department focused on probable violations of the Johnson Act of 1934 and the Neutrality Act of 1939, both of which prohibited loaning money to those who had defaulted on financial obligations to the United States or to active belligerents, since the German government was in essence receiving a loan of dollars in return for a promise to pay back marks to the Rückwanderer at some future date.[98] Conviction based on the Johnson Act would mean penalties of fines up to $10,000 or five years' imprisonment. Conviction under the Neutrality Act of 1939 would carry a penalty of $50,000 or five years' imprisonment. Each bank officer or broker involved was subject to the same penalty.[99]

On August 11, 1941, the Rückwanderer mark case was presented to a federal grand jury for the Southern District of New York. The prosecution focused on the five permit holders, as well as the largest wholesalers such as Hautz & Co. and Hans Utsch & Co.[100] Subpoenas and search warrants were issued to officers and employees of more than twenty companies. Over seventy file cabinets of records were received immediately, including those of the Deutsche Handels- und Wirtschaftsdienst, stored in a private warehouse after the German principals had fled the country. A call was also issued for Justice Department officials who could read German.[101] The subpoena to Chase National was issued later and with special care so as not to expose the FBI informants Weis and Kelley.[102] After the discovery that five firms dealt in Rückwanderer marks in return for straight commissions, prosecution of these dealers for violations of the 1917 Espionage Act and the 1938 Foreign Agents Act were considered, as well. Chase National and the others had clearly acted as agents of the German government without informing the Department of State, as was required by law. For a time, the Department of Justice considered a conspiracy charge, too.[103]

The FBI wanted very much to prosecute, since, as Hoover said, "the Bureau had put a tremendous amount of work in this case." The Justice Department moved to prosecute Chase and placed McNulty and Frederick Rarig, an Associate Attorney at the Trial Section, at the head of the prosecution team. Though McNulty and Rarig were under strong pressure from the Justice Department and the FBI to move quickly, Rarig, an eager twenty-five-year-old, needed little pressure. According to Treasury officials, he "was quite excited about the whole thing."[104] Rarig's brief on the issue argued passionately that "indictment and prosecution will . . . serve the public purpose of demonstrating to appeasement-minded business interests that they cannot flout the interests of a democratic government with impunity."[105] To Rarig, the prosecution of Chase was a matter of "high policy."[106] The State Department and Treasury Department quickly approved moving forward. The Treasury Department had already shut down Robert C. Mayer & Co. and seized its records while freezing the overseas activities of the travel agencies in question.[107]

Yet one man, Mathias Correa, the U.S. Attorney for the Southern District of New York (where the grand jury was impaneled), objected to prosecution. Correa registered what were called "strenuous objections [not specifically justified] to any indictment of the Chase National Bank." To sidestep Correa's objections, McNulty and Rarig talked about moving the case from New York to Washington, D.C.[108] On June 9, 1942, however, Berge informed Hoover that after consultation with Correa, Attorney General Francis Biddle (appointed September 5, 1941, after

WB:KNA:mhb

DEPARTMENT OF JUSTICE
WASHINGTON, D. C.

June 9, 1942

Mr. Tolson
Mr. E. A. Tamm
Mr. Clegg
Mr. Glavin
Mr. Ladd
Mr. Nichols
Mr. Rosen
Mr. Tracy
Mr. Carson
Mr. Coffey
Mr. Hendon
Mr. Kramer
Mr. McGuire
Mr. Quinn Tamm
Mr. Nease
Miss Gandy
Misc.

MEMORANDUM FOR THE DIRECTOR,
FEDERAL BUREAU OF INVESTIGATION.

Re: Rueckwanderer marks

Reference is made to your memorandum of May 29, 1942, inquiring whether prosecution will or will not be undertaken in this case.

The Attorney General has examined the case and after conference with United States Attorney Correa, has decided that no prosecution will be had under the Johnson or Neutrality Acts.

The information gathered has been and will continue to be of great value in the enforcement of the laws relating to National Defense and I take this occasion to thank you for the excellent results obtained through your efforts.

Respectfully,

WENDELL BERGE,
Assistant Attorney General.

RECORDED
&
INDEXED

65-7262

JUN 11 1942

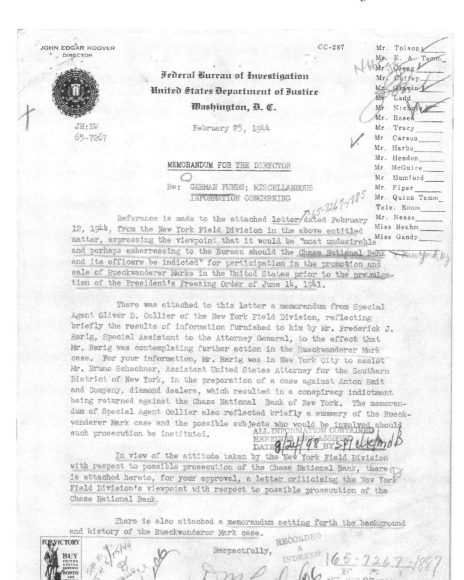

Left: Memorandum from the Assistant Attorney General to Hoover stating that the office will not take action against Chase National Bank for its involvement in the Rückwanderer mark scheme (Berge to Hoover, 9 June 1942, NA, RG 65, 65-7267-80-1703, box 96). Above: Memorandum from FBI NY field office to the Attorney General stating that prosecution of Chase could be "embarrassing" to the FBI (Ladd memorandum to Hoover, 25 Feb. 1944, NA, RG 65, 65-7267-87-1887, box 99).

Jackson became a Supreme Court Justice) had decided not to prosecute under the Johnson or Neutrality Acts.[109]

In 1944, Rarig, evidently on orders originating with Biddle himself, tried to re-open the prosecution of Chase Bank. Rarig again met with FBI agents of the New York field office.[110] But in February 1944, the FBI's New York field office, without the approval of headquarters, expressed the sentiment to the U.S. Attorney's Office in New York that it would be "most undesirable and perhaps embarrassing to the Bureau should the Chase National Bank and its officers be indicted" since information "was obtained by groups of Agents of this office . . . in the evening when members of the Foreign Department were not present."[111] The New York office did not wish to expose Weis or Kelly, whose cooperation with the FBI was still unknown to their superiors at the bank even after the grand jury investigation.[112]

Hoover was furious with the New York field office and with its attempt to influence policy. It was true, Hoover told New York Special Agent-in-Charge E. E. Conroy, that certain Chase officials had ". . . rendered valuable assistance . . . by allowing our agents to review the records of the Foreign Department of the Bank in the evening for the purpose of preparing lists of individuals who had purchased . . . Rückwanderer marks." Evidence concerning the prosecution of Chase bank officials involved in the high end of the Rückwanderer business was another matter. Here, Hoover said, the key evidence to be used at trial had come not from inside sources at Chase, but through the subpoena of testimony and documents before the grand jury. The grand jury inquiry had been under the purview of the U.S. Attorney's Office, not the FBI. In fact, the decision to prosecute or not was never within the purview of the FBI. "As you are well aware," Hoover chastised Conroy,

> it has been a long established policy of the Bureau not to influence any discussions relating to prosecution, but to merely present the facts . . . and from there let the chips fall where they may . . . The Bureau, therefore, is unable to account for the consternation by your office in regard to possible prosecution of officials of the Chase National Bank . . . unless overtures relating to compromises or promises regarding possible prosecution were made by Agents of your office who were engaged in procuring the lists of Rückwanderer mark purchasers at Chase National Bank . . . In view of the sentiments expressed by your office, which are unprecedented in Bureau procedure, the Bureau can only deduce . . . that overtures of compromise relating to possible prosecution were made to . . . officials of the Chase National Bank.[113]

Conroy quickly and emphatically denied that any deals had been made, but he did point out the following: Chase National was already under indictment for other unrelated violations of the June 1941 executive order on the freezing of funds.[114] The bank had chosen its lead attorney wisely. He was John D. Cahill, "one of the best lawyers in the country," according to the FBI, but more importantly, a former U.S. Attorney in the Southern District of New York, where the grand jury investigation of Chase had occurred. Cahill was thus well acquainted with the federal government's Rückwanderer mark case and with the fact that the FBI had attained a great deal of information in secret with the cooperation of Chase officials. He also knew that some of this information had been shared with Army and Navy intelligence. On learning that the Justice Department was again considering prosecution, Cahill privately yet firmly apprised Department officials of his awareness that Chase officials had cooperated directly with the Bureau, as well as Army and Naval Intelligence. "It is not known," said Conroy, ". . . to what extent Mr. Cahill will make use of the circumstances," but Cahill had strongly indicated to the U.S. Attorney's Office that he would indeed do so.[115]

Thus, Hoover's expectation that only information attained by subpoena would be used in the prosecution was dashed. The secrecy of FBI sources and methods, to say nothing of Army Intelligence sources and methods, was now at stake. The Department of Justice decided that no FBI agents could be placed in a position where they might have to testify in open court.[116] Despite Hoover's own eagerness to see Chase National's officials prosecuted, he did not challenge this decision. The case simply died. Over a decade after Frederick Rarig's death in the 1980s, his wife remembered that the failure to prosecute the Rückwanderer case was the biggest disappointment in her husband's life.[117]

In a supreme irony, Chase officials who had cooperated with the FBI had unwittingly protected other Chase executives who had cooperated with Nazi Germany. Thanks to Chase National's shrewd choice of attorneys, the extraordinary story of Chase National's simultaneous cooperation with the Nazi government and the FBI has remained mostly buried to this day.

Notes

1. Chase's involvement is well known and was first made public during the war. See Excerpt from Pearson and Allen Broadcast of Sunday Evening, 12 Apr. 1942, NA, RG 131, box 174, folder–Germany-Rückwanderer Marks. See also "Travel Marks Led 923 into FBI Net," *New York Times*, 1 Nov. 1943. A superficial treatment of the issue is in Charles Higham, *Trading with the Enemy: An Exposé of the Nazi–American Money Plot, 1933–1949* (New York: Dell, 1984), 44–45. While a full account of American business dealings with Nazi Germany is lacking, a good account for Great Britain is Neil Forbes, *Doing Business with the Nazis: Britain's Economic and Financial Relations with Germany 1931–1939* (Portland, OR: Frank Cass, 2000).

2. For German imports and exports by country for 1939 alone see the secret report by the Statistisches Reichsamt, "Der Außenhandel Deutschlands—Ergänzungsheft I 1939," NA, RG 242, T-71, roll 108, frames 611210ff. Information on US-Germany trade begins on frame 611301 (page 89 of report).

3. The law creating Reich Office for Foreign Exchange Control, dated 18 Dec. 1933, is in Germany, *Reichsgesetzblatt*, 1933, Teil I, 1097. There were also twenty-seven local foreign exchange offices in Germany, known as *Devisenstellen*. The office went out of existence on 9 April 1938, when its functions were transferred back to the RWM. Schacht's policies and how they affected Jewish emigration from Germany are discussed in Albert Fischer, *Hjalmar Schacht und Deutschlands "Judenfrage": der "Wirtschaftsdiktator" und die Vertreibung der Juden aus der deutschen Wirtschaft* (Cologne: Böhlau, 1995), 104–223. See also Avraham Barkai, *From Boycott to Annihilation: The Economic Struggle of German Jews, 1933–1943*, trans. William Templer (Hanover, NH: University Press of New England/Brandeis University Press, 1989), 59–63.

4. As per Runderlass 53, DSt., 16 Mar. 1935, reprinted and explained in Report by H.S. Bruninga, 20 May 1942, NA, RG 65, 65-7267-78-1665, box 96, 26.

5. These policies are explained in report by H.J. Bruninga, ibid., 24ff.

6. For a full explanation of blocked Jewish accounts see Raul Hilberg, *The Destruction of the European Jews*, rev. and definitive ed., vol. 1 (New York: Holmes and Meier, 1985), 139–144. The prohibition against any German, Jewish or not, taking liquid assets out of Germany dated from August 1931 and aimed to thwart currency speculators. It remained in force after 1933 so that Jews wishing to emigrate from Germany could not transfer their assets, lest the Reich have to pay in foreign currency for the amount of Reichsmarks taken abroad. Hilberg lists twelve methods by which emigrating German Jews could salvage something of their assets, but immigrants who did not manage to take their liquid assets abroad lost them to blocked (*Sperrmark*) accounts. Local foreign exchange offices controlled these accounts, not their owners. The blocked mark accounts could be used by Jews for a few things, such as the purchase of German real estate or for credits to Aryans, so in theory and practice Jews could sell the blocked mark accounts, though at a significant loss, sometimes up to 80 percent. In certain cases, Jewish relief agencies purchased blocked mark accounts to pay for the emigration of Jews who had no financial means. See S. (Shalom) Adler-Rudel, *Jüdische Selbsthilfe unter dem Naziregime, 1933–1939: im Spiegel der Berichte der Reichsvertretung der*

Juden in Deutschland (Tübingen: Mohr, 1974), 177–81. Generally, however, the German state came to control the vast majority of such accounts. See Barkai, *From Boycott to Annihilation,* 99–106, which points out that the Reich sold blocked marks for foreign currency first at 50 percent of the mark's value, and ultimately, by 1939, at 4 percent. In addition, Jews leaving Germany had to pay a flight tax of 25 percent on all assets worth more than RM 50,000.

7. Memorandum by Wendell Berge to the Attorney General, 30 Apr. 1942, NA, RG 65, 65-7267-85-1803, box 98.

8. Biographical information on Potts is in Report by D. E. Goubleman, 22 Oct. 1941, NA, RG 65, 65-7267-68-1337, box 93.

9. See his comments in "Reich Lures Many with Special Currency Rate," *New York World–Telegram,* 25 Aug. 1936. Cited in Report by H. J. Bruninga, 7 July 1941, NA, RG 65, 65-7267-54-1052, box 88.

10. Report by H. J. Bruninga, 20 May 1942, 12–13, NA, RG 65, 65-7267-78-1665, box 96. New York Overseas, in spite of its business, would steadily lose money. In April 1939, all shares were transferred to Hans Utsch and Co.

11. See NA–BDC, RG 242, NSDAP Zentralkartei, roll T162. Ziegra joined the party while still living in Rio de Janeiro.

12. $938,000 was paid against these 312 applications. Report by H. J. Bruninga, 20 May 1942, NA, RG 65, 65-7267-78-1665, box 96, 25–6.

13. The FBI did not notice the story until its full investigation into the matter in the summer of 1941. See Report by Report by H. J. Bruninga, 7 July 1941; and Report by H. J. Bruninga, 4 June 1941; in NA, RG 65, 65-7267-54-1052, box 88.

14. Decree No. 104 of 20 July 1936 issued by the German Minister of Economics, printed in Report by H. J. Bruninga, 7 July 1941, NA, RG 65, 65-7267-54-1052, box 88, 53–5; Runderlass, Nr. 104/D. St., 20 July 1936, printed in Report by H. J. Bruninga, 20 May 1942, NA, RG 65, 65-7267-78-1665, box 96, 37–8; for the 11 Aug. 1936 letter, see ibid., 41–2. The full German text is provided in Report by Collier, 11 Nov. 1941, NA, RG 65, 65-7267-68-1358, box 93.

15. The impression made by Hitler's Olympics the same summer had inspired Robert C. Mayer employee Hans Schlieper to join the Nazi Party. New York Overseas and Robert C. Mayer & Co. no longer exist. J. Henry Schroder Banking Corporation, chartered in New York in 1929, took the name IBJ Whitehall Bank and Trust Company in January 1999 after merger deals in 1978 and 1993. The use of Schroeder as New York Overseas' bank of deposit had come at the behest of the German authorities, who insisted during the initial permit that New York Overseas transfer funds through a reputable bank in order to build confidence with Rückwanderers. The president of Robert C. Mayer & Co. was August T. Gausebeck, a resident alien and Nazi Party member. See Report by H. J. Bruninga, 16 Sept. 1941, NA, RG 65, 65-7267-64-1283, box 91.

16. Report by H. J. Bruninga, 20 May 1942, NA, RG 65, 65-7267-78-1665, box 96, 25–6, 184.

17. There were about ninety subcontractors (wholesalers and retailers) in all, with about forty located in New York City. According to FBI figures, the busiest wholesalers were Hautz & Co. (New York and Chicago), Hans Utsch & Co. (New York), American Railway Express Co.

(New York), Amerop Travel Service (New York), North German Lloyd (New York), Hamburg America Line (New York), and Weniger & Walter (Philadelphia). See Memorandum by P. E. Foxworth, 22 July 1941, NA, RG 65, 65-7267-61-1204, box 90.

18. A copy of the forms over time are in Report by H. J. Bruninga, 20 May 1942, NA, RG 65, 65-7267-78-1665, box 96, 27–9, 47–50, 67–68, 98–106.

19. See the numerous cases included in NA, RG 242, T-71, rolls 89–90, frames 593826–958.

20. Robert C. Mayer deposited the dollars it collected in the Gold Discount Bank's account in the Bank of Manhattan. Hans Utsch & Co., Amerop, and Deutsche Handels- und Wirtschaftsdienst also deposited a portion of their re-immigrant dollars there so that from July 1940 to January 1941, over $2.1 million in Gold Discount Bank foreign exchange was deposited. This was more than at Chase National during the same months. SAC B. E. Sackett to Hoover, 25 Feb. 1941, NA, RG 65, 65-7267-29-650, box 76. The FBI was incorrect, though, when assuming in April 1941 that the Bank of Manhattan was actually in the Rückwanderer mark trade. From January 1937 to March 1941, the total dollars paid in Rückwanderer transactions was over $6.79 million. See Hoover to Berle, Hoover to Morgenthau, 14 Apr. 1941, NA, RG 65, 65-7267-39-812, box 81; Hoover to Berle, Morgenthau, 17 May 1941, NA, RG 65, 65-7267-42-864, box 82.

21. Report by H. J. Bruninga, 20 May 1942, NA, RG 65, 65-7267-78-1665, box 96, 137ff.

22. Ibid., 44ff.

23. Ibid., 139ff. In August 1937, Dr. Wilmanns was in Referat A6 of the Reichsstelle für Devisenbewirtschaftung, in charge of legal questions concerning foreign exchange. See Reichsstelle für Devisenbewirtschaftung, 7 Sept. 1937, NA, RG 242, T-71, roll 80.

24. Letters printed in Report by H. J. Bruninga, 20 May 1942, NA, RG 65, 65-7267-78-1665, box 96, 44–5.

25. E. O. Detlefsen, Foreign Department, Chemical Bank and Trust, to Hermann Kollmar, 21 Sept. 1936, photostat enclosure in Report by H. J. Bruninga, 7 July 1941, NA, RG 65, 65-7267-54-1052, box 88, 70. These photostats were made available by confidential informant H. W. Gottwald of the Chemical Bank and Trust Foreign Department.

26. Kollmar to E. O. Detlefsen, Foreign Department, Chemical Bank and Trust, 28 Aug. 1936, photostat enclosure in ibid.

27. Memorandum by H. W. Gottwald, Foreign Department, Chemical Bank and Trust, 1 Oct. 1937, Photostat enclosure to Report by H. J. Bruninga, 7 July 1941, NA, RG 65, 65-7267-54-1052, box 88; Report by H. J. Bruninga, 20 May 1942, NA, RG 65, 65-7267-78-1665, box 96, 4.

28. Report by H. J. Bruninga, 20 May 1942, NA, RG 65, 65-7267-78-1665, box 96, 111–12.

29. Ibid., 191–2.

30. Ibid., 174–5.

31. Ibid., 185.

32. Report by H. J. Bruninga, 20 May 1942, 56ff, NA, RG 65, 65-7267-78-1665, box 96. Dr. Daniel in September 1937 was the Gruppenleiter of Group A of the Reichsstelle für Devisenbewirtschaftung and was therefore the superior of Marwede and Willmanns. Group A handled foreign exchange control and money and capital exchange; see Reichsstelle für Devisenbewirtschaftung, 7 Sept. 1937, NA, RG 242, T-71, roll 80.

33. M. Stoltz, Berlin Office, J. Henry Schroeder to New York Office, J. Henry Schroeder, 9 Feb. 1938, quoted in report by H. J. Bruninga, 20 May 1942, NA, RG 65, 65-7267-78-1665, box 96, 64–65.

34. Letter of 9 Feb. 1938 quoted in ibid., 56ff.

35. Report by H. J. Bruninga, 20 May 1942, NA, RG 65, 65-7267-78-1665, box 96, 65.

36. Ibid., 69.

37. This figure was greater than the Jewish emigration for the previous five years combined, and the financial loophole wherein Jews were allowed to take goods and merchandise valued up to RM 1000 and to pay for passage in German currency was closed in the wake of Kristallnacht. Schacht, still Reichsbank President, worked on plans after Kristallnacht to make possible the emigration of 400,000 Jews in three to five years, with Jewish assets being retained by Germany, save that fraction needed to pay for emigration itself. Jewish organizations abroad understood the aim. The Jewish Central Information Office in Amsterdam (an organization of German-Jewish immigrants) commented: "German governmental offices are sparing no effort to utilize the moneys pilfered from the Jews to . . . expand German export trade and reduce German foreign debts . . . It is of the greatest importance that other countries, in full knowledge of the German policy of plunder, voice their resolute opposition to such policies." See Barkai, *From Boycott to Annihilation*, 138–146.

38. The meeting is discussed in a letter dated 5 Dec. 1938 from J. Henry Schroder's Berlin representative, Hans Zeuner, to the New York office, printed in Report by H. J. Bruninga, 20 May 1942, NA, RG 65, 65-7267-78-1665, box 96, 71.

39. Ibid.

40. Ibid., 76–7.

41. Report by H. J. Bruninga, May 20, 1942, NA, RG 65, 65-7267-78-1665, box 96, 72. Marwede, the FBI would later surmise, exaggerated these percentages in order to pressure the five permit holders into drumming up more business. The FBI, on investigating the matter in 1942, found evidence of but a tiny number of direct applications. P. E. Foxworth to Hoover, August 18, 1942, NA, RG 65, 65-7267-84-1727, box 98.

42. Minutes of meeting of 15 Feb. 1939, printed in ibid., 78–9; also in NA, RG 131, box 174, File–Germany: Rückwanderer Marks.

43. Memorandum from Rarig to McNulty, 10 Jan. 1942, NA, in ibid.

44. Report by H. J. Bruninga, 20 May 1942, NA, RG 65, 65-7267-78-1665, box 96, 105–6. On Chase totals from 1936 to 1941, see also Hoover to Berge, 10 July 1941, NA, RG 65, 65-7267-60-1173, box 90.

45. Foxworth to Hoover, 21 May 1942, NA, RG 65, 65-7267-77-1663, box 96.

46. See the reports on individual purchasers in NA, RG 131, box 174, File–Germany: Rückwanderer Marks.

47. Memorandum to the Attorney General, 30 Apr. 1942, NA, RG 65, 65-7267-85-1803, box 98.

48. On the other hand, the German government responded to the freezing order by freezing American assets in Germany in a decree of 26 June 1941. Reichswirtschaftsminister V. Dev. 6/19401/41, 30 June 1941, NA, RG 242, T-71, roll 81, frames 583215–7.

49. Memorandum by Gass, Division of Monetary Research, 16 Jan. 1941, NA, RG 131, box

174, File–Germany: Rückwanderer Marks.

50. Deutsche Golddiskontbank to Walter Funk, Nr. 23463, 31 Dec. 1943, NA, RG 242, T-71, roll 82, frames 584347–8.

51. As mentioned above, *The New York World–Telegram* ran stories on New York Overseas in 1936. When questioned by the FBI in 1941, J. Henry Schroder Bank Vice President Ernest H. Milei claimed that in 1936 the matter was freely discussed with members of the U.S. Embassy in Berlin and with Erwin G. May, the Treasury attaché there. T. J. Donnegan to Hoover, 21 July 1941, NA, RG 65, 65-7267-60-1198, box 90.

52. Captain E. B. Nixon, Office of Naval Intelligence to E. A. Tamm, FBI, 30 Sept. 1939, NA, RG 65, 65-7267-1-1, box 66.

53. Memorandum for E. A. Tamm, 5 Dec. 1939, NA, RG 65, 65-7267-1-12, box 66; Memorandum for the File, 7 Dec. 1939, NA, RG 65, 65-7267-1-23, box 66; memorandum of 26 Sept. 1940, NA, RG 65, 65-7267-14-291, box 70.

54. On J. P. Morgan's involvement with the Dawes Plan, see Stephen Schuker, *The End of French Predominance in Europe: The Financial Crisis of 1924 and the Adoption of the Dawes Plan* (Chapel Hill: University of North Carolina Press, 1976).

55. Report by Special Agent Joseph A. Genau, December 29, 1939, NA, RG 65, 65-7267-2-51, box 66; SAC P. E. Foxworth to J. Edgar Hoover, 2 Jan. 1940, NA, RG 65, 65-7267-2-54, box 66.

56. Gausebeck was a German citizen and resident alien in the United States. See Hoover to Henry Morgenthau, 10 May 1940, NA, RG 65, 65-7267-5-97x, box 67; memorandum by Hoover, 9 May 1940, NA, RG 65, 65-7267-5-102x, box 67; memorandum for Tamm, 17 May 1940, NA, RG 65, 65-7267-5-104x, box 67. Gausebeck is also known for his lobbying against the Wagner-Rogers Bill of 1939, which aimed to bring 20,000 Jewish children to the United States. See David Aretha, ed. *The Holocaust Chronicle* 1 (Lincolnwood, IL: Publications International, 2000), 157–8.

57. FBI Chicago to Director, SACs Milwaukee, New York, 26 Aug. 1940, NA, RG 65, 65-7267-17-398, box 71; Memorandum of 29 Oct. 1940, NA, RG 65, 65-7267-17-389, box 71. Among Hautz's more important clients was Ernst Wilhelm Bohle, head of the German Auslands Institute. On Heinicken's Nazi contacts, see Memorandum of 5 Dec. 1940, NA, RG 65, 65-7267-21-479, box 72. Later the Treasury Department incorrectly claimed that it tipped off the FBI on the Rückwanderer scheme. See J. C. Wiley to Morgenthau, 5 Mar. 1941, NA, RG 131, box 174, File–Germany: Rückwanderer Marks.

58. Memorandum for the Director, 28 Oct. 1940, NA, RG 65, 65-7267-17-399, box 71; Tamm to Hoover, 1 Nov. 1940, NA, RG 65, 65-7267-17-415x, box 71.

59. Memo to Hoover, 20 Nov. 1940, NA, RG 65, 65-7267-19-436, box 72.

60. Report by Collier, 5 Nov. 1941, NA, RG 65, 65-7267-68-1358 box 93.

61. See Foxworth to Hoover, 9 July 1942, NA, RG 65, 65-7267-80-1709, box 96.

62. Johannes Bähr, *Der Goldhandel der Dresdner Bank im zweiten Weltkrieg* (Leipzig: Kiepenheuer, 1998); Michael Hepp, *Deutsche Bank und Dresdner Bank: Gewinne aus Raub, Enteignung und Zwangsarbeit 1933–1944* (Bremen: Stiftung für Sozialgeschichte des 20. Jahrhunderts, 1999).

63. See for example Memorandum from Rubenstein to Tamm, 30 Dec. 1940, NA, RG 65,

65-7267-23-549x, box 73, which describes arrangements struck with bank employees to photograph forms and receipts; Report by C. A. Herring, NA, RG 65, 65-7267-24-573, box 74, 7; Report by A. H. Gunsel, 24 Jan. 1941, NA, RG 65, 65- 7267-27-604, box 75; Report by A. H. Gunsel, 9 Apr. 1941, NA, RG 65, 65-7267-37-776, box 80.

64. Report by H. J. Bruninga, 20 May 1942, NA, RG 65, 65-7267-78-1665, box 96, 45.

65. Potts sold all shares to Utsch because New York Overseas was losing money. New York Overseas kept its separate identity from Hans Utsch & Co., but moved its offices to 29 Broadway, where Hans Utsch & Co. was located. Utsch kept Hans Ziegra as the nominal president of New York Overseas because of his Berlin connections. Report by H. J. Bruninga, 20 May 1942, NA, RG 65, 65-7267-78-1665, box 96, 14–15. On the export of strategic material to Germany and Japan from Brazil, see Sumner Welles to Morgenthau, 30 Apr. 1941, NA, RG 131, General Correspondence, box 174, File–Germany: Rückwanderer Marks.

66. Hoover to SAC New York, 10 Oct. 1941, NA, RG 65, 65-7267-65-1289, box 92. Previously released documents concern the financial relationship between Hans Utsch & Co. and Robert Hautz & Co. with the German American Bund and the desire of both firms to conceal the full extent of the relationship. See Hautz & Co. memo to Fred Heinicken, 1 Nov. 1938, NA, RG 131, box 174, File–Germany: Rückwanderer Marks.

67. For this complicated relationship, see Report by H. J. Bruninga, 20 May 1942, NA, RG 65, 65-7267-78-1665, box 96, 117ff.

68. Sackett to Hoover, 23 Nov. 1940, NA, RG 65, 65-7267-19-453x, box 72; Sackett to Hoover, 3 Dec. 1940, NA, RG 65, 65-7267-19-458, box 72.

69. B. E. Sackett to SACs, 6 Jan. 1941, NA, RG 65, 65-7267-74-1519, box 95.

70. Hoover to SACs, 30 Mar. 1942, NA, RG 65, 65-7267-74-(1531–1577), box 95. Hoover to SAC New York, 21 Apr. 1942, 65-7267-74-1602, box 95.

71. Memorandum to the Attorney General, 7 Dec. 1940, NA, RG 65, 65-726-21-479, box 72. In a memorandum, Hoover listed the five biggest wholesalers, including Hautz & Co. and Utsch & Co., noted that dollar transactions to Chase for Rückwanderer marks from July to October 1940 totaled about $1.6 million dollars, and pointed out that "large sums of American capital can be immediately transferred [to] the German Government in this manner." See, Hoover to the Attorney General and to the Treasury Secretary, 27 Dec. 1940, NA, RG 65, 65-7267-23-545, box 73.

72. Report by C. A. Herring, 4 Jan. 1941, NA, RG 65, 65-7267-24-573, box 74.

73. Report by C. A. Herring, 19 Mar. 1940, NA, RG 65, 65-7267-35-741, box 80; on the Bank of Manhattan Rückwanderer files, Report by H. J. Bruninga of 9 May 1941, NA, RG 65, 65-7267-42-864, box 82; Memorandum from Rubenstein to Foxworth, 12 May 1941, NA, RG 65, 65-7267-45-916x, box 84; Report by H. J. Bruninga, 4 June 1941, NA, RG 65, 65-7267-51-1018, box 87.

74. See for example SAC B. E. Sackett to Hoover, 28 Jan. 1941, NA, RG 65, 65-7267-26-592, box 75.

75. Sackett letter of Dec. 1940, NA, RG 65, 65-7267-19-458, box 72.

76. Hoover Memorandum of 26 Dec. 1940, NA, RG 65, 65-7267-23-551x, box 73. By May 1942, the Department of Justice had made the purchase of Rückwanderer marks a chief

criteria in cases involving the revocation of U.S. citizenship and repatriation to Germany. See Berge to Hoover, 23 May 1942, NA, RG 65, 65-7267-79-1668, box 96. R.C. Suran, (SAC Cincinnati) to Hoover, 2 June 1942, NA, RG 65, 65-7267-79-1678, box 96. The DOJ prepared questions in March 1942 so that Enemy Alien Hearing Boards and courts (for naturalized citizens) could determine the true intent of the purchaser. See Berge to Hoover, 26 Mar. 1942, NA, RG 65, 65-7267-80-1697, box 96.

77. Edward J. Ennis, (Director, Enemy Alien Control Unit) memorandum to U.S. Attorneys and Members of Alien Enemy Hearing Boards, Circular 3651, 7 Mar. 1942, NA, RG 65, 65-7267-79, box 96.

78. Foxworth to Hoover, 14 Apr. 1942, NA, RG 65, 65-7267-75-1593, box 95; Foxworth to Hoover, 24 Apr. 1942, NA, RG 65, 65-7267-75-1623, box 95; Foxworth to Ladd, 2 May 1942, NA, RG 65, 65-7267-77-1650, box 96; Hoover to SAC New York, May 9, 1942, ibid.

79. Memorandum by Horn, 25 Feb. 1944, NA, RG 65, 65-7267-87-1887, box 99.

80. Strickland memorandum to Ladd, 2 May 1942, NA, RG 65, 65-7267-77-1650, box 96.

81. Strickland memorandum to Ladd, 22 Apr. 1942, NA, RG 65, 65-7267-75-1621x, box 95.

82. Sears to Hoover, 12 Aug. 1942, NA, RG 65, 65-7267-84-1725, box 98.

83. For publicity see *The Philadelphia Record*, 12 Aug. 1942; *The Philadelphia Inquirer*, 12 Aug. 1942. See also D.M. Ladd memorandum to Hoover, 12 Aug. 1942, NA, RG 65, 65-7267-84-1730, box 98.

84. Gausebeck, who testified for the grand jury and would have been a key defendant in any Rückwanderer mark case, was allowed to leave the country and return to Germany. Two other possible defendants allowed to leave thanks to Swiss intervention were Hermann F. Jahn of the Hamburg Amerika Line and Eugene C. Rieflin of Hans Lloyd International Commercial Travel Service. Foxworth to Hoover, 1 May 1942, and Hoover to Berle, 13 May 1942 both in NA, RG 65, 65-7267-75-1635, box 95.

85. Hoover to SACs, 11 Nov. 1943, NA, RG 65, 65-7267-87-1872, box 99. Memo by Horn, 25 Feb. 1944, NA, RG 65, 65-7267-87-1887, box 99.

86. Memorandum by P.E. Foxworth, 22 June 1941, NA, RG 65, 65-7267-61-1204, box 90.

87. Military Intelligence Division also pointed out that the Gestapo raised dollar exchange through the ransoming of Jews who had family in the Unites States. Lt. Col. S.V. Constant, Acting AC of S, G-2, Memo of 16 July 1941. NA, RG 65, 65-7267-60-1187, box 90.

88. "List of Nazi Mark Purchasers Leads FBI to Arrest 923," *The Washington Post*, 1 Nov. 1943.

89. This meant denaturalization for naturalized citizens. By October 1943, 30 of the 119 naturalized Germans who had been denaturalized had purchased Rückwanderer marks. Hoover to Berge, 8 Sept. 1942, NA, RG 65, 65-7267-84-1747, box 98; Berge to Hoover, 28 Sept. 1942, NA, RG 65, 65-7267-84-1759, box 98; Hoover to Berge, 15 Oct. 1942, NA, RG 65, 65-7267-84-1765, box 98; Hoover to SACs 11 Nov. 1943, NA, RG 65, 65-7267-87-1872, box 99.

90. Strickland memorandum to Ladd, 18 Sept. 1942, NA, RG 65, 65-7267-84-1752, box 98. Strickland memorandum to Ladd, 21 Apr. 1943, NA, RG 65, 65-7267-84-1856, box 98; NA, RG 65, 65-7267-87-1872, box 99.

91. Memo by Horn, 25 Feb. 1944, NA, RG 65, 65-7267-87-1887, box 99. Between 14 March

and 14 June 1941 alone, Chase and its sub-agents such as Hans Utsch & Co. pocketed over $130,000 in commissions from the German government. Report by H. J. Bruninga, 4 June 1941, NA, RG 65, 65-7267-51-1018, box 87. This seems to have been the first realization by the FBI that Chase itself was earning commissions on Rückwanderer mark transactions; Report by H. J. Bruninga, 7 July 1941, NA, RG 65, 65-7267-54-1052, box 88.

92. Report by H. J. Bruninga, 7 July 1941, Report by H. J. Bruninga, 4 June 1941, NA, RG 65, 65-7267-54-1052, box 88, 7a.

93. Memorandum from J. C. Wiley to Morgenthau, 5 Mar. 1941, NA, RG 131, General Correspondence, box 174, File–Germany: Rückwanderer Marks; Morgenthau to Jackson, draft, ibid. By this time, Treasury estimated that the FBI had already traced between $10 and $12 million from Germans in the United States to German government accounts, in addition to $8 million in the food package business. See also Morgenthau's enclosed memorandum to Jackson dated 7 Mar. 1941, on the applicability of the Johnson and Neutrality Acts, ibid. The memorandum was requested by Hoover himself.

94. Hoover Memorandum to the Attorney General, 11 Jan. 1941, NA, RG 65, 65-7267-26- 579, box 75.

95. Klaus to Rubenstein, 5 Apr. 1941, NA, RG 65, 65-7267-39-790, box 81. The Gold Discount Bank was originally founded in 1924 to link the internal Rentenmark, which was issued to end the great inflation, to the world's foreign exchange markets. See the long explanatory report on the Gold Discount Bank by Carl A. Herring, 22 May 1941, NA, RG 65, 65-7267-45-901, box 84. In 1940, Walter Funk was President of both the Reichsbank and the Gold Discount Bank, as well as Reich Economics Minister. This was considered the definitive report on the issue and Hoover forwarded it to the Treasury Department and the Attorney General in June.

96. Report by H. J. Bruninga, 7 July 1941; Report by H. J. Bruninga, 4 June 1941; Report by H. J. Bruninga, 7 July 1941; Report by H. J. Bruninga, 4 June 1941, all found in NA, RG 65, 65-7267-54-1052, box 88.

97. Aldrich was the son of Senator Nelson Aldrich (R-RI) and brother-in-law of John D. Rockefeller. Aldrich to Morgenthau, 12 May 1941, NA, RG 131, box 174, File–Germany: Rückwanderer Marks.

98. Memorandum by George A. McNulty, Special Asst. to the Attorney General, to Wendell Berge, 23 May 1941, NA, RG 65, 65-7267-60-1157, box 90.

99. Memorandum by P. E. Foxworth, 22 June 1941, NA, RG 65, 65-7267-61-1204, box 90.

100. Rubenstein to Foxworth, 24 July 1941, NA, RG 65, 65-7267-60-1154, box 90.

101. Memorandum for P. E. Foxworth from Rubenstein, 5 July 1941, NA, RG 65, 65-7267-60-1149, box 90; Hoover to Morgenthau and Berle, 10 July 1941, NA, RG 65, 65-7267-60-(1171–2), box 90; Rubenstein to Foxworth, 13 Aug. 1941, NA, RG 65, 65-7267-61-1230, box 90; S. S. Rubenstein to P. E. Foxworth, 19 Aug. 1941, NA, RG 65, 65-7267-62-1242, box 91.

102. Foxworth to Hoover, 9 July 1942, NA, RG 65, 65-7267-80-1709, box 96. The FBI was still using Vice President Sherrill Smith as a confidential source on the tracing of German consular accounts even during the grand jury investigation. See Foxworth to Hoover, 17 Nov. 1941, NA, RG 65, 65-7267-69-1389, box 93.

103. Penalties for Espionage Act violations included fines up to $5,000 or five years in jail. See Report by Collier, 11 Nov. 1941, NA, RG 65, 65-7267-68-1358, box 93; J.C. Strickland memorandum to Ladd, 1 Apr. 1942, NA, RG 65, 65-7267-74-1578, box 95; Berge to Hoover, 4 Apr. 1942, NA, RG 65, 65-7267-74-1585, box 95.
104. Report by H.J. Bruninga, 24 Oct. 1941, NA, RG 65, 65-7267-67-1322, box 92. See also Berge to Bernard Bernstein, Associate Counsel, Treasury Department, 18 Apr. 1942, NA, RG 131, box 174, File–Germany: Rückwanderer Marks; Morgenthau to Biddle, April 14, 1942, ibid; Memo of 12:30 PM, 8 Apr. 1942, ibid.
105. Memorandum from Rarig to McNulty, 10 Jan. 1942, NA, RG 131, box 174, File–Germany-Rückwanderer Marks.
106. Ibid.
107. Memorandum by Bernard Bernstein, 2 Feb. 1942, ibid.; Bernstein to Samuel Klaus, 18 Aug. 1941, ibid.
108. F.D. Vechery Memorandum to Ladd, 26 Feb. 1942, NA, RG 65, 65-7267-74-1525, box 95; D.M. Ladd memorandum to Hoover, 24 Apr. 1942, NA, RG 65, 65-7267-75-1625, box 95; Memorandum by Horn, 25 Feb. 1944, NA, RG 65, 65-7267-87-1887, box 99. There was some skepticism within the Treasury Department as to whether senior officials could be prosecuted or whether "the case will . . . be confined to the minor officials within Chase Bank who ran the Rueckwanderer business." Yet these minor officials were indeed senior names within the Foreign Department such as Kuhlman, Barth, and Rovensky. Memo by Quint, 31 Mar. 1942, NA, RG 131, box 174, File Germany–Rückwanderer Marks.
109. Berge to Hoover, 9 June 1942, NA, RG 65, 65-7267-80-1703, box 96.
110. Memorandum by Horn, 25 Feb. 1944, NA, RG 65, 65-7267-87-1887, box 99.
111. SAC E.E. Conroy to Hoover, 12 Feb. 1944, NA, RG 65, 65-7267-87-1885, box 99. Ladd memorandum to Hoover, 25 Feb. 1944, NA, RG 65, 65-7267-87-1887, box 99.
112. Foxworth to Hoover, 9 July 1942, NA, RG 65, 65-7267-80-1709, box 96.
113. Hoover to SAC New York, 2 Mar. 1944, NA, RG 65, 65-7267-87-1885, box 99.
114. The case was United States v. Leonard J.A. Smit, Chase National Bank, et al. and involved Smit's sale of diamonds to the Germans with the help of Chase officials.
115. Conroy to Hoover, 10 May 1944, NA, RG 65, 65-7267-87-1890, box 99.
116. Ladd to Mumford, 12 Apr. 1945, NA, RG 65, 65-7267-87-1907, box 99.
117. 2000 IRE Awards entry form for NBC Dateline, "Mark of Dishonor?" attained from *Dateline NBC*, 3.

8

The Ustaša: Murder and Espionage

Norman J. W. Goda

A NUMBER OF U.S. INTELLIGENCE RECORDS declassified under the Nazi War Crimes Disclosure Act of 1998 provide new evidence and insight into the activities of officials of the Independent State of Croatia, a wartime ally of Nazi Germany. Under the leadership of Ante Pavelić, the Ustaša (oo-sta-shə) regime in Croatia persecuted and carried out atrocities against Jews and Serbs while maintaining amicable relations with the Vatican. At the end of the war, the Ustaša regime collapsed, but Pavelić, after a number of mysterious episodes, was able to escape to Argentina in 1948. Meanwhile the United States Army used Father Krunoslav Draganović, a senior Ustaša functionary who had helped suspected war criminals to escape from Italy after the war, as an agent against the Communist government of Yugoslavia.

Background: The Ustaša and the War

Ante Pavelić began his career as a Croatian separatist in the multi-ethnic, Serb-dominated Yugoslav kingdom established after World War I. Pavelić went into exile in 1929, when King Alexander proclaimed a royal dictatorship in Yugoslavia. In 1930, at age forty, Pavelić founded the Croatian Liberation Movement—also known as the Ustaša ("rebels")—a group of Croatian émigrés pledged to conspiracy and terrorism in the aim of an independent Croatia. The Ustaša received financial and logistical support from Fascist Italy and Hungary, both enemies of Yugoslavia that expected to gain territorially if that state were destroyed.[1] The most famous prewar Ustaša success was the assassination of King Alexander of Yugoslavia in October 1934 in Marseilles—an attack that also killed French Foreign Minister Louis Barthou. Sheltered in Mussolini's Italy, which refused to extradite him, Pavelić never stood trial. Throughout 1940, Italian Foreign Minister Count Galeazzo Ciano schemed with Pavelić for the dismemberment of Yugoslavia in return for long-coveted territories on the Adriatic. After the Germans seized control of Yugoslavia in April 1941, Pavelić, with the help of German agents in Zagreb and of Mussolini personally, was installed as the Chief of State (*Poglavnik*) of the Independent State of Croatia—an enlarged country that, despite territorial concessions to Italy, consisted of Croatia itself, Bosnia-Herzegovina, and portions of Dalmatia.[2]

Pavelić and his Ustaša cohorts immediately began a process of "ethnic cleansing." In a blizzard of new laws promulgated from April to July 1941, Serbs (who represented 30 percent of the new state's population), Jews, and Gypsies—along with their property—were denied legal protections in the new state.[3] Croatia was to be completely emptied of Orthodox Serbs, through forced conversion, forced emigration, or murder. More than 100,000 Serbs were forcibly expelled without their property beginning in the spring of 1941. Thousands more fled on their own accord. Massacres of Serbs began less than three weeks after the proclamation of the Independent State. According to the most careful and least polemical estimates for the entirety of the war, between 330,000 and 390,000 Orthodox Serbs (including Orthodox clerics) were murdered, and roughly 32,000 Jews were killed either directly by the Ustaša or through delivery to the Nazis.[4] In the concentration camp system of Jasenovać, consisting of five camps in all, 42,000 to 52,000 Serbs and 8,000 to 20,000 Jews were murdered.[5]

Ustaša methods were so lawless and chaotic that Italian and German officials criticized them. The Ustaša had triggered broad Partisan resistance that jeopardized German economic interests and the safety of ethnic Germans living in Croatia. Yet Adolf Hitler refused to curb the Ustaša and registered no complaints in his meetings with Pavelić in June 1941 and September 1942. In the first meeting, Hitler advised Pavelić that a policy of national intolerance in Croatia "had to be pursued for fifty years" if Croatia were to become "really stable."[6] And in 1942, Hitler continued to promise a free hand to Pavelić's Ustašas to continue a war of extermination.[7]

As German power in the Balkans collapsed in 1945, so did that of the Ustaša. Its leadership, including Pavelić, fled to Austria in early May, hoping to escape the reach of the Partisans under Josip Broz Tito, against whom they hoped to fight another day. Tito's regime was unforgiving to Nazi and collaborationist war criminals. General Alexander Löhr, the Commander of German forces in southeastern Europe, was tried as a war criminal and executed in 1946. Alojzije Stepinać, the Archbishop of Zagreb, was tried the same year and sentenced to sixteen years at hard labor.[8] In May 1945, the Partisans annihilated thousands of Croatian refugees after their surrender to Partisan forces by British authorities in Austria, though the numbers cannot be precisely established.[9]

New Information on Archbishop Stepinać of Zagreb

The Catholic Church's special bond with Croatia began in the late fifteenth century, when Croats formed the Christian barrier to Ottoman expansion into Austria and Italy itself. In the early twentieth century, leading Catholic functionaries in the region viewed Eastern religious influence and Communism as new threats, so the Vatican maintained a close relationship with the loyal Catholics of the Ustaša regime. Most scholars who have written on the Church in Croatia during World War II have shown that most Croatian clerics viewed the Serbs as schismatics and the Jews as foreigners; many clerics were even active accomplices in Ustaša crimes against Serbs and Jews. Even on occasions when bloody Ustaša excesses triggered clerical alarm, such crimes never caused a church rupture with the state. Despite the fact that no de jure relations existed (the Vatican did not recognize states created in wartime), de facto relations were established quickly between the Vatican and Zagreb. Historian Michael Phayer has recently confirmed that the Vatican knew of Ustaša atrocities in detail. Yet despite its discomfort, Rome made no public protest, for as one senior Vatican official said, "Croatia is a young state [and] youngsters often err because of their age." Pavelić was even received by Pope Pius XII in a de facto act of recognition in May 1941.[10]

Equally controversial was the stance of Croatia's senior cleric, the Archbishop of Zagreb, Monsignor Alojzije Stepinać. After his arrest by Tito's regime, Stepinać was the chief defendant in a broadly publicized and one-sided show trial in Zagreb in October 1946. Stepinać was charged with treason, and specifically, with welcoming, sympathizing with, and collaborating with the Ustaša regime, particularly in the persecution of Serbs. Another charge involved plotting with the Ustaša and other reactionary elements to overthrow the "people's government." The fact that Stepinać greeted Pavelić when he arrived in Croatia from exile in April 1941, that he had attended government functions in which Ustaša and German dignitaries were present, and that he had served as military vicar to the Ustaša regime did not help his defense,[11] nor did his refusal in court to answer many questions while providing curt answers to others. Forced conversions, massacres, and the like, he said bluntly, all occurred without his approval, and his conscience, he said repeatedly, was clear. The court could do with him what it liked. And indeed it did.[12]

In subsequent years, Stepinać's reputation in the non-Croatian parts of Yugoslavia has not improved.[13] Outside Yugoslavia, accounts more sympathetic to the Archbishop appeared in the years immediately following the trial, including two that received official Vatican approval: Fiorello Cavalli's *Il processo dell'Arcivescovo di Zagabria* (1947) and Richard Pattee's *The Case of Cardinal Aloysius Stepinac* (1953). Both argue that during the war Stepinać had tried to curb Ustaša excesses. They include in his defense several of his wartime sermons and certain letters to the Ustaša authorities and even to the German Plenipotentiary in Zagreb, Edmund Glaise-Horstenau.[14]

Despite their postwar political context of Vatican anti-Communism, these published documents remain instructive in attempting to understand the ambiguity of Stepinać's position in Croatia during the war. Though the Archbishop never broke with the Ustaša leadership, he was disturbed enough by its brutality and inhumanity to say as much on a number of occasions. But what did the Archbishop's statements really mean? Was Stepinać simply a bit bolder than his superiors in the Vatican while supporting the Croatian state in principle

206 ℱ U.S. Intelligence and the Nazis

through his continued service? Israeli historian Menachem Shelah argues, based on these documents, that Stepinać did not disapprove of the state's aims, only its methods.[15] The most recent account by the late Balkan historian Jozo Tomasevich notes that Stepinać's protests to Pavelić were easy for the government to disregard and thus were effortlessly ignored. Stepinać's arguments, Tomasevich adds, only became impassioned in October 1943, when the Germans shot his own brother as a Partisan.[16] Stepinać's biographer, Stella Alexander, is more charitable, arguing that "it was some time before [Stepinać] could bring himself to believe the worst about [the Ustaša]." He was "a conscientious and brave man, of deep piety and considerable intelligence but with a blinkered world view . . . In the end one is left feeling that he was not quite great enough for his role."[17] Phayer reaches a conclusion with similar nuance. "In comparison with other eastern European church leaders," he says, "Stepinać showed courage and insight in his actions." On the other hand, Phayer concludes that Stepinać's responses remained limited and belated because both "the Holy See and Stepinać wanted to see a Catholic state succeed in Croatia."[18]

OSS records declassified under the Nazi War Crimes Disclosure Act add important details to this story. Early on, the OSS depended on British reports to follow Ustaša excesses as they were occurring. "There is a good deal of killing by Ustaša bands," said one newly declassified British report from the fall of 1941, which also noted that "the Croats intend to expel in all 2,000,000 Serbs from Croatia."[19] By 1942, the OSS had developed a number of its own sources from Croatia, including members of the Pavelić government who had become disillusioned and fled, members of the Catholic clergy within Croatia, and diplomats who had served in Zagreb and still maintained contacts there.[20]

One of the most important OSS sources was Monsignor Augustin Juretić, a Croatian Catholic priest. Before Germany's invasion of Yugoslavia, Juretić had worked under the Archbishop of Belgrade. Into 1942, he served the Catholic Episcopal Conference in the Independent State of Croatia. On the urging of Archbishop Stepinać himself, Juretić left Croatia for good in September 1942. He settled in Switzerland, where he remained until his death in 1954. Before the war, Juretić was sympathetic to Vlatko Maček's moderate nationalist Croatian Peasant's Party, which had favored greater Croatian autonomy within Yugoslavia through democratic means. He was very uneasy with the Ustaša. Once in Switzerland, Juretić served as an intelligence source, receiving secret envoys from Zagreb and then reporting on Croatian affairs to Maček's followers within the Yugoslav government-in-exile in London.

Juretić made several of his reports available to the Allies, too. One of these, a lengthy written report by Juretić on June 10, 1942, was described recently by Tomasevich. This June 1942 "Juretić Report" revealed to the Allies the extent of Ustaša atrocities, particularly at the Jasenovać camp. "The concentration camp at Jasenovać," Juretić wrote, "is a real slaughterhouse. You have never read anywhere—not even under the GPU or Gestapo—of such horrible things as the Ustaša commit there . . . The story of Jasenovać is the blackest page of the 'Ustashi' regime, because thousands of men have been killed there."[21]

A new fifteen-page report has now come to light.[22] Juretić wrote "The Catholic Episcopate in Croatia" in French in June 1943 and relayed it to the OSS in December specifically for the eyes of Allen Dulles.[23] Juretić's report makes no secret of its aim, namely the maintenance of Archbishop Stepinac's reputation: "The brief expose . . . has no other goal [than to] refute . . . erroneous and tendentious opinions, which, in these painful times . . . [make it difficult to] achieve the tasks, which fall on to [the Archbishop] in accordance with his educational and pastoral mission."

The report contains short and long excerpts from a number of Stepinać's sermons and as well as letters from Stepinać to Croatian government officials from 1941 to 1943, all of which question and attack the regime's persecution of other races, religions, and nationalities. Most of the statements by Stepinać included in "The Catholic Episcopate" are not new, having been published by Cavalli or Pattee five decades ago and quoted at length by Shelah, Tomasevich, and others. Parts are new, however, and the report as a whole, which contains editorial comments by Juretić, reveals fascinating trends. First, it is difficult to imagine that whole texts of Stepinać's sermons and private correspondence with Ustaša Interior Minister Andreija Artuković, among others, reached Juretić without the approval of the Archbishop himself. Stepinać had sent Juretić abroad in the first place. Stepinać probably intended for Croatian leaders in exile to see his statements, and for the British and Americans to see them, too.

It is hard to say exactly why Stepinać would make known to the enemies of the Croatian government his moral objections to that same government. Perhaps he was not convinced that the Ustaša regime in Croatia would last. Perhaps he hoped to confirm a respectable place for the Catholic Church in the minds of Croatians and other Yugoslavs living abroad. The leading Catholic publication in the Croatian language, *Katholiki List*, was taken over by the government when Pavelić came to power, thereby becoming a state rather than a church organ, and the state press even criticized papal encyclicals and pronouncements on a number of occasions (a hitherto unfamiliar fact which needs further study).[24] Understanding that his powerful moral position outweighed his far lesser capacity to alter the murderous actions of the present regime, perhaps the Archbishop simply wanted to go on record before the wider world. Alexander has already shown that Stepinać was dismayed by criticisms of him in 1941 and 1942 broadcasts by the BBC. He was also familiar with the tools of espionage, having knowingly allowed a British wireless radio set— left by a Croatian Jew in 1941—to operate from within his bishopric. Alexander also discovered that Stepinać had met five times starting in April 1942 with Lieutenant Stanislav Rapoteć of the Royal Yugoslav Army and Yugoslav government-in-exile. Smuggled into Croatia via British submarine in January, Rapoteć met with the Archbishop after hearing his praises from underground Serb and Jewish figures. In their meetings, Stepinać spoke wistfully of a new federated postwar Yugoslav state as advocated by Maček's followers.[25]   If Stepinać wanted his opinions on the discrepancies between Christian teaching and Ustaša policies known to a broader audience, which is likely, then Juretić provided an excellent channel.

"The Catholic Episcopate in Croatia" reveals a set of general humanist ideals noteworthy for its breadth amidst chaos. Stepinać, to be sure, remained on very safe religious and political ground in his sermons—he spoke of Ustaša crimes only in the vaguest sense and he conveyed his disagreements publicly within the context of Holy Scripture. It was clear, though, that he rejected any ideology, from the left or right, which on the basis of race, religion, or class degraded the dignity and rights of the individual. In accordance with scripture, the Fascism of Hitler and Pavelić and Communism of Stalin and Tito were equally abhorrent. In one of many condemnations of racism, Stepinać said the following on the Feast of Christ the King on October 25, 1942:

> We affirm then that all peoples and races descend from God. In fact, there exists but one race. Its genealogy is explained in the Book of Genesis, where it is written why the hand of God built the first man from the dust of the earth, and that He inspired to him the soul of life. As he gave him a partner and as he blessed them and said, "Be fruitful, multiply, subdue the earth" (Gen 1, 28). All members of this race have in common and will have in common until the end of time: the arrival in this world and the exit from this world, because it is written without exception for all: You are dust and to dust shall you return." (Gen 3, 19). The members of this race can be white or black,—they can be separated by oceans or live on the opposing poles, [but] they remain first and foremost the race created by God who must serve God, according to the precepts of natural law and positive Divine law as it is written in the hearts and minds of humans or revealed by Jesus Christ, the son of God, the sovereign of all peoples.[26]

Political violence was another *bête noire* for Stepinać.   In a hitherto unpublished statement, he publicly ridiculed the Minister for State Education Mile Budak by name on June 21, 1942, after Budak's publication of the short story "Revolutionary Blood." He did not as a rule take issue with government ministers in public, but Budak went too far:

> Not a long time ago we were struck [by] a magazine article under the title "Revolutionary Blood." We read it, and we were very affected by the words that we found there: "Pacifism should be destroyed." "It is necessary to progress on the new path." And the last words of the story: "We are and we remain a pack of wolves."
>
> We believe, first of all, that the author . . . did not think much on what he wrote. If he had wanted to stress that we have the duty to defend our fatherland, we could still understand, because the love of the Fatherland is a precept of God. But if the intention is to say that any man can do what one [sic] likes and that there

is no limit to what we allow and what we do not allow—we ourselves stand in the presence of one of the greatest aberrations, which can generate nothing good. With regard to [Budak's] words, "Pacifism should be destroyed," Christ instituted the principle "Blessed are the peacemakers for they will be called the Children of God" (Math. 5, 9).

Finally, Juretić's report contains the text of an intriguing letter, dated March 6, 1943, from Stepinac to the Croatian government. A slightly different version of the same letter is printed in Cavalli's 1947 volume. The cause of the letter was the earlier Croatian government decree that all non-Aryans—which included all Jews married to Catholics, Jews who had converted to Catholicism, and half-Jews—register with the Croatian authorities. By now, most Croatian Jews not married to "Aryans" had already been interned or murdered. The Germans had recently decided to round up Berlin's German Jews in mixed marriages amid some public protest, so well-informed observers in Zagreb understood clearly that now Croatian Jews in mixed marriages were endangered.[27]

The situation in Croatia was anomalous however, because Pavelić himself and Armed Forces Commander Slavko Kvaternik were married to half-Jews, and other senior Croatian officials were married to full Jews.[28] Stepinac pledged that if mixed marriages were to be dissolved, "I will raise my voice as a representative of the Church"—an indefinite mix of protest and threat. He objected chiefly to Croatian meddling in thousands of Church-sanctioned marriages, which would contravene Church law. The version of Stepinac's letter published by Cavalli is addressed specifically to Pavelić himself, but Juretić's version is to the Croatian government as a whole. While Cavalli's Italian-language version points out:

> No power of the state has the right to dissolve marriages. If the state wishes to avail itself of physical force, it must admit to itself that it does nothing other than gross violence, from which nothing good can come. For the rest, I know that marriages [exist] among exponents of the government, but in contrast to these, such marriages are protected.[29]

Juretić's French-language version reads:

> Consequently, no capacity of the state has the right to dissolve them. If, nevertheless, the State would take recourse to physical coercion, such would constitute an arbitrary act, *which would involve fatal consequences. [For] it is known that such marriages exist within the community of very high dignitaries of the state,* and these are sheltered from persecutions.[30]

The latter version thus contains much stronger language, even to the point of an implicit threat to make a public issue of mixed marriages within the highest echelons of government. The textual differences are especially notable in that

Juretić was generally precise when quoting the Archbishop. (Two letters from Stepinać to Interior Minister Andreja Artuković, both quoted in Juretić's report, are carefully noted as such, and Juretić's French translations of various excerpts are true to the texts in Cavalli's and Pattee's books.)[31] Juretić was similarly careful with passages quoted from Stepinać's sermons. Only the March 6, 1943, letter on Jewish spouses shows a strong discrepancy. Could it be that that the document that was forwarded to Juretić was never sent in that form? Or could it be a more accurate translation of a lost or still-hidden Croatian-language original text? It is impossible to say, but one of these versions surely carries historical significance. Nazi officials noted by April 1943 that actions against Jews in mixed marriages and against many half-Jews were encountering obstacles since many Croatian leaders were related to Jews.[32] As Mile Budak soon sulkily informed the papal legate, Abbot Giuseppe Marcone, "mixed marriages in Croatia are protected and no measures will be taken against them."[33]

What did the aggregate of Stepinać's commentaries and letters mean during the war itself? For Jews unprotected by mixed marriages, it meant nothing. Despite the Archbishop's sermons and letters, a new sweep for Jews occurred in May 1943, in which Dr. Hugo Kon, the president of Zagreb's Jewish community and Miroslav Freiberger, Zagreb's Chief Rabbi and a personal friend of Stepinać, were arrested. Neither was heard from again.[34] But Juretić made the argument to his OSS contacts in December 1943 that the Archbishop had increasingly risked his own safety by the fall of 1943 by intervening for others:

> The courageous attitude of the Archbishop of Zagreb, Monsignor Stepanić [sic], his energetic intervention in favor of the persecuted, his condemnation of the execution of hostages, of massive deportations, of scorched earth methods, etc., have dug an insuperable ditch between him and the Quisling government and the German authorities . . . The entire population of Croatia thinks of their Archbishop with pride. The churches are full, and religious life intensifies day by day. The clergy are following . . . the example of the Archbishop. More than one hundred priests have been arrested . . . The only real motive is that these priests have distributed the sermons of the Archbishop.[35]

Ironically, according to this report, Stepinać was accused by some Ustaša officials of being in league with the Partisans, who would eventually put him on trial.[36]

Historians will surely continue to debate Stepinać's part in the Croatian genocide of World War II. But the new material from OSS records demonstrates once again the difficulty of placing Roman Catholicism's senior clerics together into easy moral categories.

The Escape of Croatian War Criminals to South America

A high percentage of Ustaša leaders escaped from Europe to South America in the immediate postwar years. An Argentine government-sponsored commission recently placed the number of senior Ustaša leaders who reached Argentina at fifty-two, while also noting that the number of Ustaša overall might have gone as high as 115 by 1947.[37] Some of these men arrived on their own from Genoa or from ports in Spain; some arrived with the aid of the so-called "ratline" created by Father Krunoslav Draganović.

Like many Croatian clerics, Draganović was a nationalist as well as a theologian. He would later candidly say that he "placed his country before his church."[38] His prewar doctoral thesis was used later to justify forced conversions from Orthodoxy to Catholicism.[39] Soon after the proclamation of the Croatian state, Draganović became the Vice Chief of the Ustaša's Bureau of Colonization, which was responsible primarily for the redistribution of property taken from dead or deported Serbs. He also participated in forced conversions and served as Army chaplain at the Jasenovac concentration camp. Draganović carried out his state functions in the uniform of an Ustaša lieutenant colonel.[40] In mid-1943, Archbishop Stepinać sent Draganović to Rome in a move which U.S. Army analysts would later call a model example of "kicking a man upstairs."[41] In Rome, Draganović lived and worked in the Collegio San Girolamo degli Illirici (College of St. Jerome of the Illyrians), a hospice and church where for nearly five centuries young Croatian clerics lived while studying at Vatican institutions. Not part of the Vatican itself (the land was donated by Pope Nicholas V in 1453), the college was (and remains) under Vatican protection. Draganović soon became the leading figure there.

After the war ended, Draganović helped to create an Ustaša political nerve center called the Committee of Croatian Refugees in the College of San Girolamo. He also helped wanted Ustaša leaders escape to South America by obtaining false identity papers from the Red Cross and the International Refugees Association. The money for the documents as well as for passage seems to have come from a number of sources. Draganović raised some of it by selling travel documents to other refugees. He might also have drawn from a treasury of loot stolen from Croatian Jews and Serbs, though this has never been proven.[42]

In a 1983 U.S. government report on its intelligence relationship with Klaus Barbie (the "Butcher of Lyon"), Allan Ryan explained how agents from the U.S. Army Counterintelligence Corps (CIC) paid Draganović in October 1951 to smuggle Barbie to South America so that he could avoid arrest by the French authorities.[43] Ryan posits that the "CIC may have been involved in—at least it contemplated the possibility of—assisting Draganović with the escape of Croatian war criminals," and he notes that at the very least the money the CIC paid Draganović for assisting with the escape of Soviet defectors paid for the escape of Croatian fugitives.[44]

Newly declassified records from the CIC and the CIA reveal that, as early as 1947, the CIC grasped Draganović's functions in providing an escape route for Croatian war criminals. But thanks to the diplomatic immunity enjoyed by visitors to Vatican institutions and to Draganović's own skill in hiding his compatriots through false identity and travel documents, the CIC was unable to plug this ratline effectively.

In the fall of 1945, the Strategic Services Unit (a smaller successor of the OSS) learned that Draganović was "undertaking political activity in Rome in connection with the collection of Croatian emigrants."[45] By October 1946, the CIC became aware that Draganović was in touch with Pavelić (then in Austria), that he was sending sabotage teams into Yugoslavia, and that he was sending war criminals wanted by the British to South America.[46] The rumors prompted CIC Special Agent Robert Clayton Mudd to place an agent in the College at San Girolamo "to find out if possible if . . . the place was as had been alleged, namely that it was honeycombed with cells of Ustashi operatives." This was no easy task. Armed Ustaša youth formed guards within the college and even stood before certain individual chambers. Passwords were required to move from one room to the next, newcomers were interrogated extensively, and Ustaša "salutes" were given and received continually. Mudd's infiltrator actually had to suspend his work "abruptly when it became too dangerous . . . for the agent." In the meantime, however, the CIC established that at least nine senior Ustaša ministers were "either living in the college, or living in the Vatican and attending meetings several times a week at San Geronimo [sic]."[47] To move between the Vatican and the college, they used a chauffeured car several times a week with *Corpo Diplomatico* license plates issued by the Vatican. "Subject to diplomatic immunity," said Mudd, "it is impossible to stop the car and discover . . . its passengers." "Draganović's sponsorship of these Croat Qusilings [sic]" said Mudd,

> definetly [sic] links him up with the plan of the Vatican to shield these ex-Ustashi nationalists until such time as they are able to procure for them the proper documents to enable them to go to South America. The Vatican, undoubtedly banking on the strong anti-Communist feelings of these men, is endeavoring to infiltrate them into South America in any way possible to counteract the spread of Red doctrine.[48]

Later in the year, Mudd procured photostats of Draganović's personal files that revealed further the scope of his operations. The files also indicated the presence of twenty more Croatian war criminals in the college. These included most notably Ivan Oršanić, the leader of the Ustaša Youth.[49]

By this time, the CIA had become better acquainted with the Ustaša exodus to South America, as well. "Ustaša emigration to Argentina," said a CIA report of October 1947, "has been particularly intense." Documents received by the CIA from London suggested that the Ustaša leaders indeed expected to fight another day in Yugoslavia.[50] "The possible tie-up of the Vatican with this organization," the CIA report continued in a suitable understatement, "is interesting." But even the CIA was not able to penetrate Draganović's organization entirely. They could not identify with complete certainty the Ustaša ministers who had made it to Argentina other than to say that they had confirmed the identity of some. "Owing to the delicate nature of this matter," said an Army Intelligence report in November, "more precise details could not be obtained."[51] Pavelić himself, the biggest catch of all, had yet to surface.

Pavelić's path immediately after the war remains murky. Published theories, based on interrogations with Pavelić's retinue taken and then stored in Titoist Yugoslav archives, postulate that he had prearranged his escape to Austria, where he successfully hid from Allied forces there until his escape to Italy.[52] United States Army records indicate that U.S. authorities indeed hoped to arrest him and hand him over to Tito for trial, and most probably execution. Although most Yugoslav extradition requests were received with skepticism,[53] there was no doubt whatever of Pavelić's guilt.

The Strategic Services Unit maintained contact with other Croatian nationalists who were enemies not only of Tito, but of Pavelić as well. Primary among them was Vlatko Maček, exiled leader of the Croatian Peasants' Party, and his top military supporter, Colonel Ivan Babić, a former Yugoslav General Staff officer who had escaped on one of Pavelić's private airplanes to the Allies in January 1944. Though the United States would not support Maček's desire to launch a full rebellion against Tito, it held him as a trump card in reserve, particularly for intelligence purposes.[54] As long as Pavelić remained at large, however, the former Poglavnik could discredit any U.S. effort associated with Croatian nationalists. The United States thus had a political interest in seeing Pavelić brought to justice.

The Yugoslav government, which had pressed repeatedly for Pavelić's extradition since 1945, was convinced that the Allies were protecting him. "The Yugoslavs believe," said Walter C. Dowling in the State Department's Division of Southern European Affairs in May 1947, "quite sincerely, that he is in our custody or that at least we know where he is and are protecting him. Of course he isn't. And as for us, we don't and aren't."[55] "If Pavelić is in Rome," said Colonel J. W. Fisher, U.S. Army Intelligence assistant chief of staff in August 1945, "he should be apprehended and arrested if possible."[56] Pavelić was not yet in Rome. Special Agent William Gowan, who headed the Pavelić case in Rome in 1947, reported that in May 1945 Pavelić was "in British-guarded and requisitioned quarters" in Austria.[57] As late as 1946 he was thought to be still in Austria, though only classified British records may reveal whether British occupation forces protected him there.[58]

The Holy See was not of one mind where Pavelić and the Collegio San Girolamo were concerned. The advance of atheistic Communism into Central Europe was a principal fear of the papacy throughout the war. The Yugoslav Communist domination of the Adriatic was alarming too, especially given the ways in which Tito's Partisans dealt with Catholics in Croatia. The Partisan slaughter of nine thousand Croatian refugees (returned to Yugoslavia by the British authorities in Austria in May 1945), the high-tension dispute between Italians and Partisans over the future of Trieste in the summer of 1945, the highly publicized Yugoslav trial and conviction of Archbishop Stepinać in 1946, and Belgrade's general persecution of the Catholic Church in Croatia after the war all added to the Vatican's apprehension about Yugoslavia's new government.

On the other hand, there were those such as Cardinal Eugene Tisserant of the First Congregation, who were clearly appalled and embarrassed by Vatican ties with the Ustaša. When, in April 1946, Vladimir Stakić, a former solicitor in Belgrade, confronted Tisserant in his own palace, the latter was at least straightforward. How, asked Stakić, could the pope have received and shaken the hands of Ante Pavelić? Tisserant answered that the Croats had displayed inferiority in spite of their Catholicism. For "the crime they had committed, [they] were condemned by the Catholic Church . . . You may have my full assurance that we have the list of all the clergymen who participated in these atrocities and we shall punish them at the right time to clean our conscience of the stain with which they spotted us . . . Finally," Tisserant continued, "I can assure you that neither I nor the Vatican know the whereabouts of Pavelić; if we did we should denounce him to the Allied police."[59]

Pavelić arrived in Rome disguised as Catholic priest Don Pedro Gonner in the spring of 1946. He stayed in various Vatican residences, but apparently not in the College of San Girolamo. Once apprised of Pavelić's possible location, U.S. authorities hoped to act. Pavelić, argued Mudd in January 1947, "tops the list of Quislings whom the State Department and the Foreign Office have agreed to hand over to the Yugoslavs for trial [and he] is not a criminal in just the ordinary sense." Giving him to Belgrade would silence Yugoslav propaganda, which "has on several occasions accused the Anglo-Americans of hiding Pavelić to further their own aims."[60] Gowan added that Pavelić's arrest and extradition were a precondition "if . . . Croat democratic and resistance forces are ever to be recognized by the United States."[61]

Yet the arrest of Pavelić was in large part a diplomatic problem. The CIC could not exclude the possibility that British intelligence was indeed protecting Pavelić. Gowan and his colleague, CIC Special Agent Louis Caniglia, thought that Pavelić was still "closely linked to the British . . . though [the] degree is unknown." Both were positive that the British were at least protecting Pavelić's family, all of whom were known to be living undercover in Florence (family members could not live on Vatican grounds).[62] Thus, though British Foreign Office representatives in Rome agreed on the need to arrest Pavelić, it remained unclear how such an arrest would be managed.[63] In addition, Gowan and Caniglia assumed Vatican non-cooperation. Pavelić, they said,

is receiving the protection of the Vatican whose view of the entire "Pavelic Question" is that since the Croat state does not exist and, since the Tito regime cannot be expected to give anybody a fair trial, the Subject should not be turned over to the present Yugoslav Regime with the excuse of bringing him to justice. The extradition of Pavelic would only weaken the forces fighting atheism and aid Communism in its fight against the Church . . . Pavelic's crimes of the past cannot be forgotten, but he can only be tried by Croats representing a Christian and Democratic Government, the Vatican maintains. While Pavelic is allegedly responsible for the death of 150,000 persons, Tito is the agent of Stalin, who is responsible for the deaths of tens of millions of persons in the Ukraine, White Russia, Poland, the Baltic and the Balkan states over a period of about twenty-five (25) years.[64]

They would add later that, "Pavelic's contacts are so high and his present position is so compromising to the Vatican, that any extradition . . . would deal a staggering blow to the Roman Catholic Church."[65] And if Pavelić were to be arrested, the arrest would have to occur after he had left Vatican precincts on his own. Brigadier General J. D. A. Anderson, deputy chief of staff to the Acting Supreme Allied Commander Lieutenant General John Lee, noted that the arrest "will be an extremely tricky operation requiring elaborate co-ordination between U.S., British and Italian authorities and the maintenance of absolute secrecy."[66]

The most important new document from the CIC file on Pavelić, declassified in 2001, concerns a long meeting on August 11, 1947, at the British Embassy in Rome between Lieutenant Colonel George F. Blunda, of the U.S. Army's Intelligence Division, and two British officers using the names Bendall and Verschoyle.[67] Verschoyle was a British intelligence officer and his name, said Blunda, was probably a cover. Their conversation with Blunda suggests what British intelligence knew, where Pavelić was located, and what went wrong with the arrest. Verschoyle claimed to know the exact room in which Pavelić lived on Vatican property. Verschoyle insisted, however, that the United States should arrest Pavelić without British participation. Blunda refused, stating later that it "would not [be] to our best interests as a number of Croats have been used as informers by U.S. intelligence agencies [and a number of them] are known to be loyal to Pavelic's anti-Communist activities and Catholic fanaticism."[68] Since neither ally wished to have its fingerprints on Pavelić's arrest, it was agreed that the Italian police would take Pavelić into custody. Verschoyle agreed to arrange a pretext for Pavelić to leave Vatican grounds, after which a squad of Italian police would make the actual arrest under the supervision of selected U.S. and British officers. Such a scheme held promise, since according to Verschoyle, Pavelić, in a monk's habit with his hair cut short, had left Vatican territory as recently as July.

Yet the arrest never occurred. When asked why in November 1947, Verschoyle claimed that he was unable to lure Pavelić out of Vatican territory. The failure might have been due to a serious medical procedure which Pavelić, according to sources close to Draganović, was said to have undergone in early September—an operation which he barely survived.[69] It might also have been due to unelaborated reluctance on the part of British intelligence to implement the scheme, though it is impossible to say for sure without British records on the subject. According to CIA sources, Pavelić stayed at a monastery near the pope's summer home at

Castle Gandolfo in the summer and fall of 1948. In November 1948, he arrived in Buenos Aires aboard an Italian merchant ship. He wore a heavy beard and mustache, which he shaved thereafter. Gowan said years later that Pavelić's escape was facilitated not only by the Vatican, but also by British intelligence, though he was unable to say why the British would aid Pavelić's escape.[70]

Pavelić became active politically from the moment he reached Buenos Aires. He held two long conferences with Branco Benzon, the former Ustaša Minister to Berlin and then Bucharest and a member of Pavelić's inner circle during the war. Benzon informed Pavelić that the latter would have the "full help and cooperation" of the Argentine government. Pavelić then met with former ministers Vrancić, Josip Dumandzić, Oskar Turina, Lovro Susić and others. "Pavelic's first steps upon arrival in Argentina," said a CIA source in Buenos Aires, "indicate that he plans to become politically active . . . Pavelic is convinced that he has a mission to perform, and . . . he and his followers still regard him as the 'Poglavnik.'"[71] In subsequent years, he maintained numerous liaisons with Draganović in Rome.[72] He also conducted a private foreign policy: his associates told Italian representatives in Buenos Aires that Italy could count on "eternal Croatian friendship" and "recognition of the legal Italian claims concerning the Adriatic."[73] In the late 1950s, Pavelić still commanded the personal loyalty of 3,500 Croatian émigrés in Italy and Germany, though his extreme rightist leanings stymied the formation of a united Croat émigré movement.[74] In April 1957, after he was shot twice in a failed assassination attempt in Buenos Aires, Yugoslav officials demanded his extradition, as did the French press, which still remembered the Marseilles murders of 1934. Yet just as the Argentine Ministry of the Interior ordered his arrest, he disappeared. He died in Spain in December 1959.[75]

The Ustaša Spy: Draganović as a U.S. Intelligence Source

In the years following Pavelić's escape, Draganović maintained his position within the College of San Girolamo, helping Klaus Barbie, among others, escape justice. Yet he increasingly became an irritant for certain Vatican officials. Officially, the College of San Girolamo was under the protection of Cardinal Pietro Fumasoni-Biondi, who, according to a CIA report in August 1952, never gave approval for the non-religious work that occurred there. Draganović's ardent pro-Ustaša sentiments did not even spare fellow priests. Draganović, said the report, was "without love for that segment of his fellow man who does not nourish Ustasha ideology, in short, [he is] an uncompromising and dangerous extremist." The same report claimed that "[Draganović's] work is well known to the Vatican Secretariat of State, in an unfavorable light,"[76] though a report in Draganović's IRR file suggests that the Secretariat's objection was primarily to his exploitative financial dealings.[77] "The church," said a later report, "sometimes looks at him with suspicion as it is alleged that the Franciscan Fathers in Yugoslavia owe more allegiance to him than they do the church."[78] Draganović himself would later argue that his removal from the college was due to the feeling within the Vatican that Tito would not allow Croatian priests to come to the college so long as Draganović was there.[79]

The death of Pope Pius XII in October 1958 finally brought action. Immediately after the election of Pope John XXIII, the new Secretary of State, Cardinal Domenico Tardini, asked Draganović to leave the college.[80] Draganović, who had boarded at San Girolamo, took up a new address within Rome and obtained Austrian citizenship. Thanks to strong support among the Croatians within the college, he maintained his standing there unofficially; in fact, the Croatian Committee, a Croatian nationalist and separatist organization, survived there as well.[81] Draganović was further engaged by the Vatican as the Secretary of the Croat Committee of the Pontifical Commission on Yugoslav Refugees because, as Vatican sources put it, Draganović was "the most knowledgeable individual on Yugoslav affairs."[82] With Pavelić's death in 1959, Draganović also worked harder to reconcile Croatian exile groups, primarily the former followers of Pavelić and the more moderate followers of Maček. He remained, as his Army handlers repeatedly mentioned, passionately committed to Tito's ouster.

The U.S. Army Intelligence Division recruited Draganović in May 1959 after the Vatican itself had lost patience with him. A retiring Irish priest who had served in the Vatican for thirty-seven years and who had helped U.S. intelligence in Italy since early in World War II recommended him to Army Intelligence.[83] Draganović, said Captain Bruno Francazi (code named "Franco"), the U.S. Army agent who recruited him as a source for the 168th Military Intelligence Battalion, enjoyed "excellent coverage of Yugoslav activities." He would be of "extreme value to this unit."[84] Overwhelmingly, Army Intelligence was interested in order of battle information for specific locales within Yugoslavia, but general economic and political information was desirable as well.[85]

Yugoslavia seemed to be in political transition. Starting in 1954, Nikita Khrushchev worked to restore the bonds of friendship with Yugoslavia that Joseph Stalin had destroyed in 1948. This meant that Yugoslavia would not join a proposed Balkan Bloc with new NATO allies Greece and Turkey. It also meant that in a war, Tito's troops could fight on the side of the Warsaw Treaty Organization (founded in 1955) by invading Italy.[86] By 1959, moreover, East-West tensions over the Allied presence in West Berlin had reached a dangerous pitch.[87]

The Army reimbursed Draganović handsomely, though not, as he had wanted, with a signed U.S. government agreement concerning the political future of Croatia and a meeting with a U.S. Senator, preferably a Catholic.[88] (Army Intelligence was also aware when first they recruited Draganović that he was still in contact with Pavelić, although the latter would soon be dead).[89] The relationship between the Army Intelligence Division and Draganović, code named "Dynamo" (and "Dottore Fabiano" for financial transactions), lasted for over two years. Draganović used his clerical connections in Switzerland, Germany, Italy, France, and Croatia, his refugee camp contacts in Trieste,[90] his underground Croatian associates in Yugoslavia, and even a contact within the

Gehlen Organization to provide detailed bimonthly reports on everything from the Yugoslav order of battle to the location of anti-aircraft batteries to political, social, economic, and scientific developments. He even claimed at one point to have inside information on the pressure exerted by Khrushchev on Tito.[91] In one case, when Draganović felt that the Vatican might become too friendly with Tito's regime, he provided the United States with secret Vatican diplomatic information.[92]

Despite its close ties with Draganović from 1959 to 1961, Army Intelligence became disenchanted with the Croatian priest. Draganović never concealed that his motives were financial and that his first allegiance was to the Croatian cause against Tito. Therefore, he insisted on heavy U.S. financial support for Croatian nationalist organizations. Some of his schemes, such as the formation of a Croat legion under the command of General Rafael Trujillo of the Dominican Republic, were harebrained. Once the legion was formed, said Draganović, ironically not long before the Bay of Pigs fiasco, "the United States would not have to worry about Castro . . . as the [Croatian] Legion would take care of this problem without the United States getting involved.[93] After Pavelić's death, Draganović worked incessantly toward a reconciliation of former Ustaša followers and Peasant Party adherents of Maček, even though U.S. Army Intelligence understood that "Pavelic and the Ustashi are to most Croats, an anathema."

Draganović was loath to reveal his sources, a problem for Army Intelligence. Draganović's most valuable source in 1959 and 1960, a Croatian agent code named "Mr. X" in Trieste, who claimed to receive his information from a Yugoslav army colonel, had worked for the Italian government, and the CIA had received the same reports originating from Mr. X.[94] Other Draganović sub-sources turned out to be intelligence peddlers with dubious bona fides. One, who was also working for West German intelligence, recklessly reported through Draganović that the Soviets had stationed atomic weapons in Yugoslavia.[95] Others had simply been compromised by Yugoslav intelligence. A CIA evaluation of Draganović warned Army Intelligence as follows:

> Quite a bit of information on file shows a history of dubious allegiances and actions, and indicates that his leads are blown or penetrated. Aside from the possibility of present or future Yugoslav [intelligence] control, such individuals seem to represent organizations who have a vested interest in gaining U.S. government support . . . In short, we believe that the security hazards represented by the backgrounds of the individuals and the organizations they represent pose a greater threat to American interests in Yugoslavia and Austria than the circumstances warrant . . . We would [also] like to point out that [Draganović] as well as other members of Croatian nationalist organizations in other parts of Europe have been seeking American support ever since 1945. We have learned from sad experience that involvement with them leads to more sorrow than truth.[96]

Army Intelligence concluded that "the [Draganović] operation has neither been clandestine nor controlled."[97] Draganović, in the meantime, had come to learn too much about the U.S. intelligence structure.

Finally, in August 1961, during the East-West crisis over the construction of the Berlin Wall, Draganović seemed to blow a fuse. He complained bitterly to his handler that the United States was not helping the Croat cause enough (while helping Tito too much) to justify his own help to U.S. intelligence.[98] Later he even claimed that Serbs were controlling the Pentagon.[99] In January 1962, Draganović was dropped "with prejudice" thanks to his demands for "outrageous monetary tribute and U.S. support of Croat [organs] as . . . payment."[100]

After being dropped by U.S. Army Intelligence, Draganović lived in seclusion in a monastery at Pressbaum near Vienna. There he worked on a book on the Partisan shooting of Croatian returnees in May 1945. He also continued to prepare propaganda against Tito's Yugoslavia, and might have helped in the preparation with sabotage activities as well.[101] In September 1967, however, Draganović, now sixty-four years old, suddenly disappeared during one of his routine visits to Trieste. Incredibly, he reappeared in Sarajevo, where he would live until his death in 1979 at age eighty-three.

On his disappearance, the Croatian émigré community and the Austrian press quickly charged that Yugoslav agents had secretly abducted the priest. The Yugoslav press countered with lengthy verbatim statements allegedly from Draganović himself that his return had been completely voluntary, that he wished to dissociate himself once and for all from Croatian émigrés and their terrorist activities, and that he could not get over how fantastic Tito's Yugoslavia looked.[102] Clearly the statements were prepared and not surprising in their profligacy. The real surprise, according to CIA observers, was that a Roman Catholic priest had seemingly been kidnapped without a single protest from the Vatican. On the contrary, the CIA noted, "the Vatican stated flatly that Father Draganovic returned to Yugoslavia voluntarily and that the Vatican is not interested in the matter any further."[103]

It did not take long for the CIA to posit an explanation for these strange events. It was tied, they said, to the recent Concordat between the Vatican and Yugoslavia, signed in June 1966. The agreement between Belgrade and the papacy, now under Pope Paul VI, had been a long time in the making. Yugoslavia had broken relations with the Vatican in 1952 when Pope Pius XII responded to Archbishop Stepinac's postwar struggles in Yugoslavia by making him a Cardinal.[104] Talks leading to a rapprochement between the Vatican and Belgrade did not begin until 1964, with an agreement not to be reached for two more years. The 1966 agreement would ostensibly protect the spiritual interests of Catholics in Yugoslavia.[105] Yet in return for the Yugoslav recognition of Vatican jurisdiction over the Catholic Church there, the Vatican agreed to the principle that the functions of Catholic clerics must take place solely in an ecclesiastical setting. Political activity by priests, in other words, was prohibited. The Holy

See also promised to investigate certain cases of political activity by priests that Belgrade found especially harmful. Draganović was a continuing embarrassment to the Yugoslav government. "It is obvious," said a CIA assessment,

> that the position of Monsignor Draganovic and that of numerous other Yugoslav clergymen who are involved in the activities of organizations of anti-Communist refugees, which activities are often of an exclusively political nature and even go so far as sabotage in Yugoslavia and terrorism inside and outside their homeland; these activities now find themselves in conflict with the pledges of the Vatican and with certain new policies of the Catholic Church toward Socialist countries.

This analysis also noted that the Yugoslav authorities who still had Draganović's name on their list of wanted war criminals would not try or punish him. "The fact that he is at liberty," noted the CIA analysis, "is eloquent." And the first officials in the West who knew about Draganović's return to Yugoslavia were indeed members of the Vatican Executive Council. The Vatican, the CIA concluded, was somehow involved in Draganović's kidnapping. The only surprise registered within the Catholic Church itself was that his return had even become a matter for public discussion.[106]

Ironically, Tito's attempt to placate Croatian Catholics and to put the past to rest by allowing Draganović to travel to Zagreb in November 1967 backfired. The Croatian Communist Party leadership commented that Draganović's freedom of movement provoked "justified revulsion" while the Croatian Catholic Church maintained a "studious silence." The American Consul in Zagreb reported that "the initial handling of the Draganović case by Yugoslav federal authorities has not produced . . . the desired propaganda coup." Indeed, the last voices in the world calling for the freedom of Father Draganović were, paradoxically, U.S. and Canadian citizens of Croatian descent, who lobbied their governments to rescue a man for whom even the Vatican had no more use.[107]

Notes

1. For the Ustaša's early history, see Jozo Tomasevich, *War and Revolution in Yugoslavia, 1941–1945: Occupation and Collaboration*, (1985; Stanford, CA: Stanford University Press, 2001), 30ff. The best account of the Ustaša regime as a whole is Edmond Paris, *Genocide in Satellite Croatia 1941–1945: A Record of Racial and Religious Persecution and Massacres*, trans. Lois Perkins (Chicago: American Institute for Balkan Affairs, 1961).

2. Tomasevich, *War and Revolution*, 50–60.

3. Ibid., 380–87.

4. Figures are from the United States Holocaust Memorial Museum, www.ushmm.org.

5. Figures are from the United States Holocaust Memorial Museum exhibit. Smaller numbers are presented in Tomasevich, *War and Revolution*, 592ff.

6. On Glaise-Horstenau, see Tomasevich, *War and Revolution*, 278, 404. For Hitler's comment, Germany, Auswärtiges Amt, *Akten zur deutschen auswärtigen Politik, 1918-1945*, Series D, vol. 12 (Goettingen: Vandenhoeck and Ruprecht, 1979), document 603.

7. Percy Ernst Schramm, gen. ed., *Kriegstagebuch des Oberkommandos der Wehrmacht (Wehrmachtführungsstab)* 2, part 1, (Munich: Bernared and Graefe, 1982), 137.

8. On Germans tried by the Yugoslavs, see Josef Foltmann, and Hanns Möller-Witten, *Opfergang der Generäle*, 3rd ed. (West Berlin: Bernard and Graefe, 1957).

9. On the myths and realities of the British surrendering Croatian refugees to Partisan forces, see Tomasevich, *War and Revolution*, 759–66. See also Nikolai Tolstoy, *The Minister and the Massacres* (London: Century Hutchinson, 1986); Robert Knight, "Harold Macmillan and the Cossacks: Was there a Klagenfurt Conspiracy?" *Intelligence and National Security* 1, no.2 (1986).

10. Michael Phayer, *The Catholic Church and the Holocaust, 1930–1965* (Bloomington: Indiana University Press, 2001), 37; Paris, *Genocide in Satellite Croatia*, 74–78.

11. On these issues, see Paris, *Genocide in Satellite Croatia*, 55–58, 63–67, 165–67, 203–5.

12. See Stella Alexander, *The Triple Myth: A Life of Archbishop Stepinać* (Boulder: East European Monographs, 1987), chapter 12.

13. Vladimir Dedijer, *The Yugoslav Auschwitz and the Vatican: The Croatian Massacre of Serbs during World War II* , trans. Harvey L. Kendall (Buffalo, NY: Prometheus, 1992).

14. Fiorello Cavalli, *Il processo dell' Arcivescovo di Zagabria* (Rome: La Civiltà Catolica, 1947); Richard Pattee, *The Case of Cardinal Aloysius Stepinać* (Milwaukee: Bruce Publishing Company, 1953). The making of myth surrounding Stepinać from the Serb and Croatian sides is discussed in Alexander, *Triple Myth*, 3–5.

15. Menachem Shelah, "The Catholic Church in Croatia, the Vatican, and the Murder of the Croatian Jews," in *Remembering for the Future: Working Papers and Addenda, vol. 1: Jews and Christians During and After the Holocaust*, ed. Yehuda Bauer, et al. (New York: Pergamon Press, 1989).

16. This prompted the pastoral letter of 31 Oct. 1943, against the shooting of hostages, which resulted in the arrests of several dozen Croatian priests. Tomasevich, *War and Revolution*, 536–38, 556–58; Shelah, "Catholic Church in Croatia," 276.

17. Alexander, *Triple Myth*, 3, 5.

18. Phayer, *Catholic Church and the Holocaust*, 34–36.

19. "Conditions in Yugoslavia," 10 Sept. 1941, NA, RG 226, entry 16, box 3, folder 338-373.

20. See the report to Allen Dulles, 28 Dec. 1943, NA, RG 226, entry 210, box 94, proj. 974345.

21. Quoted in Tomasevich, *War and Revolution*, 400. On Juretić himself, see Tomasevich, *War and Revolution*, 525n27.

22. "L'Episcopat Catholique en Croatie: Son point de vue à l'égard du racime–Son attitude à l'égard de la persecution des Orthodoxes–Son activité charitable," NA, RG 226, entry 210, box 94, proj. 974345.

23. Memo from Lagrange to Dulles, 28 Dec. 1943, in ibid.

24. On the takeover, see Alexander, *Triple Myth*, 82. On the criticism of papal pronouncements, see "The Catholic Episcopate," 8–10.

25. Alexander, *Triple Myth*, 92–5.

26. "L'Episcopat Catholique en Croatie." Another very small part of this long sermon is printed in Pattee, *Cardinal Aloysius Stepinać*, 205, as part of the defense statement of 8 Oct. 1946.

27. The Croatian "racial" definition of Jewishness was modeled on Nazi definitions but was more severe. See Raul Hilberg, *The Destruction of the European Jews*, rev. and definitive ed., vol. 2 (New York: Holmes and Meier, 1985), 710. On the Berlin roundup of German Jews in mixed marriages and the resulting protests from spouses, see Nathan Stoltzfus, *Resistance of the Heart: Intermarriage and the Rosenstrasse Protest in Nazi Germany* (New York: Norton, 1996).

28. Tomasevich, *War and Revolution*, 593–4. The following officials were married to full Jewish women: Pavelić's military advisor General Ivan Percević; Ustaša Youth Leader Ivan Orsanić; and Minister to Italy Milovan Zanić.

29. Translation mine. "Nessun potere dello Stato ha il diritto di sciogliere dei matrimoni. Se lo Stato vuole servirsi della forza fisica, deve dirsi che esso non compie altro che una violenza volgare, da chi nessun buon frutto può venire. So d'altra parte che di tali matrimoni ve ne sono anche fra gli esponenti del Governo, ma, nei contronti di questi, tali matrimoni sono protetti."

30. Emphasis my own. "Par conséquent, aucun pouvoir étatier n'a la droit de les dissoudre. Si, cependant, l'Etat aurait recours à la coërcition physique, il commettrait de ce fait un acte arbitraire, qui entrainerait des consequences fatales. Or, il est connu que de tells mariages existent dans les millieux de plus hauts dignitaires de l'Etat,—et quils sont à l'abri des persecutions."

31. Cavalli, *Il processo*, 218, 253–56; Pattee, *Cardinal Aloysius Stepanić*, 300–302.

32. Tomasevich, *War and Revolution*, 595–96.

33. Marcone to Cardinal Luigi Maglione, 31 May 1943, *Actes et Documents du Saint Siège Relatifs à la Seconde Guerre Mondiale* 9, Le Saint Siège et les Victimes de la Guerre, Janvier–Décembre 1943 (Rome: Libreria Editrice Vaticana, 1975), documents 211 and 324.

34. Shelah, "Catholic Church in Croatia," 275.

35. Note no. 1: Informations fourniers par Mgr. Juretić (Décembre 24 [1943]), NA, RG 226, Proj. 974345, box 94.

36. Ibid.

37. Dennis Reinhartz, "Huida de los Ustaša a la Argentina después de la Segunda Guerra Mundial," in the report of the Comisión para el Esclarecimiento de las Actividades del Nazismo en la Republica Argentino, http://www.ceana.org.ar.

38. Headquarters, Detachment "B," APO 168, U.S. Army, XOR: 0-0214, 2 May 1959, NA, RG 319, IRR, entry 134B, Krunoslav Draganović.

39. Tomasevich, *War and Revolution*, 390, 539–40. For the thesis, see Krunoslav Draganović, "Massenübertritte von Katholiken zur 'Orthodoxie' im kroatischen Sprachgebiet zur Zeit der Türkenherrschaft." PhD diss., Pontifical Institut, Rome, 1937.

40. See, for example, CIA report "Yugoslav Émigré Personalities" No. [excised], 19 Nov. 1953, NA, RG 263, Krunoslav Draganović Name File; Paris, *Genocide in Satellite Croatia*, 220. Reports from World War II also stated that Draganović was responsible for massacres of Serbs and the forcing of Serbs into labor battalions. See [excised] to [excised], No. [excised], 12 Dec. 1958, NA, RG 263, Krunoslav Draganović Name File.

41. Tomasevich, *War and Revolution*, 557–58; Paris, *Genocide in Satellite Croatia*, 175. For the Army comment, see Report by Special Agent Robert Clayton Mudd, 12 Feb. 1947, HQ, CIC, NA, RG 319, IRR, entry 134B, Krunoslav Draganović.

42. William Slany, *U.S. and Allied Wartime and Postwar Relations and Negotiations with Argentina, Portugal, Spain, Sweden, and Turkey on Looted Gold and German External Assets and U.S. Concerns about the Fate of the Wartime Ustaša Treasury: Supplement to Preliminary Study on U.S. and Allied Efforts to Recover and Restore Gold and Other Assets Stolen or Hidden by Germany During World War II* (Washington, DC: Government Printing Office, 1998), 141–57.

43. Allan A. Ryan, Jr., *Klaus Barbie and the United States Government* (Frederick, MD: University Publications of America, 1984), 135ff.

44. Allan A. Ryan, Jr., *Klaus Barbie and the United States Government: Exhibits to the Report to the Attorney General of the United States* (Washington, DC: U.S. Department of Justice, 1983), 138–40.

45. Saint Rome to Saint Washington, Memo JZX 4080, 18 Sept. 1945, RG 266, entry 108B, box 607, folder 8.

46. CIC Report of 10 Oct. 1946, 314–16, NA, RG 319, IRR, entry 134B, Krunoslav Draganović.

47. These included Dr. Vjekoslav Vrancić, head of the Political Section of the Croatian Foreign Ministry and one-time propaganda chief who was decorated by the Germans; Dr. Lovro Susić, the Secretary General of the Ustaša Organization who served as Political Commissar with German troops in Lika; and Colonel Vilko Pecnikar, a senior Ustaša military officer who also served as leader of Pavelić's personal bodyguard and Commander of the Croatian Gendarmerie. Biographical material in "Jugoslav Basic Handbook. Supplement No. 1, Part 1: List of Personalities," Jan. 1944, NA, RG 266, entry 120, box 478, folder 4.

48. Report from Robert Clayton Mudd to AC of S, G-2, AFHQ, February 12, 1947, NA, RG 319, IRR, entry 134B, Krunoslav Draganović.

49. Report by Mudd to G-2 Trust, y-3019, 5 Sept. 1947, ibid.

50. Chief, Foreign Branch T to Chief [excised], dispatch No. [excised], 27 Oct. 1947, NA, RG 263, Krunoslav Draganović Name File.

51. AFHQ Liaison Office IAI, RAAC, to AC of S, G-2 (C-I, AFHQ, 26 Nov. 1947, ibid.

52. Tomasevich, *War and Revolution*, 755–6.

53. See for example NA, RG 466, Records of OMGUS retained by HICOG, Records relating to CROWCASS, Administration of War Crimes Trials, box 23.

54. SSU to Director, Operations, X-2, 22 Jan. 1946, RG 226, entry 210, box 119, folder 518 (3 of 3). See also the FBI File on Maček: NA, RG 65, 100-148034, box 30.

55. Walter C. Dowling to J. Graham Parsons, American Embassy, Rome, NA, RG 59, entry

1068–Myron Taylor Collection, box 17, folder 16.

56. Fisher to Commanding Officer, Rome Zone CIC Detachment, 8 Aug. 1945, NA, RG 319, IRR, entry 134B, Ante Pavelić.

57. CIC, Rome Detachment, Zone Five, Case No. 5650, 29 Aug. 1947, NA, RG 319, IRR, entry 134B, Ante Pavelić. Another CIC report by Special Agent Robert Clayton Mudd, dated 30 Jan. 1947 and also in this file, cites a reliable source to the effect that Pavelić stayed specifically in the village of Celovać (Klagenfurt) near the Austro-Yugoslav frontier.

58. "Whereabouts of ex-Croat Leaders," 11 Oct. 1946, NA, RG 263, Krunoslav Draganović Name File. Originating agency redacted, but most information came from General Miodrag Damjanović, a Chetnik General living in exile in Rome. Paris, *Genocide in Satellite Croatia*, 259, mentions that the Americans had told the Yugoslav Government that the British had arrested Pavelić.

59. Secret: Interview between Vladimir Stakić and Cardinal Tisserand [*sic*], 7 Apr. 1946, Rome, NA, RG 59, entry 1068–Myron Taylor Collection, box 28, folder 14. This document has also been declassified as part of the Nazi War Crimes Disclosure Act. For Tisserant's similar views during the war, see Alexander, *Triple Myth*, 76.

60. Memo by Robert Clayton Mudd, 30 Jan. 1947, NA, RG 319, IRR, entry 134B, Ante Pavelić.IRR, entry 134B, Ante Pavelić. It might have been the possibility of arresting Pavelić that prompted Mudd to place an agent in the Monatery of San Girolamo in the first place.

61. CIC, Rome Detachment, Zone Five, Case No. 5650, 29 Aug. 1947, NA, RG 319, IRR, entry 134B, Ante Pavelić.

62. Ibid. For the tense relations between London and Belgrade in 1945 and 1946, particularly over the issue of Trieste, see Ann Lane, *Britain, the Cold War, and Yugoslav Unity, 1941–1949* (Brighton, UK: Portland, OR: Sussex Academic Press, 1996), chapters 4 and 5. See also Ann Lane, "Putting Britain Right with Tito: The Displaced Persons Question in Anglo–Yugoslav Relations, 1946–47," *European History Quarterly* 22 (2) April 1992: 217–46.

63. P. W. Scarlett, British Political Adviser to Supreme Allied Command, Mediterranean Theater, 47/166/2A, 2 Aug. 1947; and Joseph N. Greene, Acting U.S. Political Adviser, SACMED, 29 July 1947, both in NA, RG 319, IRR, entry 134B, Ante Pavelić.

64. CIC, Rome Detachment, Zone Five, Case No. 5650, 29 Aug. 1947, ibid.

65. CIC, Rome Detachment, Zone Five, Report of 12 Sept. 1947, signed by Gowan and Caniglia, ibid.

66. Memo by Brigadier J. D. A. Anderson, Deputy Chief of Staff, AFHQ, to Chief of Staff Major General L. C. Jaynes, 7 Aug. 1947, ibid. This document was declassified in June 2000.

67. Lt. Col. G. F. Blunda, GSC, HQ, Mediterranean Theater of Operations, Office of the Assistant Chief of Staff, G-2, to Col. Carl F. Fritzsche, Assistant Deputy Director of Intelligence, HQ. European Command, U.S. Army, 8 Nov. 1947, NA, RG 319, IRR, entry 134B, Ante Pavelić.

68. Ibid.

69. CIC, Rome Detachment, Zone Five, Report of 12 Sept. 1947, signed by Gowan and Caniglia, ibid.

70. Phayer, *Catholic Church and the Holocaust*, 174.

71. CIA Report No. [excised], 2 Dec. 1948, NA, RG 263, Krunoslav Draganović Name File.

72. See the report of the discussion between Draganović and the CIC Agent code named "Sardi," dated 29 May 1959, NA, RG 319, IRR, entry 134B, Krunoslav Draganović.

73. See card dated 18 Oct. 1954 in NA, RG 319, IRR, entry 134B, Ante Pavelić.
74. This information came from Draganović, who pointed out that these 3,500 émigrés had sworn personal loyalty to Pavelić. See XOR 0-0209, 26 Mar. 1960, NA, RG 319, IRR, entry 134B, Krunoslav Draganović.
75. See the reports in NA, RG 65, 105-11194-A, box 125.
76. CIA Report of 24 July 1952, NA, RG 263, Krunoslav Draganović Name File. Pius XII had no Secretary of State after 1944 with the death of Cardinal Luigi Maglione. He acted as his own Secretary of State until his death in 1958.
77. "It was reported in August 1953 that . . . for some time Draganovic had realized about 25,000 lire from each Yugoslav refugee, on the promise that he would arrange for their emigration. At that time, reportedly, he had lost face in political civilian and ecclesiastical circles, including the Vatican Secretariat of State. It was also reported in September 1954 that Draganovic had received a contribution of 186,000 lire in March 1954, to be distributed among Croat refugees and having used the money (received from World Council of Churches) to help only a few refugees of Ustashi leanings." Francis G. Coleman to Research and Development Agency, 16 Apr. 1959, NA, RG 319, IRR, entry 134B, Krunoslav Draganović.
78. Setaf 41–Dynamo, [excised] 1961, ibid. Draganović's later American handler, "Franco," commented in December 1959 that "it is well known that Dynamo [Draganović] has a very strong hold over Franciscan priests inside Yugoslavia." XOR: 0-0712, 23 Dec. 1959, ibid.
79. NA, RG 319, IRR, entry 134B, Krunoslav Draganović.
80. Report by [excised] 11 Dec. 1958, NA, RG 263, Krunoslav Draganović Name File.
81. Convinced that Tito would attempt to kidnap or kill him, Draganović had several addresses in Rome. See XOR: 0-0214, 2 May 1959, NA, RG 319, IRR, entry 134B, Krunoslav Draganović.
82. Setaf 41–Dynamo, Date excised, 1961, ibid.
83. Colonel Richard G. Ciccolella, AC of S, G2/G3 to Deputy Chief of Staff, Intelligence, U.S. Army, Europe, AESE-CBC-MIB, 10 June 1961, ibid.
84. Franco to HQ, Department B, U.S. Army, XOR: 0-0214, 2 May 1959, ibid.
85. Sardi to HQ, XOR-0-0271, 29 May 1959, ibid.
86. Svetozar Rajak, introduction to "New Evidence from the Former Yugoslav Archives: The Tito-Khrushchev Correspondence, 1954" *Cold War International History Project Bulletin*, Issue 12/13, Fall/Winter 2001, 315–24.
87. Hope Harrison, *Ulbricht and the Concrete Rose: New Archival Evidence on the Dynamics of Soviet–East German Relations and the Berlin Crisis, 1958–1961*, Cold War International History Project Working Paper No. 5 (Washington, DC: CWIHP, 1993).
88. Franco to HQ, XOR-0-0399, 3 Aug. 1959, NA, RG 319, IRR, entry 134B, Krunoslav Draganović.
89 Sardi to HQ, XOR-0-0271, 29 May 1959, ibid.
90. Draganović created nets within the refugee camps in the Trieste region and would pick up information during his frequent visits to the camps, ostensibly to hear confessions. See the handwritten report on the La Fraschette camp, [excised] to [excised], No. [excised], 28 Apr. 1955, NA, RG 263, Krunoslav Draganović Name File.
91. XOR 0-0364, 13 July 1959; and XOR 0-0399, 3 Aug. 1959, both in NA, RG 319, IRR, entry 134B, Krunoslav Draganović.

92. Franco to HQ, XOR: 0-0859, 15 Dec. 1960, ibid. Along with a number of Order of Battle reports, Draganović supplied what he called a top secret copy of an official Vatican proposal made through the twenty-one Catholic Bishops in Yugoslavia to the Yugoslav government for closer relations between the Vatican and Yugoslav government.

93. Franco made no comment. See for example Franco to HQ, XOR: 0-0026, 13 Jan. 1960, NA, RG 319, IRR, entry 134B, Krunoslav Draganović.

94. Operational Plan, 28 Aug. 1959, 236–9; and Franco to HQ, XOR: 0-0490, 7 Sept. 1959, in NA, RG 319, IRR, entry 134B, Krunoslav Draganović. After much pressing, Draganović revealed Mr. X's name on 17 Jan. 1960, but the name is redacted. Franco to HQ, XOR: 0-0031, 18 Jan. 1960, ibid. Mr. X had worked for Italian Intelligence until 1949. Army Intelligence concluded in September 1961 that Draganović's refusal to reveal his sources raised "the inherent danger of 'paper-milling.'" Report to CO, 163rd Military Intelligence Battalion, 13 Sept. 1961, ibid.

95. Report to CO, 163rd Military Intelligence Battalion, 13 Sept. 1961, ibid.

96. Ibid. The CIA had never trusted Draganović and noted in December 1958 that "it is fairly evident in the case of Draganovic that his sponsorship of . . . Ustashi elements stem from deep-rooted conviction that the ideas espoused by this arch-nationalistic organization, half logical, half lunatic, are basically sound concepts." It was also clear to the CIA by this time that some of Draganović's "most trusted henchmen" were members of Yugoslav intelligence and that at one point a Yugoslav agent posing as an Ustaša refugee had penetrated Draganović's organization. See [excised] to [excised] No. [excised], 12 Dec. 1959, NA, RG 263, Krunoslav Draganović Name File.

97. Report to CO, 163rd Military Intelligence Battalion, 13 Sept. 1961, NA, RG 319, IRR, entry 134B, Krunoslav Draganović.

98. Marty to HQ, XOR 0-0542, 17 Aug. 1961, ibid.

99. Marty to HQ, XOR 0-0565, 31 Aug. 1961, ibid.

100. Ibid., 281ff.

101. For the suspicion that Draganović was involved in sabotage in these years, see Memorandum to Headquarters Chief by [excised], No. [excised], 16 Nov. 1967, NA, RG 263, Krunoslav Draganović Name File.

102. "Quisling Voluntarily Returns to Sarajevo," Belgrade Tanyug International Service, 10 Nov. 1967; "Émigré Priest Denied Forced Return Charge," Zagreb, Vjesnik, 12 Nov. 1967, both in NA, RG 263, Krunoslav Draganović Name File.

103. "Re: Father Krunoslav Dragonovic" [excised], 28 Dec. 1967, ibid.

104. Archbishop Stepinać was sentenced to twelve years in prison 1946 and served part of his sentence in Lepoglava prison. In December 1951, he was released due to poor health but remained under house arrest. He died in Krasic in February 1960.

105. The official name of the agreement is The Protocol of Discussions between the Representatives of the Socialist Federal Republic of Yugoslavia and Representative of the Holy See. Formal relations were reestablished when envoys were exchanged in 1970. On March 29, 1971, Tito made a formal state visit to Pope Paul VI.

106. Memorandum to Headquarters Chief by [excised], No. [excised], 16 Nov. 1967, NA, RG 263, Krunoslav Draganović Name File.

107. FBI records on these groups are included in NA, RG 263, Krunoslav Draganović Name File.

9

Nazi Collaborators in the United States: What the FBI Knew

Norman J. W. Goda

Thou gav'st us a haven,
Thou open'st the gates
To the blessed soil
Of the United States!

— "We Lift our Hearts: Hymn of the Refugees,"
words and music by Frederick C. Nagy, 1953[1]

NEWLY DECLASSIFIED FBI FILES, supplemented by files of other agencies, provide new insight into the activities of Eastern European émigrés who had collaborated with the Nazis in the murder of Jews and other ethnic groups before relocating to the United States under the 1948 Displaced Persons Act. Many have concluded that the arrival and naturalization of war criminals in the United States was the fault of the Immigration and Naturalization Service, which has been portrayed as understaffed and even incompetent.[2] Yet the INS was not as negligent as has been assumed. The FBI, as the nation's chief law enforcement agency, knew much about the criminal backgrounds of many émigrés, but it never acted on what it knew, nor did it assist other agencies that wished to act, including the INS.

The FBI's indifference must be understood in context. In the 1950s it was widely held that the threat to American security came not from Nazis or their collaborators, but from the Soviets and theirs. Communism had been a target of FBI operations since 1917, and such remained the case during World War II despite the FBI's surveillance of Nazi-related activities.[3] Postwar FBI counterintelligence directed against Communism was similarly broad in scope.[4] War crimes, on the other hand, generated considerably less FBI interest. The past crimes of Nazi collaborators were difficult to prove, and collaborators committed no new Nazi-related crimes after having settled in the United States. Moreover, in some cases, collaborators could be used as anti-Communist bulwarks in their own émigré communities. Yet, even in cases where the immigrant in question was not a major anti-Communist figure in the émigré community, the FBI was apathetic as to whether or not the accused was a war criminal. As a result, the FBI did not dig deep for the truth, and in some cases it even protected former collaborators while using them as sources or allowing other agencies to do so.

This chapter presents six case studies. These particular cases were chosen because their criminality is not in doubt. Two, John Avdzej of Byelorus and Andrija Artuković of Croatia, were "quiet criminals" who held normal jobs and tried to live inconspicuously. The FBI ignored the evidence of criminality for both. Two others, László Agh of Hungary and Viorel Trifa of Romania, were important anti-Communist figures in their communities. The FBI withheld incriminating evidence in each case during the 1950s that might have resulted in their deportation. Russian Vladimir Sokolov and Ukrainian Mikola Lebed were also leaders in their respective émigré communities. The FBI ignored the crimes of both, using the former as a source and allowing the latter to work extensively for the CIA.

Agh was ordered deported in 1960 after a long INS investigation, but remained in the United States after he appealed. Trifa and Avdzej both were obliged to leave the country and renounce their U.S. citizenship in 1984. Sokolov had his citizenship revoked in 1986. Artuković was ordered deported in 1952, but for reasons described below was not extradited to Yugoslavia until 1986. He died in 1988 awaiting execution. Lebed died in the United States in 1998 at age 88, and his criminality was clear to everyone who knew his background.

The FBI and the "Quiet Criminals"
John Avdzej

John Avdzej (or Awdziej) was a Byelorussian collaborator who surrendered his U.S. citizenship in 1984 rather than face legal denaturalization proceedings. Avdzej spent the war years in Stolpce, claiming to have been a farmer, tradesman, and road engineer. After telling the U.S. authorities in Frankfurt that he had arrived in Germany as a forced laborer, he received an immigration visa in 1950 and came to the United States. He held skilled labor jobs while living in Passaic, New Jersey, and became a naturalized U.S. citizen in 1959.[5]

Evidence surfaced against Avdzej in 1954 when his brother Alexander, six years John's junior, applied for a visa to immigrate to the United States. Information garnered by the 66th Army Counterintelligence Corps (CIC) and furnished to the FBI liaison in Heidelberg indicated that John Avdzej went to Germany with the separatist White Russian Committee in 1939 when the Germans attacked Poland; that after working with this committee in Warsaw he was transferred in 1942 by the SD to Baranowicze (then in German-occupied Byelorus); and that the Germans made him mayor of the Niasvizh district the same year. The CIC report noted that John's first act was to remove all Poles from administrative posts. He also helped engineer the arrest of members of the Polish intelligentsia, including journalists, professors, priests, and former military officers. According to the report, John submitted a list of 120 politically dangerous Poles to the SD in

Baranowicze and physically participated in their execution in Gajki. John also was said to have participated in the executions of thousands of Jews in the Niasvizh area. According to the CIC, John Avdzej had been labeled a war criminal not only by Polish and Soviet radio in 1945 and 1946, but also by the anti-Communist Polish Home Army, which had sentenced him to death in absentia.[6]

Newly released material shows that the Visa Division of the Department of State had seen the CIC information and contacted the INS in October 1954 with the comment that the "highly derogatory information [in the CIC report] concerning one [John] Avdzej" indicated that he "may have entered the country illegally."[7] The INS took the case seriously and contacted the CIA for additional information on Avdzej, but the CIA had none beyond what the INS knew.[8] The INS also contacted the Newark field office of the FBI in March 1955 to discover whether an INS investigation of Avdzej would "interfere with any action you contemplate."[9]

The FBI looked into John Avdzej. In July 1955, the Newark office interviewed Waclaw Wisniewski, a Polish immigrant to the United States from Stolpce who also lived in New Jersey. Wisniewski would provide information which, when fully developed, would show that the CIC had confused the Avdzej brothers. Alexander had been the mayor of Niasvizh. However, John was also implicated, having been the German-picked mayor of Stolpce. Wisniewski could not say whether the brothers had physically participated in executions, but he knew both had "collaborated with the Germans in carrying out their decrees, were friendly toward them, and were sympathetic toward their political beliefs."[10] Based on this information, Alexander would never be allowed into the United States. As for John, the FBI field office in Newark noted that he "may have entered the country illegally."[11]

By October the Newark field office had enough information to interview John personally in order to determine "whether or not [he] is a threat to the internal security of the United States." But before the FBI interviewed him, the Newark office sent a separate message to FBI headquarters "requesting authority to re-contact the subject as a potential security informant or double agent," possibly to infiltrate Byelorussian immigrant circles in New Jersey.[12] Hoover was uninterested in investigating Avdzej for deportation or in using him as an FBI source, commenting that "since the war there have been a great number of complaints that people aided the Germans during the war in persecuting the Jews. Interviews in other cases have developed no substantiation of the allegations." Hoover added that since a review of Avdzej's file revealed neither "substantial subversive activity" nor "sound indication of any informant potential," the case was to be closed.[13]

It was true that in the immediate postwar years the FBI had received reports of war criminals living in the United States from eyewitnesses who claimed to know their identities. It was also true that in such cases it was hard to confirm the identity of the accused based on eyewitnesses alone.[14] The evidence against Avdzej, however, was worth pursuing, especially since one of the reports came from Army

Intelligence and since the INS and the State Department were convinced that an investigation was worth doing. Avdzej did not leave the United States until nearly three decades later.

Andrija Artuković

Andrija Artuković was the Interior Minister of the Independent State of Croatia during the war. He authorized anti-Serb and anti-Jewish legislation as well as mass shootings, deportations, and the creation of Croatia's concentration camps. When Archbishop Stepanić became alarmed in 1941 about Ustaša racial hatred, it was Artuković that he addressed. OSS had been fully aware of Artuković's stature, too.[15] Like most leading Ustaši, Artuković fled Croatia before the Partisan advance in 1945. Rather than flee to Argentina like Ante Pavelić and others, Artuković joined his brother in southern California in the summer of 1948. He entered the United States illegally under a false name, and then overstayed his temporary visa. In 1949, the INS, with the help of the State Department, discovered that Artuković was indeed no refugee.[16]

Yugoslav attempts to have Artuković extradited throughout the 1950s were stymied. Neither the Justice Department nor the State Department wished to deport or extradite him to Tito's Yugoslavia, where he would surely be executed. The Yugoslav government filed an extradition request in August 1951, but the federal circuit court in Los Angeles (where his case was heard) was also sympathetic to Artuković, who had the noisy backing of the Croatian American community there. By 1959, after much legal maneuvering, he was allowed to remain in the country.[17]

The FBI's main concern in the Artuković case was propagandistic. After a Yugoslav request for Artuković's extradition in August 1951, the Yugoslav Information Agency funded and distributed to American press agencies an eighty-five-page booklet, *This is Artuković*. The booklet contained graphic photographs of corpses at Jasenovać, letters from Stepanić to Artuković, and excerpts from Artuković's own speeches. But the FBI (and Army Intelligence) viewed the booklet as simple Communist propaganda.[18] The only facet of the Artuković case investigated by the FBI in 1951 was the origins of the pamphlet. Hoover warned, "The Yugoslav Embassy . . . is very anxious to have the American press build up this story."[19] The FBI indeed traced the pamphlet's origins back to the embassy, which confirmed Hoover's belief that "Artuković is believed to possess great potential propaganda value inasmuch as appropriate action taken against him would greatly impress Yugoslav citizens who do not trust the Tito regime."

The Israeli trial of Adolf Eichmann in 1961 triggered new Yugoslav hopes that Artuković could be extradited. The CIA reported that Belgrade would send documents to Israeli prosecutors linking Artuković to Eichmann. If the documents were used at trial, then Yugoslavia would open the extradition case again in the United States based on the validity of their evidence in the Israeli case.[20] But anti-Communist suspicion continued to dominate FBI thinking.

After renowned journalist and FBI bête noire Drew Pearson published "Facts on Himmler of Yugoslavia" in *The Washington Post* in June 1962, the FBI's assessment, possibly based on phone taps, was that "Pearson is more than friendly with Yugoslav officials in the U.S." The FBI even tipped President Kennedy's press secretary Pierre Salinger so that Kennedy could sidestep questions having to do with Artuković at his June 7, 1962, press conference.[21]

Artuković was never an FBI informant in the 1960s, but the FBI questioned him on matters pertaining to Croatian terrorism in the United States. The Bureau also contacted him when it received rumors of Serb or Israeli assassination plots against the former Ustaša minister. In one interview in his California home, Artuković expressed "his deep appreciation of the FBI's interest in his safety."[22] Justice for Artuković was delayed for decades. In 1986 he was finally extradited to Yugoslavia, where he received the death sentence after his trial.

Émigré Leaders

László Agh

A fascinating story concerns the Hungarian Warriors Comradeship Association (MHBK), a global society led by former Hungarian Arrow Cross officers who had served Ferenc Szálasi's collaborationist government.[23] In 1950, the CIA and Army Intelligence put the story of the Hungarian Warriors together as follows:[24] With the Red Army pushing into Hungary, leading Hungarian SS officer Károly Ney ordered the General Staff to create a stay-behind network of special combat and intelligence forces known as *Kopjas* (pike men). They were ultimately organized by General Andras Zako, whom Szálasi made Chief of military intelligence on October 15, 1944.[25]

Many Kopjas fled into Austria with the Soviet occupation. Zako arrived in Innsbruck in 1947, and the following year the Kopjas became the "Hungarian Warriors Comradeship Association." United States Army Intelligence thought Zako aimed to become war minister in a new Hungarian government, but his group was an "organization of extreme rightists and nationalists with racial bias." Most post-1945 Hungarian exiles were loathe to identify with Zako, afraid to lose support of the Western European and U.S. governments.[26] In the meantime, he forged an intelligence relationship with French.[27]

The MHBK also intended to help with Western military operations in Hungary (should they occur) by providing Hungarian troops. It thus kept tabs on Hungarian refugees with representatives in Austria, Germany, France, Great Britain, Spain, Switzerland, Latin America, and the United States.[28] The MHBK distributed a worldwide publication called *Central Bulletin* (*Kozponti Tajekoztato*) known after May 1950 as *The Way of the Warrior* (*Hadak Utjan*). The politics of the MHBK leadership were clear to the CIA, which said that it was "composed of a clique of former Hungarian officers who were members of the Arrow Cross and are still sympathetic to its fascist principles."[29]

FBI interest in the MHBK focused on Dr. László Agh. Agh came to the United States in 1947 and became the U.S. MHBK president in 1949. Agh ingratiated himself with the FBI from the start. He wrote to the New York field office on September 8, 1949, to introduce himself as the MHBK representative in the United States, describing the MHBK as centered in Austria but "friendly to the United States." The *Central Bulletin,* Agh said, was friendly, too, and he promised to send a copy of each issue to the FBI for approval before distribution in the United States.[30]

Agh appeared at the FBI New York field office twice—on September 28, 1949, and on March 31, 1950. When first questioned, Agh said that he was a lawyer in Budapest before the war and that in 1938 and 1939 his reserve artillery regiment was called up to help occupy Slovak territory awarded to Hungary when Czechoslovakia was dismembered. In 1942, he said, his regiment was sent with the Second Hungarian Army to the eastern front on the Don. He said he was wounded in 1943, hospitalized in Budapest, and spent the remainder of the war uneventfully in Hungary. He fled as the Soviets advanced on Budapest, lived first in Austria as a refugee and then in Italy, and entered the United States in 1947. Living in Newark as of 1950, Agh registered Hungarian veterans and distributed MHBK literature for General Zako. Familiar with the Foreign Agents Registration Act of 1938, he registered his organization with the Department of Justice in December 1949, listing Zako as the foreign agent for whom he worked.

This registration—which indicated that Agh and the MHBK at the very least leaned to the extreme right—followed by Agh's visits to the FBI New York office triggered the FBI's investigation of Agh in 1950.[31] The INS Enforcement Division described the MHBK as "an organization of former Hungarian Nazis and pro-Nazis now abroad."[32] A reliable FBI informant added that the MHBK was led by pro-German Hungarian officers whose aim was "to organize and maintain contact to fight against Russia and communism when the occasion arises." The informant wondered "whether . . . the organization would not then turn toward some Nazi form of government."[33]

Agh understood American sensitivities. He registered the MHBK with the Justice Department as the Collegial Society of Hungarian *Veterans,* avoiding the more belligerent term *Warriors,* which was the accurate Magyar translation. He told the FBI that CIC and U.S. consular representatives in Austria had screened all Hungarian veterans in the United States for war crimes, though Agh, INS would later discover, lied that he came from Slovakia rather than Hungary so that his name could not be checked. At his March 1950 visit to the FBI, Agh offered his services as an FBI informant. Hoover would later note that "Agh is in periodic contact with [the New York] office as a source of information."[34] This visit brought another key statement, since Agh had to counter recent accusations in *Az Ember,* the newspaper of the Hungarian National Committee. In September 1949, he denied any wartime political affiliation, yet he now admitted that he had been an Arrow Cross member and connected with Counter Espionage and Intelligence at the War Ministry. The FBI had also begun translating MHBK literature. One issue of *Central Bulletin* claimed that the MHBK would shoulder "the task of driving back into the sewer the Moscow-worshipping rats."[35]

Hoover wanted *The Way of the Warrior* read regularly to see whether the MHBK was a disruptive force in Hungarian émigré politics. Yet Hoover was not interested in what Agh had done during the war. Agh's anti-Communist credentials and his willingness to spot Communists made his organizations an asset. As the New York field office reported:

> Investigation . . . has failed to reveal any pro-Communist activities on the part of this organization; on the contrary, because of the numerous members therein of pro-Nazi (Arrowcross) background, predominantly former Hungarian Army and gendarmerie officers, the organization is considered by some observers to be the most active group opposed to the Hungarian Communist regime.[36]

Agh bolstered his status by sending the FBI publications that emphasized the MHBK's loyalty to the United States. A 1953 booklet, *Hungarian Fidelity*,[37] claimed that the MHBK had 12,500 members in 24 countries and 21 U.S. cities, that 51 members currently served in the U.S. Army, that 18 served in Korea, and that the MHBK had raised 532 pints of blood for the American Red Cross.[38] Whitewashing the Hungarian past and the leadership corps of the MHBK, Agh added:

> Our special salute goes to President Eisenhower and to all citizens of the United States, whose consideration and good will have made it possible for us freely to plan and organize the liberation of our native land. . . .
> In fondness, we think of General Zako and his aids, who, in defiance of all the hateful attacks and vilifications that had been hurled at them, were first to lift the Hungarian soldier's flag then disgraced and dragged through the mud [and] built up what has become the largest Hungarian emigrant organization in the world.
> The members of the [MHBK] are composed mainly of refugees who fought against Communist Russia during World War II . . . We all honestly wish to take part in the fight against Bolshevism, in accordance with the intentions of the wise leadership of American statesmen.[39]

The booklet also contained a reproduction of "The Two Bells," a mural by painter Steven Juharos that was commissioned by the MHBK and presented as a formal gift to the Hall of Presidents at Gettysburg at its formal opening in June 1957. The painting is a prime example of appropriated historical memory. Surrounding a portrait of Eisenhower in his general's uniform were scenes from Hungary's heroic past, most notably the 1456 Hungarian victory "over the pagans at Nandorfehervar," and the delivery of Pope Callixtus III's proclamation that church bells be rung each day in commemoration. While Hungary's bells were now silent, Agh explained, the American Liberty Bell still represented freedom.

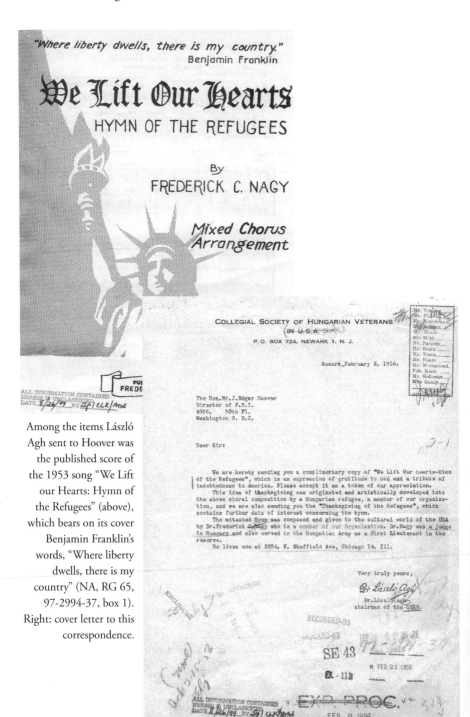

Among the items László Agh sent to Hoover was the published score of the 1953 song "We Lift our Hearts: Hymn of the Refugees" (above), which bears on its cover Benjamin Franklin's words, "Where liberty dwells, there is my country" (NA, RG 65, 97-2994-37, box 1). Right: cover letter to this correspondence.

Eisenhower had become the new guardian of a heroic Hungarian identity, and even the American shrine at Gettysburg was co-opted by the Hungarian émigré right in 1957. "As the freedom for which American soldiers died at Gettysburg was achieved," said Agh, "so will the freedom for which the Hungarians died [in 1956] be achieved. This is the meaning of . . . *The Two Bells*."[40] The White House found the painting odd enough that Bernard Shanley, the special counsel to the president, requested that the FBI perform a new check on the MHBK.

The FBI replied that an investigation had been carried out in 1950, but discontinued "inasmuch as it failed to reflect any pro-Communist activities on the part of this organization."[41] When asked by the Cincinnati field office in 1955 whether there should be an investigation of that city's MHBK branch, Hoover replied that though "several leading members [of the MHBK] are known to have been connected with the Hungarian Nazi Party" and that the MHBK "is considered on the extreme right," there was no need to investigate. "The major effort of this group in the United States," he said "is to distribute a monthly publication . . . which exhorts its leaders to be good American citizens and to report all Communist and subversive activities to the FBI."[42] Agh had done his job. The MHBK had become a desirable part of the American landscape.[43]

In July 1951, the INS began investigating whether Agh should be deported as a war criminal. Many leads came from *Az Ember*, which claimed to have uncovered twelve witnesses who could testify "as to the anti-Semitic atrocities committed by Laszlo Agh."[44] *The Way of the Warrior* answered that *Az Ember* was engaging in a Communist smear campaign.[45] But INS investigators collected dozens of witness statements and affidavits from the New York area, Israel, and even South America. Agh, everyone said, had been in charge of a Jewish forced labor detachment at the Frigyes Barracks in Komáron in 1942. Witnesses cited a speech he made to Hungarian guards in which he ordered that the Jews should be treated so harshly that ten would die and be tossed on the garbage heap each day. Others cited the sadistic punishments that Agh would inflict on Jewish prisoners, including the performance of calisthenics to the point of unconsciousness, the forced eating of non-kosher food, burial up to the neck, and the eating of one's own feces. The most terrible punishment involved the order for Jewish laborers to throw themselves on a piece of ground studded with partially buried bayonets.[46] According to the chief INS investigator:

The evidence of record indicates [Agh] was the prime mover in the commission of atrocities on inmates of a forced labor camp in Hungary during World War II. The evidence consists of depositions sworn to by witnesses who are now in all parts of the world. One witness who resides in Chile appeared personally and withstood several hours of cross-examination and remained unshaken in his testimony and in his identification of [Agh] as the perpetrator or the man who ordered the perpetration of atrocities . . . The evidence . . . would appear to indicate that [Agh's] activities . . . at the forced labor camp in Hungary showed such a state of moral depravity that [Agh] should never be admitted to citizenship of the United States.[47]

The INS' problem lay not in the discovery of evidence pertaining to Agh's activities in Hungary, which was plentiful, but in U.S. law, which provided a five-year statute of limitations protecting applicants for naturalization. Agh applied in 1955. Since the crimes had occurred over a decade before his application and since Agh had been a law-abiding resident of the United States since his arrival in 1947, the INS could deport him only with evidence that he had broken the law since his arrival or that his character was the same as before his arrival and within five years of his petition.[48] In INS hearings Agh "vehemently denied under oath" that he had ever been a member or affiliate of the Arrow Cross. Yet on March 31, 1950, Agh had admitted to FBI Special Agent Elmer Roth at the New York field office that he had indeed been an Arrow Cross member. The INS could use the statement to show "that [Agh's] character had not changed since his residence in the United States and that he had testified falsely for the purpose of facilitating his naturalization."[49] The FBI thus held the key to the case.

In July 1958, the INS asked if Roth would testify in an INS hearing and if his report dated June 22, 1950, could be admitted as evidence. Roth, said the INS, was "a necessary witness" whose testimony "is the only matter delaying the completion of this case."[50] Roth remembered Agh's comments. But in September 1959, after numerous delays, Hoover announced that Roth would not testify. "We are taking this position," Hoover said, "because of the lack of protection afforded our Special Agents when they testify in INS hearings." Specifically, Hoover referred to a recent hearing in San Francisco, where an FBI agent "was subjected to unfair and uncalled for criticism."[51]

The INS eventually lost patience. On October 8, 1959, the INS informed the FBI that they now had enough evidence without Roth to warrant a deportation proceeding.[52] In the initial INS hearing in March 1960, Agh was ordered deported after a flood of corroborative witness testimony. Agh's own witnesses did not help his case. One insisted that Hungary had a Jewish problem and that Szálasi had been a good Christian in trying to ship Jews out. Another claimed that Agh in 1939 had written an Arrow Cross pamphlet titled "We Shall Do Hanging." Agh, meanwhile, could only insist that the case was one of mistaken identity, that he had never lied to a United States official, and that everyone testifying against him was part of a Communist plot.[53]

Yet the deportation was overturned by the Board of Immigration Appeals in April 1961. The Board excluded most witness testimony and argued—based on information found in the *Encyclopedia Britannica*—that since the Germans did not invade Hungary until March 1944, mistreatment of Jews could not have occurred before that date.[54] Before the 1961 appeal, INS officials had worried that too much of their case depended on witness testimony. Much would hinge, they said, on Agh's documented lie that he had never told a U.S. government official that he had been a member of the Arrow Cross.[55]   Special Agent Roth remained a key figure, but he did not testify. It is difficult to avoid the conclusion that Hoover could have made Roth available had he wished. Partly as a result of the FBI's non-cooperation, Agh, a war criminal identified by dozens of his own victims, remained in the United States.

Viorel Trifa

A case of more overt FBI protection is that of Viorel Trifa, a war criminal from Romania who immigrated to the United States in 1950. A one-time theology student, Trifa was a leading member of the Fascist, anti-Semitic Iron Guard. Under its leader Horia Sima, the Iron Guard shared power with Romanian dictator Marshal Ion Antonescu from September 1940 to January 1941. Anti-Jewish legislation and terrorist incidents inspired by the Iron Guard abounded, but an Iron Guard revolt on the night of January 20, 1941, sought to oust Antonescu and create a more radical Guardist dictatorship. The revolt failed, but not until the Jewish portion of Bucharest was subjected to one of the war's worst pogroms.

Before the 1941 revolt, Trifa edited the anti-Semitic newspaper *Libertate*, which railed against the Jewish presence in Romania. On Sima's recommendation, Trifa also became president of the National Union of Romanian Christian Students, a post giving him control of all university student groups. On the night of January 20, Trifa helped precipitate the revolt and the Bucharest pogrom by railing before a massive student rally and signing a public manifesto posted throughout the city. He called for an Iron Guard government while praising Hitler, damning England, and condemning the Jews. He thus helped ignite mob action in which hundreds of Jews were brutally murdered, their shops destroyed, and their synagogues burned. After the Romanian Army put down the revolt, German SD agent Otto von Bolschwing spirited the Iron Guard leaders out of Romania and into Germany, where they lived in a comfortable protective custody. After the war, Iron Guardists in Europe under Horia Sima would hire themselves out as intelligence agents to the Americans, British, and French.[56]

Trifa fled to Italy, where he served as a committee member for Constantin Papanace, the leader of an Iron Guard intelligence group supported by the Vatican.[57] He arrived in New York as a displaced person in July 1950 and went to Cleveland, where he edited the official organ of the Romanian Orthodox Episcopate in the United States, *Herald (Solia)*. By this time, he had already been tried in absentia twice in Romania: in 1941 the Antonescu government sentenced him to life at hard labor, and in 1946 the People's Court in Cluj sentenced him to death for crimes amounting to genocide under the Romanian penal code.[58] As early as August 1951 the CIA and the State Department were familiar with the "Trifa Manifesto" of January 1941 and so understood that Trifa "may have misrepresented the facts of his career in obtaining a visa."[59] By March 1952, State Department officials had found "scads of info on [Trifa]," none of it good.[60]

Trifa's presence in the United States and the FBI's involvement must be understood within the context of Romanian Cold War politics. Before World War II, the Romanian Orthodox Church in the United States was headed by a bishop appointed by the Patriarch of the Romanian Church, who performed his functions from an estate known as the *Vatra Romaneasca* in Grass Lake, Michigan. The post was vacant when the war ended, and the de facto head of the church was Reverend John Trutza, a financially ambitious cleric who became president of the Romanian Episcopate Council. This body voted in March 1947 to break with the Romanian Patriarch and become autonomous. FBI investigations revealed a number of facts about Trutza's desire to control the Vatra and other Romanian church assets in the United States, and they also showed him to be a strong anti-Communist. Trutza sponsored Trifa's arrival in the United States in 1950, and arranged his job at *Herald*.[61]

In November 1950, a small number of Romanian clerics responded to Trutza's actions by electing a new bishop—Romanian-born Reverend Andrei Moldovan, who came to the United States in the 1920s and was naturalized in 1943. Nothing concerning Moldovan's elevation to the post was normal, particularly his secret trip to Romania (via Canada) in November 1950, where he was invested with his office by the Romanian Patriarch Justinian. Before the trip, Moldovan lied to his parishioners that he was going to Arkansas. He lied when attaining his U.S. passport, telling State Department authorities that he was going to France. He also arranged the trip to Romania with the financial and administrative help of the Romanian legation in Washington and was invested in the presence of the Romanian Minister of Cults and Religion, Stanciu Stoyan.

United States authorities immediately suspected that Moldovan was a Communist agent. Secretary of State Dean Acheson warned the American legation in Bucharest that "[Moldovan's] elevation . . . and the arrangements connected with it [could] have potentially significant consequences [and] possibly prejudicial national interests."[62] The CIA warned that Moldovan's consecration in Romania was part of a plan elaborated in a secret meeting of Orthodox bishops in Moscow to invest bishops who had a pro-Communist disposition in an effort to sway Orthodox Christians, even those in the United States.[63] Consensus even among Moldovan's enemies was that he was an unwitting stooge of below average intelligence used by the Romanian Communist party to gain traction in the United States.[64] Justinian's "pastoral letters" concerning alleged U.S. biological warfare against North Korean civilians and Moldovan's attempt to lead a "peace tour" to Romania did not help his legitimacy in the eyes of anti-Communists in the United States.[65]

Trutza completed the growing schism when he called a meeting of the Romanian Episcopate Council in Chicago, which narrowly chose his nominee, Viorel Trifa, as the new Romanian Orthodox bishop. The nomination was breathtaking in its audacity. Trifa was a known Iron Guardist, a war criminal, and not even an ordained priest. The FBI questioned two Catholic sources highly knowledgeable about the Romanian Church—Monsignor Gerald P. O'Hara in Ireland and Monsignor John C. Kirk in Madrid. Both commented that while it was true that the Patriarch Justinian was "a complete Communist" and a "tool of Moscow," Trifa was unprepared for a bishopric "either from the standpoint of intelligence, spiritual inspiration, or morals." He was the cat's paw of Trutza.[66]

The FBI also had a source from within the Romanian National Committee in Washington, D.C., who added that Trutza had no easy time before that committee on September 25, 1951:

> [The Council] pointed out to Reverend Trutza the awkward position in which he was placing the members of the Rumanian Orthodox faith by insisting on having a former member of the Iron Guard as Bishop of the church . . . [They] warned Reverend Trutza of the vulnerable position in which he was placing the church insofar as [a] Communist propaganda attack was concerned . . . It was pointed out to Reverend Trutza that Rumanians as a whole knew the connection that Trifa had with the Iron Guard Students Movement in Rumania. This particular movement was the strongest organization in the Iron Guard . . . As leader of this movement, Trifa advocated and called for anti-British and anti-Semitic activities on the part of his followers and . . . proclaimed the benefits of . . . Hitler and Mussolini . . . Trutza was warned that this background of Trifa made him undesirable as a church leader in the United States.[67]

Trutza insisted that Trifa was "a repentant sinner" who "now realizes the wrongs of the Rumanian Iron Guard Movement" and that Trifa was "now willing to serve in every way possible and promote the ends of democracy." Trutza further assured the committee that he "could prevent any trend in the United States . . . toward a return of the Iron Guard movement" and that "he personally [could] always handle Trifa [who] will be a substantial contributor to the solidification of Rumanian Americans who today are troubled over the recent imposition of the Rumanian Communist Bishop Moldovan."[68] The National Committee was unconvinced.

Trifa's consecration was not easy. He had to be ordained as a sub-deacon, a deacon, and a priest, and take orders as a monk before he could become a bishop. Archbishop John Theodorovich, Metropolitan of the Ukrainian Orthodox Church in the United States, consecrated him after three other archbishops refused. Theodorovich, who claimed he was the last surviving bishop among those elected in Russia in 1921 (the rest, he said, were purged), was eager to insult the Russian Orthodox Church. In March 1952, Theodorovich received a telegram from the Romanian Orthodox Episcopate Council warning that Trifa was "a Nazi collaborator morally responsible for the murderer [sic] of thousands of Rumanian Jews on . . . 21–23 January 1941."[69] Insisting that evidence of Trifa's crimes against Jews was nothing more than "Communist intervention,"[70] Theodorovich invested Trifa with his new office on April 27, 1952, and Trifa took the name Bishop Valerian. *Herald* reported the consecration with the headline "The Bells Shall Ring and the Hearts Shall Leap with Joy."[71] Trifa and Trutza also won an ongoing legal battle with Moldovan later that year. Moldovan's series of lies regarding his 1950 consecration in Romania convinced the U.S. District Court in Cleveland to award Trifa control over the Vatra and all assets of the Romanian episcopate. Moldovan was enjoined from using the title of bishop and would hold little sway in the Romanian community. He died in 1963.[72]

The FBI followed this controversy; both Trifa and Moldovan became the subjects of FBI investigations in the 1950s. Plenty of evidence surfaced on Trifa. But Hoover was obsessed with getting the names of Romanian priests who followed Moldovan; with obtaining the names of individuals who wished to travel with him to Romania in order to see family members; with tracking penicillin shipments Moldovan made to Romania through Canada; and above all with discovering whether Moldovan took a loyalty oath to the Romanian government while in Bucharest.[73]

Hoover's fixation on the loyalty oath lay in the fact that it was the best legal ground for Moldovan's denaturalization and deportation as a foreign agent. It was on this basis that Hoover approved an FBI interview of Moldovan in Detroit in April 1953. If Moldovan could be fooled into admitting that he took the oath—and sources said he was not very smart—then this information would be forwarded to the INS and deportation proceedings could begin.[74] Although FBI agents in Detroit caught Moldovan in a number of lies concerning his November 1950 trip to Romania, Moldovan insisted he took no loyalty oath and that he was a loyal anti-Communist citizen of the United States.[75] The Detroit field office thus suggested closing the Moldovan investigation, while the Attorney General's office urged Hoover to get information that could prove that Moldovan "is engaging in any form of political activity," since the Foreign Agents Act under which he could be deported exempted purely religious pursuits as foreign agent activity.[76]

The FBI meanwhile protected Trifa from a great deal of evidence, including that from the FBI's own (and only) Romanian translator, Mathew J. Cazan, who reported in 1950 that "Trifa was instrumental in the Iron Guard movement and organizations attached thereto throughout [Romania]."[77] The State Department reported to the FBI the following year that Trifa had been adjutant to Iron Guard leader Horia Sima and that he probably got into the United States through fraud. The FBI had a translated copy of the Trifa Manifesto with its call "Death to the Masons and the Jews," with Trifa's name on the bottom.[78] The CIA reported (based on its own discussions with Monsignor O'Hara) that Trifa was "a leading Iron Guardist in Romania," and that "reports from various sources indicate that [he] participated in large scale massacres of Jews... notably the burning and looting of the Dudesti and Vacaresti sections of Bucharest in 1941," and that the Romanian newspaper *Universul* in January 21, 1941, carried the full text of Trifa's speech from the night before which praised Hitler for confronting the Jewish threat to Europe.[79] Well-informed Romanians and others who were in no way Communists also provided information on Trifa to the authorities. The comments of the Romanian National Committee to Trutza, about which the FBI was fully informed, have already been mentioned. Even a former member of the Iron Guard living in Oregon told the FBI that Trifa was a key member of the Iron Guard and that he issued his famous manifesto.[80]

None of this swayed Hoover. The Romanian Episcopate in the United States published a lot of anti-Communist literature, all of which was sent for Hoover's approval. *Communistic Attempts to Gain Control over American Church Organizations* (1952), for example, argued that the Kremlin was trying to infiltrate émigré groups in the United States, that the Romanian state was using Patriarch Justinian in this regard, and that the Romanian Church in the United States was a free outpost for Romanian Orthodoxy to which "liberty and justice-loving people look" for leadership against Justinian, who was "anxious to serve the interests of pro-Soviet politics and . . . Communist ideology throughout the Church." Part of this campaign, the pamphlet said, was to accuse Bishop Trifa of war crimes. "It is our humble but considered opinion, read the conclusion,

> that the machinations of Andrei Moldovan and the activities of anyone directly connected with him in his attempt to obtain control over the Romanian Orthodox Episcopate of America and its assets, are part of a huge Communistic plan designed to gain inroads to our American way of life and thereby subject it to the domination of Moscow.[81]

Hoover thought enough of the pamphlet to forward it to the State Department's Office of Security and the Attorney General's office with the comment that it "contains a detailed analysis of the factional dispute presently existing within the Romanian Orthodox Church." While there was consensus that Justinian was a tool of the Romanian government, Hoover's insistence on accepting Trifa's stilted version of the schism—and most notably Trifa's argument that the wartime evidence against him was simply a Communist attempt to smear an upstanding American bishop—was tantamount to FBI protection of a known war criminal.[82]

The FBI's version of events surprised even the CIA. In response to Hoover's comment in late 1953 that the denunciations against Trifa reflected nothing more than "the bitter animosity exhibited by the Communists toward Trifa," the CIA's Deputy Director of Plans made a rare historical corrective:

> Without wishing to enter into the merits of the long-standing dispute within the Rumanian Orthodox Church . . . we would like to point out that despite the emotionalism and mutual name-calling indulged in by both sides, there is a body of fact to support both contentions. As far as Subject is concerned, there is, for example, a well-known inflammatory document known generally as the "Trifa Manifesto," which Subject issued during the time of the Iron Guard uprising,

in which he calls for reprisals against the British for the alleged assassination by their orders of a German officer in Bucharest. In this Manifesto he states, among other things: "Cerem guvern legionary" which, translated literally, means "I call for a Legionnaire (Iron Guard) Government." There are official records of Trifa's participation, as one of the moving spirits, in the 1941 Iron Guard Rebellion, as well as evidences of his having been given sanctuary in Nazi Germany when the attempted coup failed. His adherence to Horia Sima, Iron Guard leader, was a matter of common knowledge in Rumania.[83]

None of this was substantial enough for the FBI, which counted the 1955 interrogation of Trifa himself as bona fide exculpatory evidence. The interrogation was undertaken only as a result of reports that Communists might have been able to infiltrate Iron Guard members in the United States and Canada and that Trifa might be a conduit for Communist party funds. Though the FBI field office in Detroit was skeptical of this charge, it recommended an interview since Trifa "was an official in the Iron Guard" and that "if Trifa is truthful, he could continue to supply information regarding the Iron Guard in the United States and Canada and on Rumanian immigrants."[84]

Trifa's interview, which took place over three days in February 1955, showed that he was a better liar than Moldovan. He argued that he was nothing more than the leader of a democratic students group in Romania; that he was never a member of the Iron Guard; that Horia Sima wrote the Trifa Manifesto and put Trifa's name on the bottom; that he attended the student demonstrations in the hope of keeping them orderly; that the speech he gave on the night of January 20, 1941, was also foisted on him by Sima; and that he was arrested by the Gestapo after the demonstrations, whereupon he spent the remainder of the war in a series of German concentration camps. Moldovan and his Communist friends had manufactured the war crimes charges, which, Trifa said, went unanswered because the episcopate lacked the money for a political war of words. It was an imaginative performance and one the FBI never questioned despite all evidence it had received to the contrary.[85]

The most disturbing episode of Trifa's presence in the United States came on May 11, 1955, when he delivered the convocation prayer in the United States Senate. On the same day, he met with Vice President Richard Nixon and asked for Nixon's support on behalf of Romania and "our brothers in Bessarabia," now under Soviet rule.[86] This was too much for Nicholas Neamtu Martin, an American citizen of Romanian descent. For the past five years, Martin had supplied the FBI Detroit field office with information regarding Trifa. Included in Martin's research was the location in Ontario of a former Romanian Army officer named Stavro Jianu, who had himself interviewed a number of Jewish victims of the Iron Guard who could identify Trifa. All had lost family members in the Bucharest pogrom of January 1941. Martin had no special ecclesiastical axe to grind, since he was not associated with Moldovan in 1955.[87] After the convocation prayer,

Martin contacted journalist Drew Pearson, who used Martin's information for his radio broadcast of May 30, 1955, as well as columns in the *Washington Post*, *Washington Herald*, and *Detroit Free Press*. Martin also told the FBI Washington field office that Pearson was in the process of arranging a meeting between him and Nixon, wherein Martin would tell the vice president the truth about Trifa and his illegal entry into the United States.[88]

Hoover scotched the interview in a brief note to Nixon, belittling the charges as nothing more than the result of a "factional schism within the Rumanian Orthodox Church of America" while smearing Martin as a "follower of Reverend Moldovan." Hoover included no information on Trifa's career in Romania other than to say, "Bishop Trifa, in an interview with agents of this Bureau, denied actual membership in the Rumanian Iron Guard . . . There has been no known activity of this type on the part of Bishop Trifa since his entry into the United States." Hoover also told Nixon that sources "have reported Mr. Martin to be a braggart and of questionable moral character."[89]

Later the same year, more information reached the FBI concerning Trifa's orders during the pogrom of January 1941 that the tongues of three Jewish clothiers were to be cut out. But in 1957, the Detroit field office recommended that Trifa's case file be closed based on the 1955 interview with Trifa. "A review of the file," the field office reported, "reveals no indication that [Trifa] still adheres to the Nationalist teachings of this organization. Trifa has stated that he is ready to do all in his means to defend the American way of life. There is no indication that Trifa's activities are inimical to the United States, therefore, this case is being closed."[90]

A relationship of sorts continued between Trifa and the FBI well into the 1960s. Anti-Communist pamphlets published under Trifa's auspices and pointing to Communist attempts to infiltrate émigré groups and churches continued to be sent to the FBI and continued to pique Hoover's interest. Trifa's reputation, however, induced Hoover to dissociate FBI headquarters from the bishop, ordering that the receipt of Trifa's information not be acknowledged in writing and that the Detroit Field office should "tactfully suggest in the future that [Trifa might] desire to contact [the] Detroit office directly." Such would avoid what Hoover called "embarrassment" to the Bureau.[91] Regardless, Trifa understood clearly the debt that he owed to the FBI. Rumors that President Lyndon Johnson would replace Hoover as FBI Director in 1963 prompted a letter to the president from the bishop himself, which claimed in the strongest terms, "The American people need men like J. Edgar Hoover."[92]

Émigré Agents

Vladimir Sokolov

The case of Vladimir Sokolov, aka Vladimir Samarin, also demonstrates how anti-Communist credentials could outweigh a collaborationist past. But Sokolov was more than an émigré leader; he was a willing Nazi collaborator who slipped into the United States by lying about his wartime past. He was naturalized in 1957.

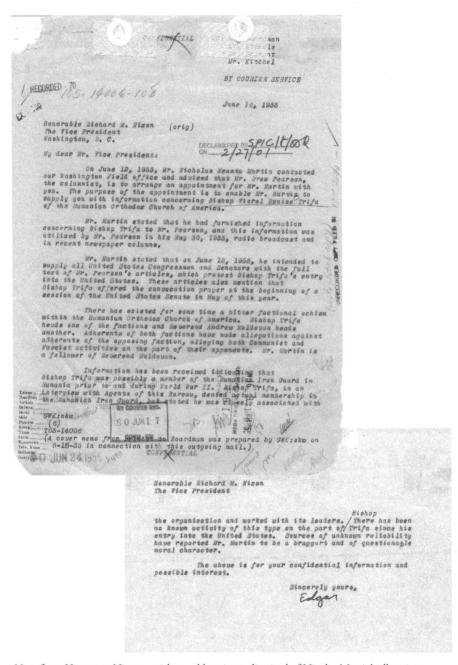

Note from Hoover to Nixon—with an ad hominem dismissal of Nicolas Martin's allegations against Trifa—opposing a Nixon interview by a journalist covering the story (Hoover to Nixon, 16 June 1955, NA, RG 65, 105-14006-4-108, box 159).

The FBI used Sokolov to spy on potential Communists and Soviet agents in the United States.

Sokolov was born in Orel, Russia, in March 1913 and worked as a teacher under the Soviet system from 1936 to 1942. The Germans occupied Orel from December 1942 to August 1944. Orel's strategic importance and large population meant that Russian collaborators were key elements to German control. SS Sonderkommando 7b, which hunted and murdered Jews in the region, needed various forms of local support. Sokolov voluntarily collaborated with the Germans as a senior editor and writer for *Speech* (*Rech*) a German-controlled, Russian language newspaper, and his contributions combined older Russian anti-Jewish tradition with the Nazi idea that Bolshevism was the latest manifestation of Jewish conspiracy. "The Kikes," he once wrote representatively in *Speech*, "will be destroyed thoroughly and decisively." According to Sokolov, Jews surrounded Joseph Stalin; Jews had started the current war; Jews controlled President Roosevelt; and the Germans with their allies "were fighting the Kikes of the world."[93] The Germans thought highly of Sokolov and decorated him with medals in 1943.[94]

Retreating with the Germans, Sokolov continued to serve them. As a displaced person in the British zone of Germany after the war, he worked for more discreet anti-Communist publications such as the weeklies *Put* and *Possev*. The latter newspaper was the official organ of the NTS (National Alliance of Russian Solidarists), an organization with its own collaborationist history. Founded in the 1930s by Russian émigrés of extreme rightist and anti-Semitic feeling, the NTS collaborated closely with the Nazis in Russia, providing local administrators, propagandists, and informants. The NTS rebuilt itself on purely anti-Communist grounds in 1945, first in Limburg an der Lahn and then in Frankfurt.[95]

In June 1951, Sokolov entered the United States as a displaced person after signing an affidavit that he had "never advocated or assisted in the persecution of any person because of religion, race, or national origin."[96] Under the pen name Vladimir Samarin, he became active in Russian émigré organizations. He worked as a proofreader for the Russian language Chekhov Press, which, funded by a $3 million Ford Foundation grant, published roughly two hundred Russian language books, including classics banned in the USSR. He contributed several articles to *New Russian Word* (*Novoye Russkoye Slovo*) and other émigré publications. He worked under Dr. Ivan London of Brooklyn College as a researcher for the Inwood Project, which studied Soviet propaganda. He contributed papers for the Columbia University Research program on the USSR, funded by the Ford Foundation and administered by the noted expert on the Soviet Union, Professor Alexander Dallin. Finally, Sokolov joined the North American Branch of the NTS, headquartered in New York City, and soon became branch president.[97] The NTS by this time remained a staunch anti-Communist organization with tight discipline and secret methods. It spread Russian language anti-Soviet propaganda even within the USSR.[98]

The FBI first became interested in Sokolov when conflicting reports emerged on him in 1954 before his naturalization. On the one hand, the FBI received a tip that a man named Vladimir Sokolov had been an NKVD (Soviet Secret Police) agent. This lead was a case of mistaken identity.[99] At the same time, the FBI received information from another Russian émigré who had known Sokolov in Orel that Sokolov had worked for *Speech* in 1943, that Sokolov had shared the views of this publication, and that he had collaborated with the Gestapo in Orel.[100] Though the mistaken NKVD charge had been a cause of great concern, the charge of collaboration with the Nazis seems to have been outweighed for the FBI by the fact that the informant did not like Sokolov and by Sokolov's anti-Communism. The same FBI report contained the assessment of another informant who described Sokolov as "a burning anti-Communist," who as the head of the NTS North American branch had even written Secretary of State John Foster Dulles on behalf of Dr. Alexander Truchnovich, a Russian who had recently been kidnapped by the Soviets in Berlin.[101] The FBI assessment of Sokolov as a "sincere, outspoken anti-Communist," was only enhanced in November 1957 when he was arrested while demonstrating outside the Park Avenue residence of the Soviet delegation to the United Nations and charged with assault.[102]

A more in-depth check of Sokolov was completed only after his naturalization in 1958 and 1959, when Sokolov applied for an announcer's position with The Voice of America. Though the State Department and the U.S. Civil Service Commission performed the checks, and though Sokolov was not hired as a VOA announcer, the FBI took a direct interest in the results of the check because, as Hoover said, "It is contemplated that we may interview [Sokolov] as a potential source" regarding the reliability of NTS members in the United States and possible Soviet penetration of other émigré organizations. The rumor that Sokolov had been an NKVD agent still hung in the air. Another FBI informant had said that "the Soviets have been able to obtain voluminous information from captured Gestapo files relating to Samarin," and that Moscow intended to make the information public. Moreover, the Soviets had published a photograph in August 1957 that included Sokolov's in-laws in Russia, possibly as a method by which to intimidate or pressure him.[103]

State Department checks on Sokolov ranged from the perfunctory to the incompetent. One researcher performed a brief check of agencies that might have had information on Sokolov including the CIC, the Berlin Documents Center, and Army Intelligence, but not the CIA, which might have had more information about NTS leaders than any other agency. He found nothing.[104] Another State Department agent interviewed one of Sokolov's NTS colleagues in Frankfurt, who naturally emphasized Sokolov's anti-Communist credentials. In this context, Sokolov was "absolutely reliable politically, intelligent, and decent in all respects."[105] The checks from the Civil Service Commission (USCSC) were, for the most part, also superficial.[106]

One USCSC report, however, by Harold Palatsky, found much more. Amid more interviews that confirmed Sokolov's aversion to the Soviet system, Palatsky found "derogatory information . . . in that subject allegedly collaborated with the Nazis during the German occupation of Russia from approximately 1942 until August of 1944, and in Germany, from approximately August of 1944 until the end of the war."[107] Vera Schwartz, the editor in chief at Chekhov Press who had supervised Sokolov for four years, related the following:

He had been Editor in Chief of a German sponsored Russian paper in Orel, Russia. This paper served the purposes of Hitler. In Germany, I would assume that Vladimir was probably in the Nazi propaganda organization. Whatever his work was in Germany before the end of the war, you cannot escape the fact that he was in the service of the Germans in Germany . . . [Sokolov] is probably absolutely loyal to the United States, as his destiny is tied to the free democratic world. However, I can't help but feel that a man who once switched to the Nazis could do it again. Other Russians who helped the Nazis have admitted their mistake but not Mr. Sokolov.

A thoughtful assessment also came from Mark Weinbaum, the editor of *New Russian Word*:

He was a conscious, ardent collaborator. He felt it was the thing to do—that the Nazis would help free Russia from the Communists.

The Russians in the United States, including myself, who are anti-Nazi, had to decide as to [the] degree of collaboration undertaken by such men as Sokolov. We had to make this decision when the United States Government allowed these people to come to this country. Of course, those who helped to murder Jews and Poles were rejected by us. That is why I spoke to Samarin and I will say that his past is "clouded." I will not say whether it is good or bad. It is up to the United States Government to question him about his past. He told me that he was an ardent anti-Communist and that he looked upon Germany as the liberator.

The most serious assessment might have come from the Columbia University history professor, Alexander Dallin, who was at the time the leading academic authority on the German occupation of Soviet territory during the war. His book, *German Rule in Russia* (1957), though revised in the 1980s, was the standard work on the German occupation,[108] and he also had worked with Sokolov on Columbia's Research Program on the USSR. "Mr. Samarin," Dallin said, "was a teacher in Russia."

He was later a newspaper editor under the Germans. The Editor in Chief of that newspaper [*Speech*] was Michael Oktan, who was one of the leading . . . Fascists in Orel, Russia.[109] My impression is that the N.T.S. placed responsible people in good positions under the German Occupation. I do not know whether or not Sokolov agreed with Oktan, who was an out and out Nazi sympathizer and collaborator. I have no reason to feel that Sokolov was enthusiastic about what the Nazis were doing, but I will say that he was prepared to work with them whatever mental reservations he had . . . I feel certain that he must have written some articles of which he is not overly proud today.

I would have no reason not to recommend him for work involving . . . national security. However, I will say to you that I am not too enthusiastic about his political attitudes and development.

Finally, the FBI studied the statements of Sokolov himself, who was interviewed in April 1957 in connection with his desire for a reentry permit following a political conference in Amsterdam.[110] If anything, Sokolov's comments foreshadowed those of Schwartz, Weinbaum, and Dallin. He admitted that he had been the literary editor and then deputy editor of *Speech* for nearly two years from December 1942 to August 1944. Yet he emphasized nothing more than its anti-Communism, which he knew would please his interrogators. "I wrote against the Communists," he argued, "because it was an anti-Communist paper . . . I am writing against Communists for the last fifteen years." Yet when he was pressed as to the more overtly anti-Semitic tenor of *Speech*, Sokolov had to be more forthcoming. "Under German occupation," he said,

there were many Russian newspapers published . . . and we were forced to assume certain political lines. We Russians fought the best way we could, but under the ever-present danger of being shot to death on the spot, we had to put in . . . Fascist and Anti-Semitic [remarks] to please the Germans . . . As to anti-Semitic remarks, there may have been some to which I was forced.

Sokolov then explained how he left Russia for Germany in August 1944, and how he "wrote against Communism" in the Vlassovite paper *Vola Narodna*, then edited *Put* and *Possev* during the Allied occupation of Germany.[111]

Hoover was indifferent to these revelations. "The results of the United States Civil Service Commission investigation of the subject," said Hoover, "contained no unfavorable information. A few persons who were interviewed stated that they knew [Sokolov] worked for the Germans during World War II and they indicated that they were uncertain as to whether he willingly cooperated with the Nazis." Hoover continued, however, that in view of "the lack of any factual derogatory information . . . [Sokolov's] cooperation will be sought regarding information concerning NTS activities in the United States and his knowledge of any Soviet infiltration into Russian anti-Communist organizations in the United States."[112] The FBI performed no further checks concerning Sokolov's actions from 1942 to 1945.

Due to post-1958 redactions in the FBI's file on Sokolov, it is hard to say how effective a source Sokolov was for the FBI. Perhaps he was a disappointment at first. Though willing to speak in general terms to the FBI about Soviet interest in the émigré community, Sokolov would divulge little concerning the NTS membership, organization, and activities. The furthest Sokolov went was to permit one NTS subordinate to speak with the FBI from time to time due to what the FBI called the increased amount of known Soviet activity in the émigré field.[113]

Later in 1959, Sokolov gained a position on the faculty of Yale University teaching Russian language and literature. How a man with no high academic credentials suddenly procured such a prestigious position is a mystery. It is clear that the FBI used him as an informant while at Yale, possibly to report on Russian students or on faculty in the 1960s.[114] It is clear from this case that the Army Counterintelligence Corps and the CIA were not the only U.S. agencies that made active use of Nazi collaborators.

Mikola Lebed

Mikola Lebed is one of the better-known cases of a former collaborator living in the United States. Newly released FBI records, together with Lebed's CIC file, CIA Name File, and INS dossier, make it possible to reveal his history with greater detail.[115] Before and during World War II, Lebed was a leading member of the younger, more radical wing of the Ukrainian Nationalist Organization (OUN) under Stephan Bandera (OUN-B) and its military/terrorist arm, the Ukrainian Insurgent Army (UPA). Based in Galicia, a region of Ukraine that was located in Poland from 1919 to 1939, the OUN had long called for an independent greater Ukraine. OUN counted among its enemies those that had denied Ukrainian independence (Poles, Soviets) and those in the Ukraine who had failed to assimilate (Jews).[116] During the Polish government's repression of the OUN in Galicia, Lebed helped plan the assassination of Polish Interior Minister Bronislaw Pieracki in Warsaw. In 1936 he was jailed by the Polish government for his role. Following the German attack on Poland in September 1939, he escaped from a column of prisoners.

In its work to destabilize the Polish state, the OUN's ties with Germany extended back to 1921. These ties intensified under the Nazi regime as war with Poland drew near.[117] Galicia was allotted to the Soviets under the August 1939 Nazi-Soviet Non-Aggression Pact, and the Germans welcomed anti-Polish Ukrainian activists into the German-occupied General Government. In 1940 and 1941, in preparation for what would become the eastern campaign, the Germans began to recruit Ukrainians, particularly from Bandera's wing, as saboteurs, interpreters, and police, and trained them at a camp at Zakopane near Cracow. In the spring of 1941, the Wehrmacht also developed two Ukrainian battalions with the approval of the Banderists, one code named "Nightingale" (*Nachtigall*) and the other code named "Roland."

Germans and Ukrainian units reached Lvov four days after the eastern campaign began, and on June 30, 1941, OUN-B officials proclaimed an independent Ukrainian state under a government of OUN-B members who

250 ⌒ U.S. Intelligence and the Nazis

hoped the Germans would accept the fait accompli. But though the Germans hoped to use the Ukrainians against the Poles, Soviets, and Ukrainian Jews, they had no intention of allowing even a semi-independent Ukraine. The Germans arrested Bandera and other OUN-B leaders and moved them to Sachsenhausen.[118] On July 16, the Germans absorbed Galicia into the General Government.

When the Germans arrested the OUN-B leadership, Lebed slipped through the German police net and became the de facto leader of the OUN-B. In October 1941, the German Security Police issued a wanted poster with Lebed's photograph. The following year he would form the underground terror wing, the UPA (Ukrainian Insurgent Army), which would initially fight German imperialism in the Ukraine but which also settled scores with rival Ukrainian leaders, Poles, Communists, and Jews.[119] Indeed, the Banderists sent a manifesto to the Gestapo in Lvov that Hitler had deceived them but which also proclaimed, "Long Live greater independent Ukraine without Jews, Poles and Germans: Poles behind the San [River], Germans to Berlin, Jews to the gallows."[120] There are numerous survivor testimonies concerning the Banderist murder of Jews who had escaped to the forests in Galicia in 1941 and 1942.[121]

From the fall of 1941, German police officials in the western Ukraine had nagging problems with Banderist sabotage and anti-German Ukrainian nationalist propaganda issued by the OUN-B. Certain German police reports even mention Banderist aid to Jews in the form of false papers, most likely for Jewish doctors or skilled workers who could help the movement.[122] Only in 1943—the year in which German police units carried out a major campaign against the UPA—did OUN-B leaflets suggest that for the moment participation in anti-Jewish actions would make the OUN-B "a blind tool in foreign hands."[123] In the long run, the OUN-B's chief enemies remained the Soviets, who were more likely to regain control of Galicia with the German retreat from the Ukraine in 1943 and 1944. Red Army POWs told their German captors in 1944 that the UPA, led by Lebed and made up of "fanatic" Banderists, was a "terror" for Red Army units in the Ukraine to the point where the Soviets viewed them as German agents. A war of extreme atrocities thus raged between the Red Army and the UPA, with former Ukrainian Nazi collaborators backing the UPA but eventually suffering Red Army counter-insurgency methods. With the advance of the Red Army, Jews serving the UPA were murdered either by the UPA or by the Germans, and by September 1944 German Army officers in northern Ukraine told their superiors in Foreign Armies East that the UPA was a "natural ally of Germany" and "a valuable aid for the German High Command."[124] Himmler himself authorized intensified contacts with the UPA.[125] Though UPA propaganda emphasized that organization's independence from the Germans, the UPA also ordered some young Ukrainians to volunteer for the Ukrainian SS Division "Galicia," and the rest to fight by guerrilla methods.[126] Lebed still hoped for recognition from the Germans. In July 1944 he helped form the Supreme Ukrainian Liberation Council (UHVR), which would claim to represent the Ukrainian nation while soon serving as a theoretical government-in-exile. The leadership positions in the UHVR tended to be held by OUN-B members, since more moderate Ukrainian nationalists had drifted away earlier in the year.[127]

With the war lost, Lebed adopted a strategy similar to that of General Reinhard Gehlen—he contacted the Allies after escaping to Rome in 1945 with a trove of names and contacts of anti-Soviets located in the western Ukraine and in displaced persons camps in Germany. The contacts theoretically made him very useful in the postwar intelligence world, and CIC took the bait. Though CIC noted in July 1947 one witness's claim that "[Lebed] is a well known sadist and collaborator of the Germans," it used him in 1947 and 1948 because he could provide complete information on Ukrainian groups within the U.S. zone of Germany, information on Soviet activity within the U.S. zone, and information on Ukrainian and Soviet activities outside of occupied Germany.[128]

In late 1947, the danger arose that the Soviets, who had recently ordered Lebed's arrest, would kidnap him from Rome, especially should U.S. occupation forces withdraw from Italy. "Should such an eventuality arise," said the American authorities, "the interest of the U.S. would suffer an indirect damage in as much as [Lebed] is in possession of vital information regarding the Ukrainian resistance activities . . . in the Ukraine."[129] In addition, Lebed's safety would reassure Father Ivan Hrynioch (Hirnyj), a wartime collaborator of Lebed who was now the Chief of the UHVR Political Section and a provider of counterintelligence to American authorities. Hrynioch requested Lebed's movement to safety.[130] The CIC therefore smuggled Lebed and his family from Rome to Munich in December 1947.

By late 1947, Lebed had thoroughly sanitized his prewar and wartime activities for American consumption. In his own rendition, he had been a victim of the Poles, the Soviets, and the Germans—he would carry the Gestapo "wanted" poster for the rest of his life to prove his anti-Nazi credentials.[131] Though he admitted to U.S. authorities his involvement in the 1934 Pieracki assassination, he blamed Pieracki. Lebed characterized his participation in the proclamation of the Ukrainian State in Lvov in June 1941 as having taken "part in the Ukrainian independence demonstration." After the June 1941 house arrest of OUN-B leaders, Lebed said, he began to organize resistance against the Germans while becoming the "spiritual father" of the UPA. For this, he said, the Gestapo and NKVD both placed a price on his head, and the Gestapo took his family to Buchenwald and Auschwitz in an attempt to force him to surface. In 1947, he was the official Foreign Minister of the UHVR, and he presented his manufactured credentials via mail to Secretary of State George C. Marshall and British Foreign Secretary Ernest Bevin. He also published a 126-page booklet on the UPA, which chronicled the heroic struggle of Ukrainians against both Nazis and Bolsheviks, while calling for an independent, greater Ukraine that would represent the human ideals of free speech and free faith. The UPA, according to the booklet, never collaborated with the Nazis, nor is there mention of the slaughter of Galician Jews or Poles in the book.[132] The CIC considered the booklet to be the "complete background on the subject."[133] The CIC overlooked the fact that under its own watch an OUN Congress held in September 1947 had split, thanks to Lebed's own criticism of the creeping democratization of the OUN.[134] This was also overlooked by the CIA, which began using Lebed extensively in 1948.[135]

Despite living under an assumed name (Roman Turan) in Munich, Lebed was still in danger of being found by his Stalinist enemies. He hoped to immigrate to the United States, but, unlike most Nazi collaborators, he became familiar enough with U.S. immigration law to be "loath to perjure himself and face deportation after . . . passing false [information]."[136] He managed anyway. In June 1949, after Assistant CIA Director W. G. Wyman notified the INS of the fact that Lebed "has been rendering valuable assistance to this Agency in Europe," the CIA smuggled him into the United States with his wife and daughter under the legal cover of the Displaced Persons Act.[137]

After his arrival, Lebed reverted to his real name and began speaking to immigrant groups in New York, which triggered Justice Department interest in him. The INS began investigating Lebed the same month he arrived in the United States. It reported to Washington in March 1950 that numerous Ukrainian informants had spoken of Lebed's involvement in the Pieracki assassination and of his role as "one of the most important Bandera terrorists." During the war, these informants said, the Banderists were trained and armed by the Gestapo and responsible for "wholesale murders of Ukrainians, Poles and Jewish [sic] . . . In all these actions, Lebed was one of the most important leaders."[138] At some point during the investigation, the INS learned of the CIA's interest in Lebed, and in 1951 top INS officials apprised the CIA of its findings along with the comment that Lebed would likely be subject to deportation. The CIA countered on October 3, 1951, that all of the charges were false and that the Gestapo "wanted" poster of Lebed proved that he "fought with equal zeal against the Nazis and Bolsheviks." Lebed's deportation, added the CIA, would damage national security.[139]

INS officials were willing to suspend the investigation but they remained uncomfortable. In the first place, they noted that the CIA note of October 3 "does not . . . dispose of the allegations." Additionally the INS worried that "this is the sort of case that can be exploited by commentators of the [Walter] Winchell variety," especially since Ukrainians that knew Lebed could contact the press on their own. "We will [then] be in no position," said W. W. Wiggins, the Chief of the INS Investigative Section, "to explain our failure to investigate."[140] INS officials asked the CIA to notify them when their need for Lebed's services would end so that the INS could "pursue our investigative responsibilities."[141] The CIA sidestepped the question. Instead, the Agency pressed the INS in February 1952 to grant Lebed reentry papers so that he could leave and reenter the United States at will.[142]

This was too much for Argyle Mackey, the Commissioner of the INS. He contacted Attorney General J. Howard McGrath to ask for guidance. "We have always cooperated whole-heartedly with the Central Intelligence Agency within the permissible limits of the law," Mackey said, "and have in this case suspended further investigation of what appears to be a clear-cut deportation case." But should Lebed leave the country and apply once again for readmission, said Mackey, "I do not see how we can give the requested assurance." Mackey gave the same reply to the Director of the CIA, Walter Bedell Smith. A reentry permit for Lebed, he said, brought "no guarantee of readmissability," since for non-U.S. citizens each re-entry was legally a new entry under which the subject had to be investigated. In other words, if Lebed left the country on CIA business, he would likely not get back in.[143]

Mackey's comments are notable in light of the notion that the INS was careless in allowing war criminals into the United States, and his warning that Lebed might not get back into the country showed there were limits beyond which the INS could not comfortably go. His statement that the INS had "always cooperated with the CIA" suggests, moreover, that there might have been similar cases.

Regardless, the CIA would not be denied Lebed's services. In a decisive letter to Mackey of May 5, 1952, Allen Dulles, then Assistant Director of the CIA, said that Lebed was the "authorized Foreign Minister of the Ukrainian Supreme Council of Liberation (UHVR), an underground organization within the USSR," and his contacts as such "have been of inestimable value to this Agency and its operations." Dulles added:

> In connection with future Agency operations of the first importance, it is urgently necessary that subject be able to travel in Western Europe. Before [he] undertakes such travel, however, this Agency must . . . assure his reentry into the United States without investigation or incident which would attract undue attention to his activities.

Dulles claimed that Lebed's 1936 trial in Poland could be discounted because it "was largely influenced by political factors and this Agency has no reason to disbelieve subject's denial of complicity in this assassination." This statement contradicted all information on Lebed, who had not denied his role in the killing.[144] Dulles also wanted Lebed's legal status changed to that of "permanent resident," under Section 8 of the CIA Act of 1949, since his continued availability, as Dulles said, was "essential to the furtherance of the national intelligence mission and is in the interest of national security." Thus Lebed would be able to come and go from the United States as he pleased. Dulles also wanted Lebed's application for permanent residence status backdated to October 1949, when Lebed had first entered the United States. Since Section 8 of the Act provided legal cover for permanent residence without regard to existing immigration laws, the INS had no choice but to comply even though, as Wiggins later said, Lebed's "deportability would be established" if the INS should investigate further.[145] They never did—Lebed became a naturalized U.S. citizen in March 1957.

The FBI, meanwhile, was very familiar with Lebed. In May 1951, the CIA asked Hoover if the Bureau wished to use Lebed, who, the Agency said, was "active for many years in Ukrainian resistance movements."[146] Since this seems to be a rare case of the CIA offering to share an agent, the Agency might have been hoping to enlist the FBI's aid against a snowballing INS investigation. The FBI looked into Lebed's past as best it could by retrieving information it received in 1943 from British intelligence concerning Ukrainian terrorism and Lebed's role in the Pieracki assassination. It also examined a small trove of captured German General Staff documents from 1943 and 1944, which revealed German appreciation with the work of the UPA while mentioning Lebed by name.[147] The New York field office also questioned a Ukrainian informant, Peter Jablon, a former member of the OUN security service, who claimed that Lebed was a German collaborator and assassin who would "use American intelligence for his own benefit."[148]

Still, Hoover gave orders that Lebed, owing to his anti-Communism, should be interviewed with a view toward possibly "developing [him] as a potential source of information concerning Ukrainian groups . . . in the United States." When questioned, Lebed gave the FBI a sanitized version of his past.[149] When asked about Jablon's charges, Lebed said that Jablon was a "strange man" who seemed to be pathologically ill.[150]

There is no evidence that the FBI ever used Lebed, but there is no evidence that it helped the INS much, either. When asked in May 1951, the Bureau told the INS that they had no objection to the latter's investigation of Lebed, and Jablon's statements of a year earlier were even provided to the INS.[151] Later, when Dulles requested permanent resident status for Lebed, the INS forwarded the Dulles letter to Hoover and asked Hoover to reply to the INS "with any comments you desire to make."[152] Since the FBI had already shared the Jablon statements, INS surely expected a measure of support. Hoover, however, replied that "based on the available information [the FBI] has no comments to make."[153] Hoover could have shared a great deal of information from German staff records and from British intelligence, but these are not in Lebed's INS file.

In the following months, the FBI continued to collect information on Lebed, including interviews with Jablon in 1953. The FBI also found Army Intelligence reports that confirmed parts of Jablon's statements, which the FBI sent to the CIA but not to the INS.[154] Lebed, meanwhile, continued to work for the CIA. The full extent of his activities as "Foreign Minister" may never become known, but FBI surveillance of him gives some idea. Partly, Lebed lectured at prestigious universities such as Yale on such topics as biological warfare used by the Soviet government in the Ukraine.[155] From 1956 to the mid-1960s, Lebed was active as the chief of a firm in New York called the Prolog Research and Publishing Association, which apparently directed agents in Eastern Europe and which, according to some, received its funding from the CIA. In any event, Lebed does not seem to have read any manuscripts for the press.[156]

FBI files on Nazi collaborators in the United States are an important source of information about the wartime and postwar activities of these figures, most of whom are not mentioned prominently, if at all, in secondary literature or even in German wartime records. For example, there is more information on the wartime activities of Lebed in FBI records than in the records of the German General Staff itself.

Examining these records, one can reach conclusions about the FBI's position—and that of other U.S. agencies—regarding Nazi collaborators after the war. The Bureau was vigilant during World War II in watching Axis officials, spies, bank accounts, and businesses in the entire Western Hemisphere. After the war, it remained vigilant only to a point.[157] The newly released records do not demonstrate that the FBI planned or condoned the immigration of lesser Axis officials and collaborationists who had slipped into the United States. Nevertheless, once these men were in the United States, the FBI, as the nation's chief federal law enforcement agency, did not create for itself an especially distinguished record.

Notes

1. This was the official Hymn of the American Branch of the Hungarian Warriors Comradeship Association, described in this chapter.

2. Such was the tenor of Congressional discussions leading to the Holtzman Amendment of 1978 and the creation of the Office of Special Investigations within the Department of Justice in 1979. Both steps aimed to correct INS mistakes. Allan A. Ryan, *Quiet Neighbors: Prosecuting Nazi War Criminals in America* (New York: Harcourt Brace Jovanovich, 1984), chapter 2.

3. FBI records from the war years contain voluminous material on FBI investigations of Nazi spies, German businessmen, and German sympathizers in the United States and in Latin America during the war. Such records are beyond the scope of this study, but they make possible significant new scholarship on German activity in the Western Hemisphere.

4. For the most part, records involving these operations were not declassified under the Nazi War Crimes Disclosure Act unless suspected Nazi war criminals were involved.

5. Report by Fred R. Woodward, 11 Mar. 1955, NA, RG 65, 105-35311-2, box 71.

6. The CIC report was received by the FBI Newark field office on 5 Nov. 1954. FBI (Newark field office) memo to INS, 28 Oct. 1954, NA, RG 65, 105-35311, box 71; Report by Fred R. Woodward, 11 Mar. 1955, NA, RG 65, 105-35311-2, box 71; Report by Robert E. Mangan, 6 May 1955, NA, RG 65, 105-35311-7, box 71.

7. Eli Rosenbaum (Director, United States Department of Justice, Criminal Division, Office of Special Investigations), interview with author, 13 Nov. 2003.

8. Ibid.

9. Ibid.

10. Report by Mervyn E. Hogan, Newark field office, 12 Aug. 1955, NA, RG 65, 105-35311-9, box 71.

11. Report by Robert E. Mangan, 6 May 1955, NA, RG 65, 105-35311-7, box 71. Information garnered later determined the following: John had become mayor of the Stolpce region when German occupation forces arrived there in late June 1941. He served at the pleasure of the Germans until their retreat in July 1944. During John's mayoralty, Jews were confined to a ghetto that John—at the German behest—ordered built in the fall of 1941. He identified Poles who could be a political threat to the Germans. He passed German orders, such as the Jewish star decree, to lesser mayors in the Stolpce region. He was also in office as the entire Jewish population of the Stolpce region was used for slave labor and executed in shooting operations carried out by the Germans and Byelorussian auxiliaries between 1941 and 1943. Indeed, by August 1943, the Germans on the spot could report that "The District of Stolpce is . . . free of Jews." Schultz (Hauptwachmeister d. Schutzpolizei u. Posternführer, Stolpce) to Gebietsführer Baranowitsche, 8 Aug. 1943, United States Holocaust Memorial Museum, RG 002M, roll 4. For the context of this document in the case of John Avdzej, I benefited from an interview with Eli Rosenbaum, 28 Oct. 2003.

12. SAC Newark to Hoover, 10 Oct. 1955, NA, RG 65, 105-35311-10, box 71.

13. Hoover to SAC Newark, 1 Nov. 1955, ibid.

14. See, for example, the case of Ludwig Miechciski, who was accused of having collaborated with

the Germans in the killing of Jews in Podhajce, Poland. The FBI questioned him thoroughly, but in the face of his denials, they could take the case no further. NA, RG 65, 105-10074, box 65.

15. See chapter 8.

16. Summary in Ryan, *Quiet Neighbors*, 142–153.

17. Artuković received bail in September 1951, which would have allowed him to flee the United States had he wished. He also received the benefit of the doubt when he denied all responsibility for Ustaša crimes. In addition, he was granted the argument that the 1901 U.S. extradition treaty with Serbia was void owing to the federal status of Yugoslavia. Most importantly, he was granted a stay of deportation on the argument that the crimes of which Yugoslavia had accused him were "political" in nature and that he would suffer political (i.e., Communist) persecution if he were to return; Ryan, *Quiet Neighbors*, 155–85.

18. Hoover to [excised] 9 July 1951, NA, RG 65, 100-361810-EBF 123, box 75. Copies of *This is Artuković* are included in this FBI file. See also "FBI Accuses Titoists of Smearing," *The Register* (Santa Ana, CA), 17 June 1958; and "Reds Want Him," *The Washington Post*, 19 Sept. 1957.

19. Hoover to [excised], 11 May 1951, NA, RG 65, 100-361810-123, box 74–75.

20. See the CIA Current Intelligence Digest of 13 Apr. 1961, NA, RG 65, 100-361810-1, box 74.

21. On Pearson and Salinger, see W. R. Wannall to Asst. Director William C. Sullivan, 7 June 1962, NA, RG 65, 100-361810-56, box 74–75. For "Facts on Himmler of Yugoslavia," see *The Washington Post*, June 25, 1962. The FBI had on occasion listened in on Pearson's telephone conversations and read his letters. See Athan Theoharis, *From the Secret Files of J. Edgar Hoover* (Chicago: I. R. Dee, 1991), 205–08; 279–80, 342.

22. Los Angeles field office report, LA Report, 8-14-63, NA, RG 65, 100-361810-2, box 74–75.

23. On the Szálasi government and the Holocaust in Hungary in general see Randolph L. Braham, *The Politics of Genocide: The Holocaust in Hungary*, 2 vols., condensed edition, (1981; Detroit, Wayne State University Press, 2000.)

24. Three lengthy background reports on the MHBK's activities in Europe are as follows: CIA Intelligence Report of 11 Oct. 1950, NA, RG 65, 97-2994-14, box 1; Brigadier General John Weckerling, Chief Intelligence Division, Department of the Army to Director, FBI, undated, NA, RG 65, 97-2994-12, box 1; CIC Memo of 20 Aug. 1953, "Activities of Vienna Intelligence Branch of Hungarian Émigré Organization (M.H.B.K.)," NA, RG 65, 97-2994-23, box 1.

25. On the organization of the Kopjas, see also the Strategic Services Unit report from X-2, Italy, "The Kopjas Movement," 13 June 1946, which states that at that time, some Kopjas were in Austria. NA, RG 226, entry 211, box 48, folder 5, field HQ file, JRX-3547 WN-20455.

26. CIC Memo of 20 Aug. 1953, "Activities of Vienna Intelligence Branch of Hungarian Émigré Organization (M.H.B.K.), NA, RG 65, 97-2994-23, box 1.

27. CIA to Director, FBI, 21 June 1950, NA, RG 65, 97-2994-5 box 1; CIA Intelligence Report of 11 Oct. 1950, NA, RG 65, 97-2944-14, box 1; Saint Washington to Saint London, 8 Nov. 1945, NA, RG 226, entry 109, box 146; "First Detailed Interrogation Report on Lt.

General Vasvary, Josef, 1 SC/CSDIC/SD 50, 27 Dec. 1945, NA, RG 226, entry 109, folder XX10561-79; FBI memorandum of 15 Jan. 1959, NA, RG 65, 97-2994, box 1.

28. Report by Elmer M. Roth, 22 June 1950, NA, RG 65, 97-2994-4, box 1. Report by Elmer Roth, 3 Nov. 1950, NA, RG 65, 97-2994-10, box 1.

29. CIA to Director, FBI, 21 May and 21 June 1950, NA, RG 65, 97-2994-5, box 1. According to the CIA, the MHBK maintained a strategic office under General Lajos Nadas, a former member of the Hungarian General Staff of German (Swabian) Heritage who, according to a reliable FBI informant, "exhibited most rabid pro-Nazi tendencies during World War II." In fact, OSS had known in 1945 that Nadas had been Szálasi's military adviser. Report by James L. Startzell, 2 June 1950, NA, RG 65, 97-2994-3, box 1; British "Detailed Interrogation Report," 6824 DIC (MIS)/EI 36, 11 June 1945, NA, RG 332, box 93. Six sources were interrogated.

30. The text of the letter is reproduced in SAC New York to Director, FBI, 28 Sept. 1949, NA, RG 65, 97-2994-64, box 1.

31. By 1955 the MHBK had eighteen such offices, most notably in Chicago, Cincinnati, Cleveland, Denver, Detroit, Los Angeles, New York, Pittsburgh, San Francisco, and St. Louis. See NA, RG 65, 97-2994-33, box 1.

32. W. F. Kelley, Assistant Commissioner, Enforcement Division, Central Office, INS to Director, FBI, 20 Feb. 1951, NA, RG 65, 97-2994-16, box 1.

33. Report by James L. Startzell, 2 June 1950, NA, RG 65, 97-2994-3, box 1.

34. See Hoover's handwritten note on Agh to Hoover, 9 May 1955, NA, RG 65, 97-2994-33, box 1.

35. Report by Elmer M. Roth, 22 June 1950, NA, RG 65, 97-2994-4, box 1.

36. SAC New York to Director, FBI, 6 Feb. 1951, NA, RG 65, 97-2994-15, box 1.

37. Received by the FBI in Feb. 1954, NA, RG 65, 97-2994-20, box 1.

38. Agh had in fact sponsored a Hungarian blood drive on the radio as early as 1951. Hennrich to Bellmont, 1 Nov. 1951, NA, RG 65, 97-2994-20, box 1.

39. Speech printed in *Hungarian Fidelity*, 6–7. The final paragraph is from Agh's description of the MHBK, 2.

40. For the explanation, see Agh's invitation, sent to the FBI Philadelphia field office, NA, RG 65, 97-2994-38, box 1. The mixture of Hungarian and U.S. symbols was present in other MHBK publications sent to the FBI.

41. Belmont to Ladd, 25 Jan. 1954, NA, RG 65, 97-2994-26, box 1; FBI to Shanley, 28 Jan. 1954, NA, RG 65, 97-2994-27, box 1.

42. Hoover to SAC Cincinnati, 27 June 1955, NA, RG 65, 97-2994-34, box 1.

43. Though the FBI files contain little on Agh's other governmental contacts, it is clear that Agh lobbied others, even within the Congress, possibly for money that could be used for intelligence gathering in Europe. In April 1952, Congressman Charles J. Kerstein of Wisconsin wrote a friendly letter to Agh, claiming, "I cannot over estimate the value of your work. It is most important to register . . . individuals who have had substantial experience in warfare against the Soviets. And also, it is highly important to keep information compiled on military preparations behind the Iron Curtain." Kerstein to Agh, 23 Apr. 1952, NA, RG 65, 97-2994-68, box 1.

44. FBI to Shandley, 28 Jan. 1954, NA, RG 65, 97-2994-27, box 1. See also NA, RG 65, 105-11669-88, box 1.
45. FBI to Shanley, 28 Jan. 1954, NA, RG 65, 97-2994-27, box 1.
46. Numerous witness testimonies corroborate one another. For details, see United States Department of Justice, INS, file A-6-801-064, Newark, 7 Oct. 1960, report by William B. Taffett, Special Inquiry Officer. I am indebted to the staff of the Office of Special Investigations, Department of Justice, for providing me with this report.
47. J. Goldberg, Asst. Dist. Director for Citizenship, DOJ, INS, to SAC Newark, 25 May 1959, NA, RG 65, 97-2994-51, box 1.
48. Ibid.
49. Ibid. It is difficult to say how INS investigators learned of the admission to Roth. INS investigators in Newark learned it from the FBI field office there. See Goldberg to Hoover, 14 July 1958, NA, RG 65, 97-2994-42, box 1.
50. For the initial inquiry, see Goldberg to Hoover, 14 July 1958, NA, RG 65, 97-2994-58, box 1. For the comment on Roth's testimony, see SAC Newark to Hoover, 17 Nov. 1958, NA, RG 65, 97-2994-48, box 1.
51. Hoover to Yeagley, 14 Sept. 1959, NA, RG 65, 97-2994-60, box 1.
52. Donahoe to Belmont, 13 Oct. 1959, NA, RG 65, 97-2994-65, box 1.
53. United States Department of Justice, INS, file A-6-801-064, Newark, 7 Oct. 1960, report by William B. Taffett, Special Inquiry Officer. I am indebted to the staff of the Department of Justice Office of Special Investigations for providing me with this report.
54. United States Department of Justice, Board of Immigration Appeals, 11 Aug. 1961. The Department of Justice Office of Special Investigations kindly provided me with this report.
55. Examining Officers Memorandum Re: Laszlo Agh, 2 Dec. 1959; Examining Officers Memorandum Re: Laszlo Agh, 21 Apr. 1961. I am indebted to the staff of the Office of Special Investigations, Department of Justice, for providing me with these documents.
56. CIC, Trieste, 16 Jan. 1950, NA, RG 263, Viorel Trifa Name File.
57. On his role in Italy, see ibid. For summary, see Ryan, *Quiet Neighbors*, chapter 8.
58. U.S. Embassy Bucharest to Secretary of State, No. 2280 of 12 Apr. 1979, NA, RG 59, Viorel Trifa Collection, DQ-017.
59. EE-J.C. Campbell to VD, 6 Aug. 1951, NA, RG 263, Viorel Trifa Name File.
60. [excised] to [excised] 25 Mar. 1951, NA, RG 263, Viorel Trifa Name File.
61. Trutza's own commentary is in Report by Anthony S. Fernandez, Cleveland field office, NA, RG 65, 100-225319-1-37, box 31.
62. Acheson was convinced on good evidence that the Patriarch Justinian himself was completely subservient to the Communist government in Romania. Acheson to U.S. Legation Bucharest, 19 Oct. 1950, NA, RG 65, 100-225319-1-2, box 31.
63. Report by Robert W. McCaslin, Washington field office, 23 June 1951, NA, RG 65, 100-225319-1-21, box 31.
64. James Ganterbein, Chargé d'Affaires, Bucharest, to Acheson, 28 Nov. 1950, NA, RG 65, 100-225319-1, box 31. See also Trutza's assessment, Report by Anthony S. Fernandez, Cleveland field office, NA, RG 65, 100-225319-1-37, box 31.
65. On Justinian, SAC Washington field office to Hoover, 5 June 1953, NA, RG 65, 100-225319-

3-87, box 31; Report by Paul M.W. Sterner, 24 Aug. 1953, NA, RG 65, 100-225319-3-93, box 31. On the peace tour, NA, RG 65, 100-225319-1, box 31.

66. O'Hara was the former Regent of the Apostolic Nunciature in Bucharest. Expelled by the Romanian Government in 1950, he now served in that capacity in Dublin. Kirk was the former head of the Roman Catholic Mission for Europe. See Hoover's correspondence with the Legal Attaches in London and Madrid, of Apr., May, and Nov. 1952 in NA, RG 65, 100-225319-2, box 32.

67. SAC Washington to Hoover, 6 Oct. 1951, NA, RG 65, 105-14006-1- 5, box 158.

68. Ibid.

69. Telegram received by Archbishop Mstyslav Skrypnyk and John Theodorovich, 19 Mar. 1952, NA, RG 263, Viorel Trifa Name File.

70. The State Department attempted to delay the consecration ceremony after receiving information on Trifa from Dr. Charles Kremer, President of the United Romanian Jews of America. Theodorovich refused to delay the ceremony, however. See Washington field office to Hoover, 23 Apr. 1952; Hoover to Assistant Attorney General James McInerney, 26 Apr. 1952; State Department Memorandum of Conversation between Father John Hundiak and A.G. Sherer (East Europe Desk), 8 Apr. 1952; all in NA, RG 65, 105-14006-25-(31–34), box 158.

71. NA, RG 65, 105-14006-2-(42-43), box 158.

72. SAC Cleveland to Hoover, 25 Sept. 1952, NA, RG 65, 105-14006-3-(58-59), box 159.

73. Hoover to Legal Attaché London, 24 Apr. 1952, NA, RG 65, 100-225319-2, box 32.

74. SAC Detroit to Hoover, 19 Nov. 1952, Hoover to SAC Detroit, 22 Jan. 1953, NA, RG 65, 100-225319-2-69, box 32; W.A. Brannigan to A.H. Belmont, 16 Jan. 1953, NA, RG 65, 100-225319-2-72, box 32.

75. Report by Edgar A. Begholtz, 30 Apr. 1953, NA, RG 65, 100-225319-81, box 32.

76. Warren Olney III, Assistant Attorney General, Criminal Division, to Hoover, 26 Aug. 1953, NA, RG 65, 100-225319-3-94, box 32; SAC Detroit to Hoover, NA, RG 65, 100-225319-3-99, box 32.

77. Guy Hottel, SAC, Washington to Hoover, 12 Dec. 1950, NA, RG 65, 105-14006-1-1, box 158.

78. Memo by J.C. Campbell (East European Desk) 6 Aug. 1951, forwarded to FBI, NA, RG 65, 105-14006-1- 2, box 158.

79. [Excised], Acting Assistant Director, CIA, to Commissioner, INS, 25 Sept. 1951, NA, RG 65, 105-14006-1, box 158; SAC Washington to Hoover, 31 Mar. 1952, NA, RG 65, 105-14006-1-24, box 158.

80. Report by Julius A. Bernhard, Portland, OR, 15 Apr. 1952, NA, RG 65, 105-14006-1-25, box 158.

81. The text of the pamphlet, *Communistic Attempts the Gain Control Over American Church Organizations: The Facts Behind the Romanian Orthodox Missionary Episcopate in America*, published in 1952 by the Public Relations Office of the Romanian Orthodox Episcopate in America, is in the Episcopate's communication to Hoover, 31 Mar. 1952, NA, RG 65, 105-14006-3, box 159.

82. Hoover to John W. Ford, 30 Apr. 1953, NA, RG 65-105-14006-3, box 159. On the

Romanian Government's use of Church positions in 1953, the CIA reported in June that the 1948 appointment of Archimandrite Martinian Ivanovici in Paris by the Romanian Ministry of Cults was backed by the former head of Romanian intelligence, Emil Bodnaras. See NA, RG 65, 105-14006-3-73, box 159.

83. CIA Deputy Director of Plans to Hoover, 16 Oct. 1953, NA, RG 65, 105-14006-3-80, box 159.
84. Detroit field office to Hoover, 20 Oct. 1954, NA, RG 65, 105-14006-3-92, box 159.
85. The seventy-page report by Paul E. Bowser of the Detroit field office containing the Trifa interview of 19–21 Feb. 1955 is dated 10 May 1955, NA, RG 65, 105-14006-4-102, box 159.
86. SAC Washington to Hoover, 1 June 1955, NA, RG 65, 105-14006-4-105, box 159.
87. FBI Washington to Hoover and Detroit field office, telegram of 28 Apr. 1955, NA, RG 65, 105-14006-3-97, box 159; SAC Washington to Hoover, 13 May 1955, NA, RG 65, 105-14006-3-100, box 159.
88. Washington field office to Hoover, 12 June 1955, NA, RG 65, 105-14006-4-108, box 159.
89. Hoover to Nixon, 16 June 1955, ibid. There are no actual reports of Martin's moral character, but the FBI file on Trifa does point out that, since September 1951, there had been twenty-two reports based on Martin's information received by the FBI, NA, RG 65, 105-14006-4-110, box 159.
90. SAC Detroit to Hoover, 27 Dec. 1956, NA, RG 65, 105-14006-4-126, box 159.
91. Hoover to SAC Detroit, 1 Apr. 1957, NA, RG 65, 105-14006-4-127, box 159.
92. Trifa to Johnson, 3 Dec. 1963, NA, RG 65, 105-14006-4-145, box 159.
93. See the excellent analysis of *Rech* and Sokolov in Robert E. Hertzstein, "Anti-Jewish Propaganda in the Orel Region of Great Russia, 1942–1943: The German Army and its Russian Collaborators," *Simon Wiesenthal Center Annual* 6, chapter 2.
94. Vladimir Sokolov, et al., *Petitioner v. United States of America*, U.S. 87-323 (1987).
95. Alexander Dallin, *German Rule in Russia, 1941–1945: A Study of Occupation Policies*, 2nd ed. (1957; Boulder, CO: Westview, 1981), 525–27; Christopher Simpson, *Blowback: America's Recruitment of Nazis and its Effects on the Cold War* (New York: Weidenfeld and Nicolson, 1988), 220–22; United States, Department of State, Office of Intelligence and Research, "NTS–The Russian Solidarist Movement," External Research Paper Series 3, No. 76, 1951; Boris Dvinov, *Politics of Russian Emigration* (Santa Monica, CA: Rand Corporation Study No. P-768, 1955), 113–94.
96. Vladimir Sokolov, et al., *Petitioner v. United States of America*, U.S. 87-323 (1987).
97. The basics of Sokolov's biography can be pieced together in his FBI file, NA, RG 65, 100-100-409764 (and enclosures), box 39.
98. SAC New York to Director, FBI, 8 Mar. 1966, NA, RG 65, 100-409764-11, box 39. See also the report to the Director, FBI, 17 Apr. 1959, NA, RG 65, 100-409764-8, box 39.
99. SAC New York to Director, FBI, 19 Nov. 1954, NA, RG 65, 100-409764-4, box 39.
100. SAC New York to Director, FBI, 2 July 1954, NA, RG 65, 100-409764-2, box 39.
101. Ibid.
102. Sokolov was released the same evening. See NA, RG 65, 100-409764-5, box 39.
103. Hoover to SAC New York, 23 Mar. 1959, NA, RG 65, 100-409764-7, box 39.

104. Report by Robert J. Jackson, 22 Jan. 1959, NA, RG 65, 100-409764-6, box 39.
105. Report by Helmut C. Labusch, 20 Jan. 1959, ibid.
106. Report by William T. Ryan, 2 Dec. 1958, ibid.
107. The comment as well as those from Vera Schwartz, Mark Weinbaum, and Alexander Dallin, are in Report by Harold Palatsky, 21 Nov.–2 Dec. 1958, ibid.
108. Dallin, *German Rule in Russia*.
109. Oktan, and in this case Sokolov as well, were part of abortive efforts by the German Ministry of Propaganda to establish a basis of Nazism within Russian groups. Oktan, a former Soviet journalist-turned-collaborator, led the League for the Struggle against Bolshevism. See Dallin, *German Rule in Russia*, 525n1.
110. In this connection, Sokolov's rather speedy naturalization on 21 May 1957 also raises interesting questions. For his sworn statement of 19 Apr. 1957, see Report by Harold Palatsky, 21 Nov.–2 Dec. 1958, NA, RG 65, 100-409764-6, box 39.
111. For the Sokolov interrogation, see the Palatsky reports cited above, 15–18.
112. Hoover to SAC New York, 23 Mar. 1959, NA, RG 65, 100-409764-7, box 39.
113. Report by Special Agent Paul Garrity, 16 June 1959, NA, RG 65, 100-409764-9, box 39; SAC New York to Director, FBI, 1 Dec. 1959, NA, RG 65, 100-409764, box 39.
114. Most of the documentation on Sokolov's FBI activity while at Yale is either redacted or withheld as irrelevant to the Nazi War Crimes Disclosure Act. See, however, Director, FBI to SAC New Haven, 25 May 1959, NA, RG 65, 100-409764-12, box 39.
115. Simpson, *Blowback*, discusses the Lebed case with the aid of the dossier kept on Lebed by Army CIC (part of which was provided by FOIA requests, all of which is now declassified thanks to the Nazi War Crimes Disclosure Act), a dossier on Lebed kept in the Israeli Holocaust archive at Yad Vashem provided by Lebed's former ally Mykyta Kosakivs'kky, and interviews conducted with Lebed himself.
116. The variety of Ukrainian nationalist groups and the split within the OUN between the more radical Bandera faction and the more moderate Mel'nyk faction is discussed in detail in John A. Armstrong, *Ukrainian Nationalism, 1939–1945* (New York: Columbia University Press, 1955), 31ff.
117. On OUN contacts before the war and in 1939, see Dallin, *German Rule in Russia*, 114-19; Armstrong, *Ukrainian Nationalism*.
118. For the Declaration of the Ukrainian State Government sent to Adolf Hitler under a congratulatory letter of "sincere gratitude and admiration for your heroic army," see Ukrainische Regierung, No. 1/41, 3 July 1941, Bundesarchiv (Berlin) R 43 II/1500. See also Dallin, *German Rule in Russia*, 119–22.
119. German police reports dated October 1941 report that "fanatic" Bandera followers, organized in small groups, were "extraordinarily active" against Jews and Communists. See Philip Friedman, "Ukrainian-Jewish Relations during the Nazi Occupation," *YIVO Annual of Jewish Social Science* 12 (1958–1959) 266n12.
120. Ereignismeldung UdSSR Nr. 126, 29 Oct. 1941, document 4134 of the unpublished materials in *United States vs. Otto Ohlendorf*, quoted in Friedman, "Ukrainian-Jewish Relations," 268n15.
121. Friedman, "Ukrainian-Jewish Relations," 283n54.

122. See the Einsatzgruppen reports from the West Ukraine from July 1941 to July 1943 in Bundesarchiv (Berlin), R 58/219, R 58/221, R 70/31, R 58/220, R 58/217, R 58/215, R 58/698, R 70/204, R 58/220, R 70/31. On the use of Jews by the UPA, see Friedman, "Ukrainian-Jewish Relations," 284–85.

123. Armstrong, *Ukrainian Nationalism*, 102–7, 117.

124. Belmont to Hennrich, 5 June 1950, NA, RG 65, 105-12528-2, box 128. The German originals of this material are in NA, RG 242, T-76, roll 565, frame 673ff. The translated version studied by the FBI are in Turner to Whitson, 11 May 1945, NA, RG 65, 105-9571-17, box 126. See also Frontaufklärungskommando 305 bei Heeresgruppe Nordukraine Br. B. Nr. 2399/44g, 21 Sept. 1944, Bundesarchiv (Berlin), R 70. On the murder of Jews connected with the UPA see Friedman, "Ukrainian-Jewish Relations," 285–86, and n. 61

125. Reichsminister for the Occupied Eastern Territories Nr. P 918 a/44g., 18 Sept. 1944, NA, RG 242, T-78, roll 565.

126. Frontaufklärungskommando 305 bei Heeresgruppe Nordukraine Br. B. Nr. 2399/44g, 21 Sept. 1944, Federal Republic of Germany, Bundesarchiv (Berlin), R 70. See also Armstrong, *Ukrainian Nationalism*, 128–32.

127. On the formation of the UPA and UHVR, see Dallin, *German Rule in Russia*, 620–22; and Armstrong, *Ukrainian Nationalism,* chapter 6. By the fall of 1943, the Bandera group was in control of the country districts of Volhynia and southwestern Polessia, while the Germans controlled the towns in the region. The Soviets advanced into Volhynia in February 1944.

128. Card Ref D 82270, 22 July 1947, NA, RG 319, IRR, entry 134B, Mikola Lebed.

129. CIC memo of 10 Nov. 1947, ibid.

130. GID/OPS/CIS D-201967, 21 Nov. 1947, ibid.

131. Eli Rosenbaum, interview with author, 28 Oct. 2003.

132. For this rendering of the facts, see the memo by Special CIC Agent Camille S. Hadju of the 970th CIC Detachment, 17 Nov. 1947, with enclosures, NA, RG 319, IRR, entry 134B, Mikola Lebed. A translated synopsis of Lebed's booklet *UPA* was ordered by the FBI and can be found in NA, RG 65, 105-12528-9, box 128.

133. Ellington D. Golden, HQ Counterintelligence Corps Region IV, 970th CIC Detachment, IV-2872, 18 Nov. 1947, NA, RG 319, IRR, entry 134B, Mikola Lebed.

134. Memo by R. F. Carroll, NA, RG 319, IRR, entry 134B, Mikola Lebed; Memo by Special CIC Agent Daniel Barna, 19 Apr. 1948, ibid.

135. The date is confirmed in Dulles to Mackey, 5 May 1952, NA, RG 263, Mikola Lebed Name File.

136. Munich to Special Operations, [excised], 18 May 1949, ibid.

137. CIA [excised] to Commissioner for Immigration and Naturalization, 20 June 1949, ibid.

138. Mitchell S. Solomon, Investigator, INS, to T. Avery, Asst. Chief, Investigations Section, 20 Mar. 1951, NA, RG 85, INS File–Lebed, A7 320 118.

139. CIA, Col. Sheffield Evans to Commissioner INS (Attn. W. W. Wiggins), 3 Oct. 1951, NA, RG 85, INS File–Lebed, A7 320 11.

140. W. W. Wiggins, Chief, Investigation Section, to W. F. Kelley, Asst. Commissioner, Enforcement Division, 4 Oct. 1951, NA, RG 85, INS File–Lebed, A7 320 118.

141. W. F. Kelley to Director CIA, 12 Oct. 1951, ibid.

142. Edwards to Wiggins, 9 Feb. 1952, ibid.
143. Commissioner for Immigration and Naturalization to Attorney General, 13 Feb. 1952, NA, RG 85, INS File–Lebed, A7 320 118; Argyle Mackey to Director CIA, 27 Feb. 1952, ibid.
144. Dulles to Mackey, 5 May 1952, NA, RG 263, Mikola Lebed Name File. There is a copy of this letter in Lebed's FBI file, as well. For Lebed's admission to the Pieracki assassination, see the MI-5 records in the FBI file. Lebed would deny complicity when questioned by the INS in April 1952. See Questionnaire Submitted to Mr. Lebed, 8 Apr. 1952, NA, RG 263, Mikola Lebed Name File.
145. Wiggins to Kelley 13 May 1952, NA, RG 85, INS File–Lebed, A7 320 118.
146. Robert A. Schow, Assistant Director, CIA, to Director, FBI, 1 May 1950, NA, RG 65, 105-12528-1, box 129.
147. Belmont to Hennrich, 5 June 1950, NA, RG 65, 105-12528-2, box 128. The German originals of this material are in NA, RG 242, T-76, roll 565, frame 673ff. The translated version studied by the FBI are in Turner to Whitson, 11 May 1945, NA, RG 65, 105-9571-17, box 126.
148. Belmont to Hennrich, 5 June 1950, NA, RG 65, 105-12528-2, box 128. See also FBI report of 2 Feb. 1951, NA, RG 65, 105-12528-6X, box 128.
149. FBI Report of 3 Aug. 1950, NA, RG 65, 105-12528-4, box 128.
150. FBI Report of 2 Feb. 1951, NA, RG 65, 105-12528-6X, box 128.
151. C. H. Pennington, Chief, Investigations Section, to Mackey, 17 May 1951, NA, RG 85, INS File–Lebed, A7 320 118.
152. Kelley to Hoover, 13 May 1952, ibid.
153. Hoover to Mackey, 20 May 1952, ibid.
154. A translation of the 24 July 1952 article, "A Tragic Anniversary," *Novoye Russkoye Slovo* (*New Russian Word*) is in NA, RG 65, 105-12528-14, box 128; FBI New York Report of 5 June 1953, NA, RG 65, 105-12528-15, box 128; Hoover to Director, CIA, 12 Aug. 1953, NA, RG 65, 105-12528-18, box 128; see unsigned report "Mykola Lebid" in Albert H. Mackenzie to Brigadier General Mark McClure, Deputy Chief of Staff, G-2, Department of the Army, 22 Sept. 1953, NA, RG 65, 105-12528-19, box 128.
155. "Underground Ukraine War Bared Here," *New Haven Journal–Courier*, February 14, 1951; Jaro Halat, "The Assassin and the Admiral," *The New Leader*, 28 July 1951, 10. Halat was another pseudonym for Peter Jablon.
156. Director, FBI to SAC New York, 20 June 1962, NA, RG 65, 105-12528, box 39; Director, FBI to SAC, New York, 28 June 1965, ibid. On CIA funding, see Joe Conason, "To Catch a Nazi," *Village Voice*, Feb. 11, (1986), 21.
157. On German youth see NA, RG 65, 100-197219. On Bormann, see NA, RG 65, 65-55639.

10

The Nazi Peddler:
Wilhelm Höttl and Allied Intelligence

Norman J. W. Goda

No CASE ILLUSTRATES THE MORAL, political, and operational complexities in the postwar intelligence world better than that of Wilhelm Höttl, an SD intelligence officer. Höttl established contacts with the Office of Strategic Services (OSS), the Army Counterintelligence Corps (CIC), the West German Defense Ministry, and even the KGB. The release of his voluminous CIA Name File, which comprises over 1600 pages, along with previously withheld OSS records, substantially fills out what has been known about Höttl from Army Counterintelligence records. Höttl was an unapologetic Nazi who helped to expropriate assets from and annihilate Jews, particularly in Hungary in 1944. He was, furthermore, an unusually corrupt man who wove intricate lies as he built contacts, stashed secret funds, and enhanced his personal standing. He maintained these traits his entire life. Höttl's career serves as a mirror, reflecting the nature of each intelligence organization that had contact with him. In the end, U.S. intelligence agencies determined to crush him professionally and bury all evidence of contact with him once the possibility was clear that he was working for the Soviets and that his past association with the United States could become public knowledge.

Höttl's Nazi Background

Höttl's SS personnel records comprise one of the longest SS officer files.[1] Born in Vienna in 1915, Höttl became a dedicated Nazi even as a student. His association with Nazi groups began illegally in Austria—even before Hitler's takeover in Germany. In 1931, at age 16, Höttl joined the NS-Schülerbund; he joined the SS at age 18. In March 1934, he became an SS student leader and soon did illegal work for the SD in Vienna. Long before he received his doctorate in history from the University of Vienna in 1937, he had cast his lot with the Nazis. After Germany annexed Austria, Höttl continued his SD work in Vienna, now legally, working on anti-Jewish and Freemason issues. Thanks to what his SS file labels as "outstanding achievements," he was charged with the leadership of Referat VI (intelligence) in the Vienna SD office in December 1940.[2]

Here Höttl's corruption and influence peddling quickly began to irritate his SS superiors, especially his repeated intervention on behalf of American-born countess Dorothy Pálffy. Whether the countess provided Höttl with his initial entrée into the Pálffy family is hard to say, but count Fidél Pálffy—leader of the pro-German, Nazi-style United National Socialist Party—later became a chief contact for Höttl in Budapest.[3] For the moment, the countess was one of Höttl's best intelligence sources, and he tried to return the favor by working through German authorities in Upper Austria, Cracow, and Warsaw to secure confiscated Jewish property for her. "I have known this woman for many years," he said, "and can confirm that she is anything but a friend to the Jews, [though] her anti-Semitism as a full-blooded American is naturally different than is ours . . ."[4] When Höttl got into trouble for his efforts, he claimed that Reinhard Heydrich himself had sanctioned this intelligence relationship.[5] Already dead, Heydrich could neither confirm nor deny this claim. In addition, large sums had disappeared from an SD bank account in Vienna while Höttl was there.

Höttl's superior, SS-Sturmbannführer Friedrich Polte, took these matters to higher channels in October 1941. Höttl was a fine intelligence officer in terms of his eagerness and volume, Polte said, but he was also "the typical troublesome Viennese—a liar, a toady, a schemer, and a pronounced operator."[6] Höttl was removed from SD duties and assigned to the eastern front as a war correspondent. He remained there for most of 1942, defending himself against a snowballing investigation. He had been a loyal Nazi since 1931, he said, risking even the gallows before 1938 as he "worked for the liberation of the Ostmark [Austria]." After listing his many Hitler Youth decorations, he concluded, "I have had recognized successes in the struggle against the Church, Jews and Freemasons."[7]

Höttl's deliverance came with the appointment of fellow Austrian Ernst Kaltenbrunner as chief of the RSHA in January 1943. By the following month, Höttl was back in the RSHA in Berlin on Kaltenbrunner's insistence, and the investigation was dropped. Höttl's recall was due in part to Kaltenbrunner's need to create a core of loyal Austrians within the RSHA to counteract Walter Schellenberg's close relationship with Heinrich Himmler.[8] And Höttl's expertise on southeastern Europe, Kaltenbrunner said, made him indispensable.[9]

Höttl's rise under Kaltenbrunner was noteworthy. He served as chief of the Italian Desk for SD Foreign Intelligence, and he played a role in Mussolini's rescue in September 1943 by working with the German embassy in Rome.[10] He also assisted in the German capture of count Galeazzo Ciano's diplomatic notes in January 1944, shortly before Ciano's execution.[11] Höttl's reward came in October 1943, when Kaltenbrunner insisted that he be promoted to the rank of SS-Sturmbannführer, despite the fact that he had yet to reach the requisite age of 30. The reason, Kaltenbrunner said, was Höttl's role in bringing Amt VI (Foreign Police Intelligence) into the Mussolini rescue, which the Führer himself had recognized. The promotion was made retroactive to September 11, 1943, the day before the rescue operation.[12]

Höttl was most devastating in Hungary, where he had built contacts with members of the pro-Nazi Hungarian right. He generally avoided Ferenc Szálasi's Arrow Cross party, since Höttl suspected that Szálasi would pursue Hungarian rather than German interests. His contacts lay rather with people and parties who would happily hand Hungary's Jews over for destruction, such as Count Pálffy's United National Socialists and Béla Imrédy's Party of Hungarian National Life. These ties became even more valuable after the German occupation of Hungary in March 1944.

Kaltenbrunner himself arrived in Budapest on March 19 with the aim of establishing a new Hungarian government that would help Adolf Eichmann and his subordinates to round up, deport, and destroy Hungary's 725,000 Jews. The new Prime Minister was Hungarian Lieutenant General Döme Sztójay, Hungarian Ambassador to Berlin since 1935. His interior ministry was dominated by Höttl's protégés, Lászlo Baky and Lászlo Endre, two leading Hungarian National Socialists. "This was a government," noted historian Ronald Zweig, "streamlined to do exactly what Höttl and his [SS] superiors in Berlin had been planning for years." Indeed, Höttl remained in Budapest as more than 400,000 Hungarian Jews were deported to Birkenau and gassed between April and June 1944.[13]

Höttl and OSS

Like several SS officers, Höttl tried to ingratiate himself with the Americans toward the war's end. He had two primary motives. First, he hoped to avoid prosecution as a war criminal and perhaps even become part of a transitional Austrian government.[14] Second, he hoped to get his hands on a hoard of stolen Jewish loot.

Höttl had had a lengthy association with Colonel Árpád Toldi, who became Hungary's Commissioner for Jewish Affairs under the Szálasi regime in October 1944.[15] In February 1945, Toldi was in charge of the famous Hungarian Gold Train, which was loaded with tons of valuable Jewish belongings confiscated by the Hungarian government. With the Red Army fanning out across Hungary, Toldi needed to find a safe place to hide the train in Austria. Höttl knew all about the Gold Train; so did an Austrian friend of his, Friedrich Westen, who profited from expropriations of Jewish property and Jewish slave labor.[16]

In February 1945, Höttl had Westen make contact with Allen Dulles, the OSS representative in Bern. Dulles was intrigued by the chance that Höttl, as Kaltenbrunner's representative, might help with a separate Austrian peace while acting as a wedge within the SD. In early March 1945, Dulles arranged for an intermediary to meet Höttl at the Swiss-Austrian border.[17] Höttl made several trips to Switzerland in the spring of 1945, posing as Kaltenbrunner's "peace envoy" to the OSS. Kaltenbrunner never reconciled Höttl's Swiss contacts with his own loyalty to Hitler. Though it was clear to the OSS that Höttl had played a role in Hungary during the Jewish deportations there,[18] his closeness to Kaltenbrunner might offer a key to the so-called Alpine Redoubt.

The redoubt was a supposedly impregnable fortress into which the Germans were to pour their last reserves for a final, bloody stand, but in the end it was "a sink-hole that sucked in the odds and ends of a dying regime."[19] The Allies, thanks to aerial photography, knew of the extensive preparations to fortify and supply the area. The Allies also received overblown SD reports designed to give an impression of the redoubt's impregnability in order to draw the Allies to the negotiating table. Given the intelligence mistakes that had preceded the Allied disaster in the Ardennes in December 1944, such information had to be taken seriously.[20]

Höttl understood and exploited Allied concerns. In mid-April, more than ten days before the German surrender in Italy, Höttl reported to the OSS that a number of senior generals would retreat to the redoubt, including High Command of the Armed Services (OKW) Chief Wilhelm Keitel, Field Marshal Ferdinand Schörner, and Field Marshal Albert Kesselring, the last of whom had become notorious by now for not cooperating with SS-Obergruppenführer Karl Wolff's surrender plans in Italy. "[Field Marshal Alexander] Löhr's men from Croatia are almost certain to get there," said the same OSS report based on Höttl's intelligence. Höttl added that *Werwolf*, the inchoate Nazi guerrilla movement, should be taken seriously, too. It had been well organized for the past two years with concealed arms depots, explosives, ample hidden funds, and 100,000 reliable SS men under Otto Skorzeny, another Austrian.[21]

But there was a solution. Höttl told his American interlocutors that Kaltenbrunner had entrusted him with contacting Austrian anti-Nazi (and anti-Communist) circles and that he had indeed contacted numerous worker and Catholic opposition leaders. Höttl said he was chosen because his father, Karl Höttl, was a well-known socialist Austrian school reformer.[22] OSS Chief William Donovan argued that "I am convinced [that Höttl] is the right hand man of Kaltenbrunner," and thus a key contact to develop.[23] Höttl's comments, Donovan said, lay "well within the range of possibility," for if "certain SS elements are trying to save their skins by turning to the West . . . to follow [a] line which will obviate [the] necessity of their joining [the] die-hards in [a] last-ditch struggle [then] these trends offer [the] possibility of checkmating any future organization of [the] German reduit." Donovan even postulated that Himmler himself was "pulling the strings . . . and possibly preparing himself to desert the die-hards."[24]

Höttl was lying. An OSS check on Karl Höttl revealed that he was indeed a social democratic reformer, but that he was not related to Wilhelm.[25] A source in London further commented that Höttl was "long identified with [the] extremist clique" and that Kaltenbrunner could hardly send him on his mission to Switzerland without the news reaching Schellenberg and Heinrich Himmler. It seemed more likely that Höttl was a tool for "embroiling [the] Western Powers with [the] Russians since negotiations [are] likely to become known."[26]

One senior OSS officer, Edgeworth Murray Leslie, viewed Höttl's ambiguity as an asset that could help end the war. "[Höttl] is, of course, dangerous . . ."

He is a fanatical anti-Russian and for this reason we cannot very well collaborate with him . . . without informing the [R]ussians. But I see no reason why we should not use him in the furtherance of [common] interests . . . namely, the hastening of the end of the resistance in Austria by the disruption of the Réduit.

To avoid any accusation that we are working with a Nazi reactionary . . . I believe that we should keep our contact with him as indirect as possible. . . .

I think . . . that he takes it for granted that we will take into account his present services when judging his past activities. Furthermore, I believe that he hopes that he and his associates will be able to play a political role in the future Austria as a result of his present activities. To make our position clear on these points, I told him that no man need fear for his security, provided he was not guilty of any war crime . . .[27]

Dulles agreed that "this type of source requires utmost caution."[28] After meeting several times with Leslie during his trip to Switzerland in the second week of April, Höttl (now code named "Alperg") was told—based on his own offer—to proceed to the Alpine Redoubt and from there, via wireless transmitter, to send information to the Americans through the Swiss military police on German war potential and to make suggestions for Allied propaganda.[29] Unbeknown to the OSS, the Gold Train arrived within the borders of the planned redoubt on April 8.[30] Höttl did not tell them. Dulles assumed only that Höttl wished to avoid prosecution: "Hoettl's record as [an] SD man and collaborator [of] Kaltenbrunner is of course bad," reported Dulles on April 21, "but I believe he desires to save his skin and therefore may be useful."[31]

Events outstripped Höttl's viability with the OSS as well as his hope to use the redoubt to hide the stolen Jewish loot. On April 27, Social Democrat Karl Renner proclaimed an independent Austria in Soviet-occupied Vienna with a left-leaning coalition government.[32] On April 29, Karl Wolff's representatives signed the secret "Sunrise" surrender at Caserta, which went into effect on May 2.[33] Höttl worked on a "legitimate Austrian government" to present to the Allies in opposition to that of Renner, while Kaltenbrunner worked on the redoubt, but all to no avail.[34] Höttl finally informed Leslie about the Gold Train in the redoubt area.[35] But he was making plans to hide a share for himself. Colonel Toldi had already placed the Gold Train's most valuable gold and jewelry in numerous crates, which he was trying to remove from the train and hide. Höttl met with Toldi at Feldkirch on April 29 and struck a deal whereby Höttl and Westen would transport the crates into Switzerland (which Toldi had been unable to do) in return for 10 percent of the valuables.[36]

Believing he had saved his loot, Höttl hoped to save his skin. But on his final trip to Switzerland in the first week of May, the French military had advanced to the Swiss-Austrian border, so Höttl got only as far as Liechtenstein. He failed to set up a meeting he desired between Dulles and Kaltenbrunner. Left in the cold of defeat and having to hide from Hungarians in Austria who knew his murderous

DaT: 17.4.45

~~SECRET~~   *april 17-1945*

CONCLUSIONS.

1. I believe that in their different ways both H. and W. are important contacts, well worth developing.

H. is, of course, dangerous. He is a Nazi and an admitted associate of such men as Glaise-Horstenau and Meindl. He is a fanatical anti-Russian and, for this reason, we can not very well collaborate with him - at least not without informing the Russians. But I see no reason why we should not use him in the furtherance of interests common both to the United Nations and to him and his associates, namely, the hastening of the end of resistance in Austria by the disruption of the Réduit. I feel that we should make full use of the Nachrichtendienst which he is organizing, of the propaganda services which he is setting up, and of the material which he can supply for this propaganda. I fully concur with him that psychological warfare must play a tremendously important rôle in combatting the Réduit. Further, I feel that we should encourage him in his attempts to create opposition groups within the Réduit. Although it is impossible to have any real sympathy for a man of his type, he nevertheless made a favourable impression on me. I believe he is sincere and to be trusted, provided we give him a certain measure of confidence. There is considerable evidence of his good will in his rescuing of such men as Seitz and Messner, and in his bringing out a man like W. There is also W.'s opinion of him, and G.'s trust of him as reported by W.

To avoid any accusation that we are working with a Nazi reactionary and a fanatical anti-Russian, I believe that we should keep our contact with him as indirect as possible. A., L., and possibly Grimm should be the people to deal with him, if and when he comes out again (and he expects to do so very shortly). I might possibly see him again but not alone and only in the capacity of an interested observer at his discussions with A. and Co. In such a capacity, I can always give him the encouragement he seeks without committing us in any way to any direct form of collaboration.

In this connection, it is amusing that H. told me that upon his return to Germany, he would have to show his Nazi masters something for his visit here. He stated that he would like to say that he had managed to obtain contacts with the Americans and had discovered from them that their divergencies with the Russians were very real. I told him that if he made any such reports, there was no question of my ever seeing him again, nor I imagine, of any collaboration with the Austrian group here. A., who was present, fully confirmed this. H. then asked me if I could provide him with any material to pass on his Nazi masters - something less harmful, such as reports of difficulties we were having with

To:
From:
Dispo: 17.4.45   ~~SECRET~~   NWJC - 001556   the German

Page from a memorandum from an OSS officer to Allen Dulles, arguing that Höttl would be a valuable source despite his past [Leslie to 110 (Dulles), 17 Apr. 1945, NA, RG 263, Wilhelm Höttl Name File, vol. 1].

record, he turned himself in to the 3rd U.S. Army Counterintelligence Corps at Kirchdorf, hoping through his OSS contacts to rebuild his position.[37]

With no cachet as a peacemaker, Höttl could count on no legal favors. He speedily worked to forge another type of relationship with the Americans. He explained his Nazi past by posing as a Catholic scholar who joined the Nazi Party in May 1938 from fear of Bolshevism. Heydrich ousted him from the SD, he said, because he was too friendly with Jews. Kaltenbrunner reinstated him, he said, because he was a fellow Austrian. Austria's future, Höttl told his American captors, lay in a strong alliance with the West against Communism. Höttl also offered something of value to the United States—a "permanent" intelligence chain into southeastern Europe reaching into Budapest, Bucharest, and Zagreb, which he said had survived intact from the war.[38] "Hoettl claims," said his CIC interrogators, "that his is the only information net of Amt VI that has come out of the general disorganization attending Germany's defeat basically intact. He believes that all existing nets have been damaged beyond repair, but some of their lines could possibly be reactivated in the course of time."

When asked why the United States would want to employ such a former SD net in southeastern Europe, especially since the United States and USSR were allies, Höttl was matter of fact:

> From my activities in the South-East, extending over years, I know that the American information services in that area are still in their formative phase and that, in some countries, there are none at all. On the other hand [I have] been able to ascertain from various sources that the British have a well-established . . . information net, which, even during the German occupation, has never been fully destroyed, nor, most likely, will it be destroyed during the period of the Russian occupation. Inasmuch as the organization of an information [net] inside of Soviet Russia proper would meet with considerable difficulties, it appears logical . . . to use the neighboring countries now occupied by Russia as a window into Soviet-Russia.

Höttl added that the SD Referat leaders in southeastern Europe were loyal to him and staunchly anti-Soviet.[39] As for himself, Höttl offered his services "unreservedly" and "altruistically," but above all, pragmatically:

> The USA cannot run its intelligence service in Germany . . . only with former opponents of the National Socialist Regime . . . In their own interest, the USA will also have to use former adherents of National Socialism . . . Through the death of our Fuehrer and Reichsfuehrer SS, we are released from our oath as SS men . . . I believe that I can be of considerable benefit to the interests of the USA . . . more help than if my experience . . . against the Soviet Union would be left unused in an internment camp. . . .
>
> For this reason I have voluntarily reported to the U.S. Army . . . on my own accord, without making use of the possibility of disappearing, confident that as an

honorable officer, who has never acted against the principles of international law and morals, I will be treated honorably.[40]

Continued interrogation of Höttl on his trips to Switzerland and his southeastern European net brought the same story. Höttl claimed numerous contacts with the moderate left in Austria, whom, he said, agreed with Höttl on the need for an independent and now democratic Austria. He also said that he had a wireless station in the village of Steyrling that had been designed to feed information to the Allies on the redoubt and *Werwolf*, the plans for which, he continued to argue, were fully developed.[41]

The OSS and the CIC assessed Höttl as someone whose dedication to Nazism was transformed into the postwar aim of splitting the East-West alliance. So despite the Army's conclusion that Höttl was "one of the most intelligent SD functionaries in the field of foreign affairs,"[42] it was also true that his motives, whatever they were,

cannot necessarily be differentiated from the long standing German wish to see the Western Allies embroiled with Russia, an embroilment which could not help but to restore some of Germany's lost power. To obscure this, Hoettl would have us believe that he has long been politically suspect in Germany; to ingratiate himself, he claims as well to have been partially instrumental in securing the surrender of the southern German armies who were to have defended the Redoubt.[43]

Höttl's former associates were interrogated to ascertain his bona fides. In Germany, his former secretary Hildegard Beetz was questioned and even sent to meet Höttl (their conversation was recorded) "to find out . . . what he considers the purpose of his present collaboration with us, and what his plans are for the future of Germany and himself." Correspondence between Höttl and Beetz suggested that Höttl planned to work for the United States, but Beetz warned her U.S. Army interrogators that Höttl "is not a man to be completely trusted." Her interrogators came away with the clear sense that "if we saw to use him we should beware of his retaining connections with the underground . . . that she had on several occasions heard from RSHA officials . . . discussing post defeat plans such as [using] the American service as a cover for their own operations."[44] Beetz, said OSS in July 1945, "suggested the likelihood of Höttl playing a double game."[45]

Höttl's former intelligence associates had little good to say, either. Willy Goetz, a former Abwehr officer in Budapest, charged that Höttl had threatened in April 1941 to report him for having a Jewish mistress if Goetz refused to spy for the SD against the Abwehr and supply Höttl (then in Vienna) with political reports from Hungary.[46]

The negative information was too much for the OSS. United States authorities quickly located and activated Höttl's wireless transmitter station in Steyrling in early July. Masking their identity, they contacted Höttl's agents

in Budapest and Bucharest, who reported from both cities. U.S. officials soon suspended these operations "due to necessity of consulting Russian authorities" because "careful exploitation of existing facilities should prove of great value to completely eliminate the organization."[47] By late July, the OSS (with Dulles' help) had contacted the Soviets to roll up the Höttl network. Officials from the U.S. zone of Germany commented that the Höttl case "is probably [the] most important one in [the] European theater because of its many implications of liaison with Russian intelligence."[48] Far from dividing the Americans and Soviets, Höttl spawned rare intelligence cooperation.

Records in Höttl's U.S. Army Counterintelligence file shows that in August 1945 the Joint Chiefs of Staff and the War Department had expressed certain "misgivings" about him.[49] At best, he could be used as a witness for the Nuremberg trials of the major war criminals, one of which was to be Kaltenbrunner.[50] His most notable statement there concerned the numbers of Jews killed by the Nazis. Eichmann, Höttl claimed, had made the estimate of six million in the summer of 1944—a round number that remained fixed in the public imagination while seemingly cementing Höttl's supposed value as a witness.[51] But the fact that Höttl was released for such tasks at Nuremberg was proof that though he might be allowed to save his life, the United States had little use for him in the intelligence field. He would not return to Austria until October 1947.

Höttl and Army Counterintelligence

After Höttl was of no further use at Nuremberg, the U.S. Army transferred him to Upper Austria in October 1947. In Klessheim prison camp in Salzburg he awaited his trial before the Austrian People's Court in Vienna. But even in Klessheim, Höttl ingratiated himself with the CIC, convincing the CIC office in Gmunden and particularly the Chief for Upper Austria, Thomas A. Lucid, that he was a valuable intelligence operative.

Uninformed and under-motivated, Lucid took everything Höttl said at face value, thinking that Höttl's past as a former SD officer was a great advantage. "During the past twelve months that Hoettl has been in contact with this office," Lucid would later write,

> he has proven to be an excellent source for ideas, both concrete and theoretical, on the expansion of American intelligence in Austria. His background as a former Deputy Chief of Amt VI RSHA for southeast Europe enables him to evaluate incoming reports on the Soviets with fairly complete accuracy.[52]

As a result, the Army released Höttl from Klessheim in December 1947 and agreed not to bind him over to the People's Court provided that Höttl kept Army Intelligence appraised of his activities. As of July 1948, however, he had not done so.[53] Instead, taking advantage of the Central European tensions triggered by the Berlin Blockade, Höttl created a new intelligence net in southeastern Europe in order to offer his service to the U.S. authorities "at a price." According to those who knew him, Höttl was contacting former SD and other former intelligence operatives, including one who now worked for the Gehlen Organization in Western Germany, who told the U.S. authorities that Höttl was already telling prospective agents that he was working for the Americans and that he had high contacts within the Republican Party.[54]

Two nets created by Höttl were approved and activated that year by the CIC. In July, Lucid activated a net code named "Montgomery," which Höttl constructed to penetrate Hungary and obtain military information. Montgomery's agents included Austrians and Hungarian refugees living in Austria. Lucid predicted that Montgomery would be "very fruitful" and that it would soon represent the CIC's "central effort" at garnering intelligence in Hungary, Romania, and the Ukraine.[55] In October, "Mount Vernon," Höttl's second approved net, was activated at an initial cost of 25,000 Austrian schillings per year (it eventually cost more than 33,000 schillings) and aimed at the Soviet occupation zone of Austria. Höttl's thirteen major contacts in the Soviet zone included a lawyer, a chief engineer, a wholesaler, an oil foreman, a railroad official, and even a well-placed Communist, and as of May 1949 there would be four wireless sets in the Soviet zone.[56] "It is felt," said Lucid, echoing his prediction for Montgomery, "that this will make a very fruitful net . . ."[57] Sub-sources were said to have included a secretary in the Cominform's Vienna Branch and an interpreter at Soviet Army headquarters at Baden bei Wien.[58]

The moment Lucid's superiors in Army Counterintelligence and CIA operatives in Austria learned that Höttl was in U.S. employ, warnings emerged complete with the recognition that Höttl's background presented moral as well as operational problems. An unsigned memo to Lieutenant Colonel James Berry, the Commanding Officer of the United States Forces in Austria, warned that

> it is well known that [Höttl] was not one of the few decent representatives of the former SD . . . Knowing Hoettl's past, his own dubious character as well as of his co-workers and the most questionable political intrigues of Hoettl and his circle . . . warning must be given. . . .
>
> Should it eventually become known that Hoettl is being used by the Americans, this would be incomprehensible to all decent Germans and Austrians.[59]

The warning should have been heeded, for there were many things wrong with Montgomery and Mount Vernon. First, Höttl's finances seemed illegitimate. Circumstantial evidence (which later would be the stuff of legend) suggested that Höttl financed himself through a large cache of RSHA-controlled stolen foreign currency, which he had hidden in Switzerland at the end of the war at Kaltenbrunner's behest. "Very few people know," said one U.S. notation on a French request to interrogate Höttl in early 1948, "that Hoettl was responsible for the transfer of Kaltenbrunner's assets into Switzerland.[60] Iris Scheidler, wife of Kaltenbrunner's former adjutant Arthur Scheidler, told U.S. authorities that Höttl had "a seemingly unlimited supply of money."[61] Further sources included Kaltenbrunner's widow, who said that before her husband's execution he had told her that Höttl would care for her financially, as would Friedrich Westen, who admitted to having the conduit through which the assets were transferred to that country. The Austrian Police in Linz pursued the case without success in 1949.[62] So did French military intelligence in Austria, which interrogated Höttl on several occasions in September and October with regard to the missing crates of Jewish treasure from Hungary. While everyone speculated, Höttl embezzled large amounts of money provided by the CIC earmarked for his own agents.[63]

Károly Ney

Meanwhile, Höttl's Montgomery and Mount Vernon subordinates were as compromised as Höttl. Most notorious was Montgomery's first Operations Chief, Károly Ney. A Hungarian of German descent, Ney was an artillery officer in the Hungarian Army until 1943. In 1944, he became an SS officer owing to his services to Höttl and Obergruppenführer Otto Winckelmann, the Highest SS and Police Leader in Budapest. In September 1944, under the supervision of Otto Skorzeny, Ney formed the SS Kampfgruppe Ney, a collection of German and Hungarian SS units "whose job was the liquidation of Jews, defeatists, saboteurs, and others inside Hungary."[64] In 1946, Ney was sentenced to life in prison by the U.S. military tribunal in Salzburg for the execution of five U.S. fliers by his Kampfgruppe at Bor. Three of his co-defendants were hanged, but Ney was soon pardoned and released from prison at the behest of the CIC in upper Austria. Three years later, senior officials remarked,

> The circumstances under which Ney was released from American custody months after his life-sentence was imposed, are greatly puzzling in view of the fact that a crucial Hungarian witness arrived in Salzburg three days after the trial of Ney and company . . . with enough damaging eyewitness testimony of Ney's role in the execution of the fliers to have sent him to the gallows . . . A persistent but unconfirmed report circulating in 1947 among American military intelligence circles in Austria indicated that Ney was quietly released upon high-level intervention from the United States, and that Vatican contacts had much to do with his release.[65]

Ney had been in discreet contact with the CIC in 1947. In Munich by May 1948, Ney claimed to be at the head of a CIC project to re-establish a partisan underground in Hungary.[66] By the summer of that year, Höttl recruited Ney for the Montgomery net. Ney always had his own agenda. As the head of the Hungarian Union of Veterans of the War against the Soviet Union, Ney used intelligence jobs to raise money for his project of leading an underground anti-Communist group in Hungary. While working for Höttl and the CIC, Ney strove to be financially independent of both. Evidence emerged that Ney, while part of Montgomery, ran Hungarian agents for French intelligence, and that he had twice met the French military governor in Germany, General Pierre Koenig.[67] He was dropped from Montgomery for what was euphemistically labeled "operational incompetence," but he continued to work for French intelligence while trying to find and recruit former members of his Kampfgruppe.[68]

Erich Kernmayer

Erich Kernmayer was another dubious Montgomery operative. Like Höttl, he was a member of the illegal Austrian Nazi Party as early as 1934, after which he joined the illegal SA in 1935 and became the editor of the Nazi Party's *Oesterreichischer Beobachter* as well as the editor for a number of formerly Jewish-owned newspapers after the *Anschluss*. In 1941 he joined the SS, directing propaganda against Tito and eventually serving as an assistant to Otto Skorzeny in Budapest. Captured by the Americans, he served as an informant to CIC Salzburg until he joined Montgomery at its inception. Within Montgomery, Kernmayer was Ney's press chief, writing propaganda on Hungary for the Austrian press. Kernmayer became operational head of Montgomery after Ney was fired.[69]

Karl Kowarik

Mount Vernon's operations chief was no better. Karl Kowarik was another Viennese who joined the Nazi Party in 1930. He once proclaimed proudly that his father was a devoted follower of the famous Austrian anti-Semite Georg von Schönerer.[70] Kowarek became the Hitler Youth leader for Vienna in 1934, fled to Germany under Austrian police threats, and then returned a year later to run the entire illegal Hitler Youth in Austria. In April 1939, Kowarek was made an SS officer after his evaluation "as an old National Socialist of outspoken ideological conviction."[71] Now listed as a journalist in Mount Vernon, Kowarik spent much of his time contacting and financially supporting his former Hitler Youth subordinates.[72]

Finally, Höttl's intelligence circle dabbled openly in postwar Austrian politics. Höttl and Kernmayer formed the newspaper *Alpenländischer Heimatruf*, aimed at former Nazis in Austria.[73] Höttl himself was a major participant at a secret meeting between high-ranking members of the Austrian People's Party and former Nazis in Gmunden on May 27, 1949, the object of which was to form a cooperative relationship in connection with the forthcoming elections. Höttl left the meeting with the assignment of disrupting the political activities of Dr. Albert Kraus, the Chief of the Association of Independents, who himself was the chief of four nets working for the CIC.[74] "We have warned him time and again," CIC Operations Chief Major J. V. Milano later said, "that it is impossible for him to work as an intelligence operative and be mixed up with local politics."[75] And since either Höttl or Kraus could easily have exposed the other's activities, Lucid had to broker an arrangement between the two.[76] A CIA officer very familiar with Höttl was blunt. "If [Höttl is] slated for a political role in Austria," he said,

[it] would have to be viewed with grave concern . . . Höttl is a born intriguer and dyed-in-the-wool Austrian Nazi with a veneer of "Wienerische Graziösität" . . . He is bound to attract desparadoes [*sic*] of the type that surrounded Kaltenbrunner. Their political program [is] the re-establishment of Austrian ascendancy in the Balkans . . . Yet I wouldn't rule out that Dr. Höttl, on purely opportunistic grounds, might decide to play ball with the Russians.[77]

Höttl might even then have been working for the Soviets. As early as January 1949, the CIC learned that Höttl had contacted a person from his university and wartime years, Dr. Tarias von Borodajkewycz, who was classified as a Nazi "offender" by the Austrian People's Court. Borodajkewycz was a researcher for the Moscow Academy of Sciences under a Soviet Colonel named Stern, who also served in the Austrian Communist Central Committee.[78] Borodajkewycz, it was later learned, also received Soviet funding for his business enterprises in western Austria. Following the Borodajkewycz lead, U.S. authorities also learned that Höttl "was in contact with Soviet intelligence" through at least four known Soviet penetration agents. The British would later be convinced that Höttl had given one of their agents over to the Soviets in 1952. And the CIC would eventually conclude that "part of the information [received from Höttl] was . . . actual and deliberate deception aimed at misleading American intelligence."[79]

The CIC began to lose patience with Höttl and his networks in the spring of 1949, when Höttl insisted that his subordinates be protected from Austrian court proceedings. Dr. Hubert Hueber, a former Gestapo chief in Salzburg, was now, according to Höttl, "one of the best experts on the Communist movement in Western Austria." When the Austrian People's Court wanted to try Hueber for illegal membership in the NSDAP before 1938, Lucid arranged to have Hueber placed under CIC house arrest with his mother in Windischgarten, though he was to be available when his trial came up. Helmuth Hecke, another illegal Nazi who acted as Höttl's secretary for Mount Vernon, was less fortunate. Höttl's request that the CIC "get hold of [Hecke's] records at the People's Court *at once* and hold them for some time" ran aground. When Lucid asked a superior if the CIC could place him under a more benign house arrest, he received the blunt answer, "Nothing doing!"[80]

In the aggregate, Höttl's problems were too great for the CIC to retain him for long. After a high level meeting of officers within the 430th CIC Detachment in August 1949, both networks were soon dropped. "Hoettl," said Major Milano,

is considered an excellent intelligence man, but an extremely dangerous one. We have been requested many times by other U.S. intelligence agencies in Europe to discontinue our support of Hoettl since he was an SD leader and is feared by all present intelligence factions representing the Abwehr or non-German sources. The reason that he is feared is that he was an excellent intelligence man in his day and actually was a war criminal who was exonerated at Nuremberg due to the fact that he became a State's witness.

Despite Höttl's past, Milano conceded that it was Höttl's political maneuverings, his dishonesty with his CIC handlers, and the decline in the quality of his reports that had brought matters to a head. His reports over the past several months had been especially poor. The CIC did not believe that their intelligence on Austria and Hungary would suffer as a result of dropping Höttl and his networks. Surprisingly, the CIC did not fear that Höttl would work more for the Soviets. Milano reported, "We will watch Hoettl very closely . . ."[81] Ever smooth, Höttl accepted his termination with grace, asking for a month of severance for both nets and commenting that "I shall continue my efforts for a mobilization against the Bolshevist world-enemy."[82] Many of Höttl's subordinates from Mount Vernon and Montgomery quickly offered their services to the CIC for a third of their earlier pay.[83]

Höttl, West German Intelligence, and the CIA

In 1950, despite prohibitive costs, Höttl opened his own publishing house in Linz, Niebelungen Verlag. He had mentioned this project as a possible front for espionage activities while still working for the CIC. Everything about the press was irregular. Höttl's name appeared nowhere in the ownership or operation, and his wife, Elfriede, held legal power of attorney.[84] Niebelungen Press published Höttl's first book, *Die geheime Front*, under the pseudonym Walter Hagen, which brought Höttl a financial success (it was among the first to discuss German secret operations in World War II). The book was also an advertisement for Höttl, who could not resist revealing his identity. While mentioning nothing of German war crimes in Italy, Hungary, or anyplace else, the book exaggerated Höttl's "genius" as a political analyst and secret operative as well as his anti-Soviet and pro-Western credentials. He masterminded the plan to rescue Mussolini; his advice to leave Horthy in power in Hungary in October 1944 would have stabilized the Carpathian front against the Red Army (which in Höttl's version seems to have committed the only atrocities in Hungary); he had worked for a peace with the West since 1943 only to be thwarted by Hitler and Roosevelt; and his own contact with Dulles had saved Austria from a bloody military campaign and Communist takeover, thus ensuring the democratic transition and independent Austria that he supposedly favored all along.[85] Thanks in part to Höttl's success as an author, Niebelungen Press provided jobs for a number of Höttl's associates. The book's arguments—and here we must remember that the self-serving memoirs of Hitler's followers were read and believed by a wide German public in the 1950s—also might have helped to ensure his future employment with other intelligence groups.[86]

In 1950, Höttl was in contact with French intelligence through former SS-Sturmbannführer Werner Göttsch, another SD official whom the French jailed in

1945 and then used for intelligence purposes. Through Göttsch, Höttl resold to French intelligence copies of reports that he had already sold to the CIC in 1949, even while the French were interrogating him on the hidden crates of Hungarian Jewish loot. French intelligence in Austria was impressed enough with Höttl to protect him from Russian criminal investigators in 1950 and to offer Höttl permanent employment through another French agent in Austria, Raimund Strangl, also a pre-1938 Austrian Nazi.[87] Strangl, it turned out, had himself been the source of many of Höttl's reports to the CIC, which Höttl rewrote and passed off as original. They had been based mostly on newspapers and uncoded Hungarian radio broadcasts, which the Americans could hear themselves.[88]

Evidence was also plentiful of Höttl's contacts with Soviet agents, including Russian representatives in Vienna. The CIC thought that Höttl had been enlisted to establish a Soviet-controlled apparatus within West German intelligence.[89] Höttl indeed met frequently with Dr. Emmerich Offczarek, a former classmate at the University of Vienna who was the Gehlen Organization's most senior official in Austria. It is difficult to say what these meetings concerned, but Höttl came away angry, stating that Offczarek was one of the dumbest intelligence men in Central Europe. If Höttl had contacted Offczarek to procure a job with the Gehlen Organization, he failed.[90]

Höttl's main desire, however, was to work for West German intelligence in such a way that he would be invulnerable to the Americans, who had made clear their distrust. The partial sovereignty of West Germany in 1949 and the discussion of rearmament that followed the outbreak of the Korean War in 1950 also opened the question in Bonn of who would head a new West German intelligence agency—Reinhard Gehlen, whose organization had been officially under U.S. control, or someone else. In 1950, Chancellor Konrad Adenauer created the Zentrale für Heimatdienst (ZfH), an umbrella organization of four detachments charged with national defense. The third branch of the ZfH was Information und Nachrichtendienst under Achim Oster, the son of Hans Oster, the Abwehr officer who was executed for his part in the 1944 plot to kill Hitler. The operative chief of the branch was another former Abwehr officer, Friedrich Wilhelm Heinz, whose influence was such that the detachment became known as the Friedrich-Wilhelm-Heinz-Amt (FWHA). Charged with gathering intelligence from East Germany and the other Soviet satellites, it would build nets into Eastern Europe but would also have a presence in Italy and Austria.

The very existence of the FWHA was secret. Its administrative offices were outside of Bonn in Bad Godesberg, and only the Chancellor himself could determine how information gathered by the office would be used. In October 1950, the entire ZfH was placed under the so-called Amt Blank, which would become the official West German Ministry of Defense in 1955.[91] These developments had the full attention of Gehlen—who hoped to remain the head of whatever intelligence service emerged from West German sovereignty—and of Gehlen's sponsors in the CIA. Both were well informed about Heinz's activities. The CIA was in direct contact with Heinz, using a code name either for Heinz himself or for his office, and Gehlen would later penetrate the Heinz organization.[92]

The CIA was able to monitor Höttl through Army CIC Detachment 35 of United States Forces Austria. One of the CIC agents who provided a considerable amount of information on Höttl was Karl Theodor Haas, another former SD official. In 1951, the CIC and the CIA both learned that Höttl approached Haas to work for him in the Heinz office.[93] The two met at Bad Ischl in January 1952. Höttl told Haas that he had been hired by Heinz to head the southeast section of the new German intelligence service, which, Höttl said, would be truly independent and not, like the Gehlen Organization, dependent on the United States. Höttl said that his own West German citizenship process was underway and that Haas, if he were to join, would work in Milan under a commercial cover as head of the Italian subsection. Höttl claimed to have found section chiefs for the other southeastern states as well. He introduced Haas to Baron Heinrich Mast, a disaffected Gehlen employee who was now Höttl's "Chief of Staff," and who would be fired by the Gehlen Organization for this reason in March 1952.[94] Haas told the CIC about the meeting, and also that he was tempted by Höttl's offer to become a German civil servant with a high monthly salary (Höttl promised 1,000 deutsche marks per month).[95]

CIC Detachment 35 showed concern because Höttl was "a definite security threat." His very presence in the Heinz's organization discredited that office in American eyes.[96] More cynical CIA officials toyed with leaving Höttl in place within the Amt Blank because "a well-documented case of [Heinz's] use of unacceptable RSHA types such as Hoettl could very well give us sufficient leverage to resolve any [Gehlen–Heinz] differences . . . to our advantage."[97] But this assessment assumed that the Heinz office could firmly control Höttl; ultimately, the CIA placed little stock in this hope. The CIA expressed its concerns to Heinz in April 1952. Heinz told the CIA Chief in Frankfurt that though Höttl was "uncouth and characterless," and although much of his reportage was worthless, Höttl provided valuable political reports on Austria. These reports were then sent to Blank and distributed in the West German Chancellery itself. Heinz said he had actually received a handwritten commendation from Adenauer for his reporting on the French and Austrian political scenes, the latter of which had originated with Höttl.[98] In the meantime, Höttl was trying to extend his net into Trieste, Slovakia, North Africa, and even the Vatican.[99]

By now, the CIA had learned that Höttl was employing the same sorts of men he used in Montgomery and Mount Vernon. One was former SS-Hauptsturmführer Rupert Mandl, who served the Nazi regime in Rome and Zagreb. Another was the infamous Otto von Bolschwing, who helped to engineer the failed Iron Guard coup in Romania in January 1941.[100] And Höttl's intelligence from the operations standpoint seemed just as suspect as it had in 1948. Several CIA operatives in Vienna commented that despite Adenauer's commendation, Höttl's analysis of Austrian politics was "distinguished more by its rhetoric than by its profundity." Despite Heinz's conviction that Höttl had a source within the Austrian government, CIA readers of his reports were struck by the low quality of information, which "does not require the talents of a very astute operator." Höttl, they noted, "can turn out a sizable volume of such information without interrupting his regular pattern of coffeehouse conversations." Any support for Höttl, they concluded, "is a Bad Thing."[101]

Höttl also had a corrosive effect in Austria, where in the summer of 1952, Major Victor Tuliszewski, the Commanding Officer of the U.S. Military Intelligence Service, paid 3,000 schillings for a sheaf of reports on the Soviet zone of Austria and Hungary, and then demanded reimbursement from the CIC. Both the CIA and the CIC identified the reports as coming from Höttl. Furious, the CIC insisted that the CIA tell Heinz to sever all contacts with Höttl. "If persuasion is not enough, and the Germans persist in using Hoettl," said Army Intelligence, "USFA is planning some unfavorable publicity for Hoettl and would not feel reluctant to mention his present connections with [the German government] along with elaboration of his past scurrilous record," which, they seemed to have momentarily forgotten, included a stint with the CIC.

The CIA agreed that "the elimination of Hoettl . . . would be to the general good of intelligence in Austria."[102] Colonel Heinz, however, refused to cut off Höttl, possibly because anyone who could help earn him a handwritten commendation from Adenauer also bolstered his position against Gehlen. "[Heinz] is fully aware of Hoettl's reputation," reported the CIA, "but finds him a useful man."[103] The CIA said later, "I did not fail to point out to Heinz that his continued relations with Hoettl would in the end discredit the entire [West German Intelligence] office."[104] On October 2, 1952, Heinz finally relented, dropping Höttl for supplying false reports. Höttl protested to Heinz and then to Blank himself in November, arguing that it was the Americans who forced him back into retirement. Not until Höttl's home was searched in March the following year and his correspondence read was the CIA convinced that West German intelligence had really dropped Höttl.[105]

A Soviet Agent? Höttl and the Ponger-Verber Affair

In January 1953, U.S. authorities in Vienna arrested two naturalized U.S. citizens living in that city—Kurt Ponger and his brother-in-law, Walter Verber—for Soviet espionage. Both men were Jewish natives of Vienna who had come to the United States in 1938 and soon after secretly joined the Communist Party of the United States. Because of their language skills, both had served U.S. intelligence during the war, and Ponger had worked as an interrogator at Nuremberg. Afterwards, they returned to Vienna where they lived in the Soviet municipal sector and established the Central European Press as a cover for espionage activity on behalf of the Soviet Union. The U.S. Army's 430th Counterintelligence Corps, based in Vienna, placed them under surveillance in 1949 and compiled more than two thousand top-secret reports on them.[106]

The CIA tracked a connection between the two Communist agents and Höttl. A Gehlen Organization section chief stated that in late October 1952 he had seen Höttl together with Ponger and Ponger's associate Walter Lauber on an auto trip through West Germany—all four happened to stop at the same highway rest stop. During this West German trip, Höttl, Ponger, and Lauber separated for a time, and Höttl met with Wilhelm Krichbaum, the wartime head of the German Army's Geheime Feldpolizei and now a senior Gehlen official. Krichbaum later claimed that Höttl was asking all of his contacts in West Germany about the possibility of a job with the Gehlen Organization.[107] When the CIC arrested Lauber, they found a handwritten copy of Höttl's address book containing the names of numerous CIA and Gehlen operatives.[108] On April 14, Ponger, about to plead guilty to espionage, said that he had cultivated both Höttl and Krichbaum as penetration agents against the Gehlen Organization.[109] In 1963, the CIA discovered—likely thanks to a West German investigation—that Krichbaum had been working for the Soviets as early as 1950.[110] The fact that Höttl had contact with Ponger and Lauber opened up the possibility that, wittingly or unwittingly, he was being used as a Soviet penetration agent against West German intelligence.

The first challenge for the CIA was to assess the level of damage, which meant evaluating the nature of the connection between Höttl and the Gehlen Organization. Senior Gehlen officials emphatically denied an operative relationship with Höttl, and CIA liaisons with Gehlen believed these denials. "[We] have made such strong representation [at] all levels of Zipper [Gehlen Organization code name] [in the] last four months that they would not risk flaunting us especially since they knew we [were] well informed on Hoettl's dealings from other sources."[111] Others were less sure. On March 4, one CIA employee went over the case with Gehlen personally and charged his organization with "intentionally withholding information of vital interest." Gehlen's Austrian elements, said this CIA liaison, were once again a source of "considerable friction" between the CIA and the Gehlen Organization.[112] The only way to assess the nature of Höttl's connections would be through a full interrogation of Höttl, preferably by a CIC agent well acquainted with Austria but not compromised by the Montgomery or Mount Vernon fiascos.

Höttl conceded nothing in a CIC interrogation in February 1953. His contacts with Ponger, Verber, and Lauber, he suggested, were all about his journalistic projects and the procurement of photographs from Ponger's wartime collection. Ponger and Verber, Höttl said, probably had ties to Israeli intelligence, but they always had seemed anti-Communist to him.[113] The CIA was sure that Höttl was lying. After the CIA sent information on Ponger and Verber to Army Intelligence suggesting that Ponger and Verber had indeed tried to penetrate the Gehlen Organization through Höttl and that Ponger had tried hard to get Höttl employment with Gehlen, the Army agreed to re-arrest and re-interrogate Höttl. This time, the interrogation would be less friendly because Höttl was "very adept at lying and evasion" and because the CIC now believed that Höttl was a witting agent of Ponger. They "strongly suspected" that Höttl also tried to use his contacts in the Gehlen Organization to assist Ponger in making contacts. Moreover, Höttl possessed records from Mount Vernon and Montgomery—records that by now "could constitute a source of embarrassment to the Command and [which] should be retrieved." Höttl was therefore lured by CIC Special Agent Rolf Ringer to Salzburg, where he was arrested on March 25 and interrogated on March 26 and 28, and then, after being held in solitary confinement, again on April 3. The interrogations themselves filled seven reels of audiotape.

Höttl remained a tough nut to crack. "When faced . . . with the two alternatives," said the preliminary interrogation report,

> that he was a witting member of the Soviet-controlled [Ponger] complex or that he was a complete dope, Hoettl refused to accept either alternative. Being a proud man, he argued at length against the accusation that he must have been a fool to be taken in by Ponger and at the same time maintained that he never in any way tumbled to the true affiliations of the Verber-Ponger family although he was aware that the Pongers resided in [the] Soviet sector of Vienna.[114]

Instead, Höttl threw suspicion onto Krichbaum, stating that Ponger had used Krichbaum to get Höttl a job with Gehlen, but that Ponger never tried to recruit Höttl himself. Höttl said he did not think Krichbaum was a Soviet agent, but implied that it was a possibility. "This off-hand or indirect type of slander," reported the interrogator, was "characteristic of all Hoettl's remarks concerning previous colleagues."[115]

In the end, it was impossible to tell whether Höttl was a Soviet agent. Even Höttl's voluminous correspondence of more than thirty thousand pages, which was seized and partially microfilmed, offered no sure answers. Correspondence from Höttl to Baron Mast professed shock at the Ponger-Verber affair, while further implicating Krichbaum as one of Ponger's closest contacts. Höttl insisted in this correspondence that his own longstanding connections with Ponger were only in the journalistic field. This correspondence could itself have been a fabrication left conspicuously for the eventuality that Höttl was arrested. After all, once Ponger and Verber were arrested, Höttl could have concluded that his turn would come. The CIC feared that more incriminating correspondence could be hidden in another cache, which might also have included his Montgomery and Mount Vernon correspondence, none of which had been found.[116] But if Höttl's anti-Communist correspondence were a clever fabrication, it revealed traces of his Nazi colors. Ponger, he said in a letter to Rupert Mandl, "felt himself much more Jew than American," and that "this entire espionage case has been set up in certain Jewish circles in order . . . to indicate how innocent these 'new Americans' . . . are and how they have been persecuted."[117]

CIA evaluators gave Höttl the benefit of the doubt. One agent familiar with the case was:

inclined to offer odds of ten to nine, or perhaps twenty to nineteen, that Hoettl is not under Soviet control and was unaware that Ponger and Verber were Soviet agents. His function in the affair may have been to act as [an] unwitting red herring, so that if Ponger's travel in Western Austria and Germany should come to the attention of an anti-Soviet service, attention would be diverted to everybody's normal curiosity about Hoettl's activity. It is also conceivable that Ponger, who made a persistent attempt to build Hoettl into Zipper, was . . . setting up an approach which was to be made at some later date . . . after Hoettl had begun to function as a Zipperite.[118]

For the moment, this was as close to the truth as anyone would get. After the second interrogation, the CIA concluded that "[Höttl] is determined to hold out under heavy pressure and appear ridiculous if necessary, rather than yield one inch of the story he has prepared. He does not really fear us, nor can he be readily intimidated by us."[119] In fact, Höttl spent his time in solitary confinement writing an article on Walter Schellenberg, which he would later try to sell to the German press. "I was Hitler's Master Spy," another Höttl article partially based on this work, was published later in the year. CIA analysts found the article more "amusing" than accurate.[120] Amazingly, during his captivity Höttl also offered to work for U.S. intelligence again as a double agent who would expose Ponger and Verber's Soviet contacts. "All readers of this report will be overwhelmed with relief," said the second interrogation report, "that the interrogator did not accept Hoettl's offer."[121]

The need to scotch Höttl's intelligence activities once and for all was handled in connection with his release during the second week of April. Two days before, a press release implicated Höttl in the Ponger-Verber affair. Such would "ensure that our version of the story would appear first, while making Höttl too suspect for use either by Gehlen or the Soviets."[122] Such did not dissuade agencies lured by Höttl's supposed expertise, however. Yugoslav intelligence tried in the summer and fall of 1953 to recruit Höttl for work in Trieste (presumably against the likes of Draganović), and Höttl tried to get the backing of the Gehlen Organization for this project. Gehlen turned down the proposal, but agents within the organization maintained contact with Höttl well into the following year. "We have pointed out the disadvantage to Zipper of having so close a connection to the eternal Willi, but, naturally without avail."[123]

The real surprise came in the years to follow. A former KGB staff officer named Anatoly Golitsin who defected in 1961 and who carried a CIA code name, commented during debriefing in 1963 that Höttl had been a "Soviet agent of long standing," having worked as a KGB counterintelligence agent in Vienna. Another defector, Peter Deriabin, confirmed that Höttl operated under the Soviet code name "Cheka" and was "the highest paid [Russian intelligence] agent [Deriabin] knew of."[124] The possibility that Höttl was still an active Soviet agent did not appear to bother the CIA, however. "If Hoettl has ever been a highly paid Soviet agent," said one CIA Chief of Station, "then he managed to defraud the [Soviets] along with his other employers."[125]

By this time, Höttl had actually taken to defrauding his fellow citizens. As the headmaster of a private middle school in Alt Aussee, Höttl presided over a bankruptcy when the school went 15 million schillings in debt in February 1964 following a number of questionable building contracts.[126] Höttl landed on his feet. In 1955 he had published a second book (*Hitler's Paper Weapon*) concerning Operation Bernhard.[127] His expertise in this fascinating story landed him Austrian television appearances. This notoriety in turn helped to protect him when the Hungarian government demanded his extradition. Höttl, the Hungarians said, had helped to plan the occupation of Hungary, had been behind the arrest of Hungarian resistors, and had helped in the deportation of Hungary's Jews. The Hungarian demand was denied. In the following decades Höttl continued to pose as an intelligence expert uncompromised by his Nazi career or his connections with Communists. As a parting shot, in 1997 he published self-serving memoirs under his own name.[128] He died two years later.

Höttl's career is valuable in supplementing our understanding of the relationship between Allied intelligence and the Nazis in the early postwar years. Knowledgeable people—including Germans who had served Hitler—tempted some U.S. intelligence officials, who overlooked Nazi pasts if the individuals seemed especially valuable. We will never know whether it was Höttl's shameful record as an SS officer or his fundamental dishonesty as a swindler and security risk that hurt him more in Americans eyes. It appears that if Höttl had shown more candor and supplied better intelligence, his U.S. patrons might have continued to protect him, despite their awareness of the risks posed by his Nazi past. There were those in the CIA, after all, who hoped to use Höttl's SS past as a political lever in the West German intelligence struggle.

Many postwar intelligence agencies were tempted by Höttl's smoothness at one time or another, but only the least competent and most vulnerable succumbed. The OSS was willing to keep a channel open to Höttl if such a channel could weaken the Alpine Redoubt, but once the war was over, Höttl's lines to the East were shut down. Three years later, East-West tensions had reached the point that local CIC officials in Upper Austria were willing to clutch at any straw to provide additional security for the western Austrian zones. Even then, those Army and CIA officers familiar with Höttl's background demonstrated moral misgivings over his use, though Höttl's dubious contacts and financial/political shenanigans brought about his termination. How Höttl found employment in the Amt Blank awaits the opening of German intelligence records. For now we can assume that his Austrian reports impressed someone in Bonn enough to provide Friedrich Wilhelm Heinz with some leverage against his political opponents. The CIA and the CIC saw Höttl as a moral as well as an operational risk to the new West German state. Ultimately, however, it took Höttl's association with the Soviets, rather than with the Nazis, to ruin his cachet in the Western intelligence world for good.

Notes

1. Höttl SS Officer File, NA–BDC, RG 242, A-3343, SSO, roll 105A, frame 536ff.
2. Ibid.
3. Ronald W. Zweig, *The Gold Train: The Destruction of the Jews and the Looting of Hungary* (New York: William Morrow, 2002), 19.
4. Höttl to Untersturmführer Wöbling, 23 Oct. 1940, Höttl SS Officer File, NA–BDC, RG 242, A-3343, SSO, roll 105A.
5. 1. I. D. 2 Disz. L. Nr. 1921/42, 20 Oct. 1942, "Vorlage SS-Gruppenführer Streckenbach," Höttl SS Officer File, NA–BDC, RG 242, A-3343, SSO, roll 105A.
6. Polte's letter is quoted in Der Inspekteur der Sicherheitspolizei und des SD in Wien, I D 2 B. Nr. 588/41 Dr. St./Zr., 17 Aug. 1942, Höttl SS Officer File, NA–BDC, RG 242, A-3343, SSO, roll 105A, frame 615f.
7. Höttl to SS Gruppenführer und Generalleutnant der Polizei, Heinrich Streckenbach, Berlin, 5 July 1942, Höttl SS Officer File, NA–BDC, RG 242, A-3343, SSO, roll 105A, frame 637ff.
8. Peter R. Black, *Ernst Kaltenbrunner: Ideological Soldier of the Third Reich* (Princeton, NJ: Princeton University Press, 1984), 178.
9. Chef der Sicherheitspolizei und SD, VI/V. B. Nr. 2090/42, 12 Dec. 1942, Höttl SS Officer File, NA–BDC, RG 242, A-3343, SSO, roll 105A, frame 555; RSHA, I D 2 Disz. L. Nr. 1921, 29 Mar. 1943, ibid., frame 554.
10. In his SS file, Höttl's exact role is unclear. His own version is discussed in his memoir, *The Secret Front: Nazi Political Espionage 1938-1945*, trans. R. H. Stevens (New York: Praeger, 1954), chapters 13–15.
11. Black, *Kaltenbrunner*, 185–6.
12. RSHA, IA5 a AZ. 2 749, dated 25 Oct. 1943, Höttl SS Officer File, NA–BDC, RG 242, A-3343, SSO, roll 105A, frames 542–3, 546.
13. Zweig, *The Gold Train*, 39–42. Kaltenbrunner said after the war that his best information on Hungary came from Höttl, who remained in Budapest as the chief SD intelligence man and was political adviser to Edmund Vessenmayer, the Reich Plenipotentiary in Hungary. CI War Room incoming telegram, Ref. 410, 25 May 1945, NA, RG 226, entry 119A, box 55, folder 1602; War Room incoming telegram, Ref. 413, sent 26 May 1945, ibid. Black, *Kaltenbrunner*, 228.
14. In postwar interrogations Höttl falsely claimed to have developed contacts with moderate Austrians and to have floated peace feelers to the West since 1943. Black, *Kaltenbrunner*, 223ff.
15. Zweig, *Gold Train*, 69.
16. Ibid., 261n68.
17. Neal H. Petersen, ed., *From Hitler's Doorstep: The Wartime Intelligence Reports of Allen Dulles, 1942–1945* (University Park: Pennsylvania State University Press, 1996), documents 5-45 and 5-48.
18. Petersen, *Hitler's Doorstep*, document 5-66; Zweig, *Gold Train*, 93.
19. Timothy J. Naftali, "Creating the Myth of the Alpenfestung: Allied Intelligence and the

Collapse of the Nazi Police State," *Contemporary Austrian Studies* 5 (1996): 203-56; Perry Biddiscombe, *Werwolf! The History of the National Socialist Guerilla Movement, 1944–1946* (Toronto: University of Toronto Press, 1998), 177ff; Bradley F. Smith and Elena Agarossi, *Operation Sunrise: The Secret Surrender* (New York: Basic Books, 1979), 22–25.

20. Smith and Agarossi, *Operation Sunrise*, 22–25. See also Kaltenbrunner's comments relayed in CI War Room telegram Ref. 413, no date, NA, RG 226, entry 119A, box 55, folder 1602.
21. Leslie to 110 (Dulles), 17 Apr. 1945, NA, RG 263, Wilhelm Höttl Name File, vol. 1.
22. William Donovan to Secretary of State, unnumbered, 24 Mar. 1945, ibid.
23. This is based on a comment from Dulles. See Petersen, *Hitler's Doorstep*, document 5-75. For Donovan, see Donovan to Secretary of State, unnumbered, 24 Mar. 1945, NA, RG 263, Wilhelm Höttl Name File, vol. 1.
24. Donovan to Secretary of State, 24 Mar. 1945, NA, RG 263, Wilhelm Höttl Name File, vol. 1, again based on Dulles's report of the same day. See Petersen, *Hitler's Doorstep*, document 5-75.
25. Donovan Telegram to Dulles, No. 1264, 29 Mar. 1945, NA, RG 263, Wilhelm Höttl Name File, vol. 1. Höttl's actual father, Johann, was an Austrian financial official.
26. Telegram to U.S. Legation Bern, No. 1576, 7 Apr. 1945, ibid.
27. Leslie to 110 (Dulles) 17 Apr. 1945, ibid.
28. Dulles report of 13 Apr. 1945, Petersen, *Hitler's Doorstep*, document 5-98.
29. Top Secret report, authorship unknown, copied by SCI, 12th Army Group, 31 May 1945, NA, RG 319, IRR, entry 134B, box 617, Wilhelm Höttl.
30. Zweig, *Gold Train*, 99–100.
31. Dulles report of 21 Apr. 1945, Petersen, *Hitler's Doorstep*, document 5-107.
32. Günther Bischof, *Austria in the First Cold War, 1945–1955: The Leverage of the Weak* (New York: St. Martin's Press, 1999).
33. Smith and Agarossi, *Operation Sunrise*, 155–57.
34. Black, *Kaltenbrunner*, 247–50.
35. Zweig, *Gold Train*, 95.
36. Ibid., 112–17, 124–25. Westen seems to have hidden the crates in Switzerland, but they vanished soon after and were never recovered. Westen died in June 1951 after a bizarre incident in which he tried to prove the corruptibility of Austrian policemen. Höttl, it was reported, subsequently suffered a breakdown owing to the fact that he had not been able to locate the stolen Jewish assets that they had taken together; ibid., 210.
37. Top Secret report, copied by SCI, 12th Army Group, 31 May 1945, NA, RG 319, IRR, entry 134B, box 617, Wilhelm Höttl.
38. Third U.S. Army SCI Detachment Report, 21 May 1945 to CO, SCI 12th Army Group, NA, RG 226, entry 119A, box 55, folder 1602.
39. Top Secret Report, copied by SCI, 12th Army Group, 31 May 1945, NA, IRR, entry 134B, box 617, Wilhelm Höttl. Höttl was captured along with his chief assistant and technician Paul Neunteufel; Kurt Auner, the Amt VI E head of the Romanian sector; Yugoslav expert Rupert Mandl; Hungarian expert Josef Deworezky; Bulgarian expert Bruno Klaus; and two wireless transmitter operators. See War Room incoming telegram from Paris X-2, sent 27 May 1945, Ref. 415, NA, RG 226, entry 119A, box 55, folder 1602. While little was

known about the others, it was clear that Neunteufel had helped Höttl combat the Polish underground during the war. See Summary of Traces, 29 May 1945, NA, RG 226, entry 119A, box 55, folder 1602.

40. SCI Agent Nathan Plung, study of 28 July 1945, enclosed in Lt. Col. Andrew H. Berding (A.C. Chief, OSS/X-2), to Chief, CIB, USFET, 30 July 1945, NA, RG 226, entry 108A, box 287, folder LWX-005-1945–1946.

41. Special Interrogation of Höttl, 20 June 1945, NA, RG 319, IRR, entry 134B, box 617, Wilhelm Höttl.

42. HQ, 3rd U.S. Army Intelligence Center, Interrogation Section, "The SD and the RSHA," 9 July 1945, ibid.

43. SCI Agent Nathan Plung, study of 28 July 1945, enclosed in Lt. Col. Andrew H. Berding (A.C. Chief, OSS/X-2), to Chief, CIB, USFET, 30 July 1945, NA, RG 226, entry 108A, box 287, folder LWX-005-1945–1946. Plung cited several cases in this study of German intelligence efforts to plant fake Soviet spies behind Allied lines in the effort to hasten a split between the United States and the USSR.

44. L. E. de Neufville, Civ, SCI, report of 17 June 1945, SCI Detachment Weimar, NA, RG 319, IRR, entry 134A, box 59, Red Orchestra, vol. 4, file 3, 559.

45. OSS Mission to Germany for SCI 3rd Army, 6 July 1945, NA, RG 319, IRR, entry 134B, box 617, Wilhelm Höttl. A microphone was to be used to tape their conversation.

46. For Goetz's comments, see document bundle covered as Höttl, PF. 602, 139, NA, RG 226, entry 119A, box 55, folder 1602.

47. Saint Washington to 109 (Donovan), London, 5 July 1945, NA, RG 319, IRR, entry 134B, box 617, Wilhelm Höttl.

48. Spearhead Amzon (Lt. Col. Andrew H. Berding, Asst. Chief of Staff, OSS/X-2 Germany) to Saint London, 30 July 1945, ibid.

49. Berding to Dulles (Berlin), 18 Aug. 1945, ibid.

50 AB 12, 3rd Army to AB Amzon, 12 Sept. 1945, ibid.

51. See for example "Die Unklarheiten über die Zahl der getöteten Juden," bundle dated 24 Nov. 1948, vol. 2, ibid.

52. For this quote and the facts above, see the CIC bundle on Montgomery dated 5 Jan. 1950 and designated [excised] by the CIA, NA, RG 263, Wilhelm Höttl Name File, vol. 3.

53. Summary of Information dated 12 July 1948, sent to Deputy Director of Intelligence, European Command, 6 Aug. 1948, NA, RG 319, IRR, entry 134B, box 617, Wilhelm Höttl.

54. Summary of Information dated 12 July 1948, sent to Deputy Director of Intelligence, European Command, 6 Aug. 1948, RG 263, Wilhelm Höttl Name File, vol. 8; 263 FS Section 55/L of 23 Aug. 1948 to Styria District Security, HQ (Austria), on Kungel, Adalbert, NA, RG 263, Wilhelm Höttl Name File, vol. 9.

55. The July 10, 1948, activation date for Montgomery is according to a CIC Report on Montgomery, 5 Jan. 1950, NA, RG 263, Wilhelm Höttl Name File, vol. 3; see also Thomas A. Lucid, Chief CIC, Land Upper Austria, to Chief, CIC, USFA, Memo. Re. Proposed Hungarian Network, 20 July 1948, ibid; Bundle titled Net Project Montgomery, NA, RG 263, CIA Subject File, Army/CIC Nets in Eastern Europe.

56. Bundle titled Net Project Mount Vernon, NA, RG 263, CIA Subject File, Army/CIC Nets in

Eastern Europe.

57. Lucid to Chief, CIC, USFA, 3 Sept. 1948, NA, RG 263, Wilhelm Höttl Name File, vol. 3.

58. Lt. Col. J. J. Irvin, GSC, Chief IB, Memo on "Project Mt. Vernon," 11 Oct. 1948, ibid.

59. Unsigned memo to Lt. Col. James Berry, Commanding Officer, USAF, HQ European Command, 16 Oct. 1948, ibid.

60. HQ, European Command, Office of the Deputy Director for Intelligence to Director of Intelligence, OMGUS, 16 Mar. 1948, NA, RG 319, IRR, entry 134B, box 617, Wilhelm Höttl.

61. Summary of Information dated 12 July 1948, sent to Deputy Director of Intelligence, European Command, 6 Aug. 1948, ibid.

62. CIA memo received 20 Mar. 1952, NA, RG 263, Wilhelm Höttl Name File, vol. 4; CIA Dispatch, 6 Oct. 1949, Chief [excised] Vienna to Chief Foreign Branch M, NA, RG 263, Wilhelm Höttl Name File, vol. 2; Memo iII Ag of 19 Sept. 1949, NA, RG 263, Wilhelm Höttl Name File, vol. 9.

63. On embezzlement, Höttl, Dr. Wilhelm, Summary from Files, 27 Feb. 1952, NA, RG 263, Wilhelm Höttl Name File, vol. 9.

64. Chief [excised] to Chief [excised], No. [excised], 8 July 1948; [excised] to [excised], 15 Feb. 1949; Chief [excised] Karlsruhe to Chief [excised], 18 Feb. 1949; Chief [excised] to Chief [excised], No. [excised], 13 Sept. 1949; all in NA, RG 263, Karoly Ney Name File.

65. Chief [excised] to Chief [excised], No. [excised], 13 Sept. 1949; 34.3, No. 331, 9 Oct. 1948; [excised] to [excised], 11 Feb. 1949; all in ibid.

66. [Excised] to [excised], 15 Feb. 1949; and Chief [excised] to Chief [excised], No. [excised], 13 Sept. 1949, ibid.

67. See the CIA report Subject: Dr. Wilhelm Höttl, dated Jan. 1949 and enclosed in Chief [excised] to Chief [excised], 5 Jan. 1950, NA, RG 263, Wilhelm Höttl Name File, vol. 3.

68. See [excised] Card dated 5 Nov. 1948; and Heid [excised] to Karl, 24 Feb. 1949; in NA, RG 263, Karoly Ney Name File.

69. Unsigned memo to Lt. Col. James Berry, Commanding Officer, USAF, HQ European Command, 16 Oct. 1948; CIA report Subject: Dr. Wilhelm Höttl, Jan. 1949 in Chief [excised] to Chief [excised], 5 Jan. 1950; CIC Report on Montgomery in CIA, 5 Jan. 1950; in NA, RG 263, Wilhelm Höttl Name File, vol. 3.

70. Kowarik SS Officer File, NA–BDC, RG 242, A-3343, SSO, roll 105A, frame 366.

71. Ibid., frame 391.

72. Subject: Dr. Wilhelm Höttl, Jan. 1949 (report on Mount Vernon and Montgomery), in Chief [excised] to chief [excised] 5 Jan. 1950, NA, RG 263, Wilhelm Höttl Name File, vol. 3.

73. Unsigned memo to Lt. Col. James Berry, Commanding Officer, USAF, HQ European Command, 16 Oct. 1948, (redesignated on 8 Feb. 1951), ibid.

74. Memo for the Record by Lt. Col. T. G. Carey, GSC, Chief Ops, 9 June 1949, NA, RG 263, Wilhelm Höttl Name File, vol. 9; Memo by Carey, "CI Sources," 13 June 1949, ibid; Major J. V. Milano, Chief of Operations, to Deputy Director of Intelligence, undated, ibid., vol. 3.

75. Memo by Major J. V. Milano to Deputy Director of Intelligence, undated, enclosed in CIA bundle on Montgomery and Mount Vernon, redesignated [excised], 5 Jan. 1950, NA, RG 263, Wilhelm Höttl Name File, vol. 3.

76. Memo by Carey, CI Sources, 13 June 1949, NA, RG 263, Wilhelm Höttl Name File, vol. 9.

77. Chief [excised] Station to Chief [excised], 21 June 1949, No. [excised]–2558, NA, RG 263, Wilhelm Höttl Name File, vol. 3.

78. "Subject: Dr. Wilhelm Höttl," Jan. 1949 (report on Mount Vernon and Montgomery), enclosed in CIA [excised] Vienna to Chief, Foreign Division, 5 Jan. 1950, ibid.

79. Höttl, Dr. Wilhelm, Summary from files, 27 Feb. 1952, NA, RG 263, Wilhelm Höttl Name File, vol. 9; on his Soviet contacts, see Report No. [excised]–2952, [excised] to [excised], 25 July 1952, NA, RG 263, Wilhelm Höttl Name File, vol. 4.

80. Höttl note of 23 Mar. 1949, NA, RG 263, Wilhelm Höttl Name File, vol. 9. Höttl note to Lucid and Morrison, 23 Mar. 1949, ibid., and attached notes. Hecke received a sentence of one year in prison and confiscation of all property.

81. Memo by Major J. V. Milano to Deputy Director of Intelligence, undated, enclosed in CIA bundle on Montgomery and Mount Vernon, redesignated [excised], 5 Jan. 1950, NA, RG 263, Wilhelm Höttl Name File, vol. 3.

82. Höttl to Milano, 31 Aug. 1949, ibid., vol. 9.

83. [Excised] to [excised], eyes only, 2 Dec. 1949, ibid., vol. 3.

84. On Niebelungen, see Reports by John K. Allen and Karl Kittstein, 430th CIC Sub Detachment Land Upper Austria, 16 Jan. 1950 and 6 Feb. 1950, ibid., vol. 9.

85. The expanded English translation is *The Secret Front: The Story of Nazi Political Espionage* (New York: Praeger, 1954).

86. The continuing popularity of the memoirs of Hitler's generals is a case in point. See Geoffrey P. Megargee, *Inside Hitler's High Command*, (Lawrence: University Press of Kansas, 2000).

87. Report by Zigmund C. Yanecko, Gmunden field office, Land Upper Austria Sub Detachment, 430th Detachment CIC, 16 Mar. 1950, NA, RG 263, Wilhelm Höttl Name File, vol. 9; CIA Chief [excised] to Chief [excised], Dispatch [excised], 28 Apr. 1950, ibid., vol. 3; CIC Vienna Report No. [excised], 25 Oct. 1950, ibid; CIA Chief [excised] to Chief, [excised], 22 Nov. 1950, ibid.

88. Report by Lt. Col. J. W. Dobson, Chief of Operations, G2, HQ, USFA, XOD-3098, 29 Nov. 1951, NA, RG 263, Wilhelm Höttl Name File, vol. 3; CIA Chief [excised] to Chief [excised], 28 Nov. 1951, ibid., vol. 1.

89. Höttl, Dr. Wilhelm, Summary from files, 27 Feb. 1952, ibid., vol. 9; [excised] to Special Operations, IN 36344, 7 Aug. 1950, ibid., vol. 1.

90. CIA report Verbindung Höttl-Offczarek, 16 May 1950, ibid., vol. 2; Memo, HQ CIC, 430th Detachment, Vienna Sub Detachment, "Höttl, Dr. Wilhelm–Intelligence Activities," 28 June 1950, ibid., vol. 9.

91. Susanne Meinl, "Der politische Weg von Friedrich Wilhelm Heinz," *Vierteljahrshefte für Zeitgeschichte*, (January 1994): 39ff; Meinl, "Im Mahlstrom des kalten Krieges: Friedrich Wilhelm Heinz und die Anfänge des westdeutschen Nachrichtendienstes, 1945–1955," in *Spionage für Frieden: Nachrichtendienst in Deutschland*, ed. Wolfgang Krieger und Jürgen Weber (Munich , 1997), 247–66. In general see Bodo Wegmann, "Friedrich W. Heinz: Der unbekannte Geheimdienstchef," http://www.ifdt.de/111299/Artikel/Wegmann.htm.

92. The penetration was through Gerhard Schacht, a Gehlen section leader who had given the appearance of having defected to Heinz's group. It was through this connection in early 1952 that Gehlen and then the CIA re-learned that Heinz had employed Höttl for its Austrian

and Italian reporting. CIA Pullach Operations Branch to Special Operations, 9 Jan. 1952, NA, RG 263, Wilhelm Höttl Name File, vol. 3; CIA Chief [excised] to Chief [excised], No. [excised], 10 Jan. 1952, ibid., vol. 4.

93. Salzburg to Special Operations, [excised], 6 Jan. 1952, NA, RG 263, Wilhelm Höttl Name File, vol. 3; Chief [excised] to Chief [excised], 3 June 1952, ibid. vol. 4, folder 1. Haas was also known by Nazi-hunter Simon Wiesenthal for his anti-Semitic activity in Austria.

94. Salzburg to Special Operations, No. [excised] 6 Jan. 1952, NA, RG 263, Wilhelm Höttl Name File, vol. 3; HQ, USFA, Office of the Chief of Staff, G-2 Staff Group, Detachment 35, XOD-44, 10 Jan. 1952, ibid., vol. 4.

95. HQ, USFA, Office of the Chief of Staff, G-2 Staff Group, Detachment 35, XOD-44, 10 Jan. 1952, NA, RG 263, Wilhelm Höttl Name File, vol. 4.

96. When Höttl offered the CIA what he called new information on Croatia and Russia in August 1951, the CIA demurred. XOR: 2274, 29 Aug. 1951, NA, RG 263, Wilhelm Höttl Name File, vol. 3.

97. Chief [excised] to Chief [excised], No. [excised] 18 Feb. 1952, NA, RG 263, Wilhelm Höttl Name File, vol. 1, folder 1.

98. Chief [excised] to Chief [excised], Operational, 9 Apr. 1952, NA, RG 263, Wilhelm Höttl Name File, vol. 4.

99. CIC Report, [excised] 4321, Control No. L/26435, 1 July 1952; CIA Salzburg to Operations, No. [excised], 9 July 1952; CIA Station Chief [excised] to Chief [excised], No. [excised], 21 May 1952, all in ibid.

100. No. [excised], "West German Intelligence Operatives Active in Austria," 16 July 1952, NA, RG 263, Wilhelm Höttl Name File, vol. 1. This is a CIC report forwarded to Chief EE from [excised] Vienna.

101. Chief [excised] Vienna to Chief [excised], No. [excised]-1678, 21 May 1952, NA, RG 263, Wilhelm Höttl Name File, vol. 4.

102. Chief [excised] to Chief [excised], No. [excised] 1960, 11 Aug. 1952, ibid.

103. Chief [excised] to chief [excised] 18 Sept. 1952, ibid.

104. Chief [excised] to Chief [excised], No. [excised], 29 Sept. 1952, ibid. By mid-summer 1952, when Heinz's organization was incorporated into the Gehlen Organization with Heinz as a section Chief, Höttl was maintained as an operative for southeast Europe. Gehlen told CIA contacts that the DM 50,000 that Heinz's group received from Bonn was actually supplemented by the British government thanks to the expenses inherent in Höttl's operations in Italy, North Africa, and southeast Europe. Note from Salzburg for Höttl File, [excised], 14 July 1952, ibid.

105. Attachment B to [excised], 16 Oct. 1952, NA, RG 263, Wilhelm Höttl Name File, vol. 4; Chief [excised] to Chief [excised], No. [excised], 25 Nov. 1952, ibid., vol. 4; Chief [excised] to Chief [excised], No. [excised], 4 Feb. 1954, ibid., vol 5.

106. Paul B. Brown, "Analysis of the Name File of Wilhelm Krichbaum," http://www.archives.gov/iwg/declassified_records/rg_263_cia_records/rg_263_krichbaum.html.

107. Extract from Files, No. [excised] 30 Jan. 1953; and [excised], 4 Mar. 1953, NA, RG 263, Wilhelm Höttl Name File, vol. 1.

108. Chief [excised] to Chief [excised], No. [excised], 10 Mar. 1952, ibid., vol. 4.

109. Director Central Intelligence to SR Rep Vienna, Out No. 53974, 14 Apr. 1953, ibid.

110. Brown, "Wilhelm Krichbaum."

111. SR Rep Pullach to Director CIA, No. [excised], 27 Feb. 1953, NA, RG 263, Wilhelm Höttl Name File, vol. 4.

112. Extract of [excised], 10 Mar. 1953, ibid.

113. SR Rep Salzburg to Director CIA, [excised], 26 Feb. 1953, ibid.

114. Interrogation of Dr. Wilhelm Höttl: Preliminary Report, 1 Apr. 1953, attachment to [excised], Chief [excised] Vienna to Chief EE, 8 Apr. 1953, ibid.

115. Ibid.

116. Interrogation of Dr. Wilhelm Höttl: Preliminary Report, 1 Apr. 1953, attachment to [excised], Chief [excised] Vienna to Chief EE, 8 Apr. 1953; SR Rep Salzburg top Director, CIA, [excised], 30 Mar. 1953; Höttl to Mast, [dated] 23 Jan. 1953, in Chief [excised] Vienna to Chief EE, [excised], 8 Apr. 1953, ibid.

117. See also Höttl to Rupert Mandl, enclosed in Chief [excised] Vienna, 8 Apr. 1953, ibid., which also incriminates Krichbaum.

118. Chief [excised] Vienna to Chief EE, EAVA-2251, 3 Apr. 1953, ibid., vol 4.

119. Chief [excised] Munich to Chief EE, 9 Apr. 1953, EGMA-4869, ibid., vol 4.

120. Interrogation of Dr. Wilhelm Höttl: Reaction to Solitary Confinement, 20 Apr. 1953, CIC record forwarded from Chief [excised] to Chief [excised], No. [excised], 21 Apr. 1953, NA, RG 263, Wilhelm Höttl Name File, vol. 5. See also note of 17 Nov. 1953.

121. Interrogation of Dr. Wilhelm Höttl: Reaction to Solitary Confinement, 20 Apr. 1953, CIC record forwarded from Chief [excised] to Chief [excised], 21 Apr. 1953, NA, RG 263, Wilhelm Höttl Name File, vol. 5.

122. Interrogation of Dr. Wilhelm Höttl: Reaction to Solitary Confinement, 20 Apr. 1953, CIC record forwarded from Chief [excised] to Chief [excised] Salzburg, [excised], 21 Apr. 1953, ibid.

123. Chief [excised] to Chief [excised], [excised], 11 Mar. 1954, ibid.

124. Memorandum for the file, 5 Apr. 1963, NA, RG 263, Wilhelm Höttl Name File, vol. 5; [excised] to Chief EE, [excised]-5929, 7 Jan. 1964, ibid., vol 5. I am grateful to Timothy Naftali for the names of Soviet defectors.

125. ACOS addendum to Chief of Station [excised] to Chief EE, [excised]-3334S, 28 Feb. 1964, NA, RG 263, Wilhelm Höttl Name File, vol. 5.

126. "Mit 15 Mill S in Konkurs Privatschule geschlossen," *Wiener Kurier*, 17 Feb. 1964, ibid., vol. 5.

127. Wilhelm Höttl, *Hitler's Paper Weapon*, trans. Basil Creighton (London: R. Hart-Davis, 1955).

128. Wilhelm Höttl, *Einsatz für das Reich* (Koblenz: Bublies, 1997).

11

Tracking the Red Orchestra:
Allied Intelligence, Soviet Spies, Nazi Criminals

Norman J. W. Goda

DID THE MOST RENOWNED Soviet spy network in World War II, the Red Orchestra, offer vital clues to understanding Soviet espionage in the postwar period? The FBI, the U.S. Army Counterintelligence Corps (CIC), and the CIA, as well as British, French, and West German intelligence were all convinced that the answer was yes. Nazi Germany's Gestapo had gathered a great deal of information about the Red Orchestra, which put former Gestapo officials in the position of perceived experts who were ready to serve new masters in the postwar milieu. FBI, Army, and CIA documents newly declassified by the IWG reveal how a number of war criminals managed to get recruited by intelligence agencies and how they failed in their new capacity, for they never knew much as they claimed to know about the Red Orchestra.

"Red Orchestra" (*Rote Kapelle*) was a Gestapo term describing Soviet espionage networks in Western Europe directed by Red Army Intelligence (Glavonoye Rasvodyvatelnoye Upravalenie, or GRU).[1] In Berlin, the Soviets depended on information from well-placed officials in the German government. Harro Schulze-Boysen, the grand nephew of Grand Admiral Alfred von Tirpitz, headed one net from within the German Air Ministry. Arvid Harnack, the scion of a famous academic family and a senior official in the Reich Ministry of Economics, headed another net. Both networks were diverse collections of espionage amateurs—academics, artists, and writers united by leftist sympathies and antipathy to Nazism.[2]

Professional Soviet agents ran the Western European networks. Leopold Trepper, a Polish Jew trained in Moscow, arrived in France in December 1936 as a technical adviser for Soviet nets in Western Europe and Scandinavia. With Leon Grossvogel, a Jewish businessman with Communist sympathies, Trepper soon created a cover firm known as Le Foreign Excelente Reincote (The Foreign Excellent Raincoat Company) in Brussels. The firm exported rainwear and served as cover for espionage activities in several countries.

The term "Red Orchestra" implies that the Soviet nets operated as a whole, but in fact the Red Orchestra comprised smaller networks that were designed to remain watertight so that penetration of one would not lead to the betrayal of all. Its operations had flaws, however, and in 1941 the Gestapo began to dismantle the network in Berlin and elsewhere in Europe.

The Gestapo's Berlin investigations of the Red Orchestra were conducted by the Sonderkommission Rote Kapelle, a Gestapo detachment headed by Obersturmbannführer Friedrich Panzinger, head of the Gestapo department focused on Communism and Marxism. The Commission's daily work was headed by Panzinger's subordinate, Kriminalrat Horst Kopkow, head of Gestapo-Sabotage and a former Nazi brawler who had joined the SS in 1932 and the Gestapo in 1934. Kopkow personally arrested leading Red Orchestra personalities, including Harro Schulze-Boysen, and sanctioned torture to learn names of other Soviet agents.[3] By the end of October 1942, 119 people had been arrested in Germany, 77 to be tried in nineteen separate secret proceedings before the Reich Court-Martial from December 1942 to July 1943.[4] It appeared that Nazi Germany's police and judicial machinery had neutralized this mortal threat.

Following arrests of other Red Orchestra agents in Western Europe, the aim of the Sonderkommando Rote Kapelle was to "play back" captured agents against Moscow. The GRU would continue to receive information—some genuine, most not—in hopes that the Gestapo would learn more about Communist cells and Soviet espionage in Western Europe while sending the Soviets damaging disinformation. By November 1942, the Gestapo played back the agents captured in the low countries, where four wireless beams communicated with Moscow.[5]

But was the Red Orchestra really dead? From 1945 to 1949, British counterintelligence (MI-5) studied the Red Orchestra more systematically than any other agency.[6] In all, MI-5 composed three lengthy reports on the Red Orchestra: a preliminary report in April 1946, the second draft in November 1946, and the final report with appendices in 1949.[7]

Even the preliminary report frightened all who read it. MI-5 deduced that

> it is clear that the Russian organizations concerned were not . . . a wartime creation, but derived directly from the Russians' pre-war network in Europe. There is evidence that up till 1940 or even 1941 this network . . . was working not against Germany but against this country [England] and perhaps also against the USA.[8]

Sources for the report included Nazis such as Horst Kopkow, whom the British captured in May 1945.[9] An important non-Nazi source was Igor Gouzenko, a cipher clerk for the Soviet military attaché in Canada. In September 1945, Gouzenko defected from the Soviet embassy in Ottawa with records on GRU activities.

Gouzenko's records revealed Red Orchestra financial links running through New York to the Red Three (*Rote Drei*), a Soviet espionage network in Switzerland.[10] During the war, GRU operations in Switzerland were headed by

Alexander Rado, a Hungarian (code named "Dora").[11] Rado used three radio operators after 1941: Alexander Foote, a British adventurer; and two native Swiss, Marguerite Bolli and Edmond Hamel.[12] But Rachel Duebendorfer (code named "Sissy"), a Polish Jew who joined Rado in 1941, was the key to Rado's nets.[13] Her prized source was Rudolf Roessler (code named "Lucy").[14] Roessler had access to high-quality German military intelligence, which he forwarded to Duebendorfer through Swiss cutout Christian Schneider (code named "Taylor"). Duebendorfer passed it to Rado for transmission by Foote. Duebendorfer never divulged Lucy's identity even to her superiors, despite Moscow's irritation.[15] The Swiss Federal Police disrupted the Rote Drei for a time with the arrests of Hamel, Bolli, and Foote in October and November 1943 (Rado fled the country).[16] But the Germans could never destroy GRU operations in Switzerland. It thus remains the least understood of the Soviet nets.

In May 1945, Hans von Pescatore, an Abwehr and later SD Foreign Police official in Switzerland, was arrested by Swiss Federal Police for espionage and then smuggled into Italy on the request of Allen Dulles, head of the OSS mission in Bern. Pescatore had told the British that the Red Orchestra's Duebendorfer net could become active again. Hence, the FBI became interested in the Rote Drei.

The FBI and the Search for Spies in the United States
MI-5 concluded by 1949 that Rudolf Roessler, unlike most Soviet agents, was a true mercenary: he demanded thousands of Swiss francs per month with cash on delivery. His information cost between SF 33,000 and SF 48,000 over the course of his service.[17] Moscow's insistence that the link to Lucy be maintained, combined with Duebendorfer's refusal to reveal his identity, meant Duebendorfer was constantly short of money to pay Roessler.[18] The British and Americans were aware in 1946 of financial links that kept Soviet espionage afloat in Switzerland, but the details were murky because they had never been clear to the Germans, on whose information they relied. "Moscow," Pescatore said, "found numerous technical difficulties in getting money to Switzerland, and suggested various ways to Rado . . . Large sums did come from the U.S.A., though how they came remained a mystery."[19]

Financial links from North America to Switzerland were partially revealed during the Gouzenko case, and the FBI followed them up. Germina Rabinowitz, a Lithuanian Jew with a doctorate from the University of Heidelberg, had worked in the International Labor Office (ILO)—an organization with diplomatic immunity—in Geneva from 1929 to 1940. She knew Duebendorfer (who had also worked for the ILO) in Geneva before moving to the ILO in Montreal from 1941 to 1944. Duebendorfer contacted Rabinowitz via the ILO mail pouch in November 1943 and again in April 1944 asking for money.[20] Rabinowitz contacted the Soviet embassy in Ottawa to secure funds. Military attaché Nikolai Zabotin provided $10,000.[21] Rabinowitz transferred the money through the Helbros Watch Company of New York, whose director, William Helbein, was a naturalized U.S. citizen born in Russia. During the war, Helbros was a buyer of Swiss watches for American forces and could "transfer without mention almost unlimited sums of money to Switzerland," despite U.S. regulations. Helbein also had contacts in Switzerland through his sister-in-law Berthe Helbein, another Russian émigré. Berthe was a friend of Duebendorfer, and, according to Swiss authorities, a Soviet agent herself.[22]

The Central Intelligence Group (CIG), the immediate predecessor of the CIA, was given access to MI-5 reports on the Red Orchestra. CIG feared the Soviets had used Helbros to transfer money throughout the war; now Helbein "may be coerced by the Russians into additional espionage activity . . . "[23] FBI chief J. Edgar Hoover was not yet convinced. "The only information we have," he said, was the "deposit of $10,000 to . . . Duebendorfer in Geneva."[24] Helbein was interviewed by FBI agents in New York in 1946 and again in 1947, but they learned nothing substantive.[25]

The following year, the FBI acquired information on Berthe Helbein from CIG, which described her as "a disagreeable woman with some very expensive jewelry."[26] Claiming that she thought she was helping a Soviet relief organization, Berthe Helbein loaned Duebendorfer nearly SF 10,000 during 1943. On November 3, 1944, she gave Duebendorfer SF 28,500, which was the equivalent of $10,000 minus the money loaned to Duebendorfer in 1943. The existence of the $10,000 in New York was revealed to her by William Helbein, then in Lisbon.[27]

Duebendorfer's letters to Rabinowitz, as well as the $10,000 money transfer to Switzerland, both went through a cutout named Alexander Abramson (code named "Sascha"), a Lithuanian Jew and ILO employee in Geneva.[28] In 1946, the British and FBI knew little about Abramson thanks to his ILO diplomatic status, but he was clearly connected with Swiss Communists. Swiss police thought he was the chief Soviet agent in Switzerland after the war.[29] When Abramson left the ILO in 1947, Swiss police interrogated him and the information made its way to the FBI. Abramson admitted to being Germina Rabinowitz's cousin and to being Duebendorfer's friend. He admitted sending Duebendorfer's letters to Rabinowitz through the ILO pouch because Duebendorfer had told him that the money requested was for Soviet POWs. The Swiss police, unconvinced by Abramson's insistence that he consciously did no work for Soviet intelligence, argued that "he is without doubt deeply implicated in the whole affair."[30] Abramson moved to Paris before implicating himself further.[31]

The FBI ran down all leads in New York provided by the CIA and MI-5.[32] The British interrogation of Foote in 1947 and an examination of Foote's personal notebook revealed an earlier financial connection between RKO Radio Films representatives and the Soviet network in Geneva. The president of RKO film distribution in Geneva was Armand Palivoda, a Polish Jew who had been in Switzerland since 1907. MI-5 and the CIA believed by 1947 that Palivoda was an active Soviet agent because "his financial status appears too good to be entirely brought about by his job."[33] Foote's written materials noted a $4,000 deposit into the RKO Swiss branch account in the Irving Trust Bank in New York in July 1941, whereupon Palivoda handed over the equivalent sum in Swiss francs to an intermediary of Foote's. Foote claimed that these transactions via RKO representatives occurred into 1943.[34] In 1948, when Palivoda applied for a U.S. visa, the CIA and FBI agreed that he was a security risk who would not be admitted into the country.[35]

Nothing more was learned about a Red Orchestra presence in the United States. But the FBI maintained a close watch on anyone in the United States who had any connection, familial or otherwise, with Soviet wartime networks in Europe. Marguerite Barcza's family is a case in point. Barcza herself was a Jewish Czech refugee who became the wartime mistress to Anatoli Gurevitch, a top Red Orchestra operative in Brussels and then Marseilles. Barcza's mother, Else Singer, and her brother, Bederich Singer, were both Jewish refugees who came to the United States and resided in New York before and after the war, respectively. Barzca's mother received a gift of $100 during the war through Gurevitch, which the FBI followed up as far as it could before closing the file. The FBI kept a file into the 1950s on Bederich Singer, whom the British thought had been part of the Gurevitch network in France.[36] Marguerite Barcza was not allowed into the United States when she applied for a visa in 1947, though the CIA searched her room in Brussels and found nothing incriminating.[37]

Other Jewish refugees connected with the Soviet networks were also watched closely. Two of the three Jewish directors of the Belgian rainwear firm Au Roi de Caoutchouc, who were also financial partners in Leon Grossvogel's Le Foreign Excelente Reincote, had come to the United States as refugees in 1941. They were Abraham Lerner and Maurice Padawer, both originally Polish Jews. Once it was learned that Grossvogel, their one-time partner in Brussels, was to have come to the United States in the interest of Soviet espionage, the FBI checked both men and placed them under surveillance.

The FBI remained vigilant even after receiving the final MI-5 report on the Red Orchestra in 1949. "[There] are at the present time," said Hoover,

a number of persons residing in the United States who were either involved in espionage activities in Europe in the Rote Kapelle or Rote Drei espionage networks, or were closely associated with or are relatives of individuals who so operated . . . [T]he information thus far obtained has not resulted in determining whether the individuals residing in the United States are presently active as espionage agents or assisting . . . in gathering data for foreign principles.[38]

Such scrutiny with known and suspected Soviet agents is understandable. With information from decrypts and other sources, by 1949 the FBI had helped to uncover a number of Soviet spies in the United States. Most of these spies, however, were American Communists who, like Alger Hiss, spied for the Soviets out of misguided idealism.[39] Wartime Jewish refugees who fought against Nazism before the United States entered the war would seem to be in another category, especially since those investigated by the FBI had only the loosest of ties with Soviet wartime intelligence in Europe.

The CIC and the Red Orchestra: Justice, Ineptitude, and Gestapo Criminals

The U.S. Army Counterintelligence Corps was added to the Red Orchestra information loop late.[40] The British asked the CIC for help in locating relevant records and personalities in 1946.[41] But not until January 1948 did the 970th CIC Detachment fully comprehend that "British intelligence is greatly interested in the investigation of Rote Kapelle and has assigned at least two case officers to work on it exclusively," or that "British intelligence has extensive information . . . on Rote Kapelle."[42] By that time, MI-5 was producing their final report, complete with organizational charts, personality indices, and interrogations. MI-5 also concluded that the best sources on the Red Orchestra had been Soviet agents and their associates—not the Germans who tracked them—and that the wartime Red Orchestra was not especially relevant for understanding postwar Soviet espionage.[43] Yet the CIC did not receive a copy of the 1949 report until 1952.[44]

When stumbling onto the Red Orchestra in 1947, the CIC thought it had discovered an entirely new story. The CIC's interest was triggered by German Red Orchestra survivors' call for the trial of Dr. Manfred Roeder, judge advocate general and chief legal officer of Air Region III (Berlin), and the chief prosecutor to Red Orchestra spies arrested in Berlin. Later known as "Hitler's Bloodhound," Roeder secured Hermann Göring's agreement to try the defendants before a military court-martial and demanded the death sentences that were handed down, even to many whose roles were incidental. Roeder prepared his cases with Gestapo help. He was ruthless in court, arguing that the Schulze-Boysen and Harnack nets were unprincipled, financially corrupt, and composed of sexually perverted scum who acted from the basest of motives. He thus started an argument in Germany that lasts to this day.[45]

Roeder had been in U.S. custody as a Nuremberg witness since May 8, 1945.[46] By January 1947, Army prosecutors had heard accusations that Roeder was a war criminal.[47] In June he underwent a long interrogation by American prosecutor Robert Kempner in which he was dramatically confronted by Adolf Grimme, a socialist minister from the Weimar period and Harnack group survivor now living in the West.[48] In May, Roeder was re-categorized from a witness to "Defendant A"—"a prisoner who is to be indicted and tried" by the Office of the Chief of Counsel for War Crimes. Repeated orders said Roeder was not to be released from custody even for family leave.[49]

The CIC was more intrigued with Greta Kuckhoff, an outspoken Communist survivor of the Harnack net whose husband, Adam, had been executed by the Nazis. Kuckhoff aimed to justify the networks as resistors, rather than traitors, through a public trial of Roeder.[50] United States authorities in Berlin intercepted a telephone call in which Kuckhoff said she was in touch with Red Orchestra survivors who were collecting evidence against the former prosecutor.[51] Günther Weissenborn, a playwright and Harnack group survivor, suggested a public survivors' meeting to present evidence of Roeder's criminality. Kuckhoff wanted actual records but said "I am afraid . . . that the Gestapo orders for torture . . . won't be there."[52]

The CIC did not help Kuckhoff, but instead dispatched Special Agent Hans Johnson, who posed as an American leftist, to speak with her in order to learn the names of other Soviet agents. "Greta Kuckhoff," Johnson reported,

> is in possession of material giving the full story of the Rote Kapelle and its members who were engaged in high-level penetration attempts of the Nazi regime. She knows the full story of the . . . trial, the penetration of Rote Kapelle by the Gestapo and the final liquidation of the organization. She also knows that the organization was active in France, Belgium and Holland. It is believed that Greta Kuckhoff also has knowledge of the present activities of the members of Rote Kapelle in Berlin, in the U.S. Zone of Germany and in Western Europe.[53]

In fact, the CIC could learn nothing from Kuckhoff that had not been known to MI-5 (and thus the FBI and CIA) for some time. Even the names she provided were listed in the 1943 Gestapo Final Report on the Red Orchestra, which the British had found more than a year earlier.

By mid-1947, the CIC in Regensburg launched a full investigation[54] based on the assumptions that Red Orchestra survivors in Germany were still working for the Soviets and that former Nazis were those best suited to discover who and where they were.[55] The CIC Special Agent Benjamin Gorby led the investigation. Roeder, a wanted war criminal, would be the key source. The CIC reasoned, "Since Roeder was in charge of the prosecution of the military members of the ring (and was promoted for his handling of it), he undoubtedly could supply information in great detail."[56] On December 23, 1947, the CIC took custody of Roeder right after his jailers received orders that he was wanted by the Legal Division of OMGUS in Berlin.[57] On arrival in Neustadt, where the CIC took charge, Roeder received the code name "Othello."

Roeder had his own agenda: avoiding prosecution. All year he had insisted that his accusers were traitors and that he was guilty of no crimes, since Göring had ordered him to prosecute the Red Orchestra cases (in fact, he had insisted to Göring that he try it). Further, Roeder claimed that "the Führer decreed that everyone who took part in the Rote Kapelle were to be sentenced to death immediately."[58] This claim was manifestly untrue; the Gestapo had "played back" some captured agents.

The 970th CIC Detachment also borrowed a senior Gestapo official held by U.S. war crimes authorities, Walter Huppenkothen, assigning him the code name "Fidelio." During the Polish campaign, Huppenkothen was Army liaison officer for Einsatzgruppe I; in October 1939 he served as Commander of the Security Police in Cracow, and in February 1940 he was transferred to the same position in Lublin. In July 1941, he succeeded Walter Schellenberg as head of the Gestapo unit A-3 (Reactionaries and Liberals), and in February 1945 he was promoted to Gruppenleiter of Gestapo unit A (Enemies). Captured in Gmünden with the remnants of the Waffen-SS division Leibstandarte Adolf Hitler on April 26, 1945, he told his American captors that his last advice from Gestapo Chief Heinrich Müller was, "It's only a matter of time until the Americans will want you in their coming fight against the East. In the meantime, do your best to remain in obscurity."[59] Huppenkothen listened. "[He] is very tightlipped," said one war crimes interrogator, "When questioned about anything involving him personally, he speaks extremely slow, as though he were aware that every word would be counted against him."[60] Huppenkothen insisted, for instance, that his job in Cracow and Lublin was to fight banditry and that he knew nothing about the "Jew Camps."[61]

Huppenkothen had nothing to do with the Red Orchestra case, but in October 1947, Gorby learned that Huppenkothen would soon be extradited to Poland. Gorby suspected a Soviet maneuver, since Huppenkothen as a former Gestapo counterintelligence head knew a lot about Soviet espionage. United States authorities had to get to him first. CIC headquarters agreed with Gorby's assessment that "an attempt should be made to prevent [Huppenkothen's] extradition."[62] Therefore, Roeder and Huppenkothen were housed "in such a place and manner as to convince [them] of the sincerity of CIC's intentions, and the desire of U.S. authorities that [they] be treated commensurate with the quality of information required."[63]

Once in the CIC's care, Roeder took advantage, noting that the Red Orchestra "is still alive and active in more than one country." This comment drove further investigation.[64] Gorby quickly insisted that the interrogation, originally envisioned for three weeks, now become a project of six months or more that would include not only Roeder and Huppenkothen, but also "other personalities who possess a wealth of information and experience in the field of counterespionage and who, to the best knowledge of this Headquarters, have not . . . been fully exploited."[65] Roeder provided names from the Schulze-Boysen net. One of his lists was based on newspapers and included old enemies such as Kuckhoff, Weissenborn, Grimme, and others who could testify against him. The CIC missed the trend, stating instead that these people were all prominently mentioned in the Communist press as democrats and anti-Fascists, but "any [mention] of their connections with the R/K [Red Orchestra] organization had been carefully avoided." Another list included those who, according to the CIC, "belong to the more interesting group of R/K survivors from a counter-intelligence point of view . . . Some of [them] are well trained agents and it can be assumed that they are again secretly active." A third included agents Roeder and the CIC thought had been turned, such as Gurevitch and Trepper (the Gestapo arrested Gurevitch on November 12, 1942, and Trepper on December 5, 1942).[66] But the names Roeder provided were all available in London and Washington with more reliable biographical data. In the meantime, Roeder and Huppenkothen added that to fight the Red Orchestra, the United States would need the help of Gestapo officers who had fought it before.[67]

By May 1948, the CIC decided to sever its relationship with Roeder because "Othello . . . has been exploited to the fullest extent. Further use . . . is not recommended due to the fact that Othello is a major target for former [Red Orchestra] members and their Soviet sponsors . . . [If] Othello was ever hard pressed he might reveal his relationship to CIC in order to protect himself." Thus "if and when [Roeder] is released, his release [should] be arranged in such a manner that he will not come under the control of Soviet or Soviet-sponsored authorities."[68] This arrangement would of course preclude a trial. Ironically, the 970th CIC Headquarters, after having finally liaised with the British, "share the opinion that Rote Kapelle, as such, is not active today." The time spent with Roeder had thus been operationally worthless. He was remanded to custody to the Office of the Chief of Counsel at Nuremberg in May 1948.[69]

Huppenkothen remained in CIC custody until the end of 1948, providing a sheaf of reports on everything from Soviet intelligence in southern Germany to Soviet intelligence in Switzerland to Günther Weissenborn's activities. Even if accurate, Huppenkothen's reports contained material that was half a decade old; they were never used. Gorby complained in December that most of the reports had been neither translated nor forwarded to anyone.[70] In the meantime, Huppenkothen dreamed up ideas to protect himself and fellow Gestapo veterans from justice. His boldest proposal was for a net of former Gestapo officials under his command, which could locate German Communist Party (KPD) members that the Third Reich had once placed in concentration camps. No one, Huppenkothen said, was in a better position to keep tabs on illegal KPD members than former Gestapo officials. But, he warned, the Americans would have to treat former Gestapo officials with respect. Many would be mistrusting due to trials against former police officials, and they would have to be "given some assurances . . ."[71]

The Office of the Chief of Counsel, which thought Roeder and Huppenkothen both deserved long prison sentences, was stunned that the CIC had used them. On their return to the control of the war crimes authorities, neither man would answer questions, claiming that they were working for the CIC. "Assuming for the moment that their claims of having contacts with the C.I.C. is true," said Benno Selke, the deputy director of the Evidence Division at Nuremberg, "the mere fact that they have revealed such a relationship would in itself seriously question their usefulness." Roeder, Selke said, is "one of the most hated men in Germany . . . who could well qualify as Public Enemy No. 1 in any German democracy." Huppenkothen, he continued, "was similarly zealous with members of the German underground and . . . leader of the first Einsatzgruppe during the Polish campaign." He added,

> This office finds it hard to believe that C.I.C would knowingly enlist the aid of two such notorious, unscrupulous, opportunistic Nazis who would surely have been tried [at] Nuremberg, had the scope of the Nuremberg trials been greater. It seems that their only selling point could possibly be the fact that they are presumably anti-Communist and have knowledge in connection with Russian underground methods.

Hitler had similar anti-Communist credentials, Selke said.[72] Unfazed, the CIC stated that both remained of interest and that while neither had been ordered not to cooperate with war crimes interrogators, both had also been ordered not to divulge the details of their work for the CIC. "That specific information," said Lieutenant Colonel George Eckman of the 7970th CIC Group in Regensburg, "is not believed pertinent in the War Crimes proceedings against these two individuals."[73] This statement was nonsense. Yet the relationship of both men with the CIC, founded on poor intelligence work from the start, had indeed wrecked the chances that U.S. authorities would try either man.[74]

By 1951, Manfred Roeder had used his past as a Nazi supporter to become a West German political figure on the radical right. His relationship with the CIC in 1947 and 1948 showed him that anti-Communism offered protection from prosecution and vindicated his view of Germany's Nazi past. Though not a member of the Socialist Reich Party (SRP)—a neo-Nazi party founded in 1949 and banned in 1952—Roeder supported the SRP and was close to one of its founders, a *völkisch* writer named Fritz Dorls. On April 25, 1951, Roeder gave a speech in Lüneburg to an overflow crowd on the wartime treachery of the Red Orchestra. He attacked Adolf Grimme, now the general director of Northwest German Radio (Nordwestdeutsche Rundfunk), and Helmut Roloff, another West German survivor of the Schulze-Boysen group and now a concert pianist. The U.S.-sponsored Neue Zeitung charged that Roeder promoted a new stab-in-the-back legend.[75] Perhaps this only encouraged Roeder, in 1952, to publish the same arguments in *Die Rote Kapelle: Europäische Spionage*.

Roeder used his prominence to try his luck again with the CIC. He arranged a meeting in the Hotel Grüner Wald in Heidelberg with three special agents from the 66th CIC Detachment (the successor to the 7970th) in January 1952. In a five-hour meeting, he told the CIC agents that he could procure a cache of documents over a meter in height on the Red Orchestra as well as human intelligence from former Gestapo officials. The information, he said, contained photos, information on Red Orchestra personalities, and their present-day activities in West Germany, France, the low countries, and Switzerland. To whet the American appetite, he listed a few people that he said were still active in the Red Orchestra (again, all witnesses against Roeder should he ever stand trial). He could arrange for the Americans to copy the records and to meet former German counterintelligence figures. He could also supply the trial transcripts of the Red Orchestra courts-martial. In return, he and his associates only wished for their old salaries.[76]

The CIC officials in question, none of whom had been involved in the use of Roeder in 1948, were intrigued. They met with Roeder again in February 1952 in Hanover. The meeting was arranged by Dorls, who hoped to take part but was dissuaded by the CIC owing to the close surveillance of Dorls by the West German authorities. Instead, Roeder showed up with count Wolf von Westarp, another SRP member. Roeder explained his strong sympathies to the SRP, "the most . . . desirable party from the viewpoint of Germany" and then explained that the records to which he had access reconstructed the entire Soviet net as it operated during the war. Though all of this information had been available for years, CIC agents rated Roeder and his statements as fully reliable ("A-1"). And though the 66th CIC hoped that "a working arrangement can be established with Dr. Roeder," it is not clear what this arrangement amounted to.[77] By October, the SRP was banned by the federal German authorities. There is no further reference to Roeder in CIC files nor are there reports on the Red Orchestra that originated with him. It might have been at this time that the 66th finally received the final MI-5 report of 1949, which contained the sketches of Red Orchestra members that Roeder said that he and only he could provide.

The Return of the Gestapo

In March 1953, Rudolf Roessler was arrested in Switzerland for espionage. His November trial received international attention, and stories appeared about his wartime ring in Switzerland.[78] Roessler also told the Swiss Federal Police that he had been recruited by Czech intelligence in 1948 to rebuild the Red Orchestra and to funnel military and air information from Western Europe.[79] The Sureté Nationale in Paris, which had been convinced for years that the Red Orchestra still existed in France, believed him. It continued investigating former Red Orchestra members living in France on the assumption that "a number of the subjects are becoming active again."[80]

Roessler's arrest had implications in West Germany, too. Until October 1953, the Bundesamt für Verfassungsschutz (BfV) led West German inquiries into the Red Orchestra, but in that month the Gehlen Organization took over the Red Orchestra investigation, code naming it "Fire Tongs" (*Feuerzange*). The CIC learned that both the BfV and the Gehlen Organization believed that the World War II version of the Red Orchestra "was only partly shattered" and that "since the end of the war it has been enlarged and is very active in the Federal Republic and all of Western Europe." The Gehlen official heading up Fire Tongs, whose name the CIC never learned, thought that the threads ran all the way into the West German government ministries.[81]

CONFIDENTIAL

AGENT REPORT   ~~TOP SECRET~~   BJMG/er

SUBJECT: Proposed Use of Former Gestapo Personnel to Combat
Present Day Illegal KPD Activities

1. In the course of the series of interviews with Walter HUPPENKOTHEN
and in line with the set of EEIs prepared by Headquarters 7970th CIC to be
answered by him, a number of ideas were discussed which, it is felt by this
Agent, should be brought to the attention of higher Headquarters for consideration and possibly voluntary action. In taking such action HUPPENKOTHEN may be
of value in establishing certain initial contacts.

2. It should be pointed out that it was not HUPPENKOTHEN who took the
initiative to propose the establishing of such contacts through him. XXXXX
Therefore, his suggestions as outlined below should not be interpreted as
an attempt on his part to extend the relative security and comfortable life
enjoyed by him at this time that is due to the fact that he is in this
organization's temporary custody.

a. HUPPENKOTHEN started out by saying that, while he did not know what
amount of knowledge the American authorities possessed about the extent of
and persons involved in the illegal KP activities, he would assume that the
Americans must have the intention to gain a clear picture of the illegal
activity of the KPD, as well as other Communistic organizations in Germany
prior to 1945, their extent and persons involved. To gain such a clear
picture, however, is, in his opinion, important because points of departure
for a successful surveillance of present Communistic efforts and, furthermore,
for counter measures, will necessarily result from conclusions derived from
that picture.

b. He, HUPPENKOTHEN himself, has only a relatively limited knowledge
concerning this field (Communistic activities) to offer. Part of the Gestapo

REGRADED CONFIDENTIAL
ON 22 JUN 1984
BY DEP CDR USAINSCOM FOIPO
Auth Para 1-603 DoD 5200. 1-R

222

CONFIDENTIAL

Page from an unsigned agent report, "Proposed Use of Former Gestapo Personnel to Combat
Present Day Illegal KPD Activities," outlining Walter Huppenkothen's suggestions for using his
colleagues to combat Communism. The full report is found in NA, RG 319, IRR, entry 134B,
Walter Huppenkothen, 222–25.

94787

Confidential

4 August 1948

SUBJECT: Manfred ROEDER and Walter HUPPENKOTHEN

TO: Commanding General, EUCOM
        Office of the Deputy Director of Intelligence
        APO 403, U.S. Army

        Attention: Colonel Schow

1. Among the internees at present in the Nuremberg jail are Manfred ROEDER, former Generalrichter der Luftwaffe (Judge holding the rank of a General in the German Air Corps), and Walter HUPPENKOTHEN, former SS Standartenfuehrer in charge of Amt. IV E (RSHA - Gestapo).

2. The advisability of trying ROEDER and HUPPENKOTHEN by German authorities under Control Council Law No. 10 is at the present time under consideration by the Legal Division, OMGUS. HUPPENKOTHEN is a member of an organization found to be criminal by decision of the International Military Tribunal. Inasmuch as these two individuals are confined in the Palace of Justice jail, the Office of Chief of Counsel for War Crimes has been asked by the Legal Division, OMGUS, to assist in the investigation and interrogation of these two mentioned individuals as a prerequisite for any further action which may be taken against these two individuals.

3. The interrogations and investigations in the case of ROEDER are seriously hampered, if not completely stalemated, by the fact that he steadfastly refuses to give information, stating that he was so directed by a C.I.C. officer, Lt.-Col. Hayes of Regensburg, for whom he is presently working according to his statement. HUPPENKOTHEN has made a similar claim. It has furthermore been indicated that the C.I.C. is anxious to keep these two men from German jurisdiction, an additional factor further jeopardizing investigations of their cases.

4. ROEDER, one of the most hated men in Germany at the present time, who could well qualify as Public Enemy No. 1 in any German democracy, is a notorious former Air Force Judge, whose brutally harsh and bloodthirsty methods earned him the right to act as "investigating officer and prosecutor", not only in the "Rote Kapelle" case but also in other cases involving members of the German underground.

Regraded CONFIDENTIAL by authority of
Lt Col H. A. Reinke   by   [signature]
on   17 APR 1956   242   L. E. Phillips 2d Lt ORDC

Confidential

REGRADED UNCLASSIFIED
ON   22 JUN 1984
BY   CDR USAINSCOM FOIPO
Auth Para 1-603 DoD 5200. 1-R

First page from a memorandum from the deputy director of the evidence division at Nuremberg expressing astonishment that the CIC would hire Roeder and Huppenkothen. See Benno Selke, Deputy Director, Evidence Division, OCCWC, Nuremberg, to Commanding General, EUCOM, Office of the Deputy Director for Intelligence, 4 Aug. 1948, NA, RG 319, IRR, entry 134B, Walter Huppenkothen, 242–43.

This Gehlen official was surely Heinrich Reiser. After the German surrender, Reiser, the one-time commander of the Sonderkommando Rote Kapelle in Paris, had been captured by the French and debriefed throughout 1948 in the French occupation zone. He was then handed over to the West German authorities, who jailed him in Karlsruhe. He was released on March 30, 1950, and hired within days by the Gehlen Organization. It seemed to be a coup for West German intelligence. With Karl Giering (the original chief of the Sonderkommando) dead and Heinz Pannwitz (leader of the Sonderkommando from 1942) imprisoned in the USSR, Reiser was the senior-most former Gestapo official from the old Sonderkommando. His quick hiring by Gehlen angered the CIC, which in 1950 still considered the Red Orchestra its own domain of inquiry and had tried to recruit Reiser for itself.[82]

Reiser might have influenced West German understanding of the Red Orchestra. In 1951 he wrote a very long assessment of the Red Orchestra (257 pages of which are in CIA records) based on his contacts in France, articles and books on the Red Orchestra, and his own hunches.[83] Reiser concluded that the Red Orchestra as a GRU organization had been deliberately intertwined with other Soviet organizations, such as the Comintern and the Soviet Secret Police (NKVD), not in competition with them; that the Red Orchestra's components in France, the low countries, Germany, and Switzerland, far from being compartmentalized, had been in deliberate contact with each other; and that the Red Orchestra was not crippled under German pressure, but survived the war and continued to function in the service of global revolution.

Reiser's report showed the dangers of having a former Gestapo officer in a senior postwar intelligence position. Reiser saw conspiracies everywhere. He thought the Red Orchestra during the war permeated all German resistance groups including Wehrmacht resistance circles. Most Schulze-Boysen and Harnack network members, he thought, survived the war and continued their work via "other ways and other lines." Rudolf Herrnstadt, who had worked for Soviet intelligence before 1933 and who was now publicly active as an editor of *Neues Deutschland* and a member of the Socialist Unity Party (SED) Central Committee in East Germany, still recruited agents from that position, according to Reiser. "One can compare him," said Reiser, "with certain insects that . . . lay their eggs wherever they lie down."

Reiser's report also discussed the Red Orchestra in France. He argued that his old Sonderkommando subordinate, Willi Berg, willingly helped Red Orchestra leader Leopold Trepper to escape in September 1943. Now, said Reiser, Berg was a Soviet agent, likely in contact with Konstantin Jeffremov, another top GRU operative, in Berlin.[84] Reiser argued that Gurevitch "who is likely a type [of] Mongoloid . . . [distinguished] by his characteristically protruding lower lip," was active in the Soviet zone of Germany in 1947 and 1948 and that Trepper, "who characterized himself as a non-Jew . . . but belongs to the Jewish race or is a half-Jew" was still active, too. Both were in fact in prison in the USSR. Even Pannwitz could now well be working for the Soviets, according to Reiser. In short, the Red Orchestra, connected as it had been to Communist parties; disguised as it was through radio, courier routes, and business covers; healthy as it was through the survival of its top agents; and racially mongrelized as it was by Mongoloids and Jews, still functioned. Reiser concluded that the Red Orchestra in 1945 was "only seemingly dead" (*sheintot*); it "rose again from the ashes like the apocryphal Phoenix."

Reiser's operations for the Gehlen Organization are not in his CIA Name File, but he ran down leads pertaining to his imagined Red Orchestra. The case of Walter Klein is a case in point. Klein had been a minor Gestapo officer in the Sonderkommando in Paris during the war, responsible for watching Marguerite Barcza's ten-year-old son while Gurevitch worked with the Gestapo. He was held in French custody until April 1949 when he returned to Germany. In mid-March 1951, the French Sureté office in Mainz began paying Klein a monthly salary for which Klein was to locate former members of the Sonderkommando Rote Kapelle. The French thought that "the present [1951] activity of the [Red Orchestra] only could be cleared up with the help of persons who had already been occupied with the complex previously."[85] Armed by the Sureté with the money and travel tickets, Klein liaised with former Sonderkommando officers Willi Berg, Rolf Richter, and Heinrich Reiser. He also compiled a register of all French men and women who had worked for the Soviets during the war.[86] The French thought, based on Klein's lies, that Klein had been a senior official in the Sonderkommando and that he also would give them microfilmed records from that organization.[87]

Reiser, using a business cover, contacted Klein in July 1950, nine months before the French officially hired him, and visited him so often that Klein referred to his former Gestapo superior as "Heini."[88] In February 1951, Reiser procured a print of Klein's microfilm. He also gave Klein Willi Berg's address in West Berlin and used Klein to spy on Berg.[89] Rolf Richter, another former Gestapo member of the Sonderkommando also kept an eye on Klein as a paid source of Reiser's. Klein, who had also tried to sell information to the Soviets, thought that he was using both men.[90] The West German police arrested Klein in November 1951. Reiser eliminated him by telling the West German police, who were unaware that Reiser worked for Gehlen, that Klein was a French agent and that he "is . . . criminally inclined."[91] Richter added that "Klein . . . claims to have been active in an executive capacity [in the Gestapo] . . . only for financial reasons" and was deluded into thinking he could "become Minister of Police in a future [neo-Nazi] state."[92]

In January 1956, Friedrich Panzinger and Heinz Pannwitz returned to West Germany from Soviet captivity. Panzinger, the former head of the Sonderkommission Rote Kapelle whom the Russians captured in Linz in 1946, returned as a Soviet agent to penetrate the Gehlen Organization through his old Gestapo contacts. In return, the Soviets promised to protect him from war crimes charges resulting from his command of Einsatzgruppe A from September

1943 to May 1944. On arriving in Munich, Panzinger informed the BfV of the entire business, and the Gehlen Organization, also promising to protect him against prosecution, decided to play him back against the Soviets. Between 1956 and 1958 Panzinger made eight letter drops to a Soviet cutout in Munich. The Bundesnachrichtendienst (BND), as the Gehlen Organization was called as of April 1956, hoped to "build [the operation] up as a major deception effort against the [USSR]."[93] But Panzinger committed suicide in prison in August 1959 after missed communications within the West German government resulted in his arrest for war crimes charges.[94]

Panzinger's bizarre tale led to the suspicion in the BND that Heinz Pannwitz was also a Soviet penetration agent. Heinz Felfe, the actual Soviet spy within the Gehlen Organization, did not leave this suspicion to chance. He told anyone who would listen that Pannwitz had a Soviet mission. Pannwitz repeatedly denied such a mission, but it would remain the accepted wisdom in the BND that Pannwitz was not entirely truthful. Felfe thus diverted attention from himself by using the West German phobia of the old Red Orchestra.[95]

Regardless of its suspicions, the BND hired Pannwitz in August 1956, perhaps to keep him quarantined from the BfV and the CIA, both of which had already begun debriefings.[96] Reiser had visited Pannwitz in May to tell him that the BND alone would handle his case.[97] The BND promised to send interrogation reports to the Americans but complained instead that Pannwitz had been a tough nut to crack, leaving the CIA to wonder how the BND had failed to learn anything from such an important source.[98]

Pannwitz acted more like a disgruntled civil servant than a Soviet spy. On arriving in West Germany, he contacted Reiser and other former wartime subordinates in search of employment but insisted on senior state official rank (*Oberregierungsrat*) that would take account of his years of Gestapo service. Until May 1956 he seems to have hoped for a police job with the BfV.[99] On taking employment with the BND he immediately told the CIA his salary, hoping that the CIA would top it. Pannwitz then pressed his BND colleagues to help him avoid any denazification hearings that could affect his pension. By 1958, the BND had pulled the right strings. Pannwitz's Gestapo service, wartime promotions, and eleven years in Soviet captivity were recognized for pension purposes.[100] In February 1958, the CIA noted that Pannwitz "has now . . . achieved 95% of what he has been fighting for the past two years . . . to gain official recognition of his permanent civil service tenure and the rights associated with it."[101] When the BND gave up debriefing Pannwitz and handed him over to the CIA in 1959, Pannwitz again put money first, wanting a long-term contract from the CIA instead of month-to-month payments.[102] Pannwitz, in short, would not tell his story for free.

CIA interrogators were skeptical of Pannwitz before six months of debriefings began in mid-1959. They noted "his efforts to portray the Gestapo in a more favorable light" and his failure to acknowledge that his playback operations owed to the Gestapo's ominous reputation. The CIA also noted that Pannwitz, like Roeder, was "very emotional over the postwar effort to describe . . . the [Berlin] Rote Kapelle complex as 'anti-Nazi resistance fighters' rather than as 'traitors, spying against their native land.'" But they were sure he was no Soviet agent. After long discussion of his years in USSR prisons and camps, the CIA reported that "it is . . . safe to state that [Pannwitz] came out . . . with an intense dislike of the Soviet Communist government." "No indication of deception," they added, "was found."[103]

⟫◆⟪

Recently declassified U.S. intelligence records throw new light on the Red Orchestra itself and its manipulation by the Gestapo. Mostly though, the records demonstrate the long shadow thrown by the Red Orchestra and its legend on postwar intelligence agencies. The burning desire to understand how it worked, the scope of its success, who had been involved, and who was still active, had a significant impact on a number of intelligence agencies from Washington to Bonn, while inducing surveillance from New York to Berlin. At its worst, the shadow of the Red Orchestra helped to convince certain intelligence agencies to shelter and employ former Nazis. Men such as Pannwitz who had hoped that the Nazi counterintelligence operations could help split the Western Allies from the Soviets surely felt a certain satisfaction.

Notes

1. The best summary description is CIA, "Rote Kapelle: A Survey Report." The two volumes were written in 1973, and declassified in 1976. See NA, RG 263, Rote Kapelle Subject File. A more readable description, particularly from the German perspective (despite its age), is Heinz Höhne, *Codeword: Direktor–The Story of the Red Orchestra*, trans. Richard Barry (New York: Coward, McCann and Geoghegan, 1971).

2. The picture of Schulze-Boysen and Harnack group members as Stalinist traitors is partially a result of their trial by the Nazi state and partly a result of Cold War rhetoric in the Federal Republic of Germany. On this topic see Jürgen Danyel, "Die Rote Kapelle innerhalb der deutschen Widerstandsbewegung," in *Die Rote Kapelle im Widerstand gegen den Nationalsozialismus*, ed. Hans Coppi, Jürgen Danyel and Johannes Tuchel (Berlin: Edition Hentrich, 1994), 12–38.

3. Kopkow was so effective that Hermann Göring awarded him a gratuity of nearly 30,000; see Johannes Tuchel, "Die Gestapo-Sonderkommission 'Rote Kapelle'" in *Die Rote Kapelle im Widerstand*, 147–53 and note 46. Information from the Special Archive in Moscow shows that Göring had a special cash fund with which to reward those working on the case, amounting to 100,000 marks total. By January 1945, more than RM 67,000 had been paid out to sixty-five different officers, with Kopkow getting nearly half. Kopkow also helped himself to property once owned by the Schulze-Boysens.

4. The count varies between 117 and 119. See Norbert Haase, "Der Fall 'Rote Kapelle,' vor dem Reichskriegsgericht," in *Die Rote Kapelle im Widerstand*, 167. Records of this court-martial recently found in Prague destroy the postwar apologia that it maintained impartiality of military law. It admitted evidence secured through torture, its trials were closed to the public, the records were sealed to all but a few, and defendants were given no time to prepare their cases. Forty-five defendants received death sentence by hanging or guillotine, twelve received hard labor, and seventeen received prison sentences. Between the start of the war and February 1945, the Reich court-martial handed down 1,189 death sentences, of which 1,049 were carried out. (During the entirety of World War I, the German military justice system handed down 150 death sentences, of which 48 were carried out.) The Rote Kapelle judgments found in Prague show a clear political bent on the part of the justices, as did the Nazi insignias in the courtrooms and the bust of Hitler in the reception hall. See Haase, "Der Fall 'Rote Kapelle,'" 163.

5. Höhne, *Codeword: Direktor*, 224. CIA, Rote Kapelle, Survey Report, vol. 1:42–43 has the Belgian playbacks beginning in August.

6. There is also a long French Sureté Nationale report dated Jan. 1949 is in NA, RG 65, 100-344753-EBF 420, box 53.

7. MI-5, "The Case of the Red Orchestra: Preliminary Report," sent from Cimperman to Hoover, 9 Apr. 1946, NA, RG 65, 100-344753-1-1, box 42. MI-5, "The Case of the Red Orchestra: Second Report," sent from Cimperman to Hoover, 6 Nov. 1946, NA, RG 65, 100-344757-E 86, box 44. "The Case of the 'Rote Kapelle' Final Report" (including supplementary material, charts, personality index), sent to the FBI on 24 Oct. 1949, NA, RG 65, 100-344753-EBF 393, part 1, box 50.

8. MI-5, "The Case of the Red Orchestra: Preliminary Report," 1–2.

9. For more on Kopkow, see chapter 6.

10. They would also provide evidence against Communist wartime spies in the United States, such as Alger Hiss; see John Earl Haynes and Harvey Klehr, *Venona: Decoding Soviet Espionage in America* (New Haven, CT: Yale University Press, 1999), 168ff.

11. MI-5, "The Case of the 'Rote Kapelle': Final Report," part 2, 2.

12. Ibid., 32, 40.

13. CIA, "Rote Kapelle, A Survey Report," vol. 2, 308–10; MI-5, "The Case of the 'Rote Kapelle': Final Report," part 2, 32.

14. MI-5, "The Case of the 'Rote Kapelle': Final Report, part 2, 32, which (based on Foote's information) states that Roessler was a Czech refugee, is wrong on this point as shown by CIA, "Rote Kapelle, A Survey Report," vol. 1, 215.

15. CIA, "Rote Kapelle, A Survey Report," vol. 1, 186.

16. MI-5, "The Case of the 'Rote Kapelle': Final Report," part 2, 51–54. Roessler and Duebendorfer were arrested but held only briefly in 1944. See ibid., 61–62.

17. CIA, "Rote Kapelle, A Survey Report," vol. 1, 221–22.

18. The Swiss penetration of the Rote Drei is beyond the scope of this study. It was the Swiss Federal Police, which had its own signals-interception capability, and not German counterintelligence, that crippled the Rote Drei. In October 1943, the Swiss arrested radio operators Hamel and Bolli and in November they arrested Foote, which cut all wireless ties to Moscow from Geneva. Rado quickly went into hiding to avoid arrest. See CIA, "Rote Kapelle, A Survey Report," vol. 1, 192ff.

19. MI-5, "The Case of the Red Orchestra: Second Report," 104. This comment was also forwarded from the CIG to Hoover in CIG to Tamm, 29 Nov. 1946, NA, RG 65, 100-344753-3-89, box 43.

20. CIA, "Rote Kapelle, A Survey Report," vol. 2, 427–9. The first letter from Duebendorfer was published as part of the Royal Commission Report on Soviet Espionage in Canada.

21. MI-5, "The Case of the Red Orchestra: Second Report," 102–103.

22. Ibid. 103.

23. CIG to Tamm, 29 Nov. 1946, NA, RG 65, 100-344753-3-89, box 43.

24. Hoover to Hoyt S. Vandenberg, Director, CIG, 17 Dec. 1946, NA, RG 65, 100-344753-3-89, box 43.

25. Interrogations of Helbein are not in the FBI's Red Orchestra records but they are referenced in Hoover to SAC New York, 3 Jan. 1947, NA, RG 65, 100-344753-4-257, box 45. Before the second interview, the FBI was tracking his movements in Geneva and England.

26. Director CIG to Hoover, 8 Mar. 1948, NA, RG 65, 100-344753-7-285, box 46.

27. Hoover to SAC NY, NA, RG 65, 100-344753-5-335, box 45. This information came from a highly confidential British source who learned of an interrogation of Berthe Helbein.

28. Abramson's role here was also revealed in the Canadian spy trial in 1946.

29. MI-5, "The Case of the Red Orchestra: Second Report," 104.

30. Hoover to SAC NY, 14 June 1947, NA, RG 65, 100-344753-5-171, box 45.

31. This information came from the Department of State. Hoover to Leg. Att. Paris, 19 June 1947, NA, RG 65, 100-344753-5-175, box 45.

32. The most detailed records are of a Hungarian couple in New York named Gergely, whose address was found with Duebendorfer's effects when she was arrested in 1943. See NA, RG 65, 65-57507, boxes 221-222.

33. CIA to John F. Doherty, FBI Liaison, 28 Jan. 1948, NA, RG 65, 100-344753-7-265, box 46.

34. SAC LA R. B. Hood to Hoover, Dec. 22, 1947, NA, RG 65, 100-344753-232, box 46; [excised] No. 8791, 17 Feb. 1948, NA, RG 65, 100-344753-7-283, box 46.

35. CIA to John F. Doherty, FBI Liaison, 28 Jan. 1948, NA, RG 65, 100-344753-7-265, box 46.

36. Report by Joseph Walsh, New York, 21 Sept. 1949, NA, RG 65, 100-344753-11-388, box 50.

37. Hoover's idea to play back Barcza as a double agent was quickly dismissed by the CIA, which argued that if Barcza had applied for a visa as part of a Soviet espionage mission to the United States, she would not have done so under her own name. Hoover to Director CIA, 28 Mar. 1947, NA, RG 65, 65-57576-2, box 45; CIA Asst Director Memo to Hoover, 4 Apr. 1947, NA, RG 65, 65-57576-15.1, box 45; Hoover to SAC NY, NA, RG 65, 65-57576-6x3, box 45. See also the FBI file on Barcza, NA, RG 65, 65-57576-10-2, box 222.

38. Hoover to SAC New York, 22 June 1949, NA, RG 65, 100-344753-374, box 48.

39. See Allen Weinstein and Alexander Vassiliev, *The Haunted Wood: Soviet Espionage in America— The Stalin Era* (New York: Random House, 1999), 151ff; Haynes and Klehr, *Venona*.

40. The CIC detachment in Germany between November 1945 and June 1948 was named the 970th Counterintelligence Corps Detachment. Between June 1948 and November 1949 it was called the 7970th Counterintelligence Group. After November 1949 it was called the 66th Counterintelligence Corps Detachment.

41. Letter from J. M. A. Gwyer, London, S.F. 422/Gen/3/ADF/JMAG, 12 Apr. 1946 to Major R. V. Hemblys-Scales, British Liaison to CIC, USFET, NA RG 319, IRR, entry 134A, box 59, Red Orchestra, vol. 4, file. 2, 500–505; Int. Div/_ (a)5810/4/15, to Advance HQ, Intelligence Division, COG Berlin, Dec. 1946, NA, RG 319, IRR, entry 134A, box 59, Red Orchestra, vol. 3, file 1, 331.

42. Col. David G. Erskine, HQ, 970th CIC to Ops Br ODDI, 23 Jan. 1948, NA, RG 319, IRR, entry 134A, box 59, Red Orchestra, vol. 3, file 1, 379.

43. MI-5, "The Case of the 'Rote Kapelle': Final Report," 1.

44. MI-5, "The Case of the Rote Kapelle," (1949) is the only major study in Army CIC files and there is no cover sheet to show when the Army received it. The cover of part 3 of the MI-5 report is stamped by the 66th CIC Detachment, however, which did not exist until late 1949 and which did not look into the Red Orchestra seriously until 1952. See NA, RG 319, IRR, entry 134A, box 60, Red Orchestra, vol. 5-6, file 1–2.

45. A balanced view is given in Höhne, *Codeword: Direktor*, 178–84. For historiography see Peter Steinbach, "Die Rote Kapelle 50 Jahre danach," in Coppi et al., *Die Rote Kapelle im Widerstand*, 54–67.

46. He was used as a witness in the U.S. cases against Erhard Milch and against Nazi judges. For summaries of these cases, tried in Nuremberg by the U.S. Military Tribunal, see *Der Nationalsozialismus vor Gericht: die alliierten Prozesse gegen Kriegsverbrecher und Soldaten 1943–1952*, ed. Gerd R. Ueberschär (Frankfurt: Fischer Taschenbuch, 1999), 86–109.

47. Interrogation–no. 538, 31 Jan. 1947, NA, RG 238, entry 183, box 119.

48. Vernehmung des Manfred Roeder durch Dr. R. M. W. Kempner, 30 June 1947, NA, RG 238, entry 183, box 119.

49. See note of 28 May 1947, on card "Manfred Roeder," NA, RG 549, Judge Advocate Division, War Crimes Branch, Alphabetical Card Index, box 3; RG 549, Index to War Crimes Case Files, 1946–1947, box 27; on the categories see NA, RG 238, entry 146, box 4, Locator File. On family leave rejection, see the notes in NA, RG 238, entry 200, box 25, File–Roeder 201.

50. See Kuckhoff article in *Neues Deutschland*, 12 Apr. 1947. Kuckhoff argued this point in a report by the anti-fascist *Vereinigung der Verfolgten des Naziregimes*. See Klaus Lehmann, *Widerstandsgruppe Schulze-Boysen/Harnack* (Berlin, VVN. Verlag, 1948). Kuckhoff's call was partly a reaction to her anger at Allen Welsh Dulles' book *Germany's Underground* (New York: Macmillan, 1947), which argued that the Red Orchestra was a fundamentally unimportant band of spies. For Kuckhoff's comments, see Severin F. Wallach, Chief Special Branch Memo for the officer in Charge, HQ, COIC Region VIII, 970th CIC Detachment, 28 Aug. 1947, NA, RG 319, IRR, entry 134A, box 59, Red Orchestra, vol. 3, file 2, 417–8. In fact, she had called for Roeder's trial before the International Military Tribunal in 1945. For other calls to legitimize the Schulze-Boysen and Harnack groups as German resistance movements through the punishment of their tormentors, see also Günther Weissenborn, "Es gab eine deutsche Widerstandsbewegung," *Neue Berliner Illustrierte*, September 1947. See Elsa Boysen, *Harro Schulze-Boysen: Das Bild eines Freiheitskämpfers* (Düsseldorf, 1947); Falk Harnack, *Vom anderen Deutschland: Teilbericht über die Harnack-Schulze-Boysen-Widerstandsorganization* (Berlin, 1947). Speeches by Günther Weissenborn (1946), Greta Kuckhoff (1948) and Adolf Grimme (1947) and the remainder of the immediate postwar publications are analyzed in Jürgen Danyel, "Die Rote Kapelle innerhalb der deutschen Widerstandsbewegung," 16–17.

51. U.S. Civil Censorship Submission, Civil Censorship Division, EUCOM, A-47-12714, Dated 4 Apr. 1947, NA, RG 319, IRR, entry 134A, box 59, Red Orchestra, vol. 3, file 2, 419–20.

52. U.S. Civil Censorship Submission, Civil Censorship Division, EUCOM, CV-47-19216, 9 Sept. 1947, ibid., 414–15.

53. Severin F. Wallach, Chief Special Branch Memo for the officer in Charge, HQ, COIC Region VIII, 970th CIC Detachment, 28 Aug. 1947, ibid., 417–8.

54. HQ, CIC Region V, 970th CIC Detachment, Summary Report of Investigation, 13 May 1948, NA, RG 319, IRR, entry 134A, box 59, Red Orchestra, vol. 2, file 1, 146–53.

55. Ibid.

56. The Rote Kapelle Organization of 1942–Report by L. E. de Neufville, Civilian, SCI, Commanding, NA, RG 319, IRR, entry 134A, box 59, Red Orchestra, vol. 4, file 4.

57. Card, Manfred Roeder, NA, RG 549, Judge Advocate Division, War Crimes Branch, Alphabetical Card Index, box 3; and NA, RG 549, Index to War Crimes Case Files, 1946–1947, box 27.

58. "Aussage des Generaldichters Dr. Manfred Roeder–Bertrifft Rote Kapelle," Oberursel, 27 Feb. 1947, NA, RG 319, IRR, entry 134A, box 59, Red Orchestra, vol. 3, file 2, 421ff.

59. HQ, USFET, MIS Service Cts., CI War Room, Preliminary Investigation Report No. 76, October 1945, NA, RG 319, IRR, entry 134B, Walter Huppenkothen.

60. Ibid.

61. Ibid., 354ff.

62. HQ, CIC Region V, 970th Detachment, SA Benjamin Gorby, Memorandum for the Officer in Charge, 30 Oct. 1947, ibid., 261–3.

63. Browning, HQ, 970th CIC Detachment, Region V to CO, 970th CIC Detachment at HQ EUCOM, 31 Oct. 1947, ibid; SA L. E. Cornish, CIC, 970th Detachment, Region V to CO, 970th CIC Detachment, HQ, EUCOM, 31 Oct. 1947, ibid., 260; and Memorandum by Benjamin Gorby, Special Agent, CIC [HQ CIC Region V] Detachment, to Lt. Kirkpatrick, 31 Dec. 1947, NA, RG 319, IRR, entry 134A, box 59, Red Orchestra, vol. 3, file 2, 404–5.

64. HQ, CIC Region V, 970th CIC Detachment, Summary Report of Investigation, 13 May 1948, NA, RG 319, IRR, entry 134A, box 59, Red Orchestra, vol. 2, file 1, 146–53.

65. Memorandum by Benjamin Gorby, Special Agent, CIC [HQ CIC Region V Detachment, to Lt. Kirkpatrick, 31 Dec. 1947, NA, RG 319, IRR, entry 134A, box 59, Red Orchestra, vol. 3, file 2, 404–05.

66. On the SIMEX arrests, MI-5, "The Case of the 'Rote Kapelle': Final Report," 7.

67. MI-5, "The Case of the 'Rote Kapelle': Final Report," part 3.

68. HQ, CIC Region V, 970th CIC Detachment, Summary Report of Investigation, 13 May 1948, NA, RG 319, IRR, entry 134A, box 59, Red Orchestra, vol. 2, file 1, 146–53.

69. Major Earl S. Browning for Col. Erskine, 970th CIC, to Commanding Officer, CIC Region V, 20 May 1948, NA, RG 319, IRR, entry 134A, box 59, Red Orchestra, vol. 1, file 2, 131; Card, Manfred Roeder, NA, RG 549, Judge Advocate Division, War Crimes Branch, Alphabetical Card Index, box 3; NA, RG 549, Index to War Crimes Case Files, 1946–1947, box 27.

70. Gorby to CO, 7970th CIC Group, Regensburg, 10 Dec. 1948, NA, RG 319, IRR, entry 134B, Walter Huppenkothen, 226–7.

71. Unsigned agent report, "Proposed Use of Former Gestapo Personnel to Combat Present Day Illegal KPD Activities," ibid., 222–25.

72. Benno Selke, Deputy Director, Evidence Division, OCCWC, Nuremberg, to Commanding General, EUCOM, Office of the Deputy Director for Intelligence, 4 Aug. 1948, ibid., 242–43.

73. Lt. Col. George Eckman, Deputy Commander, HQ, 7970th CIC Group to Ops. Br., 26 Aug. 1948, ibid., 240.

74. In October 1948, Selke had Roeder turned over to local German authorities on the hope that he would be arrested and tried. Selke to Sutton, Prison Ops, 25 Oct. 1948, NA, RG 238, entry 200, box 25, File–Roeder 201. Though a case was assembled against Roeder by the West German judicial authorities in Lower Saxony between 1949 and 1951, Roeder would never be brought to justice. Dr. Hans-Jürgen Fink, the local prosecutor, suspended the investigation in November 1951, convinced by Roeder's own argument that the members of the Red Orchestra deserved no better and that the charges against him were fueled by Communist intrigue. The disillusioned mother of Harro von Schulze-Boysen wrote Günther Weissenborn that "the important thing is that Roeder is silenced." Shareen Blair Brysac, *Resisting Hitler: Mildred Harnack and the Red Orchestra* (New York: Oxford University Press, 2000), 385–86. Huppenkothen would be tried by the Landesgericht in Munich in 1950, but the verdict was set aside in 1952 by the Bundesgerichtshof. In October

1955 he was retried and sentenced in West Germany to seven years imprisonment for being an accessory to murder. Both court proceedings against Huppenkothen were for his roll in the April 1945 executions at Flossenbürg of five conspirators involved in the 20 July plot, including Canaris, Oster, and Hans von Dohanyi. Huppenkothen was never tried for his activities in Poland.

75. "Demagogen einer neuen Dolchstoßlegende," *Neue Zeitung*, No. 110/111, 12 May 1951, 3. On the *Neue Zeitung*, see Jessica C. E. Gienow-Hecht, *Transmission Impossible: American Journalism as Cultural Diplomacy in Postwar Germany, 1945–1955* (Baton Rouge: Louisiana State University Press, 1999).

76. Lt. Col. John R. Guenard, Co. Region II, 66th CIC to HQ, 66th CIC Det., 29 Jan. 1952, NA, RG 319, IRR, entry 134A, box 59, Red Orchestra, vol. 1, file 1, 36ff.

77. Region II, 66th Detachment, Report of 11 Feb. 1952, ibid., 32–33.

78. *Sunday Dispatch*, 29 Mar. 1953, *Schweizer Illustrierte Zeitung*, 17 Apr. 1953.

79. Hoover to Legal Attaché Paris, 29 Sept. 1953, NA, RG 65, 100-344753-14, box 55.

80. Legal Attaché Paris to Hoover, 27 Nov. 1953, ibid.

81. Jack H. Lenz, U.S. Consul General, Munich to 66th CIC, Benjamin, BAV-140, 20 Aug. 1954, NA, RG 319, IRR, entry 134A, box 59, Red Orchestra, vol. 1, file 1, 12.

82. Reiser worked for GV-L but there is little in his CIA Name File on his actual activities. See his brief dossier, undated, in NA, RG 263, Heinrich Reiser Name File.

83. The report is in NA, RG 263, Heinz Pannwitz Name File, vol. 1, and is referenced as Reiser's in Frankfurt to Director, No. [excised], 14 June 1956, NA, RG 263, Heinz Pannwitz Name File, vol. 1; and Chief of Base Pullach to Chief, Frankfurt Operations Base, No. [excised] 14 June 1956 in the same file.

84. Reiser's belief may owe to the fact that he approved the trip by Berg and Trepper into Paris the day Trepper escaped. Pannwitz would say in 1959 that Berg was "honestly very upset" by the escape and had to be placed on suicide watch, and that he was a loyal Gestapo agent with a close relationship with Müller, since he was Müller's cigar supplier during the war. Pannwitz attributed the escape to the fact that Berg trusted Trepper too much. Pannwitz also said that during his captivity in Moscow, "the Soviets attempted to convince me that Willi Berg was a close, trusted friend of Trepper and a Moscow agent." Att A (para 53, 57) to Chief Munich Base to Chief EE and Chief SR, 17 Aug. 1959, NA, RG 263, Heinz Pannwitz Name File, vol. 2.

85. Bundeskriminalamt (BKA) testimony of Walter Klein, Bonn, 14 Jan. 1952, NA, RG 263, Heinrich Reiser Name File. See also Sureté Nationale, "The Rote Kapelle Network," 89ff.

86. BKA Interrogation of Klein, Weissenthurm, 29 Nov. 1951, NA, RG 263, Heinrich Reiser Name File; Bundeskriminalamt, Interrogation of August-Wilhelm Berg, Berlin–Charlottenburg, 10 Jan. 1952, ibid.

87. BKA Interrogation of Walter Klein, Neuwied, 28 Nov. 1951; and BKA Interrogation of Klein, Weissenthurm, 29 Nov. 1951, ibid.

88. BKA Interrogation of Walter Klein, Neuwied, 26 Nov. 1951; and BKA, Interrogation of Walter Klein, Bonn, 14 Jan. 1952, ibid.

89. BKA Interrogation of Walter Klein, Weissenthurm, 29 Nov. 1951, ibid.

90. BKA Interrogation of Walter Klein, Bonn, 14 Jan. 1952, ibid.

91. BKA Interrogation of Heinrich Reiser, Karlsruhe, 16 Dec. 1951, ibid.

92. BKA interrogation of Rolf Richter, Koblenz, 12 Dec. 1951; and BKA Interrogation of

Marianne Muckert, 13 Dec. 1951, ibid.

93. Chief, EE to Chief [excised], No. [excised]–34599, 6 June 1958, NA, RG 263, Friedrich Panzinger Name File. Panzinger's CIA Name File is sketchy about his arrest in Linz. Since Linz was in the U.S. occupation zone, it is possible the Soviets kidnapped (rather than arrested) him.

94. From September 1943 to May 1944, Panzinger was the SD and Sicherheitspolizei Commander in Riga, and was promoted personally by Himmler for his service there in fighting partisan activity. He also approved in November 1944 the use of prisoners for medical experiments. See NA–BDC, RG 242, A-3343, SSO, roll 364A; and Chief, EE to [excised], No. [excised]–6514, 8 Aug. 1958, NA, RG 263, Friedrich Panzinger Name File. Both the Soviets and the Gehlen Organization on separate occasions pledged to protect him from arrest, but due to missed communications with the Bavarian authorities, he was arrested anyway, whereupon he took a lethal dose of poison on arriving in prison; see Chief [excised] to Chief, EE, No. [excised]–45916, 12 Nov. 1959, NA, RG 263, Friedrich Panzinger Name File.

95. For Felfe's accusations and Pannwitz's denials, see Frankfurt to Director, No. [excised], 14 June 1956, NA, RG 263, Heinz Pannwitz Name File, vol. 1; Chief Stuttgart Liaison Office to Chief Munich Liaison Base, No. [excised], 20 May 1965, ibid., vol. 2.

96. For BND suspicion see Chief Munich Liaison Base to Chief EE, No. [excised], 6 May 1965, NA, RG 263, Heinz Pannwitz Name File, vol. 2. For his partial debriefing by CIA and hiring by the West Germans, see Director to COB Pullach, No. [excised], 10 Aug. 1956; Chief of Station Germany to Chief EE, No. [excised], 14 Aug. 1956 and attachment A; COB Pullach to Director, No. [excised], 14 Aug. 1956, NA, RG 263, Heinz Pannwitz Name File, vol. 1; and Chief Munich Operations Base to Chief EE, No. [excised], 5 Mar. 1959, NA, RG 263, Heinz Pannwitz Name File, vol. 2. The name of the German agency that hired Pannwitz, effective September 1, 1956, is redacted in CIA records.

97. Amcongen Stuttgart–Reports Section to CO, 66th CIC Region IV, APO 108, 6 July 1956, NA, RG 319, IRR, entry 134B, file FE591032, Heinz Pannwitz; J.E. Catlin, Jr. (DAD Liaison Officer) to C.O., HQ 66th CIC Detachment, 12 July 1956, ibid.

98. COB Pullach to Chief EE, No. [excised], 13 Sept. 1957; COB Munich to Chief EE, No. [excised] 5 Mar. 1959, both in NA, RG 263, Heinz Pannwitz Name File, vol. 2.

99. Amcongen Stuttgart–Reports Section to CO, 66th CIC Region IV, APO 108, 6 July 1956; and J.E. Catlin, Jr. (DAD Liaison Officer) to C.O., HQ 66th CIC Detachment, 12 July 1956; both in NA, RG 319, IRR, entry 134B, file FE591032, Heinz Pannwitz.

100. COB Munich to Chief EE, No. [excised], 5 Mar. 1959, NA, RG 263, Heinz Pannwitz Name File, vol. 2.

101. Ibid.

102. Stuttgart to Director, No. [excised], 19 Mar. 1959, ibid.

103. Chief Munich Base to Chief SR, Chief EE, No. [excised], 14 July 1959, ibid.

12

Coddling a Nazi Turncoat

Robert Wolfe

IT IS A COMMONPLACE in the documents declassified under the Nazi War Crimes Disclosure Act of 1998 that U.S. intelligence services employed and protected selected Axis war criminals in order to employ them as purveyors of (often untrustworthy) human intelligence. That protection also derived in some cases from a principled sense of obligation for services already rendered, however self-serving for the enemy turncoat and only putatively beneficial to the United States. This sense of U.S. obligation survived even when there was little expectation that such hirelings would be of use in the future.

The case of SS-Standartenführer Eugen Dollmann is a classic example of a U.S. intelligence agency perforce coddling a war crimes suspect who was no longer a useful source. Dollmann had played a prominent role in Operation Sunrise, the timely and opportunistic surrender of German forces in Italy on May 2, 1945, one week before the VE-Day capitulation of the remainder of the German armed forces.[1] For U.S. intelligence, failure to shield Dollmann would risk embarrassing public disclosure of continued covert anti-leftist operations by the United States in postwar Italy. Furthermore, it could deter more skilled Nazi intelligence sources from trusting U.S. spymasters' promises of unending protection.

Dollmann's case also illustrates the setbacks to scholarship that resulted from the half-century delay in the declassification of Counterintelligence Corps (CIC), Office of Strategic Services (OSS), CIA, FBI, and Army documentation of war crimes and intelligence dossiers of war criminals. Documents released under the Nazi War Crimes Disclosure Act allow us to fill in some historical gaps and amend otherwise reliable accounts.[2]

Dollmann's Career before Operation Sunrise

Eugen Dollmann was born on August 8, 1900. In the summer of 1918, he served as a volunteer in the 7th Bavarian Field Artillery Regiment.[3] Thereafter, he matriculated at the Ludwig Maximilian University in Munich, majoring in art history and literature, and he was awarded a doctorate magna cum laude in 1926. Since he was a Protestant, his dissertation on "Lazarus von Schwendi and the Political Problems of the German Counter-Reformation" was a fortuitous preparation for his future liaison with Pius XII's Vatican.[4]

Supported by a research grant, Dollmann spent 1927 to 1930 at various Italian universities studying the Farnese dynasty of Parma in the context of the Italian sixteenth century. On the death of his mother in 1934, this seemingly perpetual student had to earn his living. Apparently, his mother had also supported him during his years of study, but he was an incorrigible spendthrift, perpetually strapped for cash.[5] His first gainful employment was as an editorial trainee at the *Münchener Neueste Nachrichten,* after which he was assigned to Rome as a foreign correspondent. He joined the Nazi Party in February 1934, and his Third Reich career took off in 1935, when he became press leader of the Roman Party chapter.[6] In 1937, he graduated to the staff of the Hitler Youth Leader in Italy. He also served as Roman representative of *Wille und Macht* (*Will and Power*), a publication of the Reich Youth Leader. Having translated Marshall Pietro Badoglio's World War I memoirs, Dollmann was best able to analyze the situation after Badoglio defected to the Allies in September 1943.

Dollmann applied for membership in the SS in November 1937.[7] Displaying what appears to be a lifelong penchant for embellishing official forms with surnames that do not appear on his birth certificate, in his SS application, Dollmann gave his mother's maiden name as "von Fischer," suggesting an aristocratic standing.[8] He was accepted within one month as an SS-Mann and simultaneously given the rank of SS-Obersturmführer, an uncommon but not unknown procedure.[9] He was assigned to the Personal Staff of the Reichsführer SS, whose chief of staff was SS-Obergruppenführer Karl Wolff. Dollmann later served as an aide to Wolff, who was the ranking SS officer in northern Italy after 1943.

Although stationed in Rome and assigned to Himmler's personal staff throughout his SS career, Dollmann's ascent in rank was steady: Hauptsturmführer, September 1938; Sturmbannführer, April 1939; Obersturmbannführer, March 1941; Standartenführer, November 1943. He served as Himmler's liaison first to the Royal Italian government and then to Mussolini's Fascist republic. He also served as Wolff's liaison to Mussolini's republic and to the Vatican, and acted as interpreter between the Nazi and Fascist dictators on some occasions.[10]

An entry in Dollmann's CIA file describes him as "very temperamental with a vivid personality and a great sense of humour, but egoistic and a bad organizer: speaks fluent English and Italian and a little French: talks with a slight Munich accent."[11] Whatever his administrative and personal shortcomings, the multilingual Dollmann was an able liaison officer and keen observer, with a talent for rhetoric. Colleagues, acquaintances, interrogators, and interviewers considered Dollmann handsome and charming. After Allen Dulles met him face-to-face in the spring of 1945, he remarked,

[Dollmann] had long black hair, combed back Italian style, and almost effeminate gestures . . . He was an intellectual, highly sophisticated, somewhat snobbish and cynical . . . As the situation in Italy changed in 1943 . . . he now became a kind of top liaison officer between the Germans and the Italian officials, and the church . . . In short, he was everybody's man, but only in high places . . . It is no wonder, then, that later he was also one of the first Germans to appear as emissary to the Allies.[12]

Dollmann's affinity and affection for Italians, although acquired, was genuine. Italy was his post and playground, its language his métier. Often mufti-clad by preference, he not only combed his hair but also wore his suits Italian style. After the defeat of Germany, he repeatedly attempted to pass himself off as an Italian. Dollmann no doubt hoped to save his own skin by propitiating the victors. His promotion of an early surrender may have also been urged by a desire to avert the devastation of northern Italy, his cultural home.

The military situation in March 1944 found the Allied armies inching toward Rome. The political situation was much more complex: the Pope was attempting to convince the belligerents to make Rome an "open city" from which the Germans would withdraw and which the Allies would bypass. This would keep Rome in control of Mussolini's Fascist regime (derisively dubbed the "Republic of Salo") and the pope as its bishop, preventing the leftist partisan takeover so feared by Pius XII. The German commanders in Italy, contrary to Hitler's orders to fight for every foot of Roman soil, sought only to make a safe withdrawal, sparing their troops to fight another day.

On March 23, 1944, Nazi officials were considering a range of reprisals to the ambush of an SS police unit by Italian partisans in Rome's Via Raselli, during which 32 SS police were killed and many others maimed and wounded. Unable to apprehend the culprits, on the following day the SS shot and entombed in the ancient Ardeatine catacombs 335 imprisoned Romans, including some 75 Jews, none of them involved in the ambush. The Nazi officials also applied the excruciating psychological punishment of "night and fog" (*Nacht und Nebel*), refusing for weeks to divulge the names of the victims or let anyone enter the Ardeatine caves.[13]

Dollmann foresaw the Roman population's outraged backlash against the reprisal still being planned by his colleagues. He hastened to his longtime Vatican contact, the head of the Order of Salvatorians, Padre Pancrazio (his Bavarian compatriot, born Pankratius Pfeiffer), who was the designated liaison between the Vatican and the German occupiers. At once, Padre Pancrazio consented to appeal to the Pontiff for intervention, and the Vatican *did* make a diplomatic inquiry about the impending executions to Ernst von Weizsäcker, the German ambassador to the Holy See.[14] The Germans replied that this "terrorist" action by Italian partisans could hamper German consent to declare Rome an open city.[15] Pius XII then chose to condemn the "Communist" Italian attackers, rather than the German reprisals.[16]

A persuasive summation of the Pope's motivation deserves repetition here:

[The] Vatican's silence in occupied Rome . . . [a] *moral* failure . . . based on Pius XII's committing one of the great misreadings of history, is evidenced by the relationship between the Vatican and the German occupiers—a Faustian pact by definition. The papal obsession with protecting the physical integrity of the Vatican City-State by any means, against enemies less real than imagined, was fulfilled in exchange for papal silence, not one silence, but one following another, a whole range of silences for the whole range of Nazi and Fascist brutality.[17]

Concerning Dollmann's ideological leanings, a perhaps too-favorable Allied assessment described Dollmann as "unusually vivacious for a German . . . extremely intelligent and alert of mind. He is vain and probably without a great deal of principle but has a sense of form that would prevent his sinking to the depths of cruelty and cowardice of many of his colleagues . . . He undoubtedly used the SS as a means to a pleasant, easy existence without ever believing in National Socialism."[18]

An anti-Semitic remark attributed to Dollmann is found in a report sent on May 13, 1943, by a visiting Nazi diplomat to a friend in Paris. That diplomat quoted Dollmann as saying that "the Italian armed forces are still riddled with full Jews and innumerable half-Jews."[19] This exaggeration could be taken as Dollmann's subtle discouragement to instituting deportations of Roman Jewry to "the East"—such as were then underway in France—which would not go down well with Germany's still-useful Italian military allies.[20] Whether it was so intended by Dollmann can only be surmised in the context of his overall behavior.

Hitler's "Tea Party"

On occasion, declassification of federal records under the Nazi War Crimes Disclosure Act yielded serendipitous historical connections and new perceptions about previously accepted scholarship. One such instance is an intriguing document vividly portraying the impromptu "tea party" at Adolf Hitler's Rastenburg field headquarters, code named "Wolf's Lair" (*Wolfsschanze*), immediately after the failed July 20, 1944, assassination attempt on Der Führer.[21] As SS liaison officer to Mussolini's Italian Social Republic, Dollmann escorted Il Duce to the so-called tea party, acting as interpreter between the two dictators, as extant photographs attest. This unique event in Dollmann's experience presumably sowed the seed of Operation Sunrise.

For more than a half-century, most nonfiction and media renditions of that bizarre tea party have drawn on its portrayal in Sir Hugh Redwald Trevor-Roper's *The Last Days of Hitler*.[22] An Oxford (and later Cambridge) don and medieval historian before the Second World War, Major Trevor-Roper served as a British intelligence officer assigned at war's end to investigate Hitler's possible survival. Describing his source as "perhaps overdrawn; but not improbably," Trevor-Roper did not identify his human source or cite the origin of his documentary source (although some direct quotations are ascribed to Hitler and Foreign Minister Joachim Ribbentrop). Presumably, the formidable British Official Secrets Ac dictated suppression of proper scholarly attribution.[23] Since he could not have been an eyewitness to Hitler's tea party, and there is no other contemporaneous primary documentation, the precise source—and therefore accuracy—of Trevor-Roper's account remained an unchallenged mystery.

A 1945 SHAEF Combined Services Detailed Interrogation Center (CSDIC) report released under the Nazi War Crimes Disclosure Act gives us Trevor-Roper's source.[24] The report contains an English translation of the German transcription of a surreptitiously recorded conversation on July 20, 1945—exactly one year after the tea party—between Dollmann and SS-Standartenführer Georg Elling, both then in a British prisoners-of-war cage in Italy.[25] As SS officers, they were in the Allies' "automatic arrest" category and were personally susceptible to indictment as members of an organization declared guilty of war crimes by the Nuremberg International Tribunal (IMT). Dollmann had served as SS police attaché at the German Embassy in Rome during 1941–43, and Elling during a corresponding period as SS police attaché at the German Embassy to the Vatican. Their closely parallel assignments in Italy may partially explain why Dollmann imparted to Elling the experience that made him turn his coat.

Here follows a comparison of the two transcripts.

Dollmann Transcript

At five o'clock there was a big tea party; it was amazingly interesting, all of them were there, in the Fuehrer's GHQ, and over tea they all began arguing and shouting at one another, and each one putting the blame on the other because the war had not yet been won!

Ribbentrop raved against the Generals, because they had betrayed us to England, Doenitz raved against the Generals, and the Generals raved in their turn against Ribbentrop and Doenitz! The Fuehrer kept quiet the whole time, and Mussolini was very reserved too. Graziani began telling him about his adventures in Africa, when all of a sudden someone happened to mention the 30th of June 1934 [The so-called Röhm Purge during which the SA leadership and various other perceived opponents of the Nazis were liquidated]; the Fuehrer leaped up, in a fit of frenzy, with

Trevor-Roper Account

It was five o'clock when the tea party began, and the whole court assembled in the Fuehrer's headquarters. Conversation was naturally about the Fuehrer's escape, but it quickly deteriorated into recrimination. Voices were raised in high-pitched and bitter argument; and everyone in turn each blamed because the war had not yet been won. Ribbentrop and Doenitz raved against the generals because they had betrayed Germany to England, and the generals raved in reply against Ribbentrop and Doenitz. All the time Hitler and Mussolini sat quiet and reserved, as if mere spectators of the scene, while Graziani told them of his African adventures. Then, quite suddenly, someone mentioned that other famous "plot" in Nazi history— the Roehm plot of 30th June 1934, and the bloody purge which followed it. Immediately, Hitler leaped up in a fit of frenzy, with foam on his lips, and foam on his lips, and yelled out that he would be revenged on all traitors, that Providence had just shown him once more that he had been chosen to make world history, and shouted about terrible punishments for women and children, all of them would have to be put inside concentration camps!

He shouted about an eye for an eye and a tooth for a tooth for everyone who dared set himself against divine Providence. It was awful, and it went on for about half an hour! I thought to myself, the man must be mad. I don't know why I didn't go over to the Allies there and then.

Mussolini found it most unpleasant. Meanwhile more tea was served by the footmen in white, and Graziani started discussing with Keitel the question of AA troops we wanted from the Italians.

Then a call came through from Berlin, to say that order had not yet been restored there. The Fuehrer answered the call, and started yelling again, gave full powers for shooting anyone they liked, why wasn't Himmler there yet, and so on.

Then came the lovely bit: "I'm beginning to doubt if the German people is worthy of my great ideas."

At that of course there was a tremendous to-do, they all wanted to convince the Fuehrer of their loyalty. Doenitz and Goering came out with all they had done, Doenitz told him about the blue-eyed boys in blue—damned rubbish—and Goering started

shouted that he would be revenged on all traitors. Providence has just shown him once again, he screamed, that he had been chosen to make world history; and he ranted wildly about terrible punishments for women and children—all of them would be thrown into concentration camps—an eye for an eye, and a tooth for a tooth—none should be spared who set himself against divine Providence. The court fell silent as the Fuehrer raged for a full half-hour; the visitors thought he must be mad,—"I don't know" said one of them, [undoubtedly Dollmann, according to Dollmann!] "why I didn't go over to the Allies there and then."

Mussolini looked embarrassed, and said nothing; Graziani sought feebly to break the spell by beginning a technical discussion with Keitel; and all the time footmen, dressed in white, circulated with teapots among the gaping worshippers.

This scene was interrupted by a call from Berlin, where order had not yet been restored. Hitler seized the telephone and shouted his orders into the mouthpiece, giving full orders to shoot anyone and everyone. Why hadn't Himmler arrived yet?

Then came the portentous statement of the megalomaniac: "I'm beginning to doubt whether the German people is worthy of my great ideals."

These words broke the spell of silence. At once the entire court competed to speak, each protesting his loyalty. In grovelling terms Doenitz sang the praises of the German Navy. Goering began a violent quarrel with Ribbentrop and made a pass at having a row with Ribbentrop, and Ribbentrop shouted at him: "I am still the Foreign Minister, and my name is von Ribbentrop!" Goering made a pass at him with his Field Marshal's baton. I'll never forget that scene!

The Fuehrer was in a very peculiar state at that time. It was the time when his right arm began to develop a tremor. He sat there almost the whole time eating his colored pastilles [vitamin pills].

him with his field-marshal's baton; and the voice of Ribbentrop was heard above the tumult protesting, "I am still Foreign Minister and my name is von Ribbentrop."

Only Hitler was silent now. The parts in the comic opera were reversed, and the prima donna ceased while the chorus discordantly sang. He sat still; in his hand he had a tube of brightly colored pastilles which he sucked.

Thanks to Trevor-Roper's influential *imprimatur*, as well as the British Official Secrets Act and American deference thereto, for over a half century Dollmann's unacknowledged and untested one-year-old recollections—"perhaps overdrawn but not improbably"—have been accepted as an accurate depiction of the tea-party scene. Since then, virtually all extant accounts of the tea party, whether print, documentary, or docudrama and other genres of historical fiction, unwittingly closely track Eugen Dollmann's remarkable recollection of the circumstances—vivid despite the intervening most turbulent full year of his life. It has also fostered a prevailing presumption that Adolf Hitler was a ranting psychopath, when more likely he was a cunning fanatic.

Although the undocumented English translation of the CSDIC's near-verbatim text had already been made public by Trevor-Roper in 1947, it remained classified for more than a half century, until made available by the IWG under the Nazi War Crimes Disclosure Act.

Operation Sunrise

It is a compelling surmise that Dollmann's resolve to spur the negotiations that led to Operation Sunrise, which saved an uncountable number of American, Italian, and German lives, was prompted by his dismay at Hitler's appalling behavior at the *Wolfsschanze* tea party, a dismay already aroused by Hitler's order for the massacre of 335 innocent Roman citizens during the Ardeatine massacres just four months before. That Dollmann contemplated turning his coat on departing the *Wolfsschanze* on July 20, 1944, can be inferred from his recounting to Elling, exactly one year later: "I thought to myself . . . [Hitler] must be mad. I don't know why I didn't go over to the Allies there and then."

Immediately on his return to Italy, still during the last week of July, Dollmann cautiously began to trim sail, canvassing both Germans and Italians about the possibility of a separate surrender of German armed forces in Italy. He was the realist who first broached to Karl Wolff the suggestion that eventually led to the

TOP SECRET

Excerpt from CSDIC/CMF/X 194

Conversation held on 20 July 1945,
between DOLLMANN and ELLING.

1. A STORM AT THE FUEHRER'S GHQ.

DOLLMANN : A year ago today exactly I escorted the DUCE from
FLORENCE to GERMANY. The train was scheduled to
leave at one o'clock on the 20th of July. We were
in the station, when suddenly an air raid alarm
was given and the whole train had to be blacked out.

ELLING : But it was daylight, surely?

DOLLMANN : Yes, it was broad daylight, and all the same the
whole train had to be blacked out, all the windows were
covered over and we sat there in the dark! When we
arrived at the station - we were going to the
FUEHRER's GHQ - the FUEHRER was there to meet us,
white as a sheet, and his whole staff. HIMMLER,
GOERING, KEITEL, RIBBENTROP, and so on, they were
all there. I got out after the DUCE, and heard
HITLER saying to him: "I've just had the greatest
piece of luck I've ever had", and then he went on
to tell him about the attempt on his life. Afterwards the FUEHRER and MUSSOLINI and myself went to
have a look at the place where it happened. It was
a mass of debris.

At five o'clock there was a big tea party; it was
amazingly interesting, all of them were there, in
the FUEHRER's GHQ, and over tea they all began arguing and shouting at one another, and each one
putting the blame on the other because the war had
not yet been won! RIBBENTROP raved against the
Generals, because they had betrayed us to ENGLAND,
DOENITZ raved against the Generals, and the Generals
raved in their turn against RIBBENTROP and DOENITZ!
The FUEHRER kept pretty quiet the whole time, and
MUSSOLINI was very reserved too. GRAZIANI began
telling him about his adventures in AFRICA, when all
of a sudden someone happened to mention the 30th
of June 1934: the FUEHRER leapt up, in a fit of
frenzy, with foam on his lips, and yelled out that
he would be revenged on all traitors, that Providence
had just shown him once more that he had been chosen
to make world history, and shouted about terrible

Translation of a transcript of a German conversation between Elling and Dollmann,
surreptitiously recorded while the two were in a POW camp in Italy, which was the
unacknowledged source of Trevor-Roper's account of Hitler's infamous tea party (NA, RG 226,
entry 190C, box 7, folder 95).

opportunistic premature surrender of German forces in Italy. Later, during a "scientifically conducted interrogation"[26] on August 20, 1946, Dollmann related that he discussed the advisability of beginning negotiations with the Allies with the German air attaché in Italy, Luftwaffe General Ritter von Pohl, "during July 1944"—presumably within days after his return from the July 20 tea party.[27]

By late 1944, Dollmann pursued several possibilities on Wolff's behalf, directly with the Italian Resistance, but also (through Ildefonso Cardinal Schuster of Milan) with Mussolini and the Fascist regime. He was also parleying with the Italian partisan forces, which were still awaiting recognition from the Allies.[28] Wolff's purpose was to negotiate tolerable surrender conditions for the German forces in Italy, which included buying clemency for himself and his SS subordinates. Cardinal Schuster was simultaneously dickering with the Germans, the Fascists, and the partisans, seeking the best bargain to avert ravage of his diocese. The pope was mainly concerned with preserving his temporal authority over the Vatican City-State as well as preventing a partisan "Communist" takeover of Rome and Italy—as, to be sure, were the Allies.[29]

Perhaps it was the ambience of the locale, but Operation Sunrise closely resembled a performance from the *Commedia dell'Arte*, replete with mistaken identities, missed connections, surprise entrances and exits, with everything falling into place just in time for the final curtain. Much of that fantastic story is based on postwar interrogations, interviews, and memoirs, in which numerous German, Italian, and Swiss military and civilian actors claimed a key role in its successful outcome.

By the end of the year, Dollmann was urging Wolff to begin negotiations with the Allies. During an indiscreet conversation about the necessity of a negotiated surrender, Dollmann was overheard by SS-Obersturmbannführer Guido Zimmer. Zimmer thereupon introduced Dollmann to Baron Luigi Parilli, an industrialist who had at one time represented the American Nash-Kelvinator refrigerator company, and who feared that a Communist takeover of northern Italy would endanger his financial interests. He contacted an old friend, Dr. Max Husmann, headmaster of a boys' school in Switzerland. Husmann enlisted the cooperation of Major Max Waibel, a Swiss intelligence officer who made the contact to Allen Dulles, the OSS chief agent in Bern. Waibel provided the indispensable cover for Wolff and his emissaries' clandestine incursions into Switzerland.[30]

On February 28, Parilli and Husmann met with Dulles' OSS deputy, American Gero von Schultze-Gaevernitz, in Lucerne. Dollmann was not at that first meeting. But on March 3, 1945, Dollmann, Parilli, and Zimmer were taken in hand at the Swiss border by Husmann and, as a stand-in for Waibel, Swiss Lieutenant Friedrich Rothpletz, who provided security escort to Lugano. Gaevernitz was not there.[31] Instead, the Axis delegation was met by OSS agent Paul Blum, who obviously had instructions only to listen, except to request the release of imprisoned partisan leader Ferruccio Parri and Antonio Usmiani of Royal Italian Intelligence as a test of Wolff's bona fides.[32]

On March 8, Wolff, Dollmann, Parilli, Zimmer, and his adjutant, SS-Sturmbannführer Eugen Wenner, slipped across the border to Lugano, where they were met by Rothpletz and Husmann. Encouraged by the liberation of Parri and Usmiani, Dulles decided to meet with Wolff alone at an OSS secret house in Zurich. Dulles arrived with Gaevernitz in tow.[33] The discussion went so well that on April 23 Wolff dispatched Dollmann to the supreme German commander in Italy, Field Marshal Albert Kesselring, to secure his concurrence in the surrender.[34]

Meanwhile, it had become necessary to coordinate negotiations with Allied Forces Headquarters (AFHQ), Field Marshal Harold Alexander's Allied command in Italy. On March 18, Alexander's American deputy at AFHQ, Major General Lyman Lemnitzer, and British Major General Terence Sydney Airey, AFHQ intelligence chief, arrived at Ascona. Dulles and Gaevernitz introduced them to Wolff, who was accompanied by Wenner and Zimmer. The ubiquitous Parilli and Husmann, as well as the indispensable Waibel, were also there. Dollmann had been left behind at Wolff's headquarters to cope with any emergencies that might arise.[35]

At that inauspicious moment, on April 26, 1945, Kesselring, who had succeeded Rundstedt in the shrinking western command in March, was now elevated to supreme command of the entire western and southern fronts, by now condensed to the western borders of Germany, but also including northern Italy and the remaining foothold in the Balkans. Upon this prearranged escalation to the pinnacle of his military career, the notoriously ambitious Kesselring reverted from a grudging tolerance to angry disapproval of negotiations for a separate Italian surrender. Wolff simply ignored him. Kesselring's successor, General Heinrich von Vietinghoff-Scheel, at first balked but then acquiesced to the inevitable. The capitulation terms were signed on April 29 by Wolff's adjutant Wenner, and Colonel Viktor von Schweinitz on behalf of Vietinghoff, culminating in the May 2 surrender of all German forces in Italy.

On the day following, perhaps the most fitting tribute to Operation Sunrise was sent by secret telegram to Dulles from the OSS headquarters in Washington by his colleague, John Magruder, Deputy Director of the OSS: "Countless thousands of parents would bless you were they privileged to know what you have done. As one of them privileged to know, and with a boy in the mountain division, I do bless you."[36]

After such an accolade, it is not surprising that Dulles and the OSS, especially its Special Services Unit (SSU), Central Intelligence Group (CIG), and CIA successors, felt some obligation to the Nazi war crimes suspects whose turncoat cooperation, whatever their motives, made Operation Sunrise feasible and provided the feather in Dulles' cap that led to his appointment as Director of the CIA.

The Pitfalls of Assuming Obligations Toward Nazi Turncoats

Dollmann's postwar career as a would-be U.S. protégé illustrates the vexatious thicket that entrapped the victors when they assumed obligations toward turncoat war crimes suspects. There can be no doubt of the salient role Dollmann played in Operation Sunrise, but thereafter, as an intelligence peddler, he proved to be worthless. His career had sharpened his natural talent for liaison work, not intelligence. Yet, he incessantly offered dubious information and promoted harebrained schemes because he needed money. Nevertheless, after the war, the United States protected him from prosecution as a war criminal.

On May 7, 1945, while they were still at their respective stations in Italy awaiting roundup into Allied captivity, Wenner had anxiously written to Dollmann: "What happens to those members of the Security Police designated as war criminals? Should something be undertaken against this . . . [in view of Field Marshal] Alexander's radio assurance that Wehrmacht, Waffen-SS, Ordnungspolizei, Sicherheitspolizei are to have the same conditions?"[37] Despite their collaboration with the Allies during Operation Sunrise, Wenner and Dollmann remained subject to automatic arrest as SS officers.

The uniform treatment SS personnel hoped to read in General Alexander's radio message—let alone special rewards—was not forthcoming, so Wenner and Dollmann surrendered to British forces at Bolzano on May 13, 1945. They were confined in a POW cage at Modena until October 7, 1945,[38] when they were transferred to a British compound at Ancona. Angered by the "rough treatment" they received, they escaped on December 20, 1945.[39]

Harbored in an insane asylum near Milan, Dollmann received a false identity card from the Italian Military Intelligence Service (SIM), purportedly in return for recruiting two German scientists for the Italian Navy.[40] Perhaps disoriented by their deranged surroundings, Dollmann and Wenner succumbed to threats to turn them over to the Italian courts on war crimes charges unless they endorsed Cardinal Schuster's fraudulent claim to have negotiated the May 2 surrender.[41]

In August 1946, Dollmann and Wenner were kidnapped and taken into custody by the SSU, a short-lived successor of the OSS. They were allowed a limited mobility, and an Italian police officer recognized Dollmann on the street early in November 1946, just when Dollmann and Wenner were about to be moved to a monastery.[42] The SSU successor and CIA predecessor agency, the CIG, promptly took Dollmann and Wenner into custody and moved them to Rome, issuing them IDs signed with the cover name "Major O'Brien."[43] Dollmann's was a "phoney document using same name already on his Italian ID: 'Ammon.'"[44]

On November 13, 1946, James Angleton deemed it necessary to justify his characteristically high-handed actions with respect to Dollmann and Wenner. In a memorandum to G2 of the U.S. Army Mediterranean Theater, he wrote that "military honor dictated that we should honor the promises made to these men." As aides to General Wolff in consummating Operation Sunrise, they had benefited U.S. interests by averting such threats as

a redoubt in Austria, which may have resulted in a Tito or Russian occupation of parts of Venezia Giulia as well as much of the present Allied zones in Austria . . . a "scorch[ed] earth" policy in North Italy . . . to render it impossible for the

Allies or the Italians to restore . . . a bankrupt Italy [which] would have resulted in severe political disturbances [and] costliness in Allied lives.[45]

On January 14, 1947, preparatory to the trial of Field Marshal Kesselring, Italian warrants were issued for the arrests of Dollmann, SS-Obersturmbannführer Herbert Kappler, and SS-Hauptsturmführer Erich Priebke and Kurt Schutz.[46] Of these, only Dollmann was in U.S. custody, and he was ill with an infected ear and kidney.[47] An inter-Allied debate ensued whether under such an invidious spotlight it was prudent to protect him in appreciation for his role in the Operation Sunrise surrender.[48]

In a statement printed in the Italian and world press, General Airey had denied any Dollmann role in Operation Sunrise.[49] But Airey, representing AFHQ, had been brought into the surrender negotiations with Dulles and Gaevernitz only as of March 17, 1945, after Dollmann's last direct participation on March 8. Allen Dulles and Major General Lyman Lemnitzer, the principal American negotiators, however, confirmed Dollmann's early participation. Unfortunately, it was too late to avert AFHQ publication of Airey's denial.[50]

Airey's erroneous announcement was assiduously disseminated by Italian leftists. The assumption that Dollmann was a war criminal dogged him during his lifetime. Perhaps also because he had spent so much time associating with Italians, he had become a symbol of the Nazi occupation to the Italian Left. A May 16, 1945, article in *L'Epoca* described him as an "ill-famed, snake-like . . . man of the nine months of Rome, of the subsequent 10 months of the north . . . the tyrant of the Fascist Ministry of Interior, the messenger of Himmler."[51] That reputation persisted, for example, in *Blowback*, Christopher Simpson's classic indictment of U.S. coddling of Nazi and Nazi-collaborator war criminals. In deploring Allen Dulles' solicitous attitude toward SS war criminals who contributed to the success of Operation Sunrise, Simpson mentioned Dollmann, but the available information allowed him to say no more than that Dollmann was "instrumental in the killing programs directed at Italian Jews," and was "in American hands in 1947 yet managed to escape to Switzerland in the early 1950s."[52]

By the time of Simpson's 1993 reprise, *The Splendid Blond Beast*, more information had become available and Dollmann figures more substantially. However, aside from quoting Dollmann's self-serving observations, Simpson reiterates the incorrect passage on Dollmann's involvement in the deportation of Italian Jews.[53] As we have seen, Padre Pancrazio attested that Dollmann had gone to some risk in vainly seeking papal intervention to avert the Ardeatine Caves massacre.

Conversely, there is abundant newly declassified evidence that Dollmann was not only "in American hands in 1947," as *Blowback* had it, but was impartially shielded from British, Italian, and German prosecution. He was also tolerated successively by the OSS, SSU, CIG, and CIA throughout 1945 to 1954 in his attempts to peddle various absurd intelligence schemes.

Dollmann was undoubtedly a rogue, a wastrel, and a former SS officer, but he was neither a brute nor a killer. The initial Allied reservations about shielding Dollmann against Italian charges of war crimes in the Ardeatine cave case had soon been alleviated. His otherwise personal adversary, SS-Obersturmbannführer Herbert Kappler, as a prosecution witness on the first day of the first Ardeatine trial of Generals Hans von Mackensen and Kurt Mälzer (November 18, 1946), exonerated Dollmann of Ardeatine involvement.[54] Although no promises had been made to any of the Germans involved in Operation Sunrise, CIG feared Axis intelligence sources would dry up unless some protection were offered to Germans who had risked their lives in making a separate surrender.

Against much opposition and consequent delay, in April and May 1947, U.S. military authorities obtained State Department concurrence for Dollmann and Wenner to be taken into U.S. custody and released into the American zone of occupied Germany, subject to its denazification courts.[55] Not daring to show its hand during this process, which lasted many months, the CIG nevertheless wanted to insure, after the fact, that the beneficiaries of these favors were aware of the identity of their benefactors. So, in July 1947, they wrote to EUCOM Special Operations in Heidelberg:[56]

1. Following forwarded for your information on Dollmann and Wenner who were turned over to G2, EUCOM on 19 May by [sanitized]
2. D. W. case taken out of our hands by G2 AFHQ and 46.
Both held in local MP jail under difficult circumstances. During this period CIG made every effort to prevent
   a. turnover of D to Italians
   b. return of Wenner and Dollmann to British custody, and to obtain their removal from this theater.
   With Washington backing this finally carried out. MP detention resulted on souring both; therefore we made no effort to contact them during their detention. Both have information which would place present Italian political regime in bad light if published. We solicit your aid in assuring expeditious rehabilitation and preferential treatment within sep regulations now in force. Desire, if possible they be informed directly of our part in achievement program outlined paragraph 2, above . . .
4. Would like from them some address at which they could be contacted in event future necessity. Also we hold certain articles of clothing and books of Dollmann which desire to forward.
5. Our real names we believe still unknown to them. Name Major O'Brien adequate for recognition.[57]

This attempt to propitiate both beneficiaries "soured" by the "difficult circumstances" of their sojourn in an MP jail was sufficiently transparent so that certainly the clever Dollmann was encouraged to apply subtle blackmail whenever his shrunken exchequer required.

Attempting to shed further responsibility for Dollmann, EUCOM ran him through the standard process during June 1947. He filled out a German registration form and a denazification form, both cluttered with characteristic biographical embellishments contrary to fact, and was discharged from the Waffen-SS on June 30.[58] But he was detained until October 24, 1947, at Oberursel for intelligence exploitation by EUCOM CIC, particularly about Italian political factions, during which his American captors continued to disagree about whether Dollmann, as well as Wolff and staff, had actually risked their lives for Operation Sunrise.[59] He was given US$450 worth of Swiss francs, papers for residence in the American zone of Germany, and ordered to report weekly to CIC Munich.[60]

Perpetually short of cash, Dollmann had been involved since 1945 in several clandestine ex-Nazi organizations attempting to peddle intelligence. To prospective backers, he hawked a yarn about a cache of German armored equipment buried by the Brandenburg Regiment in a cave in Austrian-Tyrol by the gauleiter of Tyrol, Franz Hofer.[61] While attempting an illegal border crossing into the French occupied zone of Austria in January 1948, in pursuit of this purported "Hofer cache," Dollmann was arrested by French military police. Only with some embarrassment did the American liaison at Innsbruck obtain his release.[62]

In January 1950, CIA agents in Italy received an eleven-page report in Italian, purportedly from Dollmann. Bad as were most of the reports submitted by intelligence peddlers trying to earn a dishonest day's pay, this one is saturated with name-dropping, gossip, and insinuations calculated to interest CIA agents. In a sense, both agents and sources were dependent on these reports for income, careers, and promotion. But if this was the best a desperately impecunious Dollmann could produce, it proved that the erudite scholar and cultured, adroit liaison emissary was a total loss as an intelligence source.[63]

In 1951, Dollmann departed Germany for Lugano, Switzerland,[64] only to be expelled to Italy on February 8, 1952, as a war criminal bearing a false Italian passport under the alias "Ammon."[65] He was also alleged to have engaged in homosexual acts, perhaps only as a pretext for his expulsion, but he never denied the allegation. His American protectors soon characterized him with a "reputation for blackmail, subterfuge and double-dealing . . . a homosexual," although the last assumption may have been based purely on hearsay.[66]

In March 1952, he reached Spain via the "ratline," the U.S. Army's system for smuggling fugitives out of Europe. In Spain, Dollmann allegedly came under Skorzeny's "protection."[67] A December 6, 1952, article in the magazine *Epoca*, based largely on an interview with Dollmann, quotes him as claiming to have personally opened two crates containing "the Führer's treasures: golden cigarette cases with his autograph, watches with his initials, pearl and diamond pins" subsequently buried by Franz Hofer near Innsbruck.[68] Dollmann, who had spent considerable time with his Führer, undoubtedly knew that Hitler was adamant in refusing to allow smoking in his presence. Obviously strapped for cash as usual, Dollmann was recklessly appealing to greed in his desperate trolling for backers.

Dollmann returned to Germany in October 1952 on a fatuous mission to locate and excavate the buried treasure trove he had already bruited about to various European newspapers during 1952. Now he added to the temptation of avarice a well-timed lure for U.S. Cold War propagandists. He averred that this buried trove consisted not only of Hitler memorabilia, but of special files on the 1939 Nazi-Soviet Pact purportedly also buried by Gauleiter Hofer. Although Dollmann's description of the special files was adequate, their alleged location was literally far afield, and their excavation by American troops had occurred years before.[69]

On October 7, 1952, he disembarked in Frankfurt Rhein-Main airport from a KLM flight from Madrid bearing a passport in the name of Enrico Larcher, on which the embossed seal had been replaced with a photograph. During a court hearing on the matter the following day, Dollmann did not contest the charges that he falsified the passport. He was sentenced to sixty days in Frankfurt's Hammelsgasse prison.[70]

In August 1954, the impoverished Dollmann approached Vice Consul Alan James at the U.S. Consulate General in Munich with an offer to plant an agent in the Soviet zone of Germany. He presented himself as "Dollmann von Fischer," the bogus title of nobility with which he embellished his mother's maiden name in his SS membership application years before.[71] Presumably assuming he still could blackmail his U.S. intelligence protectors, Dollmann asked James to forward—to President Eisenhower no less—for American review and comment galleys of his forthcoming Italian language memoirs revealing his OSS contacts.[72]

Dollmann was a man of many talents, marred by many character flaws, possessed of superb liaison skills, but a flop as an intelligence agent. An opportunist inhibited by occasional moral twinges, he was trapped in a time and place that ultimately thwarted fulfillment of those talents, while magnifying those flaws. He died in Munich in 1985.

Notes

1. Between the May 2 surrender and the VE-Day surrender of May 8, there were two other partial surrenders: on May 5, German armies cut off in northern Germany surrendered to Montgomery's 21st Army Group; on May 5–6, Heeresgruppe G in southeastern Germany and Austria surrendered to Dever's 6th Army Group. For more on the Nazi occupation of Rome and Operation Sunrise, see chapter 3.

2. For a glaring example, see Elizabeth Wiskemann, *The Rome–Berlin Axis: A History of the Relations between Hitler and Mussolini* (NY: Oxford University Press, 1949), listing both Trevor-Roper (1946) and Allen Dulles (1947) in her bibliography and correctly identifying the former's unidentified and the latter's identified source of their descriptions of the tea

party as "coming from Dollmann later in captivity" (p. 334, n.3), which asserts without a source that the "German Reign of Terror was organized by . . . the indispensable Dollmann" (pp. 325–6). She makes no reference whatsoever to SS-Obersturmbannführer Herbert Kappler, who as a prosecution witness at the first Ardeatine Cave trial on November 18, 1946, had already exonerated Dollmann of any Ardeatine involvement, who in fact had attempted to inhibit the reprisals (see pp. 319 and 328–9).

3. He was the son of Stefan and Paula (née Schummerer) Dollmann. See birth Register Regensburg No. 959/1900, 66th Group, memo of 4 Aug. 1953, cited in NA, RG 319, IRR, entry 134B, box 40, Eugen Dollmann. This CIC Personal File is more precise and more reliable than his CIA Name File (NA, RG 263, Eugen Dollmann Name File) presumably because in the first years of occupation, military government had direct custody of German official files.

4. Eugen Dollmann, "Lazarus von Schwendi und die politischen Probleme der deutschen Gegenreformation" (dissertation, Ludwig Maximilian University in Munich, 1926).

5. Fully one-half of Dollmann's sixty-page SS Officer File consists of accounts which show that during his well-paid SS service he was always in advance of salary and in arrears on repayment.

6. Nazi Party Member No. 349254.

7. SS No. 289 259.

8. Biographical data on Dollmann through 1937 are from his official Third Reich SS Officer File, specifically his holograph vita written in applying for SS membership. See Dollmann's SS Officer File, NA–BDC, RG 242, SSO, roll 159. For Dollmann's career until war's end, see John Toland, *The Last 100 Days* (New York: Random House, 1965); Allen Welsh Dulles, *The Secret Surrender* (New York: Harper and Row, 1966); Robert Katz, *Death in Rome* (New York: Macmillan, 1967), as well as his *The Battle for Rome: The Germans, the Allies, the Partisans, and the Pope*, (New York: Simon and Schuster, 2003); Bradley F. Smith and Elena Agarossi, *Operation Sunrise: The Secret Surrender* (New York: Basic Books, 1979); Christopher Simpson, *Blowback: America's Recruitment of Nazis and Its Effects on the Cold War* (New York: Weidenfeld and Nicolson, 1988). Toland offers a wealth of detail, but is too prone to accept Dollmann's account, as does Katz. Dulles verifies Dollmann's role in Operation Sunrise, but thereafter merely mentions his escape from internment.

9. Dollmann SS Officer File, NA–BDC, RG 242, SSO, Roll 159.

10. Ibid. Hence, the title of his memoirs: *Dolmetscher der Diktatoren* (Bayreuth: Hestia, 1963).

11. Typewritten card undated and source sanitized, NA, RG 263, Eugen Dollmann Name File. In his November 1937 SS application, Dollmann claimed competency in French, Italian, and Spanish, but not English, possibly to support his preference for assignment to Italy or at least the Mediterranean area.

12. Dulles, *Secret Surrender*, 56–57. The description reflects Dulles' respect and even admiration for Dollmann. However, Dollmann struck Dulles' OSS subordinate, Paul Blum, as "a slippery customer . . . with his dark look, his long black hair combed straight back and curling a little over his ears"; ibid., 75.

13. The most thorough account of the Ardeatine cave affair is Katz, *Battle for Rome*. The mostly favorable references to Dollmann are much as in Katz's earlier work, relying chiefly on Dollmann's published accounts and his self-serving statements to Allied interrogators. In a brief supplement, "Pacelli v. Katz et al." (*Battle for Rome*, 353-54), an account of Katz' trial for defamation of Pius XII, which with appeals ran from 1974 to 1978, Katz reinforces his previous appreciation that Dollmann, although a prosecution witness, supported Katz's defense by revealing the warning to the

Pope through Padre Pancrazio of the incipient Ardeatine reprisals. Other than that postscript, Katz's new book does not deal with Dollmann's postwar vicissitudes, except to refer to him–mistakenly as contended in this essay–as "a source for Allied intelligence" (*Battle for Rome*, 24).

14. Katz, *Death in Rome*, 67, 79–80, 87–90; *Battle for Rome*, 232n10-14. Katz quoted Dollmann as complaining of Pius XII's passivity during the Ardeatine cave massacres, which Dollmann initially denied. Dollmann had refrained from mentioning his approach to the Vatican in his memoirs because he believed Padre Pancrazio was still alive, but he confirmed it after learning that the Padre had died in an automobile accident (*Death in Rome*, 247–48). Konstantin (Prince of Bavaria), independently states that Padre Pancrazio corroborated the fact and purpose of Dollmann's visit in his book *The Pope: A Portrait from Life*, trans. Diana Pyke (NY: Roy Publishers, 1956), 257. During an interrogation of Dollmann conducted by British intelligence on August 20, 1946, however, Dollmann denied being in Rome during the Ardeatine massacres; see Angleton memo of 13 Nov. 1946, NA, RG 319, IRR, entry 134B, box 40, Eugen Dollmann, 4. This was either an attempt to deny any involvement, or an attempt to protect Padre Pancrazio from exposure to Vatican rebuke, a protection Dollmann maintained until learning of the Padre's death.

15. Monsignor Alberto Giovannetti, *Il Vaticano e la Guerra* (Vatican City: Libreria Editrice Vaticana, 1960), 255. Quoted in Katz, *Death in Rome*, 121; *Battle for Rome*, 231-2, 379n11.

16. Katz, *Death in Rome*, 121; *Battle for Rome*, 242-43, 257-58 and particularly 260-61 quoting the article headlined "the deeds in Via Rasella" in the *Osservatore Romano* of March 25, 1944.

17. Katz, *Battle for Rome*, 345-6.

18. Preliminary Interrogation Report, dated 12/28/52, NA, RG 319, IRR, entry 134B, box 40, Eugen Dollmann.

19. Dr. Carltheo Zeitschel to Dr. Heinrich Knochen, commander of Security Police in France, quoted in Raul Hilberg, *Die Vernichtung der Europäischen Juden: Die Gesamtgeschichte des Holocaust* (Berlin: Olle and Wolter, 1982), 460n954. The translation is mine.

20. Mussolini's ouster on 25 July 1943 removed whatever inhibitions remained on the German roundup and deportation of Roman Jews to Auschwitz, which commenced in October 1943. Pius XII said nothing, failing to follow up an independent initiative undertaken by his Vatican subordinates, Padre Pancrazio and Bishop Alois Hudal. For a comprehensive account of the deportation of the Roman Jews to Auschwitz and the Pope's failure to intervene, see Katz, *Battle for Rome*, 61-85, 100-116.

21. The meeting was held in a teahouse on the Wolf's Lair compound in lieu of the conference hut devastated by the assassin's bomb. While other men of power entertained guests at their home bars, teetotaler Hitler frequented or maintained a teahouse at every property he occupied or owned before and after coming to power, including those at several of his wartime field headquarters.

22. H. R. Trevor-Roper, *The Last Days of Hitler* (New York: Macmillan, 1946), 31–32.

23. The Geneva Conventions prohibit eavesdropping of conversations between unsuspecting prisoners-of-war, but permit a direct interrogation if its protection requiring that they yield only name, rank, and serial number is waived.

24. NA, RG 226, entry 190C, box 7, folder 95. This document is an extract of a CSDIC report that Allen Dulles obtained from G2 SHAEF at the OSS Mission in Berlin in September 1945, apparently for use in writing *Germany's Underground* (New York: Macmillan, 1947), his book on the German resistance and the events of July 20, 1944. In his book, Dulles

cryptically alluded to this CSDIC report: "Dollmann has given a vivid description of the macabre meeting." See *Germany's Underground*, 9–11.   Dulles paraphrased Dollmann's account, and, unlike Trevor-Roper, avoided near-plagiarism of its English translation.

25.   In his memoirs, Dollmann presented a discursive, self-serving, less vivid, but essentially similar account of the tea party, unaware that his 1945 conversation with Elling had been surreptitiously recorded. See *The Interpreter: Memoirs*, trans. J. Maxwell Brownjohn (London: Hutchinson, 1967), 320–25.

26.   Memorandum dated 20 Nov. 1946, NA, RG 263, Eugen Dollmann Name File, 8. This is evidently a euphemism for a lie detector test, as opposed to an "unscientifically" conducted third degree grilling.

27.   In a deposition signed "Max Ritter von Pohl" on August 15, 1945, while he was held in a prisoner-of-war cage at Cinecittà near Rome, Pohl placed this first political "discussion" at his headquarters near Florence "at the end of June 1944"; see Dollmann, *Interpreter*, 312–14.

28.   See the accounts in Smith and Agarossi, *Operation Sunrise*, and Dulles, *Secret Surrender*.

29.   Katz, *Battle for Rome*, 345-46.

30.   Toland, *Last 100 Days*, 239–40, contains an excellent sketch of these personal connections, which is verified by reports in the NA, RG 263, Eugen Dollmann Name File and other pertinent documents declassified under the Nazi War Crimes Disclosure Act.

31.   This was a disappointment to Dollmann, who had spent an evening à trois with Gaevernitz in autumn 1940 at the Roman home of German Embassy attaché Carl F. Clemm von Hohenberg, a friend of the part-Jewish Gaevernitz (by then an American citizen) from shared years in the United States during the 1920s. Clemm's notes are quoted in Dollmann, *Interpreter*, 174–75.

32.   NA, RG 263, Eugen Dollmann Name File; and Dulles, *Secret Surrender*, 77–78, 91, 94–95.

33.   Dulles, *Secret Surrender*, 95–99.

34.   No date, WC 000757. NA, RG 263, Eugen Dollmann Name File. According to Dollmann's "scientifically conducted" interrogation of August 20, 1946, he caught up with Kesselring on August 26 at Pullach, near Munich, when American troops were only fifty miles north. See Dulles, *Secret Surrender*, 223. For more on these events, see chapter 4.

35.   Dulles, *Secret Surrender*, 105–16.

36.   Facsimile, 3 May 1945, RG 226, entry 190C, box 7.

37.   National Archives Microfilm Publication, RG 242, T175, roll 225, frames 2736802–3. The translation is mine. During my service with an American Historical Association team describing captured German records to be microfilmed for deposit in the National Archives, I encountered a personal communication on Wenner's letterhead (as Karl Wolff's adjutant) dated 7 May 1945, signed "Eugen," and addressed to "Eugen." My description in *Guides to German Records Microfilmed at Alexandria, Va., Records of the Reich Leader of the SS and Chief of the German Police (RFSS)* No. 39, page 8, reads in part: ". . . sent to a friend by Stubaf. Eugen Wenner"; obviously, I was then unaware of the significance in that context of the identity of the recipient, Eugen Dollmann.

38.   Summary of Information, 10 Dec. 1951, NA, RG 319, IRR, entry 134B, box 40, Eugen Dollmann, 2. It was during that confinement that Dollmann's portrayal of Hitler's bizarre tea party to Elling was surreptitiously recorded.

39.   Memo dated 20 Nov. 1946, NA, RG 263, Eugen Dollmann Name File, 1–2.

40.   Memo dated 27 Nov. 1951, ibid, 1. Dollmann promptly made a copy of his false ID on the shrewd assumption that it would some day be confiscated; see memo dated 7 May 1952, NA,

RG 263, Eugen Dollmann Name File, with attached reproductions of that passport. Two German physicists, Hermann Oberth, rocket propulsion expert, and Gottfried Koch, chemist and vice director of the Buna plant in Schkopau, were employed by the Italian Navy in La Spezia. See memo CIA to AC of S, G-2, re: Eugen Dollmann, 17 Nov. 1951, NA, RG 263, Eugen Dollmann Name File, 2. Whether Dollmann had been the go-between, or this was just a pretext for issuing him the false passport, is a matter for conjecture.

41. Telex dated 20 Nov. 1946, NA, RG 263, Eugen Dollmann Name File, 1–2. Monsignor Gregario Bicchieri, Schuster's aide, and Captain Ghisetti of SIM fraudulently claimed for Cardinal Schuster—and thus for the Catholic Church—the credit for negotiating the surrender. This was probably an attempt to prop up Pius XII's justification for remaining neutral, purportedly because he was on the verge of securing designation of Rome as an open city. That way he would avoid the calamity of an "atheistic Communist" takeover of Rome, his very own bishopric. See also Dollmann, *Interpreter*, 340–41.

42. 20 Nov. 1946, NA, RG 263, Eugen Dollmann Name File, 5.

43. "Major O'Brien" was a cover name for the famous (or for many, notorious) James Angleton, who served with the OSS in Italy, 1944–45. He was the SSU agent who "directed the kidnapping of Dollmann and Wenner," (see Angleton memo of 13 Nov. 1946), and was CIG station chief for Italy in 1946–47, and Chief of CIA Counterintelligence, 1954–74. See Timothy J. Naftali, "Artifice: James Angleton and X-2 Operations In Italy" in George C. Chalou, ed., *The Secrets War: The Office of Strategic Services in World War II* (Washington, DC: National Archives and Records Administration, 1992), 218–245; Memoranda of 22 Apr. (p.2), and 20 May (p. 1), 1947, read: on 19 Nov. 1946, "Angleton promptly wired his headquarters in Washington explaining the whole situation." NA, RG 319, IRR, entry 134B, box 40, Eugen Dollmann.

44. Telex dated 20 Nov. 1946, NA, RG 263, Eugen Dollmann Name File, 3.

45. Angleton memorandum of 13 Nov. 1946, NA, RG 319, IRR, entry 134B, box 40, Eugen Dollmann.

46. See translation of *Ministro della Difessa* warrant in ibid; see also memo of 15 May 1947, ibid., 1.

47. Memo of 20 May 1947, ibid., 2.

48. Ibid., 21.

49. Memo dated 20 Nov. 1946, NA, RG 263, Eugen Dollmann Name File, 6.

50. Memo dated 5 Dec. 1946, NA, RG 263, Eugen Dollmann Name File, 1–2. Dulles does not mention this contretemps, presumably to avoid embarrassing Airey; see *Secret Surrender,* 107–8.

51. Translation of this article is found in NA, RG 319, IRR, entry 134B, box 40, Eugen Dollmann.

52. Simpson, *Blowback*, 93n†.

53. Christopher Simpson, *The Splendid Blond Beast: Money, Law, and Genocide in the Twentieth Century* (New York: Grove Press, 1993), 236. Vatican officials Padre Pancrazio and Bishop Alois Hudal attempted in vain to prevent these deportations, possibly through Dollmann in his official liaison role. See Katz, *Death in Rome*, 88, unnumbered note, and his *Battle for Rome*, 106-08.

54. Report of 20 Nov. 1946, NA, RG 263, Eugen Dollmann Name File, 7.

55. The CIG, the State Department's U.S. Political Advisor in Germany Robert Murphy, and Allen Dulles collaborated to shield Wolff, Dollmann, and Wenner from prosecution by the Italian government and even by the U.S. authorities in Germany. EUCOM actually smuggled the three SS officers out of Italy on May 16, 1947. See memorandum of 10 Dec.

1951, NA, RG 319, IRR, entry 134B, box 40, Eugen Dollmann, 4.

56. Memo dated 7 July 1947, NA, RG 263, Eugen Dollmann Name File, 1–2.

57. See note 40 above for the CIG's earlier resort to the pseudonym "Major O'Brien."

58. See his *Meldebogen* [report form], *Fragebogen* [questionnaire] and discharge papers from Prison of War Enclosure 10E, NA, RG 319, IRR, entry 134B, box 40, Eugen Dollmann.

59. 10 Dec. 1951, NA, RG 319, IRR, entry 134B, box 40, Eugen Dollmann, 4–6, based on information forwarded by U.S. Chief of Counsel at Nuremberg, Telford Taylor, drawing on Judge Michael Musmanno's interrogation of Karl Wolff.

60. Ibid.

61. Extract from report dated 20 July 1950, ibid.

62. 20 Dec. 1951, bid., 1, 6.

63. English translation of the 11-page report dated 8 Feb. 1950, NA, RG 263, Eugen Dollmann Name File.

64. CIC Daily Summary, 6 Aug. 1951, ibid.

65. Memo of 24 Feb. 1952, ibid. It is unclear, given his propensity for making copies of his own fake IDs, whether this was the false ID issued him in 1946 by Roman authorities at the request of the Italian Navy, or the substitute in the same name furnished by the CIG.

66. Memo dated 23 Apr. 1952, ibid., 2.

67. So that his Italian escorts could slip him into Spain in March 1952, a passport was issued to him in the name of "Francesco Venzoni," which they thereupon confiscated. But he meanwhile had taken careful note of its content, which he later used to report his "lost" passport, for which Italian officials issued a replacement. Evidently, he had learned something from the intelligence operators among his SS colleagues. In pursuit of the buried treasure, he reportedly entered Austria by way of Germany, giving his name as Enrico Fälscher, meaning "falsifier," which exactly fit the situation.

68. A translation of that article in *Epoca* magazine of 6 Dec. 1952, was sent by an American agent to the U.S. Commissioner of Narcotics; Charles Siragusa to Harry Anslinger, 3 Dec. 1952, NA, RG 263, Eugen Dollmann Name File. Similar articles had already appeared earlier in 1952 by Charles Foley in the *British Daily Express*, as well as in the *Corriere della Sera* and the *Hamburger Abendblatt*.

69. Nazi microfilm of records of the negotiations and terms of the Nazi-Soviet Pact, scheduled by Hitler and Ribbentrop for destruction along with the original paper records, were excavated by American forces from the slope of a pine forest about 300 yards from Schönberg Estate, which was about twelve miles from Mühlhausen in Thuringia. German Foreign Office official Karl von Loesch, who had secretly buried the microfilm, guided them to the site of the cache. See British Col. R. R. Thomson's report 1945 (PRO London, copy in U.S. files); State Department 1945 reports and telegrams printed in FRUS/originals in NA; Interrogations of Karl von Loesch, August 1945. See also, C-Span coverage of Robert Wolfe, "Surviving Microfilm Documenting the Nazi-Soviet Pact," at Heritage Foundation, September 1994, in NA, RG 242, T 120, F-serials, rolls 1–26 (the so-called Loesch series).

70. 7–8 Oct. 1952, NA, RG 319, IRR, entry 134B, box 40, Eugen Dollmann.

71. James Memorandum of Conversation, 6 Aug. 1954, NA, RG 263, Eugen Dollmann Name File.

72. Ibid.

13

The CIA and Eichmann's Associates

Timothy Naftali

On may 23, 1960, Israeli Prime Minister David Ben-Gurion rose in the Knesset, the Israeli parliament, to make a stunning announcement. "Adolf Eichmann," he revealed, "one of the greatest Nazi war criminals, is in Israeli custody." Nearly two weeks earlier, Israeli officers had nabbed Eichmann on a quiet street in a suburb of Buenos Aires as he walked home from work. Eichmann, who once lamented to SS colleagues that only 6 million Jews were murdered under his supervision, had been living under the alias Richard Klement for a decade after the war. Once he realized the Israelis would not shoot him on the spot, Eichmann admitted his real identity.

Eichmann's abduction came as a complete surprise to the U.S. government.[1] The Israelis had given no warning to the CIA (the principal point of contact between the Israeli intelligence community and Washington since 1951) that they had tracked down the most famous living Nazi war criminal and would summarily bring him to justice. In the final days of World War II, Allied counterintelligence officers had assumed that Eichmann would take his own life rather than risk capture. But by late 1945, based on the testimony of two former SS men, the Allies concluded that he had somehow escaped their dragnet and was on the run. The Israelis decided that his fifteen-year odyssey had to end.[2]

Documents released in response to the Nazi War Crimes Disclosure Act of 1998 reveal that had the Israelis not made the effort to capture Eichmann, he might well have ended his years in peace in Argentina. Despite the intensity of U.S. interest in finding Eichmann in the immediate aftermath of World War II, by the 1950s the hunt had faded into the background.[3] With a war raging in Korea and a covert struggle for military secrets and political influence underway throughout Europe and the rest of Asia, U.S. intelligence resources were stretched thin, and there was no political will to divert any of it toward finding the last of Hitler's henchmen. In 1953, when a congressional request to determine whether Eichmann was hiding in the Middle East led to a brief flurry of official interest in the fugitive, the CIA explained to interested U.S. senators that it was no longer responsible for tracking down Nazi fugitives, even the notorious Eichmann. "While CIA has a continuing interest in the whereabouts and activities of individuals such as Eichmann," explained a CIA officer with the approval of the Deputy Director of Central Intelligence, "we are not in the business of apprehending war criminals[;] hence[, we are] in no position to take an active role in this case."[4] The senators apparently accepted this mission statement. Noting that "'the Hill' was satisfied" with the CIA's position on the Eichmann matter, the Agency then queried its stations in the Middle East for information about his possible whereabouts.[5] Finding none, the inquiry was suspended in 1954.[6]

The U.S. Army's Counterintelligence Corps (CIC) shared the CIA's view that the pursuit of Nazi war criminals was incompatible with meeting the demands of the Cold War. As the only intelligence service with the power of arrest in occupied Germany and Austria, the CIC had spearheaded the hunt for Eichmann in the late 1940s. Under the pressure of its new Cold War mission, however, it, too, lost interest in him. "At this time, 1952, the apprehension of war criminals is no longer considered a mission of CIC," the 430th Detachment wrote to higher headquarters in the U.S. Army in Austria, adding, "It is also believed that the prosecution of war criminals is no longer considered of primary interest to U.S. authorities . . . Therefore, it appears the Salzburg police authorities should be advised that the arrest of [Adolf Eichmann] and [his] transfer to CIC is no longer desired."[7] United States Army commanders did not fully agree with the decision of Detachment 430 to wash its hands of the responsibility for dealing with Eichmann. Nazi war criminals remained on a watch list, and if the Austrians were to pick up Eichmann, he would have to be handed over to the CIC. But there would be no new U.S. efforts to track him down.[8]

⇒◆⇐

It should come as no great surprise that an unfinished mission from World War II, even one as important as punishing the perpetrators of the Holocaust, got short shrift in the U.S. struggle with the Soviet Union. Yet, the Israeli capture of Eichmann did more than refocus attention on those men who had managed to elude justice in the chaos of the immediate postwar period; for the CIA, this unexpected event would force a re-examination of some of the former Nazis it had recruited in the rush to produce intelligence results in the 1950s. Some of Eichmann's associates, it turned out, had worked for the CIA.

From the moment word of Ben-Gurion's announcement reached Washington, the CIA was eager to learn how the Israelis had scored their coup. The Agency was not even sure where Eichmann had been arrested and by which of Israel's famed secret services.[9] There were rumors that he had been caught in Kuwait, and there was also some reason to believe that he had been found in Argentina.[10] Just as the CIA was preparing a congratulatory note to the Mossad, its Israeli counterpart,[11] the Counterintelligence (CI) Staff of the Directorate of Operations launched a research operation to scour U.S. government sources for information on Eichmann that might be used to get the Israelis to talk about the operation.[12]

Headed by James Angleton since its inception in 1954, the CI Staff would later be described in various secondary accounts as the CIA's holiest of holies, with Angleton playing the role of keeper of the secrets to a succession of CIA directors in the 1950s and 1960s.[13] The truth was much less grand. In 1960, the CI Staff was a backwater with neither full access to operational materials nor a team of agents to run any operations on its own. The one exception was the CI Staff's leading role in U.S.-Israeli relations: Angleton and his colleagues were exclusively responsible for the CIA's liaison with Israel's Mossad and Shin Bet, its domestic security service. It was in support of this liaison that the CI Staff took it upon itself to do some extra digging to locate materials in U.S. archives on Eichmann.

It did not take them long to find what they needed. Their inquiry took them across the Potomac to a former torpedo factory in Alexandria, Virginia, where five miles' worth of captured Nazi records had been stored for over a decade.[14] Originally under the control of the U.S. Army, these documents—which came from the German Army as well as the SD—were in the process of being declassified. Among the millions of pages of material was a passel of documents detailing the activities of the first Jewish Affairs Department staffed by the SS. Established in 1936 under the supervision of Leopold von Mildenstein, the Department would eventually design policies for the elimination of Jewish influence from German life. This office was the forerunner of the murderous anti-Jewish unit in the Gestapo that Eichmann would later run. Available to the CIA for over a decade but left unexploited until June 1960, these documents listed the names of Eichmann's associates in the persecution of German and Austrian Jews.

On June 15, 1960, the CI Staff handed the Israelis the documents found among the captured records in Alexandria.[15] "In order to assist you in your interrogation of [Eichmann] and for the preparation of your case in court," the CIA explained to the Israelis, "we have been ransacking the captured German documents . . . for material relating to [Eichmann]." Earlier, the CI Staff had sent an urgent request to the Berlin Document Center (BDC) for any files it might have on the names mentioned in the Eichmann materials.[16] Controlled by the U.S. Department of State mission in Berlin, the BDC held the SS personnel files captured at the end of World War II. (The Nazis had fastidiously maintained detailed files on the career paths and family backgrounds of each member—including foreign members—of the SS.) Meanwhile, the acting chief of the CI Staff, S. Herman Horton, sent a memorandum to Director of Central Intelligence Allen Dulles outlining the preliminary results of the Staff's "concentrated search" for materials on Eichmann.[17]

Horton's memorandum set off alarms on the top floor of the CIA headquarters, for unknown to the CI Staff, a few of the names which they were now investigating in Berlin and sharing with the Israelis were or recently had been CIA assets. On June 17, Dulles' office sent a cable to CIA stations in Frankfurt, Hamburg, and Munich explaining the new Eichmann problem and advocating caution. Headquarters' initial concern was strictly operational, not moral or even political: If the Soviets had somehow already figured out that these CIA assets had been mixed up in anti-Jewish work, would they not have tried to blackmail these agents into switching sides? The association with Eichmann, CIA headquarters advised the stations that had worked with these agents, would have made them "very vulnerable and could have eased RIS (Russian Intelligence Service) recruitment."[18] If this were not enough of a headache for Dulles and his team, the West German police had just sent word to the State Department that as a result of the Eichmann capture, they had arrested Leopold von Mildenstein, who was seeking immunity on the grounds that he was a U.S. intelligence agent. The West Germans hinted that they were prepared to drop the charges if indeed Eichmann's old ally was a U.S. asset.[19] The Eichmann capture had yanked several skeletons out of the closet.

Whereas the CIA immediately wondered whether these assets might have been blackmailed by the Soviets, more compelling questions linger four decades later: Why did the CIA have any postwar relationships at all with individuals who had worked alongside Adolf Eichmann in persecuting and exterminating millions of people? Under what circumstances could individuals with these records be considered acceptable agent material? Leaving aside the moral dimension for a moment, what operational value could these veterans of the war against the Jews have had in the clandestine struggle with the Soviet Union? The organization for which they worked, the SD and later the Reich Security Main Office (RSHA), was the intelligence arm of the SS and of the Nazi Party. Like most intelligence services in totalitarian regimes, the SD was more the watchdog of ideology than of truth. The fact that some of these men were in the anti-Jewish office of this already ideological service should have made their intelligence credentials even more suspect.

Yet the CIA was in postwar contact with at least five men who had been significant participants in Hitler's war upon the Jews. Their names are Leopold von Mildenstein, Otto Albrecht von Bolschwing, Erich Rajakowitsch, Theodor Saevecke, and Aleksandras Lileikis. Mildenstein, Bolschwing, and Rajakowitsch had served with Eichmann in the prewar Jewish Affairs Department.[20] Mildenstein had been Eichmann's boss in the SS before World War II. Bolschwing, who also worked for Mildenstein, had been Eichmann's tutor on Zionism and the politics of Palestine in the mid-1930s and then his ally in persecuting the Jews of Austria. Rajakowitsch, who had also worked with Eichmann in prewar Austria, later represented Eichmann's wartime anti-Jewish bureau in occupied Holland, where he participated in organizing the deportation of 80 percent of that country's Jews to the death camps. Saevecke and Lileikis, though not formally associated with Eichmann's office, also participated in implementing aspects of the Final Solution. Saevecke was an SD officer who sentenced prisoners to death in a concentration camp in Poland, chased down Jews for slave labor in Tunisia, and supervised Jewish deportations from northern Italy to the death camps in the East. Lileikis, a Lithuanian security police chief, ordered the deaths of thousands—if not tens of thousands—of Jews in his hometown of Vilnius. None of these five men figured prominently at the Nuremberg war trials; they were the local chiefs whose individual acts of cruelty reflected the murderous policies of their superiors. Each of these men was either employed by the CIA or was considered an acceptable target for postwar recruitment. Before the Nazi War Crimes Disclosure Act, scholars and the interested public had only fragmentary knowledge about the CIA's relationship with Bolschwing. The story of the Agency's encounters with the other four are new to the public record and told here for the first time.

This chapter seeks to explain how and why these war criminals were given employment, assistance, and, in two cases, U.S. citizenship by a nation that had lost over 300,000 lives in World War II and whose moral compass had inspired an international commitment to prevent further crimes against humanity. This is not the story of a dark conspiracy, nor is it one of well-meaning innocence. Each man was contacted separately and by different CIA officers. In some cases, Agency representatives understood the full extent of the criminal past of the individual at the time of recruitment; in others, they did not. In every case, however, unless a court had already convicted the individual for major war crimes, the CIA assumed the tainted man could be exploited without consequences. The CIA did not bother to look deeply into the background of those it was interested in recruiting. As seen now in the thousands of pages of newly released materials on Nazi war criminals, the CIA and its representatives consciously chose to fight the Cold War in an amoral environment where recruitment decisions rested primarily on the perceived operational utility of an agent. As these five representative cases demonstrate, the CIA's approach to the recruitment of former Nazis produced operational failures, moral turpitude, and the risk of severe political damage. The Nazi war criminal consistently got the better end of the deal in his relationship with U.S. intelligence.

Leopold von Mildenstein

Before the Israeli capture of Eichmann, Leopold Eduard Stephen von Mildenstein was more a West German embarrassment than an American one. After leaving the Jewish Affairs Department in 1937, he joined Joseph Goebbels' Propaganda Ministry, where he spent the war designing virulent anti-Allied and anti-Semitic tracts primarily for use among Arabs in the Middle East.[21] After the war, he parlayed his experience with Goebbels into an attractive résumé for jobs in marketing. Coca Cola's West German unit hired him as its press secretary. Mildenstein spoke excellent English, having lived in New York City between November 1923 and April 1925, just after completing his university studies in Germany. He also maintained superb contacts among the German political elite. Despite his Nazi past, Mildenstein was a respected member of the Free Democratic Party (FDP), the libertarian political party that was popular among the country's business class. In May 1956, he was elected deputy chairman of the press committee of the FDP.[22]

Mildenstein wanted to establish a relationship with the U.S. government, probably with the CIA itself. He had visited the United States in July 1954. At the request of an unidentified "foreign government"—probably the West German government—Mildenstein was granted a U.S. visa despite his known wartime affiliation with the SS. In January 1956, Mildenstein himself approached the political officer at the U.S. embassy in Bonn for help in securing a U.S.-sponsored exchange grant for journalists. Although told by the State Department that "his Nazi background" plus the fact that he "was not an active journalist" made him ineligible for the grant, Mildenstein continued to visit the U.S. Embassy.[23] Finally, in May 1956, following his election to the FDP's press committee, he told a U.S. foreign service officer that he had "useful and valuable info[rmation] . . . which he [was] willing to exchange for unspecified consideration."[24]

Mildenstein's interest in serving as a U.S. agent reached the CIA, and the station in Frankfurt opted to consider him as a potential "operational contact." Frankfurt requested traces—a search for any relevant information—on Mildenstein from other CIA field stations and the headquarters in Washington. The local CIA officers already understood the nature of the man they were considering. Mildenstein was an "unsavory type," they cabled Washington, "and probably has [a] continuing relationship with [a foreign government]." Nevertheless, a certain foreign government official who provided this information believed that Mildenstein was the type of man "with whom [a] coldly calculated business relationship" could be maintained "without undue operational effort."[25]

There was little activity following this request. The CIA station in Stuttgart advised Frankfurt that Mildenstein had been a prewar propaganda agent for Goebbels in the Middle East, where he also wrote articles for the Nazi press. It also noted some evidence that he had been in the SS and "possibly [the] SD," but there were no specifics. The trace request drew no other CIA comment on his SS past, let alone any reference to the Jewish Affairs Department. Headquarters, it seems, had nothing to add. In any case, the CIA station in Frankfurt decided not to pursue the case any further.

Mildenstein next turned up in Egypt working for the government of Gamal Abdul Nasser. In December 1956, the Turkish press reported that he had been hired by Egypt's powerful "Voice of Arabs" radio station along with other former associates from Goebbels' organization.[26] Mildenstein's experience in inciting the Arabs against Jews in the Second World War was highly prized in Egypt. This was confirmed by a CIA report from Cairo, which listed him among a group of influential former Nazis who were shaping the actions of the Nasser government.[27]

It seems unlikely, given the released information, that the CIA recruited Mildenstein in Egypt or anywhere else following its brief dalliance with him in the summer of 1956. It was therefore with some surprise that the CIA learned in June 1960 that Mildenstein was seeking immunity as a U.S. intelligence agent. CIA Frankfurt, whose personnel had changed since the last time that Mildenstein had been of any interest, cabled Washington to find out whether he should be protected. "No indication [of] Kubark [CIA] interest since [redacted] 15 June 1956," Washington replied, and "unless further information is available [in the] field[,] no current HQS interest exists."[28] There remains the possibility that another U.S. intelligence service did have some contact with Mildenstein. If this happened—and Mildenstein was not simply blowing smoke in June 1960 to save his hide—then it was probably in Egypt, where the U.S. military attaché in Cairo was in contact with some of the former SS officers who were serving the Egyptian government.[29]

The CIA had reason to be concerned that Mildenstein claimed an operational relationship to weather the storm that followed the capture of Eichmann, but it had no reason to be surprised. CIA headquarters knew very well that the Agency had hired Nazis even more odious than Mildenstein.

Otto Albrecht von Bolschwing

When Otto Albrecht von Bolschwing heard the news that Israel had captured Eichmann, he contacted one of his former case officers in U.S. intelligence, who had since retired from the CIA.[30] Although he was a respected U.S. citizen with a good job at the drug company Warner-Lambert, Bolschwing feared the wrath of the Israelis. He told his former case officer that he might also be abducted. The retired U.S. intelligence officer, who had only a superficial knowledge of Bolschwing's actual career in the SS, could not understand his former employee's anxiety—it was inconceivable that the Israelis would try to snatch Bolschwing on U.S. soil—and so he turned to an acquaintance in the CIA's Counterintelligence Staff to learn more about him. Once Bolschwing's former case officer saw the captured German records found in the torpedo factory, he was shaken, saying that neither he nor others had known about Bolschwing's past, and asserting that "we would not have used him at that time had we known about it."[31] Some of what this intelligence officer did not remember knowing had been known by others in the CIA from the moment Bolschwing was hired.

Bolschwing's Criminal Past

The case begins in prewar Palestine, where in the mid-1930s Bolschwing operated as an SD agent, first undercover as a monk in Nazareth and then under commercial cover in Haifa.[32] His reports were sent to a bureau in the SD that studied the activities of Freemasons and Jews; under his friend Leopold von Mildenstein, this bureau was later transformed into the Jewish Affairs Department.

Born in 1909 the second son of Junker nobility, Bolschwing inherited only a facility with languages and an aristocratic demeanor. Anti-Semitism was not a birthright of Junkers, but it certainly would be expected of members of the Nazi Party, which Bolschwing joined in 1929. Bolschwing's anti-Semitism was largely a matter of cynical opportunism. Jews whom he later met in Palestine actually believed that he was sympathetic to Zionism, seeing in the establishment of an

344 ☞ U.S. Intelligence and the Nazis

anti-Communist and anti-British Jewish state in the Middle East a useful ally for a powerful Germany."[33]

This period in Palestine brought the first stirrings of Bolschwing's enthusiasm for political operations. He tried to meet secretly with Arab tribal leaders to encourage them to assist the Jews in ridding the area of the British. Bolschwing hoped the Arabs would stage a diversion of their own to coincide with a Jewish revolt against the British authority.[34] Nazi Germany wanted to make Palestine ungovernable for Great Britain. Although the term had yet to be invented, the twenty-six-year-old Bolschwing was already aspiring to be one of his country's greatest covert operators.

When the British threw the meddlesome Bolschwing out of Palestine in mid-1936, Mildenstein brought him back to Berlin to assist the Jewish Affairs Department. Bolschwing refused to take a regular position in the office, which would have meant accepting an entry-level rank in the SS and respecting a formal chain-of-command. Instead he insisted on being named a consultant. This decision would later make it easier for Bolschwing to hide this phase of his career. At the time, however, it was seen as a sign that the young aristocrat was too big for his boots.[35]

Despite his haughty manner, Bolschwing worked hard to be relevant in the office. Only a few weeks into his new post, he produced a study of Palestine that attracted the attention of SS Chief Heinrich Himmler himself. Seeing that the office's principal concern was what to do with the Jews of Germany and less the future of Palestine, Bolschwing quickly showed that he could be useful in this regard, too. He drafted a policy document outlining how to solve "the Jewish problem."[36]

The document left no doubt where Bolschwing stood on the Jewish question. He advocated reducing Jewish influence in Germany both by forcing Jews to leave and by limiting the economic power of those who stayed. To get Jews to leave, Bolschwing advocated the use of terror:

> A largely anti-Jewish atmosphere must be created among the people in order to form the basis for the continued attack and the effective exclusion of them . . . The most effective means is the anger of the people leading to excesses in order to take away the sense of security from the Jews. Even though this is an illegal method, it has had a long-standing effect as was shown by the "Kurfurstendamm riot". . . . Psychologically, this is even the more comprehensible since the Jew has learned a lot through the pogroms of the past centuries and fears nothing as much as a hostile atmosphere which can go spontaneously against him at any time.[37]

And if the terror proved insufficient, Bolschwing suggested the licensing of all Jewish businesses as a precursor to their expropriation. Bolschwing's ideas echoed those of Adolf Eichmann and others in the department. When Austria joined the Third Reich in 1938, Bolschwing was invited to assist Eichmann in developing a program for expropriating Jewish property and forcing Austrian Jews to emigrate.

In March 1940, probably as a reward for his work in the Jewish Affairs Department—which by this point had been transferred to the Gestapo under the command of Adolf Eichmann—Bolschwing received a plum foreign posting. He was named Himmler's representative in Romania, responsible for all SD activity in the country. The paper trail leaves unclear what, if any, political mission he carried with him. Bolschwing, however, acted as if he were in Bucharest expressly to enhance the power of the ultra-Fascist Iron Guard movement, which, despite the Fascist leanings of Romania's pro-German strongman Marshal Antonescu, had been shut out of any government positions. Initially, Bolschwing's efforts were greeted with success. In October 1940, the Romanian dictator Marshal Antonescu joined with the Iron Guard in forcing the Romanian king to abdicate. Certain members of the Iron Guard were then brought into the new government. Bolschwing's success was marked in another, even more pernicious way. Following this government shakeup, the Romanian government issued a series of anti-Jewish edicts. For the first time, Jewish property had to be registered. Having shaped German anti-Jewish laws and participated in their extension to Austria, Bolschwing was well suited to serve as the Iron Guard's advisor on how to do the same in Romania.[38]

Whether because of Bolschwing's advice or not, the Iron Guard subsequently overplayed its hand in Romanian politics. The relationship with Antonescu was never easy, but by early 1941 both sides understood that there was little reason to expect it to continue. When the Iron Guard struck first, Antonescu responded with military force. Bolschwing's immediate response was to support his clients. He moved the top thirteen men of the Iron Guard movement, including its head, Horia Sima, into the SD's residence in the German Embassy compound. Himmler supported the protection of the Iron Guardists, but the Hitler regime, in general, disapproved of Bolschwing's meddling in Romanian internal affairs. The Iron Guard rebellion was not in line with Nazi foreign policy, whereas the support of the existing Romanian government was considered paramount, especially in light of Hitler's plans to attack the Soviet Union later that year. Before the rebellion was put down, the Iron Guard gave the Romanian people a horrific demonstration of their hatred of the Jews. The capital's Jewish quarter was fire bombed. Synagogues were destroyed, and as many as six hundred Jews were killed, some hung on meat hooks in a gruesome attempt to defile orthodox butcher shops.

Bolschwing did everything he could to protect the perpetrators of the Bucharest pogrom. As he had argued in 1937, he viewed pogroms as useful tools to discipline Jewish behavior. When Antonescu sought to arrest Horia Sima, Constantin Papanace, and the rest of the men who had challenged his leadership and launched the pogrom in Bucharest, Bolschwing organized an operation to exfiltrate the men to Germany. He had to work quickly because the Romanian government wanted Himmler's people—especially Bolschwing himself—out of Bucharest. Before leaving the country, Bolschwing was able to lay the groundwork for getting Sima and the others out. A few weeks later, the top thirteen Iron Guardsmen escaped from Romania via Bulgaria.[39]

Bolschwing's criminal activities, however, did not end with the protection of the leaders of the Bucharest pogrom. After serving less than a year in a Gestapo prison in 1942–43 (probably as punishment for his insubordination in Bucharest, or perhaps for some other reason), Bolschwing went back into the Jewish extortion business. He participated in expropriating from its Jewish owners a major Hamburg medical supply company called Pharmacia.[40] After stealing 20 percent for himself, he relinquished some control of the Vienna office of Pharmacia to German military intelligence for use as a cover.[41]

Otto von Bolschwing

Bolschwing and the United States
As the war drew to a close, Bolschwing understood that the days of the Thousand Year Reich were numbered. He needed to find a way to survive. His second marriage to an Austrian woman gave him an opportunity to reinvent himself. His new brother-in-law was a member of O-5, the Austrian resistance movement that sprang up in 1943 when the Allies announced that Austria would be treated as a separate country. In late 1944, Bolschwing, who had by now brought his family to Salzburg, began working for the O-5 unit in the Tyrolian Alps. For a less pliable man, the transformation from Junker aristocrat to Tyrolian underground operative would have been too difficult to pull off. But Bolschwing played his new role so well that the leader of the local resistance unit would sign an affidavit attesting to Bolschwing's career in the Austrian resistance.[42]

Fortunately for Bolschwing, the first U.S. Army officers whom he encountered were in military government and not intelligence, for Bolschwing was not completely unknown to Allied intelligence. In 1940, the Poles had reported to their British allies on a Bolschwing, code named "Ossie," who was heading German intelligence in Bucharest.[43] This information appeared in the German primer, a biographic register of all known German intelligence officers, compiled by the British and shared with the Office of Strategic Services (OSS) and the U.S. Army's CIC. Beside Bolschwing's name in the primer was the note, "traveled to Palestine in 1934 in the hope of discovering a treasure chest believed to have been buried by the German Army in 1918."[44]

The reference to Palestine was not the only indication in these early portraits that Bolschwing might have had something to do with the Nazi persecution of the Jews. At the end of the war, some other information emerged that placed Bolschwing as an advisor to the Iron Guard at the time of the pogrom. In August 1945, a captured SS officer named Heinz Jost described him as a captain in the

SS who had not only been a leading player in the Iron Guard affair but also had single-handedly smuggled Horia Sima and the others to Germany.[45] These interesting tidbits aside, Bolschwing was considered a minor figure and no one in the Allied counterintelligence community bothered to investigate further. No search was made for any relevant captured Nazi documents, and nothing more on him was sent to the field. Meanwhile, the U.S. Army did not do any background tracing of him on its own. Instead it relied on an autobiography supplied by Bolschwing, which skipped over the years 1936–1940.

In April 1945, Bolschwing became "closely affiliated" with the headquarters of the 410th Infantry. There he cultivated a relationship with his first American patron and protector, Lieutenant Colonel Ray F. Goggin. Bolschwing, wrote Goggin in the first of his testimonials, "materially assisted the armed forces of the United States during its advance through Fern Pass and western Austria prior to the surrender of the German Army." Goggin credited Bolschwing with capturing over twenty high-ranking Nazi officials and fifty-five officers and also with "leading patrols that led to the capture of many more."[46]

Well aware of his own role in the persecution of the Jews, Bolschwing was eager to create a sense of obligation on the part of Germany's new occupiers that would insulate him from prosecution. He worked for the U.S. military administration in southern Germany into 1946. Sensing, however, that his greatest long-term value would be in the field of intelligence, Bolschwing deftly moved into a contractual relationship with the Gehlen Organization, a U.S.-subsidized German foreign intelligence service under U.S. Army supervision.[47] Bolschwing had tried for direct recruitment by the Central Intelligence Group (CIG), the immediate precursor to the CIA. But when CIG officers in Vienna took a look at Bolschwing in early 1947, they decided he was not worth recruiting.[48]

This initial rejection by the CIG would be an unusual event in Bolschwing's charmed career. He usually made an excellent first impression. Almost every intelligence officer, American or German, who encountered Bolschwing left thinking that he was exceedingly bright.[49] The impression was helped by Bolschwing's facility with languages: besides his native German, he spoke flawless French and English. But the CIG man in Heidelberg, Henry Hecksher, was as experienced an agent handler in Central Europe as one could find. Once he and his colleagues in Heidelberg and Vienna looked beyond the sales pitch, they found an unreliable man.[50] The key to their immunity to Bolschwing's charm was that they did not bother to socialize with him. Instead, they evaluated him strictly on what they knew of his Nazi career. In this spirit, a contemporaneous CIA assessment of Bolschwing explained, "Most evaluations of B (based without exception on study of biography rather than personal association) run as follows: self-seeking, egotistical; and a man of shifting loyalties."[51]

Bolschwing, however, was good enough for the Gehlen Organization, which in 1947 was expanding rapidly. Keen to acquire secret sources in the Balkans, the Gehlen Organization hoped Bolschwing would be able to use his contacts to reconstruct the old SS networks, comprising ethnic Germans in Romania (*Volksdeutscher*) and Iron Guardsmen (or Legionnaires). He was assigned to a unit that specialized in operations in Romania. Bolschwing was one of several former SS men hired by the West Germans for this work in 1947 and 1948.[52]

Bolschwing was not especially successful as an agent recruiter for Gehlen. Despite their loyalty to him for his efforts in 1941, the leaders of the Iron Guard had little interest in working as intelligence gatherers for Bolschwing. Horia Sima and Constantin Papanace were more interested in fighting each other for predominance among the refugees of the Iron Guard movement than in making a small contribution to containing the Soviet Union. Within about a year, the West Germans realized that the smooth-talking Bolschwing was an operational blowhard, not worth the black market gas, cigarettes, and U.S. dollars required to pay him.[53]

Ironically, just as Gehlen was preparing to oust Bolschwing for poor performance, political events in Central Europe introduced a new factor that would bring the CIA, despite its predecessor's earlier misgivings, into the case. The surprise split between Stalin and Marshal Tito of Yugoslavia in 1948 had created a possibility for agreement among the four Allied Powers on what to do about Austria. Since 1946, the talks had been deadlocked by Yugoslavia's demand, as supported by Moscow, for the cession of the southeastern provinces of Austria. But with Tito now considered an enemy, the Soviets announced in late May 1949 that they would accept the British, French, and American position on the borders of the new Austria.[54] While important issues still remained, there was reason to believe that an agreement which would end the military occupation of the country might be around the corner.

The prospect of an independent Austria forced the CIA to think hard about the future of its operations in the country. Since 1945, the U.S. civilian espionage services—the OSS, the Strategic Services Unit (SSU), and then the CIA—had been the least funded and ultimately the least established of the agencies collecting intelligence for the United States in Austria. The CIC, though initially designated to follow matters of security, became the largest collector of political information. By 1946, there was yet another entrant in this competition. The Gehlen Organization was permitted to collect information in Austria on behalf of the U.S. military. The Gehlen Organization (called "Ausodeum") had extensive contacts in the displaced persons camps in Austria and among Germans who had fled to Austria from Eastern Europe.

In the fall of 1949, the CIA undertook a series of measures designed to prepare for the end of military occupation in Austria.[55] The Agency recruited Thomas Lucid, the former chief of operations of the CIC 430th Detachment, the main U.S. military security unit in all of occupied Austria.[56] The hiring of Lucid coincided with the initiation of a penetration operation to determine the nature of all CIC operations in Austria.[57] The Agency intended to keep those networks that were worthwhile and drop those that were not. Concerned about the rebirth of German nationalism in Austria, the Agency also decided to displace Ausodeum and co-opt some of its assets.[58] James Critchfield, the chief of the CIA's Pullach base in Bavaria, played a pivotal role in deciding which of the CIC's and Gehlen's agents in Austria the CIA would acquire. Bolschwing's name had come to Critchfield as a possible recruit to salvage from Ausodeum. For some time, Bolschwing had been making noises to the CIA station in Salzburg that he wanted to transfer from the Gehlen Organization to the CIA.

Once again Bolschwing managed to sell himself as a useful intelligence asset, though this should have been impossible. From 1934 through 1949, his intelligence career had amounted to very little. He had been thrown out of both Palestine and Romania, and he managed to so anger his own government that he spent nearly a year in jail in 1942–43 and was demoted to SS sergeant in 1945. What's more, he had produced very little for Gehlen. An ill-fated covert operator and ineffectual agent-controller, if looked at objectively, Bolschwing had little to offer the CIA. Moreover, leaving aside his questionable value as an intelligence asset, the man was a political problem. At the very least he was known to have harbored the perpetrators of three nights of terror, which left hundreds of Romanian Jews dead and their neighborhoods destroyed.

At this point, however, his value as an asset was not conceived in terms of his ability as an agent. His recruitment was supported on the assumption that he had access to large groups of Iron Guardsmen and Austrian personalities. Before giving his approval, Critchfield requested a detailed background report on Bolschwing. A short while later, he received a two-page document that retold the familiar tale of Bolschwing in prewar Palestine and a discussion of his role in encouraging and then protecting the Iron Guard in Romania.[59] In retrospect, this trace can at best be described as sloppy. The CIA sent information from only its field stations, along with what was readily available at headquarters; no one bothered to check the captured German records in the old torpedo factory in Alexandria, Virginia, to ensure that the CIA knew all that it could about him.[60]

Evidence of the connection between Bolschwing and Eichmann might not have automatically disqualified Bolschwing, but it would have raised hard questions about his truthfulness, since he continued to conceal his prewar service in the Jewish Affairs Department. Critchfield knew, and there was no dispute, that Bolschwing had advised and then assisted the perpetrators of the pogrom of Bucharest. Had the hint of war criminality been a litmus test of sorts for the CIA, this alone would have disqualified Bolschwing. The information about Eichmann, however, could have awakened the CIA to the fact that Bolschwing was a liar who was as unreliable about the present as he was about his own past. In September 1949, Bolschwing had written an autobiography for the CIA that did not mention his having worked for the SD's Jewish Affairs Department in the 1930s.[61] The field representatives did not push very hard to uncover unfavorable information on Bolschwing; they needed him to achieve operational changes in

Austria. Meanwhile, CIA headquarters was too busy or too uninterested to task anyone to do some digging in the files.

Even without the Eichmann material, the CIA knew that Bolschwing was notorious enough that he might become an embarrassment if some precautions were not taken. Bolschwing had never been formally denazified by a German or Austrian court. He was still maintaining that he had never actually joined the Party. Banking on his interrogator's assumptions about his previous life as a Prussian aristocrat, Bolschwing concocted a story that he had paid his brother's butler, who was a member of the Nazi Party, to retroactively make him a member back to 1932. The CIA in Pullach knew that Bolschwing's BDC file effectively discredited this story. These files showed that he was a formal member of the SS and had even been a formal member of the RSHA, which supervised his work in Romania.

The CIA station in Pullach decided that the BDC file had to be cleansed to prevent outsiders from using this information to undermine Bolschwing's position. In late 1949, Bolschwing claimed an expertise in Austrian politics and seemed to be viewing that as the next area for political action.[62] Early in 1950, the Austrian government was starting to ask questions about Bolschwing's status in the country.[63] Despite some misgivings on the part of the CIA chief in Berlin, Critchfield received the support of CIA headquarters and the incriminating files were removed from the BDC.[64] If the Austrians or even another U.S. agency asked for traces on the man, they were to be told that there was "no file available."[65]

In lieu of attempting to stop him from cleansing the Bolschwing files, one of Critchfield's colleagues in the field cautioned:

> At the end of the war we tried to be very smart and changed the name[s] of several members of the SD and Abwehr in order to protect them from the German authorities and the occupation authorities. In most cases these persons were so well known that the change in name compromised them more than if they were to face a denazification court and face the judgment which would have been meted out to them. In the meantime, the developments in Germany and probably also in Austria have been such that membership in the SS, or in the SD, or in the Abwehr no longer is regarded as a strike against any personality. Since I regard it impossible to keep secret such associations, except in cases where a person was a clandestine agent of a given organization, I request you to reassess the advisability of withholding information available in the Berlin Documents Center.[66]

The moment the CIA acted to whitewash Bolschwing's past, this Nazi war criminal gained enormous leverage over the U.S. government. Given that he had worked for a wholly owned subsidiary of U.S. intelligence for two years, Bolschwing was already a potential disposal problem. But the fact that support was now coming directly from the CIA meant that Bolschwing could one day become a major political problem if not managed carefully.

NAZI WAR CRIMES DISCLOSURE ACT

Declassified and Approved for Release
by the Central Intelligence Agency
Date: 2001

EXEMPTIONS Section 3(b)
(2)(A) Privacy ☐
(2)(B) Methods/Sources ☑
(2)(G) Foreign Relations ☐

Bolschwing

Form No. 35-5
April 1947

INCOMING CLASSIFIED MESSAGE

(750)

CENTRAL INTELLIGENCE GROUP

~~SECRET~~

PAGE No.

FROM: PULLACH

TO: SPECIAL OPERATIONS

ACTION: BRLN

INFORMATI: [ ]

ROUTINE

18 JAN 50

[ ]

[ ]

Paraphrase Not Required. Handle as ~~SECRET~~ Correspondence per Pars. 51 (1) 60A AR-380-5

PULL [ ]

TO: BRLNF   INFO: KARLF, WASHF   CITE: PULLF

1. AUSTRIA MINISTRY INTERIOR REQUESTED BRLN DOCUMENT FOR FILE ON A.A. OTTO VON BOLSCHWING BORN 15 OCTOBER 1909.

2. IF NOT ALREADY SENT AUSTRIA CAN YOU MANAGE DOC CENTER REPLY NO FILE AVAILABLE?

3. BOLSCHWING O.S.S. TIES END OF WAR PROBABLY PREJUDICIAL OUR POSSIBLE PLANS BOLSCHWING AUSTRIA.

4. WE WOULD APPRECIATE COPIES RECORD IF AVAILABLE.

Who requested this? This may have been the beginning of all our difficulty.

[ ]

TOR: JAN 50

~~SECRET~~

Copy No.

IT IS FORBIDDEN TO MAKE A COPY OF THIS MESSAGE

BEST AVAILABLE COPY

Cable suggesting that Austrian prosecutors be told that there is "no file available" on Bolschwing. Someone at the CIA headquarters jotted, "Who requested this? This may have been the beginning of all our difficulty." CIA Pullach to Special Operations, Action Berlin, 18 Jan. 1950, NA, RG 263, Otto von Bolschwing Name File.

In an attempt to remove any misgivings at the stations in Berlin or Karlsruhe over hiding Bolschwing's SS personnel records, Richard Helms, the chief of German operations in Washington, had explained to the field that the secret had to be kept at least until August 1950: "Consider it essential [that] Usage [a Bolschwing code name] maintain [his] present position and freedom of movement. [The] [d]ecision to withhold or release Berlin file must be based [on] the consideration [of] which action [is] least likely restrict his activities [for the] next ninety days."[67]

Critchfield himself cabled to Washington in April that "[I] feel we should go [to] any length to help Usage."[68] Yet within a few months, Critchfield had evidently tired of Bolschwing.[69] The CIA Name File is silent on what Helms and Critchfield had expected to happen by August 1950, but whatever it was, it did not happen.[70] By mid-1951 Pullach had transferred Bolschwing to the responsibility of the CIA in Austria. "There appears to be little hope," Critchfield concluded in 1951, "that he will ever develop into a first-class agent."[71]

For CIA Austria, this second-class agent was now expected to revive the Iron Guard networks that he had once tended for the Gehlen Organization. Gehlen had closed the Romania networks in November 1951, perhaps under U.S. pressure, leaving the field wide open to the United States.[72] In January 1952, CIA headquarters authorized operational clearance for CIA Austria to use Bolschwing as a principal agent.[73]

Despite consistently underperforming as a reports officer and case officer, Bolschwing continued to be promoted. Part of the problem was that the people he encountered had little knowledge of Austria or Romania and therefore had no way of evaluating his material. Thus, the chief CIC intelligence officer James Milano, who saw what Bolschwing had given Gehlen, could tell Critchfield in all honesty that Bolschwing wrote the "best reports available [to the] USFA [United States Forces, Austria]."[74]

The last phase of the Bolschwing story holds an additional surprise. In 1953, a year into its new contract with Bolschwing, CIA Austria decided that it was time to close down his Romanian networks. But instead of merely firing him, the CIA station did something unimaginable. It chose to reward this incompetent by helping him achieve his long-term goal: the CIA decided to help him become a U.S. citizen.[75]

The CIA's continuing unwillingness to declassify operational details of the work done by the Nazi SS officers whom it employed after the war makes it difficult to determine the exact reasons for CIA Austria's blunder. Scattered comments in the declassified record suggest that Bolschwing had once again managed to convince some intelligence officers that he was a great political operative. In July 1953, CIA Austria recommended to Washington that Bolschwing be given U.S. citizenship so that he could return to Austria as a CIA officer.[76] Washington agreed with half of these recommendations. The CIA believed that U.S. citizenship was appropriate payment for "six years['] service" to the nation,[77] but unless "[a] more specific plan

[were] presented for future work upon return to Austria," Washington thought it was time to cut Bolschwing loose.[78]

The ease with which Bolschwing managed to enter the United States warrants a study of its own. At root, the Department of Justice, which oversaw the Immigration and Naturalization Service (INS), knowingly violated U.S. law to permit Bolschwing to enter the United States. The McCarran Act of 1950 excluded from the United States any immigrants who were Communists or who belonged to organizations deemed a threat to U.S. public security. In light of its obligations under the McCarran Act, the INS initially balked at granting the visa, but when the CIA asked that the INS "waive [its] objections," the INS did so and granted the visa.[79] "His entry was in effect accomplished," a CIA internal review of its files on the case later concluded, "by the CIA statement that his services on our behalf were of a such a nature as to override his otherwise undesirable background as defined by the McCarran Act."[80]

Bolschwing's membership in the Nazi Party and his wartime SD work in Bucharest were well-known facts among those helping him to become a U.S. citizen; the only real skeleton in Bolschwing's closet was his prewar work with Eichmann in the Jewish Department. For seven years he had managed to work with various American groups without the Eichmann question being posed. He had written documents for Mildenstein, Himmler, and Eichmann that would have immediately betrayed his true face. But until 1953, no U.S. intelligence official had ever bothered to ask him about Eichmann, let alone look for those documents.

As the Agency was pressuring the INS to bring Bolschwing into the country, some final checking by CIA Austria turned up two agent reports that placed Bolschwing in Eichmann's office before the war.[81] Of course, had CIA Austria asked headquarters to check with the archivists at the torpedo factory, the mystery would have been solved immediately. But checks on Bolschwing continued to be half-hearted. The CIA team in Austria had already decided to help Bolschwing become an American. Nevertheless, this serious lead had to be followed, so Bolschwing underwent what appears to have been a polygraph. Finally asked whether he had known Eichmann, Bolschwing lied and said he had met him only twice.[82] Bolschwing's effort at deception was detected, but the administrator of the test decided to explain the entire thing away. The conclusion: Bolschwing was hiding only "a minor point," and it could be left at that.[83]

Thus, Bolschwing became a U.S. citizen. His work for the CIA ended the moment he left Austria, and the idea that he could become a political analyst of sorts died with his operational clearance. But Bolschwing refused to melt away. After working menial jobs for a short while, he parlayed his language skills and his charm into employment at the pharmaceutical company Warner Lambert, ultimately becoming assistant to the vice president in charge of foreign exports.[84] His interest in playing politics had not dimmed, however. By 1961, he was seeking a position with the predecessor of the U.S. Agency for International

Development. Having cultivated some politicians in New Jersey, Bolschwing got himself nominated to a State Department post in India.[85]

When Israel and the U.S. Justice Department did not go after him in 1960, Bolschwing thought the secret of his supporting role in the Nazi persecution of the Jews was safe. The CIA, however, understood that Bolschwing was a major problem. In 1961, at the height of the Eichmann trial, the CIA explained to him that although he had lied about his role in the persecution of the Jews, the CIA would not turn him in to the U.S. Department of Justice or to the West Germans.[86] He had become a potential political embarrassment, and the CIA wanted to hide its role in bringing him to the United States. However, Bolschwing was told that if questions were raised, the CIA would not lie on his behalf. The CIA did make one request of Bolschwing.[87] He was advised not to pursue the U.S. government job in India, and he complied. As a result of this understanding, it was not until the early 1980s that Bolschwing would finally be exposed by the Department of Justice Office of Special Investigations as the war criminal that he had long been. He was denaturalized but avoided deportation. He was already suffering from a terminal illness at the time of his denaturalization and was allowed to die in the United States in 1982.

Theodor Saevecke

Unlike Otto von Bolschwing, Theodor Saevecke did not try to hide from his CIA handlers the fact that he was a committed Nazi. The initial phase in the relationship between Saevecke and the U.S. government remains unclear, despite new releases under the Nazi War Crimes Disclosure Act. Declassified CIA documents suggest that Saevecke was recruited by what became the CIA's Berlin Base (Kubark Berlin). The date of the recruitment is unknown; however, there is an indication that as early as 1946 Saevecke was under the protection of U.S. intelligence and that he was assisted in avoiding a British prison sentence for war crimes in 1947.

Born in 1911 in Hamburg, Saevecke joined the Nazi Party in 1929. He brought with him two years of experience as a teenage member of the Freikorps Rossbach, a paramilitary organization that terrorized German citizens in the Weimar Republic. After a stint in the German Navy, he became a criminal commissar, a Kripo (Criminal Police) officer in the storied Hanseatic League city of Lübeck with the mission of fighting "Jewish and Marxist" influences there.[88] He later moved to Berlin in the same capacity. At the start of the war, he was reassigned to the Sipo (Security Police) in Poznan, Poland, where he remained until June 1940. During this period he served at a concentration camp near Poznan, where he was one of three individuals authorized to approve executions of Poles, Russians, Gypsies, and Jews.[89] Returning to Berlin later that year, Saevecke remained two years before once again being sent out, this time to North Africa.

It was in Tunisia that Saevecke's SS career took off. He came under the wing of Walter Rauff, an SS Major who helped perfect the *Sauerwagen*, the execution trucks in which people were killed through the rerouting of carbon monoxide from the engine's exhaust. Rauff took to the younger Saevecke, who shared his intense dislike for Jews and his commitment to National Socialism.[90] When the November 1942 Allied invasion of North Africa prompted the Nazis to wrest control over the crumbling French North African empire, Rauff organized the SD team in Tunisia into an Einsatzkommando. The Jews of the area, who had enjoyed a mild immunity from persecution, witnessed a dramatic change in their treatment. Rauff used Saevecke to round up Jews for forced labor. About a hundred died as a result of mistreatment or murder. Saevecke's next port of call was southern Italy, where he served only a month before the Allied landings at Salerno in September forced him north to Milan. Once again he served under Rauff, this time as second in command with direct administrative responsibility for the Kripo and the Gestapo.

In northern Italy, Saevecke committed innumerable war crimes. As head of the Sipo and SD in Milan, he personally supervised the rounding up of Italian resistance fighters. When some resistance fighters killed an SS officer in the village of Corbetta, he took ten of his men to the village. There, they picked up three men, none of whom confessed but each of whom they shot. The next day, Saevecke accompanied Rauff and a group of twenty SS men and a hundred Italian collaborators to Corbetta. They surrounded the village and ordered the entire male population into the town square. Five men were chosen and shot in front of the rest. The dwellings of these men were then burned to the ground.[91] In Milan, following repeated acts of sabotage by the resistance, Saevecke selected fifteen political prisoners at random and they were all publicly shot in the city's Piazza Loreto.[92] Saevecke's cruelty also extended to the local Jewish population. He supervised the deportation of at least seven hundred Jews from the region to the extermination camps in the East. In the last months of the war, when more politically versatile men were trying to wash their hands of any role in the Final Solution, Saevecke was still using his authority to press for additional deportations. After discovering that an SS group from Trieste was bartering with Jews to save them, Saevecke had his SS colleagues punished, despite the fact that it was April 1945 and the war was essentially over.[93]

Saevecke did not try to hide from his American captors in late April 1945 that he was in the SD.[94] Although he was careful not to mention any responsibility for killing Jews, he did claim that he had been justified in killing Italian resistance fighters, all of whom he considered Communists. Under interrogation, he told the stories of Corbetta and the Piazza Loreto. Rauff also revealed under interrogation his deputy's specific responsibilities.[95]

At this point Saevecke came under the protection of U.S. intelligence. After somehow managing to leave U.S. internment, he turned up in Berlin, where he was recruited as agent "Cabanjo" by what would become the CIA's Berlin base.[96] Whatever he did was very well regarded. In a brief but heavily redacted discussion of his work, the CIA credited him with at least one major recruitment. The CIA knew that he was an unreconstructed Nazi with a dangerous past. "Saevecke still hankers back after the days when the Party was in the saddle," wrote one of his

CIA handlers. "He is convinced that the principles of National Socialism were sound."[97] Nevertheless, Saevecke was considered a very useful intelligence asset. He was the only member of his CIA team "with practical intelligence experience," and his "comprehension of [U.S.] intelligence objectives" was described to headquarters as "complete and settled."[98]

Saevecke's immunity from prosecution for war crimes was first tested in 1947. He was spotted by the British, who wanted him for a murder committed in Italy. United States intelligence was unable to prevent his extradition to the British zone in early October, but a finger was placed on the scale of justice to protect agent Saevecke.[99] Just a month later he was released as "of no further interest to British War Crimes Group, S.E. Europe."[100] In his defense, Saevecke wrote that he had never belonged to the SS, claiming only to have been a simple police officer in Berlin throughout the war. Although it was the British who had overseen SS-Captain Saevecke's interrogation in Italy in June 1945, the British War Crimes Commission released Saevecke. The Commission asserted that he "did not fall under the Nuremberg judgment" because he had never belonged to any organization deemed criminal by the international tribunal.[101] But at Nuremberg the SS had in fact been so designated. Clearly, there had been a whitewash. Saevecke would soon be working for the CIA.

United States intelligence certainly knew that Saevecke had been involved in war crimes. In 1950, for example, the CIA in Karlsruhe reported to Berlin that besides being chief of the Sipo and SD Aussenkommando in Milan, something CIA Berlin had already suspected, Saevecke had earlier been "concerned with the recruitment of Jews for forced labor" as assistant to the notorious Walter Rauff in Tunisia.[102]

Saevecke's role as a U.S. asset changed in the early 1950s. Initially, neither Saevecke nor the CIA thought that he could return to working for a German police force. "[Saevecke] realizes that his chances of ever getting back into the German civil service are exceedingly slim," wrote CIA Karlsruhe in August 1951, "[however,] he is grateful to us for having provided him with an opportunity of making a decent living in a position akin to his former job."[103] Yet an opportunity arose for him to join the West German federal police service through the *freie Mitarbeiter* system, a covert program designed to secure the employment of former SS personnel by skirting the formal channels of the German civil service. In 1952 or 1953, Saevecke became such an employee for the Federal Criminal Police Service (BKA).[104] Declassified CIA records indicate that a sizeable number of former Gestapo officials were employed by the West German government in this way.[105] These men—who included other veterans of Gestapo operations in Poland besides Saevecke—were paid off the books until they could be transferred to regular government employment. By 1953, Saevecke had risen to be chief of the "Operational Group" of the Sicherheitsgruppe (Security Group) of the BKA in Bonn. This former Gestapo officer was now responsible for the investigation of espionage, treason, and political crimes in a democratic Germany.

Saevecke was a ticking time bomb for the Allies. With state sovereignty not yet returned to the West Germans, the fact that this war criminal was in a position of wide authority in the "new" German federal police was a potential source of enormous political embarrassment. The CIA's decision to turn a blind eye to the *freie Mitarbeiter* system that had furthered not only Saevecke's but other Nazis' postwar careers, added to the dangers. In 1953, the chief of the CIA's Berlin base wrote somewhat defensively that "[Saevecke] disavows all part in atrocities, and painstaking Allied investigations [have] failed to buttress charges to the contrary." The CIA officer added that Saevecke still refused to apologize for his harsh treatment of Italian partisans. "[T]o him partisans were Communists and those Allied services which supported them were woefully misguided. There is no sense in arguing this point with him, especially since history may prove him right." Fearing that Washington might doubt his own political philosophy because of his continued commitment to Saevecke, the CIA's Berlin chief explained that though he knew Saevecke to be a hardened Nazi, "in discussing Nazism, a topic best avoided, I don't feel any compulsion to humor Subject. I have never made intellectual sacrifices in voicing my opinions about the creed and its representatives, about SS, SD, and RSHA and concentration camps."[106]

A year later, Saevecke came under scrutiny for the second time in his CIA career, this time because of the partisan issue. Some Italians claimed that he had committed war crimes in their country, and they sought his arrest. Sensitive to the bad press that this represented, and hopeful that the rest of the world would see the hiring of Saevecke as the exception not the rule, the West German Ministry of the Interior suspended him from the BKA and launched an investigation.[107]

The CIA tried to help Saevecke. It pulled together its file on the helpful British whitewash of November 1947 and sent those documents to the West Germans. As the case lingered, CIA headquarters noted that "it was hard to see how [Saevecke] can escape [the] onus for brutal interrogations in Milan. Doubtless [Saevecke's] role in [the] Einsatzkommando in North Africa supervising deportation [of] Jews to Germany will be noted."[108] The Director of Central Intelligence, Allen Dulles, could not recall Saevecke, who claimed that he had helped the OSS end the war early in northern Italy, but headquarters was prepared to assist him if possible: "Our attitude on [Saevecke] will depend on how bad he really was. If his past [is] in any way defensible, we will pass [to the West Germans] summary reports with our opinion [that] Cabanjo [is] politically suitable. If not, we will keep out."[109] Washington even held out the possibility of maintaining a relationship with Saevecke should the West Germans decide they had to fire him. "If Cabanjo [is] bounced," it was suggested, "[the CIA] may want [to] stake him to [a] private detective agency as insurance against rightist resurgence in [the] future."[110]

In the meantime, Saevecke was told not to reveal that he had CIA backing. Washington was afraid that its efforts to exonerate him would fail if Bonn understood that the United States was trying to keep one of its moles in the West German security system. "[This] may queer the whole plan," Washington noted.[111]

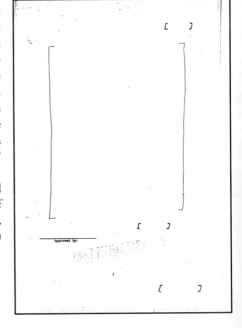

A three-page memorandum released by the CIA under the Nazi War Crimes Disclosure Act of 1998 in which a CIA officer writes of Theodor Saevecke: "Subject took a very prominent part in warfare waged by the German security service against Italian partisans during 1944 and 1945 . . . He knows that it needed a lot of persuading on the part of [excised] to make us accept him as a "Mitarbeiter."

Blank space in brackets indicates text deleted by the CIA prior to public relase. (Chief Berlin to Chief [excised] Bonn, 8 Jan. 1953, NA, RG 263, Theodor Saevecke Name File.)

Although it would take until 1955, Saevecke was cleared for lack of sufficient evidence linking him to war crimes. CIA Frankfurt later took credit for saving Saevecke's job and perhaps keeping him out of prison. "We were able to provide from Amer[ican] files, a body of Info[rmation] which helped serve to exonerate him from the charges . . . That information was passed direct[ly] to the Ministry of [the] Interior."[112]

The capture of Eichmann ushered in a new crisis for Saevecke. It was inevitable that the trial in Jerusalem, which revived general interest in the punishment of Nazi war criminals, would once more cast the harsh light of scrutiny on Theo Saevecke. In 1963, Saevecke became the subject of critical press stories. He asked the CIA, through a Sicherheitsgruppe official, to determine who had asked for information about his Nazi background. Uncertain that it could pass on this information to him, the CIA nevertheless decided to track down who was trying to discredit Saevecke.[113] The CIA's concerns had shifted since the mid-1950s. The recent case of Heinz Felfe, a former SD officer and postwar Gehlen counterespionage chief who had been recruited by the KGB, increased concerns that the other Nazi war criminals hired by the West might have fallen victim to Soviet counterespionage. Agency officials now began to ask themselves how someone who had committed crimes in Poland could have resisted notice by the Soviets in the Cold War game of spy versus spy.

The CIA watched carefully as Saevecke came under scrutiny, this time for his wartime actions in Tunisia. When East German newspapers joined the chorus of disapproval, Saevecke's bona fides as a true-blue Western agent seemed to be established. This time, the Agency took a less direct role in ensuring that he survived the investigation. When Saevecke escaped prosecution in 1964, again for lack of evidence pinning him to a particular Jewish murder, the CIA noted that Saevecke had reached an agreement with his West German employers. He would maintain a low profile for another seven years until he was eligible for retirement from the civil service at the age of 60.[114] And this is what happened. The retired policeman, who lived to enjoy a West German pension, died of old age in 1988.

Erich Rajakowitsch

Erich Rajakowitsch had taken as his life's mission the use of the law to rid the German people of all Jews. Born in Trieste in the waning years of the Austro-Hungarian empire, Rajakowitsch dreamed of union with Germany to restore Austria's former greatness. After completing his legal training at the University of Graz in the Austrian province of Styria, he went to Vienna where he joined the underground Nazi movement.

Rajakowitsch was a lawyer in Vienna at the time of the *Anschluss*. Like Bolschwing, Rajakowitsch had thought about measures to limit the economic sphere of Jews in Austria. Rajakowitsch and his ideas soon came to the attention of Adolf Eichmann, who was impressed. Rajakowitsch, Eichmann wrote, is "somebody who puts himself at the disposal of the cause with heart and soul, a National Socialist of the purest race."[115]

Once the war began, Rajakowitsch was drafted and served with the SS in Poland before becoming chief of the Sipo and SD office in Prague. Transferring in December 1939 to the RSHA, the headquarters of the SS intelligence service, he stayed in Berlin until April 1941.[116] At that time, Eichmann sent him to occupied Holland to be his representative in the Hague. Berlin believed it was losing control of the internal situation in Holland and wanted to manage Jewish affairs separately from general occupation matters. A general strike had broken out among dock workers in February, and there was increasing resistance among Dutch Jews to the introduction of anti-Jewish measures. Rajakowitsch was among those sent to help restore some order in the management of the "Jewish problem" in Holland.[117] In May 1941, all Nazis responsible for Jewish affairs in Holland met to begin preparing for the expropriation of Jewish property so that it could be "placed at the disposal of the financing of the Final Solution."[118] The concentration of Dutch Jews in half a dozen camps around the Netherlands began in January 1942. Four months later, Dutch Jews were ordered to wear the Yellow Star of David. On June 11, 1942, along with Eichmann's representatives in Paris and Brussels, Rajakowitsch participated in a meeting where it was decided that in the first phase of extermination 15,000 Jews would be deported to the death camps from Holland, 10,000 from Belgium, and 100,000 from France.[119] The first trains carrying Dutch Jews left for Auschwitz on July 15, 1942.[120] On August 12, 1942, Rajakowitsch himself cabled a message to the SS in Paris informing the office of the order to deport all Dutch Jews resident in France.[121] Within a month of receiving Rajakowitsch's message, the SS in France deported eighty-three Dutch Jews to Auschwitz, among whom were ten children, ages three to ten.[122] Rajakowitsch left the Netherlands in 1943 to attend an SS officer's school, and he spent some time on the eastern front before the war ended.

The CIC was the first U.S. agency to encounter the name Rajakowitsch. In the course of its investigation of Eichmann in 1946, the CIC developed a lead on a former mistress of Eichmann who had benefited financially from the expropriation of a factory owned by Jews in Austria. The lawyer who handled this transaction for the SS was an associate of Eichmann's named Rajakowitsch.[123] In 1947, the CIC went looking for Rajakowitsch again in connection with an Austrian request to find him to help with restitution cases initiated by Austrian citizens who had lost their properties before the war because they were Jewish.[124]

Rajakowitsch was not far away. In 1953, he came to the attention of the CIA. He was living in Milan under the name Enrico Raja or Enrico Rajakowitsch. He owned Enneri & Company, an import-export firm that controlled a significant share of the trade between Italy and Communist East Germany.[125] Enneri's participation in the export of mercury to Czechoslovakia—mercury was considered a strategic material—led to the placement of Rajakowitsch and Enneri on a U.S. government watch list in January 1954.[126] From Italian sources, the CIA learned that in business Rajakowitsch was "a man of few scruples who is capa[ble] of going into any activity if it is worth his while."[127] But the CIA concluded there was no evidence that he was a political threat of any kind and seemed to have no curiosity about what this middle-aged man had done during the war. The CIA accepted at face value Rajakowitsch's statement to the Civil Police of the Free Territory of Trieste, which the Agency acquired through a liaison, that after being drafted by the German Army he had served as a simple soldier on the eastern front.[128] Despite its continuing interest in this man, the CIA neither requested a check of the SS personnel files at the Berlin Documents Center nor requested possible traces on him from the U.S. Army, which had first investigated Rajakowitsch in 1946.

Despite his role as Eichmann's representative in the Hague, Rajakowitsch had largely escaped notice when the Allies assembled lists of wanted Eichmann staff at the end of World War II. General histories of the Holocaust produced in the 1950s focused on the activities of Eichmann's principal deputy in Holland, Willem Zoepf.[129] There was no cache of neglected documents in U.S. records about Rajakowitsch. The French appear to be the only Allied power with captured materials linking Rajakowitsch to the Final Solution, and they had turned this material over to the International Center for Jewish Documentation in Paris. Consistent with its postwar policy on Nazi war crimes, the CIA never took the time to check these files for information on Rajakowitsch.[130]

Still unaware of Rajakowitsch's SS past, a CIA officer approached Rajakowitsch in Milan in June 1959 in an attempt to recruit him for work against the East Germans and the Communist Chinese. Rajakowitsch was no friend of the United States, but he was civil to the American officer. He discussed the trip he had taken to the trade fair in Canton, China, in 1958 and even handed over the visiting cards of the people he had met and talked with there. But, as described in the CIA cable summarizing this contact, "Subj[ect] was not receptive [to the] officer's efforts [to] elicit his cooperation in accepting specific questions prior [to] his next trip [to] Canton in [19]59."[131] From the heavily redacted materials, it appears that the CIA remained intensely interested in Rajakowitsch's ongoing commercial relationship with the Eastern Bloc. Rajakowitsch had turned down the offer to cooperate; so the CIA instead used an unnamed foreign businessman to indirectly monitor Rajakowitsch's activities and penetrate his trading relationship with the Eastern Bloc. Given the redactions in available documents, however, the nature and scope of the CIA's indirect link to Rajakowitsch in the early 1960s remains unclear.

The Eichmann trial forced the CIA to consider Rajakowitsch in a different light. In May 1962, the Agency learned from the State Department that the Austrian government had sent the Israelis a list of questions on Erich Rajakowitsch to ask Eichmann before his execution.[132] The next month, presumably, the West German government requested whatever the CIA had on Rajakowitsch. The West Germans described him as a former SS officer who had served in Holland. His wartime SS superior in Holland, Wilhelm Harster, had even once recommended Rajakowitsch to the Gehlen Organization as an agent, though apparently he had not been hired. The CIA now assumed that Enrico Rajakowitsch of Milan was probably identical with this Rajakowitsch who had been in the SS.[133]

Eichmann refused to testify against his old colleague Rajakowitsch.[134] Nevertheless, the CIA told its indirect contact to Rajakowitsch in early 1963 to "disengage" from him. Rajakowitsch had previously given the foreign businessman 30,000 Swiss francs to invest, and at the request of the CIA, its agent returned this money to Rajakowitsch.[135]

In mid-1962, the famous Nazi-hunter Simon Wiesenthal announced that he was looking for Rajakowitsch.[136] By the spring of 1963, the European press had taken an interest in him. Fearful that the Italians would throw him out, especially as stories about him appeared in the Italian press, Rajakowitsch left for Switzerland on April 9, 1963. He told a CIA informant that he had millions of Swiss francs on deposit there and a villa in one of the southern cantons.[137] The Swiss, however, were not very welcoming. Within a few days, Rajakowitsch determined he had no real option other than to take his chances on Austrian justice. In mid-April he crossed the border and turned himself in to the Austrian police.

Rajakowitsch had some hope that he might be fully exonerated.[138] Karl Silberbaum, the Gestapo officer who had arrested Anne Frank, the most famous victim of the Nazi persecution of the Dutch Jews, had been found not guilty by an Austrian court.[139] In that case, the Court had accepted the argument that this man was not a war criminal because he had had no idea where Anne Frank and her relatives were being taken.

The CIA did not place any bets on the length of Rajakowitsch's jail time, but it seems to have had an interest in eventually letting him resume his East-West commercial activities in Italy. In December 1964, someone, perhaps even a CIA officer, approached the Italian authorities to see whether Rajakowitsch would be allowed to return to Italy. Once Rome agreed, the Agency planned for the likelihood that Rajakowitsch would be able to continue his activities. "As a matter of information," a CIA officer cabled in December 1964, "should Raja be freed by the Austrians, [a foreign official] plans to debrief Raja under a [code word] and in [redacted] home.[140]

As Rajakowitsch had hoped, the Austrian justice system protected him. Although Rajakowitsch stayed in an Austrian jail perhaps longer than he had expected, he ultimately received a light sentence. He was sentenced to two and a half years, but the duration of the trial was considered time served. The court found the evidence that Rajakowitsch had ordered the deportation of eighty-three Dutch Jews from France to the death camps as insufficient to charge him with anything other than "having with malicious forethought created a situation which brought about danger of life for human beings and which resulted in their death."[141]

Following this slap on the wrist, Rajakowitsch returned to Milan. In spite of all that it now knew about Rajakowitsch's role in the Holocaust, the CIA attempted to restore contact with him. Knowing that the anti-American Rajakowitsch would not willingly work for the United States, the Agency opted to use a false-flag recruitment to gain Rajakowitsch's assistance.[142] In March 1966, an unnamed foreign service requested an unnamed individual to get Rajakowitsch to

> prepare a list of names connected with the Communist world with whom he had had commercial rapport. Subject has promised to furnish [redacted] additional documentation, however, Subject would have to consult his notes at home and office in Milan. Subject said that he could not trust his memory in compiling such a listing. Subject also made known to [redacted] that he would also add numerous names of persons to this listing who are openly regarded as Communists and are, instead, pro-West. Subject made it known that this latter listing should be treated with the utmost secrecy.[143]

Rajakowitsch was not to be told that the CIA was his ultimate consumer. Although it is likely that this indirect contact continued, the publicly available CIA records are silent on what happened to Rajakowitsch after 1966. It is likely he escaped full punishment for his war crimes.

Aleksandras Lileikis

Aleksandras Lileikis was the Sipo chief in Vilnius during the German occupation.[144] After the war, he turned up as a displaced person in a camp in Bamberg, Germany. He came to the attention of the CIC in May 1947, when he was identified as "chief of the Lithuanian political security police in Vilna [Vilnius] during the German occupation, and . . . possibly connected with the shooting of Jews in Vilna."[145] The CIC had poor records on Lithuanian collaborators, and the 930th CIC Detachment could find no evidence that he was on any "wanted" lists. The 930th CIC referred the case to higher authority. Apparently, the Office of the Chief Counsel for War Crimes had equally poor records on Lithuanian war criminals. In June 1947, the CIC was informed that the Office had no interest in Lileikis.

Lileikis had relatives in the United States and wanted to emigrate here. In 1950 he applied for a U.S. visa for the first time. The U.S. Displaced Persons Commission, which received a report on his wartime activities from the CIC, unanimously rejected him, arguing that men in authority in the Sipo were there "because of their known Nazi sympathies."

In 1952, contact was established between the Munich base of the CIA and Lileikis. The declassified CIA records are silent on how or by whom Lileikis approached U.S. intelligence. The materials indicate, however, that the CIA was fully aware of the derogatory information that had prevented the Displaced Persons Commission from granting Lileikis a visa. In August 1952, CIA Munich asked CIA headquarters to approve the use of Lileikis in Germany. In November, Agency officers checked CIC records at Fort Holabird and noted that Lileikis had commanded the Sipo in Vilna and had possibly been responsible for the deaths of many Jews there. Nevertheless, on March 5, 1953, headquarters granted an operational clearance to use Lileikis. At the time, Lileikis was described as a member of the Lithuanian National Union.

If viewed in a vacuum, the decision to hire as a simple recruiter someone who had probably killed many innocent human beings might seem inexplicable. But when viewed next to the cases of Bolschwing, Saevecke, and Rajakowitsch, a pattern emerges of CIA callousness in the mid-1950s to the issue of justice and the Holocaust. War criminality did not bring automatic disqualification for recruitment, however heinous the crime. As interest ebbed in finding Eichmann, the need to be careful about hiring his associates disappeared.

Like most every other Nazi war criminal hired by the CIA, Lileikis was a failure in the field. Lileikis did not even want to play spy.[146] Instead, he sought to exploit the CIA's interest in him and get the Agency to whitewash his past so that he could join his family in the United States. In 1955, apparently without CIA sponsorship, Lileikis once again applied for a U.S. visa. The CIA, which wanted to keep him in Germany for operational reasons, gave negative information about him to the State Department. Yet, for some unknown reason, this time he was granted a U.S. visa. In response, the CIA terminated its "oral agreement" with Lileikis for work in Germany, but it retained its operational clearance for him, presumably in case he proved useful in the United States. The CIA indeed remained interested in him. He was observed at Lithuanian émigré conventions, and when the INS sought to hire Lileikis as an informant in the Lithuanian community in 1956, the CIA told the DOJ that it retained an interest in the man. In July 1957, the operational clearance for Lileikis was formally terminated. The Soviet Division of the CIA's Directorate of Operations noted in making this decision that, having immigrated to the United States, Lileikis is "no longer of operational use to this branch."

Lileikis would ultimately become a U.S. citizen. The Eichmann trial seems to have had no effect on the way he conducted his life. Only in the 1990s would he be discovered by the DOJ Office of Special Investigations and denaturalized for his role in committing crimes against humanity. He died in Lithuania in 2000 while on trial.

What did the Recruitment of Nazi War Criminals Achieve?

In an interview in 1991, Richard Helms explained that the CIA had never prevented its field stations from recruiting members of the SS, despite the Nuremberg judgment that it was a criminal organization.[147] He did not specifically include participants in the persecution of the Jews, but the recently declassified material makes startlingly clear that the CIA did not consider even this level of criminality a bar from recruitment. As dramatized by these five cases, in its zeal to collect information on the Soviet Bloc, the CIA chose to overlook the Nazi past of an agent. In the cases of Bolschwing, Saevecke, and Lileikis, the Agency hired the war criminal despite ample evidence that they were probably responsible for war crimes. In the case of Rajakowitsch, though recruitment did not happen because the war criminal himself refused, the CIA sought at least an indirect contact even after the Eichmann disclosures. Mildenstein was the only one who was not actively recruited, though it is not clear that his past was what prevented his recruitment. The CIA's central concern was not so much the extent of the criminal's guilt as the likelihood that the agent's criminal past could remain a secret.

And what was the value of these contacts? In return, the CIA got very little. Bolschwing was as incompetent an agent for CIA Austria as he had been for CIA Pullach, for the Gehlen Organization, and even for the SD itself. Lileikis appears to have had little interest in spying; but the lure of U.S. protection kept him in the game for two years. Of the five, only Saevecke was ultimately considered a worthwhile asset by the CIA and, given the lack of information available on what he achieved, even that tepid assessment is in doubt.

What were the costs of these Faustian deals? With the exception of the Bolschwing case, which received media attention in the late 1970s and 1980s, the role of the CIA in the postwar careers of these men remained a secret until after their deaths. But the absence of political embarrassment—made possible because the CIA withheld important information even from U.S. law enforcement agencies—does not mean that the hiring of war criminals lacked a corrosive effect. The whitewashing of Bolschwing's file was dismaying to a number of CIA officers in the field in Germany and made the Agency vulnerable to Bolschwing's need for protection later on. The Saevecke case involved the United States in a West German scheme to hide at least a dozen Gestapo officers who were given covert jobs in the postwar German police, which opened the West to Soviet propaganda and possibly to penetration by Soviet intelligence. Evidence on the *freie Mitarbeiter*, whose existence is revealed in the IWG material for the first time, is fragmentary; due to the lack of documentation here and in the former Soviet Bloc, the extent of Soviet penetration of that group remains unknown. The corrosive effect that Lileikis may have had on the postwar Lithuanian community in the United States is difficult to judge, but the presence of this mass murderer in the general population sent a signal to fellow veterans of the secret police in Nazi-occupied Lithuania that Cold War America was forgiving of these murders. The full extent of Lileikis' role in recruiting his colleagues in Germany and perhaps helping them to come to the United States cannot yet be determined.

These five were the most telling cases of CIA recruitment of Nazi war criminals in the Cold War, but they were by no means the only ones disclosed through the Nazi War Crimes Disclosure Act.[148] An additional twenty-one instances of the recruitment of Nazi war criminals or men with unproved but suspiciously criminal pasts highlight this troubling dimension of the early history of the CIA. There was no CIA program specifically designed to recruit Nazi war criminals. Nor was there any conspiracy to protect Hitler's willing executioners. Yet all of these cases demonstrate the mood of an era in which the rush to understand a new enemy encouraged a cynical amnesia regarding an earlier foe. More importantly, they are a stark reminder that rarely can any good result when a country's guardians divorce themselves from the morality of the people they are seeking to protect.

Notes

1. Evidence of U.S. surprise is found both in Eichmann's CIA file (NA, RG 263, Adolf Eichmann Name File) and in his FBI file (NA, RG 65, 65-65842, box 25).
2. NA, RG 263, Adolf Eichmann Name File.
3. U.S. documents make no reference to efforts by the British, French, or Soviets to capture Eichmann in the 1950s. However, materials recently released regarding Canadian discussions with the FBI about Eichmann in the 1950s suggest that though the Canadians remained interested in finding Eichmann, there was no coordinated Allied effort. NA, RG 319, IRR, entry 134B, Adolf Eichmann (1 of 2).
4. Deputy Chief, Near East Division to Chief, Near East Division, 20 Oct. 1953, "Appeal to DCI by Mr. Adolph Berle [*sic*] and Rabbi Kalmanowitz for CIA Action to 'deal' with Nazi War Criminal Karl Eichmann [*sic*]," NA, RG 263, Adolf Eichmann Name File.
5. Ibid., and Director to [excised], 20 Oct. 1953, NA, RG 263, Adolf Eichmann Name File.
6. Because it was assumed that Eichmann was in the Middle East, Kermit Roosevelt, the Chief of the Near East Division of the Directorate of Operations, oversaw what few queries were made about Eichmann. In early 1954, Roosevelt wrote, "Please bear in mind that while we are interested in the whereabouts and activities of Eichmann, it is not within the Kubark [CIA] jurisdiction to take any action in connection with his status as a war criminal." Roosevelt to Chief, [excised], 6 Jan. 1954, NA, RG 263, Adolf Eichmann Name File.
7. Memo, HQ 430th CIC Opns to AC of S, G-2 U.S. Army, 31 Mar. 1962, "Eichmann, Adolf–War Criminal wanted by Austrian and U.S. Authorities," NA, RG 319, IRR, entry 134B, Adolf Eichmann (1 of 2).
8. Memo to the Files, Henry A. Fuchs, Chief of Operations, CIC Salzburg, 11 July 1945, "Austrian police officials were verbally notified . . . that, in general, all denazification type personalities are of no further interest to USFA inasmuch as denazification was relegated to Austrian authority. However—war criminals are to be continued on Wanted Lists until specifically recalled." Evidently CIC Salzburg had had its wrist gently slapped by suggesting that Eichmann be dropped from the watch list. NA, RG 319, IRR, entry 134B, Adolf Eichmann (1 of 2).
9. Memo for the Record, "Meeting with [excised]," 26 May 1960. The CIA officer explained that he had "specifically arranged the meeting to elicit from him whatever I could on the capture of Eichmann. Richard Helms has expressed an interest in receiving all possible details to pass to the Director;" NA, RG 263, Adolf Eichmann Name File.
10. In 1958, the West German intelligence service indicated to the CIA that it had information that Eichmann had been living in Argentina under the alias Clemens since 1952. Chief, Munich to Chief, EE, [excised] Near Eastern Connections, 19 Mar. 1958, NA, RG 263, Adolf Eichmann Name File. From the context, it is evident that this is a reference to Gehlen [alias "Utility"] and the BND's sources in the Middle East. Eichmann was not believed to be one of their sources.
11. Director to [excised], 3 June 1960; Memo for the Record, "Meeting with [excised] on 15 June 1960," NA, RG 263, Adolf Eichmann Name File. Despite the redactions, this document is clearly the record of a meeting of a CIA representative in Washington with a liaison officer

from the Israeli government.

12. Memcon, "Luncheon Meeting with [excised] at Rive Gauche [excised] 1960," 1 June 1960. The CIA participant told the Israeli representative that the United States had already found documents that could help in Eichmann's prosecution; NA, RG 263, Adolf Eichmann Name File.

13. See Tom Mangold, *Cold Warrior: James Jesus Angleton: The CIA's Master Spy Hunter*, (New York: Simon and Schuster, 1991).

14. Author conversation with Robert Wolfe, July 2003. Dr. Wolfe was an archivist/historian with the Captured German Records Project in June 1960.

15. Blind Memo, "Subject: Adolf Eichmann," 15 June 1960, NA, RG 263, Adolf Eichmann Name File. It is unclear why it took this long to deliver the materials to the Israelis. By June 1, the archivists at the torpedo factory had pointed out the documents to the CIA.

16. Director to Berlin, [CI was originating unit], 24 May 1960, NA, RG 263, Adolf Eichmann Name File. This was a priority cable to be given "immediate handling" in Berlin.

17. Acting Chief, CI Staff to DCI, "Adolf Eichmann," [No Date], NA, RG 263, Otto Von Bolschwing Name File. Horton's role in replacing Angleton, who was on an extended medical leave in this period to recuperate from tuberculosis, comes from Raymond Rocca, former Deputy Chief CI Staff, interview with author, 10 Mar. 1992.

18. Director to Frankfurt, 17 June 1960, NA, RG 263, Adolf Eichmann Name File.

19. Cable, Frankfurt to Director, 1 June 1960, NA, RG 263, Leopold von Mildenstein Name File.

20. Franz Alfred Six was another alumnus of Department II Section 112 whose postwar employment became an issue once Eichmann was captured. Hired by the Gehlen Organization in the mid-1950s, he was only indirectly employed by the CIA. Six would ultimately become the head of Gehlen's GV-H department, though this may have occurred after the CIA ended its stewardship of the Gehlen Organization. See NA, RG 263, Franz Six Name File. On the CIA's relationship with the Gehlen Organization, see chapter 14.

21. Chief [excised] to Chief, Bonn. 14 Feb. 1961, NA, RG 263, Leopold von Mildenstein Name File. Von Mildenstein was referent for the Middle East press and chief of the Near East, India/Japan Section, Foreign Press Section of the Propaganda Ministry.

22. 3 June 1960, CIA Trace Request, NA, RG 263, Leopold von Mildenstein Name File.

23. Cable, CIA Frankfurt to Director, 15 June 1956, ibid.

24. Ibid.

25. Ibid.

26. Director to Frankfurt, 10 June 1960, ibid.

27. Cable, [excised] to Director, 3 Jan. 1957, "Combined Allied-Israeli Invasion of Egypt," ibid. The report cites informants in Egypt.

28. Director to Frankfurt, 10 June 1962, ibid.

29. See Friedrich Voss and Joachim Deumling Name Files, NA, RG 263. In 1958, the U.S. Army tried to recruit Deumling, a wartime Gestapo officer and Einsatzgruppe member in Croatia, who was then serving as an advisor to Egyptian military intelligence.

30. Memorandum for the record, 4 June [19]70 [handwritten], CI [excised]. NA, RG 263, Otto von Bolschwing Name File. This memo begins with a discussion of events in 1960.

The name of the U.S. intelligence officer contacted by Bolschwing is redacted. This person recruited Bolschwing in Austria shortly after the end of the war and remained a friend after Bolschwing came to the United States. The U.S. intelligence officer later joined the CI Staff in the CIA but was out of the Agency by 1960. This person may have been Colonel Ray Goggin, who had been in the CIC in Austria and may have recruited Bolschwing for the CIC. He later sponsored Bolschwing for immigration to the United States. It is not known whether Goggin later left the U.S. Army to join the CIA, though this was a well-worn career path for CIC officers in the late 1940s.

31. Ibid.

32. See Allan Ryan, *Quiet Neighbors: Prosecuting Nazi War Criminals in America* (San Diego: Harcourt Brace Jovanovich, 1984) for a complete discussion of Bolschwing's SS background, the manner in which he came to United States, and his subsequent denaturalization. Ryan, who headed the OSI at the time the case was investigated, could not go into any discussion of Bolschwing's intelligence career for the United States. Christopher Simpson, *Blowback: America's Recruitment of Nazis and its Effects on the Cold War* (New York: Weidenfeld and Nicolson, 1988) was the first serious study of that aspect of the case, which successfully used materials declassified through the Freedom of Information Act to piece together some of Bolschwing's intelligence career. A fuller discussion of the CIA's relationship with Bolschwing appeared in 1998 as a classified article in the CIA's in-house journal, *Studies in Intelligence*. Authored by CIA historian Kevin Ruffner, the article was pathbreaking, raising operational questions hitherto only vaguely understood. The article and many of the documents consulted by Ruffner were released in 2001 under the Nazi War Crimes Disclosure Act. Unfortunately, Ruffner's article on this seminal case was redacted and his footnotes were heavily censored.

33. Eli Rosenbaum (Director, United States Department of Justice, Criminal Division, Office of Special Investigations), interview with author, August 2003.

34. Ibid.

35. Ryan, *Quiet Neighbors*, 220-25. Evidence that Höttl recalled Bolschwing as "too big for his boots" comes from Eli Rosenbaum, interview with author, August 2003.

36. Bolschwing, "Zum Judenproblem" [On the Jewish Problem]," 12 Jan. 1937. Bundesarchiv, R58/956, fol. 2-19.

37. Ibid.

38. For a useful introduction to the rebellion of Jan. 1941 and the events preceding it in Romania, see Radu Ioanid, *The Holocaust in Romania: The Destruction of Jews and Gypsies under the Antonescu Regime, 1940–1944*, (Chicago: Ivan R. Dee, 2000), 43–61.

39. See 26 Feb. 1941 memorandum from Manfred von Killinger, the German Minister in Romania, to the German Foreign Ministry, "Report to the Foreign Minister regarding participation by Reich Germans in the attempted revolution by the Legionnaires," Documents of German Foreign Policy, vol. 12, 171-76. In this document, Killinger complains about Bolschwing hiding nine Iron Guardists in the legation without informing him. See also a letter from Antonescu to Killinger dated 1 March 1941 declaring Bolschwing persona non grata, NA, RG 242, T-120, roll 185, frames 89557-58. Evidence that Bolschwing saved thirteen Iron Guardists comes from page 5 of an undated list of available information on Bolschwing, NA, RG 263, Otto von Bolschwing Name File. See Also Ryan, *Quiet Neighbors*, 229-32.

40. Chief [excised] Salzburg to Chief, EE, "Otto von Bolschwing–Local Traces," 28 Sept. 1953, ibid.

41. Bolschwing told the Austrian police that he owned 20 percent of this expropriated company. See "Date of Report: 11 November 1950," ibid.

42. "Copies of photos[tat]ed letters," [no date], ibid.

43. Card from central registry, "Bolschwing, Alfred Otto von (Known as 'Ossie')," [no date], ibid.

44. Ibid.

45. The interrogation of Jost was sent to OSS (X-2) London as document XX-8719, where it became part of the Allied central files on German personalities in the summer of 1945. It was summarized for the CIA's station in Pullach in July 1949 as an extensive response to a trace request on Bolschwing. Undated, "Bolschwing, Alfred Otto von," NA, RG 263, Otto von Bolschwing Name File.

46. Goggin, 7 June 1945, NA, RG 263, Otto von Bolschwing Name File.

47. The Gehlen Organization is discussed at length in chapter 14.

48. Security Control Division [CIG Counterintelligence Division], Austria to Chief, FBM [Richard Helms], "Otto Albrecht Alfred Bolschwing," 19 Apr. 1947, NA, RG 263, Otto von Bolschwing Name File.

49. Eli Rosenbaum, interview with author, August 2003. Höttl was Bolschwing's colleague in the SD.

50. AB-43 to AB-51 [Hecksher], "Bolschwing, Otto Albrecht Alfred," 26 Mar. 1947, NA, RG 263, Otto von Bolschwing Name File. After talking to a few of the U.S. Army officers in military government who had worked with Bolschwing in Munich, CIA Heidelberg determined that Bolschwing was "unreliable and of negative character." After receiving this information from Heidelberg and apparently some from Washington, the counterespionage group at CIG Vienna (code named "Security Control Division" in this period), decided "not to use Subject in any capacity." Security Control Division, Austria to Chief FBM [Richard Helms], 19 Apr. 1947, "Otto Albrecht Alfred Bolschwing," NA, RG 263, Otto von Bolschwing Name File. The information sent by CIA HQ to Vienna in April 1947 was not found among the released documents in the Name File. Evidence that Hecksher is AB-51 comes from NA, RG 226, entry 108A, box 287, 1wx-002-1017b. He was chief of Security Control, AMZON, headquartered in Heidelberg [lwx-002-1017c]. In later years, James Critchfield would recall that Bolschwing was "very charming." James Critchfield, interview with author, November 2002.

51. Memo, "Unrest (Bolschwing) Files," [undated, but probably late 1949], NA, RG 263, Otto von Bolschwing Name File.

52. Other SS veterans recruited to work on Romania and Hungary were Kurt Auner and Josef Urban. See Kurt Auner and Josef Urban Name Files in NA, RG 263.

53. Memo, "Unrest (Bolschwing) Files," [undated, but probably late 1949], NA, RG 263, Otto von Bolschwing Name File. See also NA, RG 263, Horia Sima Name File.

54. John W. Wheeler-Bennett and Anthony Nicholls, *The Semblance of Peace: The Political Settlement after the Second World War* (New York: St. Martin's Press, 1972), 474–76.

55. Ultimately it would take another five years and the death of Josef Stalin to negotiate the

Austrian State Treaty. The CIA did not anticipate this delay in 1949.

56. James Critchfield, interview with author, 17 Aug. 2002.

57. James Critchfield, *Partners at the Creation: The Men Behind Postwar Germany's Defense and Intelligence Establishments* (Annapolis, MD: Naval Institute Press, 2003); Kevin Ruffner, "The Case of Otto Albrecht Alfred von Bolschwing," *Studies in Intelligence* (1998), NA, RG 263, CIA Subject File.

58. Memo, "Unrest (Bolschwing) Files," [undated, but probably late 1949], NA, RG 263, Otto von Bolschwing Name File. The memo makes the point that having figured this goal out, Bolschwing was using it to cozy up to the CIA.

59. "Bolschwing, Otto Alfred von," [No date but the handwritten notation "Pouch to Pull, 1 July 49"], NA, RG 263, Otto von Bolschwing Name File.

60. See Blind Memo, "Subject: Otto Albrecht Alfred von Bolschwing," 10 Apr. 1961 for evidence that the material relating to Bolschwing at the torpedo factory was seen by the CIA as a result of the hunt for documents on Eichmann, NA, RG 263, Otto von Bolschwing Name File.

61. Bolschwing, "Statement of Life History," 14 Sept. 1949, NA, RG 263, Otto von Bolschwing Name File.

62. Memo, William Philp, 1 Sept. 1949, Philp collection, the Hoover Institution. Colonel Philp discussed the future of Austria with Bolschwing, whose views garnered enormous respect from U.S. military and intelligence officials, despite the fact that Bolschwing was not Austrian and had lived there for only five years.

63. Ruffner, "The Case of Otto Albrecht Alfred von Bolschwing," *Studies in Intelligence* (1998), NA, RG 263, CIA Subject File.

64. CIA Berlin to Special Operations, Action Pullach, 27 Jan. 1950, NA, RG 263, Otto von Bolschwing Name File.

65. CIA Pullach to Special Operations, Action Berlin, 18 Jan. 1950, ibid.

66. Chief [excised] Karlsruhe to Chief, Pullach, 24 Apr. 1950, ibid.

67. Special Operations to Pullach, Karlsruhe, Berlin, 16 May 1950, ibid. Bolschwing also carried the code name "Grossbahn."

68. Pullach to Special Operations, 25 Apr. 1950, ibid.

69. Ruffner, "The Case of Otto Albrecht Alfred von Bolschwing," *Studies in Intelligence* (1998), NA, RG 263, CIA Subject File.

70. One possibility is that Helms and Critchfield were moved to protect Bolschwing because of a rare opportunity to gain Soviet cryptographic information. On the basis of interviews done in the 1980s, Mary Ellen Reese wrote that Bolschwing was involved in a CIA effort to buy Soviet ciphers in Vienna in the spring of 1950. Reese, *General Reinhard Gehlen: The CIA Connection* (Fairfax, VA: George Mason University Press, 1990), 114–18. In Reese's account, one of Bolschwing's agents in Austria had provided the lead to the cipher material. This CIA case—without any reference to Bolschwing—was first mentioned in the memoirs of Peer de Silva, an officer at the CIA station in Pullach. De Silva, *Sub Rosa: the CIA and the Uses of Intelligence* (New York: Times Books, 1978), 42–52.

71. Ibid.

72. [Undated] Trace results, NA, RG 263, Ernest Schlandt Name File. Schlandt, a former liaison officer in the SS Amt VI-Z Ost, was also a postwar member of GV-A. It appears he was not

picked up with Bolschwing.

73. Chief [excised] Salzburg to Chief [excised] Germany, "Grossbahn–U.S. Visa," 24 July 1953, NA, RG 263, Otto von Bolschwing Name File; operational clearances for Bolschwing were signed off by the CIA's Deputy Director, Plans. See "Project Termination," 22 Dec. 1953, ibid.

74. Blind memo, [traces, circa 1951], NA, RG 263, Otto von Bolschwing Name File.

75. Memo, "Unrest (Bolschwing) Files," [undated, but probably late 1949], ibid.

76. Chief [excised] Salzburg to Chief, EE; Attn [excised], "Grossbahn–U.S. Visa," 14 Aug. 1953, NA, RG 263, Otto von Bolschwing Name File. This document refers to a July document on the same topic.

77. This is how Salzburg put Washington's explanation of the gift of citizenship to Bolschwing. Cable, Senior Representative, Vienna to Director, CIA, 18 Sept. 1953, NA, RG 263, Otto von Bolschwing Name File.

78. Cable, Director, CIA to Senior Representative, Vienna, 28 Aug. 1953, ibid.

79. Ibid. This cable provides evidence of the CIA request to INS that it break the law.

80. Blind Memo, [undated], NA, RG 263, Otto von Bolschwing Name File. Bolschwing also benefited from the good relationship that the CIA representative in Munich had with the local State Department Consular official, who was very helpful; see Chief [excised] Salzburg to Chief, EE, Attn: [excised], 14 Aug. 1953, "Grossbahn–U.S. Visa," ibid.

81. One of the remaining mysteries of this case is why the CIA did not circumvent the INS entirely. According to the National Security Act of 1947, the Director of Central Intelligence has the right to bring up to one hundred aliens into the country per year if deemed in the national interest. Bolschwing, however, was determined to be "ineligible" for this blanket provision. No explanation was given in the file. See Cable, Director CIA to Senior Representative, Austria, 28 Aug. 1953, NA, RG 263, Otto von Bolschwing Name File.

82. A decade later Eichmann would testify to the many discussions he had had with Bolschwing about Zionism and Palestine.

83. Ruffner, "The Case of Otto Albrecht Alfred von Bolschwing," *Studies in Intelligence* (1998), NA, RG 263, CIA Subject File, 68.

84. Ryan, *Quiet Neighbors*, 243; and Chief [excised] Vienna to Chief, EE, 26 July 1955, NA, RG 263, Otto von Bolschwing Name File.

85. C/CI to Chief/CI/[excised], 2 Feb. 1961, "Otto Albrecht Alfred von Bolschwing," 2 Feb. 1961, ibid.; Gordon M. Stewart, Chief EE, to Chief of Operations, DDP, [Richard Helms], "Otto Albrecht Alfred von Bolschwing," 10 May 1961, ibid.

86. CI [excised] to Chief, EE [excised], "Otto Albrecht Alfred von Bolschwing," 15 May 1961, ibid.

87. Ibid.

88 Saevecke, "Lebenslauf," NA, RG 263, Theodor Saevecke Name File.

89. Chief, EE to Chief, Germany and Chief, Bonn, 6 Jan. 1964, ibid. A CIA informant related the story that "Whenever one of the inmates was executed, a form notice would appear on the bulletin board with a check-mark in the square which designated death by either firing squad or hanging. These forms contained three signatures, one of which was often Saevecke's."

90. See NA, RG 263, Walter Rauff Name File.

91. CSDIC, H.T. Shergold, First detailed Interrogation report on Five PW From the Sipo and

SD Aussenkommando Milan, 4 June 1945, NA, RG 263, Theodor Saevecke Name File.

92. Ibid.

93. Ibid.

94. Saevecke, who appeared on page 91 of the CROWCASS list of Nazi war criminals, did not need to. Dachau Detachment 7708 War Crimes Group, 9 Sept. 1947, NA, RG 263, Theodor Saevecke Name File.

95. NA, RG 263, Walter Rauff Name File.

96. TC Hughes to CO, Hdqs. 66th CIC Group, 19 July 1954, NA, RG 263, Theodor Saevecke Name File. This code name would stick with him throughout his CIA career. The released materials do not clarify exactly when Saevecke was recruited by U.S. intelligence.

97. Chief, [excised] Karlsruhe to Chief, Foreign Division "M" [Richard Helms], 6 Aug. 1951, NA, RG 263, Theodor Saevecke Name File.

98. Ibid.

99. See NA, RG 263, Ludwig Nebel Name File for evidence of how indicted war criminals could be shielded from extradition if they had cooperated with Allied intelligence.

100. Major John C. Boyd, Chief, Apprehension Section, Dachau Detachment, 7708 War Crimes Group, U.S. Army to CO, War Crimes Enclosure, Dachau, U.S. Army, 10 Nov. 1947, NA, RG 263, Theodor Saevecke Name File.

101. Memo, "Saevecke, Theo," 12 Dec. 1947, ibid.

102 Chief, Karlsruhe to Chief [excised] Attn: Berlin, 24 Oct. 1950, ibid. But this did not disqualify him for intelligence recruitment.

103. Chief, [excised] Karlsruhe to Chief, Foreign Division "M" [Richard Helms], 6 Aug. 1951, NA, RG 263, Theodor Saevecke Name File.

104. Chief, Berlin to Chief [excised] Bonn, 8 Jan. 1953, ibid. It appears that the idea to make him a *freie Mitarbeiter* did not come from the CIA. The Chief of the Berlin Base wrote in January 1953 that "it needed a lot of persuading on the part of [foreign businessman] to make us accept him as a 'Mitarbeiter.'"

105. See the Karl Gustav Halswick and Oskar Hein Name Files, NA, RG 263.

106. Chief Berlin to Chief [excised] Bonn, 8 Jan. 1953, NA, RG 263, Theodor Saevecke Name File.

107. Memorandum to Richard Helms, Chief of Operations, DD/P, 8 July 1954, ibid.

108. Director, CIA to Senior Representative Bonn, Frankfurt, 12 July 1954, ibid.

109. Ibid.

110. Ibid.

111. Ibid.

112. Cable, CIA Frankfurt to Director, 28 Feb. 1963, ibid.

113. Chief, Bonn to COS/G EE Division, 30 Apr. 1963, ibid.

114. CIA Frankfurt to Director, 29 Jan. 1964, ibid.

115. Cited in "End of the Chase," *Time Magazine*, 26 Apr. 1963, NA, RG 263, Erich Rajakowitsch Name File.

116. Chief [excised] to Chief [excised] Austria, "Traces on Dr. Erich Rajakowitsch," 12 Mar. 1963, ibid., vol. 1; Source [Austrian Police], "Translation," 28 Jan. 1949, ibid.

117. Time, "End of the Chase," 26 Apr. 1963, ibid., vol. 2; On Jewish resistance in the Netherlands

in 1941 and the Nazi response, see Leni Yahil, *The Holocaust: The Fate of European Jewry, 1932–1945*, trans. Ina Friedman and Haya Galai (New York: Oxford University Press, 1990), 176. Rajakowitsch was in Eichmann's Amt IV B 4, the Jewish section of the Gestapo.

118. Yahil, *Holocaust*, 337–39.

119. Captured German document [French translation], Paris, 15 June 1942, NA, RG 263, Erich Rajakowitsch Name File. Rajakowitsch is not referred to by name in the document. His attendance is assumed, given that the document refers to the fact that "those responsible for the Jewish sections in Brussels and the Hague" attended the meeting in Paris where these decisions were made.

120. Yahil, *Holocaust*, 391.

121. French Ministry of the Interior, "Note au sujet des deportations de Juifs Neerlandais" [Memorandum regarding the deportations of Dutch Jews] 21 Aug. 1963, NA, RG 263, Erich Rajakowitsch Name File.

122. Ibid. Only one of these eighty-three Jews survived the war. See Cable, Department of State, Vienna to Washington, "Raja Trial Verdict," 5 Mar. 1965, NA, RG 263, Erich Rajakowitsch Name File.

123. See NA, RG 263, Adolf Eichmann Name File.

124. NA, RG 319, IRR, entry 134B, Erich Rajakowitsch, file XA019421.

125. The CIA Name File on Rajakowitsch contains two reports on "Enrico" Rajakowitsch (alias Enrico Raja) and the Enneri Company from Apr. 1953. A 25 Feb. 1959 list of traces mentions a 16 Feb. 1953 report on him and Enneri, but none earlier. See NA, RG 263, Erich Rajakowitsch Name File.

126. Trace list, "Raja, Enrico," [No date but reference to Memo from Acting Chief, SE to Chief, RI, 11 Jan. 1954], NA, RG 263, Erich Rajakowitsch Name File.

127. Report No. [excised], "Enrico Rajakowitsch (Alias Raja) and the Enneri Co., Trieste," 11 Apr. 1953, NA, RG 263, Erich Rajakowitsch Name File.

128. Chief WE to Chief [excised], 27 Mar. 1959, ibid.

129. See, for example, Gerald Reitlinger, *The Final Solution: The Attempt to Exterminate the Jews of Europe, 1939-1945* (South Brunswick, NJ: T. Yoseloff, 1968), 360–63.

130. See Attachment 1, Chief [excised] to Chief [excised], 23 Dec. 1964, NA, RG 263, Erich Rajakowitsch Name File. This French-language document appears to have been generated by individuals sympathetic to Rajakowitsch. His allies argued that Rajakowitsch was too far down the chain of command to be held responsible for the extermination of the Jews of Holland and, in any case, was not likely to have known that deportation meant death. The document is useful because it discusses the provenance of the documents introduced in court by the Austrian prosecutor.

131. Cable, CIA HQ to CIA Vienna, 4 Mar. 1963, NA, RG 263, Erich Rajakowitsch Name File. Initially, information about the attempted recruitment in 1959 was redacted from the materials turned over to the IWG by the CIA. In response to an IWG request for a re-review of thirteen files, including that on Rajakowitsch, the CIA declassified a paragraph summarizing this approach, which appeared in this 4 Mar. 1963 cable to the field. Other paragraphs on the approach which appear in Dispatch, Chief, EE to Chief, Munich, 16 July 1962; and in Dispatch, Chief [excised] to Chief [excised], 12 Mar. 1963, both in the Erich

Rajakowitsch Name File, remain classified. No documents from 1959 describing the project for which Rajakowitsch was considered a suitable lead or the actual report on the CIA's meeting with him have been released.

132. Telegram, State Tel Aviv to Sec. State, 7 May 1962, NA, RG 263, Erich Rajakowitsch Name File.

133. Munich to Director, 29 June 1962, NA, RG 263, ibid. The identity of the service that requested the traces is redacted in the file. It is assumed this is the West German government, given the nearby location of the West German foreign intelligence service's [BND] headquarters; "Traces on Dr. Erich Rajakowitsch," 12 Mar. 1963, ibid.

134. Cable, Director to [excised] Vienna, 4 Mar. 1963, ibid.

135. CIA Cable, 9 Apr. 1963, ibid.

136. "Traces on Dr. Erich Rajakowitsch," 12 Mar. 1963, ibid.

137. CIA Cable, 12 Apr. 1963, ibid.

138. Dispatch, Chief [excised] to Chief [excised], 23 Dec. 1964, "Eric Rajacovich aka Raja aka Erick Rajokowic aka Enrico Raja," ibid.

139. This is mentioned in the brief supportive of Rajakowitsch acquired by the CIA. See Attachment 1, Chief [excised] to Chief [excised], 23 Dec. 1964, ibid.

140. Dispatch, Chief [excised] to Chief [excised], 23 Dec. 1964, "Eric Rajacovich aka Raja aka Erick Rajokowic aka Enrico Raja," ibid. This document, with the substitute language "foreign official" and "codeword," was released as the result of an IWG request for a re-review of the Rajakowitsch Name File in 2002.

141. Cable, Vienna to DOS, 5 Mar. 1965, ibid.

142. A false-flag recruitment involves making the agent assume he is working for an intelligence service other than the one that is actually doing the hiring.

143. Dispatch, 4 Mar. 1966, Chief [excised] to Chief [excised], "Reference [excised]; Subject: Erik Raja [excised]," NA, RG 263, Erich Rajakowitsch Name File.

144. Unless otherwise noted, all quotations come from materials in Lileikis' CIA file: NA, RG 263, Aleksandras Lileikis Name File.

145. See the Pincer Report, "Former Official of Lithuanian Political Police under German Occupation /Gestapo/now in Bamburg/M50-024," 10 Apr. 1947.

146. The precise nature of Lileikis' work for the CIA remains unclear, but the duration alone and the fact that the CIA did not help him get into the United States suggests that Lileikis was not the recruiter that he was expected to be.

147. Richard Helms, interview with author, 12 Mar. 1991.

148. Among the 743 Name Files released by the CIA are other examples of CIA Cold War recruitment of former SS men. See the Robert Ancans, Heinrich Bandholz, Friedrich Carstenn, Eduard Fischer, Karl Otto Jobke, Hans Otto, Nikolai Poppe, Hans Rues, Hans Seebolde, Eberhard Tellkamp, and Helmut Vogt Name Files, all in NA, RG 263. The Arturs Brombergs, Xhafer Deva, Hasan Dosti, Jose Garrette, Wilhelm Gruenwaldt, Peteris Janelsins, Mikola Lebed, Walter Mehnert, Radislaw Ostrowsky, and Stanislaw Stankiewicz Name Files provide examples of individuals recruited by the CIA who, though not SS veterans, nevertheless had criminal pasts in World War II.

14

Reinhard Gehlen and the United States

Timothy Naftali

THERE COULD BE NO MORE AMERICAN an event. It was the sixth and final game of the 1951 World Series. The New York Yankees, who came into this game leading the Giants three games to two, would ultimately win the championship, 4-3. Years later, sports fans would refer to 1951 as "the season of changes." This was the year that Joe DiMaggio, the Yankee Clipper, decided to retire. And it was also the season that introduced a new generation of ballplayers led by future hall-of-famers Mickey Mantle and Willie Mays.

There were 61,000 individual stories in the stands that day. Most of the men were World War II veterans. The women cheering alongside them might well have worked in a factory to keep the bombers flying and the ammunition dumps overseas filled. Some had lost loved ones in the war; indeed, there was probably no one at the game who did not know a family who had experienced a death. All were grateful that the war was over and that they were now sharing some peacetime prosperity.

Not everyone who saw DiMaggio play his last game had fought on the same side in the Second World War. Wearing tinted glasses and feeling somewhat uncomfortable at his first baseball game was a trim, well-dressed, middle-aged man of average height sitting with a group of similarly well-dressed middle-aged men. His visa indicated that he was a German businessman who specialized in international patent issues. What it did not say was that seven years earlier, Adolf Hitler had promoted this man to generalmajor (brigadier general) for his intelligence work on the eastern front. His documents also did not record that he was in the United States as the guest of the CIA, which for over two years had been subsidizing him in the expectation that he would one day become the first chief of a centralized West German intelligence service.

Reinhard Gehlen would never again be as anonymous as he was at Yankee Stadium in October 1951. The next year, his name began appearing in some Western newspaper accounts, which revealed his ties to U.S. intelligence and his ambitions for the future.[1] These first Western reports were merely the prelude to a massive Soviet propaganda campaign that would make Gehlen the poster child of an alleged postwar alliance between the NATO powers and the military leadership of the collapsed Third Reich. Even after his retirement from West German intelligence in 1968, Gehlen continued to inspire some fascination as Europe's greatest mystery man of the postwar period. To this day, his name is linked with neo-Fascist movements, Nazi war criminals, and even the KGB.

Beginning with those newspaper reports in the 1950s, there has been no lack of information about Gehlen in the public domain. In the 1970s, these reports were supplemented by books and a memoir by Gehlen himself.[2] Over a decade ago, researcher Mary Ellen Reese used materials declassified under the Freedom of Information Act and some expert interviewing to paint the first detailed picture of how Gehlen came to be employed by the United States, as well as why and under what circumstances Washington decided to reconstitute German intelligence using veterans of the Nazi era. Reese did a superb job, but there were serious gaps in the information she received.[3] Recently, Gehlen's CIA case officer, James Critchfield, published his memoirs of the eight years he worked with the German spymaster.[4] That book offered a very personal look at the development of the relationship between Reinhard Gehlen and the United States, but important questions remained unanswered.

Materials released by the CIA and the Defense Department under the Nazi War Crimes Disclosure Act of 1998 permit a thorough analysis of the origins, implications, and results of the U.S. government's postwar sponsorship of Reinhard Gehlen and of the organization that became the Bundesnachrichtensdienst (BND), the West German Secret Service, in 1956. Four broad conclusions emerge from the thousands of pages of new documentation, which will be explored in this chapter. First, despite being the principal source of funding for Gehlen's activities for close to eleven years, the U.S. government never achieved the control over Gehlen's operations that it had expected, sought, or should have had. Second, Reinhard Gehlen often acted in bad faith in his dealings with the United States. He deceived a generation of U.S. intelligence officers about the details of his operations and violated the basic agreements that were designed to undergird the system of cooperation. Third, a substantial number of former members of SD Foreign Intelligence, the Gestapo, and the Waffen-SS were recruited into the organization when it was being funded by the U.S. government. Gehlen's recruitment of these individuals was not done at the behest of the U.S. government; however, after Washington learned about Gehlen's use of war criminals, it opted to do nothing about it. Finally, the CIA did not hold Gehlen and his organization in high regard as intelligence assets. The Agency's major goals in the Gehlen affair were to facilitate U.S. penetration of a future West German intelligence community and to ensure that neither Gehlen nor any of his subordinates turned their highly nationalistic and secret organization against the West.

Gehlen's recruitment of SD and Gestapo officers is a particular focus of this chapter. From the U.S. Army's sponsorship of Gehlen in July 1945 through the end of CIA supervision in April 1956 (when Gehlen's organization was brought into the open as the BND), war criminals on Gehlen's payroll were technically employed by the U.S. government. Since the Heinz Felfe scandal of 1963—in which a former SD officer turned out to be a KGB mole in the BND—the Gehlen Organization was known to include at least a handful of former SD and Gestapo officers, and over the years it has been suspected that there were a great many more war criminals associated with this operation. Christopher Simpson, who successfully ferreted out the stories of several Nazi war criminals who received U.S. sponsorship, wrote in 1988 that "at least a half dozen—and probably more—of his first staff of fifty officers were former SS or SD men."[5] But it has never been clear whether these were isolated cases. With the Gehlen Organization numbering four thousand people at its height during the period of U.S. sponsorship, it seemed an open question whether these few bad apples constituted a source of malevolent influence, a systemic problem, or were simply the result of a few stupid decisions in the field. Equally unknown with any precision was the extent of U.S. knowledge of these recruits.

Newly released information from the CIA and the Army make it possible to assess the extent of Gehlen's recruitment of former officers of the SD and Gestapo. It turns out that it was widespread. At least one hundred of Gehlen's officers and agents had served with the SD or the Gestapo, and the number may in fact be significantly higher.[6] Although these recruits did not represent a significant percentage of the Gehlen Organization, some of those hired had participated in the worst atrocities committed by the Nazi regime, and a couple of them reached postwar positions of authority. In addition, the evidence strongly suggests that Reinhard Gehlen himself knew the background of many of these recruits. The new materials also paint a complex picture of U.S. neglect and acquiescence, raising questions about the U.S. Army's and then the CIA's handling of the moral and security issues surrounding this experiment in institution-building in occupied Germany.

Gehlen and German Military Intelligence

Reinhard Gehlen was a professional military officer, who, in the 1920s, was commissioned in the small army permitted Germany by the Versailles powers after World War I. He served as a company commander and then joined the German Army's General Staff just before the outbreak of World War II. Excelling at staff work and endowed, it seemed, with inexhaustible energy, Gehlen rose to become chief of the Fremde Heere Ost (FHO), or Foreign Armies–East, a research and analysis unit that studied the Soviet armed forces. Unlike some of the men whom he would hire in the early postwar period, Gehlen was largely a manager and analyst with no operational authority. The FHO wrote reports using intelligence collected by the Abwehr, the intelligence service of the German armed forces. With the dissolution of the Abwehr in mid-1944, however, the FHO for the first time acquired direct responsibility for intelligence gathering on the eastern front.

Gehlen was promoted to generalmajor later that year, but his service as a general in the Third Reich did not last long. In April 1945, he was fired for exhibiting a defeatist attitude.[7]

Despite Reinhard Gehlen's meteoric rise in the German General Staff and his reputation for knowledge about the Soviet armed forces, it would take a remarkable series of events to explain how the U.S. government ever came to repose any confidence in him. Arguably, at the end of World War II, senior officials in the Allied intelligence community knew more about the personalities and capabilities of Nazi intelligence than any combatant has ever known about an enemy in the history of warfare. Thanks to the weakness of German communications security and the ingenuity of British code breakers, by 1944 the Allies were reading thousands of German intelligence messages a week, primarily the communications of the Abwehr. This intelligence triumph, commonly known as Ultra, set up the possibility of identifying, capturing, and subsequently turning into double agents most of Germany's spies in areas under Allied control.[8] By the end of the war, the Allies determined that they had controlled all but three of the principal spies reporting to German military intelligence.[9] With most of German intelligence under Allied control, the Nazis fell prey to deliberate military deception on both the eastern and western fronts.

Postwar analyses of captured German records confirm that Gehlen's FHO performed only marginally better than the average German intelligence unit in World War II. Its reports on the strength and composition of Soviet forces—so-called order of battle information—were quite good; what Gehlen and the FHO lacked was strategic imagination. FHO analyses of Soviet intentions, for example, showed a tendency to believe in German superiority. In his assessments of the battle of Stalingrad, Gehlen guessed wrong about the line of attack that the Soviets would take, consequently underestimating the precariousness of the position of the German 6th Army. In 1944, he predicted "a calm summer" because he believed the Soviets lacked the tactical ability to attack the two largest German army groups in the center and the north of the front. Yet on June 22, 1944, the Soviets launched their largest offensive of the war.[10]

To understand how the U.S. government found itself in the position of championing the cause of a barely mediocre intelligence chief and his second-rate intelligence service, one must look at the politics of U.S. intelligence as World War II ended. From the moment the last shot was fired, the U.S. military and the Office of Strategic Services (OSS) entered into a competition for authority in occupied Germany that the OSS and its successor organization, the Strategic Services Unit (SSU), lost.[11] Until 1949, the U.S. Army was solely responsible for administering the American occupation zone. Accordingly, the military determined the operating conditions for rival intelligence services, favoring its own G-2 and Counterintelligence Corps (CIC). The SSU, which retained a corps of officers who had participated in the fabulously successful Anglo-American wartime counterespionage campaign, was denied a significant operational role.

Decisions about the nature and shape of postwar German intelligence would be made by newly deployed U.S. military intelligence officers who were ignorant of Ultra and had no idea how incompetent German intelligence had been during World War II. As a result, they would accord Nazi spy managers like Gehlen far more respect than their wartime record warranted.

Combined with this misperception of the quality of German intelligence was a real ignorance about Soviet capabilities and intentions. United States intelligence—the OSS as much as the intelligence components of the U.S. Army and Navy—had very little information on the Soviet Union. It had been U.S. policy, enforced with conviction from the White House on down, not to spy on the Soviets during World War II because they were an ally. The FBI and the code breakers of the U.S. Army had circumvented this prohibition, but as of 1945 they had little to show for their efforts.[12] The OSS, on the other hand, had tied itself up in knots over whether to conduct operations against the Soviets. Its counterintelligence service, X-2, had to shut down its tiny Soviet intelligence collection project at the insistence of the White House in 1944.[13]

When veterans of the Allied counterespionage war, most of whom had found their way into the CIA after 1947, discovered that the U.S. Army was intentionally trying to revive the woeful German intelligence service under Reinhard Gehlen, these professionals would try futilely to end U.S. sponsorship of this ill-conceived experiment. It was bad enough that Gehlen lacked any understanding of operational security or reports assessment; worse, Gehlen himself was never briefed about the weaknesses of his own service in World War II. Not realizing how bad German intelligence had been, he would bring a cavalier attitude to the problems of operations and operational security in the early Cold War.

Gehlen and Major Boker

At some point in early 1945, Gehlen started planning for a world without Hitler. He directed his staff to prepare eight large collections of intelligence files and send them to various secret depots in southwestern Germany. Later, he claimed that he did so with the express purpose of providing this material to the Americans for use in the inevitable war against the Soviet Union. Gehlen's later behavior suggests that he, as a German nationalist, was also hiding it for a future German General Staff. Gehlen was captured by the U.S. Army in May 1945 and sent to the 12th Army Group Interrogation Center in Wiesbaden.

A month later, Captain John R. Boker, Jr., an ambitious junior officer and interrogator in the U.S. Army, was assigned to the Wiesbaden camp. Even before the European war had been won, Boker anticipated a future conflict between the United States and the Soviet Union. Boker cut his teeth interrogating and then protecting a group of German Luftwaffe officers who had reconnaissance photographs of Soviet strategic targets to offer. A self-starter who was not inhibited by matters of rank, he sensed that he had a role to play if the U.S. Army was not to waste the intelligence potential of the many interned Nazis who knew something about the Soviet Union. "Now was the ideal time to gain intelligence of the Soviet Union if we were ever going to get it," he later recalled.[14] Nosing around the camp for Soviet experts, Boker made a point of interviewing Gehlen, who was known in the camp to have been the head of the German military intelligence service that dealt with the Soviets.

Gehlen warmed to the American, who apparently wasted no time in sharing with the German general his own belief that a clash with the Soviet Union was inevitable.[15] Gehlen revealed to Boker that he had placed key FHO files in safekeeping with the goal of eventually transferring them to the conquering Americans. Having already successfully schemed to protect the documents of the German air force intelligence officers, Boker knew exactly what to do. He told Gehlen to say nothing more to anyone else about the documents while he sought support from a higher authority to find Gehlen's former assistants and reconstitute the FHO's files.

The chief of the USFET (U.S. Forces European Theater) intelligence center at Wiesbaden, Colonel W. R. Philp, was as important as Boker in the initial creation of a relationship between Gehlen and the U.S. government. Philp had supported Boker's work with the German airmen, and he understood that Gehlen might be an even more productive source. To prevent the Soviets or the British from asking after Gehlen, Philp removed Gehlen's name from the list of POWs in U.S. custody. He also permitted Boker to track down Gehlen's key associates outside the regular channels for locating POWs. Sometime in the summer of 1945, Boker and three American colleagues moved into a separate house in Wiesbaden, where Gehlen was also permitted by Philp's order.[16]

By mid-July, Boker and his team had recovered seven of the eight batches of documents hidden by Gehlen's people.[17] In the same period, they were able to locate and bring to Wiesbaden all of Gehlen's key members and staff. Even at this time, Boker and Gehlen were discussing a much broader operation. Gehlen told Boker that he had been able to establish contact with Oberstleutnant Hermann Baun, who ran the intelligence networks on the eastern front (known as Walli) that had fed reports to FHO during the war.[18]

Boker and Philp sold the idea to the U.S. Army that Gehlen and his former staff could write useful historical studies for the U.S. Army, so in August 1945, Gehlen and his associates were flown to the United States along with many of their documents to work with a Pentagon team that was writing a history of the Soviet-German war.[19] Baun stayed behind in Germany. The U.S. military intelligence chiefs intended to use him to see what could be recovered of the Walli wartime intelligence networks.

This effort by a group of determined U.S. Army officers in Wiesbaden initially escaped the notice of the OSS and the SSU. In October 1945, however, the team working with Baun approached the chief of the SSU's German mission, requesting advice on improving the security of this new operation.[20] Astonished by the U.S. Army's audacious quest to reconstitute the German intelligence service's lines into the East, and miffed at not having been told before, the local SSU viewed the Army's operation warily.

Concern in the field about this operation extended beyond the veterans of the OSS. The Army's own counterintelligence service, the CIC, had also not been briefed about Boker and Philp's project. Increasingly, former Nazi intelligence agents carrying U.S. documents were caught by the CIC. In each case, the CIC—whose job it was to arrest former German intelligence officers—were told to let these men go free because they were working for the United States.[21]

Rusty

Gehlen returned to U.S.-occupied Germany in July 1946 with authorization to reconstitute the FHO, including the Walli networks that Baun had been pulling together.[22] From the moment Gehlen returned through July 1, 1949, the U.S. Army was his principal sponsor. In this period, the Gehlen project acquired the code name "Rusty" and grew from a few hundred veterans of the FHO and the remnants of the Walli networks to encompass about four thousand officers and agents.[23] Rusty's operations, which Baun continued to supervise for Gehlen, also spilled out from the eastern zone of Germany to the French zone of occupation, to occupied Austria, Italy, and Soviet-controlled Poland and Romania.[24]

Newly released documents from this period indicate that, despite the exponential growth in Rusty's activities and payroll, the number of U.S. Army officers assigned to monitor the organization remained at two.[25] United States supervision, such as it was, in effect meant U.S. control over the logistical and financial transfers to Gehlen. His U.S. minders took care that he had the chocolate, women's cosmetics, gas, and cigarettes needed to barter on the black market for additional operational money and the U.S. dollars that would also be traded at a profit for the still-used Reichsmark. As for operational control, there was none.[26]

What did the United States get in return? The U.S. Army in Germany considered the Gehlen Organization their "most dependable and prolific source of information on Russian military intentions and strength."[27] These Germans were a stopgap measure for a U.S. military intelligence system that was poorly trained and understaffed. Gehlen offered continuous tactical coverage of the Soviet armed forces in what would become East Germany. Lacking any agents in the Kremlin or the Soviet military headquarters, Gehlen relied on mundane but effective techniques to build a picture of the enemy's force. Gehlen agents loitered along key rail lines, watching for the movements of Soviet troops and noting the serial numbers of equipment and weapons. The patches on Soviet uniforms also gave away the formations that were in the area. Descriptions of these, too, were added to the mosaic until a pattern emerged. Having few German speakers or people with deep knowledge of German cities and towns, the U.S. Army could not replicate the tactical team that Gehlen appeared to have at his fingertips.[28]

Besides this basic information on Soviet deployments in eastern Germany, the Gehlen Organization made itself useful by providing coverage of Soviet radio communications, especially transmissions of the Soviet air force. In the difficult fiscal climate of the early postwar period, the U.S. military had limited resources to mount a signal intelligence campaign against the Soviets. The U.S. Army, for example, would not establish a radio listening station of its own in West Germany until the mid-1950s. Until that time, the U.S. Army relied on the British for high-level cryptographic work and on Rusty for the day-to-day listening on radio frequencies used by Soviet pilots, tankers, and grunts. The latter traffic was lightly encoded if at all, but in the event of a major offensive careful listening might pick up hints of what was to come.[29]

This arrangement suited Gehlen very well. The Army increased its demand for reports from the Germans and left Gehlen alone to expand and recruit as he saw fit.[30] Although Gehlen's principal minders in the U.S. Army asked him whether he had any war criminals at headquarters, they did not require that he submit biographical data on his field personnel and the agents they recruited. Gehlen refused to volunteer the real names of his employees, and he had them register for U.S. gas coupons and food rations under assumed names.[31]

Under these lax conditions, Gehlen was able to employ a sizeable number of Nazi war criminals without U.S. interference. He hired much of the SD's Balkan network, including the leadership of the Iron Guard, the Romanian Fascists whom the SD had protected in exile. The leader of these Balkan operations (which carried the code name "General Agency 13") in the Gehlen Organization was Otto von Bolschwing, who would later become a notorious employee of the CIA after Gehlen dropped him for incompetence.[32] Bolschwing was himself a war criminal, having served in the SD's anti-Jewish office with Adolf Eichmann in the 1930s and as an SD advisor in Bucharest during the anti-Jewish pogroms of 1941. Among Bolschwing's agents when he worked for Gehlen was Horia Sima, the former chief of the Iron Guard who had inspired the anti-Jewish pogrom, and former SS Romanian experts Kurt Auner, Ernst Schlandt, and Joachim Vacarescu.[33]

Gehlen also turned to SD and Gestapo officers to create a counterintelligence service, headquartered in Karlsruhe. Newly released CIA materials confirm that there were at least eleven former SD or Gestapo men who worked for this section, known initially as "Dienststelle [substation] 114," then as GV-L.[34] For example, Herbert Boehrsch, whom Gehlen used as a contact to German-speaking expatriates from the Sudetenland, had been with the SD in Prague; Walter Otten had been an SS-Sturmbannführer working in the SD office in Bremen; and Otto Somann, with the exalted rank of SS-Oberführer, had served as Inspekteur of the SD and Sicherheitspolizei (Sipo) office in Wiesbaden before being seconded to the Gestapo. Personal participation in wartime atrocities might have been difficult to prove for some of these men, though they all belonged to criminal organizations. But the criminal behavior of Emil Augsburg, who joined GV-L in October 1948 (when it still had the cover name Dienststelle 114), is beyond doubt. Augsburg, who fancied himself an expert on Slavs and the eastern front, was detailed to a Sipo unit for "*spezialle Aufgaben*" ("special duties") in Poland in 1939–40 and the western USSR in 1941. *Spezialle Aufgaben* was a euphemism for the execution teams that killed Jews and suspected Communists.[35]

Remarkably, the more criminal elements of Rusty were neither in the Romanian operation nor in GV-L, but belonged to Dienststelle 12 or GV-G, an office that organized penetrations of the Soviet zone through Berlin. CIA material reveals that a number of men who had played roles in the Holocaust worked for Gehlen in Dienststelle 12. The chief of GV-G was Erich Deppner, a deputy to SS-Brigadeführer Wilhelm Harster, the SD and Sipo commander in the occupied Netherlands.[36] Deppner at the very least witnessed the deportation of over 100,000 Dutch Jews to extermination camps. He also was personally responsible for executing Soviet prisoners of war interned in wartime Holland. The chief of Dienststelle 12's Berlin station was another SS man, Ernst Makowski, who had been a Gestapo officer in southwestern Germany.[37] Also in the Berlin office was Obersturmbannführer Karl Guse, who had been chief of the Gestapo in Rome before the German invasion in 1943, and Werner Krassowski, an SS-Hauptsturmführer who served in Poland as a concentration camp guard with an SS Totenkopf (Death's Head) regiment in 1939–41 and then served with an SS unit in the Baltics.[38]

The man with the most blood on his hands in the Gehlen Organization was perhaps Konrad Fiebig, who had served with the Einsatzkommando 9 of Einsatzgruppe B in the Belorussian town of Vitebsk and was later charged with the deaths of 11,000 Jews.[39] Before ending his Nazi career, Fiebig was named a judge in the Sondergericht judicial system, which was used by the SS to kill political enemies. Despite his past, Fiebig was hired in 1948 as a Rusty courier in Stuttgart and worked for West German intelligence into the early 1960s.[40] Fiebig was not the only Einsatzkommando veteran in Gehlen's organization. Walter Kurreck had been in Einsatzgruppe D in 1942.[41] He had worked on Operation Zeppelin, a scheme for sabotage and assassinations behind Soviet lines and for the executions of political commissars in Russian POW camp. Equally tainted, though not a veteran of an Einsatzkommando, was Alexander Doloezalek, who had worked in the Race and Settlement Office in Poznan and Lodz.[42] His office was responsible for recycling the clothing and other property taken from Jews deported to death camps. Doloezalek was a case officer for Dienststelle 62 and was important enough to be placed on a Gehlen emergency evacuation list in 1959. Friedrich Frank had been with the Gestapo in Cracow and later with Harster in the Netherlands.[43]

It is impossible to know without access to intelligence materials from the Federal Republic of Germany whether and in which cases Gehlen himself was aware of the backgrounds of the men his subordinates had hired. Hermann Baun had established a decentralized recruitment system at the start of Rusty, which Gehlen did not change. The files of personnel, including their real and assumed names and a biography, were kept at the field station that hired them. They were not sent to Gehlen's headquarters; this material was also not collated at the Dienststelle level. Gehlen later explained that the system would prevent Soviets from rolling up all of his networks in the event they captured his headquarters.[44]

What's more, Gehlen's headquarters may not have known about some of the worst recruitments because a number of these war criminals attempted to conceal their wartime pasts. Fiebig, for example, was retired by the BND in 1962 for having falsified the autobiography that he submitted when he was hired.[45] But there can be little doubt that Gehlen knew the background of the man he chose to be the head of his organization's Combined Reports, Translation and Editing Office. Erich Ulich Kayser-Eichberg was a psychologist who had spent his professional career until 1945 deploying his scientific training on behalf of the SS.[46] While professor of psychology at the University of Danzig, Kayser-Eichberg was seconded as an SS-Sturmbannführer to the Race and Settlement unit in the Waffen-SS Alpenland in 1942–43, and then to the Race and Settlement department of the Higher SS and Police Leader's office in Bohemia in 1944. Besides Kayser-Eichberg, Gehlen certainly knew the truth about Emil Augsburg, whom he promoted to a very high position as an advisor on Soviet intelligence because of his experience on the eastern front. And he must have known the backgrounds of Erich Deppner and Otto von Bolschwing, who ran two of his key operational units in the Soviet Bloc.[47] Years later, once the BND was established, Gehlen would demonstrate the consistency of his lack of concern for hiring war criminals by making a section leader out of the notorious Franz Six, who had overseen Einsatzkommando work on the eastern front before directing an anti-Semitic SS think tank.[48]

Gehlen's comfortable relationship with the U.S. Army lasted two years. By the end of 1947, new constraints emerged that threatened to impose limits not only on Gehlen's ability to recruit whomever he wished, but also on his ability to recruit in general. The first constraint came in the person of Colonel Willard K. Liebl, whom the U.S. Army named in the fall of 1947 to supervise the Rusty operation. Unlike his predecessor, Liebl was determined to force Gehlen to turn over the names of his hires. In his memoirs, written after he retired, Gehlen explained his disagreement with Liebl as a struggle to defend West German sovereignty: "The disputes with Colonel L— finally culminated in my flatly refusing to obey an order he issued in March 1948, since it would have cost the organization its hard-won independence."[49] Gehlen later recounted that he did not feel bound to accept any orders or suggestions from his U.S. supervisor unless "they would serve the mutual interests of Germany and the United States."[50]

Gehlen easily won this battle. Liebl's message was much stronger than the messenger himself. Liebl's wife and some of his associates were implicated in black market dealings, evidence of which Gehlen used to force Liebl to return to the United States.[51] Gehlen got a new U.S. commander.[52] It was his old friend Colonel Philp.

The other constraint involved was money. Liebl's arrival had coincided with the German currency reform arranged by the three Western powers. The effect of this reform was to sharply reduce the purchasing power of Gehlen's U.S. subsidies. Rusty was funded in U.S. dollars, and Gehlen saw the street value of this money plummet over 40 percent within one year without an increase in the U.S. Army's appropriations.

Despite winning the battle over giving his officers' real names to the U.S. Army, the money issue and lingering suspicions about the competence of U.S. military intelligence provoked Gehlen to seek a new U.S. sponsor. He was aware of changes in the U.S. national security community. Of special interest to him was the development of a new centralized intelligence service in Washington in 1947. The CIA, Gehlen felt, would be a much better patron for his organization. He hoped that the CIA would not only understand the needs of his organization better than the U.S. Army had, but that it would also be willing to pay for it.[53]

CIA: The Reluctant Patron

Given the rising costs of Rusty, as early as 1946 the U.S. Army was looking for a way to push these expenditures onto another organization without losing access to the tactical intelligence Gehlen produced. The Gehlen Organization cost the U.S. Army $42,367 in cash and the equivalent of $5,000 in rations per month, or about half a million dollars a year.[54] The Germans were asking for much more. They believed that short of receiving $2.5 million a year, they could not reach their potential for intelligence collection in Europe.[55] In the fall of 1946, the Army suggested a cost-sharing arrangement to the newly formed Central Intelligence Group (CIG), which had acquired the assets of what was left of the OSS.[56]

The Army's offer of Rusty stirred a debate within the fledgling CIG. Veterans of the counterintelligence campaign were especially wary of Gehlen and his organization. The sense that the U.S. Army might be offering a Trojan horse extended beyond the CI experts. In a review prepared for CIG director General Hoyt S. Vandenberg, the writers outlined various reasons for leaving the German organization alone. First, there was the concern that, due to the Army's lax attitude toward Gehlen's rapid recruitment and expansion, the entire organization might have been penetrated by the Soviet intelligence services. "It is considered highly undesirable," a CIG reviewer wrote to headquarters, "that any large-scale U.S.-sponsored intelligence unit be permitted to operate under even semi-autonomous conditions."[57] There was also the sense that participation in the Gehlen Organization represented an unnecessary moral compromise. "One of the greatest assets available to U.S. intelligence has always been the extent to which the United States as a nation is trusted and looked up to by democratic-minded people throughout the world," warned the SSU's report on Rusty in October 1946.[58] For those who were prepared to risk moral tarnish for the sake of a good intelligence operation, there was even doubt that Rusty would pay off. "There is no evidence whatsoever," it was argued, "which indicates high-level penetration into any political or economic body in the Russian-occupied zone."[59]

The supporters of acquiring Rusty refused to give up, however. They successfully convinced General Vandenberg to send an officer to do a more in-depth field study of the network.[60]   In March 1947, Samuel Bossard, an OSS veteran who had worked in the counterintelligence branch X-2 and had used Ultra materials alongside the British in London, was given the mission of determining which, if any, components of Rusty should be acquired by the CIG and which should be left with the Army or disbanded. This survey represented the first time in the two-year U.S. relationship with Gehlen that anyone with sufficient knowledge of Germany's wartime intelligence networks was given the task of evaluating this effort at reconstituting German military intelligence.[61]

Bossard's message was that the CIG had to take the Gehlen Organization very seriously. "The magnitude of responsibility either to continue or liquidate has not been exaggerated," Bossard cabled to Washington in April 1947 in advance of his report.[62] Unlike the U.S. Army, which emphasized Rusty as a producer of information, the CIG had to be concerned with the political implications of what Gehlen had managed to create under U.S. military sponsorship. "Operation Rusty," Bossard concluded, "has become less a clandestine intelligence operation directed by American authorities than a *potential resistance group* supported and fed by the U.S. Government."[63] Numbering about three thousand people in the spring of 1947, the organization was loosely organized, secretive, and widespread. Its agents extended from Stockholm and Paris to Prague and Rome and could easily be spread to the Middle East, the Far East, and the Western Hemisphere.

Bossard believed that the Germans were preparing to fight against the Soviet occupation of their country. Nevertheless, he advised Washington not to assume that this secret organization would inevitably act in the interests of the United States. He described the leadership as anti-Communist and anti-Soviet. The alliance with the United States was a matter of convenience, undertaken because "they consider [the United States] their most effective champion."[64] However, if the United States should abandon the Gehlen Organization, "this group could constitute a source of political embarrassment to the U.S. Government and a security menace to American overt as well as covert activities in Germany." Bossard discovered that already the Gehlen people had "plans for camouflage which can provide the personnel with an opportunity to continue their operations independently of American support."

Although Bossard identified the risks of losing control of the Gehlen Organization, he was just as emphatic about the potential rewards in trying to take it over. He accepted the U.S. Army's judgment that the Germans were producing "high-grade tactical intelligence."[65] And though a CIG analysis of the counterintelligence information produced by Gehlen was very negative, Bossard wrote with respect of "the full potentialities of this German intelligence machine."[66]

Bossard believed that the insecurity of the organization had been exaggerated. "There is no evidence to show that any section of the operation has suffered penetration, defection or compromise from a hostile agency," he wrote.[67] He did not explain the reasons for his confidence. Rusty had extensive recruits among the refugees from the Soviet Union. In his report, Bossard noted that there were seven hundred Georgian, Ukrainian, Polish, and White Russian agents in one operational group and another eight hundred White Russians in yet another group under Gehlen's command. Bossard was also not worried about the types of Germans whom Gehlen had hired: "I have been unable thus far to discover anything in the records of any of the German operating personnel or in any German section of the operation which for security reasons would eliminate them from consideration for future employment."[68] Bossard noted that, as Gehlen's chief of operations, Baun had recruited heavily among veterans of German military intelligence, the Abwehr. Bossard also noted that there were people whose files he had not been able to see. He believed the organization had probably recruited "outlaws" from among the anti-Communist refugees and even former SS officers, though Bossard did not note any in leadership positions. He recommended that once the CIG took over Rusty, these "outlaws" should be evaluated on a case-by-case basis. He believed that no former member of the Nazi party or the SS should be employed above the level of field agent. "Not only is such a policy a necessary safeguard of the best American interests," Bossard explained, "but it will preserve the unity and idealism of those individuals who have clean political records, high professional qualifications, and the same motives."[69]

The explanation for the fact that Bossard could be both confident of the wisdom of taking Rusty yet aware of its acute dangers lay in his assessment of Reinhard Gehlen. The CIG officer was favorably impressed with Gehlen, whom he found was "in every way the Prussian Staff officer."[70] Gehlen charmed Bossard, and cleverly shifted U.S. suspicions to Baun. Giving him his "word of honor that any responsibility placed in him will not be betrayed," Gehlen confessed a mistrust of Baun to Bossard. He mentioned that, unlike Baun, he intended to make Rusty strictly align with "American interests." As a result, Bossard came to blame Baun for all of the organization's darker characteristics. It was Baun who was behind the plans for a Europe-wide, anti-Communist resistance movement that could operate eventually without U.S. financial support. It was Baun who was the fanatical anti-Soviet with little interest in American values. Although he never said this explicitly, Bossard probably also blamed Baun for the hiring of any outlaws by the organization. In comparison with Baun, Gehlen looked like a reasonable client. "[E]very effort should be made on the part of the American authorities to allow G[ehlen] to dominate the organization at the expense of B[aun]," Bossard concluded. "G is more the statesman, and can become a spokesman for American interests while B, the professional intelligence man, should be reduced to the status of a high-level operator with little, if any, executive power."[71]

In part due to this confidence in Gehlen, Bossard wrote that he believed that the CIG should take the entire organization over and then determine which elements to keep and which to liquidate. Despite the lack of thorough supervision by the

U.S. Army, Bossard concluded that Gehlen had run his operation very effectively. "[A]t present the purposes and needs of G-2 [U.S. Army] intelligence are so well comprehended," he wrote, "that the operation can be said to 'conduct itself' to the satisfaction of G-2 Frankfurt with a minimum of direct operational guidance from that headquarters."[72]

Bossard's recommendation that the CIG seriously consider replacing the Army and taking control of Gehlen landed with a thud in Washington. The spring of 1947 had been a busy time for U.S. intelligence. By the provisions of the National Security Act of 1947, the new Central Intelligence Agency replaced CIG. Vandenberg was gone, and the CIA's first director, Rear Admiral Roscoe Hillenkoetter, disliked the idea of taking over Gehlen.[73] Bossard's report had some effect nevertheless. His interpretation of Gehlen's importance planted a seed at CIA headquarters. Bossard's immediate superior, the director of the Central European Desk of the Office of Special Operations, Richard Helms, disagreed with Hillenkoetter's decision to keep Rusty outside the Agency's control.[74]

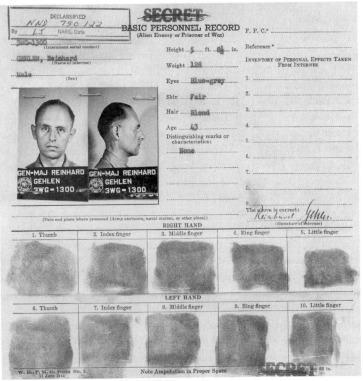

Reinhard Gehlen's Personnel Record, created when he was interrogated by the U.S. Army as a POW in August 1945 (NA, RG 238, National Archives Collection of World War II War Crimes Records, entry 160, Interrogation Records, microfilm publication M 1270, roll 24, Gehlen, Reinhard, box 26).

Less than a year later, Helms authorized a second assessment of the Gehlen operation, this time by James Critchfield. Critchfield was a celebrated colonel in the U.S. Army who had fought in North Africa and France and was now a new recruit in the Agency. Time was a factor—the Army was eager to get rid of this responsibility—so Critchfield was given only a month to visit with Gehlen and survey his operation. As would later become clear, this was not enough time to get a real feel for the nature of Gehlen and his organization. But Critchfield nevertheless produced a long document by mid-December 1948.[75]

In much the same way as Bossard had eighteen months earlier, Critchfield argued that the U.S. government had no choice but to contend with the Gehlen Organization. Critchfield knew how starved the U.S. government was for continuous tactical information from the closed Soviet zone, and he was impressed with Gehlen and with the intelligence potential of his organization. He also saw the political advantages of supporting Gehlen and his organization. Like Bossard, Critchfield was impressed with Gehlen's apparent commitment to American goals. Gehlen, he wrote, was motivated by the "conviction that the time of nationalism is past and [that the] only hope lies in [a] Western European and Atlantic Union."[76] By the fall of 1948, Gehlen had won his bitter struggle with Baun. Baun had been sidelined into strategic planning and was no longer a major factor. Gehlen was master of his own house.[77]

Gehlen allowed the American to visit some of his field stations. Critchfield was then carefully introduced to members of the stations and shown biographical data on them. Critchfield later recalled asking about the recruitment of former SS men and being told that there were none in Rusty. "I was told this in November 1948 by Gehlen, by several of his top associates," Critchfield wrote in 2002, "and by Captain Eric Waldman of the G-2 staff in Pullach."[78]

The newly declassified documents neither confirm nor contradict Critchfield's recollection. Unlike Bossard, who addressed in 1947 the problem of SS men in the Gehlen Organization, Critchfield did not discuss the matter in his long report of December 1948. His investigation, however, had brought him very close to some of Gehlen's SS men. He visited Dienststelle 114, which had four hundred people and eight field stations and was home to quite a few former SS men.[79] The month before Critchfield's visit, Emil Augsburg had been hired by this counterintelligence unit and given the alias Dr. Alberti. In his report on Dienststelle 114, Critchfield said that he was permitted to see the "agent control" or personnel records for the group, but he mentioned nothing about Augsburg or any other former SS men on the payroll. The possibility exists that the Gehlen Organization provided the CIA investigator with a carefully selected group of agent biographies to satisfy his curiosity.[80]

Although Critchfield may not have met with former SS men in Dienststelle 114, he did encounter and would later write about a Gehlen officer with a criminal background. Paul Hodosy-Strobl was chief of the *Tschardas* (Hungarian group) in Dienststelle 114. Hodosy-Strobl, who had originally been recruited by the CIC from a POW camp in 1947, had been selected by the Nazis as the chief of the Hungarian state police, the Gendarmerie, following the German invasion in March 1944. Although Critchfield noted for Washington that the work of this Hungarian group had come under suspicion within Dienststelle 114, he did not raise a flag about the political or moral problems of the CIA associating with Hodosy-Strobl. Two years later, Critchfield described Hodosy-Strobl, who tried to emigrate to the United States in 1950, as having "a dubious and somewhat odious background." In 1948 he said nothing.[81]

Critchfield did make note of some problem areas. He noticed that Gehlen's operations far exceeded the terms of the operational charter established in October 1948 between the U.S. Army and Rusty. According to that agreement, Gehlen was not to undertake any intelligence operations within the Western zones of Germany. Outside of Germany, Gehlen was to restrict any counterintelligence operations to those specifically designed to protect Gehlen's ongoing spying. Inside or outside the country, Gehlen was also not supposed to mount any penetrations of the Communist Party of Germany (KPD) lest lines get crossed with the U.S. Army's Counterintelligence Corps, which had the KPD as one of its principal targets. Critchfield discovered that in one way or another Dienststelle 114 managed to violate all three of these prohibitions. Gehlen had instructed his men to spy on the activities of the West German Communist Party and to keep an index of all "known Communists" at his headquarters in Pullach.[82] Despite the breach of trust that these violations implied, Critchfield recommended that Washington consider how the CIA might benefit from these operations anyway.

There was more skepticism about Gehlen in Washington, even among advocates of a takeover by the CIA. Richard Helms wrote that Rusty was "at best a controversial intelligence package" about which the CIA did not know a lot.[83] Helms overruled Critchfield's request that assessments of Gehlen's operations be made in the field by a future CIA liaison unit with Rusty. Helms wanted Washington, with its access to better information, to be making the call about which of Gehlen's operations would be kept.[84] Helms and his own boss, Assistant Director for Special Operations Donald N. Galloway, insisted that the CIA would first have to discover "detailed characteristics of the organization for which it is assuming responsibility . . . Without being able to run traces on the personnel and examine specific details of the operations with Army assistance and personnel, we might well lay [the] CIA open to wholesale penetration by the Rusty organization."[85] Despite this note of caution, Helms at least remained confident that if handled correctly, the Gehlen group "should be a great intelligence producer."[86]

Helms and Critchfield together planned the CIA takeover. The CIA would have to establish its authority over Rusty early on. The organization would be treated as a subordinate unit within the CIA. It would be stripped of all intelligence operations that might conceivably represent a threat to U.S. interests or which might prove more productive under direct CIA control. Gehlen was to be given a fixed budget for his overhead and his operations in the Soviet zone of Germany and such programs as had already proved productive. Although Helms and Critchfield had confidence in Gehlen's ability to produce intelligence in eastern Germany, they agreed that Gehlen should be encouraged to cut back on the number of operations he was running there "while attempting to raise the level of penetration."[87] As for Rusty's operations outside of eastern Germany, they wanted stringent controls to go into effect immediately. The CIA should fund only Gehlen's activities in the Soviet satellite countries, the so-called strategic operations, on a project-by-project basis. Funding decisions would be made in Washington after scrutiny of agent control and other operational materials for each operation. Given that half of the four thousand or so reports that Rusty produced per month for the Army already came from these operations outside eastern Germany, the CIA was intending to scrutinize a significant portion of Gehlen's work.[88] Hopeful that Gehlen would agree, Critchfield expected that this would "give us a degree of control and an insight into their operations which has been non-existent in the past."[89]

Beyond Helms, however, hostility to the idea of assuming responsibility for Gehlen remained in the CIA. Veterans of the counterintelligence war were loud in their belief that the United States would be hurt by this alliance with the discredited German intelligence service. Besides a sense that these Germans were not going to be much help in the Cold War intelligence struggle, the in-house critics reminded the CIA leadership that there was no guarantee that Gehlen and his colleagues represented the "good" Germans. Before Critchfield was sent to Germany, the anti-Gehlen lobby had summarized its argument in this way:

> [T]he general consensus is that Rusty represents a tightly knit organization of former German officers, a good number of which formerly belonged to the German general staff. Since they have an effective means of control over their people through extensive funds, facilities, operational supplies, etc., they are in a position to provide safe haven for a good many undesirable elements from the standpoint of a future democratic Germany.[90]

By early 1949, however, the critics had clearly lost the debate over assuming responsibility for Gehlen. Two factors served to tip the balance in Gehlen's favor. First, the international situation was very different from what it had been in 1947 when Hillenkoetter had rejected Bossard's recommendation that the CIA take Gehlen over. In 1948, Josef Stalin imposed a blockade on all overland communication to West Berlin, causing the start of what would be an eleven-month air-supply operation by Western air forces. In the first months of the Berlin airlift, the Allies had feared the real possibility of a Soviet attack on Western Europe. In this atmosphere, sources on the East, however imperfect their makeup, were welcome. The second factor was some subtle extortion by the U.S. Army, which in the midst of the Berlin crisis announced plans to cut almost all funding for the Gehlen operation. If the CIA wanted to prevent the untimely collapse of Rusty, it had to act fast. In addition, high-level support existed outside the Agency for the transfer. Both the Chairman of the Joint Chiefs General Omar Bradley and the Secretary of Defense James Forrestal approved of the idea.[91] Convinced by Helms and Critchfield and reassured by Bradley and Forrestal, Hillenkoetter went along with it.

The Zipper Problem

The CIA discovered almost immediately after deciding to take the project over from the U.S. Army that Reinhard Gehlen had a sharply different vision for the new relationship. Difficulties with the German chief of the Rusty project—rebaptized "Zipper" by its new sponsor—emerged even before the formal handover. The trouble started in June 1949, when Critchfield informed Gehlen that the CIA would not be increasing his budget for the moment. At that time, Critchfield also explained that the Agency expected Gehlen to eliminate his operations in Austria, Hungary, Bulgaria, and Yugoslavia, as well as those in Scandinavia. In order to proceed with a project-by-project review, Washington wanted to see the true names and operational details for all of his remaining and prospective intelligence projects outside the Soviet zone of occupation in Germany.[92]

Gehlen balked. Critchfield's proposals were not news to him. In his months spent flirting with the CIA, Gehlen had vaguely promised to close some of his less productive operations. Now that the CIA was committed, however, Gehlen rejected the budget figure he was given and showed little interest in curtailing his operations as dramatically as the CIA had proposed. Gehlen also performed a dramatic about-face with regard to sharing agent information. While making his field survey in the fall of 1948, Critchfield had been told that the agent control files would be open to the United States.[93] Now that the CIA was asking for them, Gehlen's position changed. In August 1949, he sent a letter to Critchfield explaining that it was impossible for the Germans to hand over the names of their personnel.[94] Gehlen argued that the CIA would have to earn the trust of his employees before they would be willing to take this risk.

The CIA held its ground and achieved some results. When Critchfield insisted that turning over the names was a precondition for CIA support for any of the 120 operations that Gehlen hoped to maintain outside of eastern Germany, the German relented a little. Gehlen handed over a list of 150 individuals on his headquarters staff.[95] He also permitted some sharing of minimal information about operations outside the Soviet zone of Germany.

The relationship only worsened as the CIA began analyzing this operational data. When the CIA subjected Gehlen's strategic operations to scrutiny—something the U.S. Army had lacked the ability to do—it found the entire program amateurish and wasteful. The Gehlen Organization was simply incapable of handling serious intelligence penetrations. Despite Critchfield's enthusiastic description in December 1948 of the value of the Gehlen Organization, CIA headquarters concluded in mid-1949 that 90 percent of the 120 projects were quite worthless and recommended their disbandment.[96]

Gehlen refused to accept this verdict and sent a harsh letter to Critchfield telling off the Americans for assuming they could teach the Europeans how to spy.[97] "It is quite clear to me that a mechanical application of American principles to our work," he explained, "would deprive the organization of its principal source of efficiency, the initiative of the single individuals in all fields." He resented having to wait for Washington to approve his projects. He disliked the intrusiveness of the CIA's request, and he hated, most of all, being second-guessed by intelligence officers whom he did not consider his equals. "Only due to the fact that in the past I had full freedom to set up our organization in accordance with our war experiences, " Gehlen lectured Critchfield, "I was able—in spite of the known difficulties—to develop the organization to a very high level of efficiency." He believed that Americans had a very naïve view of intelligence. Their history and geography had insulated them from the rough and tumble of international politics, where decisions had to be made quickly on the basis of imperfect information from imperfect sources. By contrast, he crowed, for Germans "the fundamental principal has always been that it is better to act wrongly instead of not acting at all, even if this would result in occasional damage."[98]

Once Critchfield understood that Gehlen would not budge on divulging the names of his agents, he knew of only two ways to solve the problem. He could seek Gehlen's removal, which he was not prepared to do in 1949, or he could begin a program of penetrating Gehlen's organization without the general's permission. Critchfield recruited Tom Lucid, a former CIC officer whom he had met when both were serving in Austria in 1946, to establish a counterintelligence group.[99] When the CIA acquired responsibility for Zipper in July 1949, Critchfield opened the Pullach Operations Base (POB), a liaison operation in the small town south of Munich where Gehlen had his headquarters. POB and Zipper shared a courtyard in a manorial residence that had served as one of Joseph Goebbels' wartime headquarters. To improve his counterintelligence capabilities, Critchfield arranged for a camera to be placed in the CIA's building so that everyone who entered Gehlen's building across the courtyard could be photographed for later identification.[100] The CIA has not declassified any information regarding this operation, making it difficult to determine with precision when the POB identified any particular Gehlen employee. Using the biographical summaries included as a response to trace requests, however, it is possible to see that, starting in 1949, the CIA acquired information about some of the SD and Gestapo officers that were under Gehlen's protection.

The Romanian Operation, known to Gehlen as General Agency 13, was the first cluster of SS men in Zipper to be identified by the CIA. It is possible that this information was not derived from Lucid's counterintelligence operation because in the fall of 1949 Gehlen was handing over some information to Critchfield on his operations outside of Germany. By whatever means, the CIA knew as of late

1949 that the former SS representative in Bucharest, Otto von Bolschwing; the former chief of the Iron Guard, Horia Sima; and lesser SS-types Kurt Auner, Ernst Schlandt, and Joachim Vacarescu were all being paid as part of Zipper.[101]

There was no internal CIA policy against hiring Nazi war criminals. SD or Gestapo candidates for CIA employment were judged on a case-by-case basis, following trace requests and police investigations in their neighborhoods.[102] Once a candidate was found to have access to information deemed important for U.S. national security or was believed to have skills of use to the United States, the key question for the CIA was not what the individual had done during World War II, but whose side he or she was on once the Cold War began. The sole exception was that the Agency was unlikely to hire an individual whose Nazi crimes were well known because of the difficulty involved in maintaining a covert existence for that person. Otherwise, even personal participation in the Holocaust was not an immediate disqualifier for employment.[103]

Nevertheless, the CIA had an interest in holding Gehlen to his word about not hiring SS men. The Agency was concerned that SD or Gestapo personnel hired by Gehlen might open the U.S. government to criticism that it was sponsoring a criminal organization in West Germany. These recruits would also complicate Zipper's absorption into the West German civil service later on, once the Federal Republic was fully sovereign.[104]

Threatened by the CIA's interventionism, Gehlen did not restrict his reaction to stern letters and firm resistance to U.S. efforts to vet his organization. Just as he had done only two years earlier when he found that he disliked the U.S. Army's requirements, Gehlen went looking for new political allies in the fall of 1949. This time he did not turn to a different part of the U.S. government for help, but instead he sought contacts among the emerging West German leadership. In September 1949, seventy-three-year-old Konrad Adenauer had become chancellor of West Germany. Although not yet fully independent, the Federal Republic of Germany was permitted by the French, British, and U.S. authorities to establish its own government. Gehlen was not personally known to Adenauer, a prewar mayor of Cologne with impeccable anti-Nazi credentials, but this did not stop the German spy chief from attempting to establish lines of communication to the new chancellor and his entourage.[105]

Gehlen tried to keep his political lobbying from the CIA. But U.S. sources in the emerging West German political community were reasonably good. By the end of 1949, the Agency was not only well aware of what Gehlen was doing but was actively discouraging him from freelancing.[106] Although the CIA intended that Gehlen should eventually become the chief of West German intelligence, it did not want that to happen before it had thoroughly penetrated his operation. "By official recognition of any individual or element of the [Gehlen] operation before the proper counterintelligence controls were firmly established," the CIA wrote in May 1950, "the Western German government would find itself able to rob us of our intelligence assets and with serious strategic or political consequences turn them against us."[107]   Ironically, at this moment of concern about Gehlen's dependability, the CIA assigned Gehlen a special cryptonym: in CIA cables he became the stalwart "Utility."[108]

Gehlen ignored Critchfield's advice about not meddling in German domestic politics.[109]   His efforts were much too successful to give them up.   Gehlen became the leading candidate to become the first chief of a new domestic intelligence service planned by the Adenauer government. The Bundesamt für Verfassungsschutz (Federal Office for the Protection of the Constitution, BfV) was to have the same duties as the FBI. Although Gehlen had no background in domestic security or police work, the fact that he had overseen the formation of Dienststelle 114, which did counterintelligence and security work in the Zipper organization, gave him some credibility. From the perspective of the Adenauer government, Gehlen was also attractive because he was one of very few experienced intelligence managers from the war who seemed acceptable to the Americans. The Western occupying powers retained the right to veto any selection to head the BfV.

In early 1950, Adenauer surprised the French, British, and Americans by announcing at a closed-door meeting of the Allied High Commission that Reinhard Gehlen was the leading candidate to lead the BfV.[110] The CIA reeled at the news that Gehlen might get the job of domestic spy chief. In conversations with Critchfield before the BfV job was a possibility, Gehlen had expressed the view that Germany needed a service that did both foreign and domestic intelligence.[111] Critchfield had debated this point with him, making the argument that this powerful organization might pose a threat to German democracy. News that Gehlen's name was being put forward for the domestic job signaled that Gehlen had not listened to CIA advice and still had the formation of a super-agency in the back of his mind.

The British—who knew very little officially about the U.S. arrangement with Zipper but through their own sources understood that there was a strong connection—mistrusted Gehlen and wanted their own man, Otto John, to get the job heading the BfV.[112] The CIA found it convenient to let the British scuttle Gehlen's plans. In a May 1950 memorandum for the record, a CIA analyst wrote that "from the standpoint of our control of future German intelligence, Utility is too powerful in his own right to be allowed to accept the [BfV] position."[113]

By the summer of 1950, as the U.S. government sat back and watched approvingly, the British vetoed Adenauer's candidate and pushed for Otto John to take the post instead. The BfV episode was but the first in a series of events over the course of 1950 that would gradually tip the balance against Gehlen in the ongoing debate over him in the Agency.[114] An additional problem for the CIA was that Zipper operations were often turning out to be second rate and not really worth U.S. taxpayers' money. Having eclipsed Baun, Gehlen held the reins of his organization so tightly that it was appropriate that he bore the balance of the blame for the many shortcomings of Zipper.

In an effort to shake up Gehlen and give him a chance to satisfy his critics at the CIA, James Critchfield "bluntly" informed him in July 1950 that though Zipper was "a credible tactical collection and military evaluation agency . . . it was, with some exceptions, definitely second class in [executing] intelligence activities of a more difficult or sophisticated nature."[115] Critchfield warned that if Gehlen wanted support for anything other than his low-level tactical intelligence teams in East Germany, he "would have to institute radical changes in personnel, procedures, and attitudes."[116]

Outwardly Gehlen took the criticism well. Privately, however, Gehlen stepped up his efforts to use the Adenauer regime to create a separate power base for Zipper. In the summer of 1950, he arranged meetings with Adenauer's most powerful assistant, State Secretary Hans Globke. Globke, described by the CIA as the "eminence grise" of the Adenauer government, was a shrewd choice.[117] Globke and Adenauer were both from the Rhineland, which helped give the younger man the chancellor's ear. Globke was also a severely compromised figure in West German politics. As a civil servant in the Jewish Department of the Interior Ministry he had helped interpret the Nuremberg Laws of the 1930s that eliminated Jewish civil rights. During the war he had repeatedly been in contact with the Gestapo's Adolf Eichmann on Jewish matters in the occupied territories. Gehlen's many compromised employees were less of an issue to Globke than they might have been to a German with a clean past.[118]

By the end of December 1950, Gehlen felt sure enough of his new alliance with the Chancellor's office that he told the CIA what he really thought of their new guidance. In a dramatic three-hour showdown in Critchfield's office on December 28, Gehlen harangued Critchfield.[119] Speaking from prepared notes, he denounced U.S. "interference in Zipper internal affairs." Apparently unconcerned about any U.S. retaliation, he informed Critchfield that he was planning to fire members of his staff who were too pro-American. He also threatened to resign if the CIA continued to tell him how to run his organization.

This outrageous performance by a man who owed his freedom of maneuver in postwar Germany to U.S. goodwill stoked the internal debate within the CIA on the wisdom of the Zipper project. It quickly became apparent that Gehlen had clearly overplayed his hand. A consensus formed at CIA headquarters that Gehlen's declaration of independence was a disaster for the Agency, ensuring that Zipper would never be a secure organization or submit to U.S. control. Washington decided that "we should overlook no opportunity to kick Gehlen upstairs into the service of the Bonn government."[120] The CIA hoped to remove Gehlen without the drama of firing him. The CIA would instead exploit Gehlen's overweening ambition by maneuvering him into a German defense position where "in all probability [he] would not continue to exert an undesirable influence on Zipper." As for Gehlen's replacement, Washington decided that "the best solution would be . . . a forthright Army general with no political ambitions." Sentiment shifted against Gehlen also within the small U.S. liaison unit at Pullach. Two of

Critchfield's top assistants, Henry Pleasants and Peer de Silva, marched into his office and told him that Gehlen had to be fired.[121]

As is well known, Gehlen was not fired. In fact, by the end of 1951, he would be in an unassailable position and Zipper itself would be the closest it had ever come to a position of equality in its relations with the CIA. Two factors contributed to saving the day for the embattled Gehlen. The most important was that the Chancellor's office, especially Hans Globke, wanted Gehlen to stay in his job and hoped that someday Zipper would become the official foreign intelligence service of a sovereign West Germany. In March and May 1951, Gehlen was invited to brief the West German chancellor on the structure of his organization.[122] Larger events had also played a role in Gehlen's political survival in Bonn. Following the surprise North Korean invasion of South Korea in June 1950, there had been a noticeable shift in the West German chancellor's thinking on West German security issues. In the first years after World War II, Adenauer had expected that West Germany would not need to rearm. The Korean War convinced him, however, that the Cold War was too dangerous and West Germany too vulnerable to dispense with having an army.[123] Gehlen was a proven commodity who could be helpful in this national emergency.

The other factor was the will and energy of James Critchfield, who did what he could to help Gehlen make his case in Bonn. The CIA officer obtained a copy of the U.S. National Security Act of 1947 for Gehlen to use in offering Adenauer possible models for the future German foreign intelligence service.[124] Critchfield was equally adept at smoothing over the ruffled feathers in Washington, where he reported that Adenauer and Globke supported Gehlen.

Critchfield made a calculated political decision to rescue Gehlen. Although he was well aware that the General had betrayed the trust of the United States, Critchfield believed that the advantages of working with the troublesome Gehlen outweighed the disadvantages.[125] He viewed the Gehlen matter through the lens of European power politics.[126] The state system on the Continent had been inherently unstable since Chancellor Otto von Bismarck unified the German Reich in the 1860s–70s. The lesson learned from two world wars was that peace hinged on properly managing the Germans, providing them with a role that accommodated their self-respect without undermining the confidence of Germany's neighbors. Critchfield had analyzed the German Army General Staff. He considered the top 130 to have been criminals and was determined not to see these people play a role in rehabilitating the country as a European power.[127] But the next tier of German military leaders included many professionals who accepted the importance of tying Germany's future to the Western alliance. Quite a few of these men were consultants to Gehlen and Zipper. Critchfield believed that though Gehlen himself was unreliable and decidedly weak as an intelligence manager, he was a useful bridge to this next generation of German military leaders. In Critchfield's eyes, Zipper was just as important as a laboratory for nurturing this generation as it had been as a stopgap measure for U.S. Army Intelligence in the early days of the struggle with the Soviet Union. Trying to isolate Gehlen from this emerging German national security elite, therefore, would entail heavy costs, which Critchfield believed unnecessary. "I think it would be politically inept of us," Critchfield wrote in June 1951, "to equivocate in the treatment we give Utility in the United States simply because of our well-documented reservations about him."[128] While others were pulling away from Gehlen, Critchfield became his champion, inviting Gehlen to the United States to raise his stature within the U.S. government and perhaps soften Gehlen's resistance to U.S. advice.

Gehlen's fate as the CIA's liaison partner was sealed in August 1951, when a high-level officer from the CIA traveled to West Germany to determine for himself the extent of Globke and Adenauer's commitment to Gehlen. The CIA was prepared to dump him, but only if the nascent West German government agreed. At a private meeting, the CIA envoy put the delicate question to Globke: "Is Gehlen acceptable to Adenauer?"[129] Globke answered affirmatively, in what was reported to Washington as a "direct and emphatic way."[130] Although doubts remained at the CIA, Gehlen had made too many influential allies in the Federal Republic for the U.S. government to discard him.

The visit by the CIA chieftain paved the way for Gehlen's trip to the United States in the fall of 1951. The chance to see Joe DiMaggio's last game at Yankee Stadium was but one of the cultural stops on a red-carpet tour of the country. Not all was sweetness and light, however. Gehlen received a frosty reception from General Walter Bedell Smith, the Director of Central Intelligence. Smith, who had been Dwight Eisenhower's Chief of Staff at the Supreme Allied Headquarters in Europe, was among those in the CIA who never warmed to the idea of flattering Gehlen's personal and professional ambitions.[131] Nonetheless, symbolic of the Agency's grudging acceptance of Gehlen was the fifteen-minute visit and handshake that Gehlen's boosters arranged with Smith.

After Yankee Stadium

Just as it was for major league baseball, 1951 turned out to be the season for change in the CIA-Gehlen relationship. After Gehlen returned from Washington, the tensions in the relationship noticeably relaxed. The change was not due to anything on Gehlen's part. He would remain as stubbornly committed to keeping the CIA's nose out of his business as ever. But there was a marked change in Washington's handling of the Zipper account. The CIA gradually gave up on its original objective of controlling Gehlen's organization. Over the remainder of 1951 and into 1952, the CIA began to accept Zipper as more of a sovereign organization with which it had a close relationship than as a wholly owned subsidiary. In December 1952, Smith, who only fourteen months earlier had been reluctant to show any favor to Gehlen, wrote the German spy chief of his hope that the West German government would transform Zipper into the official German intelligence service in "the near future."[132] Smith signaled that, in anticipation of that day, Washington was already prepared to expand the relationship into a worldwide partnership of equals. "Believing that our cooperation in intelligence matters can, to our mutual advantage, be extended," he wrote, "I have instructed Mr. Critchfield to explore with you our related interests in a number of activities in areas outside of the framework of our present cooperation in the production of intelligence on the Soviet Bloc."[133]

In this new situation, what might have been a sore point for the two services passed without creating a stir. By the end of 1951, Critchfield's penetration operation was increasingly turning up evidence that, in defiance of his promise not to hire war criminals, Gehlen had been stacking his organization with SS men.

Bolschwing and his Romanians had been found two years before, very early in the process. In 1951, the CIA discovered a much larger cluster of SS men in the counterintelligence section GV-L. As can best be determined from the new documents, the first evidence that GV-L contained SS men arrived at Pullach in the fall of 1951, when the CIA penetration operation picked up information on Henry Paul Opitz and Walter Vollmer.[134] Both men had been in the Gestapo, and Vollmer had been the head of the Gestapo office in Chemnitz. Sometime in 1951, it seems, the CIA also learned about Cornelius Van Der Horst, who operated agent chains in Poland for the GV-L.[135]

As Gehlen drew closer to the regime in Bonn, CIA counterintelligence opportunities increased. It appears that the CIA had better sources in the civilian offices of the West German government than in Zipper. One especially productive operation involved learning the names of Gehlen agents through analysis of Zipper's internal financial records, which apparently neither the U.S. Army nor the CIA had ever been officially permitted to see.[136] In the summer of 1952, Bonn sent two accountants to Pullach to begin checking the books of the Gehlen Organization so that eventually its employees could formally join the West German civil service. Some, perhaps all, of what they discovered was also seen by the CIA. Using travel receipts and salary payments, Critchfield's agents painstakingly pieced together Gehlen's widespread organization. GV-L's roster filled out. The CIA discovered that SD men Heinz Felfe and Carl Schuetz had been hired in 1951.[137] The CIA also learned that Zipper was employing the war criminals Emil Augsburg, Erich Deppner, and Konrad Fiebig.[138] Of the three, Augsburg was the most prominent because it became clear that Gehlen had selected him to be Zipper's chief specialist on the structure and tactics of the Soviet intelligence services.[139]

With the CIA expecting the Adenauer government to legalize Zipper in short order, it was now Agency policy to consider these politically sensitive recruitments as an internal German matter. There is no evidence of any effort by Washington or Critchfield at the CIA station in Pullach to press Gehlen to fire any of these discovered SS men because of their pasts. By the early 1960s, the CIA came to view former SS men as likely targets for Soviet penetration, but this was not the Agency's belief in the early 1950s. Indeed, in the second half of 1951, the

CIA was itself hiring former SS men for a paramilitary operation designed by the Office of Policy Coordination.[140] Newly released information identifies at least three former SS men—Friedrich Carstenn, Karl Otto Jobke, and Eberhard Tellkamp—who were recruited for this operation. At least two of these men had probably committed crimes against humanity.[141] Besides the fact that Jobke and Carstenn were employed through February 1953 and Tellkamp through November 1954, the precise duration and nature of this paramilitary operation organized by the OPC remains classified.[142]

Consistent with its own view that few risks were involved in hiring former members of the SD and Gestapo, the Agency opted to complain to Gehlen only about those SS veterans on whom it had information of a possible Soviet connection. One of those SS men was Wolfgang Paul Hoeher. In June 1952, the CIA warned Zipper that he might be a Soviet agent.[143]

The 1953 Crisis

Wolfgang Paul Hoeher merits a footnote in the history of the Cold War. Hoeher, the head of GV-L's office in West Berlin, disappeared into East Germany on February 13, 1953. Zipper promptly informed the CIA that Hoeher had been drugged and kidnapped across the border into East Berlin. But Hoeher had not been kidnapped. The CIA had been right to question this man's loyalty.[144] He had defected after serving as an East German mole in the Zipper organization. Hoeher's defection, six months after the warning from the CIA, ushered in a year of setbacks for Zipper that postponed legalization by Bonn for another four years and forced Gehlen to take U.S. concerns about security a little more seriously.

In October 1953, the Gehlen Organization was hit by an even more dramatic defection. Hans Joachim Geyer, who had worked for Gehlen since 1952 as an agent handler in East Berlin, defected to the East Germans when he thought the West Berlin police might arrest him. All along Geyer had been a double agent for the East German Security Service.[145] In the immediate aftermath of Geyer's departure, the East German Security Service arrested what has been described as hundreds of alleged Gehlen agents throughout the Soviet zone. Geyer then appeared at a press conference organized by the East Germans to denounce Gehlen. Two weeks later, a man linked to Gehlen was arrested as he tried to lay a communications cable along one of the canals that formed the boundary between East and West Berlin. This was followed by another press conference, where the East Germans showed off the cable layer, as well as Geyer and Hoeher.

The defections and the revelations that followed stung Gehlen. He understood that he could not hold out any longer on revealing to the CIA the names in the compromised GV-L. He needed Critchfield's help with the huge counterintelligence task he faced to ensure that there were no more Communist agents in this group. Cooperation in counterintelligence between the CIA and Gehlen had already intensified after Hoeher's defection, and by the end of the year, as the Soviets began their most concentrated propaganda campaign against

Gehlen, the CIA was quite convinced that Hoeher and Geyer could not be the only moles in Zipper. In December 1953, Gehlen finally handed Critchfield a list of the officers and agents attached to GV-L.[146] He also promised his American liaison partner that the GV-L would be "dissolved" and its agents reassigned or placed under cover as Dienststelle 150. (It was likely from this list that the CIA learned that Emil Augsburg, the former Nazi expert on the East who had also participated in "special duties" in Poland and Byelorussia, was the man known as "Dr. Alberti" in the GV-L.)[147] Gehlen informed Critchfield that, as a result of the reorganization of the GV-L, Augsburg would be transferred to Gehlen's headquarters in Pullach. The CIA apparently made no effort to encourage Gehlen to fire any of the former members of GV-L—not even the war criminal Augsburg—in the wake of the events of 1953.[148]

Even in this moment of shared concern, Gehlen was constitutionally incapable of being forthright with the CIA. Although he permitted one of his counterintelligence specialists to discuss his concerns about additional Soviet penetrations, he did not reveal to the CIA that the GV-L had itself launched a mole hunt. The SS men in the GV-L had formed a social and professional network that inspired suspicion on the part of those in the organization who had never belonged to a criminal organization. The non-SS men initiated an investigation into what they termed "the SD clique."[149]

The U.S. Army vs. Zipper

The U.S. Army's relationship with the Gehlen Organization became more adversarial as Gehlen's relationship improved with the CIA. The Army's Counterintelligence Corps reacted with as much alarm to the events of 1953 as did the CIA and Gehlen himself. Like the counterintelligence experts in both the Zipper and the CIA units at Pullach, the CIC was deeply concerned that there were more East German or Soviet sources in the discredited GV-L.

In the fall of 1954, the CIC recruited a source within the GV-L counterintelligence unit in Zipper. Ludwig Albert, a former police officer in the Nazi period, was a security representative in the province of Hesse. Albert claimed that the entire Gehlen Organization counterintelligence network in the Soviet zone was neutralized by the Hoeher case. Albert promised to help the U.S. Army because, as his CIC case officer explained, "[H]e sees in the possibility of American pressure on General Gehlen directly the only chance to save his organization from becoming an impossible quagmire."[150]

Albert was an excellent source for following the mole hunt within the GV-L (now Dienststelle 150). In November 1954, Albert passed to the CIC a list of people in sensitive positions in the Gehlen Organization who "either represent security risks and/or threats, or have backgrounds or records which have not been sufficiently clarified to satisfy minimum security considerations."[151] He also informed the CIC that within the security group in the Gehlen Organization there was the increasing sense that the East Bloc's propaganda campaign of December

1953 was not the product of Hoeher's defection but was a sign of some excellent penetration of the Gehlen Organization by the Soviets. He said that suspicion had fallen on the SS men in the organization, especially on an ambitious officer named Heinz Felfe. "The impression that Heinz Felfe and the SD clique which followed him into the organization are 'enemies' has been growing steadily."[152] Albert noted that Felfe traveled around from Gehlen office to Gehlen office where he "had no grounds for being present . . . each time asking for something or other . . . only to retreat then, stating he was in the wrong office."[153]

The CIC opted not to tell the CIA what it had learned from Albert about Heinz Felfe and the other members of the SD clique. Indeed, after the 66th CIC, the main CIC group in West Germany, initiated a full-fledged investigation of Felfe and the other GV-L veterans, it instituted a policy of keeping the CIA as far away from its penetration as possible. The CIA had a liaison officer stationed at the 66th CIC, who posed a possible threat to this policy. Writing as if this CIA man represented a foreign power rather than the United States, the CIC commander in charge of the operation laid down the reasons why he had to be contained: "His continuous presence and use of the central registry, albeit through headquarters case sections, represents a possible source of embarrassment should he determine anything more than casual interest on the part of this headquarters in the [Gehlen Organization].[154]

The CIA, however, did not need any help from the CIC. It learned about the Gehlen Organization's internal security investigation on its own.[155] It also knew that former SS men, in particular Heinz Felfe, were at the center of the controversy. In October 1954, the CIA received information that Heinz Felfe and Karl Schuetz were "the major suspects in the Gehlen Organization security leak." The CIA also discovered that Felfe was considered the "main organizer and central figure of the SD clique.[156] The CIA had known about Felfe since 1952, though this was the first time that there was any hint that he was considered a security risk.

The CIA's initial reaction was to downplay the derogatory information against Felfe.[157] James Critchfield's counterintelligence specialists had been working increasingly closely with Felfe, and, despite the GV-L debacle of 1953, had come to view him as a very dependable ally in the war against Soviet intelligence and intrigue. In 1956, when his file was being reviewed before Felfe took his first liaison trip to the United States, the CIA officer who had "known and dealt closely with [Felfe] for about a year and a half," wrote that Felfe "is a man who apparently ties his personal future to the West and has made the decision to fight Communist ideologies and practice within the best framework available to him, i.e. [Zipper]."[158] Felfe's CIA liaison partner predicted that in the years to come, Felfe would be a key player in the BND.[159] He did not predict that Felfe would be among the most damaging KGB penetrations of the entire Cold War. Although the CIC could be blamed for not coordinating its efforts with the CIA, the CIA had only itself to blame for not looking into Felfe earlier and more closely than it did.

Above: Allen Dulles
Left: James Critchfield

Mutual Suspicions and Damage Control

The ever-widening investigation of the security of the Gehlen Organization did nothing to disrupt the CIA's interest in strengthening the relationship. In September 1954, CIA director Allen Dulles visited the future chief of West German intelligence at his headquarters. Behind the symbolism of the meeting there was substance. Dulles raised the possibility of cooperation outside Eastern Europe. In late 1952, Smith had permitted Critchfield to discuss expanding cooperation beyond the Soviet zone (which in 1949 became the German Democratic Republic, or East Germany). Apparently, however, little had come of this overture, and Dulles stressed to Gehlen once more the need for this cooperation. Although the particular region of which Dulles spoke has been redacted in pages released by the CIA, from the historical context it is reasonable to speculate that Dulles discussed activities in the Near East, where in 1952-53 former Nazi military officers had been invited by the Syrian and Egyptian governments to train their military and intelligence establishments.[160]

Later, Gehlen hinted in his memoirs that his operations in the Middle East were both successful and of great importance to Bonn. "This is a region of vast importance for Europe," he wrote. "Both bridge and pivot," he continued, "it confronts the southern flank of NATO and borders on the Mediterranean, the domination of which has always been one of the great Soviet ambitions."[161] As of the mid-1950s, Gehlen's officers had "decided to establish a network of contacts there for the service in order to provide a continuous flow of intelligence reports."[162]

Something else in Gehlen's memoirs suggests that the CIA not only participated in these operations but also knew that they involved some notorious Nazi figures. Gehlen wrote in the early 1970s that he had employed some of "the few former SS members" in Zipper in the Middle East with "the full approval" of the United States.[163] "We found the Arab countries particularly willing to embrace Germans with an ostensibly 'Nazi' past," he wrote.[164] By implication, so, too, was the United States. A former CIA officer in the region, Miles Copeland, then identified former SS-Sturmbannführer Otto Skorzeny as the principal player in this operation. In World War II, Skorzeny had achieved near legendary status by leading a dramatic paratroop operation to spirit former Italian dictator Benito Mussolini out of detainment by the Italian government that had surrendered to the Allies in 1943. In 1944, Skorzeny had trained the guerrilla warriors who infiltrated the Allied lines dressed in U.S. uniforms so as to disrupt communication when Hitler launched his desperate final offensive in the Ardennes. According to Copeland, Gehlen approached Skorzeny with the plan that he would go to Egypt in 1953 to train the Egyptian army. Skorzeny understood that the money for this operation would come from the CIA, and that he and the other SS men he recruited as instructors would be responsible for spying on the Egyptians.[165]

Records released in response to the Nazi War Crimes Disclosure Act cast doubt on Copeland's story and suggest that the operations Gehlen was writing about did not involve the CIA. The evidence is quite clear that the CIA and Gehlen did not cooperate regarding Skorzeny or any other of the dozens of aging Nazis who did indeed trek to Cairo in the first years of Nasser's reign to prepare the Arabs for battle with the new Jewish state.[166] If Gehlen was involved with those men, this was kept from the CIA.[167] To the extent that the CIA detected any official West German hand behind these work projects for former Nazis, it seems that it was the embryonic German defense ministry under Heinz Blank, the so-called Amt Blank, which was the sponsor of some of these men. In any case, the CIA was not a sponsor, just an interested onlooker.

One area of joint cooperation, however, was the investigation of the circumstances surrounding the defections and releases of 1953–54. In 1954, a Soviet defector named Petr Deriabin had revealed to the CIA that the KGB ran two agents in the BND. The defector could only provide code names for these men: "Peter" and "Paul."[168] Only in 1957 did the CIA take seriously that Felfe could be either Peter or Paul. From that year until the case was closed with Felfe's arrest in 1961, the CIA and the Gehlen Organization worked on this counterintelligence problem in the cooperative manner that it deserved.[169] Until his arrest, however, Felfe continued his steady rise in West German intelligence. As chief of all counterintelligence operations against the Soviets, his final position with the BND, Felfe was able to reveal to Moscow every Gehlen operation in the Soviet Bloc.

During the investigation of the Felfe case, the CIA discovered that there were other high-level Soviet moles in the BND, not all of whom could be identified. Two that could be identified were Hans Clemens and Wilhelm Krichbaum, both of whom had at one time or another recruited other agents for the BND and the Soviets.[170] Clemens and Krichbaum had collaborated in recruiting Felfe for the KGB in 1951. At the very least, Zipper's and later the BND's entire counterintelligence campaign in the 1950s was an open book for Moscow.

In April 1956, the Adenauer government formally legalized the Gehlen Organization as the BND. While the Chancellor had been relying on it as his foreign intelligence service since 1951, the U.S. government continued to pay the salaries of Gehlen's headquarters personnel and much of Zipper's operational costs until Gehlen's staff officially joined the West German civil service.[171]

What must have been a moment of shared glory for the CIA and the new BND was oddly bittersweet. Although they had never been personally close, Critchfield and Gehlen experienced a severe falling out in 1955. The cause of the problem was Gehlen's discovery of the CIC penetration into his organization, for which he blamed Critchfield and the CIA. In July 1955, Gehlen informed Critchfield that two American men had been identified as covering West German government figures and the Gehlen Organization.[172] The West German police also determined that Ludwig Albert was involved in unauthorized activity. After he was arrested, the West German police uncovered evidence in his apartment that he had been working for CIC. Albert later committed suicide in prison.

Gehlen never accepted that one U.S. intelligence service could act independently of another in occupied Germany. When Critchfield told him that the CIA had no idea that the U.S. Army had targeted Zipper, Gehlen assumed this was one of those polite lies that make diplomatic relations possible.[173] As a result, the Albert case cast a pall over Gehlen's relationship with the Pullach group throughout the remainder of the CIA's sponsorship of Zipper. Critchfield's final days at Pullach before the CIA closed its special liaison office were difficult. Gehlen himself did not bother to visit with the American who had been his most tolerant CIA ally over eight years. Curiously—for a man who repeatedly broke his word in dealings with Americans—he refused to forgive Critchfield for the actions of the CIC.

The CIA's relationship with the BND emerged unaffected by the personal tensions between these two men. Although the newly released information does not add much to the literature on West German-U.S. intelligence cooperation after the period of CIA stewardship, there is some evidence in the public domain to suggest that at a certain point after Felfe's arrest the relationship became mutually advantageous. As for the period under U.S. supervision, the judgment cannot be positive. The CIA was never able to renegotiate the open-ended commitment that the U.S. Army had rashly made to Gehlen in 1945–46. By 1951, the CIA recognized that the strong-willed Gehlen would use every instrument at his disposal to deter U.S. control over his activities. Had Gehlen not been a wily political infighter, he would have been fired. But Gehlen had made himself too powerful to replace, even in a country still occupied by the U.S. Army. As a result, for over a decade Reinhard Gehlen was able to use U.S. funds to create a large intelligence bureaucracy that not only undermined the Western critique of the Soviet Union by protecting and promoting war criminals but also was arguably the least effective and secure in the North Atlantic Treaty Organization.

As many in U.S. intelligence in the late 1940s had feared would happen, the Gehlen Organization proved to be a back door by which the Soviets penetrated the Western alliance. Through Gehlen's careless employment of Nazi war criminals, this organization was also a back door to tranquility and fat pensions for men who had committed—or at least abetted—the worst atrocities of the twentieth century. Even though the record of intelligence-sharing remains spotty for the Army period and closed for the period of CIA sponsorship, it is hard to imagine any stream of information whose value could outweigh these two facts. It is equally hard to imagine that the United States could not have found another horse to bet on in the race to build a West German intelligence service if the decision had been made early enough. The U.S. sponsorship of Reinhard Gehlen should be an object lesson in how easily governments can lose control of the institutions they foster in foreign lands and the damaging results that can ensue.

Notes

1. The first series on Gehlen in major newspapers ran in Britain in March 1952. The articles were written by Sefton Delmer, a journalist with British intelligence connections. First the U.S. Army, then the CIA, had tried to keep their British ally in the dark about the U.S. relationship with Gehlen. Some in the CIA interpreted the newspaper series as an official British attempt to weaken Gehlen, a man whom they did not trust. Gehlen did not trust the British intelligence services, either. He considered them thoroughly penetrated by the Soviet Union. The CIA arranged the first official meeting between Gehlen and MI-6, the British secret intelligence service, after the Conservatives under Winston Churchill were returned to power in 1953. James Critchfield, interview with author, 17 Aug. 2001.

2. Heinz Höhne and Hermann Zolling, *Network: The Truth about General Gehlen and His Spy Ring*, trans. Richard Barry, (London: Secker and Warburg, 1972); E. H. Cookridge, *Gehlen: Spy of the Century* (New York: Random House, 1972); Reinhard Gehlen, *The Service: The Memoirs of General Reinhard Gehlen*, trans. David Irving (NY: World Publishing, 1972).

3. Mary Ellen Reese, *General Reinhard Gehlen: The CIA Connection* (Fairfax, VA: George Mason University Press, 1990). Two years earlier, Christopher Simpson had addressed the Gehlen-CIA relationship and added new details in *Blowback: America's Recruitment of Nazis and its Effects on the Cold War* (New York: Weidenfeld and Nicholson, 1988). Using fewer new Gehlen-related sources than Reese did, Simpson tended to overstate the OSS' and later the CIA's enthusiasm for Gehlen. Major biographies of Allen Dulles, who was director of central intelligence during the last half of the CIA's sponsorship with Gehlen, also appeared in the 1990s, but Peter Grose, *Gentleman Spy: The Life of Allen Dulles* (Boston: Houghton Mifflin, 1994) and James Srodes, *Allen Dulles: Master of Spies* (Washington, DC: Regnery, 1999) added little to the Gehlen story.

4. James H. Critchfield, *Partners at the Creation: The Men Behind Postwar Germany's Defense and Intelligence Establishments* (Annapolis, MD: Naval Institute Press, 2003).

5. Simpson, *Blowback*, 45.

6. This number is an estimate. It is based on the examination of 743 Name Files released by the CIA (RG 263). There are two reasons to believe that the number is higher than a hundred. In its declassification review, the CIA maintained an inconsistent policy on whether to acknowledge that an individual belonged to the Gehlen Organization. Some files released in 2000 and 2001 contain acknowledgements of an operational relationship with Gehlen. But re-reviews of other files later determined that in some cases, the CIA had redacted references to employment by Gehlen. By 2002, the IWG achieved an agreement that the CIA would not excise evidence that an individual worked for the Gehlen Organization during the period of U.S. sponsorship (1945–1956). By 2002, however, hundreds of Name Files had already been released, and the CIA lacked the personnel to re-review all of these released files to re-insert acknowledgements of Gehlen recruitment where they had been excised. The second reason to believe that the number is higher is that, due to Reinhard Gehlen's reluctance to turn over personality information to the CIA, it is doubtful the CIA ever knew about all of the former SS men Gehlen hired.

7. Gehlen's FHO benefited from the results of the German army's cruel program of interrogating

Soviet POWs. There is evidence that these POWs were tortured and killed, all in violation of the Geneva Convention. However, Gehlen was not in command of this program.

8. More information on Allied communication intelligence is found in the appendix.

9. These were the Ostro, Kraemer, and the Max or Klatt cases. Of these three spies not under Allied control, two were fabricators/entrepreneurs who were spinning nonsense out of newspaper articles and some contacts in neutral countries, and the third was thought to be a Soviet deception run against Berlin. For the judgment of Allied counterintelligence on these cases, see F. H. Hinsley and C. A. G. Simkins, *British Intelligence in the Second World War* vol. 4 (New York: Cambridge University Press, 1990). Although World War II was a golden age of counterintelligence, there were limits to Allied knowledge of German spying. Most of the successes were scored against the Abwehr. From the start, the communications of Heinrich Himmler's SD and Gestapo were more difficult to crack. The SD and Gestapo did not operate against the United States, and their operations against Great Britain were largely restricted to some meddling in Ireland. Only one member of Britain's network of double agents—the double-cross system—was an SD officer. See chapter 4.

10. Analysis of Fremde Heere Ost reports by Hans-Heinrich Wilhelm, "Die Prognosen der Abteilung Fremde Heere Ost 1942–1945," in *Zwei Legenden aus dem Dritten Reich* (Stuttgart: Deutsche Verlags-Anstalt, 1974), 7–75, cited in Kahn, *Hitler's Spies: German Military Intelligence in World War II* (New York: Macmillan, 1978), 440–41.

11. The OSS, an agency of the Joint Chiefs of Staff, was dissolved by executive order in Sept. 1945. Its successor, the Strategic Services Unit, reported to the War Department but was considered a civilian organization.

12. See *Venona: Soviet Espionage and the American Response, 1939–1957*, ed. Robert Louis Benson and Michael Warner, (Washington, DC: National Security Agency/Central Intelligence Agency, 1996), xi–xxii.

13. X-2 veterans James R. Murphy, interview with author, 16 Nov. 1983; and Robert Rushin, interview with author, 10 March 1988.

14. John R. Boker, Jr., Report of Initial Contacts with General Gehlen's Organization, 1 May 1952, *Forging an Intelligence Partnership: CIA and the Origins of the BND, 1945–1949* [hereafter, *CIA and the Origins of the BND*], Kevin C. Ruffner, ed., NA, RG 263, vol. 1, document 6. As a member of the CIA history staff, Dr. Ruffner compiled this superb collection of ninety-seven documents to mark the fiftieth year of CIA-West German cooperation. The collection was declassified in 2002 as part of the CIA's IWG effort.

15. Ibid.

16. Ibid.

17. Ibid.

18. The Abwehr operated Walli until 1944. After the collapse of the Abwehr following the July 1944 attempt on Hitler's life, Gehlen took over Baun's networks.

19. "Statement of Lt. Col. Duin on Early Contacts with the Gehlen Organization," [Undated], NA, RG 263, *CIA and the Origins of the BND*, vol. 1.

20. Crosby Lewis, Chief [X-2 (formerly OSS Counterintelligence) Germany] to [excised] 25 Oct. 1945, ibid.

21. Cable, Critchfield to Crosby Lewis to Richard Helms, Acting Chief of FBM, 8 Oct.

1946, enclosing Lewis to Donald H. Galloway, Assistant Director for Special Operations, Washington, 17 Dec. 1948, NA, RG 263, *CIA and the Origins of the BND*, vol. 2, document 71.

22. Debriefing of Eric Waldman on the U.S. Army's Trusteeship of the Gehlen Organization During the Years 1945–1949, 30 Sept. 1969, NA, RG 263, *CIA and the Origins of the BND*, vol. 1; HQ, USFET, MISC, Lt. Col. John Dean, Jr., to Assistant Chief of Staff, G-2, USFET, "Plan for the Inclusion of the Bolero Group in Operation Rusty," 2 July 1946, NA, RG 263, vol. 1.

23. The code name probably comes from Col. Philp, whose own longtime nickname was Rusty. Chief of Station, Karlsruhe to Chief, FBM, 4 Dec. 1948, NA, RG 263, *CIA and the Origins of the BND*, vol. 2. The figure of approximately four thousand at the time of transfer to the CIA comes from Critchfield's analysis of the Gehlen Organization in December 1948. Cable, Karlsruhe [Critchfield] to SO, 17 Dec. 1948, NA, RG 263, *CIA and the Origins of the BND*, vol. 2.

24. Chief MOB [Critchfield] to Chief, OSO, "Report of Investigation–Rusty," 17 Dec. 1948, NA, RG 263, *CIA and the Origins of the BND*, vol. 2, document 72.

25. Ibid.

26. Maj. Gen. W.A. Burress, G-2, to Lt. Gen. Hoyt S. Vandenberg, Director of Central Intelligence, "Operation Rusty–Use of the Eastern Branch of the Former German Intelligence Service," with attachments, 1 Oct. 1946, NA, RG 263, *CIA and the Origins of the BND*, vol. 1; Debriefing of Eric Waldman on the U.S. Army's Trusteeship of the Gehlen Organization during the Years, 1945–1949, 30 Sept. 1969, NA, RG 263, *CIA and the Origins of the BND*, vol. 1, document 9.

27. The U.S. Army said this to an investigator from the Central Intelligence Group in 1947. See Bossard to DCI, "Operation Rusty," 29 May 1947, NA, RG 263, *CIA and the Origins of the BND*, vol. 2.

28. Ibid. In an effort to sell the SSU on the Rusty Operation, the U.S. Army explained what the group had given them in 1945–46.

29. The Gehlen cryptographic unit was at Oberursel. The CIA reported that this unit was in close contact with the cryptographers at the Army Security Agency. Chief of Station, Karlsruhe to [excised], 18 Nov. 1948, "Rusty," NA, RG 263, *CIA and the Origins of the BND*, vol. 2. A month later Critchfield would describe this effort in more detail in his final report. Chief MOB [Critchfield] to Chief, OSO, "Report of Investigation–Rusty," 17 Dec. 1948, ibid., document 72. Confirmation of this contact with the ASA and information as to when the ASA's successor, the National Security Agency, placed its own intercept station in West Germany came from the author's interview with an NSA official who asked to remain anonymous.

30. Chief MOB [Critchfield] to Chief, OSO, "Report of Investigation–Rusty," 17 Dec. 1948, NA, RG 263, *CIA and the Origins of the BND*, vol. 2, document 72; James Critchfield, interview with author, 17 Aug. 2001. This is how Gehlen himself explained to Critchfield the rapid expansion of his organization.

31. Later CIA background checks on these individuals revealed that they had received ration coupons under assumed names.

32. See the NA, RG 263, Otto von Bolschwing Name File.

33. See NA, RG 263, Name Files on Kurt Auner, Ernst Schlandt, Horia Sima, and Joachim Vacarescu.

34. See NA, RG 263 Name Files on Emil Augsburg, Herbert Boehrsch, Hans Clemens, Heinz Felfe, Kurt Moritz, Walter Otten, Heinrich Josef Reiser, Ernst Schwartzwaller, Carl Schuetz, Otto Somann, and Cornelius Van der Horst. A twelfth person with a criminal background in the GV-L was Paul Hodosy-Strobl, a police general who became the head of the Hungarian State Police during the collaborationist Szálasi regime in 1944–45. See NA, RG 263, Paul Hodosy-Strobl Name File.

35. Richard Breitman, "Historical Analysis of 20 Name Files from CIA Records," April 2001, http://www.archives.gov/iwg/declassified_records/rg_263_cia_records/rg_263_report.html.

36. NA, RG 263, Erich Deppner Name File. Deppner was head of Abt. I of the Sipo and SD in the Hague. He was commended by Heinrich Himmler in June 1943 for his good work in Holland. See Chief, Munich to Chief, EUR, 5 Dec. 1966. Deppner ultimately served nine months in prison in 1960–61 for having shot Soviet POWs in occupied Holland. In this document, the CIA notes that despite the war crimes conviction, the BND hired him back to do "research" at home "on non-sensitive matters."

37. NA, RG 263, Ernst Makowski Name File.

38. NA, RG 263, Karl Guse and Napoleon Krasnowski Name Files. The so-called Krasnowski file covers the career of Werner Krassowski.

39. NA, RG 263, Konrad Fiebig Name File. Fiebig was acquitted in 1962 for lack of sufficient evidence, but the BND did not believe he was innocent of all crimes, so retired him.

40. Fiebig was in section GV-H.

41. NA, RG 263, Walter Kurreck Name File.

42. NA, RG 263, Alexander Doloezalek Name File,.

43. NA, RG 263, Friedrich Frank Name File.

44. James Critchfield described the recruitment procedures for Dienststelle 114 [later GV-L] after his visit to its field stations in the fall of 1948. Chief, MOB [Critchfield] to Chief, OSO, "Report of Investigation–Rusty," with annexes, 17 Dec. 1948, NA, RG 263, *CIA and the Origins of the BND*, vol. 2, document 72. In August 1949, Gehlen explained to CIA the rationale behind this system. 34 [Gehlen] to 20 [Critchfield], 22 Aug. 1949, NA, RG 263, *CIA and the Origins of the BND*, vol. 2, document 97.

45. NA, RG 263, Konrad Fiebig Name File.

46. NA, RG 263, Erich Ulich Kayser-Eichberg Name File.

47. NA, RG 263, Emil Augsburg Name File.

48. NA, RG 263, Franz Six Name File.

49. Gehlen, *Memoirs*, 137.

50. Ibid.

51. In June 1948, Gehlen wrote a letter to Liebl's superior to demand that he be sent home. Debriefing of Eric Waldman on the U.S. Army's Trusteeship of the Gehlen Organization During the Years 1945–1949, NA, RG 263, *CIA and the Origins of the BND*, vol. 1, document 9.

52. Enclosure 2a, Gehlen to General Walsh, [Critchfield] to Chief, FBM, "[Gehlen Organization]

General Policy," 7 July 1949, NA, RG 263, *CIA and the Origins of the BND*, vol. 2, document 94.

53. In August 1948, Gehlen wrote to Samuel Bossard, the CIA officer who had done the first CIA survey of Rusty in 1947, to ask him to return to West Germany to discuss "some dangerous points which have to be handled in the right way to prevent increasing disappointment and perhaps a strike of our employees." This raised concerns at the very top of the Agency. See Rear Admiral R. H. Hillenkoetter, DCI, to Lt. General S. J. Chamberlin, Dir of Intel, U.S. Army, 31 Aug. 1948, NA, RG 263, *CIA and the Origins of the BND*, vol. 2, document 64.

54. Bossard to DCI, "Operation Rusty," 29 May 1947, ibid., document 42.

55. Maj. Gen. W. A. Burress, G-2, to Lt. Gen. Hoyt S. Vandenberg, Director of Central Intelligence, "Operation Rusty–Use of the Eastern Branch of the Former German Intelligence Service," with attachments, 1 Oct. 1946, ibid., document 19. Burress explained to Vandenberg that the Germans believed it would take $2.5 million a year to run the intelligence service they were capable of in Europe. The U.S. Army claimed to the SSU in mid-1946 that it had received permission to spend $2.5 million on the project but that it could only afford to do this through the end of the 1947 fiscal year. See Crosby Lewis to Col. Donald Galloway, "Keystone Operation," 22 Sept. 1946, ibid.

56. Ibid.

57. Kevin Ruffner, "American Intelligence and the Gehlen Organization, 1945–1949," *CIA Studies in Intelligence* (1997), 73.

58. Ibid.

59. Ibid.

60. The most important supporter was General Edwin L. Sibert, who as chief of U.S. military intelligence in Germany had been Philp's commander in Europe. When he joined CIG in the fall of 1946, he briefed Vandenberg on the Rusty project and pushed for CIG to consider the Army's offer very seriously. See Report of Interview with General Edwin L. Sibert on the Gehlen Organization [undated], NA, RG 263, *CIA and the Origins of the BND*, vol. 1, document 8.

61. Bossard to DCI, "Operation Rusty," 29 May 1947, NA, RG 263, *CIA and the Origins of the BND*, vol. 2.

62. Heidelberg to SO, 8 Apr. 1947, NA, RG 263, *CIA and the Origins of the BND*, vol. 1.

63. Ibid. Emphasis in original.

64. Bossard to DCI, "Operation Rusty," 29 May 1947, NA, RG 263, *CIA and the Origins of the BND*, vol. 2.

65. Ibid.

66. CIG German mission to Bossard, 1 Apr. 1947, "Evaluation of Rusty CI Reports," NA, RG 263, *CIA and the Origins of the BND*, vol. 1. The CIG mission concluded that "if the Rusty operation aims at the development of a full-fledged CE service, then it must be in the earliest stages of organization." The CIG office rejected "a high percentage of the reports" that Bossard sent for evaluation. The Bossard quotation comes from Bossard to DCI, "Operation Rusty," 29 May 1947, NA, RG 263, *CIA and the Origins of the BND*, vol. 2.

67. Ibid.

68. Ibid.

69. Ibid.
70. Ibid.
71. Ibid.
72. Ibid.
73. Hillenkoetter to Secretaries of State, etc. [never sent], 6 June 1947, ibid.
74. James Critchfield, interview with author, 17 Aug. 2001.
75. Chief MOB [Critchfield] to Chief, OSO, "Report of Investigation–Rusty," 17 Dec. 1948, NA, RG 263, *CIA and the Origins of the BND*, vol. 2, document 72.
76. Cable, Critchfield to Special Operations, Washington, 17 Dec. 1948, ibid., document 71.
77. Critchfield hardly mentioned Baun in his report. In his memoirs, he recalls how Gehlen eclipsed this once-powerful spymaster. Critchfield, *Partners at the Creation*, 116–18.
78. James Critchfield, "The Gehlen Organization," 25 Jan. 2002, NA, IWG Administrative Files.
79. "Organization 114," an annex to Chief MOB [Critchfield] to Chief, OSO, "Report of Investigation–Rusty," 17 Dec. 1948, NA, RG 263, *CIA and the Origins of the BND*, vol. 2, document 72.
80. Shortly before his death in April 2003, James Critchfield wrote his recollections of the Augsburg case for the historians of the IWG. He recalled meeting Dr. Alberti on a number of occasions after 1953 and mentioned that the CIA, which knew that Alberti was an alias, initiated efforts to determine Alberti's real name beginning in 1949. He did not recall meeting him in 1948. Critchfield, "Case Histories," 7 Mar. 2002, NA, IWG Administrative Files.
81. Chief of Station, Karlsruhe to Chief, Foreign Division M, 3 Aug. 1950, NA, RG 263, Paul Hodosy-Strobl Name File. In July 1950, Gehlen asked Critchfield for the CIA's help in obtaining a visa for Hodosy and two other GV-L Hungarians to emigrate to the U.S. Critchfield suggested to Washington that "each case should be considered separately." Washington determined Hodosy was ineligible for emigration. He was also dropped from Zipper in 1950. See his Name File for the story of this attempted emigration in 1950. Information about Hodosy-Strobl's background and his work for the CIC also comes from his Name File. Hodosy-Strobl later went to Brazil and successfully emigrated to the United States in 1963 and was naturalized in 1970. Critchfield described the "Hungarian Group" and its chief, without naming him, in the annex on Dienststelle 114 in his report of 17 Dec. 1948.
82. Gehlen, *Memoirs*, 226.
83. Chief, FBM [Richard Helms] to Chief of Station, Karlsruhe "[Gehlen Organization]," 2 Feb. 1949, NA, RG 263, *CIA and the Origins of the BND*, vol. 2, document 79.
84. Chief, Foreign Branch M [Helms] to Chief, Karlsruhe Station, Attn [Critchfield], 9 Feb. 1949, NA, RG 263, *CIA and the Origins of the BND*, vol. 2, document 82.
85. Galloway to DCI, "Recommendations in re Operation Rusty," 21 Dec. 1948, NA, RG 263, *CIA and the Origins of the BND*, vol. 2, document 73. Helms expressed similar sentiments in February 1949. See Chief, FBM [Richard Helms] to Chief of Station, Karlsruhe. "[Gehlen Organization]," 2 Feb. 1949, ibid., document 79.
86. Chief, FBM [Richard Helms] to Chief of Station, Karlsruhe. "[Gehlen Organization]," 2 Feb.

1949, ibid., document 79.

87. Chief, Foreign Branch M [Helms] to Chief, Karlsruhe Station, Attn [Critchfield], 9 Feb. 1949, NA, RG 263, *CIA and the Origins of the BND*, vol. 2, document 82.

88. The analysis of the breakdown of the reports comes from Critchfield's 17 Dec. 1948 report. The figure for the number of reports in Dec. 1948 comes from a chart prepared by Gehlen. See [Critchfield] to Chief, FBM, "Dr. Schneider's Reply to Recent Policy Guidance Letters," 12 Oct. 1949, ibid., document 94.

89. [Critchfield] to Chief, FBM, "[Gehlen Organization]: Current Situation," 18 Apr. 1949, ibid., document 89.

90. Chief of Station, Karlsruhe to Chief, FBM, "Rusty," 19 Aug. 1948, cited in Kevin Ruffner, "American Intelligence and the Gehlen Organization, 1945–1949, *Studies in Intelligence*, 76.

91. Helms, Memorandum for the Files, "Operation Rusty," 1 Feb. 1949, NA, RG 263, *CIA and the Origins of the BND*, vol. 2, document 78.

92. Critchfield to Dr. Schneider [Gehlen], 15 June 1949, NA, RG 263, *CIA and the Origins of the BND*, vol. 2.

93. Gehlen had also promised in the fall of 1948 that "basic central records on all agent personnel" were being collected. Gehlen blamed Baun for the fact that his headquarters lacked sufficient information on the agents the organization had recruited. See Chief MOB [Critchfield] to Chief, OSO, "Report of Investigation–Rusty," 17 Dec. 1948, NA, RG 263, *CIA and the Origins of the BND*, vol. 2, document 72. By mid-1949, Gehlen would be explaining to the CIA why the Baun system could not be changed. On this point see 34 [Gehlen] to 20 [Critchfield], "Personal Data," 22 Aug. 1949, NA, RG 263, *CIA and the Origins of the BND*, vol. 2, enclosure to document 97.

94. 34 [Gehlen] to 20 [Critchfield], "Personal Data," 22 Aug. 1949, NA, RG 263, *CIA and the Origins of the BND*, vol. 2, enclosure to document 97.

95. In an interview with the author on 12 Nov. 2002, Critchfield explained that on his first visit, he had asked Gehlen for a description of his organization and for the aliases and real names of his operatives. Within a week, Gehlen had given him 150 names. On the fragmentary information turned over on the projects outside the Soviet zone, see Critchfield to Dr. Schneider [Gehlen], 20 Sept. 1949, NA, RG 263, *CIA and the Origins of the BND*, vol. 2.

96. Critchfield to Dr. Schneider [Gehlen], 20 Sept. 1949, ibid., document 96; [Critchfield] to Chief, FBM [Helms], "Dr. Schneider's [Gehlen's] Reply to Recent Policy Guidance Letters," 12 Oct. 1949, ibid., document 97.

97. Ibid.

98. Ibid.

99. Ibid.

100. James Critchfield, interview with author, 17 Aug. 2001.

101. See the NA, RG 263, Name Files for Otto von Bolschwing, Kurt Auner, Ernst Schlandt, Horia Sima, and Joachim Vacarescu.

102. For examples of the background checks the CIA undertook before hiring SS men in the early Cold War, see the NA, RG 263, Name Files for Karl Jobke and Friedrich Carstenn.

103. For more on the CIA's handling of Otto von Bolschwing, see chapter 13.

104. Bossard to DCI, "Operation Rusty," 29 May 1947, NA, RG 263, *CIA and the Origins of the BND*, vol. 2.

105. [Critchfield] to Chief, FBM, "[Gehlen Organization]–Dr. Schneider's Negotiations with Third Parties," 22 Sept. 1949, NA, RG 263, *CIA and the Origins of the BND*, vol. 2.

106. Both Gehlen and Critchfield mention in their memoirs that the CIA discouraged Gehlen's politicking in late 1949.

107. Blind Memo, "Intelligence Estimate," [handwritten date: May 1950], NA, RG 263, Reinhard Gehlen Name File, vol. 1.

108. NA, RG 263, Reinhard Gehlen Name File. The new cryptonym came into effect 20 Sept. 1949.

109. James Critchfield writes delicately about this difficult period in the U.S.-Gehlen relationship. See Critchfield, *Partners at the Creation*, 121–27.

110. [Critchfield] to Chief, Foreign Division "K," 3 Apr. 1950, "Meeting of Allied High Commission with Chancellor," with "verbatim report" attached, NA, RG 263, Reinhard Gehlen Name File, vol. 1.

111. Critchfield, *Partners at the Creation*, 126.

112. The Anglo-American tension over the emergent West German intelligence community deserves its own treatment. Despite close Anglo-American intelligence cooperation elsewhere in the world, the CIA maintained a strict policy of walling off the Gehlen Organization from the British secret services until after 1951. James Critchfield, interview with author, 17 Aug. 2001.

113. Blind Memo, "Intelligence Estimate," [handwritten date: May 1950], NA, RG 263, Reinhard Gehlen Name File, vol. 1.

114. Although an effort was made to find a reflection of attitudes toward Gehlen in High Commission and National Security Council materials, the only mention of the BfV incident is in CIA documents in the Gehlen Name File.

115. Quoted in a later summary of recent events in the CIA-Zipper relationship, Blind Memo, 4 Jan. 1951, NA, RG 263, Gehlen Name File, vol. 1.

116. Ibid.

117. Chief [excised] Karlsruhe to Chief [excised], 9 May 1950, "Dr. Hans Globke," NA, RG 263, Hans Globke Name File. In April, Globke told an officer from the U.S. High Commission in Germany that though he had not yet met Gehlen, he considered him "a competent and honest person." J. S. Arouet, "Interview with Dr. Hans Globke," 7 Apr. 1950, ibid.

118. The U.S. government was well aware of Globke's role in the implementation of the Nuremberg Laws when Adenauer elevated him to the Chancellor's office. See NA, RG 263, Hans Globke Name File.

119. Pullach to ADSO, 30 Dec. 1950, NA, RG 263, Reinhard Gehlen Name File, vol. 1.

120. Blind Memo, "Summary," [Handwritten Date: 4 Jan. 1951], NA, RG 263, Reinhard Gehlen Name File, vol. 1.

121. Critchfield, *Partners at the Creation*, 126.

122. Ibid., 156–57.

123. Ibid., 119–30.

124. Ibid., 157.

125. [Critchfield] to Chief, Foreign Division M, 30 Mar. 1951, "Zipper [excised] Complex," NA, RG 263, Reinhard Gehlen Name File, vol. 1.

126. James Critchfield, interview with author, 17 Aug. 2001; Critchfield, *Partners at the Creation*, 19.

127. Critchfield, "The Gehlen Organization," 25 Jan. 2002, NA, IWG Administrative Files.

128. [Critchfield] to Chief, Foreign Division M, 7 June 1951, "Utility's Visit to the USA," NA, RG 263, Reinhard Gehlen Name File, vol. 1.

129. Extract, " [excised]-Globke Meeting, 9 August '51," 10 Aug. [19]51, NA, RG 263, Reinhard Gehlen Name File, vol. 1. In a conversation with the author on 30 Jan. 2002, James Critchfield confirmed that Adenauer was the German official whose name is redacted from this document as declassified.

130. Ibid.

131. James Critchfield, interview with author, 18 Feb. 2002.

132. Letter, W. B. Smith to Gehlen, [no date, but cover letter is dated 13 Jan. 1953], NA, RG 263, Reinhard Gehlen Name File.

133. Ibid.

134. In November 1951, CIA Karlsruhe sent Pullach background information on these men in response to a trace request. NA, RG 263, Walter Vollmer Name File.

135. See NA, RG 263, Cornelius Van Der Horst Name File.

136. James Critchfield, interview with author, 12 Nov. 2002. See also James Critchfield, "Memorandum for the Record, November 2002," NA, IWG Administrative Files, which concerns the CIA's first vetting of Heinz Felfe in 1952.

137. NA, RG 263, Heinz Felfe Name File. On 19 September 1952, CIA Pullach requested traces from CIA headquarters on Felfe and Schuetz. The CIA discovered Felfe in September 1952, when he made an official request for information from the Ministeriums für Gesamtdeutsche Fragen on a suspect's automobile registration. The Agency then asked Zipper directly about him. See Felfe Traces, Handwritten Date, 1 Dec. 1953, ibid. When Kurt Moritz sought a U.S. travel visa in mid-1952, the Agency discovered enough to determine that this former SS-man was also in GV-L. See NA, RG 263, Kurt Moritz Name File.

138. It is difficult to determine when the CIA detected a particular individual. However, on 5 July 1951, the POB sent trace requests on Emil Augsburg and in return was sent a report that in 1950 he had been transferred from GV-L in the field to Zipper headquarters to work as chief specialist on the Soviet intelligence services. On 28 January 1953, the CIA opened a new file on Augsburg (alias Althaus), who was described as creating Zipper's handbook on the Soviet intelligence services. The CIA first traced Erich Deppner on 28 Apr. 1950 and 16 Mar. 1953. See Director to CIA Munich, 27 June 1961, NA, RG 263, Erich Deppner Name File. In February 1953, the CIA determined that the Zipper agent living under the alias Konrad Fiedler was Konrad Fiebig, who had been wanted by the CIC in 1946 for mass murder. See "Fiebig, Konrad," trace list, 29 July 1954, NA, RG 263, Konrad Fiebig Name File.

139. CIA Pullach knew his background before it knew Augsburg's Zipper alias. In 1949, the CIA was aware that Augsburg had worked with the CIC as part of the same agent network as Klaus Barbie. In August 1951, James Critchfield was told that this same individual had been with the "SD Einsatzkommando UdSSR." See Chief Karlsruhe to James Critchfield, 1 Aug. 1951,

NA, RG 263, Emil Augsburg Name File.

140. Information on this OPC operation is limited to these three Name Files released under the Nazi War Crimes Disclosure Act: NA, RG 263, Friedrich Carstenn, Karl Otto Jobke, and Eberhard Tellkamp Name Files.

141. Jobke, who had been a Gestapo officer in Danzig before the war, later served with the Einsatzkommandos in Poland before joining the SD. Tellkamp was in the Allgemeine SS before joining the Waffen-SS in 1935. During the war he was a Lt. Col. in units known to have participated in atrocities in the Balkans and Poland. The third recruit, Carstenn, had been an expert on Scandinavia and England in the SD before becoming an SS-Sturmbannführer with the SD "culture" section.

142. There is a fourth SS man hired at that time, who may have also been part of the same operation. The newly released Hans Rues Name File indicates that the field received operational clearance from CIA headquarters to run him at about the same time as the others. Given his background, which is similar to Tellkamp's, there is reason to believe he was part of the same OPC operation. Three years after joining the Allgemeine SS in 1936, Hans Rues entered the Waffen-SS. He rose to the rank of Captain in the "Prinz Eugen" division, which committed war crimes in anti-partisan activities on the eastern front.

143. NA, RG 263, Wolfgang Paul Hoeher Name File.

144. There is no indication in the CIA Wolfgang Hoeher Name File of the source of the CIA's concerns in July 1952.

145. The Geyer defection is discussed in Reese, *General Reinhard Gehlen*, 129–32; and Critchfield, *Partners at the Creation*, 171–72.

146. Critchfield to Chief, EE, "Zipper's CI/CE Agency," Dec. 1953, NA, RG 263, Emil Augsburg Name File.

147. It is clear from the Augsburg Name File that the CIA certainly knew that Emil Augsburg was the true name of Dr. Alberti in Dec. 1953, but it might have learned this earlier.

148. This conclusion is based on an examination of the eleven CIA Name Files for SS men in GV-L.

149. 66th CIC, 24 June 1954, "Felfe, Heinz," NA, RG 319, IRR, entry 149A, box 145A, Reinhard Gehlen, vol. 3.

150. 66th CIC, 22 Nov. 1954, ibid. Albert's recruitment by source X-899-HQ on 29 September 1954 is described in Lt. Col. Ira K. Ewalt to CO, 66th CIC, 29 Oct. 1954, "Gehlen Organization," ibid.

151. Section III, 66th CI group, 22 Nov. 1954, "Gehlen Organization," ibid.

152. 66th CIC, 29 Oct. 1954, ibid.

153. Ibid.

154. Col. Warren S. Leroy to Asst. Chief of Staff, USAEUR, 1 Apr. 1955, NA, RG 319, IRR, entry 149A, box 145A, Reinhard Gehlen, vol. 1.

155. In his memoirs, James Critchfield would make much of this fact. The "U.S. intelligence community never was functional in Germany," he wrote in a section blaming the CIC for the ease with which Heinz Felfe remained a Soviet mole into the early 1960s. See Critchfield, *Partners at the Creation*, 198. However, the CIA materials released under the Nazi War Crimes Disclosure Act make plain that though the CIA was kept in the dark about the CIC's

penetration project, it learned on its own about the allegations against Felfe in 1954 and did little about them until 1957.

156. Trace List, [undated, but last trace is dated 20 Nov. 56], NA, RG 263, Heinz Felfe Name File.

157. James Critchfield recalled that Felfe had been put on a list of possible moles in 1954, but this was based on flimsy information. James Critchfield, interview with author, 12 Nov. 2002.

158. Blind Memorandum for the Records, "@Friesen," [undated, but from context 1956; it was an attachment to a 14 July 1959 document on "Heinz Felfe @ Hans Friesen"], NA, RG 263, Heinz Felfe Name File; see also Memo, "Conversation with @Friesen on 28 March 1956," 29 Mar. 1956, NA, RG 263, Heinz Felfe Name File. It seems the latter was written by the same CIA officer as the undated memo cited above. Some of the same phrases appear in both memos to describe Felfe's character and motivation. The "@Friesen" also appears to be an idiosyncratic way to refer to Felfe.

159. Ibid.

160. Dulles meeting with Gehlen, Sept. 1954, NA, RG 263, Reinhard Gehlen Name File.

161. Gehlen, *Memoirs*, 344.

162. Ibid.

163. Ibid., 203.

164. Ibid.

165. Miles Copeland, *The Game of Nations: The Amorality of Power Politics* (New York: Simon and Schuster, 1970), 104.

166. A document in the CIA Eichmann Name File outlines the Agency's lack of knowledge about Gehlen's Mideast operations in 1958. See Chief [excised] Munich to Chief, EE, "[BND] Near East Connections," 19 Mar. 1958, NA, RG 263, Adolf Eichmann Name File. See also the Otto Skorzeny, Karl Radl, Joachim Deumling, Leopold von Mildenstein, Friedrich Beissner, Franz Rademacher, Otto Ernest Remer, Johannes von Leers, Joseph Tiefenbacher, and Friedrich Voss Name Files, NA, RG 263. The Deumling Name File, in particular, shows how unsure the CIA was about the nature of Gehlen's penetration of the Egyptian colony in Cairo in the mid-1950s. The CIA on its own, however, may have had some dealings with Skorzeny. Although the CIA Skorzeny Name File provides no hint of a relationship in the late 1950s, the FBI's Skorzeny file indicates that in 1959 a CIA officer in Madrid requested a visa for Skorzeny to visit the United States, characterizing the visit as being in the interest of the United States. When the State Department balked, CIA headquarters refused to back up its field officer. See NA, RG 65, Records of the FBI, World War II Collection, 98-37716–Otto Skorzeny, box 5. IWG requests for additional CIA materials on the possible relationship between the CIA in Madrid and Skorzeny in the late 1950s remained unanswered at the time this book was published.

167. James Critchfield recalled that Gehlen regularly made trips to Switzerland to meet special agents; "Gehlen," he recalled, "had special relations with the Swiss police." Critchfield, who accompanied Gehlen on some but by no means all of these trips, doubts that Skorzeny was one of these special agents. James Critchfield, interview with author, 30 Jan. 2002.

168. David C. Martin, *Wilderness of Mirrors* (New York: Harper and Row, 1980), 103.

169. In 1959, a CIA agent in Polish intelligence, Michal Goleniewsky, reported that a KGB

colleague had bragged that of the six BND officers sent to the United States for training in 1956, two were KGB moles. Felfe visited the United States in 1956. The other mole has not been publicly revealed. See Martin, *Wilderness*, 103.

170. See NA, RG 263, Hans Clemens and Wilhelm Krichbaum Name Files; see also Paul Brown, "Analysis of the Name File of Wilhelm Krichbaum," http://www.archives.gov/iwg/declassified_records/rg_263_cia_records/rg_263_krichbaum.html, National Archives, (accessed March 31, 2004).

171. A CIC report from early 1956 suggests that some CIA support for the Gehlen Organization continued after the formal establishment of the BND. Among other items, the CIA offered to share the costs of some operations and would provide logistical support for Gehlen operations in Berlin. Memo, CI Branch, G-2, USAEUR, 13 Feb. 1956, NA, RG 319, IRR, entry 134B, Reinhard Gehlen, vol. 5.

172. Cable, 66th CIC, no date, NA, RG 319, IRR, entry 134B, Reinhard Gehlen, vol. 4.

173. James Critchfield, interview with author, 17 Aug. 2001.

15

Manhunts:
The Official Search for Notorious Nazis

Norman J. W. Goda

THE SHADOW OF THE NAZI PERIOD is a long one, particularly in terms of the search for notorious Nazi criminals. The 1960 Israeli capture of Adolf Eichmann still fires the public imagination, due to the daring nature of the kidnapping and to the historic importance of Eichmann's trial.[1] Also fervent in the public imagination are those Nazi figures of singular evil who disappeared after the war and who, unlike Eichmann, managed to escape justice entirely—or at least for a far longer time. Popular books and films—historical and fictional—based on figures like Josef Mengele (the infamous Auschwitz doctor) have helped to keep the Nazi past in the public imagination.

Behind public fascination lie untold, less glamorous, and often frustrating episodes in the international hunt for such figures. Newly declassified State Department, FBI, and CIA records provide glimpses into the search by U.S. agencies for vanished figures of the Third Reich. The cases of prominent Gestapo figures Heinrich Müller, Walter Rauff, and Alois Brunner are discussed in chapter six. The cases of Martin Bormann, Klaus Barbie, and Josef Mengele follow.

A scholarly analysis of such manhunts is worthwhile. Aside from the historical meaning that war criminals carry in the context of their wartime careers, such individuals assume meaning beyond their crimes as the years pass. Like mirrors of morality, manhunts cast a poor light on nations that shelter criminals and a more benevolent glow on those that work for their capture. While satisfying an intrinsic need for judicial reckoning, manhunts also have a broader cultural meaning, which reflects their own time as well as a more painful past.

Justice Robert Jackson, the FBI, and the Search for Martin Bormann
No figure has fuelled the popular imagination as much as Martin Bormann: the chief of the Nazi Party Chancellery following Rudolf Hess' flight to Scotland in 1941, Secretary to the Führer himself after April 1943, and perhaps the most powerful member of Hitler's inner circle after that time. "Everything," Joseph Goebbels once lamented, "goes through Bormann." Reich Chancellery chief

Hans Heinrich Lammers once complained that Bormann was the true interpreter of Hitler's directives. Bormann was loyal to Hitler to the very end, helping to create Nazi guerrilla organizations toward the end of the war and informing Party leaders on April 1, 1945, that terrible justice awaited anyone "who does not fight to the last breath," helping to trigger arbitrary violence against those who recognized Germany's defeat.[2]

Unlike the bodies of Hitler, Heinrich Himmler, and Goebbels—leading Nazis who escaped the Nuremberg trials by taking their own lives—Bormann's body was not found either before or during the proceedings. The Office of Strategic Services (OSS) concluded in August 1945 that Bormann most likely died in the final battle for Berlin on May 2, 1945, but the possibility remained that he would turn up alive. He was included as a defendant in the Nuremberg indictment and a case was prepared against him. Bormann was "served" with a warrant via radio before the trial began in October 1945, tried in absentia, found guilty, and sentenced to death. The file on Bormann was never closed because the intelligence of his whereabouts was never solid. Various reports had it that he was hiding in Germany, Austria, Denmark, and elsewhere. Not until 1972 was the mystery laid to rest. Road construction workers in West Berlin unearthed a skeleton proven to be Bormann's from dental records. DNA testing in 1999 confirmed these results and the veracity of reports that Bormann, along with his doctor Ludwig Stumpfegger, had swallowed poison on May 2, 1945.[3]

Following his success as the chief prosecutor at the international Nuremberg trials, Supreme Court Justice Robert S. Jackson returned to the bench. He brought home with him a permanent mistrust of the Soviet Union based on constant friction with Soviet prosecutors. It was partially on Jackson's recommendation to President Harry Truman that a second international trial, this time of leading German business figures, was shelved. The United States, Jackson said toward the end of the first judicial venture with the Soviets, should hold subsequent trials alone.[4] Truman needed no convincing. Relations with the Soviets had already entered a tense phase that would culminate in the Berlin Blockade of 1948. By the end of the Nuremberg trials, the Soviets had yet to hold promised democratic elections in Poland, and their relationship with the Allies in occupied Germany had developed acrimoniously due partly to the favors the Soviets gave to German Communists in their zone.[5] The purported laxity of the West on the issue of war crimes trials and punishment of the guilty was a Communist propaganda theme that began in October 1946 with the Nuremberg acquittals of Hjalmar Schacht, Franz von Papen, and Hans Fritzsche and the sentencing of seven other defendants to prison instead of to death. While Western nations looked at the Nuremberg sentences with a certain satisfaction, the Communist-controlled Eastern press expressed outrage that the lives of nearly half the Nazis on trial at Nuremberg had been spared by the Allied judges.

Soviet and East German propaganda efforts drove the subsequent U.S. search for Bormann. It was not undertaken with a high expectation that Bormann would be located. Well-informed intelligence and law enforcement agencies already assumed the most likely solution to the Bormann mystery—that he was dead. But there were concerns in the highest reaches of the U.S. government that the Soviets would use Bormann's supposed presence in Argentina as a propaganda weapon against the Allies, which could in turn have repercussions in Europe, where the Cold War had entered a pivotal phase.

In early May 1948, Jackson received information from an informant named John F. Griffiths, who reached the Supreme Court Justice through contacts in the State Department. Griffiths, a former employee at the U.S. Embassy in Buenos Aires, claimed that he knew a local Argentine handyman—later revealed as Juan Serrino—who had worked on a German-owned ranch on the South Atlantic coast near La Caleta, close to the River Plate region in southern Argentina. The ranch was owned by a man named Müller and, according to Serrino, a number of Germans lived there. In the middle of 1946, Griffiths said, Müller indiscreetly told Serrino that a certain newcomer to the ranch for whom all the Germans there had shown reverence was Martin Bormann. Serrino had told Griffiths that he had never heard of Bormann before, but that he saw Bormann at the estate nearly every day while working there. Serrino, according to Griffiths, also heard that Bormann had arrived in Argentina by submarine, that Bormann returned to Europe in the spring of 1946 through Spain, and that he returned to Argentina with two large crates of documents that had been hidden in Bavaria.[6]

Jackson was skeptical, but he remembered from Nuremberg a nagging possibility that Bormann might have escaped with the help of the Soviets. When interrogating other prisoners at the U.S. Army's detention facility at Bad Mondorf (code named "Ashcan"), the Soviets had offered the Americans the chance to interrogate Bormann, but the next day they insisted that the Americans had been mistaken.[7] Now Bormann, if alive, could also have a cache of important documents. Jackson therefore told the president himself about the information, and the president, Jackson said, "was keenly interested in the Griffiths report." Truman asked Jackson to consult the FBI and then to make an informed recommendation to the president on how to proceed. On May 6, Jackson and J. Edgar Hoover spoke, and while Hoover thought the issue should be handled by the CIA, Jackson "thought perhaps it could be worked out as part of a follow-up to the Nurenberg [sic] trials [wherein] he would have the authority to carry out any additional investigations and delegate this matter as he saw fit."[8] Jackson preferred to use his old Justice Department connections.[9]

There was nothing on the face of the Griffiths report to distinguish it from the many other false Bormann sightings. The FBI had received reports that Bormann was in Argentina, Mexico, and even Nevada.[10] FBI Special Agent Francis Crosby, a former legal attaché in Buenos Aires, interviewed Griffiths on the evening of May 6, 1948, shortly after Hoover's discussion with Jackson, and said that though Griffiths was truly convinced that Bormann was on the Argentine estate, "the story is certainly on the fantastic side."[11]

Yet this story contained a political element. Griffiths had contacted Jackson through sophisticated channels. He also had a political agenda. Griffiths had been removed from the U.S. Embassy staff in Buenos Aires in mid-1946 because he was a vocal opponent of the Perón regime and friendly with Argentine labor circles and other Perónist political opponents. Soon after, Griffiths was expelled from Argentina, allegedly for trying to trigger a bank strike, and he was now living in Uruguay.[12] Given Griffiths' political sympathies and the fact that he contacted Jackson himself, perhaps the story was part of a Soviet maneuver to discredit the United States further on the war crimes issue. Immediately after the war, the Soviets had accused the British of sheltering Bormann, and on several occasions in 1945, Radio Moscow had claimed that Bormann was in Argentina. After Nuremberg, such disinformation was of additional propaganda value.[13] Jackson understood this. According to Crosby, who met with Jackson in May 1948, Jackson was most impressed "by the propaganda use which the Russians might make of real or apparent American laxity toward looking for a criminal wanted as badly as Bormann." Jackson said that the president's interest, too, focused "particularly on that aspect involving the Russians."[14]

In a long FBI memorandum on Bormann prepared to assist Justice Jackson with his report to the president, the argument was made that Soviet disinformation could have a "considerable and probably very effective" negative impact on the U.S. image in Europe. The memorandum added that there had been earlier reports that the Soviets had helped Bormann escape to Argentina. If they had, it continued, such reports "would make clear the real attitude of the Russians in their relations with the [W]estern powers and would show clearly the designs which the Russians have on the [W]estern [H]emisphere."[15]

In preparing the memorandum on Bormann, the FBI discovered something else. In March 1947, over a year earlier, the FBI had secretly received two British intercepts from an undisclosed source named "Bureau Source Two" that mentioned Bormann. They came to the attention of the FBI only by accident. "It appeared," assistant director D. M. Ladd would explain to Hoover in May 1948, that

the British were intercepting and decoding traffic over a clandestine network, [which had survived] the German defeat . . . The existence of this network. . . was said to be a closely guarded secret and traffic intercepted was handled on an "eyes only" basis . . . instead of the customary "top secret" basis on which Source Two material is handled. On the day these particular messages, dealing with Bormann, were received, the Army officer handling the "eyes only" traffic was away and the Navy got hold of the two messages. They were published as regular diplomatic traffic by the Navy . . . The British were, as usual, horrified at the lack of security [and] rumbling from the incident is still going on in the Army.

"These intercepts," continued Ladd, "unless some very pointless deception was being engaged in, are a very close indication that Bormann is alive."[16]

The two intercepts from February 1947 were suggestive. Both came from traffic between Madrid and Barcelona. The first, from February 14, said, "tell us whether you know Martin Borman [sic] personally and whether he would recognize you. Your collaboration would be necessary in order to save this person. Tell us whether you are prepared to help in this matter." The second intercept, of February 21, commented that, "The matter of Martin has been postponed. I shall tell you about it when we meet . . . Affectionate Greetings, Mariano."[17] The U.S. Consul General in Barcelona, Richard Ford, took various steps to "discover the reliability of reports that Martin Bormann had landed or would soon land at this port on his way to South America."[18] Bormann never turned up, and interest in the intercepts waned until Jackson sparked it again the following year. For the moment, even sober minds within the FBI talked about a possible investigation in Argentina. Due to the lack of available photographs that could identify Bormann, the Bureau thought that "Hitler's personal photographer, [Heinrich] Hoffmann might be such a witness . . . [It] might become necessary to take [him] to [Argentina] . . . to definitely identify [Bormann].[19]

Hoover communicated all of this to Jackson on May 14.[20] As Jackson studied the available materials, the Bureau tried to get to the bottom of the British intercepts. This was tricky. "Because of the security consideration involved," said Ladd, "it is necessary that the Bureau maintain the posture that it has no information from Source Two on Bormann. However," he suggested to Hoover, "inquiry should be made of the British, and probably could be made with some degree of success on the basis that persistent rumors are being received concerning Bormann."[21] Hoover took up the suggestion and ordered his legal attaché in London, J.A. Cimperman, to make a discreet inquiry with British intelligence. "For your exclusive information," Hoover said, "a serious indication has been received that Bormann is still alive and some details concerning this are known to the British. However, because of the manner in which this information was obtained, no indication that the Bureau possesses it may be given them."[22] Cimperman quickly received answers from both MI-5 and MI-6. "This office," replied the former, "is of the opinion that this highly important Nazi character is not alive."[23] "We have no specific information on this point," replied MI-6, "and can say only that all Allied Intelligence agencies have searched for him in vain."[24]

Such reports cooled the Bureau's ardor to investigate further. "It might . . . be of assistance to Justice Jackson, in making his recommendation to President Truman," said Ladd, "to intimate to him that the Bureau is of the opinion that running out the leads suggested by [the Griffiths] report . . . will not develop any information to disprove the British belief."[25] Soon after, however, Griffiths reported from South America that Serrino had positively identified a photo of Martin Bormann as the same man he had seen repeatedly at the Müller ranch.[26] Jackson was skeptical that Serrino could make a positive identification. But on June 14, he told Special Agent Crosby that, "regardless of [the informant's]

STANDARD FORM NO. 64

Office Memorandum · UNITED STATES GOVERNMENT

TO   : The Director   **TOP SECRET**   DATE: May 15, 1948

FROM   : D. M. Ladd

SUBJECT : MARTIN BORMANN
           War Criminal

Further reference is made to my memorandum of May 14, 1948,
discussing the two intercepts received from Bureau Source Two in March of
1947, indicating that Martin Bormann is, in fact, still alive. SA S. W.
Reynolds made inquiry at the War Department and ascertained the following:

The release of the two messages discussing Martin Bormann, as
regular Source Two messages, caused a great flurry of excitement in
British circles. It appeared that the British were intercepting and
decoding traffic over a clandestine network, a survivor of the German
defeat, with ramifications in Europe and Germany. The existence of this
network was said to be a closely kept secret and the traffic intercepted
was handled on an "eyes only" basis (i.e. for the use only of the officer
to whom addressed) instead of the customary "top secret" basis on which
Source Two material is handled. On the day these particular messages,
dealing with Bormann, were received, the Army officer handling the "eyes
only" traffic was away and the Navy got hold of the two messages. They
were published as regular diplomatic traffic by the Navy. The State
Department caused a number of photographs and descriptions of Bormann to
be printed up and circulated among various embassies. State got considerable
publicity for the allegation that Bormann was still alive. The British
were, as usual, horrified at the lack of security. Their circuit apparently
was broken up and the rumbling from the incident is still going on in the
Army. (TS)

These intercepts, unless some very pointless deception was being engaged in,
are a very close indication that Bormann is still alive. The British, apparently,
are the only ones who have precise information about the network over which the
clandestine traffic was moving. The furor caused by the above-mentioned incident
apparently restrained the Army from inquiring into Bormann's whereabouts; CIA was not
well set up at the time and the State Department's investigation was probably
perfunctory. It would thus seem that the British are the only ones who have any
real information about the possible whereabouts of Bormann, as well as about the
clandestine traffic concerning him. Because of the security consideration involved,
it is necessary that the Bureau assume the posture that it has no information from
Source Two on Bormann. However, inquiry should be made of the British, and
probably could be made with some degree of success on the basis that persistent rumors
are being received concerning Bormann. (TS)   RECORDED · 39

There is attached a proposed memorandum to the Legal Attache of the American
Embassy in London, containing a request that he contact available sources for any
information which will throw light on the question whether Bormann is still alive,
and also specific identifying data including physical description, handwriting,
fingerprints and photographs.

RECOMMENDATION: If you approve, it is suggested that the attached memorandum
be forwarded to our representative in London.

TOP SECRET

Memorandum explaining the secret source of (erroneous) information indicating that Martin
Bormann was alive in March 1947 [D. M. Ladd to Hoover, 15 May 1948, NA, RG 65, 65-55639-
(1-24), box 38].

accuracy, the possibility that the Russians might make propaganda out of any laxity in running out the report was increased by the alleged identification." He would discuss the matter with the president.[27]

It was still the propaganda concern that Jackson emphasized in his memorandum to Truman. "Circumstantial evidence," he said,

> indicates that Bormann probably is dead. But the uncertainty as to whether he may have escaped was enough so that we considered it wise to indict and convict him in absentia. Many rumors that he has appeared in various parts of the world have proved false.
>
> A complete investigation would be extensive in time and cost. In addition, it would not be possible to apprehend or interrogate suspects or witnesses without the cooperation of the governments involved. Informed opinion of the F.B.I. is to the effect that if Bormann is in the Argentine, it must be with the connivance of the Argentine government. Obviously, the situation requires discreet handling.
>
> On the other hand, to neglect entirely to investigate this lead has two dangers. First, it is possible that Bormann is there. Second, even if he is not, publicity might be given to the fact that this information was laid before United States officials who did nothing and therefore are charged to be, in effect, protecting him. This claim would have propaganda value to Russia, for Bormann in the Eastern countries was one of the most hated of the Nazis.
>
> My suggestion therefore, is that the F.B.I. be authorized to pursue thoroughly discreet inquiries of a preliminary nature in South America and to encourage and cooperate with Griffiths in developing his sources of information, to check those sources as to their probable reliability and accuracy, and to determine on the basis of the preliminary investigation whether a more thorough and full-scale investigation should be undertaken, perhaps after communication with any government affected.[28]

Truman agreed. On June 24, the president wrote to Attorney General Thomas C. Clark, commenting that "I think the suggestions of the Justice are all right and if you and Mr. Hoover think well of them, perhaps we ought to follow through on the suggestions."[29]

With the president's request, Special Agent Crosby, who had served in Argentina and who was most familiar with the case, was ordered "to proceed immediately to Argentina to run down and verify Bormann's presence."[30] He would set up his investigation from the embassy in Montevideo (to avoid problems with the Perón regime in Argentina), interview Serrino at great length, investigate whatever leads necessary "to establish that Bormann is in the River Plate area," or "to set up with sufficient certainty that Bormann is not in the Argentine in order that no criticism be made of the United States Government for any real or supposed laxity in handling the report." He would communicate with Washington through cipher.[31]

Crosby interviewed Serrino in Montevideo on July 10, 1948, in an inconspicuous café after Griffiths arranged for him to come by bus. Crosby reported that "Serrino's recital leaves much to be desired." Serrino claimed to have seen Bormann twice in Uruguay, not Argentina, and had only heard reference to the cache of documents but had never seen them. Griffiths, meanwhile, struck Crosby as "somewhat incoherent . . . He so badly wants the whole elaborate congeries of charges to be established that he has apparently failed to observe that each of the allegations is so vague that none can be established as a fact."[32] The FBI assessment was that "the story concerning Bormann has been fabricated from its inception and that the Bureau is on a 'wild goose chase.'"[33]

Crosby remained in Montevideo trying to get more definite information. In August he reported that "efforts are being made to place [Serrino] in the employ of the group of Germans with whom Martin Bormann is reported to have been hiding."[34] After a number of frustrations though, Crosby returned to Washington on August 23. He had spent two months in Montevideo.[35] Hoover told Jackson that no further investigation was justified at the moment and Jackson agreed. The American government had done due diligence.[36] By this time, the British were following leads that Bormann was in Trieste and Lisbon, and the FBI was noting rumors that Bormann was being used by the Soviets as an adviser.[37] The U.S. Army Counterintelligence Corps (CIC), meanwhile, watched the mail of Bormann's eldest son, who was living with a Jesuit order in Ingolstadt, albeit with no result.[38]

By mid-1948, the Cold War had generated an atmosphere of mistrust and uncertainty regarding Soviet policies, and anything seemed possible. For a moment, the notion that the Soviets had somehow protected Martin Bormann was believable to U.S. agencies, and the idea that they would use Bormann's ghost as propaganda against the United States during the crisis over Berlin was entirely believable to the FBI, to Justice Jackson, and to the president himself. In this atmosphere, Bormann had to be chased, even if he could not be found.

Klaus Barbie

Klaus Barbie's extradition from Bolivia in 1983 was potentially a watershed event. A native of Bad Godesberg, Barbie joined the SS and SD in 1935 and reached the rank of Obersturmführer in 1940. He was best known for his time as the Gestapo chief in Lyon from 1942 to 1944, where he brutally repressed the French resistance and deported Jews to their death.[39] In the spring of 1947, Barbie found employment with the CIC and helped run an extensive net that reported on former SS officers, French intelligence, the French occupation zone, and Soviet activities in the U.S. and Soviet zones of Germany. Barbie was deliberately protected from French arrest for his crimes and even from courtroom testimony in the treason trial of René Hardy in 1947 and afterwards, in June 1949, when the French government began to call for his extradition from the U.S. German zone. In fact, Barbie remained a CIC informant throughout 1950, living in an

Augsburg safe house, though this fact was deliberately hidden from the Office of the High Commissioner in Germany and thus from the Department of State as well. At the end of 1950, the CIC arranged to have Barbie spirited out of Europe, and Barbie, under the alias Klaus Altmann, ended up in Bolivia in 1951.[40]

Recently declassified materials contain nothing new on Barbie himself or on the U.S. intelligence use of Barbie from 1947 to 1950. They do, on the other hand, contain a variety of documents on how the United States chose to deal with the embarrassing legacy of Barbie's employment and escape from Europe. The State Department's top officials, in a recently found document, argued in 1950 that Barbie should be handed over to the French regardless of his ties to the U.S. Army. Secretary of State Dean Acheson warned in June that "Franco-American relations [would] be affected more adversely by refusal to extradite than [would] be [the] case if he is extradited."[41]

The willingness to accept embarrassment had changed somewhat by 1972. On January 28, the French Nazi-hunter Beate Klarsfeld arrived in Bolivia claiming that Klaus Altmann was in fact Barbie. She also soon claimed that the United States had refused to hand over Barbie back in 1950.[42] The French government quickly requested Barbie's extradition from the Bolivian government on February 1, 1972, and the issue rapidly became one of national sovereignty for what the U.S. Ambassador in La Paz described as "the small, proud and sensitive Bolivia . . . jealous of its sovereignty," especially under the nationalist dictatorship of Hugo Banzer Suárez.[43] Angry statements in the Parisian and Lyon press by French pressure groups, particularly old resistance fighters, only exacerbated Bolivia's resistance.[44] Beate Klarsfeld quickly wore out her welcome in La Paz with a February press conference in which she attacked the Bolivian government for its "shameful" protection of Barbie and with a March 6 demonstration in the capital.[45] "[It] is strictly a Bolivian matter," snapped the Interior Minister Adet Zamora in La Paz when assured the next day that the "U.S. has no interest in protecting Klaus Altmann aka Klaus Barbie."[46] On March 8, Washington pressed harder. Secretary of State William Rogers cabled La Paz: "While we recognize that Bolivia's disposition in the Altmann case is an internal Bolivian matter, the hope of the U.S. government is that justice will be done in this matter."[47] On the other hand, Rogers would only press so far. Nothing would be done to urge the Bolivians publicly, he said, "in view [of] traditional Bolivian hypersensitivity."[48]

But the issue in 1972 would ultimately be decided by the Department of Defense. French President Georges Pompidou had written Banzer personally about the case, and Banzer replied that Barbie could be extradited to France only through the Bolivian court system, not political pressures.[49] Thus, the matter became one of legal identification, since Barbie and his lawyers maintained that he was not Barbie and that Altmann was his given name. Even Adet Zamora argued that "Altmann is the subject's given legal name."[50] On February 25, the French Ambassador to La Paz asked U.S. authorities there for documentary support. "He believes," said Ambassador Ernest Siracusa, "that Barbie was furnished documentation for a new identity as Klaus Altmann by U.S. forces."[51] On March 9, the French embassy in Washington presented a formal note asking for the same kind of documentary support.[52] But the State Department lacked the records to establish proof that Barbie was Altmann; the records on Barbie's false identity were Army records.

Voices in the U.S. State and Justice Departments argued that it was in the "national interest" to support the French while coming clean about Barbie's past employment. But the Pentagon refused to cooperate. By mid-May, the Pentagon had received the relevant intelligence documentation from the Army and decided that "the records must retain their classification status."[53] As one senior official at the State Department put it:

> We have good reason to believe that Barbie received documentation from U.S. Army Intelligence although this fact apparently was not known to U.S. diplomatic personnel in Germany who were trying to locate him in 1950 . . . The French extradition request is now before the Bolivian courts . . . It would be extremely helpful to the French case if the U.S. were able to furnish information tending to identify Altmann as Barbie [or] to establish that he was naturalized under a false identity.
>
> In view of the seriousness of the crimes with which Barbie is charged, and the fact that the USG may have inadvertently facilitated his evasion of justice, we believe there is a strong moral responsibility to be responsive to the French request. Conceivably, there could be considerations of national security which would require maintaining the confidentiality of our information, but it is impossible for the State Department to know, as DOD has refused to disclose the material available or to offer any justification for withholding it.[54]

And so for the next eleven years, Barbie would remain free, though as Angel Baldiveso, the Bolivian undersecretary for justice noted privately, "everyone knew that Altmann was Barbie."[55]

The situation in 1983, which included a new Bolivian government and a new overall mood in Washington, was different. In Bolivia, the democratic regime of Hernán Siles Suazo of the MNRI (National Revolutionary Party of the Left) arrested Barbie in January in connection with a tax debt. On February 5, Bolivian officials transferred Barbie to French custody, bypassing the right-wing Bolivian courts that had protected him for the past decade (in fact, Barbie's case was still pending in 1983), and on February 8 Barbie arrived in Paris amid intense French press interest. There was "some evidence" immediately that leading members of President François Mitterand's French Socialist Party provided cash payments to leaders of the MNRI.[56] To be sure, transparent economic incentives, including aid packages, helped.[57] But heavy U.S. diplomatic pressure on the Bolivian government not to allow Barbie to escape justice this time is evident from the records.[58] In fact, President Ronald Reagan's Secretary of State George Shultz had the U.S. Embassy in La Paz re-endorse the March 1972 French extradition request in August 1982, months before Barbie's arrest.[59]

The Americans were irritated with the West German government for nearly botching the chance to get Barbie out of Bolivia. The West Germans had had their own extradition request pending before the Bolivian Supreme Court, and Helmut Hoff, Bonn's ambassador to La Paz, had made representations to the new Bolivian government, though French officials in La Paz had their doubts about how badly the Germans wanted Barbie.[60] In January 1983, with Barbie under arrest in La Paz, there was still some doubt whether the Bolivians would allow the French to have him. "Frankly," said one CIA analyst, "we would be surprised if the Supreme Court allowed Barbie to be extradited."[61] Yet on January 26, the Bolivian government asked whether the West Germans would like to take Barbie, and Bonn refused. CIA sources said the Germans were caught off guard by the Bolivian offer and did not feel they had a strong case against Barbie since the German witnesses they once had were dead. The Germans, said the CIA, also did not want to deal with Barbie with an election imminent in early March.[62] On learning this, the State Department showed a certain exasperation with the Germans, arguing that their fecklessness might have resulted in Barbie's release and disappearance from Bolivia altogether. The excuse from the German Ministry of Justice was that there existed no aircraft that could move Barbie non-stop from La Paz to German soil, and that the Germans worried that landing in a third country to refuel would trigger legal problems. The American Ambassador to Bonn, Arthur Burns, was visibly unconvinced.[63]

As French and American journalists began to speculate on the full nature of Barbie's connection with U.S. intelligence after the war, American policymakers also had to determine how honest Washington was to be about this particular issue. This was no easy decision. The Barbie affair was choice propaganda material for the Soviets, who had long argued that German war criminals were active in the NATO alliance, and whose state organs now charged that the Americans had raised the concealment of war criminals to "a matter of state policy."[64] At first, Washington was indecisive.[65] The Defense Department remained opposed to making the relationship with Barbie public.[66] Yet the CIA, which had never had a relationship with Barbie, thought differently. CIA General Counsel Stanley Sporkin advised Director of Central Intelligence William Casey that truth was the best policy for pragmatic reasons if no other. "We should not appear," Sporkin said,

> to be making a deep commitment to justify what took place with respect to Barbie thirty years ago. If we make such a commitment, we will begin an endeavor from which it will be difficult to extricate ourselves and will create the appearance that somehow the current Administration bears some kind of responsibility for past events. The focus of our effort must be to make clear the distance of the questionable events in time. We must all recognize, too, that it was the

documented policy of the United States to make pragmatic intelligence collection use of ex-Nazis after World War II, because we were retooling our capabilities to deal with a new enemy, the Soviet Union.[67]

This was an improvement over the advice Casey received from the CIA station in Paris, which had already woven a series of rather implausible lies to explain away Barbie's use by the CIC.[68] The State and Justice departments agreed to undertake an investigation in the interest of full disclosure, with the DOJ Office of Special Investigations (OSI) conducting the investigation.[69] The study that emerged from the OSI in August 1983, *Klaus Barbie and the United States Government*, provided the full truth based on Army counterintelligence documents. The State Department sent copies of the 1983 report to major embassies along with an apology to the French government. "The United States Government," said the State Department, "expresses its deep regrets to the Government of France for [past] actions."[70] Regrets were indeed in order.

Nevertheless, the Barbie case was a watershed for the United States and Europe. It showed that diplomatic pressure combined with economic and moral incentives could dislodge notorious war criminals from their third-world hiding places. The Barbie case was pivotal for governments in Latin America and the Middle East in more negative ways. The Siles government might have won kudos from the Western world, but at home and elsewhere in the less-developed world it was roundly criticized for giving in to European, U.S., and even Jewish pressure. "Many Bolivians [have concluded]," said a press survey, "that the government acted precipitously in the hope of quick political gains," as would "somebody who turned somebody in for a reward." Bothersome even to Bolivian democrats was "the government's hasty abandonment of [the] extradition case in the Supreme Court."[71] In short, the Barbie extradition would not be so easily repeated elsewhere, especially since the other states concerned were still under military dictatorships that remained prickly under Western pressure.

Mengele's Ghost: The Secret Manhunt of 1985
Known as the "Angel of Death," Dr. Josef Mengele was responsible for "selections" at Auschwitz-Birkenau, as well as for conducting horrible medical experiments, many on children. On June 6, 1985, in the village of Embu near São Paulo, Brazilian police with West German support discovered Mengele's remains in a grave marked for a man named Wolfgang Gerhard. West German authorities located the grave after searching the home of Hans Sedlmeier in the Bavarian town of Günzberg, West Germany. Sedlmeier had managed the Mengele family business and had served for years as a conduit between Mengele and his family. Letters found in Sedlmeier's home suggested that Mengele had died of a stroke while swimming near São Paulo in February 1979. German, American, Israeli, and Brazilian forensic experts examined letters ostensibly written by Mengele, as well as the bones. They were his.[72]

An unknown part of this Mengele story, however, is that just as his body was exhumed, the U.S. government, believing Mengele still alive, was moments from launching a clandestine search for him in Paraguay, the government of which was overtly hostile to international hunts for German war criminals on its soil. Once Mengele was caught, he would presumably be kidnapped and sent to West Germany for trial. That the U.S. government would run such diplomatic risks in Latin America over an aging war criminal was a testament to the power of Holocaust memory in the United States in the mid-1980s and the U.S. government's responsiveness to it following its handling of Barbie and Rauff.[73]

It had long been known that Mengele was in South America, though until 1985, evidence was murky as to exactly where.[74] According to the 1992 report by the OSI, *In the Matter of Josef Mengele*, he arrived in Argentina in 1949 under the name Helmut Gregor and began using his real name in 1956. In 1959, he left Argentina and became a naturalized Paraguayan citizen. After the Israeli capture of Adolf Eichmann in May 1960, Mengele moved to Brazil.[75] Legal authorities were always a step behind. In 1959 and 1960, the West German government issued a warrant for Mengele's arrest and demanded his extradition from Argentina.[76] In August 1962, the West German government again demanded Mengele's extradition, but from Paraguay. A Paraguayan judge ordered his detention, but to no avail.[77] Israeli intelligence meanwhile looked for Mengele in Paraguay until 1963, when they concluded that he had left for Brazil.[78]

In June 1979, in the wake of the elimination of the West German statute of limitations on murder, Chancellor Helmut Schmidt's government insisted that Paraguay revoke Mengele's citizenship so that he could be deported should he surface there. Paraguayan authorities claimed that they did not know of Mengele's whereabouts—in fact he had drowned in Brazil that February—but, in a move grudgingly calculated to appease Western democracies, they revoked his citizenship on August 12, 1979, based on the constitutional provision that he had forfeited it by unexplained absence from the country for over two years.[79] Even with this minor step, the proto-fascist, right-wing dictator Alfredo Stroessner saw a crypto-Jewish conspiracy. In what U.S. Ambassador Edward White described as a "rambling 20-minute monologue," Stroessner complained that Mengele was no longer in Paraguay and that the entire issue was an "international scandal . . . raised by [a] communist conspiracy out to blacken the reputation of Paraguay."[80] Stroessner's protests notwithstanding, it was true that Mengele was not there, and other leads were emerging. The West German police at one point thought that Mengele was living in Argentina and that he was scheduled to fly from Asunción to Miami on August 29, 1979. The FBI, after checking the lead thoroughly, found the tip to be false.[81]

The Mengele issue came to a head in the United States in late 1984 and early 1985. In November 1984, Brooklyn District Attorney Elizabeth Holtzman led an unofficial delegation to Asunción to urge the Paraguayan government to act.

Though unable to meet with Stroessner, the Holtzman group received promises of a new Paraguayan search. The search amounted to little, but the visit kept the issue of Mengele in the American public eye.[82] The Mengele issue became more urgent after the release of two sets of documents in January 1985. The first set, from U.S. Army records, became public after a request from the Simon Wiesenthal Center based on the Freedom of Information Act. It contained a 1947 letter from Benjamin Gorby of the 430th CIC Detachment in Vienna suggesting that the U.S. Army had arrested and detained Mengele the previous year, only to release him.[83] As a result of more public pressure, the CIA released twenty-eight pages of sanitized documents suggesting that Mengele might have been involved in drug trafficking in Paraguay in 1972. Though this information was scanty and based on unconfirmed leads, the documents were a sensation, especially in the wake of the OSI Barbie report of 1983. Rabbi Marvin Hier, Dean of the Simon Wiesenthal Center, said that the Gorby letter alone "create[s] reasonable doubts as to whether or not the U.S. had a role in the case of Joseph [*sic*] Mengele, and the only way the truth will surface is an official investigation."[84] Hier went on to suggest that "[Mengele] might have been aided by U.S. officials in his postwar escape from Germany."[85] Senators Alphonse D'Amato (R-NY) and Arlen Specter (R-PA) charged in a press conference that the government had failed to follow leads, and they demanded a worldwide search for Mengele. Forgetting momentarily that Nazism had been an episode in German history and that the Nuremberg trials had been an American initiative, Specter charged that "Nazi atrocities are a chapter in history that the United States wants to sweep under the rug . . . Nobody really gives a damn about Nazi war criminals."[86] D'Amato claimed on television that Mengele was in Portugal in 1980 (the year after he had died), and that he had even sent out Christmas cards.[87] More stories exploded onto the scene. Mengele was in Chile. Mengele was in Houston. Mengele had been an auto mechanic. Mengele had been a beekeeper. Mengele had even lived with Martin Bormann.[88]

Just as Ambassador James Theberge had warned from Santiago not to pressure Augusto Pinochet on the issue of Walter Rauff, Arthur Davis, the U.S. ambassador to Asunción, warned against pressuring Stroessner. "We should not underestimate the strength which the Mengele issue will have in the Congress," Davis had told the State Department. But Congress also had to appreciate how little was known about Mengele. "[We] do not know of any hard evidence to indicate that Mengele is in Paraguay," cautioned Davis, "and it would appear that those of our colleagues who would best be in a position to know [the Israeli and West German Embassies in Asunción] have none either."[89] And unlike the Barbie cases, in which the subject's address was known, Mengele's whereabouts had long been the stuff of rumor and legend.[90] Any demarche from the State Department would bring the well-worn answers that Mengele's location was unknown, with the additional irritation that would come from the U.S. inference that Stroessner's government was lying.

But the documents released in January 1985 were too explosive. On February 6, 1985, Attorney General William French Smith ordered the OSI to collect all available evidence on Mengele's postwar activities and, if possible, his present whereabouts so that he could be brought to justice.[91] OSI Chief Neil Sher oversaw this investigation, which resulted in the 1992 Department of Justice report *In the Matter of Josef Mengele*. More drastic, though, was the interagency search for Mengele, which quickly developed as a result of the Attorney General's order. Mengele was to be caught regardless of the diplomatic consequences, which anyone who remembered the Eichmann kidnapping of 1960 knew would be substantial.[92]

The intelligence agencies that knew Latin America best were unenthused. In response to a directive of March 2, 1985, which tasked CIA stations in South America "to acquire any information on Mengele, his activities and contacts,"[93] one CIA station, probably in Asunción, critiqued what it considered a poor use of human resources. "As HQ is aware," the CIA station reported,

> thousands of articles, accusations, and speculation—much of it nonsense—have been written about Josef Mengele and his whereabouts . . . [This] is but the latest manifestation. If a serious, concerted and systematic effort is made to localize him . . . [the CIA] will have to track him down on a world-wide basis and many hours will be expended in the process.
>
> To begin with, the nation which theoretically has prime interest in Mengele is Israel . . . From a Paraguayan perspective, it is quite clear that if Mengele [is] in Paraguay he is extremely well protected either by the Government or by Nazi sympathizers . . . It follows that overt demands will get us nowhere. [The CIA] has already . . . asked all of its assets about Mengele and the answer is that Mengele did indeed live in Paraguay—but no longer . . . Suffice it to say that we have not a clue as to [Mengele's] whereabouts or if he is even alive.[94]

A document dated March 27, 1985, however, provided the necessary marching orders. "The [U.S. government]," said a memo from Secretary of State Shultz, "has decided to mount a major effort, drawing on all available intelligence resources, to locate Nazi War Criminal Josef Mengele—if he is still alive—and have him brought to trial, most likely in the Federal Republic of Germany." The U.S. Marshals Service (USMS) was charged with gathering the necessary intelligence. They were to receive the full cooperation of the American embassies and their CIA components and legal attachés. The focus of the search would be Paraguay or any country into which Mengele might have slipped. The CIA forwarded these orders, which it labeled the "Get Mengele" program, to its stations abroad.[95]

The Marshals' lack of background on Nazi issues was palpable, but the CIA would help. On April 3, William Casey met with the marshal in charge of the case, Director of Operations Howard Safir (the future New York Police Chief), and

434 ⌐ U.S. Intelligence and the Nazis

commented that it was "readily apparent that the Marshals are . . . dealing with a vast amount of rumors, unsourced reports, and unsubstantiated information of probably dubious value . . . If we can cut through this chaff by concentrating on the clandestine collection of hard intelligence which may lead to Mengele's arrest . . . we will have made a worthwhile contribution." Casey ordered CIA stations in South America and Europe to report which assets were available and the potential for recruiting new ones. The protection of agency sources, Casey said, would not be a problem because they would not have to testify if Mengele were tried in West Germany.[96]

The USMS needed help from West German authorities, too. During the first week of April 1985, they visited the Frankfurt Prosecuting Attorney's office, where the Chief Prosecuting Attorney, Hans Eberhard Klein, welcomed them. According to the Marshals, the Germans were extremely cooperative (as they had been with the CIA's search for Heinrich Müller fifteen years earlier), having turned over six thousand documents connected with the Mengele case.[97] The Marshals never visited Israel, where there was useful information as well. The CIA therefore tasked its station there to ask—on behalf of the U.S. government—what the Israelis knew. "We are not trying to broker contact between the Marshals service and [Israel]," noted the Director of Central Intelligence (DCI), "although that may come later."[98]

Plans to catch Mengele in Paraguay were proceeding. On May 21, 1985, a Mengele Task Force met in the U.S. embassy in Asunción, chaired by Chargé d'Affaires Daniel Claire, which included the embassy's political officers; the three Marshals then leading the hunt; Stanley Morris, the director of the USMS itself; and the CIA contingent to the Embassy.[99] Though nothing could be decided without Ambassador Davis present, the Marshals were the meeting's driving force. Having reviewed all materials they had on Mengele, they were convinced that he was still alive and in Paraguay. The Marshals "began with the assumption that they could not expect cooperation from the Paraguayan government, and [that] their effort . . . would have to be entirely covert." They claimed to have "a stable of assets . . . which the USMS intends to run in its operations against Mengele." When the Marshals asked what the CIA could provide, the CIA contact at the meeting pledged that "if existing resources were not sufficient . . . we were fully prepared to seek new sources in support of this important endeavor." Only Claire seemed worried by the possibility that U.S.-Paraguayan relations could explode if the local authorities discovered what the USMS and the CIA were up to. It was "important for all concerned," he said,

> to understand the risks involved in an operation such as described by the Marshals. While the Paraguayan police and intelligence service are not omniscient they have during the years of the Stroessner regime been generally successful in discovering any kind of unusual activity within the country . . . [There] is a good chance that the Paraguayan authorities would soon become aware of at least some of the covert operations to be conducted here. . . .

[They] would certainly consider such activities to be a violation of their sovereignty. Beyond that . . . they might put an even darker interpretation on them. The Paraguayan Government, from the President on down, has repeatedly insisted that it has searched for Mengele and that he is not here. Government officials might conclude that the [U.S.] effort represented an attempt to discredit or even destabilize the Stroessner regime, by revealing embarrassing facts about Mengele's connections in Paraguay.

Hence, there would be ground rules imposed by the U.S. embassy. The Marshals would not undertake anything without consulting the embassy first, and they would seek embassy approval for the employment of all local agents. It was especially important, said Claire, "to avoid the use of persons who are political opponents of the Stroessner regime as covert agents. This would arouse the worst fears of the [Stroessner] Government."[100] Yet the hunt was to go forward, which belied Morris's comments to the *New York Times* toward the end of May: "The Marshals," Morris said, "are not out in some foreign country running an investigation."[101] In fact, the USMS had already met with officials in the State Department and decided that the headquarters for the Marshals' covert search would be Buenos Aires, since the smaller embassy at Asunción carried too high a risk of discovery. Two Marshals would arrive at the U.S. embassy there and would remain for six months "to develop and run informants on a wide basis to locate Mengele."[102] CIA suggestions that the Marshals operate under cover and that they operate from São Paulo rather that Buenos Aires (the former was closer to where the operation would be) were not taken, but the CIA would nevertheless cooperate closely, particularly in the evaluation of informants. Two days before the discovery of Mengele's remains in Brazil, the CIA had already expressed disapproval of one such source of information, noting that this potential agent was too well known as a Stroessner opponent and that his cover story would not withstand close scrutiny if he were caught and interrogated by Paraguayan police.[103]

The two Marshals charged with running the operation from the U.S. embassy in Buenos Aires, John Pasacucci and Rafael Fonseca, were to leave Washington on June 6 and arrive the next day. On the day they left, Mengele's grave was exhumed in Brazil. The two Marshals were therefore rerouted to São Paulo.[104] The remainder of the Mengele saga consisted only of identifying the remains and piecing together his postwar travels and activities, none of which were as exciting as the legends.[105]

The remaining mystery involved why the West German authorities did not inform the United States that they were close to finding Mengele. It is possible that the U.S. government's effort to distance itself from the Bitburg affair of May 5, 1985—when President Reagan and West German Chancellor Helmut Kohl visited a German cemetery containing the tombs of forty-eight Waffen-SS members—played a part. West German opinion was angry over what it felt to be American sanctimony and the president's uneasiness during the visit. How these issues affected the Mengele search is hard to say, but the earlier spirit of cooperation had surely ended. "[The] BKA [German Federal Police Office] expressed some bewilderment and annoyance," read a report to FBI Director William Webster in late May 1985,

> at the revived interest in the Mengele Case, particularly on the part of the U.S. Government . . . The BKA and other German authorities were recently "inundated" with U.S. officials visiting Frankfurt and Wiesbaden . . . [A BKA] official made the comment that they . . . [are asking] themselves why they should be reporting any information to the U.S. Government in the first place [since] there is no warrant outstanding for Mengele in the U.S., and, in fact, the only warrant . . . is the German warrant.
>
> Although not specifically stated, the Germans perceive this whole matter as a political ploy on the part of [the United States] to make it appear that they are "doing something" about Nazi war criminals, and that the German government is perhaps less interested in finding Mengele, an insinuation deeply resented by the Germans . . . which could very easily damage some excellent relations with agencies such as the BKA.[106]

The West Germans therefore opted not to tell the U.S. Marshals about the May 31 search of Hans Sedlmeier's home until after Mengele's body was discovered in Brazil on June 6. There had been no time, said German police officials in São Paulo, to inform the American authorities, even though a week had intervened between the search of the home and the exhumation of the grave. "If we were the ones who had made the breakthrough," said OSI chief Neil Sher later, "we would have shared it with the other countries before going public."[107] The release of additional records in the years ahead may shed light on the issue from the West German perspective. For the moment, one can say that the search for notorious international criminals since the war has been about something more than justice, while at the same time, it has been about something less.

If one were to argue that the official search for Martin Bormann and Heinrich Müller were pointless exercises; that Klaus Barbie's trial came too late to claim its rightful meaning; or that the government's efforts to capture Walter Rauff, Alois Brunner, and Josef Mengele were too little and too late; one would perhaps be correct. Yet such an argument misses a vital point. The official hunts, their timing, the reasons behind them, and the level of political risk that they assumed all have something to teach us. In the cases of men already dead, such as Bormann and Müller, the U.S. hunts show the value in confirming the facts, especially when the ghosts of such men remain politically charged.

Klaus Barbie's long-delayed justice demonstrates that the postponement of a trial matters not only politically but judicially as well—and not only because key witnesses might have died in the interim. In his 1987 trial, Barbie's grandstanding lawyers prepared a grotesque post-modernist defense that compared Barbie's Nazi crimes to French behavior in Vietnam and Algeria and to Western imperialism and racism in general. Barbie was found guilty despite their effort to put "the West" on trial, but the Butcher of Lyon would have received a far more poignant trial had it been conducted in the 1950s or even in the 1970s.[108] However, a thorny trial was better than none at all. And the dialogue within Washington on whether to come clean about Barbie brought the recognition by no less a figure than the DCI that the intelligence mistakes of the past could be admitted without the slightest danger to national security.

As for the searches of the 1980s, one can offer many cynical explanations. Serious hunts for Rauff, Brunner, and Mengele were pursued too late to apprehend any of them or, had these old men been arrested, to punish them with more than token prison terms. Figures in Washington surely understood that the pursuit of these notorious Nazis promised easy political benefits. Everyone understood by the spring of 1985 that the arrest of a man like Mengele would wash away the unfortunate stain of Bitburg. Even for West Germany, a trial of such men would have allowed a society obsessed with the question of its own historical responsibility to focus more easily on the most well-known monsters of the Hitler years.

Yet the searches of the 1980s were also about something more than form and public relations. The State Department and other agencies could have made a far smaller effort than they did and at far less political risk in the field. Against the advice of its agents in Santiago, Asunción, and Damascus, the U.S. government ran political risks over issues that were four decades old and over which Syria, Chile, and Paraguay could only be angered. Too late or not, the episodes show that despite the failures in judgment by U.S. intelligence officials in the early Cold War, it was the lessons of the Nuremberg trials rather than the lessons of cooperation with soulless men that were ultimately internalized in official circles—even if those lessons took four decades to sink in.

Notes

1.   On the capture of Eichmann, see Moshe Pearlman, *The Capture of Adolf Eichmann* (London: Weidenfeld and Nicholson, 1961); Zvi Aharoni and Wilhelf Dietl, *Operation Eichmann: The Truth about the Pursuit, Capture, and Trial* (New York: John Wiley, 1997); Isser Harel, *The House on Garibaldi Street* (Portland, OR: Frank Cass, 1997); Peter Z. Malkin and Harry Stein, *Eichmann in My Hands* (New York: Warner, 1990). On the significance of the trial, see Hannah Arendt, *Eichmann in Jerusalem: A Report on the Banality of Evil* (New York: Penguin, 1964); and Tom Segev, *The Seventh Million: The Israelis and the Holocaust* trans. Haim Watzman (New York: Hill and Wang, 1993).

2.   Ian Kershaw, *Hitler, 1936–1945: Nemesis* (New York: W.W. Norton, 2000), 572n60, 774, 790–1.

3.   The above is summarized from Richard Overy, *Interrogations: The Nazi Elite in Allied Hands, 1945* (New York: Viking, 2001), 111–14. On the suicide, see Jochen von Lang, *Der Sekretär—Martin Bormann: der Mann, der Hitler beherrschte* (Stuttgart: Deutsche Verlags-Anstalt, 1987), 436ff.

4.   Robert H. Jackson to President Harry Truman, 7 Oct. 1946, NA, RG 238, Office of Chief of Counsel for War Crimes, box 46.

5.   See Norman M. Naimark, *The Russians in Germany: A History of the Soviet Zone of Occupation, 1945–1949* (Cambridge, MA: Harvard University Press, 1995).

6.   DM Ladd to Hoover, 6 May 1948, NA, RG 65, 65-55639-1-20, box 38. The FBI was aware that two German submarines indeed surrendered in Argentina in June 1945 after destroying their engines. Rumors were widespread thereafter that prominent Nazis had been on the subs and escaped into Argentina, but U.S. Naval authorities noted that only the subs' crews were on these vessels.

7.   Overy, *Interrogations*, 111.

8.   Hoover to Tolson, Ladd, and Tamm, 6 May 1948, NA, RG 65, 65-55639-1-18, box 38; Ladd to Hoover, 10 May 1948, ibid., no serial; Ladd to Hoover, 1 June 1948, NA, RG 65, 65-55639-1-29, box 38.

9.   See Ladd to Hoover, 10 May 1948, NA, RG 65, 65-55639-1, box 38.

10. Edward J. Martin, Legal Attaché, Montevideo to Legal Attaché, 8 Feb. 1946, Buenos Aires, NA, RG 65, 65-55639-1-2x, box 38; American Legation, Stockholm to Department of State, A-441, 26 Dec. 1946, NA, RG 65, 65-55639-1-8, box 38. Other such reports are scattered throughout the same file.

11. Ladd to Hoover, May 6, 1948, NA, RG 65, 65-55639-1-20, box 38.

12. Ibid.

13. See FBI memo, Martin Bormann, War Criminal, 14 May 1948, NA, RG 65, 65-55639-1-22, box 38.

14. Ladd to Hoover, 10 May 1948, NA, RG 65, 65-55639-1-31, box 38.

15. Hoover to Jackson, 14 May 1947, NA, RG 65, 65-55639-1-22, box 38.

16. D.M. Ladd to Hoover, 15 May 1948, NA, RG 65, 65-55639-1-24, box 38.

17. Quoted in C.H. Carson to D.M. Ladd, 27 Mar. 1947, NA, RG 65, 65-55639-1-9, box 38.

18. Richard Ford to Secretary of State, 14 Apr. 1947, NA, RG 65, 65-55639-1-10, box 38.

19. See FBI memo, Martin Bormann, War Criminal, May 14, 1948, NA, RG 65, 65-55639-1-22, box 38.

20. Hoover to Jackson, 14 May 1948, ibid.

21. D. M. Ladd to Hoover, 15 May 1948, NA, RG 65, 65-55639-1-24, box 38.

22. Hoover to Legal Attache, London, 15 May 1948, D. M. Ladd to Hoover, 15 May 1948, NA, RG 65, 65-55639-1-23, box 38.

23. J. A. Cimperman to Hoover by Air Pouch, 14 June 1948, NA, RG 65, 65-55639-1-32, box 38.

24. Cimperman to Hoover, 15 June 1948, NA, RG 65, 65-55639-1-33, box 38.

25. Ladd to Hoover, 1 June 1948, NA, RG 65, 65-55639-1-29, box 38.

26. Ladd to Hoover, 12 June 1948, NA, RG 65, 65-55639-1-35, box 38.

27. Ladd to Hoover, 16 June 1948, NA, RG 65, 65-55639-1-34, box 38.

28. Jackson to Truman, 16 June 1948, NA, RG 65, 65-55639-1-38, box 38.

29. Truman to Attorney General, NA, RG 65, 65-55639-41, box 37.

30. Ladd to Truman, 28 June 1948, NA, RG 65, 65-55639-42, box 37.

31. Ladd to Hoover, 29 June 1948, NA, RG 65, 65-55639-43, box 39.

32. See Crosby's memo, Re: Martin Bormann, War Criminal, 14 July 1948, NA, RG 65, 65-55639-1-47, box 37.

33. V. P. Keay to Ladd, 23 July 1948, ibid.

34. Memo, Re: Martin Bormann, War Criminal, 5 Aug. 1948, NA, RG 65, 65-55639-1-55, box 37.

35. Ladd to Hoover, Martin Bormann, War Criminal, 8 Sept. 1948, NA, RG 65, 65-55639-2-67, box 38.

36. Jackson to Hoover, 13 Sept. 1948, Memo, NA, RG 65, 65-55639-2-68, box 38.

37. For these and other rumors, see NA, RG 65, 65-55639-2-(2-3), box 38.

38. Robert A. Schow, Assistant Director, CIA, to Hoover, 9 Dec. 1949, NA, RG 65, 65-55639-2-91, box 38.

39. Allan A. Ryan, Jr., *Klaus Barbie and the United States Government: The Report, with Documentary Appendix, to the Attorney General of the United States* (Frederick, MD: University Publications of America, 1984), 4–6.

40. Ryan, *Klaus Barbie*, 13–57.

41. Acheson to McCloy, 1 July 1950, NA, RG 59, Barbie Materials, DD-098.

42. U.S. Embassy La Paz to Secretary of State, No. 587, 31 Jan. 1972, NA, RG 59, DE-44 and NR-015. The roles of Nazi-hunters Beate Klarsfeld and Serge Klarsfeld in the Barbie case is recounted, rather heroically, in Beate Klarsfeld, *Partout où ils seront* (Paris: Édition spéciale, 1972), chapters 14–17.

43. Siracusa to Secretary of State, No. 1056, 25 Feb. 1972, NA, RG 59, NR-015. On the speedy French request, U.S. Embassy to Secretary of State, No. 617, 1 Feb. 1972, NA, RG 59, DE-45.

44. Siracusa to Secretary of State, No. 1047, 25 Feb. 1972, NA, RG 59, NR-016.

45. On Klarsfeld's press conference of 28 Feb. 1972, see Siracusa to Secretary of State, No. 1129, 29 Feb. 1972, NA, RG 59, DE-22. On the demonstration, Siracusa to Secretary of State, No. 1211, 7 Mar. 1972, NA, RG 59, DE-27.

46. U.S. Embassy La Paz (Siracusa) to Secretary of State, No. 1268, 7 Mar. 1972, NA, RG 59, NR-011.

47. Secretary of State to U.S. Embassy La Paz, No. 040181, 8 Mar. 1972, NA, RG 59, NR-012.

48. Rogers to U.S. Embassy La Paz, No. 033512, 10 Mar. 1972, NA, RG 59, NR-010.

49. Siracusa to Secretary of State, No. 1056, 25 Feb. 1972, NA, RG 59, NR-015; Siracusa to Secretary of State, No. 1129, 29 Feb. 1972, NA, RG 59, DE 22; Siracusa to Secretary of State, No. 1269, 7 Mar. 1972, NA, RG 59, DE-27.

50. Siracusa to Secretary of State, No. 1047, 25 Feb. 1972, NA, RG 59, NR-016. By Feb. 1973, the Bolivian Supreme Court returned the case to the La Paz District Court for legal determination of Barbie's identity. See Siracusa to Secretary of State, No. 6863, 5 Dec. 1972, NA, RG 59, DD-76; Siracusa to Secretary of State, No. 0839, 15 Feb. 15, 1973, NA, RG 59, NR-177.

51. Siracusa to Secretary of State, No. 1056, 25 Feb. 1972, NA, RG 59, NR-015.

52. French Embassy to Department of State, translated version, No. 58, 9 Mar. 1972, NA, RG 59, NR-005E.

53. Armistead I. Selden, Jr. Acting Assistant Secretary of Defense, to John Crimmins, Deputy Assistant Secretary for Inter-American Affairs, 16 May 1972, NA, RG 59, NR-007.

54. ARA Charles A. Meyer and EUR (Acting) George S. Springsteen to the Under Secretary dated 15 June 1972, NA, RG 59, NR-003. Since Barbie claimed that he was not Barbie, but rather Klaus Altmann, his identification before the Bolivian courts was paramount. The Department of State's records on Barbie were incomplete, so Army records were key for identifying him. Compare with John N. Irwin II (Under Secretary of State) to Kenneth Rush (the Deputy Secretary of Defense) undated, NA, RG 59, NR-004.

55. Siracusa to Secretary of State, No. 5657, 6 Oct. 1972, NA, RG 59, NR-018.

56. Corr to Secretary of State, No. 00881, 10 Feb. 1983, NA, RG 59, N-62.

57. Shultz to all Diplomatic Posts, No. 132640, 25 Feb. 1983, NA, RG 59, DE-94.

58. Secretary of State to Bonn and La Paz, No. 033840, 5 Feb. 1983, NA, RG 59, Barbie Materials, NO-59.

59. Shultz to U.S. Embassy La Paz, No. 076376, 26 Aug. 1982, NA, RG 59, DD-48.

60. U.S. Embassy La Paz (Corr) to Secretary of State, No. 7441, 8 Dec. 1982, NA, RG 59, N-56.

61. [CIA/LA] to [CIA/EUR], 31 Jan. 1983, NA, RG 263, Klaus Barbie Name File, vol. 2.

62. Ibid. The March 6 election of that year would give Kohl's CDU/FDP coalition a parliamentary majority.

63. Secretary of State to U.S. Embassies Bonn and La Paz, No. 033840, 5 Feb. 1983, NA, RG 59, DZ-61; U.S. Embassy Bonn (Burns) to State, No. 03244, 7 Feb. 1983, NA, RG 59, DZ-63.

64. U.S. Embassy Moscow (Hartman) to Secretary of State, No. 03410, 22 Mar. 1983, NA, RG 59, N-66.

65. Vice President George Bush, who visited Paris three days after Barbie's arrival, received only vague talking points from the State Department and CIA. The United States, Bush said, supported the prosecution of all war criminals. Concerning Barbie's past employment, however, the Vice President had not been able to keep up, owing to his recent busy travel schedule. Shultz to Paris, No. 035718, 8 Feb. 1983, NA, RG 59, Barbie Materials, DD-039; [excised] to [excised], 11 Feb. 1983, NA, RG 263, Klaus Barbie Name File, vol. 2.

66. Memorandum for the General Counsel from [CIA Associate General Counsel], 16 Feb. 1983, NA, RG 263, Klaus Barbie Name File, vol. 2.

67. Stanley Sporkin to William Casey, 16 Feb. 1983, ibid.

68. Barbie, the French press would be told, was used only to catch other war criminals, who would not have been caught otherwise. Any connection with Barbie having to do with intelligence on Communists would be denied. [CIA/EUR] to DCI, 17 Feb. 1983, ibid.

69. Secretary of State Washington to U.S. Mission Berlin, No. 053765, 8 Mar. 1983, NA, RG 59, Barbie Materials, DD-033. Secretary of State Washington to AMEMB Berlin, No. 071299, 15 Mar. 1983, NA, RG 59, Barbie Materials, DD-035.

70. Secretary of State Washington to AMEMB Paris, No. 231254, 11 Aug. 1983, NA, RG 59, Barbie Materials, DZ-071.

71. Shultz to all Diplomatic Posts, No. 132640, 25 Feb. 1983, NA, RG 59, DE-94.

72. Summarized from the U.S. Department of Justice, Criminal Division, Office of Special Investigations, *In the Matter of Josef Mengele: A Report to the Attorney General of the United States* (Washington, DC: Department of Justice, 1992), 146–52. On the forensics, see Gerald L. Posner and John Ware, *Mengele: The Complete Story* (New York: McGraw-Hill, 1986).

73. See chapter 6 on the search for Rauff.

74. The legends are described in Posner and Ware, *Mengele*.

75. U.S. Dept. of Justice, *In the Matter of Josef Mengele*, 127–30.

76. U.S. Embassy Buenos Aires to State Department, Desp. 1837, 24 June 1960, NA, RG 65, 105-98306-1-1, box 72-75.

77. Memorandum of 18 July 1962, NA, RG 263, Josef Mengele Name File, vol. 2. Mutual recriminations between Israeli intelligence and Wiesenthal are in Hella Pick, Simon Wiesenthal: *A Life in Search of Justice* (Boston: Northeastern University Press, 1996), 186–89.

78. Memorandum of 18 July 1962, NA, RG 263, Josef Mengele Name File, vol. 2.

79. U.S. Embassy Asunción to Secretary of State, 79-2918864, 12 Aug. 1979, ibid.

80. U.S. Embassy Asunción to Secretary of State, 79-2894138, 7 Aug. 1979, ibid.

81. German Embassy (Washington) to Department of State, 28 Aug. 1979, NA, RG 65, 105-98306-1-7, box 72-75.

82. Secretary of State to U.S. Embassy Asunción, 84-5657266, 8 Nov. 1982; U.S. Embassy Asunción to Secretary of State, 84-5864658, 4 Dec. 1984; U.S. Embassy Asunción to Secretary of State, 23 Feb. 1985, all in NA, RG 263, Josef Mengele Name File, vol. 2. Beate Klarsfeld had already visited Asunción in February 1984 and had a tense meeting with Paraguayan Interior Minister Dr. Sabino Augusto Montanero, who chided her for going to the Paraguayan press before asking the government what it knew of Mengele's whereabouts. At that time as well, Montanero told the press that the Mengele issue was a plot by the regime's enemies to discredit Paraguay in the world's eyes. See U.S. Embassy, Asunción, to Secretary of State, 19840223, 22 Feb. 1984, RG 263, Josef Mengele Name File.

83. For the Gorby letter see the appendix to *Matter of Josef Mengele*, 86. The issue of the Gorby letter is covered in ibid., 70–82. OSI concluded that the information was flawed and that this arrest never took place.

84. Ralph Blumenthal, "Papers Indicate Mengele May Have Been Held and Freed after War," *New York Times*, January 23, 1985.

85. Jay Mathews, "'82 Nazi Sighting Aired: Hill Panel to Hear Testimony on Mengele," *The Washington Post*, February 19, 1985.

86. Bill Peterson, "Nazi Fugitive Linked to Drug Trafficking: Two Senators Release CIA

Documents," *The Washington Post*, February 27, 1985. The CIA documents had been released upon a personal request from D'Amato to DCI William Casey. See D'Amato to Casey, 21 Jan. 1985, NA, RG 263, Josef Mengele Name File, vol. 2.

87. CIA memorandum, 22 Feb. 1985, NA, RG 263, Josef Mengele Name File, vol. 2. CIA turned up no information that Mengele or any of his aliases had been to Portugal; [excised] to [excised], 25 Feb. 1985, ibid.

88. The so-called "Mengele Trial" in Jerusalem, which ended in February 1985, also played a role in moving the Mengele search to the top of the global agenda. Here, before Wiesenthal, Nuremberg prosecutor Telford Taylor, and Eichmann prosecutor Gideon Hausner, Mengele's living victims offered their testimonials as to his war crimes.

89. Davis to Shultz, 2196, 11 Apr. 1984, NA, RG 263, Nazis in South America Subject File, vol. 1.

90. See the various stories in Posner and Ware, *Mengele*.

91. Stephen S. Trott, Assistant Attorney General, Criminal Division, to FBI Director William Webster, 19 Feb. 1985, NA, RG 65, 105-98306-1-18, box 72-75; Trott to Webster, 12 Mar. 1985, NA, RG 65, 105-98306-1, box 72-75.

92. See the records concerning the Eichmann kidnapping and the U.N. Security Council in NA, RG 59, Lot file 62, D305, box 88.

93. DCI to [CIA/LA], 2 Mar. 1985, NA, RG 263, Josef Mengele Name File, vol. 2.

94. [CIA/LA] to DCI, 5 Mar. 1985, ibid.

95. Secretary of State to U.S. Embassies Buenos Aires, Asunción, Santiago, Brasilia, La Paz, 27 Mar. 1985, ibid.

96. DCI to [CIA/LA], [CIA/EUR], 5 Apr. 1985; and Memo to DCI, 22 May 1985; ibid.

97. DCI to [CIA/EUR], 9 Apr. 1985, ibid.

98. DCI to [CIA/NE], 5 Apr. 1985, ibid.

99. The meeting is described in Secretary of State to CIA, 25 May 1985, NA, RG 263, Josef Mengele Name File, vol. 1; Memo to DCI, 22 May 1985, ibid.

100. Secretary of State to [CIA], 25 May 1985, ibid.

101. Leslie Maitland Werner, "The Mengele File: U.S. Marshals Join the Hunt," *The New York Times*, 28 May 1985.

102. DCI to [CIA/LA] 31 May 1985, NA, RG 263, Josef Mengele Name File, vol. 1.

103. DCI to [CIA/LA], 4 June 1985, ibid.

104. DCI to [CIA/LA], 6 June 1985, ibid.

105. OSI, *In the Matter of Josef Mengele*, 136–92.

106. FM Bonn to William Webster, 29 May 1985, NA, RG 65, 105-98306 4 76x2, box 72-75. The CIA has a source within the West German government involved in the Mengele search who had described West German police efforts as "unsystematic and without any real focus." Since the West Germans would soon raid the Sedlmeier home, the source was either ill informed or willfully deceiving the CIA; [CIA/EUR] to DCI, 15 Apr. 1985, NA, RG 263, Josef Mengele Name File, vol. 2.

107. Quoted in Posner and Ware, *Mengele*, 317.

108. Alain Finkielkraut, *Remembering in Vain: The Klaus Barbie Trial and Crimes against Humanity*, trans. Roxanne Lapidus with Sima Godfrey (New York: Columbia University Press, 1992); Erna Paris, *Unhealed Wounds: France and the Klaus Barbie Affair* (New York: Grove Press, 1986).

Conclusion

Norman J. W. Goda
with Richard Breitman

THE NAZI WAR CRIMES DISCLOSURE ACT OF 1998 has triggered the release of some 8 million pages of documents on a breathtaking range of wartime and postwar topics—everything from the Greek resistance to Vichy French funds in the United States to Vatican policies. The preceding chapters show, through a sampling of these records, how the new files add to what scholars have known while offering some signposts for future research.

One subject not covered in our volume is the postwar U.S. war crimes trial program. Records of these proceedings and nearly all documents about preparations for the trials had been declassified previously; new information adds little to our understanding of them. Still, a contrast between American prosecution and American intelligence activities is instructive.

The United States took the lead in the first grand experiment with postwar justice beginning with the International Trial of the Major War Criminals at Nuremberg in 1945 and 1946.[1] Following this landmark trial, the United States held twelve more trials in Nuremberg, which involved 144 high-level defendants from the German High Command, the medical profession, big business, the judiciary, government ministries, SS economic officials, and most notably, the Einsatzgruppen. More military trials were held of German camp personnel and others so that by 1949, the United States had tried more than 1,800 German suspects.[2] The U.S. war criminal prison in Landsberg had roughly one thousand inmates and bore the official name War Criminal Prison Number 1 on the assumption that there would be a War Criminal Prison Number 2. The worst SS criminals were hanged as late as July 1951, despite the virtual sovereignty of the Federal Republic of Germany, despite mass West German protests at Landsberg prison, and despite the intercession of high-ranking West Germans who would be instrumental for the rearmament of West Germany and its military alignment with NATO.[3]

Only the Soviet Union tried more German personnel. But Soviet proceedings were often for violations of Soviet criminal codes and contained a strong air of show trials.[4] Other continental European states, including West European ones, generally tried Germans only for crimes committed against their own nationals.

Thus the United States' judicial record was unique, innovative, and substantial. It was not the policy of a state sympathetic with Nazism, indifferent to the Holocaust, or soft on war criminals.

Intelligence operations represented a different facet of American policy—a cold world where *Realpolitik* trumped idealism, where the primary aim was the acquisition of raw information, and where secrets often served the most practical of ends. The sensitive nature of how information is gathered and the utterly pragmatic ways in which such information is used—or not—lie at the heart of why intelligence records are held classified for so long in the first place.

Just as democratic societies must examine past successes and failures in diplomacy, military operations, and the like so that mistakes are understood, so must intelligence operations, particularly those riddled with errors, be examined publicly. Intelligence shortcomings contributed to Pearl Harbor and, more recently, to the al-Qaeda attacks of 2001. Although World War II in Europe saw spectacular Allied intelligence successes, from the breaking of the ENIGMA codes to the deception campaign that made D-Day possible, this book has revealed mistakes in either the gathering or the use of information about the Holocaust and other Nazi crimes, which cast a long shadow.

The first major theme of this work concerns what U.S. and other Allied intelligence sources knew about the nature of Hitler's Final Solution, when they knew it, and what sorts of reactions this information triggered during the war. It has been known for many years that the Allies were not in the dark when it came to German atrocities.[5] Yet in the face of the mounting evidence of the modern world's greatest atrocity, the Allies took no bold initiatives. While rescue attempts such as the bombing of Auschwitz or the trading of Jewish lives for trucks (both in 1944) might well have been difficult or impractical from a logistical or political standpoint, explicit public statements or warnings to Jewish populations, Axis satellites, or neutral countries were never beyond the realm of possibility.[6]

Many of the newly released intelligence records, particularly from the OSS, show that Allied intelligence agencies were aware of even more detail concerning the eradication of Europe's Jews than was previously understood by historians. But they also suggest more powerfully than before that some senior intelligence officers grasped that Nazi measures amounted to a state policy of full-blown extermination. Joseph Goldschmied's long report to the OSS Oral Intelligence unit in July 1942, which argued that German policies in Prague aimed at the depletion of Europe's Jews, was deemed entirely credible by OSS officials thanks its high level of detail. The "Dear A" letters from observers stationed in Europe—letters Allen Dulles solicited before he left for Bern in November 1942—contained a notable three-part serial letter titled "Nazi Extermination of Jews," based partly on British information from Warsaw itself and eyewitness accounts from the Baltic killing fields. "Germany no longer persecutes the Jews," Dulles's source said in June 1942. "It is systematically exterminating them."

Once in Switzerland, Dulles also had a broad and reliable window to the bloody policies of Hitler's allies, particularly in Croatia, from no less a source than the Archbishop of Zagreb himself. "Jasenovać," the OSS learned repeatedly, "is a real slaughterhouse." The British-pilfered despatches from 1941 and 1942 of the Chilean Consul in Prague, Gonzalo Montt Rivas—despatches routinely shared with the Americans—were especially damning. Montt was no Jewish leader or refugee who could be said to have an axe to grind. He was an ideological ally of the Nazis who thought he was communicating with his government in complete secrecy. By March 1942 at the latest, American intelligence agencies learned from Montt's reports to Santiago that the Nazis wanted a Europe "freed of Semites" and that German victory in the war would serve that end. Montt was considered reliable enough that translated copies of some of his reports found their way to senior officials in the State Department, the FBI, and the OSS itself.[7]

U.S. intelligence agencies never undertook active study of the Final Solution or any of its components, from shooting operations to extermination camps. There was a war on. Military information and analysis that could help to shorten the war always took priority. British studies on Nazi concentration and death camps contain conspicuous mistakes, showing that those writing the studies had limited access to information available in the British intelligence community. But there *were* British studies.[8] The Soviets, stretched though their own information-gathering agencies were, actively compiled enormous mounds of evidence concerning the crimes that took place on their soil. Despite Moscow's proclivity to see Nazi crimes in Marxist terms and their insistence that bloody Soviet crimes, such as the massacre and burial of Polish officers at Katyn, either never took place or were committed by the Germans, the Soviets still compiled immense amounts of testimony and evidence on bona fide Nazi crimes from witnesses and survivors.[9] Despite the primacy of military operations, it was always possible to learn more and to analyze more.

Old and new OSS documents suggest that at least some high OSS officials comprehended the range of Nazi crimes, but the organization did not venture deeply into this area. Was it because too much attention to Nazi killings of Jews might jeopardize American consensus for the war itself? Dulles, who was as well informed as anyone, was complicit in this practice. After his arrival in Bern, he continued to receive intelligence on crimes from German mass shootings to the roundup of the Berlin Jews. Yet Dulles understood that the State Department wanted no public reckoning with German crimes against Jews, lest pressures from groups such as the World Jewish Congress for rescue operations or relaxed immigration quotas become irresistible. It is in this context that Dulles's March 1943 comment to Willem Visser t'Hooft, that OSS information on specific German roundups of Jews was not confirmed and that Allied measures to hinder German atrocities were not practical, must be understood. The political problem presented by the Holocaust may also explain the decision *not* to route Montt's information on the Final Solution to Henry Morgenthau, Jr.—Roosevelt's vocal

Secretary of the Treasury—even though Morgenthau, who was Jewish, received some copies of Montt's economic reports.[10]

Most ironically, the OSS's understanding of the Final Solution's scope helped to preclude more cooperation with Jewish groups whose interest in Nazi Germany's defeat was greater than anyone else's. On the one hand, U.S. intelligence officials had a right to be skeptical of some initiatives, such as Joel Brand's mission to Istanbul in May 1944 to negotiate a deal for Jewish lives in Hungary in return for trucks. Brand's companion Bandi Grosz was a double agent working for the Nazis, and partly through his efforts the Nazis had penetrated the American-supported Dogwood intelligence chain in Istanbul. It is not surprising that neither the British nor the Americans took Brand's mission seriously as a rescue effort, or that they interrogated Brand and Grosz rather than send them back to Budapest with a promise for Allied trucks.

On the other hand, there does not seem to have been much interest by Allied intelligence in working with Jewish groups anyway, most notably the Jewish Agency for Palestine. Though always willing to accept and use intelligence supplied by Jewish Agency sources, neither British nor American intelligence officials showed any enthusiasm for joint operations such as the dropping of Jewish commandos behind enemy lines or the use of Jewish camp inmates for anti-German activities. As one OSS official put it, Jews would fight for Jewish interests such as saving Jews (even if this meant bargaining with the Germans) or the creation of an independent Jewish state after the war. The use of Jewish agents was a dangerous policy.[11] Yet the Allied war against Nazism was full of competing agendas ranging from those of French Communists to the territorial aims of Poland's government-in-exile, all of which represented suffering national groups. The Allied principle of working the least with those suffering the most seems incongruous, especially since this coolness was still apparent late in the war when cooperation meant little more than the identification of Germans to be arrested. At the very least, such a backwards policy might have diminished the importance of the Final Solution in the eyes of U.S. intelligence officials and agencies, many of whom, like Dulles, held key posts in the postwar years.

During the war U.S. intelligence officials also misread the close relationship between Nazi intelligence and Nazi racial policies. U.S. intelligence and counterintelligence officials, perhaps using themselves as a frame of reference, seem to have understood Nazi intelligence agencies in traditional terms. Newly released FBI records are loaded with reports on German police methods, Abwehr spies and saboteurs in the United States, and SD Foreign Intelligence agents in South America, all based on the partly accurate assumption that pure information-gathering was at the heart of German intelligence. But even when the FBI began its investigation of Chase Bank in 1939, the Bureau was driven primarily by the concern that seized Jewish assets were being used to fund German intelligence operations on American soil. The fact that the assets were stolen as part of a broader process to implement Nazi racial ideology was not considered especially relevant.[12]

Gestapo counterintelligence and SD Foreign Intelligence officers, all of whom were Nazi Party members and SS officers serving within the RSHA, were not traditional intelligence men (or in rare cases, women). The conflation of Nazi racial ideology and police terror with intelligence functions in these services meant that there were very few thoughtful agents or analysts in either. Apart from the anti-Nazi elements in the Abwehr, most who dealt with the Allies were little more than ideologues, dilettantes, thugs, or thieves. The destruction of the Berlin branch of the Red Orchestra by the likes of Gestapo official Horst Kopkow was triggered more by the amateurish nature of Soviet spies in Germany and by Gestapo torture than by Gestapo intelligence acumen. Gestapo officers, moreover, botched counterintelligence operations against Soviet agents in France. The Gestapo learned only in 1942 that the Polish underground, thought to have been smashed three years before, was sending vital information to London. They seem to have known little about British or U.S. intelligence operations in occupied Europe. Those SS/SD officers who attempted "covert" actions late in the war, namely peace feelers targeted at OSS officials in Istanbul and Switzerland, aimed, based on their own ideological assumptions, to split the Western-Soviet alliance while saving their skins. New records do not at all support the notion, made prevalent after the war, that German police intelligence agencies were either especially good at intelligence or opposed to Nazi crimes or the continuation of the conflict past the point of diminishing returns.

SD Foreign Intelligence Chief Walter Schellenberg, mentioned prominently in newly declassified files, exemplifies the effort by substantial numbers of Nazi intelligence and police officials to recast their reputations late in the war or immediately afterwards. After the German defeat, Schellenberg built a reputation through extensive British interrogations and through his memoirs as a man who woke to his country's crimes and tried to engineer an early end to the conflict, while saving the lives of concentration camp inmates where he could. Sadly for him, he was blocked by the ideologues within the government such as RSHA chief Ernst Kaltenbrunner, on trial in 1945 as a major war criminal, and Gestapo Chief Heinrich Müller, who was (as we argued earlier) most likely dead.[13] But the new records show Schellenberg as a cold, calculating SS official who did not become Himmler's favorite intelligence officer for nothing. Far from being appalled by the Nazi camp system, he used it to garner information and to carry out his covert foreign policy. He made extensive use of counterfeit money produced by Operation Bernhard in Sachsenhausen (despite later calling Friedrich Schwend, the distributor of the money, a swindler). He advocated and facilitated the purchase of concentration camp barracks in Switzerland in order to cultivate intelligence connections in that country—and one of the chief beneficiaries might have been Dr. Heinrich Rothmund, who helped engineer Switzerland's restrictive policy toward Jewish refugees from 1938 to the end of the war.[14]

Schellenberg also approved the Brand mission to Istanbul in May 1944, but not as a deal to end or even to delay the destruction of Hungary's Jews. For

Schellenberg, Brand was a means by which to use the supposed connections of world Jewry to open a rift in the anti-German coalition by inducing the Allies to spare Jews by supplying equipment to be used on the eastern front. Schellenberg also tried to arrange contacts with Allen Dulles after January 1945. Yet these were hardly peace feelers. Schellenberg hoped to convince the Americans of Soviet perfidy so that the Germans could continue to fight in the East unabated by a front in the West. Despite his failure with Dulles, Schellenberg continued on Himmler's behalf the famous contacts with former Swiss president Jean-Marie Musy in Switzerland and Swedish rescuer Count Folke Bernadotte. These negotiations involved swapping the lives of camp inmates for a halt in the fighting in the West or at least very lenient justice for SS camp guards. Schellenberg was not saving lives; he was bargaining with them. His effort was not very different from the more successful and more openly extortionist channel applied by another Himmler deputy, Kurt Becher in Hungary, who openly traded Jewish lives for cash.[15]

Other German intelligence professionals and amateurs in contact with Allen Dulles in 1945 saw their efforts pay off. SS-General Karl Wolff's group helped to arrange the early German surrender in Italy, only days before the German surrender, through what Dulles named Operation Sunrise. No promises were made, but Wolff was rewarded during a U.S. military tribunal two years later with an unprecedented private meeting with the U.S. judges who declined to prosecute him thanks to his covert contacts with Dulles at the very end of the war. Evidence that Wolff had facilitated Jewish transports to Treblinka was ignored, and OSS-held evidence that he had been involved in SS reprisals against Italian resistors was seemingly not available. Wolff did not receive jail time until 1962, and then only because of West German authorities. Eugen Dollmann, Wolff's SS subordinate in Operation Sunrise, was demanded by Italian authorities in 1947 in connection with the bloody Ardeatine Caves massacre of March 1944. U.S. intelligence officials provided him with a false identity and shipped him from Rome to the U.S. occupation zone in Germany. To do otherwise, they said, would cause other agents to doubt American protection.[16]

SS Major Wilhelm Höttl, a top SD Foreign Intelligence operative who had served in Austria and Hungary, had also been in contact with the Americans in Bern on Kaltenbrunner's behalf after February 1945, spinning a web of promises for the immediate future and lies about his recent past. Dulles knew that Höttl had been in Hungary during the mass deportations of Jews from that country and that he was Kaltenbrunner's subordinate, but it was Höttl's supposed skill as an intelligence operative from the feared Alpine Redoubt by which the OSS judged him. Had the war not ended when it did, Höttl surely would have been used on the assumption that he was a highly trained, professional operative, rather than an agent of Jewish destruction. As Edgeworth Leslie said, "Höttl is . . . dangerous [but] I feel that we should make full use of his Nachrichtendienst [intelligence service], . . . of the propaganda services which he is setting up, and of the material that he can supply for this propaganda." Höttl was not put on trial. He could claim to have known Dulles (though they never met), to have worked for an early peace against Hitler's wishes, and to have been a quality intelligence operative who could be rehired later.[17]

The piles of new CIC, FBI, and CIA files reveal no overarching policy by which American intelligence agencies targeted known SS or Gestapo officers for hiring. Hiring happened on a case-by-case basis via different U.S. intelligence offices and detachments. But the records also reveal that this unfortunate practice was hardly limited to the infamous Klaus Barbie (whose hiring by CIC in 1947 became public knowledge in 1983) or a few other bad apples. How can one explain it all?

Pragmatism is part of the answer for the use and protection of war criminals. It surely explains Britain's protection of Kopkow, who escaped justice because he knew something about the Red Orchestra, justifiably a major British concern in 1945 since the Soviets had clearly spied on the British before the war. But the repeated U.S. use of Nazi criminals is not simply a case of the Cold War shifting U.S. intelligence priorities to the point where the hiring of SS and Gestapo officers became seemingly appropriate.

Avoidance of, or lack of attention to, the Holocaust and other Nazi crimes by the U.S. intelligence establishment surely played some role. Serious active study of the Final Solution as it took place might have led to more serious postwar consideration of the men who had been involved in it. Many former Nazis and collaborators were remarkably successful and even entrepreneurial in casting themselves as highly knowledgeable intelligence men with caches of vital information rather than as thugs, killers, and incompetents. Emil Augsburg, an SS "expert" on Slavic peoples who had taken part in massacres in the USSR in 1941, was hired by CIC in 1947, in part thanks to his claim to have eight [never recovered] trunks of files on the Comintern. General Reinhard Gehlen, the Chief of the German Army Staff's Foreign Armies East office, a man who had been wrong on every major prediction he made concerning the Red Army, was hired and feted by the U.S. Army immediately after the war thanks to his collection of buried intelligence files. As late as 1952, former Nazi prosecutor Manfred Roeder dazzled CIC officials with his tales of hidden intelligence records. Only in 1955 did the CIA catch on, declining an offer by former SS-Gruppenführer Otto Skorzeny to sell them a trove of what he claimed were secret Red Orchestra decodes. Skorzeny, it turned out, had already fooled the CIA once with made-up information.[18]

The biggest culprit in U.S. intelligence misjudgments in Europe may be the CIC. In the immediate postwar years the CIC was the largest U.S. intelligence organization in Germany and Western Europe. Responsible for the apprehension of Germans in automatic arrest categories and for larger issues of denazification in public German institutions such as universities, some CIC agents acquired the reputation of being "hard" on former Nazis.[19] CIC agents ran daring operations from time to time, such as the attempted penetration of Father Krunoslav Draganović's College of San Girolamo and the attempted arrest of Ante Pavelić. Other CIC agents, however, were responsible for extraordinary errors of judgment, believing that former SS and Gestapo officers could offer useful information on the new Soviet foe. Astonishing sluggishness in performing serious background checks on captured German records contributed to these errors.

CIC blunders surprised contemporaries who knew of them. U.S. Army prosecutors were stunned at the use of known criminals like Manfred Roeder and Walter Huppenkothen. CIA officials pointed to the low quality of intelligence from the likes of Höttl and Draganović, together with the security risks these men represented. And Army counterintelligence records not seen by the authors of this work may contain more cases of this kind, because the CIC seemed not to learn much over time—an indication that confusion or inexperience in the immediate postwar period was not the root of its problem. In 1947 the CIC hired SS-Gruppenführer Heinz Reinefarth, destroyer of Warsaw during the Polish rising of August 1944, thanks to his knowledge of Soviet infantry tactics. The CIC ignored repeated Polish extradition requests even though U.S. Army prosecutor Telford Taylor pressed for Reinefarth's extradition from 1947 on.[20] Even the British were surprised by U.S. stubbornness. "Much of the detail in the Polish note," said British occupation authorities in 1951, "is correct . . . [there is] a considerable amount of evidence to support the accusation that [Reinefarth] is guilty of the mass murder of Polish civilians in Warsaw in 1944."[21] But by now the State Department supported the CIC, partly because extraditing Reinefarth was in itself a security risk: "In the course of [Reinefarth's] work," a recently declassified State memorandum argued,

> . . . he is believed to have acquired too great a familiarity with American military information to make it safe to allow him to go to any area subject to Soviet domination. It may also be observed that the extradition of this man to Poland would make any further consultation with him impossible and would have the additional consequence of disturbing similar work now being conducted with other German officers who would be made apprehensive about being deported in the same way.[22]

Earlier misjudgments, in other words, had now taken on a life of their own. And as the CIC proclaimed in 1952 in connection with the missing Adolf Eichmann, they were no longer in the business of searching for war criminals anyway.

Perhaps the most extreme CIC misjudgment of a key Holocaust perpetrator came in the 1950s. Hermann Julius Höfle, a major Nazi war criminal, served the CIC briefly in 1954 as a paid informant. Höfle had served on the front lines in the Nazi war against political and racial enemies as early as 1939 as an officer with murderous police auxiliaries *(Selbschutzführer)* in the Cracow district, as the head of a forced labor camp for Jews near what would later become the Belzec extermination camp, and especially in the Lublin district, where he worked under SS and Police Leader Odilo Globocnik. Höfle held the title Head of the Main Section of *Aktion Reinhard*—the code name for the murder of Jews in the General Government, denoting most of Nazi-occupied Poland. He was Globocnik's most important subordinate, giving basic instructions to the personnel assigned to *Aktion Reinhard* and requiring subordinates to sign a declaration of secrecy. He helped clear the Warsaw Ghetto and later served as an officer at Sachsenhausen concentration camp and as a senior SS officer in Greece.[23]

Höfle later told U.S. army officials that he was arrested by British authorities in Austria in 1945 and held until 1947. In 1948 Höfle learned that the Polish government was seeking his extradition for war crimes, so he escaped to Italy, using a network of former SS associates, where he lived under an assumed name. In March 1951 he tried to enter West Germany from Austria but was arrested for unauthorized crossing of the border. Admitting his real name, Höfle told a Munich court that Poland was seeking to prosecute him and that he feared kidnapping. In April 1951 he was given West German identification documents and allowed to live there legally. After taking up contact with his old SS comrades in Bavaria, Höfle came to the attention of CIC officials as a potential source of information about far-right-wing circles and their possible infiltration by Communist elements. A CIC assessment of Höfle's character in February 1954 did not penetrate past the surface:

> Subject is punctual, militant in action, truthful and trusting in a person only after his trustworthiness has been proven. Subject has been found to be most appreciative and courteous . . . . Based on information received from subject, he can be evaluated as fairly reliable at this time. Subject is considered "usually reliable" insofar as past activity of the SS and Gestapo is concerned. It is pointed out, however, in the majority of cases that subject must be asked specific questions during meetings because he is prone to minimize an occurrence or event rather than to magnify it.[24]

Höfle had told CIC officials that during the war he had served in the Waffen-SS, that he was affiliated with the organization of partisan groups in fighting the Russians, and that he had taken part in security work in Poland in regard to German personnel. "Security work" involved the murder of some 2 million Polish Jews.

Although it was not known at the time, even among American intelligence officials, Höfle had actually reported the statistics of *Aktion Reinhard* to Adolf Eichmann during the war. In at least one case, Höfle's report was sent by coded radio message in abbreviated form and intercepted by British intelligence. This message is the most reliable source scholars have for the number of Jews killed at Belzec, Sobibor, Treblinka, and Maidanek through 1942. (The United Kingdom declassified this information only in the late 1990s.[25]) Even if the depth of Höfle's involvement in genocide was hidden, anyone with some knowledge about Nazi Germany and with access to his SS file in the Berlin Document Center could have exposed his falsehoods and evasions.

After giving the CIC information deemed of value in February 1954, Höfle received the cover name Hans Hartman and was placed on the rolls for a monthly stipend of DM 100. In June 1954, however, he was dropped without prejudice for undisclosed reasons. He thus worked for the CIC for only five months.

Höfle's newly declassified file is remarkable for what it does not contain. Although the CIC was aware that Poland wanted to prosecute him for war crimes and although there apparently was a cursory check of Berlin Document Center records about him, no one seems to have been concerned about what Höfle might have done as an SS officer in Poland. Army officials seemed content to accept Höfle's sanitized version of what can only be described as a consistent record of monstrous and barbaric crimes.

Like the CIC, the CIA flubbed some background checks and even sanitized some incriminating records. Newly declassified CIA records so far reveal direct relationships between that agency and at least thirty former Axis war criminals. Otto von Bolschwing's SD "intelligence" role in the January 1941 Bucharest pogrom and in the protection of Romanian Iron Guard leaders was common knowledge among everyone who dealt with him. The CIA did not try to understand what sort of "intelligence" von Bolschwing had performed in Romania or to learn more about von Bolschwing's work for the SD's Jewish Department. Thus von Bolschwing's self-proclaimed intelligence contacts in Austria were thought valuable, and the CIA sanitized his records of what were thought to be simple embarrassments. As James Critchfield, the CIA's head of the Pullach Operations Base, reported in 1950, "[I] feel we should go [to] any length to help [von Bolschwing]."

SD officer Theodor Saevecke was silent about his extensive record against Italian and North African Jews under the tutelage of the infamous Gestapo officer Walter Rauff, but he boasted about his bloody measures against Italian "Communists," to the point where his CIA handlers fully understood his continued devotion to Nazism. His past was sanitized as well. The CIA performed similar favors for Ukrainian nationalist Mikola Lebed, whose collaboration with the Gestapo in 1941 had led to wholesale murders in the Ukraine, and whose postwar work for the CIA with the Ukrainian underground was deemed "of inestimable value." In 1952, Allen Dulles, then Assistant Director of the CIA, denied all criminal accusations against Lebed—even the ones Lebed had admitted.

Clearly aware of the Holocaust during the war, Dulles failed to grasp what it meant morally, politically, and even in terms of postwar intelligence. Those implicated in the crimes of Nazi Germany and its allies were most unlikely to be effective sources or agents, and if used by the United States, became security risks simply by virtue of their hidden pasts. Whatever credit certain Nazi officials earned with the United States at the end of the war did not change the basic problem. Dulles had to deal with the consequences of some of his own previous mistakes. When the Israeli capture of Adolf Eichmann in 1960 refocused the world's attention on the Nazi past, Dulles—then Director of Central Intelligence—expressed operational concerns about possible Soviet blackmail of the CIA's former Nazi agents.[26]

The CIA's largest problem came in its takeover of the Gehlen Organization from the U.S. Army in 1949. Army and CIG studies as early as 1947 lamented that Reinhard Gehlen had never revealed the backgrounds of the thousands of agents and administrators in his employ and supported by the U.S. government, especially since former SS officers were clearly in top positions. Yet by December 1948, the year of the Communist coup in Prague and the Berlin Blockade, the CIA had stopped asking the tough questions. Those in the CIA who argued that the Gehlen Organization did not represent "good Germans" were overruled. Not only was the Organization "definitely second class" in the CIA's own words; Gehlen still would not reveal the names of his subordinates. The old SD network from Romania was discovered in the first year of CIA sponsorship and by 1951 Gehlen's counterintelligence group was discovered to be packed with former SS men, including notorious figures such as Emil Augsburg, Erich Deppner, and Konrad Fiebig. Given Gehlen's resistance to any CIA interference, his proclivity to find support in the new West German government, and the need for basic tactical intelligence on the Red Army thanks to the war in Korea, the presence of war criminals in the Gehlen Organization was regarded as an internal German matter.[27]

New FBI records show for the first time that J. Edgar Hoover also took the narrowest possible view of Eastern European collaborators in the United States after World War II. All were useful, he thought, in the global struggle against Communism and could at the very least hold their own émigré communities in the United States to an anti-Communist line while reporting subversion from within those same communities. Thus Hoover protected László Agh, a Hungarian camp officer who had lied repeatedly to U.S. immigration and even FBI officials about his past since entering the United States in 1949, by withholding information that could have resulted in his deportation. Agh's staunch anti-Communist work with Hungarian émigrés, Hoover thought, was more important than his crimes during the war. Viorel Trifa, a Romanian Iron Guard Leader and instigator of the bloody Bucharest pogrom in January 1941, was also protected by Hoover after Trifa entered the United States in 1950 despite the overwhelming evidence of his criminality. As the Romanian Orthodox Archbishop in the United States, Trifa played a critical role in the battle for the political soul of Romanian émigrés whose country was now under Communist rule. Even the CIA, which by this time had used a number of war criminals, was surprised by the degree to which Hoover was willing to soft-pedal Trifa's nauseating past. The FBI used Vladimir Sokolov, once a collaborator in Nazi propaganda in German-occupied Russia, to spy on the Russian émigré community in the United States despite the mountain of testimony from those who knew him, including prominent scholars of the USSR. If the CIA had not used Mikola Lebed in Cold War Ukrainian politics, the FBI would have done so. At the very least, Hoover never shared the FBI's evidence on Lebed, which came from captured German Army staff records, with the INS.[28]

Such relationships are often described as Faustian bargains, but in dealing with the Devil, Faust received the earthly delights he had been promised. Did any U.S. intelligence agencies benefit from their own moral compromises? The new records suggest they did not. Research thus far indicates that the CIC learned next to nothing from the stable of bad actors that it hired. Höttl's networks in Austria provided the CIC with information from newspapers and by dabbling in Austrian politics and with German, French, and Soviet intelligence, Höttl was a security risk besides. Roeder's polemical comments on the Red Orchestra uncovered not a single Soviet spy. Draganović provided sheaves of useless and false material while never revealing his sources to his handlers, who paid him generously.

FBI and CIA hires were no better. Sokolov was hired to provide information on Russian émigrés in the United States, and for the most part he never did so. The separatism in the Ukraine that Lebed promised finally occurred in 1991, but it had nothing to do with Lebed. Immediately after hiring von Bolschwing, CIA officials in West Germany discovered what every other intelligence agency, even the Gehlen Organization, already knew: von Bolschwing was useless. As for Gehlen himself, as far as can be determined from what has been declassified, the postwar German spymaster never provided anything more than low-grade tactical intelligence to the United States, and his counterintelligence group was thoroughly penetrated by the Soviets.

The thousands of pages of intelligence records seen by the writers of this volume contain but a very few pages that indicate important information garnered through direct relationship between a U.S. intelligence agency and a former Nazi intelligence figure. Karl Theodor Hass, for example, was used by the CIC in 1951 to provide information on Höttl's activities with West German intelligence. Former Einsatzgruppe member Friedrich Panzinger might have been of some use in sending phony intelligence to the Soviets. Heinz Pannwitz provided some interesting historical information on topics ranging from Reinhard Heydrich's murder to Gestapo playback operations from France during the war.[29] The bloodstained Theo Saevecke and Heinz Reinefarth might have provided something of use, but if they did, it is not in the CIA or CIC files. In all, former Nazis were of very little value in relation to the headaches and security breaches they created.

On the contrary, such men applied American support and American money entirely to their own agendas. The best example is Gehlen himself, whose marriage to the U.S. Army from the very start was one of convenience. In return for a half million dollars a year during the occupation, the U.S. Army received no operational control and no sense of whom Gehlen had hired. When pressed by Army or CIA officials to cooperate more while overextending himself less,

Gehlen growled at his handlers until they backed off. His main concern was his budget and his place in the West German establishment; it was never to provide intelligence for the Americans. Draganović never hid the fact that his priority lay in Croatian independence from Tito, and he was constantly irritated that the United States did not back his various schemes, one of which involved a Croatian "Bay of Pigs" invasion. Höttl, meanwhile, embezzled American funds and sold false reports to the U.S. Army while trying to find a place for himself in the West German intelligence establishment. The hiring of foreign assets by intelligence agencies always carries such risk—realism generally trumps altruism as a motive for spies. Rarely, however, is so little gained in return.

The shadow of these bargains far outlived the bargains themselves, for the potential embarrassment and security risks continued long after the intelligence relationships had officially ended. The CIC discovered this problem with every Nazi criminal with whom they dealt. Thus, Barbie had to be shipped to South America; Höttl had to be arrested and publicly neutralized on the hope that he had no records pertaining to his service for the CIC; everyone was relieved when Draganović was kidnapped by Tito's government, never to be heard from in the West again. The CIA was not so lucky. Von Bolschwing and Lebed had to be rewarded for their work with U.S. citizenship, and their embarrassing relationships had to be hidden as long as possible—not indefinitely as it turned out.

All the while, relationships between the U.S. government and known war criminals provided grist for active Communist propaganda mills while obviating much of the moral high ground that had been won by U.S. leadership in prosecuting Nazis. Trifa and Agh, for instance, were constant themes in Romanian and Hungarian government statements; and once the FBI had decided to protect such men, the Bureau became complicit in their odious statements that the evidence against them was cooked up by Communists and Jews. Soviet and East German propaganda harped repeatedly on the Gehlen problem, especially after the revelations in the wake of the Heinz Felfe affair that the Organization had been loaded with war criminals. Though the Soviets used former Gestapo and SS officers, such as Friedrich Panzinger and Heinz Felfe, for espionage as well the United States gave Moscow the ability to claim publicly as late as 1983 that the United States had raised the concealment of war criminals to "a matter of state policy." It was not the moral position that anyone had envisioned in 1945.

The United States was not the only state in this position. Though the new records come from American agencies, they reveal a not inconsiderable amount of material concerning the use and protection of war criminals by other governments and organizations in the early Cold War years. Future historians with greater access to closed foreign records will hopefully follow up on these problems. Chief among them is the Federal Republic of Germany's intelligence policy. In trying to resist CIA control, Gehlen looked for and found influential allies in Bonn. Adenauer and Globke clearly discussed the issue at length before Globke informed the CIA "in a direct and emphatic way" that Gehlen had the Chancellor's support. The

Friedrich Wilhelm Heinz Amt employed Höttl throughout 1952 despite his SD record and then circulated his reports within the Chancellery itself. Because the reports earned Heinz a commendation from Adenauer, it took extensive CIA pressure to get Heinz to drop Höttl. Ultimately, it was the moral argument that worked. Höttl's past, they said, "would in the end discredit the entire West German intelligence establishment."

The *Freie Mitarbeiter* system of the 1950s, through which former SS and Gestapo personnel worked for the Federal German Police while being paid off the books, epitomized by Theo Saevecke, needs further investigation. German police and intelligence records, if ever opened, will provide a far better sense of how many SS officers were employed in these ways and what sorts of intelligence they provided. Yet what the West German government understood about West German intelligence would also help historians to fill out the relationship of the Bonn government with the Nazi past.

OSS and CIC records continue to spark questions about the Vatican that can only be answered by greater access to Vatican archives. Why did Herbert Kappler, the SS officer who executed Kaltenbrunner's orders to deport Rome's Jews to Auschwitz in October 1943, see the Vatican as an obstacle to the logistics of roundup and deportation? Were Vatican officials providing clandestine help and warnings to the Jews of Rome? Or was Kappler simply imagining problems where none existed?[30] The degree to which Vatican officials helped Nazi and Ustaše criminals after the war has also never been fully established, but CIC records make the questions all the more poignant. British intelligence, after all, knew Ante Pavelić's exact location in the Vatican in 1947, and the CIA was sure he was at the Pope's summer residence the following year. U.S. intelligence knew that Draganović's activities in the College of San Girolamo—activities that included the hiding of Ustaše officials—were receiving at least tacit Vatican support after the war, and that only the death of Pius XII in 1958 brought Draganović's removal from the College.

The use and protection of some of the very worst Nazi war criminals by Middle Eastern and South American governments also turns up in the new records in ways that can only be supplemented with full access to the records of those states. When studying the policies of Arab states in the late 1940s and early 1950s, the CIA discovered that the Syrians actively recruited SS officers for intelligence work, perhaps hiring as many as fifty of them, including Walter Rauff, one of the most notorious Gestapo criminals. How Alois Brunner arrived in Syria remains a mystery, but CIA records place him there as early as 1957, and NSA intercepts mention his death in Damascus in 1992. Brunner and his associate Franz Rademacher, according to CIA records, advised Syrian police forces at least until the early 1960s, and the Syrian government doggedly protected him until his death. The Egyptians under Gamel Abdel Nasser were no better, having hired a virtual colony of Nazis to help train their forces, including the ubiquitous Skorzeny. Since neither Gehlen nor the CIA could do much to penetrate the Nazi group in Cairo, the truth must await the opening of records there.

Recent work on Argentina shed light on the Perónist sympathy for ex-Nazi and Ustaše officials who made homes there after 1945.[31] Chilean records may or may not illuminate Rauff's activities in that country from his arrival in 1958 until his death in 1984. At the very least, they will clarify the thinking of the Augusto Pinochet government after 1973 when the decision was made over and over again to protect him from extradition and justice. Was it a case of Latin American prickliness at repeated Western pressure, as seems to have been the case when the Bolivian government refused to hand Barbie over to the French in 1972? Or did the Chilean dictator have some sympathy for the aging Nazi criminal as did Paraguay's Alfredo Stroessner in the case of Josef Mengele?

Between the Mossad's capture of Adolf Eichmann in 1960 and the U.S. government's revelations of 1983 concerning its relationship with Klaus Barbie, Western countries gradually moved to the moral side of the war criminal issue. They tried to find and bring to justice former SS perpetrators, regardless of past mistakes in apprehending them. Gestapo Chief Heinrich Müller was never found after the war. But the West German search for him months after the Eichmann capture showed that the Federal Republic's police forces had outgrown the days of the *Freie Mitarbeiter*. Stories from the end of the war were reexamined, graves were exhumed, and family members were watched—if Müller was alive, then he would be found. In the following years and decades, the West German government continued to track down the most notorious war criminals of the Nazi period in an effort to bring them to justice. Bonn issued repeated warrants for Mengele's arrest and pressed the governments of Argentina and Paraguay to hand him over. Bonn also demanded that successive Chilean governments hand over Walter Rauff to the point in 1984 where Hermann Holtzheimer, the West German ambassador to Chile, had sharp words indeed for Pinochet's diplomats. Hans Dietrich Genscher, perhaps West Germany's greatest foreign minister, shocked Syrian President Hafez al-Assad in Damascus in 1988 when he raised the desire of his government to arrest Brunner. Assad was stunned to the point where his ambassador in Bonn made a formal protest. Whatever the determination of Chancellor Helmut Kohl to move West Germans beyond the shadow of the Nazi past in the 1980s, Bonn tried until the end to capture and try the worst of the worst.

Meanwhile, the Americans also tried to make up belatedly for the moral lapses involved in earlier intelligence gaffes. Though the Pentagon kept the Army's 1947 relationship with Barbie secret in 1972, thus precluding his extradition to France, the CIA in 1983 realized that it was time to make amends for past errors (especially since the error with Barbie was the CIC's fault anyway). Though couching its reasoning in the context of the exigencies of the early Cold War years, the CIA was nevertheless moved by the realization that the use of Nazi criminals contained a moral component, and that revealing intelligence blunders of four decades previous would not harm contemporary intelligence operation in the least. The government of a liberal democracy would look better in the public eye if it tried to remedy or apologize for past mistakes.

White House and State Department efforts to dislodge the final monsters of the Nazi regime in the mid-1980s should be seen in this context. Thanks to growing scholarship on the Holocaust, media representations of that terrible event, generations' worth of war crimes trials, and recent legal measures to deport Nazi collaborators from the United States, the U.S. used diplomatic pressure and even covert operations aimed at righting past wrongs.

The wretched, disheveled bones of Josef Mengele, unearthed in Brazil four decades after his crimes, showed that it was indeed too late to correct every mistake. Yet some criminals will always escape justice and some elements of global tragedies will always be misunderstood. Such is the nature of mankind. It is not through the attempted correction of the past, but rather through the reckoning with the past, that our nature and our mistakes are best understood. And the truest reckoning with the official past can never be complete without the full release of government records, including those concerned with intelligence. Just as intelligence successes should be celebrated, intelligence failures must be studied. Such is ultimately the point of this book and of the disclosure law that made it possible.

Notes

1. On U.S. policy, Bradley F. Smith, *The Road to Nuremberg* (New York: Basic, 1981); idem., *The American Road to Nuremberg: The Documentary Record* (Stanford: Hoover Institution Press, 1982). On international pressures, Arieh J. Kochavi, *Prelude to Nuremberg: Allied War Crimes Policy and the Question of Punishment* (Chapel Hill: University of North Carolina Press, 1998).

2. Albrecht Götz, *Bilanz der Verfolgung von NS-Straftaten* (Köln: Bundesanzeiger, 1986), pp. 9–29; Frank M. Buscher, *The US War Crimes Trial Program in Germany, 1946–1955* (Westport, CT: Greenwood Press, 1989).

3. "John McCloy and the Landsberg Cases," in *American Policy and the Reconstruction of West Germany, 1945–1955,* eds. Jeffry M. Diefendorf, Axel Frohn, and Hermann-Josef Rupieper (New York: Cambridge University Press, Publications of the German Historical Institute, 1933), pp. 433–54.

4. In general George Ginsburgs, *Moscow's Road to Nuremberg: The Soviet Background to the Trial* (The Hague: Nijhoff, 1996); Manfred Zeidler, "Der Minsker Kriegsverbrecherprozeß von Januar 1946: Kritische Anmerkungen zu einem sowjetishchen Schauprozeß gegen deutsche Kriegsgefangene," *Vierteljahrshefte für Zeitgeschichte* 52 (April 2004): 211–44.

5. Walter Laqueur and Richard Breitman, *Breaking the Silence: The German Who Exposed the Final Solution* (Hanover: The University Press of New England); Richard Breitman, *Official Secrets: What the Nazis Planned, What the British and Americans Knew* (New York: Hill and Wang, 1998).

6. For the former arguments see Michael Neufeld and Michael Berenbaum, eds., *The Bombing of Auschwitz: Should the Allies Have Attempted It?* (New York: St. Martin's, 2000); Yehuda Bauer, *Jews for Sale: Nazi-Jewish Negotiations, 1933–1945* (New Haven: Yale University Press, 1994), pp. 120ff.

7. Chapters 1, 2, and 8.

8. Chapter 1.

9. Ginsburgs, *Moscow's Road to Nuremberg,* pp. 37–40.

10. Chapter 1.

11. Chapter 2.

12. Chapter 7.

13. See most recently Reinhard Doerries, ed., *Hitler's Last Chief of Foreign Intelligence: Allied Interrogations of Walter Schellenberg* (London: Frank Cass, 2003).

14. Chapter 5.

15. Chapter 4. On Becher, see most recently Ronald Zweig, *The Gold Train: The Destruction of the Jews and the Looting of Hungary* (New York: Morrow, 2002), appendix.

16. Chapters 3 and 12.

17. Chapter 10, pp. 268–69.

18. NA, RG 263, Emil Augsburg Name File; Chapters 11 and 14. On Skorzeny, NA, RG 65, File 100-344753, Section 14.

19. Steven P. Remy, *The Heidelberg Myth: The Nazification and Denazification of a German University* (Cambridge, MA: Harvard University Press, 2002), pp. 146ff.

20. HQ 7708 War Crimes Group, European Command to HQ 970th CIC Detachment, 12 September 1947, NA, RG 319, IRR Personal Files (Optical Disc), File Heinz Reinefarth.

21. British Embassy Memorandum of 20 February 1951, 1661/4/51G, NA, RG 59, West European Affairs 41–54, Box 8.

22. Department of State Memorandum, 13 March 1951, NA, RG 59, West European Affairs 41–54, Box 8. For Reinefarth's work for the CIC, see NARA, RG 319, IRR Personal Files (Optical Disc): Heinz Reinefarth.

23. Biographical information on Höfle is available in his SS Personnel File, United States National Archives (NA), Record Group 242, Berlin Document Center, Microfilm A-3343, SSO 102A. See also Joseph Wulf, *Das Dritte Reich und seine Vollstrecker* (Frankfurt: Arani Verlag, 1984), 275–87; Yitzhak Arad, *Belzec, Sobibor, Treblinka: The Operation Reinhard Death Camps* (Bloomington: Indiana University Press, 1987), pp.19, 44–5, 54, 61.

24. IRR Files Hermann Julius Höfle, NA RG 319 AE 544 848WJ and XE 000631.

25. See Peter Witte and Stephen Tyas, "A New Document on the Deportation and Murder of Jews during 'Einsatz Reinhardt' 1942," *Holocaust and Genocide Studies*, vol. 15, no. 3 (2001): 468–86.

26. Chapters 9, 11, and 13.

27. Chapter 14.

28. Chapter 9.

29. NA, RG 263, Friedrich Panzinger Name File; Ibid., Heinz Pannwitz Name File.

30. Chapter 3.

31. Uki Goñi, *The Real Odessa: How Perón Brought the Nazi War Criminals to Argentina* (London: Granta Books, 2002).

Appendix

Western Communications Intelligence Systems and the Holocaust

Robert J. Hanyok

ONE OF THE GREATEST ADVANTAGES that the United States and Great Britain had in their struggle against Nazi Germany and Imperial Japan during the Second World War was their ability to decode or decipher the secret military and diplomatic messages of the Axis powers.[1] Although this ability was limited in many ways, it provided important intelligence about Axis military operations, Axis appreciation of the Allied strategy, and international relations during the war.

The Allied exploitation of Germany's Enigma cipher machine, referred to popularly as "Ultra," was finally revealed with the publication of F. W. Winterbotham's *The Ultra Secret* in 1974.[2] This book provided information about an aspect of the war that had only been hinted at over the thirty years since the war ended, though there had been a partial revelation years before about America's prewar exploitation of Japan's diplomatic cipher machine, code named "Purple." Many memoirs and histories followed that revealed more of the Allied code-breaking success.

Not long after these revelations, scholars began to ask what Allied code-breaking efforts revealed about the Nazi plans to eliminate Jews and others considered inferior by the Third Reich. In the early 1980s, the first histories were published that contained information about the Holocaust obtained from code breaking. These few histories were quite limited and cited no archival records, which remained classified and unavailable to the public.[3] It was not until 1996 that the National Security Agency (NSA) released to the U.S. National Archives and Records Administration its incomplete set of decrypts of German police units that had operated in the USSR. Along with the police decrypts, NSA released almost 250,000 translations of multinational diplomatic decrypts that contained further information about the Holocaust. In May 1997, the British Public Record Office (PRO) finally released the complete set of several thousand German police decrypts.[4]

Scholars found that the number of decrypts or translations of Axis or neutral radio messages related to the Holocaust held in the National Archives and the PRO was not particularly large. In the National Archives, there were about five hundred such records, while in the PRO, the number of German police decrypts containing information about police massacres in Russia or about the concentration camps represented a small percentage of the thousands that were available.

Considering the scale of the Holocaust—which involved, to a degree, all countries of Europe—and the fact that the eradication of Europe's Jews was a prime Nazi goal, the number of decrypts and translations of intercepted messages seemed meager in comparison.[5] It could be construed from this apparent shortage that a large body of classified records had not been released, or that many undecrypted messages were still held by the code-breaking agencies. However, these suggestions were disproved by the continued release of both World War II-era records by intelligence agencies and other records processed for release under the aegis of the Interagency Working Group. The fact that there were relatively few decrypts and translations was due to the way Allied code-breaking agencies operated during the war.

The Allied system for obtaining intelligence from Axis communications was known as communications intelligence or COMINT. The United States and Great Britain were the major Allied COMINT powers. The cryptologic agencies were heart of these operations: the U.S. Army Signal Intelligence Service (SIS), the U.S. Navy OP-20-G, and Britain's Government Code and Cypher School (GC&CS).[6] The United States also utilized the Coast Guard, the Office of Strategic Services, the Federal Communications Commission, and the Office of Censorship (for cable traffic), and the British used its Radio Security Service, the General Post Office, and Secret Intelligence Service (MI-6). In addition, the Commonwealth countries of Canada, Australia, and New Zealand, and Britain's colony of India provided substantial numbers of personnel, especially in the Middle East, Pacific, and Asian theaters of operation. There also were detachments from Poland, France, the Netherlands, and China. By war's end, COMINT had developed into a worldwide, interconnected system of intercept sites, processing centers, associated analysts, and linguists, with a dissemination system that delivered COMINT to the Allied leadership.[7]

Nevertheless, COMINT was unable to exploit all or even a major part of Axis and neutral communications. There were two main reasons. The first was the disparity between the size and breadth of the Axis communications networks and the Allied COMINT structure. The second reason was that there were several technical shortcomings within the COMINT system. While, on occasion, the Allies were able to completely exploit a particular Axis radio network or cipher system, the overall result was uneven.

The Allied COMINT system during World War II included four major steps: (1) determining Axis targets, (2) intercepting targeted communications, (3) analyzing and translating the decrypt, and (4) disseminating the intelligence to the Allied leadership. The steps of the system were interrelated; a significant change to one step affected all the others.

Step 1: Setting Priorities

For the Allies, the most difficult step in the COMINT system was to decide what Axis or neutral communications to target for intercept and processing. There were thousands of Axis radio terminals in hundreds of radio networks around the world supporting military, naval, diplomatic, intelligence, security, and commercial entities. They utilized hundreds of cryptographic systems, from simple hand ciphers to extensive codes and intricate machines such as Enigma, Purple, Jade, and Tunny.[8] Added to this electronic horde were hundreds of additional neutral networks and cryptographic systems.

COMINT simply could not target all Axis communications networks. The British, and later the Americans, lacked the personnel, facilities, and the technology to monitor and analyze adequately all Axis and neutral communications. This disparity between Axis communications output and COMINT capabilities meant that intelligence chiefs in Washington and London had to set priorities that they hoped would produce the intelligence that most met current and critical Allied needs. Military requirements were the highest priority for the COMINT agencies throughout the war.

In the various combat theaters, cryptologic assignments among the Allies followed de facto theater preeminence. In Europe, the GC&CS was considered the principal Allied cryptologic agency. The Atlantic was shared by the GC&CS and OP-20-G. In the Pacific, the U.S. SIS and OP-20-G supervised intercept and cryptanalytic operations. In the theater comprising India and Burma, the British dominated activities.

In July 1943, the United States and Great Britain reached an accord that divided COMINT tasks and responsibilities. Known as the BRUSA Agreement, the two countries agreed to a complete exchange of finished military intelligence.[9] Except for U-boat traffic, unprocessed or "raw" intercept was not exchanged. Diplomatic traffic was not covered by this agreement, though a separate sharing mechanism was set up in August. Theater arrangements remained in place, though integrated Allied operations were established. The British continued to collect and process all German intelligence and security-related radio traffic in Europe, including German police, SS, and SD messages that related to the Holocaust. In accordance with the BRUSA Agreement, this material was shared with the United States, specifically through the War Department's Special Branch and the OSS liaison staffs in England.

Target priorities could change during the war as the situation warranted. A good example was Switzerland. Because of Bern's historic role as a neutral, early in the war, both Allied COMINT organizations targeted Swiss diplomatic communications. However, they produced little intelligence. There were some technical reasons for this. For one, much of Switzerland's communications with Europe went by cable, which could not be intercepted. Also, Switzerland used twenty-two diplomatic manual ciphers plus a version of the Enigma. Even after the Allies broke the Swiss Enigma, they found there was little intelligence of interest.[10] So the mission languished into 1944.

The situation changed in mid-1944, when it was discovered that Swiss diplomats were reporting on conditions in Eastern Europe as the Red Army drove out German forces. Of particular interest was Hungary, which, in the late summer, had secretly approached the Allies about surrender. The government in Budapest was seized during a German-engineered coup in October. During this period, the Allies stepped up collection of Swiss messages from Budapest. These intercepts, meant to cover the political situation, provided unexpected intelligence on the Nazi roundup of Hungarian Jews supervised by Adolf Eichmann. Supplemented by reports from the U.S. Ambassador in Switzerland, the Allies received a detailed picture of the removal of about half a million Hungarian Jews and the desperate efforts by neutral diplomats in Budapest, led by Raoul Wallenberg, to save some of the victims.

In a similar fashion earlier in 1941, British cryptologists had unexpectedly obtained intelligence about massacres by German police units in the western USSR. From 1939, the British had been intercepting and decrypting police messages as a supplementary source of intelligence on administrative matters and the order of battle of the German military, as well as information about domestic conditions in Germany and occupied Europe. From a cryptanalytic aspect, German police manual ciphers also provided insight into similar German armed forces systems. The British intercepted and decrypted SS Enigma radio messages for much the same reasons. Later, it was discovered that the SS radio messages carried information about the concentration camps.[11]

This information from the police and SS decrypts was passed to, among others, the British Foreign Office, which was accumulating evidence for later possible war crimes proceedings. There is no evidence that the decrypts were used in the War Crimes Tribunals.[12] Evidence from captured documents and debriefs of SS and police personnel was often enough for conviction. Throughout the war, German police and SS radio nets that carried such information remained a lower priority target than the communications of Axis military and selected diplomatic targets.[13]

Step 2: Intercepting Enemy Messages
By the end of the war, the Allies had established about a hundred sites worldwide that performed radio intercept and related activities, such as frequency research and direction finding. In addition to targeting the radio communications of Axis and neutral radio nets, the United States and Great Britain censored all incoming and outgoing cable traffic. This effort, managed by the British General Post Office and the U.S. Office of Censorship, obtained copies of all cable telegrams, including those of foreign diplomatic stations located in both countries.

While the Allied intercept effort was extensive, it also was hampered by a number of limitations that reduced the number of Axis messages that could be collected. For example, censorship worked only if the cables passed through a terminal controlled by the United States or Great Britain. Many countries were aware of this and took measures to reduce the vulnerability of their messages.[14]

When it came to intercepting radio messages, the disparity between the number of Allied intercept facilities and the number of Axis radio stations was a major factor that affected the degree of coverage. Even the nearly one hundred intercept and direction-finding sites were not enough; the Allies had to consider every Axis military unit, plane, ship, security unit, and diplomatic facility a potential target. Precise numbers of Axis daily message levels are not available; however, some estimates from the Pacific campaign suggest that a single Japanese area army command could send as many as fourteen hundred messages a day.[15]

Other factors, such as local weather conditions or the presence of sunspots, the distance between a monitoring station and the target transmitter, terrain, and even the time of day affected the quality of intercepts. These and other environmental conditions were critical when the Allies considered locations for intercept sites.

One monitoring station, Poste de Commandement Cadix, merits a short mention because of its unique contribution to the intercept of German police messages from 1941 to the end of 1942. PC Cadix was a covert Allied intercept site located in the southeastern part of unoccupied France. It had been formed in 1939 by the head of the French Army's radio intelligence organization, Colonel Gustave Bertrand. The site was staffed by a polyglot team of Poles, exiled Spanish Loyalists, and French.

Due to peculiarities of the nighttime propagation of radio signals, PC Cadix was able to monitor German military and police radio traffic from western USSR. Among the traffic collected by Bertrand's team were over three thousand German police messages, which were eventually decrypted. The decrypts were transmitted to Bletchley Park, having first been encrypted, ironically, with a German Enigma device. PC Cadix continued to operate until early November 1942, when the German occupation of southern France forced the team to flee.[16]

Step 3: Processing Intercepts

Once messages had been intercepted, they were forwarded to a theater or national center for processing; that is, analysis and translation. In the beginning of the war, intercepts from overseas sites were sent by courier. By 1944, worldwide secure radio and cable communications linked all of the Allied stations. Intercepts encrypted in high-level systems such as Enigma and Purple were sent to the main analytic centers at Arlington Hall, Virginia; OP-20-G Headquarters in Washington, D.C., and to Bletchley Park, England. These sites were the heart of the analytic effort, staffed with thousands of people who worked many steps of the analytic process.

After an intercepted message had been received, it was reviewed by analysts who extracted intelligence from its addresses, radio frequency, message priority, and cryptographic system. Next, if the encrypted text was "clean copy," without substantial missing cipher groups, it was decrypted. This was a formidable task. Allied cryptanalysts worked against over 200 diplomatic codes and ciphers and several hundred military systems. The more a system was used, the better the chance it would be decrypted. However, despite the image of overall success created by the exploits against Enigma and Purple, many Axis and neutral systems were only partly exploited or never broken at all. The Gestapo version of the Enigma and even a Vatican cipher completely resisted Allied cryptanalytic efforts.[17]

How effective overall was Allied decryption? It is a difficult to evaluate just how much intercept was exploited by the cryptanalysts. Certainly, for some campaigns, such as the one against the U-boats, the cryptanalytic success rate may have been quite high. For one period, however, from about February to November 1942, the Allies could not exploit messages sent with new model Enigmas that were used by the U-boats.[18] Where there are statistics, the picture is one of very limited success. For example, in a July 1945 OP-20-G report, it was noted that only 10 percent of all intercepted Japanese naval messages were processed fully and disseminated.[19] In another case, in 1944, Arlington Hall noted that of 576,000 diplomatic intercepts, about 89,000, or roughly 15 percent, were solved by the cryptanalysts.[20]

Once solved by the code breakers, the revealed message texts were passed to linguists. They would produce a formal translation for use in intelligence staff reports. The Allies faced serious problems when it came to translating intercepted messages. For one, they had to account for over three-dozen languages, ranging from French to Amharic. In addition, the cryptologists had to vie for scarce linguists with other services, such as the Allied Translator and Interpreter Section (ATIS).

The few statistics available indicate that the rate of translation was not high. The Arlington Hall statistics from 1944 show that of the 89,000 decrypts, about 50,000 were translated. This is about 56 percent of the decrypts, but only 8.6 percent of the total intercepts.[21] In 1940, the Diplomatic and Commercial Section of GC&CS intercepted about 100,000 messages from cable and radio. The Section read about 70,000, but only circulated 8,000 translations, or 8 percent of the total intercepts.[22]

The difficulties enumerated above greatly affected the time it took to process an intercept, which, in turn, affected the value of the intelligence for Allied leaders. A good example involves two translations concerning the roundup of the Hungarian Jews in June 1944. Both messages were intercepted by the army site at Asmara, Ethiopia, and were received at Arlington Hall one day later. The first, a Vichy diplomatic message from Budapest to Ankara, Turkey, was intercepted on June 13 and was published as a formal translation on June 24. The second, a Hungarian diplomatic report from Budapest also to Ankara, took from June 27 to December 16 to be completely processed and published as a translation.

Any number of reasons can be found for the difference, principally that Vichy diplomatic cryptography had been exploited by Arlington Hall for almost two years prior, while Hungarian systems were still being recovered; furthermore, French was easier than Magyar to translate. The long delay does not exclude the possibility that the information in the Hungarian intercept may have been passed informally to a recipient, such as the U.S. State Department. However, the months it took to process the Hungarian intercept illustrates the difficulty the Allies faced in getting intelligence from source to user in a timely manner.

Finally, Allied cryptologists did not always know what to make of certain intelligence. To give just one example, in early January 1943, the British intercepted an SS message from Lublin (in occupied Poland) to Berlin that reported the outcome of Operation Reinhardt. In the decrypted text was a series of letters followed by numbers. This decrypt went unreported by intelligence officials probably because the significance of the numbers and the reference to Operation Reinhardt were not understood. Only recently have scholars determined that this message reported the number of victims in the death camps located in Poland—some 1,274,166 killed at Treblinka, Sobibor, Belzec, and Lublin during 1942, the first year of Operation Reinhardt, the cover name for the extermination of the Jews at these camps.[23]

Step 4: Dissemination

Once a translation was completed, the intelligence had to be given to those who needed it. It was recognized early in the war that COMINT was both the best source of intelligence about Axis plans and operations and was also the most vulnerable to compromise. To lose the ability to trust intelligence gathered via COMINT—what Churchill on one occasion called his "golden eggs"—could have seriously hampered an Allied victory.[24]

Britain and the U.S. created special staffs to securely distribute intelligence. There were the British Joint Intelligence Committee and the U.S. War Department's Special Branch. Both received intelligence from all sources: COMINT, prisoner interrogation, captured documents, diplomatic reports, and photographic intelligence. This material either was transmitted overseas to special liaison and security personnel for further distribution, or was combined into special all-intelligence reports that were disseminated within the Allied governments. COMINT easily was the most prevalent source in these reports.

Within the departments of the Allied governments, COMINT intelligence was circulated by a combination of summary-type reports and personal briefings. In the United States this first method was accomplished primarily with the "Magic" diplomatic summary. Drawn up by the Special Branch, this summary contained digests of translations based mostly on diplomatic sources. President Roosevelt also received personal daily briefings based on selected diplomatic and military translations received from the Special Branch.[25] A review of both the "Magic" summary and the translations selected for the White House indicates that very little COMINT intelligence about the Holocaust reached the White House and the rest of the U.S. government. The "Magic" summary contained less than twenty citations about the Holocaust.[26] However, FDR received much information from other sources, such as the State Department, private individuals, and the Office of Strategic Services.[27]

Churchill, because of the British exploitation of German police messages, received briefings about their atrocities in the western Soviet Union during the early phase of Operation Barbarosa, the Nazi invasion of the USSR. On August 24, 1941, Prime Minister Churchill gave a radio address that alluded to atrocities committed against the Russian civilian population by German police units. While no mention was made of Jewish victims of the police actions, the mention of the German police possibly compromised the source of Churchill's information.

On September 12, 1941, Kurt Daluege, the commander of the German police, sent a message to his units ordering the cessation of radio reports concerning the executions of Jews. Three weeks had passed since Churchill's speech, and it is probable that the German police hierarchy spent that time evaluating it. Daluege's order refers to the "danger of enemy decipherment of wireless messages."[28] Whatever the reason, while the reports did not stop right away or completely, the level of information eventually dropped off. In November 1941, the German police changed their cipher system. Ironically, the Germans adopted a system that was easier to exploit. Still, the British believed that Daluege's order and the cryptographic change were inspired, at least in part, by Churchill's speech.[29]

Notes

1. A code is a set of arbitrary groups of letters, numbers, or other symbols used to replace words, phrases, letters, or numbers for the purposes of concealment or brevity. A cipher is a method of concealing plaintext by transposing letters or numbers or by substituting other letters or numbers according to a key. Communications intelligence (COMINT) is defined as all activities, including code breaking or cryptanalysis, used to exploit the communications of Axis and neutral countries. Cryptology is the science of making and breaking codes or cipher systems.

2. F. W. Winterbotham, *The Ultra Secret* (New York: Harper and Row, 1974).

3. Walter Laqueur, *The Terrible Secret: Suppression of the Truth About Hitler's "Final Solution"* (New York: Owl Books, 1998 edition) 84–86; *British Intelligence in the Second World War,* F. H. Hinsley et al., vol. 2 (London: Her Majesty's Stationery Office, 1981) appendix 5, 669–73.

4. The police decrypts are located in NA, RG 457, Historical Cryptographic Collection (HCC), box 1386, and in the Public Record Office, HW/16, "GC&CS: German Police Decrypts." The diplomatic translations are located in RG 457, boxes 286–523. In 2003 the PRO was renamed the National Archives.

5. Gerhard Weinberg demonstrated the high priority of this Nazi intention in *A World at Arms: A Global History of World War II* (New York: Cambridge University Press, 1995) 95–96, 191–92.

6. The Signal Intelligence Service underwent several title changes during the war. From 1929 to 1942, it was the SIS. In June 1942, it was briefly renamed the Signal Intelligence Service Division. One month later it was renamed the Signal Security Division (SSD). In 1943, the SSD became the Signal Security Service. In late summer 1943, the SSS became the Signal Security Agency (SSA). It remained the SSA until September 15, 1945, when the SSA became the Army Security Agency.

7. Eunan O'Halpin, "Small States and Big Secrets: Understanding SIGINT Cooperation between Unequal Powers during the Second World War," *Intelligence and National Security* 17, no. 3, Autumn 2002), 1–16.

8. The Enigma and Purple cipher machines are well known from the literature of World War II. Less famous Axis cipher machines were also exploited for intelligence. Tunny was the cover name applied to the Lorenz Company's on-line enciphered teleprinter known to the Germans as Schluesselzusatz 40 or SZ-40. GC&CS first broke into it in late 1942.

9. BRUSA is an acronym for Britain–United States of America. For more on the BRUSA Agreement and its background see Robert L. Benson, *A History of U.S. Communications Intelligence during World War II: Policy and Administration* (Fort George G. Meade, MD: National Security Agency, Center for Cryptologic History, 1997), 97–133; and Bradley F. Smith, *The Ultra-Magic Deals and the Most Secret Special Relationship, 1940–1946* (Novato, CA: Presidio , 1993), 105–70.

10. David H. Hamer, Geoff Sullivan, and Frode Weierud, "Enigma Variations: An Extended Family of Machines." *Cryptologia* 23, no. 3 (July 1988); SSA "Effort against the Swiss Cipher Machine (SZD)"; NA, RG 457, HCC, box 1284.

11. Hinsley et al., *British Intelligence*, 669–71.

12. GC&CS "Accumulating Evidence for War Crimes," PRO HW 14/55, Oct. 1942; Stephen Budiansky, *Battle of Wits: The Complete Story of Codebreaking in World War II* (New York: Free Press, 2000), 202; Richard Breitman, *Official Secrets: What the Nazis Planned, What the British and Americans Knew* (New York: Hill and Wang, 1998), 191, 212–15.

13. Memorandum, Priorities for Operation of the Signal security Service, 8 Mar. 1943. SRH-145, "Collection of Memoranda on Operations of SIS Intercept Activities and Dissemination, 1942–1945" (Fort George G. Meade, MD, 1983) 92.

14. For example, see Lisbon (Foreign Minister) to Washington, 22 June 1944, MC-916, in which the Washington Embassy is reminded to paraphrase public text, such as speeches, so as to avoid the use of them as plaintext cribs; also, Washington (Hopenot/Baudet) to Algiers, 13 May 1944, MC-806, in which the French Committee for National Liberation is reminded that all cables can be obtained by the "enemy" and exploited because the cables were encoded with Vichy codes, NA, RG 457, HCC, box 879, "Code Instructions"; finally, Berlin (Oshima) to Tokyo, 5 Mar. 1944, CI-1813, in which the Japanese diplomats in Germany discreetly instruct Tokyo to keep new communications routes secret from the British "telegraph office." NA, RG 457, HCC, box 954, folder 2863–Japanese Message Translations Categorized as CI (Code Instructions) for Diplomats, 1943–45.

15. Edward J. Drea, *MacArthur's ULTRA: Codebreaking and the War against Japan, 1942–1945* (Lawrence: University Press of Kansas, 1992), 52–53.

16. Gustave Bertrand, *Enigma: Ou la Plus Grande Enigme de la Guerre, 1939–1945* (Paris: Plon, 1973) 118, 129–30.

17. For a complete listing of GC&CS success against the various Enigma keys, see Hinsley et al., appendix 4, 656-668; David Alvarez, *Secret Messages: Codebreaking and American Diplomacy, 1930–1945* (Lawrence, KS: University Press of Kansas, 2000), 176; "History of the Solution of Vatican Systems in SSA and GCCS, 1943–44" (Washington: Sept. 1944) NA, RG 457 HCC, box 1284.

18. In February 1942, U-boats replaced the three-wheel Enigma with a new four-wheel Enigma, which exponentially increased the work factor for decryption.

19. Memorandum, Naval Inspector General to Secretary of the Navy, Serial 001971, "Survey of OP-20-G Section of Naval Communications Division of the Bureau of Naval Personnel which Procures Uniformed Naval Personnel," 13 July 1945, NA, RG 457, HCC, box 1286, Item 23 (d).

20. Frank B. Rowlett, *The Story of Magic: Memoirs of an American Cryptologic Pioneer* (Laguna Hills, CA: Aegean Park Press, 1998), 253–54.

21. Ibid.

22. Non-notated and unsigned memorandum on diplomatic cryptanalysis for 1940, 13 Jan. 1941, HW 14/11, "Government Code and Cypher School: Directorate, Second World War Policy Papers," as cited in John Ferris, "The Road to Bletchley Park: The British Experience with Signals Intelligence, 1892–1945," *Intelligence and National Security* 17, no. 1, (Spring 2002), 53–84.

23. Peter Witte and Stephen Tyas, "A New Document on the Deportation and Murder of Jews during 'Einsatz Reinhardt 1942,'" *Holocaust and Genocide Studies* 15, no. 3, (Winter 2001), 468–86.

24. According to Ronald Lewin, *Ultra Goes to War: The First Account of World War II's Greatest Secret Based on Official Documents* (New York: Pocket Books, 1978), 210.

25. David Kahn, "Roosevelt, Magic, and Ultra," *Cryptologia* 16, no. 4, (October 1992), 289–319; SRH-111 "Magic Reports for the Attention of the President, 1943–1944" (Fort George G. Meade, MD: National Security Agency, 1980).

26. Alexander S. Cochran Jr., *The MAGIC Diplomatic Summaries: A Chronological Finding Aid* (New York: Garland, 1982).

27   Joseph E. Persico, *Roosevelt's Secret War: FDR and World War II Espionage* (New York: Random House, 2001), 315–20; Laqueur, *Terrible Secret*, 94–6; Breitman, *Official Secrets*, 150–52.

28. 13 Sept. 1941, NA, RG 457, HCC, box 1386, item 12.

29. Breitman, *Official Secrets*, 92–96; Budiansky, *Battle of Wits*, 199–201.

Terms and Acronyms

Anschluss	Germany's annexation of Austria (March 1938)
ATIS	Allied Translator and Interpreter Section
BfV	Bundesamt für Verfassungsschutz, Federal Republic of Germany Office for the Protection of the Constitution
BKA	German Federal Police Office
BND	Bundesnachrichtendienst, German Secret Service
CIC	U.S. Army Counterintelligence Corps
CIG	Central Intelligence Group
COI	Coordinator of Information
DCI	Director of Central Intelligence
Devisenbewirtschaftung	Reich Office for Foreign Exchange Control
EUCOM	U.S. European Command
FGI	foreign government information
FHO	Fremde Heere Ost, Foreign Armies–East,
Forschungsamt	Research Office, a German intelligence organization
GAO	General Accounting Office
Generalmajor	Rank comparable to U.S. Army Brigadier General
GIS	German Intelligence Service
GRU	Glavonoye Rasvodyvatelnoye Upravalenie, Red Army Intelligence
HAP	Historical Advisory Panel
ICRC	International Committee of the Red Cross
ILO	International Labor Office
IMT	International Military Tribunal
INS	Immigration and Naturalization Service
IWG	Nazi War Crimes and Japanese Imperial Government Records Interagency Working Group
JCS	Joint Chiefs of Staff
JIOA	Joint Intelligence Objectives Agency
KPD	Kommunistische Partei Deutschlands, Communist Party of Germany
Kripo	Kriminalpolizei, Third Reich criminal police
MHBK	Magyar Harcosok Bajtársi Közössége, Hungarian Warriors Comradeship Association

MID	Military Intelligence Division
MNRI	Movimiento Nacionalista Revolucionario de Izquierda, National Revolutionary Party of the Left
NKVD	Narodnyi Kommissariat Vnutrennikh Del, Soviet Secret Police
NSDAP	Nationalsozialistische deutsche Arbeiterpartei, Nazi party
NTS	Narodno-Trudovio Soiuz, National Alliance of Russian Solidarist
Oberstleutnant	Rank comparable to U.S. Army Lt. Colonel
OKW	Oberkommando der Wehrmacht, High Command of the German Armed Forces
OMGUS	Office of Military Government United States
OSI	Office of Special Investigations (Department of Justice)
OSS	Office of Strategic Services
OUN	Organization of Ukranian Nationalists
PWE	Political Warfare Executive
RSHA	Reichssicherheitshauptamt, Reich Security Main Office
RSI	Republica Sociale Italiana, Italian Social Republic
RWM	Reichswirtschaftsministerium, Reich Ministry of Economics
Schutzpolizei	municipal police
SD	Sicherheitsdienst, SS intelligence organization
SHAEF	Supreme Headquarters Allied Expeditionary Force
SIM	Servizio Informazioni Militare, Italian military intelligence service
Sipo	Sicherheitspolizei, security police, a branch of the RSHA
SS	Schutzstaffeln, Protective Corps
SS-Brigadeführer	Rank comparable to U.S. Army Brigadier General
SS-Gruppenführer	Rank comparable to U.S. Army Maj. General
SS-Hauptsturmführer	Rank comparable to U.S. Army Captain
SS-Obergruppenführer	Rank comparable to U.S. Army Lt. General
SS-Oberscharführer	Rank comparable to U.S. Army Staff Sergeant
SS-Oberstgruppenführer	Rank comparable to U.S. Army General
SS-Obersturmbannführer	Rank comparable to U.S. Army Lt. Colonel
SS-Obersturmführer	Rank comparable to U.S. Army 1st Lt.
SS-Standartenführer	Rank comparable to U.S. Army Colonel
SS-Sturmbannführer	Rank comparable to U.S. Army Major
SS-Untersturmführer	Rank comparable to U.S. Army 2nd Lt.
UHVR	Ukrainska Holovna Vyzvolna Rada, Supreme Ukrainian Liberation Council
UPA	Ukrainska povstanska armiia, Ukranian Insurgent Army
USFET	U.S. Forces European Theater
USMS	U.S. Marshals Service
WASt	Wehrmachtsauskunftsstelle, Third Reich Armed Forces Information Office
ZfH	Zentrale für Heimatdienst, a postwar German government information and education office

Selected Bibliography

Aharoni, Zvi, and Wilhelm Dietl. *Operation Eichmann: The Truth about the Pursuit, Capture, and Trial.* Translated by Helmut Bögler. New York: John Wiley, 1997.

Alvarez, David. *Secret Messages: Codebreaking and American Diplomacy, 1930-1945.* Lawrence: University Press of Kansas, 2000.

Arad, Yitzak. *Belzec, Sobibor, Treblinka: The Operation Reinhard Death Camps.* Bloomington: Indiana University Press, 1987.

Arendt, Hannah. *Eichmann in Jerusalem: A Report on the Banality of Evil.* New York: Penguin Books, 1964.

Barkai, Avraham. *From Boycott to Annihilation: The Economic Struggle of German Jews, 1933-1943.* Translated by William Templer. Hanover, NH: University Press of New England for Brandeis University Press, 1989.

Bauer, Yehuda. *Jews for Sale? Nazi-Jewish Negotiations, 1933-1945.* New Haven, CT: Yale University Press, 1994.

Benson, Robert Louis. *A History of U.S. Communications Intelligence during World War II: Policy and Administration.* Fort George G. Meade, MD: Center for Cryptologic History, National Security Agency, 1997.

Bischof, Günther. *Austria in the First Cold War, 1945–1955: The Leverage of the Weak.* New York: St. Martin's Press, 1999.

Braham, Randolph L. *The Politics of Genocide: The Holocaust in Hungary.* 2 vols. 1981. Condensed ed. Detroit: Wayne State University Press, 2000.

Breitman, Richard. *The Architect of Genocide: Himmler and the Final Solution.* Hanover, NH: University Press of New England, 1991.

———. *Official Secrets: What the Nazis Planned, What the British and Americans Knew.* New York: Hill and Wang, 1998.

Breitman, Richard, and Alan M. Kraut. *American Refugee Policy and European Jewry, 1933-1945.* Bloomington: Indiana University Press, 1987.

Brysac, Shareen Blair. *Resisting Hitler: Mildred Harnack and the Red Orchestra.* New York: Oxford University Press, 2000.

Budiansky, Stephen. *Battle of Wits: The Complete Story of Codebreaking in World War II.* New York: Free Press, 2000.

Buscher, Frank M. *The U.S. War Crimes Trial Program in Germany, 1946-1955.* New York: Greenwood, 1989.

Carpi, Daniel. *Between Mussolini and Hitler: The Jews and the Italian Authorities in*

France and Tunisia. Hanover, NH: University Press of New England, 1994.

Casey, William J. *The Secret War Against Hitler.* Washington, DC: Regnery Gateway, 1986.

Chalou, George C., ed. *The Secrets War: The Office of Strategic Services in World War II.* Washington, DC: National Archives and Records Administration, 1992.

Critchfield, James. *Partners at the Creation: The Men Behind Postwar Germany's Defense and Intelligence Establishments.* Annapolis, MD: Naval Institute Press, 2003.

Dallin, Alexander. *German Rule in Russia, 1941-1945: A Study of Occupation Policies.* 1957. 2nd rev. ed. Boulder, CO: Westview, 1981.

De Silva, Peer. *Sub Rosa: the CIA and the Uses of Intelligence.* New York: Times Books, 1978.

Drea, Edward J. *MacArthur's ULTRA: Codebreaking and the War against Japan, 1942–1945.* Lawrence: University Press of Kansas, 1992.

Dulles, Allen Welsh. *The Secret Surrender.* New York: Harper and Row, 1966.

Engel, David. *Facing a Holocaust: The Polish Government-in-Exile and the Jews, 1943-1945.* Chapel Hill: University of North Carolina Press, 1993.

———. *In the Shadow of Auschwitz: The Polish Government-in-Exile and the Jews 1939-1942.* Chapel Hill: University of North Carolina Press, 1987.

Feingold, Henry L. *Bearing Witness: How America and its Jews Responded to the Holocaust.* Syracuse, NY: Syracuse University Press, 1995.

———. *The Politics of Rescue: The Roosevelt Administration and the Holocaust, 1938-1945.* New Brunswick, NJ: Rutgers University Press, 1970.

Finkielkraut, Alain. *Remembering in Vain: The Klaus Barbie Trial and Crimes against Humanity.* Translated by Roxanne Lapidus with Sima Godfrey. New York: Columbia University Press, 1992.

Fischer, Albert. *Hjalmar Schacht und Deutschlands "Judenfrage": der "Wirtschaftsdiktator" und die Vertreibung der Juden aus der deutschen Wirtschaft.* Cologne: Böhlau, 1995.

Forbes, Neil. *Doing Business with the Nazis: Britain's Economic and Financial Relations with Germany 1931-1939.* Portland, OR: Frank Cass, 2000.

Friedman, Saul S. *No Haven for the Oppressed: United States Policy Toward Jewish Refugees, 1938-1945.* Detroit: Wayne State University Press, 1973.

Gehlen, Reinhard. *The Service: The Memoirs of General Reinhard Gehlen.* Translated by David Irving. New York: World Publishing, 1972.

Gilbert, Martin. *Auschwitz and the Allies.* New York: Holt, Rinehart, and Winston, 1981.

Goñi, Uki. *The Real Odessa: How Peron Brought the Nazi War Criminals to Argentina.* New York: Granta, 2002.

Grose, Peter. *Gentleman Spy: The Life of Allen Dulles.* Boston: Houghton Mifflin, 1994.

Gutman, Yisrael, and Michael Berenbaum, eds. *Anatomy of the Auschwitz Death Camp.* Bloomington: Indiana University Press, published in association with the United States Holocaust Memorial Museum, Washington, D.C., 1994.

Hafner, Georg M., and Esther Schapira. *Die Akte Alois Brunner.* Frankfurt: Campus Verlag, 2000.

Harris, Whitney R. *Tyranny on Trial: The Trial of the Major German War Criminals at the End of World War II at Nuremberg, Germany, 1945–1946.* 1954. Dallas: Southern Methodist University Press, 1999.

Haynes, John Earl and Harvey Klehr. *Venona: Decoding Soviet Espionage in America.* New Haven, CT: Yale University Press, 1999.

Headland, Ronald. *Messages of Murder: A Study of the Reports of the Einsatzgruppen of the Security Police and the Security Service, 1941-1943.* Rutherford, NJ: Fairleigh Dickinson University Press, 1992.

Higham, Charles. *Trading with the Enemy: An Exposé of the Nazi-American Money Plot, 1933-1949.* New York: Delacorte, 1983.

Hilberg, Raul. *The Destruction of the European Jews.* 1961. 3 vols. New Haven, CT: Yale University Press, 2003.

———. *Perpetrators, Victims, Bystanders: The Jewish Catastrophe 1933-1945.* New York: Aaron Asher Books, 1992.

Hinsley, F. H., et al. *British Intelligence in the Second World War.* 5 vols. New York: Cambridge University Press, 1979-1990.

Hoffmann, Peter. *The History of the German Resistance 1933-1945.* Translated by Richard Barry. Cambridge, MA: MIT Press, 1977.

Höhne, Heinz. *Canaris: Hitler's Master Spy.* 1976. Translated by J. Maxwell Brownjohn. New York: Cooper Square, 1999.

———. *Codeword: Direktor—The Story of the Red Orchestra*, trans. Richard Barry. New York: Coward, McCann and Geoghegan, 1971.

———. *The Secret Front: Nazi Political Espionage 1938-1945.* 1954. Translated by R. H. Stevens. New York: Enigma Books, 2003.

Ioanid, Radu. *The Holocaust in Romania: The Destruction of Jews and Gypsies Under the Antonescu Regime, 1940-1944.* Chicago: Ivan R. Dee, 2000.

Kahn, David. *Hitler's Spies: German Military Intelligence in World War II.* 1978. Cambridge, MA: Da Capo Press, 2000.

Katz, Barry M. "The Holocaust and American Intelligence." In *The Jewish Legacy and the German Conscience: Essays in Memory of Rabbi Joseph Ascher*, edited by Moses Rischin and Raphael Ascher. Berkeley, CA: Judah L. Magnes Museum, 1991.

Katz, Robert. *The Battle for Rome: The Germans, the Allies, the Partisans, and the Pope.* New York: Simon and Schuster, 2003.

———. *Black Sabbath: A Journey Through a Crime Against Humanity.* New York: Macmillan 1969.

———. *Death in Rome.* New York: Macmillan, 1967.

Kershaw, Ian. *Hitler: 1936–1945: Nemesis.* London: Penguin, 2000.

Klarsfeld, Beate. *Partout où ils seront.* Paris: Édition spéciale, 1972. English edition: *Wherever They May Be!* Translated by Monroe Stearns and Natalie Gerardi. New York: Vanguard Press, 1975.

Koblik, Steven. *The Stones Cry Out: Sweden's Response to the Persecution of the Jews, 1933–1945.* Translated by David Mel Paul and Margareta Paul. New York: Holocaust Library, 1988.

Kochavi, Arieh J. *Post-Holocaust Politics: Britain, the United States and Jewish Refugees, 1945-1948.* Chapel Hill: University of North Carolina Press, 2001.

Lamb, Richard. *War in Italy, 1943–1945: A Brutal Story.* New York: De Capo Press, 1996.

Laqueur, Walter. *The Terrible Secret: Suppression of the Truth about Hitler's "Final Solution."* Boston: Little, Brown, 1980.

Laqueur, Walter and Richard Breitman. *Breaking the Silence: The German Who Exposed the Final Solution.* Hanover, NH: University Press of New England for Brandeis University Press, 1994.

Mangold, Tom. *Cold Warrior: James Jesus Angleton: The CIA's Master Spy Hunter.* New York: Simon and Schuster, 1991.

Mares, David R. and Francisco Rojas Aravena, *The United States and Chile: Coming in From the Cold.* New York: Routledge, 2001.

Mauch, Christof. *The Shadow War Against Hitler: The Covert Operations of America's Wartime Secret Intelligence Service.* Translated by Jeremiah M. Riemer. New York: Columbia University Press, 2003.

Michaelis, Meir. *Mussolini and the Jews: German-Italian Relations and the Jewish Question in Italy, 1922–1945.* New York: Oxford University Press, 1989.

Morse, Arthur D. *While Six Million Died: A Chronicle of American Apathy.* 1968. Woodstock, NY: Overlook, 1983.

Newton, Verne W., ed. *FDR and the Holocaust.* New York: St. Martin's Press, 1996.

Overy, Richard. *Interrogations: The Nazi Elite in Allied Hands, 1945.* New York: Viking, 2001.

Paris, Edmond. *Genocide in Satellite Croatia 1941-1945: A Record of Racial and Religious Persecutions and Massacres.* Translated by Lois Perkins. Chicago: American Institute for Balkan Affairs, 1961.

Penkower, Monty N. *The Jews Were Expendable: Free World Diplomacy and the Holocaust.* Detroit: Wayne State University Press, 1988.

Persico, Joseph E. *Roosevelt's Secret War: FDR and World War II Espionage.* New York: Random House, 2001.

Petersen, Neal H., ed. *From Hitler's Doorstep: The Wartime Intelligence Reports of Allen Dulles, 1942-1945.* University Park: Pennsylvania State University Press, 1996.

Phayer, Michael. *The Catholic Church and the Holocaust, 1930-1965.* Bloomington: Indiana University Press, 2001.

Pick, Hella. *Simon Wiesenthal: A Life in Search of Justice.* Boston: Northeastern University Press, 1996.

Posner, Gerald L., and John Ware. *Mengele: The Complete Story.* 1986. New Introduction by Michael Berenbaum. New York: Cooper Square, 2000.

Reese, Mary Ellen. *General Reinhard Gehlen: The CIA Connection.* Fairfax, VA: George Mason University Press, 1990.

Rubinstein, William D. *The Myth of Rescue: Why the Democracies Could Not Have Saved More Jews from the Nazis.* NY: Routledge, 1997.

Ryan, Allan A. Jr. *Klaus Barbie and the United States Government: The Report, with*

Documentary Appendix, to the Attorney General of the United States. Frederick, MD: University Publications of America, 1984.

————. *Quiet Neighbors: Prosecuting Nazi War Criminals in America*. San Diego, CA: Harcourt Brace Jovanovich, 1984.

Schellenberg, Walter. *The Labyrinth: Memoirs of Walter Schellenberg, Hitler's Chief of Counterintelligence*. 1956. Translated by Louis Hagen. New York: DeCapo Press, 2000.

Schlesinger, Arthur M. Jr. *A Life in the Twentieth Century: Innocent Beginnings, 1917-1950*. Boston: Houghton Mifflin, 2000.

Segev, Tom. *The Seventh Million: The Israelis and the Holocaust*. Translated by Haim Watzman. New York: Hill and Wang, 1993.

Simpson, Christopher. *Blowback: America's Recruitment of Nazis and its Effects on the Cold War*. New York: Weidenfeld and Nicolson, 1988.

————. *The Splendid Blond Beast: Money, Law, and Genocide in the Twentieth Century*. New York: Grove Press, 1993.

Smith Bradley F., and Elena Agarossi. *Operation Sunrise: The Secret Surrender*. New York: Basic Books, 1979.

Stoltzfus, Nathan. *Resistance of the Heart: Intermarriage and the Rosenstrasse Protest in Nazi Germany*. New York: W. W. Norton, 1996.

Toland, John. *The Last 100 Days: The Tumultuous and Controversial Story of the Final Days of World War II in Europe*. 1965. New York: Modern Library, 2003.

Tomasevich, Jozo. *War and Revolution in Yugoslavia, 1941-1945: Occupation and Collaboration*. 1985. Edited by Novak Strugar. Translation by Margot and Bosko Milosavljević. Stanford, CA: Stanford University Press, 2001.

Weinberg, Gerhard L. *A World at Arms: A Global History of World War II*. New York: Cambridge University Press, 1994.

Weinstein, Allen, and Alexander Vassiliev. *The Haunted Wood: Soviet Espionage in America–the Stalin Era*. New York: Random House, 1999.

Wheeler-Bennett, John, and Anthony Nicholls, *The Semblance of Peace: The Political Settlement after the Second World War*. New York: St. Martin's Press, 1972.

Wiesenthal, Simon. *Justice, Not Vengeance*. Translated by Ewald Osers. New York: Grove Weidenfeld, 1989.

Winterbotham, F. W. *The Ultra Secret*. New York: Harper and Row, 1974.

Wood, E. Thomas, and Stanislaw M. Jankowski. *Karski: How One Man Tried to Stop the Holocaust*. New York: J. Wiley, 1994.

Wyman, David S. *The Abandonment of the Jews: America and the Holocaust, 1941-1945*. New York: Pantheon, 1984.

Zuccotti, Susan. *The Italians and the Holocaust: Persecution, Rescue, and Survival*. New York: Basic Books 1987.

————. *Under His Very Windows: The Vatican and the Holocaust in Italy*. New Haven, CT: Yale University Press, 2000.

Zweig, Ronald W. *The Gold Train: The Destruction of the Jews and the Looting of Hungary*. New York: William Morrow, 2002.

Record Groups Cited

RG 38	Records of the Office of the Chief of Naval Operations
RG 59	General Records of the Department of State
RG 65	Records of the Federal Bureau of Investigation (FBI)
RG 84	Records of the Foreign Service Posts of the Department of State
RG 85	Records of the Immigrations and Naturalization Service (INS)
RG 131	Records of the Office of Alien Property
RG 165	Records of the War Department General and Special Staffs
RG 200	National Archives Collection of Donated Materials (formerly RG 200)
RG 226	Records of the Office of Strategic Services
RG 238	National Archives Collection of World War II War Crimes Records
RG 239	Records of the American Commission for the Protection and Salvage of Artistic and Historic Monuments in War Areas
RG 242	National Archives Collection of Foreign Records Seized
RG 260	Records of the Office of Military Government United States (OMGUS)
RG 263	Records of the Central Intelligence Agency (CIA)
RG 316	Records of the Japan-United States Friendship Commission
RG 319	Records of the Army Staff
RG 330	Records of the Office of the Secretary of Defense
RG 332	Records of U.S. Theaters of War, World War II
RG 338	Records of the U.S. Army Commands, 1942-
RG 457	Records of the National Security Agency/Central Security Service
RG 466	Records of the U.S. High Commissioner for Germany
RG 493	U.S. Army China-Burma-India Theaters
RG 498	Records of U.S. Theaters of War
RG 549	Records of United States Army, Europe

Contributors

RICHARD BREITMAN, professor of history at American University, is the author of *Official Secrets: What the Nazis Planned, What the British and Americans Knew* and a number of other books. He serves as editor of the scholarly journal *Holocaust and Genocide Studies*, and is director of historical research for the Interagency Working Group.

PAUL BROWN, historian and employee of the National Archives, specializes in Third Reich, Holocaust, and intelligence-related subjects. Prior to his appointment to the IWG, he was a member of the Presidential Advisory Commission on Holocaust Assets in the United States. His most recent article is "The Senior Leadership Cadre of the Geheime Feldpolizei, 1939-1945" in *Holocaust and Genocide Studies*.

NORMAN J. W. GODA is an associate professor of history at Ohio University. His publications include *Tomorrow the World: Hitler, Northwest Africa, and the Path toward America* as well as numerous journal articles. He is currently completing *Tales from Spandau: Diplomacy, Symbolism, and the Nuremberg War Criminals 1947-1987*. He received his Ph.D. in European History from the University of North Carolina.

ROBERT HANYOK is a historian with the Center for Cryptologic History of the National Security Agency. He served as a special technical adviser to the staff of the IWG. Mr. Hanyok has published and lectured on various subjects in cryptologic history. He received his master's degree in history from the University of Maryland, Baltimore County.

TIMOTHY NAFTALI, an associate professor at the University of Virginia, is director of the Presidential Recordings Program and Kremlin Decisionmaking Project at the Miller Center of Public Affairs. His book reviews on intelligence history appear in various publications, including the *New York Times* and the *Los Angeles Times*.

ROBERT WOLFE was the senior reference specialist for more than thirty years for the National Archives' massive captured German and World War II war crimes trial records, as well as for the records of the postwar occupation of Germany and Austria. His publications include *Americans as Proconsuls: U.S. Military Government in Germany and Japan, 1944-52* and *Captured German and Related Records*.

Index